VICE AND VIRTUE IN EVERYDAY LIFE

Introductory Readings in Ethics

VICE AND VIRTUE IN EVERYDAY LIFE

Introductory Readings in Ethics

CHRISTINA HOFF SOMMERS
Clark University

Under the general editorship of Robert J. Fogelin
Dartmouth College

Harcourt Brace Jovanovich, Publishers

SAN DIEGO   NEW YORK   CHICAGO   ATLANTA   WASHINGTON, D.C.
LONDON   SYDNEY   TORONTO

For my father
KENNETH EUGENE HOFF

PREFACE

In the nineteenth century, moral philosophy was the most important course in a student's college career. It was taken during the senior year and was typically taught by the college president. Now, after many years, normative ethics is flourishing again. Philosophy departments are attracting unprecedented numbers of students to courses in contemporary ethical problems, business ethics, medical ethics, ethics for engineers, nurses, and social workers. We find dozens of journals, hundreds of texts and anthologies, and, according to a survey by the Hastings Center, 11,000 courses in applied ethics. It is too early to venture more than a suggestion as to what has caused the renaissance of normative ethics. Undoubtedly, the unsettling effects of rapid social and technological change are somehow implicated. But if we cannot confidently identify the cause of the renaissance, we can describe it and comment on its significance for moral education in America and England. And, without looking a gift horse in the mouth, we are permitted to criticize its direction. For not all is cause for self-congratulation.

In reading the articles for a course in applied ethics, students encounter arguments by philosophers who take strong stands on important social questions like abortion, euthanasia, capital punishment, and censorship. By contrast, they may find little to read on private individual virtue and responsibility. Many college ethics courses are primarily concerned with the conduct and policies of schools, hospitals, courts, corporations, and governments; again, the moral responsibilities of the students may be discussed only occasionally. Because most students are not likely to be personally involved in administering the death penalty or selecting candidates for kidney dialysis, and because most will never conduct recombinant DNA research or even have abortions, the effective purpose of such courses in applied ethics is to teach students how to form responsible opinions on social policies—a purpose that is more civic than personal. "Applying" ethics to modern life involves more than learning how to be for or against social and institutional policies. These are important, but they are not enough.

This anthology brings together classical and contemporary writings on such matters as courage, wisdom, compassion, generosity, gratitude, honor, and self-respect. It also includes essays on moral foibles such as hypocrisy, self-deception, jealousy, and narcissism.

vii

More standard materials are included: chapters on theories of moral conduct, free will and determinism, and contemporary social issues. The collection thereby seeks to combine the virtues of current texts on applied ethics with the virtues of more traditional survey texts. In addition, it addresses lively and important issues in personal morality.

Social ethics is only half of normative ethics. Private ethics, including the theory of virtue, is the other half. My colleague Peter Lipton has aptly characterized much of what goes on in courses in practical ethics as "ethics without virtue." I believe we need more balanced and traditional fare. Hence, this anthology.

ACKNOWLEDGMENTS

I would like to thank my husband, Fred Sommers, for the many hours he spent helping me. I owe a special debt of gratitude to Peter Lipton, who not only gave me the idea for this book, but also has been a great help throughout. I thank the Mellon Foundation and Clark University for a grant, and I am deeply indebted to my department secretary, Ethel Theodore, who has been wonderful in every way at each stage of this undertaking. I am grateful to the late Professor Hardy Jones of The University of Nebraska at Lincoln, and to Professors Arthur Caplan of the Hastings Center, Hugh Fleetwood of Western Washington University, Kenneth J. Blankmeyer of Tulsa Junior College, Donald Nolen of Parkland College, and Lynne McFall of The University of Texas at Austin for reviewing the manuscript. Finally, I would like to thank Bill McLane, Robert Fogelin, and Cate Safranek for their excellent editorial advice.

CHRISTINA HOFF SOMMERS

CONTENTS

INTRODUCTION

Why, in novels, films, and television programs, are villains so easy to distinguish from heroes? What is it about, say, Huckleberry Finn or the runaway slave Jim that is unmistakably good, and about Huck's father Pap and the Duke and King that is unmistakably bad? For generations children have loved Cinderella and despised her evil stepsisters. Our moral sympathies are in constant play. We root for the moral heroes of the primetime shows and eagerly await the downfall of the villains they pursue.

The moral dimension of our everyday experience is a pervasive and inescapable fact. In an important sense we are all "moralizers," instinctively applying moral judgment to the fictional and real people of our acquaintance and, in reflective moments, to ourselves as well. Moral philosophy seeks to make sense of this moral dimension in our lives. One objective is moral self-knowledge and self-evaluation. This is notoriously difficult. It is one thing to recognize good and evil when we encounter it in literature or even in our friends; it is quite another to recognize good and evil in ourselves. The philosophical study of morality, by its reasoned approach to the concepts that figure centrally in our moral judgments, can help us be more objective. In particular, it can help by alerting us to some of the characteristic deceptions that prevent us from seeing our own moral virtues and defects.

The philosopher's approach to concepts such as good and evil or vice and virtue differs in important ways from the social scientist's or theologian's. A sociologist or an anthropologist, for example, describes and interprets a society's mores and, in contrast to the moral philosopher, is usually careful to keep the account morally neutral. A theologian will call on us to act in a particular way and to avoid certain sinful practices. By contrast, the moral philosopher does not usually exhort to action. Instead he or she will explain what makes an act right or a person virtuous. In discussing criteria of right action and virtuous character, the philosopher will try to show why certain traits, such as honesty, generosity, and courage, are worthy, and others, such as hypocrisy, selfishness, and cowardice, are not. More generally, the moral philosopher seeks a clear and well-reasoned answer to the question, What is it to be moral?

Moral philosophers have viewed this central question in two distinct ways. Some construe it as asking what we, as responsible agents confronting decisions of right and wrong, ought to do. These moral philosophers, then, see it as their task to formulate general principles of behavior that define our duties by distinguishing right actions from wrong ones. A theory that emphasizes moral duties and actions is *action based*. A second approach—called *virtue based*—takes the central question of morality to be, What sort of person should I be? Here the emphasis is not so much on what to *do* as on what to *be*. For virtue-based theorists, the object of moral education is to produce a virtuous individual. They therefore have much to say about moral education and character development. By concentrating attention on character rather than action, the philosopher of virtue tacitly assumes that a virtuous person's actions generally fall within the range of what is right and fair.

In the modern period that goes back to David Hume and Immanuel Kant, moral philosophy has tended to be action based. The reader will learn some of the reasons for the recent neglect of virtue and character from the essays by Bernard Mayo, Anthony Quinton, and Alasdair MacIntyre. Mayo, Quinton, and MacIntyre are among the growing number of philosophers who feel that an exclusively action-based approach is inadequate. I have attempted to give equal space to virtue-based theories.

The eight chapters of this book are distinguished thematically. The opening essays highlight the crucial importance of character and of the capacity for sympathy and compassion. These essays, along with several others in the body of the book, suggest that being moral is never simply a matter of knowing how one should act. Sociopaths may be well aware of the right thing to do but, because they lack human sympathy, simply do not care enough to be moral except where a display of moral behavior serves their own purpose. All the same, knowing how to act is essential to being moral. The essays in Chapter 2 are devoted to the exposition and criticism of several action-based theories such as utilitarianism, Kantianism, and egoism.

The selections on virtue and vice in Chapters 3 and 4 range from classical to contemporary. Aristotle's (and Plato's) thesis that happiness is tied to the moral virtues is a central theme. The religious and philosophical discussions of vice and virtue differ in characteristic ways. For a theologian such as Augustine or Abelard, vice is sin construed as rebellion against the decrees of God. For a philosopher such as Aristotle or Plutarch, vice is more akin to physical illness or deformity. The selections contain representative analyses of such virtues as generosity and courage, and such vices as envy and self-deception. One essay critically examines the thesis, held in common by most philosophers and theologians, that the person of vice is necessarily unhappy.

One of moral philosophy's fundamental problems concerns the extent to which we may be held *responsible* for what we do. Some philosophers believe that we are not free because everything we do is causally determined. They argue that, since we cannot have acted otherwise, the very idea of moral responsibility is untenable. Others hold that we are free. Still others argue that freedom to act is compatible with determinism and that moral responsibility simply requires us to be free in the sense of being externally unconstrained. The essays in Chapter 5 are devoted to this very difficult question.

Of course, if we view ourselves as *forced* to do what we do, then we can hardly blame ourselves for our own shortcomings. The price for this view of ourselves is a loss of self-respect. Self-respect is an intimate part of moral consciousness; part of being moral is respecting ourselves as well as respecting others. Respect for others is bound up with self-respect since we cannot respect ourselves as moral beings unless we value ourselves for treating others respectfully. The notions of honor and shame are related to these notions of self-respect. Chapter 6 includes discussions of the roles of self-respect and honor in the development of moral character in ancient and modern times.

The essays in the last two chapters belong mainly to that part of moral philosophy called applied ethics. Here the student will encounter philosophers arguing different sides of topical moral issues such as divorce, rearing of children, and duties to one's parents, as well as more general social issues such as the morality of abortion, exploitation of animals for food and research, and the problem of world hunger. The individual's obligations in the context of a morally concerned social system raise special problems concerning the relation of private and social ethics. We tend, for example, to hold the state responsible for such things as care of the elderly, which in previous generations was primarily an individual or family responsibility. Two of the philosophers represented in the last section argue that the recent shift of responsibility to social institutions is morally backward and generally harmful. Here, too, one's view of the matter will depend on one's basic approach to morality. Action-based moralists, such as utilitarians, will not be disturbed that the elderly are cared for increasingly by the state; what primarily matters is that they *are* being cared for. But virtue-based moralists tend to be concerned with the decline of individual moral initiative that they attribute to an increasing reliance on social agency. In this controversy, as in many others throughout the book, the student will undoubtedly locate his or her own position.

What, finally, may the open-minded and careful reader of a comprehensive text on moral philosophy expect to gain? First, if not foremost, the reader will acquire a great deal of knowledge of the classical approaches to moral philosophy and, with this, some sense of the moral tradition of Western civilization as Greek and Judeo-Christian thought have influenced it. Second, the reader will become aware of some of the central problem areas in ethics and will be in a better position to approach them with the confidence that comes with historical perspective and a sharpened moral insight. Social change and novel technologies bring about new problems, each with its moral dimension. Yet morality itself is not really changed in any radical way. There will always be a right and decent way to cope with the new situations that confront us.

VICE AND VIRTUE IN EVERYDAY LIFE

Introductory Readings in Ethics

Chapter

1

GOOD AND EVIL

Much of moral philosophy is a disciplined effort to systematize and explain our most common convictions about good and evil and right and wrong. Proper ethical philosophy takes the simplest moral truths as its starting point. Almost no one doubts that cruelty is wrong. But philosophers differ on how to explain what is wrong about acting cruelly and even about the meaning of right and wrong. So we have various systems of moral theory. Inevitably we have the possibility that a philosopher may devise a pseudo-ethical doctrine that loses sight of basic intuitions about human dignity and elementary decency. When such a doctrine achieves currency and popular respectability, it becomes a powerful force for evil. For then, what passes as conventional wisdom allows the average person to behave in reprehensible but conventionally acceptable ways.

In three of the selections in Chapter 1 we find examples of the ways the moral intuitions of the individual may conflict with publicly accepted principles that are not grounded in respect for human dignity. In the first two selections, "From Cruelty to Goodness" by Philip Hallie and "The Conscience of Huckleberry Finn" by Jonathan Bennett, the moral failure of principle is easy to diagnose. A dominant group adopts a philsophy that permits it to confine its moral concern to those inside the group, treating outsiders as beyond the moral pale; their pain, their dignity, even their very lives merit no moral consideration. Huckleberry Finn, being white, is within the moral domain. His mentors have taught him that he does not owe moral behavior to slaves. Yet Huck treats Jim, the runaway slave, as if he too deserves the respect due a white person. And therein lies Huck's conflict. Everything he conventionally believes tells him he is doing wrong in helping Jim elude his pursuers.

Mark Twain's account of the conflict between official "book" morality and the ground-level morality of an innately decent and sympathetic person is one of the best in literature. Usually the conflict is embodied in two protagonists (Victor Hugo's novel *Les Misérables* is an example), but Huck Finn's conflict is within himself. And we are glad that his decency is stronger than his book morality. Both Jonathan Bennett and Philip Hallie quote the Nazi officer Heinrich Himmler, one of the fathers of the "final solution," as a spokesman for those who advocate suspending all moral feeling toward a particular group. Interestingly, Himmler considered himself all the more moral for being above pitying the children and other innocent victims outside the domain of moral consideration. Indeed, we hear stories of Germans who were conscience-stricken because—against their principles—they allowed some Jews to escape.

Our dismay at man's inhumanity to man is qualified by the inspiring example of the residents of the French village Le Chambon-sur-Lignon who acted together to care for and save 6,000 Jews, mostly children, from the Nazis. Le Chambon is said to have been the safest place in Europe for a Jew during the Second World War. From his studies of the village, Hallie concludes that Le Chambon residents successfully combatted evil because they never allowed themselves to be blind to the victim's point of view. "When we are blind to that point of view we can countenance and perpetrate cruelty with impunity." The true morality of Le Chambon drives out false and hypocritical Nazi "decencies" that ignore the most elementary moral intuitions and that permit and encourage the horrors of Himmler's and Hitler's Germany.

The example of Le Chambon is the proper antidote to the moral passivity that is the condition of many people today, and which Martin Gansberg dramatically describes in "38 Who Saw Murder

Didn't Call Police." In sharp contrast to the residents of Le Chambon, the spectators who witnessed the murder of Kitty Genovese were literally demoralized. Not only did they fail to intervene; they did not even call for help.

Richard Taylor's article "Compassion" is about the bedrock moral intuitions that are the raw data of moral theory. He presents several case studies of goodness and wickedness and points out that most people recognize goodness when they see it, even if they have never read any treatises on morality. Huck Finn would have been amazed but relieved to read Taylor's article: In it he would have found a moralist who thoroughly approves of him.

In his selection, Josiah Royce defends a morality that respects human dignity. Beginning from the axiom that we owe respect and decency to our neighbor, Royce confronts the question that the Nazi and all those who ignore the humanity of special groups pervert: Who, then, are our neighbors? Royce answers that our neighbors include anyone with feelings: "Pain is pain, joy is joy, everywhere even as in thee." Royce calls this the Moral Insight. He points out that treating strangers with care and solicitude is hardly unnatural; for each of us, our future self is like a stranger to us, yet we are naturally concerned with the welfare of that stranger.

The moral blindness that is the opposite of Royce's Insight has tragic consequences not only for the victim whose humanity is ignored, but also for those who ignore it. This theme in Shakespeare's *King Lear* is the focus of Lionel Trilling's "The Tragedy of King Lear." Out of foolish pride and moral confusion King Lear thrusts aside his youngest daughter and divides his kingdom among those who flatter him. The play depicts how he suffers the consequences of his lack of sympathy toward the innocent and decent people who have depended on him. Shakespeare, says Trilling, is fully aware that human beings are at the mercy of nature: We grow old, our powers diminish, and we die. But Lear's tragedy and that of his subjects is not the work of nature; it is the result of Lear's culpable self-deception and of the willfully cruel acts of other people. Trilling speaks of a small "precinct of freedom" in which human choice determines whether we live in a "moralized universe" or a demoralized universe of degradation and chaos. That freedom entails human responsibility for evil—both for those who do evil and for those who passively permit it. But it is also at work in the likes of Huckleberry Finn and the people of Le Chambon.

From Cruelty to Goodness

PHILIP HALLIE

Philip Hallie (b. 1922) is a professor of philosophy at Wesleyan University. His published works include *The Paradox of Cruelty* (1969) and *Lest Innocent Blood Be Shed* (1979).

Hallie considers institutionalized cruelty and finds that, besides physically assaulting its victims, it almost always assaults their dignity and self-respect. As an example of the antithesis of institutionalized cruelty, Hallie cites the residents of the French village of Le Chambon who, at grave risk to their lives, saved 6,000 Jews from the Nazis. For him the opposite of being cruel is not merely ceasing to be cruel; nor is it fighting cruelty with violence and hatred (though this may be necessary). Rather, it is epitomized in the unambiguous and unpretentious goodness of the citizens of Le Chambon who followed the positive Biblical injunctions "Defend the fatherless" and "Be your brother's keeper," as well as the negative injunctions "Thou shalt not murder or betray."

I am a student of ethics, of good and evil; but my approach to these two rather melodramatic terms is skeptical. I am in the tradition of the ancient Greek *skeptikoi*, whose name means "in-

FROM CRUELTY TO GOODNESS © Institute of Society, Ethics and the Life Sciences, 360 Broadway, Hastings-on-Hudson, N.Y. 10706. Reprinted by permission of the copyright holder.

quirers" or "investigators." And what we investigate is relationships among particular facts. What we put into doubt are the intricate webs of high-level abstractions that passed for philosophizing in the ancient world, and that still pass for philosophizing. My approach to good and evil emphasizes not abstract common nouns like "justice," but proper names and verbs. Names and verbs keep us close to the facts better than do our highfalutin common nouns. Names refer to particular people, and verbs connect subjects with predicates *in time*, while common nouns are above all this.

One of the words that is important to me is my own name. For me, philosophy is personal; it is closer to literature and history than it is to the exact sciences, closer to the passions, actions, and common sense of individual persons than to a dispassionate technical science. It has to do with the personal matter of wisdom. And so ethics for me is personal—my story, and not necessarily (though possibly) yours. It concerns particular people at particular times.

But ethics is more than such particulars. It involves abstractions, that is, rules, laws, ideals. When you look at the ethical magnates of history you see in their words and deeds two sorts of ethical rules: negative and positive. The negative rules are scattered throughout the Bible, but Moses brought down from Mount Sinai the main negative ethical rules of the West: Thou shalt not murder; thou shalt not betray. . . . The positive injunctions are similarly spread throughout the Bible. In the first chapter of the book of Isaiah we are told to ". . . defend the fatherless, plead for the widow . . ." The negative ethic forbids certain actions; the positive ethic demands certain actions. To follow the negative ethic is to be decent, to have clean hands. But to follow the positive ethic, to be one's brother's keeper, is to be more than decent—it is to be active, even aggressive. If the negative ethic is one of decency, the positive one is the ethic of riskful, strenuous nobility.

In my early studies of particularized ethical terms, I found myself dwelling upon negative ethics, upon prohibitions. And among the most conspicuous prohibitions I found embodied in history was the prohibition against deliberate harmdoing, against cruelty. "Thou shalt not be cruel" had as much to do with the nightmare of history as did the prohibitions against murder and betrayal. In fact, many of the Ten Commandments—especially those against murder, adultery, stealing, and betrayal—were ways of prohibiting cruelty.

Early in my research it became clear that there are various approaches to cruelty, as the different commandments suggest. For instance, there is the way reflected in the origins of the word "cruel." The Latin *crudus* is related to still older words standing for bloodshed, or raw flesh. According to the etymology of the word, cruelty involves the spilling of blood.

But modern dictionaries give the word a different meaning. They define it as "disposed to giving pain." They emphasize awareness, not simply bloodshed. After all, they seem to say, you cannot be cruel to a dead body. There is no cruelty without consciousness.

And so I found myself studying the kinds of awareness associated with the hurting of human beings. It is certainly true that for millennia in history and literature people have been torturing each other not only with hard weapons but also with hard words.

Still, the word "pain" seemed to be a simplistic and superficial way of describing the many different sorts of cruelty. In Reska Weiss's *Journey Through Hell* (London, 1961) there is a brief passage of one of the deepest cruelties that Nazis perpetrated upon extermination camp inmates. On a march

> Urine and excreta poured down the prisoners' legs, and by night-fall the excrement, which had frozen to our limbs, gave off its stench. . . .

And Weiss goes on to talk not in terms of "pain" or bloodshed, but in other terms:

> . . . We were really no longer human beings in the accepted sense. Not even animals, but putrefying corpses moving on two legs. . . .

There is one factor that the idea of "pain" and the simpler idea of bloodshed do not touch: cruelty, not playful, quotidian teasing or ragging, but cruelty (what the anti-cruelty societies usually call "substantial cruelty") involves the maiming of a person's dignity, the crushing of a person's self-respect. Bloodshed, the idea of pain (which is usually something involving a localizable occurrence, localizable in a tooth, in a head, in short, in the body), these are superficial ideas of cruelty. A whip, bleeding flesh, these are what the journalists of cruelty emphasize, following the etymology and dictionary meaning of the word. But the depths of an understand-

6

ing of cruelty lie in the depths of an understanding of human dignity and of how you can maim it without bloodshed, and often without localizable bodily pain.

In excremental assault, in the process of keeping camp inmates from wiping themselves or from going to the latrine, and in making them drink water from a toilet bowl full of excreta (and the excreta of the guards at that) localizable pain is nothing. Deep humiliation is everything. We human beings believe in hierarchies, whether we are skeptics or not about human value. There is a hierarchical gap between shit and me. We are even above using the word. We are "above" walking around besmirched with feces. Our dignity, whatever the origins of that dignity may be, does not permit it. In order to be able to want to live, in order to be able to walk erect, we must respect ourselves as beings "higher" than our feces. When we feel that we are not "higher" than dirt or filth, then our lives are maimed at the very center, in the very depths, not merely in some localizable portion of our bodies. And when our lives are so maimed we become things, slaves, instruments. From ancient times until this moment, and as long as there will be human beings on this planet, there are those who know this and will use it, just as the Roman slave owners and the Southern American slave owners knew it when—one time a year—they encouraged the slaves to drink all the alcohol they could drink so that they could get bestially drunk and then even more bestially sick afterwards, under the eyes of their generous owners. The self-hatred, the loss of self-respect that the Saturnalia created in ancient Rome, say, made it possible to continue using the slaves as things, since they themselves came to think of themselves as things, as subhuman tools of the owners and the overseers.

Institutionalized cruelty, I learned, is the subtlest kind of cruelty. In episodic cruelty the victim knows he is being hurt, and his victimizer knows it too. But in a persistent pattern of humiliation that endures for years in a community, both the victim and the victimizer find ways of obscuring the harm that is being done. Blacks come to think of themselves as inferior, even esthetically inferior (black is "dirty"); and Jews come to think of themselves as inferior, even esthetically (dark hair and aquiline noses are "ugly"), so that the way they are being treated is justified by their "actual" inferiority, by the inferiority they themselves feel.

A similar process happens in the minds of the victimizers in

7

institutionalized cruelty. They feel that since they are superior, even esthetically ("to be blonde is to be beautiful"), they deserve to do what they wish, deserve to have these lower creatures under their control. The words of Heinrich Himmler, head of the Nazi SS, in Posen in the year 1943 in a speech to his SS subordinates in a closed session, show how institutionalized cruelty can obscure harm-doing:

> . . . the words come so easily. "The Jewish people will be exter-minated," says every party member, "of course. It's in our program . . . extermination. We'll take care of it." And then they come, these nice 80 million Germans, and every one of them has his decent Jew. Sure the others are swine, but his one is a fine Jew . . . Most of you will know what it means to have seen 100 corpses together, or 500 or 1000. To have made one's way through that, and . . . to have remained a decent person throughout, that is what has made us hard. That is a page of glory in our history. . . .

In this speech he was making a sharp distinction between the program of crushing the Jews and the personal sentiments of indi-vidual Germans. The program stretched over years; personal senti-ments were momentary. He was pleading for the program, for institutionalized destruction.

But one of the most interesting parts of the speech occurs toward the end of it:

> . . . in sum, we can say that we fulfilled the heaviest of tasks [destroying the Jews] in love to our people. And we suffered no harm in our essence, in our soul, in our character. . . .

Commitment that overrides all sentimentality transforms cruelty and destruction into moral nobility, and commitment is the life-blood of an institution.

Cruelty and the Power Relationships

But when I studied all these ways that we have used the word "cruelty," I was nagged by the feeling that I had not penetrated into its inner structure. I was classifying, sorting out symptoms; but symptoms are signals, and what were the symptoms signals *of*? I felt like a person who had been studying cancer by sorting out brief pains from persistent pains, pains in the belly from pains in the head. I was being superficial, and I was not asking the question, "What are the forces behind these kinds of cruelty?" I felt that there were such forces, but as yet I had not touched them.

Then one day I was reading in one of the great autobiographies of western civilization, Frederick Douglass's *Life and Times*. The passage I was reading was about Douglass's thoughts on the origins of slavery. He was asking himself: "How could these whites keep us enslaved?" And he suddenly realized:

> My faculties and powers of body and soul are not my own, but are the property of a fellow-mortal in no sense superior to me, except that he has the physical power to compel me to be owned and controlled by him. By the combined physical force of the community I am his slave—a slave for life.

And then I saw that a disparity in power lay at the center of the dynamism of cruelty. If it was institutional cruelty it was in all likelihood a difference involving both verbal and physical power that kept the cruelty going. The power of the majority and the weakness of a minority were at the center of the institutional cruelty of slavery and of Nazi anti-Semitism. The whites not only outnumbered the blacks in America, but had economic and political ascendancy over them. But just as important as these "physical" powers was the power that words like "nigger" and "slave" gave the white majority. Their language sanctified if it did not create their power ascendancy over the blacks, and one of the most important projects of the slaveholders and their allies was that of seeing to it that the blacks themselves thought of themselves in just these powerless terms. They utilized the language to convince not only the whites but the blacks themselves that blacks were weak in mind, in will power, and in worth. These words were like the excremental assault in the killing camps of the Nazis: they diminished both the respect the victimizers might have for their victims and the respect the victims might have for themselves.

It occurred to me that if a power differential is crucial to the idea of cruelty, then when that power differential is maintained, cruelty will tend to be maintained, and when that power differential is eliminated, cruelty will tend to be eliminated. And this seemed to work. In all kinds of cruelty, violent and polite, episodic and institutional, when the victim arms himself with the appropriate strength, the cruelty diminishes or disappears. When Jews joined

9

the Bush Warriors of France, the Maquis, and became powerful enough to strike at Vichy or the Nazis, they stopped being victims of French and Nazi cruelty. When Frederick Douglass learned to use the language with great skill and expressiveness, and when he learned to use his physical strength against his masters, the power differential between him and his masters diminished, and so did their cruelty to him. In his autobiography he wrote:

> A man without force is without the essential dignity of humanity. Human nature is so constituted that it cannot honor a helpless man, though it can pity him, and even this it cannot do long if signs of power do not arise.

When I looked back at my own childhood in Chicago, I remembered that the physical and mental cruelties that I suffered in the slums of the southwest side when I was about ten years old sharply diminished and finally disappeared when I learned how to defend myself physically and verbally. It is exactly this lesson that Douglass learned while growing up in the cruel institution of slavery.

Cruelty then, whatever else it is, is a kind of power relationship, an imbalance of power wherein the stronger party becomes the victimizer and the weaker becomes the victim. And since many general terms are most swiftly understood in relationship with their opposites (just as "heavy" can be understood most handily in relationship with what we mean by "light") the opposite of cruelty lay in a situation where there is no imbalance of power. The opposite of cruelty, I learned, was freedom from that unbalanced power relationship. Either the victim should get stronger and stand up to the victimizer, and thereby bring about a balance of their powers, or the victim should free himself from the whole relationship by flight.

In pursuing this line of thought, I came to believe that, again, dictionaries are misleading: many of them give "kindness" as the antonym for "cruelty." In studying slavery in America and the concentration camps of central Europe I found that kindness could be the ultimate cruelty, especially when it was given within that unbalanced power relationship. A kind overseer or a kind camp guard can exacerbate cruelty, can remind his victim that there are other relationships than the relationship of cruelty, and can make the victim deeply bitter, especially when he sees the self-satisfied smile of his victimizer. He is being cruelly treated when he is given a penny or a bun after having endured the crushing and grinding of his mental and bodily well-being. As Frederick Douglass put it:

> The kindness of the slave-master only gilded the chain. It detracted nothing from its weight or strength. The thought that men are for other and better uses than slavery throve best under the gentle treatment of a kind master.

No, I learned, the opposite of cruelty is not kindness. The opposite of the cruelty of the overseer in American slavery was not the kindness of that overseer for a moment or for a day. An episodic kindness is not the opposite of an institutionalized cruelty. The opposite of institutionalized cruelty is freedom from the cruel relationship.

It is important to see how perspectival the whole meaning of cruelty is. From the perspective of the SS guard or the southern overseer, a bit of bread, a smile is indeed a diminution of cruelty. But in the relationship of cruelty, the point of view of the victimizer is of only minor importance; it is the point of view of the victim that is authoritative. The victim feels the suffering in his own mind and body, whereas the victimizer, like Himmler's "hard" and "decent" Nazi, can be quite unaware of that suffering. The sword does not feel the pain that it inflicts. Do not ask it about suffering.

Goodness Personified in Le Chambon

All these considerations drove me to write my book *The Paradox of Cruelty*. But with the book behind me, I felt a deep discontent. I saw cruelty as an embodiment, a particular case of evil. But if cruelty is one of the main evils of human history, why is the opposite of cruelty not one of the key goods of human history? Freedom from the cruel relationship, either by escaping it or by redressing the imbalance of power, was not essential to what western philosophers and theologians have thought of as goodness. Escape is a negative affair. Goodness has something positive in it, something triumphantly affirmative.

Hoping for a hint of goodness in the very center of evil, I started looking closely at the so-called "medical experiments" of the Nazis upon children, usually Jewish and Gypsy children, in the death camps. Here were the weakest of the weak. Not only were they despised minorities, but they were, as individuals, still in their nonage. They were dependents. Here the power imbalance between the cruel experimenters and their victims was at its greatest. But instead of seeing light or finding insight by going down into this hell, into the deepest depth of cruelty, I found myself unwillingly becoming part of the world I was studying. I found myself either yearning to be viciously cruel to the victimizers of the children, or I found myself feeling compassion for the children, feeling their despair and pain as they looked up at the men and women in white coats cutting off their fingertips one at a time, or breaking their slender bones, or wounding their internal organs. Either I became a would-be victimizer or one more Jewish victim, and in either case I was not achieving insight, only misery, like so many other students of the Holocaust. And when I was trying to be "objective" about my studies, when I was succeeding at being indifferent to both the victimizers and the victims of these cruel relationships, I became cold; I became another monster who could look upon the maiming of a child with an indifferent eye.

To relieve this unending suffering, from time to time I would turn to the literature of the French resistance to the Nazis. I had been trained by the U.S. Army to understand it. The resistance was a way of trying to redress the power imbalance between Hitler's Fortress Europe and Hitler's victims, and so I saw it as an enemy of cruelty. Still, its methods were often cruel like the methods of most power struggles, and I had little hope of finding goodness here. We soldiers violated the negative ethic forbidding killing in order, we thought, to follow the positive ethic of being our brothers' keepers.

And then one gray April afternoon I found a brief article on the French village of Le Chambon-sur-Lignon. I shall not analyze here the tears of amazement and gladness and release from despair—in short, of joy—that I shed when I first read that story. Tears themselves interest me greatly—but not the tears of melancholy hindsight and existential despair; rather the tears of awe you experience when the realization of an ideal suddenly appears before your very eyes or thunders inside your mind; these tears interest me.

And one of the reasons I wept at first reading about Le Chambon in those brief, inaccurate pages was that at last I had discovered an embodiment of goodness in opposition to cruelty. I had discovered in the flesh and blood of history, in people with definite names in a definite place at a definite time in the nightmare of history, what no classical or religious ethicist could deny was goodness.

The French Protestant village of Le Chambon, located in the Cévennes Mountains of southeastern France, and with a population of about 3,500, saved the lives of about 6,000 people, most of them Jewish children whose parents had been murdered in the killing camps of central Europe. Under a national government which was not only collaborating with the Nazi conquerors of France but frequently trying to outdo the Germans in anti-Semitism in order to please their conquerors, and later under the day-to-day threat of destruction by the German Armed SS, they started to save children in the winter of 1940, the winter after the fall of France, and they continued to do so until the war in France was over. They sheltered the refugees in their own homes and in various houses they established especially for them; and they took many of them across the terrible mountains to neutral Geneva, Switzerland, in the teeth of French and German police and military power. The people of Le Chambon are poor, and the Huguenot faith to which they belong is a diminishing faith in Catholic and atheist France; but their spiritual power, their capacity to act in unison against the victimizers who surrounded them, was immense, and more than a match for the military power of those victimizers.

But for me as an ethicist the heart of the matter was not only their special power. What interested me was that they obeyed *both* the negative and the positive injunctions of ethics; they were good not only in the sense of trying to be their brothers' keepers, protecting the victim, "defending the fatherless," to use the language of Isaiah; they were also good in the sense that they obeyed the negative injunctions against killing and betraying. While those around them—including myself—were murdering in order presumably, to help mankind in some way or other, they murdered nobody, and betrayed not a single child in those long and dangerous four years. For me as an ethicist they were the embodiment of unambiguous goodness.

But for me as a student of cruelty they were something more: they were an embodiment of the opposite of cruelty. And so, somehow, at last, I had found goodness in opposition to cruelty. In studying their story, and in telling it in *Lest Innocent Blood Be Shed*, I learned that the opposite of cruelty is not simply freedom from the cruel relationship; it is *hospitality*. It lies not only in something negative, an absence of cruelty or of imbalance; it lies in unsentimental, efficacious love. The opposite of the cruelties of the camps was not the liberation of the camps, the cleaning out of the barracks and the cessation of the horrors. All of this was the *end* of the cruelty relationship, not the opposite of that relationship. And it was not even the end of it, because the victims would never forget and would remain in agony as long as they remembered their humiliation and suffering. No, the opposite of cruelty was not the liberation of the camps, not freedom; it was the hospitality of the people of Chambon, and of very few others during the Holocaust. The opposite of cruelty was the kind of goodness that happened in Chambon.

Let me explain the difference between liberation and hospitality by telling you about a letter I received a year ago from a woman who had been saved by the people of Le Chambon when she was a young girl. She wrote:

> Never was there a question that the Chambonnais would not share all they had with us, meager as it was. One Chambonnais once told me that even if there was less, they still would want more for us.

And she goes on:

> It was indeed a very different attitude from the one in Switzerland, which while saving us also resented us so much.
>
> If today we are not bitter people like most survivors it can only be due to the fact that we met people like the people of Le Chambon, who showed to us simply that life can be different, that there are people who care, that people can live together and even risk their own lives for their fellow man.

The Swiss liberated refugees and removed them from the cruel relationship; the people of Le Chambon did more. They taught them that goodness could conquer cruelty, that loving hospitality could remove them from the cruel relationship. And they taught me this, too.

It is important to emphasize that cruelty is not simply an episodic, momentary matter, especially institutional cruelty like that of Nazism or slavery. As we have seen throughout this essay, not only does it persist while it is being exerted upon the weak; *it can persist in the survivors* after they have escaped the power relationship. The survivors torture themselves, continue to suffer, continue to maim their own lives long after the actual torture is finished. The self-hatred and rage of the blacks and the despair of the native

Americans and the Jews who have suffered under institutional crushing and maiming are continuations of original cruelties. And these continuations exist because only a superficial liberation from torture has occurred. The sword has stopped falling on their flesh in the old obvious ways, but the wounds still bleed. I am not saying that the village of Chambon healed these wounds—they go too deep. What I am saying is that the people I have talked to who were once children in Le Chambon have more hope for their species and more respect for themselves as human beings than most other survivors I have met. The enduring hospitality they met in Le Chambon helped them find realistic hope in a world of persisting cruelty.

What was the nature of this hospitality that saved and deeply changed so many lives? It is hard to summarize briefly what the Chambonnais did, and above all how they did it. The morning after a new refugee family came to town they would find on their front door a wreath with *"Bienvenue!"* "Welcome!" painted on a piece of cardboard attached to the wreath. Nobody knew who had brought the wreath; in effect, the whole town had brought it.

It was mainly the women of Chambon who gave so much more than shelter to these, the most hated enemies of the Nazis. There was Madame Barraud, a tiny Alsatian, who cared for the refugee boys in her house with all the love such a tiny body could hold, and who cared for the way they felt day and night. And there were others.

But there was one person without whom Le Chambon could not have become the safest place in Europe for Jews: the Huguenot minister of the village, André Trocmé. Trocmé was a passionately religious man. He was massive, more than six feet tall, blonde, with a quick temper. Once long after the war, while he was lecturing on the main project of his life, the promotion of the idea of nonviolence in international relations, one of the members of his audience started to whisper a few words to his neighbor. Trocmé let this go on for a few moments, then interrupted his speech, walked up to the astonished whisperer, raised his massive arm, pointed toward the door, and yelled, "Out! Out! Get out!" And the lecture was on nonviolence.

The center of his thought was the belief that God showed how important man was by becoming Himself a human being, and by

15

becoming a particular sort of human being who was the embodiment of sacrificially generous love. For Trocmé, every human being was like Jesus, had God in him or her, and was just as precious as God Himself. And when Trocmé with the help of the Quakers and others organized his village into the most efficient rescue machine in Europe, he did so not only to save the Jews, but also to save the Nazis and their collaborators. He wanted to keep them from blackening their souls with more evil—he wanted to save them, the victimizers, from evil.

One of the reasons he was successful was that the Huguenots had been themselves persecuted for hundreds of years by the kings of France, and they knew what persecution was. In fact, when the people of Chambon took Jewish children and whole families across the mountains of southeastern France into neutral Switzerland, they often followed pathways that had been taken by Huguenots in their flight from the Dragoons of the French kings.

A particular incident from the story of Le Chambon during the Nazi occupation of France will explain succinctly why he was successful in making the village a village of refuge. But before I relate the story, I must point out that the people of the village did not think of themselves as "successful," let alone as "good." From their point of view, they did not do anything that required elaborate explanation. When I asked them why they helped these dangerous guests, they invariably answered, "What do you mean, 'Why'? Where else could they go? How could you turn them away? What is so special about being ready to help (*prête à servir*)? There was nothing else to do." And some of them laughed in amazement when I told them that I thought they were "good people." They saw no alternative to their actions and to the way they acted, and therefore they saw what they did as necessary, not something to be picked out for praise. Helping these guests was for them as natural as breathing or eating—one does not think of alternatives to these functions; they did not think of alternatives to sheltering people who were endangering not only the lives of their hosts but the lives of all the people of the village.

And now the story. One afternoon a refugee woman knocked on the door of a farmhouse outside the village. The farmers around the village proper were Protestants like most of the others in Chambon, but with one difference: they were mostly "Darbystes," followers of a strange Scot named Darby, who taught their ancestors

16

in the nineteenth century to believe every word of the Bible, and indeed, who had them memorize the Bible. They were literal fundamentalists. The farm-woman opened the door to the refugee and invited her into the kitchen where it was warm. Standing in the middle of the floor the refugee, in heavily accented French, asked for eggs for her children. In those days of very short supplies, people with children often went to the farmers in the "gray market" (neither black nor exactly legal) to get necessary food. This was early in 1941, and the farmers were not yet accustomed to the refugees. The farm-woman looked into the eyes of the shawled refugee and asked, "Are you Jewish?" The woman started to tremble, but she could not lie, even though that question was usually the beginning of the end of life for Jews in Hitler's Fortress Europe. She answered, "Yes."

The woman ran from the kitchen to the staircase nearby, and while the refugee trembled with terror in the kitchen, she called up the stairs, "Husband, children, come down, come down! We have in our house at this very moment a representative of the Chosen People!"

Not all the Protestants in Chambon were Darbyste fundamentalists; but almost all were convinced that people are the children of God, and are as precious as God Himself. Their leaders were Huguenot preachers and their following of the negative and positive commandments of the Bible came in part from their personal generosity and courage, but also in part from the depths of their religious conviction that we are all children of God, and we must take care of each other lovingly. This combined with the ancient and deep historical ties between the Huguenots and the Jews of France and their own centuries of persecution by the Dragoons and Kings of France helped make them what they were, "always ready to help," as the Chambonnais saying goes.

A Choice of Perspectives

We have come a long way from cruelty to the people of Chambon, just as I have come a long way in my research from concrete evil to concrete goodness. Let me conclude with a point that has been alternately hinted at and stressed in the course of this essay.

A few months after *Lest Innocent Blood Be Shed* was published I received a letter from Massachusetts that opened as follows:

I have read your book, and I believe that you mushy-minded moralists should be awakened to the facts. Nothing happened in Le Chambon, nothing of any importance whatsoever.

The Holocaust, dear Professor, was like a geological event, like an earthquake. No person could start it; no person could change it; and no person could end it. And no small group of persons could do so either. It was the armies and the nations that performed actions that counted. Individuals did nothing. You sentimentalists have got to learn that the great masses and big political ideas make the difference. Your people and the people they saved simply do not exist. . .

Now between this position and mine there is an abyss that no amount of shouted arguments or facts can cross. And so I shall not answer this letter with a tightly organized reply. I shall answer it only by telling you that one of the reasons institutional cruelty exists and persists is that people believe that individuals can do nothing, that only vast ideologies and armies can act meaningfully. Every act of institutional cruelty—Nazism, slavery, and all the others—lives not with people in the concrete, but with abstractions that blind people to individuals. Himmler's speech to the SS leadership in 1943 is full of phrases like "exterminating a bacillus," and "The Jewish people will be exterminated." And in that speech he attacks any German who believes in "his decent Jew." Institutional cruelty, like other misleading approaches to ethics, blinds us to the victim's point of view; and when we are blind to that point of view we can countenance and perpetrate cruelty with impunity.

I have told you that I cannot and will not try to refute the letter from Massachusetts. I shall only summarize the point of view of this essay with another story.

I was lecturing a few months ago in Minneapolis, and when I finished talking about the Holocaust and the village of Le Chambon, a woman stood up and asked me if the village of Le Chambon was in the Department of Haute-Loire, the high sources of the Loire River. Obviously she was French, with her accent; and all French people know that there are many villages called "Le Chambon" in France, just as any American knows that there are many "Main Streets" in the United States. I said that Le Chambon was indeed in the Haute-Loire.

She said, "Then you have been speaking about the village that saved all three of my children. I want to thank you for writing this book, not only because the story will now be permanent, but also because I shall be able to talk about those terrible days with Americans now, for they will understand those days better than they have. You see, you Americans, though you sometimes cross the oceans, live on an island here as far as war is concerned. . .''

Then she asked to come up and say one sentence. There was not a sound, not even breathing, to be heard in the room. She came to the front of the room and said, "The Holocaust was storm, lightning, thunder, wind, rain, yes. And Le Chambon was the rainbow."

Only from her perspective can you understand the cruelty and the goodness I have been talking about, not from the point of view of the gentleman from Massachusetts. You must choose which perspective is best, and your choice will have much to do with your feelings about the preciousness of life, and not only the preciousness of other people's lives. If the lives of others are precious to you, your life will become more precious to you.

STUDY QUESTIONS

1. Distinguish between positive and negative moral injunctions. Do you agree with Hallie that we need both for moral decency?
2. Do you agree with Hallie that cruelty is prevalent when a serious imbalance of power exists among people? Can we be cruel to our equals?
3. Why does Hallie deny that kindness is the opposite of cruelty? What does he consider to be cruelty's opposite?
4. What does the writer Terence des Pres mean when he says of Le Chambon, "Those events took place and therefore demand a place in our view of the world"?
5. With whom do you agree more: (a) the person from Massachusetts who wrote and called Hallie a "mushy-minded moralist" who has failed to realize that the Holocaust was like a geological event that could not be stopped or modified, or (b) Hallie, who claims that Le Chambon teaches us that goodness can conquer cruelty?

The Conscience of Huckleberry Finn

JONATHAN BENNETT

Jonathan Bennett (b. 1930) is a professor of philosophy at Syracuse University. He is the author of several books, including *Rationality* (1964) and *Linguistic Behavior* (1976).

In this article Bennett considers the moral consciences of Huckleberry Finn, the Nazi officer Heinrich Himmler, and the Calvinist theologian Jonathan Edwards. He is interested in how each, in his own way, resolves the conflict between his human sympathies and the moral doctrine he is following that requires him to override those sympathies. Huck Finn develops a deep attachment to Jim, the runaway slave, but the official morality of his community does not allow for fellow feelings towards slaves. When forced to choose between his kindly feelings and the official morality, Huck gives up on morality. Himmler set his sympathies aside. Jonathan Edwards's case represents a third way out: he allowed himself no sympathies at all. Bennett finds Edwards's solution to be as bad as Himmler's, if not worse. Bennett concludes that while we should not give our sympathies a "blank check," we must always give them great weight and be wary of acting on any principle that conflicts with them.

THE CONSCIENCE OF HUCKLEBERRY FINN From *Philosophy* 49 (1974): 123–134. Reprinted by permission of Cambridge University Press.

I

In this paper, I shall present not just the conscience of Huckleberry Finn but two others as well. One of them is the conscience of Heinrich Himmler. He became a Nazi in 1923; he served drably and quietly, but well, and was rewarded with increasing responsibility and power. At the peak of his career he held many offices and commands, of which the most powerful was that of leader of the S.S.—the principal police force of the Nazi regime. In this capacity, Himmler commanded the whole concentration-camp system, and was responsible for the execution of the so-called "final solution of the Jewish problem." It is important for my purposes that this piece of social engineering should be thought of not abstractly but in concrete terms of Jewish families being marched to what they think are bathhouses, to the accompaniment of loud-speaker renditions of extracts from *The Merry Widow* and *Tales of Hoffmann*, there to be choked to death by poisonous gases. Altogether, Himmler succeeded in murdering about four and a half million of them, as well as several million gentiles, mainly Poles and Russians.

The other conscience to be discussed is that of the Calvinist theologian and philosopher Jonathan Edwards. He lived in the first half of the eighteenth century, and has a good claim to be considered America's first serious and considerable philosophical thinker. He was for many years a widely renowned preacher and Congregationalist minister in New England; in 1748 a dispute with his congregation led him to resign (he couldn't accept their view that unbelievers should be admitted to the Lord's Supper in the hope that it would convert them); for some years after that he worked as a missionary, preaching to Indians through an interpreter; then in 1758 he accepted the presidency of what is now Princeton University, and within two months died from a smallpox inoculation. Along the way he wrote some first-rate philosophy; his book attacking the notion of free will is still sometimes read. Why I should be interested in Edwards' *conscience* will be explained in due course.

I shall use Heinrich Himmler, Jonathan Edwards, and Huckleberry Finn to illustrate different aspects of a single theme, namely the relationship between *sympathy* on the one hand and *bad morality* on the other.

II

All that I can mean by a "bad morality" is a morality whose principles I deeply disapprove of. When I call a morality bad, I cannot prove that mine is better; but when I here call any morality bad, I think you will agree with me that it is bad; and that is all I need.

There could be dispute as to whether the springs of someone's actions constitute a *morality*. I think, though, that we must admit that someone who acts in ways which conflict grossly with our morality may nevertheless have a morality of his own—a set of principles of action which he sincerely assents to, so that for him the problem of acting well or rightly or in obedience to conscience is the problem of conforming to *those* principles. The problem of conscientiousness can arise as acutely for a bad morality as for any other: Rotten principles may be as difficult to keep as decent ones.

As for "sympathy" I use this term to cover every sort of fellow-feeling, as when one feels pity over someone's loneliness, or horrified compassion over his pain, or when one feels a shrinking reluctance to act in a way which will bring misfortune to someone else. These *feelings* must not be confused with *moral judgments*. My sympathy for someone in distress may lead me to help him, or even to think that I ought to help him; but in itself it is not a judgment about what I ought to do but just a *feeling* for him in his plight. We shall get some light on the difference between feelings and moral judgments when we consider Huckleberry Finn.

Obviously, feelings can impel one to action, and so can moral judgments; and in a particular case sympathy and morality may pull in opposite directions. This can happen not just with bad moralities, but also with good ones like yours and mine. For example, a small child, sick and miserable, clings tightly to his mother and screams in terror when she tries to pass him over to the doctor to be examined. If the mother gave way to her sympathy, that is to her feeling for the child's misery and fright, she would hold it close and not let the doctor come near; but don't we agree that it might be wrong for her to act on such a feeling? Quite generally, then, anyone's moral principles may apply to a particular situation in a way which runs contrary to the particular thrusts of fellow-feeling that he has in that situation. My immediate concern is with sympathy in relation to bad morality, but not because such conflicts occur only when the morality is bad.

Now, suppose that someone who accepts a bad morality is struggling to make himself act in accordance with it in a particular situation where his sympathies pull him another way. He sees the struggle as one between doing the right, conscientious thing, and acting wrongly and weakly, like the mother who won't let the doctor come near her sick, frightened baby. Since we don't accept this person's morality, we may see the situation very differently, thoroughly disapproving of the action he regards as the right one, and endorsing the action which from his point of view constitutes weakness and backsliding.

Conflicts between sympathy and bad morality won't always be like this, for we won't disagree with every single dictate of a bad morality. Still, it can happen in the way I have described, with the agent's right action being our wrong one, and and vice versa. That is just what happens in a certain episode in Chapter 16 of *The Adventures of Huckleberry Finn*, an episode which brilliantly illustrates how fiction can be instructive about real life.

III

Huck Finn has been helping his slave friend Jim to run away from Miss Watson, who is Jim's owner. In their raft-journey down the Mississippi river, they are near to the place at which Jim will become legally free. Now let Huck take over the story:

> Jim said it made him all over trembly and feverish to be so close to freedom. Well I can tell you it made me all over trembly and feverish, too, to hear him, because I begun to get it through my head that he *was* most free—and who was to blame for it? Why, *me*. I couldn't get that out of my conscience, no how nor no way. . . . It hadn't ever come home to me, before, what this thing was that I was doing. But now it did; and it stayed with me, and scorched me more and more. I tried to make out to myself that *I* warn't to blame, because *I* didn't run Jim off from his rightful owner; but it warn't no use, conscience up and say, every time: "But you knowed he was running for his freedom, and you could a paddled ashore and told somebody." That was so—I couldn't get around that, no way. That

was where it pinched. Conscience says to me: "What had poor Miss Watson done to you, that you could see her nigger go off right under your eyes and never say one single word? What did that poor old woman do to you, that you could treat her so mean? . . ." I got to feeling so mean and miserable I most wished I was dead.

Jim speaks of his plan to save up to buy his wife, and then his children, out of slavery; and he adds that if the children cannot be bought he will arrange to steal them. Huck is horrified:

> Thinks I, this is what comes of my not thinking. Here was this nigger which I had as good as helped to run away, coming right out flat-footed and saying he would steal his children—children that belonged to a man I didn't even know; a man that hadn't ever done me no harm.
>
> I was sorry to hear Jim say that, it was such a lowering of him. My conscience got to stirring me up hotter than ever, until at last I says to it: "Let up on me—it ain't too late, yet—I'll paddle ashore at first light, and tell." I felt easy, and happy, and light as a feather, right off. All my troubles was gone.

This is bad morality all right. In his earliest years Huck wasn't taught any principles, and the only one he has encountered since then are those of rural Missouri, in which slave-owning is just one kind of ownership and is not subject to critical pressure. It hasn't occurred to Huck to question those principles. So the action, to us abhorrent, of turning Jim in to the authorities presents itself *clearly* to Huck as the right thing to do.

For us, morality and sympathy would both dictate helping Jim to escape. If we felt any conflict, it would have both these on one side and something else on the other—greed for a reward, or fear of punishment. But Huck's morality conflicts with his sympathy, that is, with his unargued, natural feeling for his friend. The conflict starts when Huck sets off in the canoe towards the shore, pretending that he is going to reconnoiter, but really planning to turn Jim in:

> As I shoved off, [Jim] says: "Pooty soon I'll be a-shout'n for joy, en I'll say, it's all on accounts o' Huck I's a free man . . . Jim won't ever forget you, Huck; you's de bes' fren' Jim's ever had; en you's de *only* fren' old Jim's got now."
>
> I was paddling off, all in a sweat to tell on him; but when he says this, it seemed to kind of take the tuck all out of me. I went along

slow then, and I warn't right down certain whether I was glad I started or whether I warn't. When I was fifty yards off, Jim says:

"Dah you goes, de ole true Huck; de on'y white genlman dat ever kep' his promise to ole Jim." Well, I just felt sick. But I says, I *got* to do it—I can't get *out* of it.

In the upshot, sympathy wins over morality. Huck hasn't the strength of will to do what he sincerely thinks he ought to do. Two men hunting for runaway slaves ask him whether the man on his raft is black or white:

I didn't answer up prompt I tried to, but the words wouldn't come. I tried, for a second or two, to brace up and out with it, but I warn't man enough—hadn't the spunk of a rabbit. I see I was weakening; so I just give up trying, and up and says: "He's white."

So Huck enables Jim to escape, thus acting weakly and wickedly— he thinks. In this conflict between sympathy and morality, sympathy wins.

One critic has cited this episode in support of the statement that Huck suffers "excruciating moments of wavering between honesty and respectability." That is hopelessly wrong, and I agree with the perceptive comment on it by another critic, who says:

The conflict waged in Huck is much more serious: He scarcely cares for respectability and never hesitates to relinquish it, but he does care for honesty and gratitude—and both honesty and gratitude require that he should give Jim up. It is not, in Huck, honesty at war with respectability but love and compassion for Jim struggling against his conscience. His decision is for Jim and hell: a right decision made in the mental chains that Huck never breaks. His concern for Jim is and remains *irrational*. Huck finds many reasons for giving Jim up and none for stealing him. To the end Huck sees his compassion for Jim as a weak, ignorant, and wicked felony.[1]

That is precisely correct—and it can have that virtue only because Mark Twain wrote the episode with such unerring precision. The crucial point concerns *reasons*, which all occur on one side of the conflict. On the side of conscience we have principles, arguments, considerations, ways of looking at things:

[1]M.J. Sidnell, "Huck Finn and Jim," *The Cambridge Quarterly*, vol. 2, pp. 205–206

"It hadn't ever come home to me before what I was doing"

"I tried to make out that I warn't to blame"

"Conscience said 'But you knowed . . .'—I couldn't get around that"

"What had poor Miss Watson done to you?"

"This is what comes of my not thinking"

". . . children that belonged to a man I didn't even know."

On the other side, the side of feeling, we get nothing like that. When Jim rejoices in Huck, as his only friend, Huck doesn't consider the claims of friendship or have the situation "come home" to him in a different light. All that happens is: "When he says this, it seemed to kind of take the tuck all out of me. I went along slow then, and I warn't right down certain whether I was glad I started or whether I warn't." Again, Jim's words about Huck's "promise" to him don't give Huck any *reason* for changing his plan: In his morality promises to slaves probably don't count. Their effect on him is of a different kind: "Well, I just felt sick." And when the moment for final decision come, Huck doesn't weigh up pros and cons: he simply *fails* to do what he believes to be right—he isn't strong enough, hasn't "the spunk of a rabbit." This passage in the novel is notable not just for its finely wrought irony, with Huck's weakness of will leading him to do the right thing, but also for its masterly handling of the difference between general moral principles and particular unreasoned emotional pulls.

IV

Consider now another case of bad morality in conflict with human sympathy: the case of the odious Himmler. Here, from a speech he made to some S.S. generals, is an indication of the content of his morality:

> What happens to a Russian, to a Czech, does not interest me in the slightest. What the nations can offer in the way of good blood of our type, we will take, if necessary by kidnapping their children and raising them here with us. Whether nations live in prosperity or starve to death like cattle interests me only in so far as we need them as slaves to our *Kultur*; otherwise it is of no interest to me. Whether 10,000 Russian females fall down from exhaustion while digging an

antitank ditch interests me only in so far as the antitank ditch for Germany is finished.[2]

But has this a moral basis at all? And if it has, was there in Himmler's own mind any conflict between morality and sympathy? Yes there was. Here is more from the same speech:

> I also want to talk to you quite frankly on a very grave matter . . . I mean . . . the extermination of the Jewish race. . . . Most of you must know what it means when 100 corpses are lying side by side, or 500, or 1,000. To have stuck it out and at the same time—apart from exceptions caused by human weakness—to have remained decent fellows, that is what has made us hard. This is a page of glory in our history which has never been written and is never to be written.

Himmler saw his policies as being hard to implement while still retaining one's human sympathies—while still remaining a "decent fellow." He is saying that only the weak take the easy way out and just squelch their sympathies, and is praising the stronger and more glorious course of retaining one's sympathies while acting in violation of them. In the same spirit, he ordered that when executions were carried out in concentration camps, those responsible "are to be influenced in such a way as to suffer no ill effect in their character and mental attitude." A year later he boasted that the S.S. had wiped out the Jews

> without our leaders and their men suffering any damage in their minds and souls. The danger was considerable, for there was only a narrow path between the Scylla of their becoming heartless ruffians unable any longer to treasure life, and the Charybdis of their becoming soft and suffering nervous breakdowns.

And there really can't be any doubt that the basis of Himmler's policies was a set of principles which constituted his morality—a sick, bad, wicked *morality*. He described himself as caught in "the old tragic conflict between will and obligation." And when his physician Kersten protested at the intention to destroy the Jews,

---

[2]Quoted in William L. Shirer, *The Rise and Fall of the Third Reich* (New York, 1960), pp. 937–938. Next quotation: ibid., p. 966. All further quotations relating to Himmler are from Roger Manwell and Heinrich Fraenkel, *Heinrich Himmler* (London, 1965), pp. 132, 197, 184 (twice), 187.

saying that the suffering involved was "not to be contemplated," Kersten reports that Himmler replied:

> He knew that it would mean much suffering for the Jews. . . . "It is the curse of greatness that it must step over dead bodies to create new life. Yet we must . . . cleanse the soil or it will never bear fruit. It will be a great burden for me to bear."

This, I submit, is the language of morality.

So in this case, tragically, bad morality won out over sympathy. I am sure that many of Himmler's killers did extinguish their sympathies, becoming "heartless ruffians" rather than "decent fellows"; but not Himmler himself. Although his policies ran against the human grain to a horrible degree, he did not sandpaper down his emotional surfaces so that there was no grain there, allowing his actions to slide along smoothly and easily. He did, after all, bear his hideous burden, and even paid a price for it. He suffered a variety of nervous and physical disabilities, including nausea and stomach-convulsions, and Kersten was doubtless right in saying that these were "the expression of a psychic division which extended over his whole life."

This same division must have been present in some of those officials of the Church who ordered heretics to be tortured so as to change their theological opinions. Along with the brutes and the cold careerists, there must have been some who cared, and who suffered from the conflict between their sympathies and their bad morality.

V

In the conflict between sympathy and bad morality, then, the victory may go to sympathy as in the case of Huck Finn, or to morality as in the case of Himmler.

Another possibility is that the conflict may be avoided by giving up, or not ever having, those sympathies which might interfere with one's principles. That seems to have been the case with Jonathan Edwards. I am afraid that I shall be doing an injustice to Edwards' many virtues, and to his great intellectual energy and inventiveness; for my concern is only with the worst thing about him—namely his morality, which was worse than Himmler's.

According to Edwards, God condemns some men to an eternity of unimaginably awful pain, though he arbitrarily spares others— "arbitrarily" because none deserve to be spared:

> Natural men are held in the hand of God over the pit of hell; they have deserved the fiery pit, and are already sentenced to it; and God is dreadfully provoked, his anger is as great toward them as to those that are actually suffering the executions of the fierceness of his wrath in hell . . . ; the devil is waiting for them, hell is gaping for them, the flames gather and flash about them, and would fain lay hold on them . . . ; and . . . there are no means within reach that can be any security to them. . . . All that preserves them is the mere arbitrary will, and uncovenanted unobliged forebearance of an incensed God.[3]

Notice that he says "they have deserved the fiery pit." Edwards insists that men *ought* to be condemned to eternal pain; and his position isn't that this is right because God wants it, but rather that God wants it because it is right. For him, moral standards exist independently of God, and God can be assessed in the light of them (and of course found to be perfect). For example, he says:

> They deserve to be cast into hell; so that . . . justice never stands in the way, it makes no objection against God's using his power at any moment to destroy them. Yea, on the contrary, justice calls aloud for an infinite punishment of their sins.

Elsewhere, he gives elaborate arguments to show that God is acting justly in damning sinners. For example, he argues that a punishment should be exactly as bad as the crime being punished; God is infinitely excellent; so any crime against him is infinitely bad; and so eternal damnation is exactly right as a punishment—it is infinite, but, as Edwards is careful also to say, it is "no more than infinite."

Of course, Edwards himself didn't torment the damned; but the question still arises of whether his sympathies didn't conflict with his *approval* of eternal torment. Didn't he find it painful to contemplate any fellow-human's being tortured for ever? Apparently not:

---

[3]Vergilius Ferm (ed.), *Puritan Sage: Collected Writings of Jonathan Edwards* (New York, 1953), p. 370. Next three quotations: ibid., p. 366, p. 294 ("no more than infinite"), p. 372.

The God that holds you over the pit of hell, much as one holds a spider or some loathsome insect over the fire, abhors you, and is dreadfully provoked; . . . he is of purer eyes than to bear to have you in his sight; you are ten thousand times so abominable in his eyes as the most hateful venomous serpent is in ours.

When God is presented as being as misanthropic as that, one suspects misanthropy in the theologian. This suspicion is increased when Edwards claims that "the saints in glory will . . . understand how terrible the sufferings of the damned are; yet . . . will not be sorry for [them]."[4] He bases this partly on a view of human nature whose ugliness he seems not to notice:

The seeing of the calamities of others tends to heighten the sense of our own enjoyments. When the saints in glory, therefore, shall see the doleful state of the damned, how will this heighten their sense of the blessedness of their own state. . . . When they shall see how miserable others of their fellow-creatures are . . . ; when they shall see the smoke of their torment, . . . and hear their dolorous shrieks and cries, and consider that they in the mean time are in the most blissful state, and shall surely be in it to all eternity; how they will rejoice!

I hope this is less than the whole truth! His other main point about why the saints will rejoice to see the torments of the damned is that it is *right* that they should do so:

The heavenly inhabitants . . . will have no love nor pity to the damned. . . . [This will not show] a want of spirit of love in them . . . ; for the heavenly inhabitants will know that it is not fit that they should love [the damned] because they will know then, that God has no love to them, nor pity for them.

The implication that *of course* one can adjust one's feelings of pity so that they conform to the dictates of some authority—doesn't this suggest that ordinary human sympathies played only a small part in Edwards' life?

---

[4]This and the next two quotations are from "The End of the Wicked Contemplated by the Righteous: Or, The Torments of the Wicked in Hell, No Occasion of Grief to the Saints in Heaven," from *The Works of President Edwards* (London, 1817), vol. 4, pp. 507–508, 511–512, and 509 respectively.

VI

Huck Finn, whose sympathies are wide and deep, could never avoid the conflict in that way; but he is determined to avoid it, and so he opts for the only other alternative he can see—to give up morality altogether. After he has tricked the slave-hunters, he returns to the raft and undergoes a peculiar crisis:

> I got aboard the raft, feeling bad and low, because I knowed very well I had done wrong, and I see it warn't no use for me to try to learn to do right; a body that don't get *started* right when he's little, ain't got no show—when the pinch comes there ain't nothing to back him up and keep him to his work, and so he gets beat. Then I thought a minute, and says to myself, hold on—s'pose you'd a done right and give Jim up; would you feel better than what you do now? No, says I, I'd feel bad—I'd feel just the same way I do now. Well, then, says I, what's the use you learning to do right, when it's troublesome to do right and ain't no trouble to do wrong, and the wages is just the same? I was stuck. I couldn't answer that. So I reckoned I wouldn't bother no more about it, but after this always do whichever come handiest at the time.

Huck clearly cannot conceive of having any morality except the one he has learned—too late, he thinks—from his society. He is not entirely a prisoner of that morality, because he does after all reject it; but for him that is a decision to relinquish morality as such; he cannot envisage revising his morality, altering its content in face of the various pressures to which it is subject, including pressures from his sympathies. For example, he does not begin to approach the thought that slavery should be rejected on moral grounds, or the thought that what he is doing is not theft because a person cannot be owned and therefore cannot be stolen.

The basic trouble is that he cannot or will not engage in abstract intellectual operations of any sort. In chapter 33 he finds himself "feeling to blame, somehow" for something he knows he had no hand in; he assumes that this feeling is a deliverance of conscience; and this confirms him in his belief that conscience shouldn't be listened to:

> It don't make no difference whether you do right or wrong, a person's conscience ain't got no sense, and just goes for him *anyway*.

>If I had a yaller dog that didn't know no more than a person's
>conscience does, I would poison him. It takes up more than all of a
>person's insides, and yet ain't no good, nohow.

That brisk, incurious dismissiveness fits well with the comprehensive rejection of morality back on the raft. But this is a digression.

On the raft, Huck decides not to live by principles, but just to do whatever "comes handiest at the time"—always acting according to the mood of the moment. Since the morality he is rejecting is narrow and cruel, and his sympathies are broad and kind, the results will be good. But moral principles are good to have, because they help to protect one from acting badly at moments when one's sympathies happen to be in abeyance. On the highest possible estimate of the role one's sympathies should have, one can still allow for principles as embodiments of one's best feelings, one's broadest and keenest sympathies. On that view, principles can help one across intervals when one's feelings are at less than their best, i.e. through periods of misanthropy or meanness or self-centeredness or depression or anger.

What Huck didn't see is that one can live by principles and yet have ultimate control over their content. And one way such control can be exercised is by checking of one's principles in the light of one's sympathies. This is sometimes a pretty straightforward matter. It can happen that a certain moral principle becomes untenable—meaning literally that one cannot hold it any longer—because it conflicts intolerably with the pity or revulsion or whatever that one feels when one sees what the principle leads to. One's experience may play a large part here: Experiences evoke feelings, and feelings force one to modify principles. Something like this happened to the English poet Wilfred Owen, whose experiences in the First World War transformed him from an enthusiastic soldier into a virtual pacifist. I can't document his change of conscience in detail; but I want to present something which he wrote about the way experience can put pressure on morality.

The Latin poet Horace wrote that it is sweet and fitting (or right) to die for one's country—*dulce et decorum est pro patria mori*—and Owen wrote a fine poem about how experience could lead one to relinquish that particular moral principle.[5] He describes a man who

---

[5] I am grateful to the Executors of the Estate of Harold Owen, and to Chatto and Windus Ltd., for permission to quote from Wilfred Owen's "Dulce et Decorum Est" and "Insensibility."

is too slow donning his gas mask during a gas attack—"As under a green sea I saw him drowning," Owen says. The poem ends like this:

> In all my dreams before my helpless sight
> He plunges at me, guttering, choking, drowning.
> If in some smothering dreams, you too could pace
> Behind the wagon that we flung him in,
> And watch the white eyes writhing in his face,
> His hanging face, like a devil's sick of sin;
> If you could hear, at every jolt, the blood
> Come gargling from the froth-corrupted lungs,
> Bitter as the cud
> Of vile, incurable sores on innocent tongues,—
> My friend, you would not tell with such high zest
> To children ardent for some desperate glory,
> The old Lie: Dulce et decorum est
> Pro patria mori.

There is a difficulty about drawing from all this a moral for ourselves. I imagine that we agree in our rejection of slavery, eternal damnation, genocide, and uncritical patriotic self-abnegation; so we shall agree that Huck Finn, Jonathan Edwards, Heinrich Himmler, and the poet Horace would all have done well to bring certain of their principles under severe pressure from ordinary human sympathies. But then we can say this because we can say that all those are bad moralities, whereas we cannot look at our own moralities and declare them bad. This is not arrogance: It is obviously incoherent for someone to declare the system of moral principles that he *accepts* to be *bad*, just as one cannot coherently say of anything that one *believes* it but it is *false*.

Still, although I can't point to any of my beliefs and say "That is false," I don't doubt that some of my beliefs *are* false; and so I should try to remain open to correction. Similarly, I accept every single item in my morality—that is inevitable—but I am sure that my morality could be improved, which is to say that it could undergo changes which I should be glad of once I had made them. So I must try to keep my morality open to revision, exposing it to whatever valid pressures there are—including pressures from my sympathies.

I don't give my sympathies a blank check in advance. In a conflict between principle and sympathy, principles ought sometimes to win. For example, I think it was right to take part in the Second World War on the allied side; there were many ghastly individual incidents which might have led someone to doubt the rightness of his participation in that war; and I think it would have been right for such a person to keep his sympathies in a subordinate place on those occasions, not allowing them to modify his principles in such a way as to make a pacifist of him.

Still, one's sympathies should be kept as sharp and sensitive and aware as possible, and not only because they can sometimes affect one's principles or one's conduct or both. Owen, at any rate, says that feelings and sympathies are vital even when they can do nothing but bring pain and distress. In another poem he speaks of the blessings of being numb in one's feelings: "Happy are the men who yet before they are killed/Can let their veins run cold," he says. These are the ones who do not suffer from any compassion which, as Owen puts it, "makes their feet/Sore on the alleys cobbled with their brothers." He contrasts these "happy" ones, who "lose all imagination," with himself and others "who with a thought besmirch/Blood over all our soul." Yet the poem's verdict goes against the "happy" ones. Owen does not say that they will act worse than the others whose souls are besmirched with blood because of their keen awareness of human suffering. He merely says that they are the losers because they have cut themselves off from the human condition:

> By choice they made themselves immune
> To pity and whatever moans in man
> Before the last sea and the hapless stars;
> Whatever mourns when many leave these shores;
> Whatever shares
> The eternal reciprocity of tears.[6]

STUDY QUESTIONS

1. What does Bennett mean by a "bad morality"?
2. Does Bennett think principles play an important role in moral

---

[6]This paper began life as the Potter Memorial Lecture, given at Washington State University in Pullman, Washington, in 1972.

life? Can you suggest occasions where one's principles *should* overrule one's sympathies?
3. What are the consequences of Bennett's arguments for ethical relativism?
4. Why does Bennett claim that Jonathan Edwards's morality was even worse than Himmler's? Do you agree?
5. What are the implications of Bennett's position for the view that we must always follow our conscience?

38 Who Saw Murder Didn't Call Police

MARTIN GANSBERG

Martin Gansberg (b. 1920) is on the staff of the *New York Times*. He taught journalism at Fairleigh Dickinson University from 1947 to 1973.

In 1964, the American public was stunned by reports from Kew Gardens, Queens: Kitty Genovese was brutally stabbed while her neighbors passively witnessed the murder. Gansberg describes the incident in detail without overtly judging the bystanders.

For more than half an hour 38 respectable, law-abiding citizens in Queens watched a killer stalk and stab a woman in three separate attacks in Kew Gardens.

Twice their chatter and the sudden glow of their bedroom lights interrupted him and frightened him off. Each time he returned, sought her out, and stabbed her again. Not one person telephoned the police during the assault; one witness called after the woman was dead.

That was two weeks ago today.

Still shocked is Assistant Chief Inspector Frederick M. Lussen, in charge of the borough's detectives and a veteran of 25 years of homicide investigations. He can give a matter-of-fact recitation on many murders. But the Kew Gardens slaying baffles him—not because it is a murder, but because the "good people" failed to call the police.

"As we have reconstructed the crime," he said, "the assailant had three chances to kill this woman during a 35-minute period. He returned twice to complete the job. If we had been called when he first attacked, the woman might not be dead now."

This is what the police say happened beginning at 3:20 A.M. in the staid, middle-class, tree-lined Austin Street area:

Twenty-eight-year-old Catherine Genovese, who was called Kitty by almost everyone in the neighborhood, was returning home from her job as manager of a bar in Hollis. She parked her red Fiat in a lot adjacent to the Kew Gardens Long Island Rail Road Station, facing Mowbray Place. Like many residents of the neighborhood, she had parked there day after day since her arrival in Connecticut a year ago, although the railroad frowns on the practice.

She turned off the lights of her car, locked the door, and started to walk the 100 feet to the entrance of her apartment at 82–70 Austin Street, which is in a Tudor building, with stores on the first floor and apartments on the second.

The entrance to the apartment is in the rear of the building because the front is rented to retail stores. At night the quiet neighborhood is shrouded in the slumbering darkness that marks most residential areas.

Miss Genovese noticed a man at the far end of the lot, near a seven-story apartment house at 82–40 Austin Street. She halted. Then, nervously, she headed up Austin Street toward Lefferts Boulevard, where there is a call box to the 102nd Police Precinct in nearby Richmond Hill.

She got as far as a street light in front of a bookstore before the man grabbed her. She screamed. Lights went on in the 10-story apartment house at 82–67 Austin Street, which faces the bookstore. Windows slid open and voices punctuated the early-morning stillness.

Miss Genovese screamed: "Oh, my God, he stabbed me! Please help me! Please help me!"

From one of the upper windows in the apartment house, a man called down: "Let that girl alone!"

The assailant looked up at him, shrugged, and walked down Austin Street toward a white sedan parked a short distance away. Miss Genovese struggled to her feet.

Lights went out. The killer returned to Miss Genovese, now trying to make her way around the side of the building by the parking lot to get to her apartment. The assailant stabbed her again.

"I'm dying!" she shrieked. "I'm dying!"

Windows were opened again, and lights went on in many apartments. The assailant got into his car and drove away. Miss Genovese staggered to her feet. A city bus, Q-10, the Lefferts Boulevard line to Kennedy International Airport, passed. It was 3:35 A.M.

The assailant returned. By then, Miss Genovese had crawled to the back of the building, where the freshly painted brown doors to the apartment house held out hope for safety. The killer tried the first door; she wasn't there. At the second door, 82–62 Austin Street, he saw her slumped on the floor at the foot of the stairs. He stabbed her a third time—fatally.

It was 3:50 by the time the police received their first call, from a man who was a neighbor of Miss Genovese. In two minutes they were at the scene. The neighbor, a 70-year-old woman, and another woman were the only persons on the street. Nobody else came forward.

The man explained that he had called the police after much deliberation. He had phoned a friend in Nassau County for advice and then he had crossed the roof of the building to the apartment of the elderly woman to get her to make the call.

"I didn't want to get involved," he sheepishly told the police.

Six days later, the police arrested Winston Moseley, a 29-year-old business-machine operator, and charged him with the homicide. Moseley had no previous record. He is married, has two children and owns a home at 133–19 Sutter Avenue, South Ozone Park, Queens. On Wednesday, a court committed him to Kings County Hospital for psychiatric observation.

When questioned by the police, Moseley also said that he had slain Mrs. Annie May Johnson, 24, of 146–12 133d Avenue,

Jamaica, on Feb. 29 and Barbara Kralik, 15, of 174–17 140th Avenue, Springfield Gardens, last July. In the Kralik case, the police are holding Alvin L. Mitchell, who is said to have confessed that slaying.

The police stressed how simple it would have been to have gotten in touch with them. "A phone call," said one of the detectives, "would have done it." The police may be reached by dialing "O" for operator or SPring 7–3100.

Today witnesses from the neighborhood, which is made up of one-family homes in the $35,000 to $60,000 range with the exception of the two apartment houses near the railroad station, find it difficult to explain why they didn't call the police.

A housewife, knowingly if quite casual, said, "We thought it was a lover's quarrel." A husband and wife both said, "Frankly, we were afraid." They seemed aware of the fact that events might have been different. A distraught woman, wiping her hands in her apron, said, "I didn't want my husband to get involved."

One couple, now willing to talk about that night, said they heard the first screams. The husband looked thoughtfully at the bookstore where the killer first grabbed Miss Genovese.

"We went to the window to see what was happening," he said, "but the light from our bedroom made it difficult to see the street." The wife, still apprehensive, added: "I put out the light and we were able to see better."

Asked why they hadn't called the police, she shrugged and replied: "I don't know."

A man peeked out from a slight opening in the doorway to his apartment and rattled off an account of the killer's second attack. Why hadn't he called the police at the time? "I was tired," he said without emotion. "I went back to bed."

It was 4:25 A.M. when the ambulance arrived to take the body of Miss Genovese. It drove off. "Then," a solemn police detective said, "the people came out."

STUDY QUESTIONS

1. Two professors at the Princeton Theological Seminary designed an experiment to find out why bystanders often ignore people in distress. They told several seminary students to re-

port to the studio to record a Biblical text. The professors arranged that, on their way to the studio, the students would pass another student lying on the ground writhing and gasping. The researchers found that the only significant factor in determining who stopped was how much time students thought they had: Of those rushed for time, only 10 percent stopped; of those who had plenty of time, 63 percent. It seemed to make no statistical difference that half the students had been assigned to read the parable of the good Samaritan. Do these findings surprise you? Despite their poor showing, do you think the seminarians did better than a randomly selected group would have? Can we do anything as a society to increase the proportion of people who will stop?

2. Do you think more states should adopt a statute like the one in Vermont that legally requires bystanders to aid those in critical need when they can safely do so?

3. Do you agree with those who say that the thirty-eight witnesses to Kitty Genovese's death are accessories to murder?

Compassion

RICHARD TAYLOR

Richard Taylor (b. 1919) is a professor of philosophy at the University of Rochester. He writes in the areas of ethics and metaphysics. Among his many books are *Good and Evil* (1971) and *With Heart and Mind* (1973). He is also an expert on bees.

Illustrating his argument with several case studies of kindness and cruelty, Taylor concludes that compassion is more fundamental to morality than is a sense of duty or attention to consequences. Goodness is easy to detect; one does not need philosophical understanding. Compassion does not differentiate between races or species. Compassion should override even the sense of duty. It is the essence of virtue.

Let us first, then, bring to our minds actions of the following sort, beginning with fairly insignificant ones so that we can see moral good and evil, whether small or great.

Story 1. A boy, strolling over the countryside on his way from Sunday school, came across a large beetle lumbering over the ground. Fascinated by its size and beauty, he took a pin from his pocket, stabbed the insect through the back, ran it up to the head of the pin, and impaled it on a nearby tree. Several days later, having forgotten this, while he was going about his daily play, the boy found himself again in the same place and curiosity led him again to

COMPASSION From *Good and Evil* by Richard Taylor (Prometheus Press, Buffalo, N.Y., 1970). Reprinted with permission of the author.

the tree. There was the beetle, its legs still moving, although very slowly, against the empty air.

Story 2. A group of boys, wandering aimlessly about in search of amusement, found a dirty and emaciated old cat asleep in a barn. One of the boys was sent off with a tin can for some kerosene while the others tied the cat up in a bag and sat around waiting. The kerosene finally supplied, it was sprinkled liberally over the squirming animal, precautions being taken not to get any into its face and eyes, and then a match was applied to the tail. The effect was spectacular: a howling torch, streaking over the field, culminating in a series of wild gyrations and leaps, and finally into a twitching mass whose insides burst forth in wet sputters, the eyes bulging to the size and brilliance of agates.

Story 3. A trio of soldiers, ragged and bearded and evidently a long time away from home and hearth, was wending its way back to its encampment in recently conquered territory. The surroundings, as far as vision could see, bore the marks of recent incredible devastation by war. Coming upon the remains of a shack, they were surprised to see signs of life. They threw open what served as a door to find a bearded old man huddled in the corner, trembling from fear and cold. A Star of David inscribed on one of the walls was more than sufficient incitement for what followed. The old man was goaded outside with rifle butts, was made to scrape a crude hole in the ground, and was then bludgeoned into it with rocks and sticks. A bit of dirt was finally shoved over his still quaking body. When the soldiers had finished this work and resumed their trek a faint wail betrayed that there was an infant still in the shack. They found her at once, and soon managed to replace her crying with giggling by dangling bright objects in her face and tickling her toes. When her giggling and the laughter of the soldiers flowed freely, her skull was blown open with a single bullet, and what was left of her small body was added to the grave already dug.

Now, with the passing reminder that things of this sort happen, and with fair regularity, we must ask: What is it in stories like this that sickens and evokes revulsion?

Shall we say, with Protagoras, that man, after all, is the measure of all things, that the insensitivity or depravity that some might think they detect in these illustrations really exists only in the mind

41

of the observer, and that modes of behavior simply differ from one group to another? Surely that is not insight, but blindness, and it adds no enlightenment to remark that some courses of conduct are *better*, in terms of their consequences. It is not the *consequences* of actions like this that appall, but what is in the hearts of the agents.

Shall we then, with Socrates, say of the soldiers, for example, that they have acted from ignorance, choosing the lesser in preference to the greater good? That is altogether too tepid, and only manages to assimilate such actions to those of the fool who fails to look before he leaps. It is not the mere folly of these men that produces horror, or their inability to distinguish better and worse. It is something of a different character altogether.

Shall we say then, with Plato, that the agents whose deeds we consider have evidently failed to preserve a harmony between the rational and the appetitive parts of their souls? This seems a bit better, but it still falls far short of explaining our revulsion, which cannot have very much to do with what we take to be the inner arrangements of someone's mind or soul.

Perhaps we should say, then, that the behavior of these agents is ill-calculated to advance the maximum of pleasure for the maximum number. It is, indeed, but what has that to do with moral revulsion?

Perhaps, then, they have all acted from their inclinations rather than from duty, and what they should have done was remind themselves of this maxim, clear to any rational being: So act, that you can will the maxim of your action to be a universal law, binding on all rational beings. Surely that is pedantic. What if they had so acted? Perhaps then they would have done the same things anyway, but with a bit more ceremony and rationalization. It is difficult to see, in any case, what is *irrational* about pinning an insect, or dispatching a stray cat or a starving old man and infant. Surely the words one wants here are not irrational or undutiful, but something like heartless or cruel.

Then maybe we should say that such agents evidently overlook the theological consequences of what they do. Men may be lax in their laws and punishments, but the eye of God never sleeps. Men should remember that great happiness awaits those who conduct themselves properly, and great pain awaits those who forget. But this is only to say that they may be missing out on a good thing and taking a needless risk of going to Hell. Maybe so, but are they condemned in our eyes for *that*?

The recital of answers could go on, Aristotle perhaps noting that all these actions betray a disregard for that golden mean between excess and deficiency that honorable men prize; James observing that we should include in our accounting all of the interests and claims that are made (including, no doubt, the "claims" insisted on by the cat); and so on and on.

But clearly, all we *need* to say about these things is that they are wantonly *cruel*. That is the whole sum and substance of them all, and it is the perception of sheer cruelty or malice, of the intended infliction of injury and the delight derived from it, that fills us with that peculiar revulsion that is moral. Our perception does not stop at the irrationality of such agents, nor at their folly, imprudence, lack of wit, or intelligence. It hardly notices these things. We are not at all tempted to weigh interests against interests, to make summations of pleasures and pains, reserving our verdict until we are sure that none of these features has been overlooked. Even generally considered, it is not the consequences that gives them their moral significance. It is no disaster to the world that an insect should die, or a cat, or even an old man and baby who were destined to soon die of starvation anyway. That such things should result is doubtless an evil, but this is not what gives these actions the stamp of moral evil or distinguishes their authors as vicious. The moral perception goes straight to the heart, to the incentive that produced and was indeed aimed at producing those evils, and the one thing it sees, overriding everything else, is malice.

Compassion: The Second Class of Actions

We can now compare the foregoing with deeds of a very different kind.

Story 4. A boy, poking around in a loft where he had no business to be and looking for something to steal, came upon a cupola that had been screened off with chicken wire to prevent pigeons from roosting and nesting inside. Twenty or so of the birds were inside, however, having somehow gotten trapped there. They presented a lamentable appearance, some crawling about on the filth-encrusted floor, their wings half outstretched, and others lying about dead. They had evidently been there a long time. The boy resisted the temptation to tear off the screening and release them, for it had been put there by the owner; it would only be replaced eventually, and he might get himself into serious trouble by tampering. So he left things as they were. But that night he awakened with an image in his mind of the dumb birds up there in the dark loft, and particularly those too weakened to fly any more. He told his father about it the next day, but was firmly reproved for his trespassing and was given an unqualified order not to do it again, along with remarks about pigeons as a nuisance. He felt profoundly guilty, and the whole thing was put out of his mind until the next night, when his sleep was disturbed even more by the same images of suffering and death. Finally, on the third night, he slipped from the house before dawn armed with a flashlight and, although frightened to the bones of the darkness, he picked his way up to the high cupola. There, one by one he liberated each bird through a hole he tore in the screen, with many painful pecks to his hands and much flapping and commotion bringing constantly closer the possibility of attracting the attention of the owner or the police. He repaired the hole, and gathered the birds that were to weak to fly into a bag and carried them tenderly home. The next morning they betrayed the boy's disobedience to his father, and for this he was beaten, but with only a few deaths he nursed the sick pigeons back to strength and let them go.

Story 5. A man deeply conditioned by the traditions of his local culture was deputized as a sheriff, along with dozens more from the same community, in order to cope with the growing civil rights menace there. Like most of the others, this man thoroughly respected the law and the orderly traditions he swore to uphold. He had always respected, too, his fellow men, black or white, and his firm adherence to the conventions of separation could not fairly be ascribed to any hatred for anyone. Blacks had always worked for him and received decent wages, although he had never seen any reason to treat them as equals and had been taught from childhood not to. He was, therefore, appalled at the thought that they should vote and perhaps even hold elective office. The menace to his settled world came not, it seemed to him, from the local black community, which was peaceful enough, but from outsiders, black and white, who had for months been arousing people at mass

meetings, hiring lawyers from outside, goading blacks into disregarding all the legally erected symbols of segregation and, it
seemed to him, threatening to turn a peaceful community into a
jungle. Matters became intensely critical with the scheduling of a
massive parade onto the town hall, in defiance of the law, at which
time, it was threatened, all the blacks willing to do so would
register as voters. This man, together with a massive force of
sheriffs and deputies, went forth heavily armed to repel that assault,
and a scene of violence was quickly enacted, blacks falling bleeding
by the road, but getting in a few wounds of their own with rocks
and pop bottles and whatever came to their hands. Restraint on
both sides disappeared entirely when one sheriff and two Negroes
got killed. Our deputy then managed to seize at gunpoint one of
the blacks who was obviously a leader, and an outsider. Throwing
him into his own car, which was to serve as a paddy wagon, he
drove for about half a mile and stopped. Red and sweating with
fury and screaming "nigger," his gun in his victim's face, he began
beating him about the head and face with his weapon. Then suddenly the deputy fell to the seat, tears streaming from his eyes.
Sobbing like a child, and muttering epithets mingled with abject
apology, he helped the beaten and astonished Negro from the car,
wiped the blood and sweat from his brow, and gave him a drink of
cold water and a clean handkerchief. Then he drove home and got
drunk.[1]

Story 6.   Two soldiers found themselves marooned on a tiny
island in the Pacific. One was an American marine, the other a
Japanese, and for a day or so neither suspected the presence of the
other. The Americans had, they thought, killed or captured every
one of the enemy, who were not numerous to begin with. The
marine had been left behind when he was knocked out and lost, but
not otherwise seriously wounded, during the fighting. It was the
American marine who first discovered the other, and discovered
too, to his dismay, that his foe was armed with a rifle, luger, and
knife, while he had only a large knife. From then on he lived only
by stealth, hiding during the day, meagerly sustaining himself by

---

[1]This story is suggested by, but is not intended as an account of, an episode described
by Dick Gregory in *Nigger: An Autobiography*. (New York: Pocket Books, 1968),
pp. 171–172.

silently picking about in the darkness and covering all his traces, for he knew he would be hunted as soon as his presence was known, and that he would die as soon as he was seen. He soon began to feel stalked, a naked and helpless animal for whom no concealment was safe, and he could sleep only in brief naps, when exhaustion forced sleep upon him, not knowing but that his enemy might at that moment be at his back. He knew that the bullet that was going to kill him would be in his skull before he would hear it, and he lived almost moment to moment expecting it. He began to contrive schemes for ambushing his hunter, who he knew must have learned of him by now, but the odds were so against him in all of these that he abandoned them as futile and lived furtively, certain that it could not go on indefinitely. Thirst, hunger, and exhaustion had after many days magnified his terror and helplessness. He clutched his knife day and night, and his enemy became to his imagination a vast, omnipotent, and ineluctable spectre. But deliverance came suddenly one day when, in the early light of dawn, he stumbled upon the Japanese, lying in profound sleep, both guns at his side, and a huge knife laid out on his belly. His role as the hunted was ended, and with a single lunge he would abolish the source of his terror. His own knife raised high, he was ready to fall on his foe, when he began to shake and could find no strength in his limbs. Thus he remained for some seconds, until the knife fell from his hand. The other leaped awake, and each stood staring into the terrified face of the other. The Japanese reached slowly for his weapons, pushed them violently out of reach of both men, and then, hesitating, let his knife fall, harmless, beside the other.

The Significance of These Stories

There are no heroes in these stories. No one has earned any medal of honor, any citation from any society for the protection of animals, or any recognition from any council on civil liberties. Goodness of heart, tenderness toward things that can suffer, and the loving kindness that contradicts all reason and sense of duty and sometimes denies even the urge to life itself that governs us all are seldom heroic. But who can fail to see, in these mixtures of good and evil, the one thing that really does shine like a jewel, as if by its own light?

Are we apt to learn anything by reviewing these things in the light of the analyses moralists have provided? Who acted from a sense of duty, or recited to himself the imperative of treating rational nature as an end in itself, or of acting on no maxim that he could not will to be a law for rational beings, and so on? Nothing of this sort was even remotely involved in anyone's thinking. Nor can we talk about consequences very convincingly, or the maximization of pleasure, or of competing claims and interests, or of seeing the good and directing the will to its attainment, or of honoring a mean between extremes—in short, there is not much that is strictly *rational* in any of these actions. We are not at all struck by the philosophical acumen that somehow led these people to see what was "the right thing to do." Insofar as they thought at all about what they were doing, or consulted their duty, or weighed possible consequences, they were inclined to do precisely what they did not do. We have in all these cases a real war between the head and the heart, the reason and the will, and the one thing that redeems them all is the quality of the heart, which somehow withstands every solicitation of the intellect. It is the compassionate heart that can still somehow make itself felt that makes men's deeds sometimes noble and beautiful, and nothing else at all. This, surely, is what makes men akin to the angels and the powers of light, and snuffs out in them the real and ever present forces of darkness and evil.

If someone were to say, "This is a good and virtuous man— although, of course, he has a rather pronounced tendency to cruelty and is quite unfeeling of others," we would at once recognize an absurdity. It would be quite impossible to pick out any morally good man under a description like that. Similarly, if one were to say, "This is a truly vicious man, wholly bereft of human goodness—although he has a good heart, and is kind to all living things," the absurdity leaps up again. Virtue and vice are not evenly distributed among men; no doubt all men have some of both, and one or the other tends to prevail in everyone. Most men, however, seem to know just what human goodness is when they see it, whether they have read treatises on morality or not, or whether or not they have tried to fathom its metaphysical foundations. For the fact is, it seems to have no such foundations, and no treatises on morals or disquisitions on the nature of true justice make it stand forth with more clarity than it already has. It would be as odd to suppose that one must become a philosopher before he can hope to recognize genuine moral good and evil, as it would to suppose that no man can be overwhelmed by a sunset until he understands the physics of refraction.

The Scope of Compassion

It will, of course, appear that genuine morality is not, by this account, confined to our relations with men, but extends to absolutely everything that can feel. Why should it not? What but a narrow and exclusive regard for themselves and a slavish worship for rational nature would ever have led moralists to think otherwise? That men are the only beings who are capable of reason is perhaps true, but they are surely not the only things that suffer. It seems perfectly evident that morality is tied to the liability to suffer rather than to the strictly human capacity for science and metaphysics and similar expressions of reason.

It makes no essential difference to morality, but only a difference of degree, that in my stories it was an insect that was impaled, a cat that was burned, and common pigeons that were liberated. The incentives were quite plainly identical in my first three stories, and identical again in the latter three, and it is quite obviously this malice in the former and compassion in the latter that stirs the moral sentiment. Something very precious is lost when men die at the hands of others, but that is not the reason for its moral evil. It is perhaps far less bad that a cat should die, and almost insignificant that an insect should perish; yet, the quality of moral evil remains essentially the same in all these cases. Similarly, we can surely say of our marine in the last story, struggling to keep living and finding suddenly the threat to his life lying helpless before him, that he had a good heart. Do the words lose one bit of their force or meaning if said of the boy and his pigeons?

Most men have always recognized their kinship with the rest of creation and their responsibility to other living things, in spite of the fact that moralists in our tradition hardly so much as mention it. When the question comes up for wise men to consider, they more often than not relegate it to a footnote or an appendix, thinking it quite ancillary to any serious moral considerations, even though it has as much seriousness and urgency as any moral problem that can be raised. Enthralled by man's rational nature, and finding no sign of it among what men fondly refer to as the brutes, philosophers and moralists have tended to dismiss the latter as mere *things*. Descartes even went so far as to call them automata, implying that they do not even feel pain—an idea, one would think, that could never find lodgement in the mind of any man who had seen animals bleeding in traps. Nor has religion, in our culture, done much to offset such an error. The Christian religion, indeed, compares most unfavorably with others in this respect, and in not one of its creeds will one find the least consideration of animals generally. The theological emphasis, to be sure, is not on man's rational mind, but on his soul, which other animals are somewhat arbitrarily denied to possess. The result is the same as before, however; animals are thought of as mere things to be treated in any way that one pleases. One can hear a thousand sermons, or study the casuistic manuals of an entire theological library, without finding a word on the subject of kindness to animals. When, in fact, it was proposed to establish in Rome a society for the prevention of cruelty to animals, the effort was vetoed by Pope Pius IX on the ground that we have no duty to them.[2] His reason and theology were without doubt correct. It can be doubted, however, whether the abstract kind of duty he had in mind is owed to anything under the sun. Yet, it cannot be doubted that animals suffer exactly as men do, and they suffer unutterably because they cannot protest, cannot make their "claims," of which William James spoke, very articulate. The heart is no less evil that takes delight in the suffering of a cat, than one that extracts similar delight from the sufferings of men. The latter we may fear more, but the moral pronouncement is the same in each case.

Incentives and Consequences

Next it will be noted that on this account the consequences of one's deeds are of little relevance to pronouncing upon the moral significance of those deeds themselves. Here, again, this view is in perfect agreement with Kant, and in complete opposition to Mill. It

---

[2]Edward Westermarck, *The Origin and Development of the Moral Ideas* (London: Macmillan, 1917), Vol. II, p. 508.

is not, Kant said, what we happen to produce by our actions that counts, but why we perform those actions to begin with. But Kant, obsessed with rational nature, decided that the only acceptable moral incentive would have to be a rational one: namely, the rational apprehension of one's duty, according to the formula of the categorical imperative. My account, on the other hand, provides no such rational formula at all. Indeed, the impulse of compassion so far transcends reason that it can as easily as not contradict it. It is sometimes the very irrationality of compassion, the residual capacity to respond with tenderness and love when all one's reason counsels otherwise, that confers upon a compassionate act its sweetness, beauty, and nobility. In exactly the same way does the irrationality of malice, the *pointless* but deliberate infliction of suffering, produce its acute and revolting ugliness.

Still, Kant was surely right in directing perception straight to the incentive of action rather than to its results, and Mill quite wrong in wanting to consider only the latter. Thus, it is a great evil that men should suffer and die. Considering these effects by themselves, the evil is the same no matter what produces it. But it is not a *moral* evil. Whether a man dies from being struck by lightning, by an automobile, or by a bullet, the effect is exactly the same in each case; and, considering only the effect, its evil is the same. This, however, is no moral judgment at all. To note that a given man dies from a lightning bolt, and that this is an evil, is to make no moral judgment on the lightning, the man, or his death. It is only to make a pronouncement of good and evil, of the kind considered far back in this discussion. It is, in other words, to describe a fact and add to the description an indication of the reaction to that fact of some conative or purposeful being. This becomes all the more evident when we consider that *all* men suffer and die, simply because they are sentient and mortal beings. No one escapes this fate. Yet, no morality at all turns on it; it is simply a fact, against which men may recoil, but not one that gives rise to any moral praise or blame. Nor is the picture automatically altered when such evils are found to result from human actions. A thousand men die on American highways every week as a result of their own actions, those of others, or both, and although no one doubts that this is a great evil, it is only rarely that the question of moral evil even arises. It is a problem of good and evil not significantly different from the evil of cancer. It is an evil to cope with, to minimize, but not one that normally prompts moral condemnation. Even when we bring the matter down to particular actions that are deliberate and willed, the situation is not significantly changed. That an insect should be killed (by an entomologist, for example), or a cat (by a medical researcher), or even a man (by an enemy soldier) are in varying degrees evil, but it is not the moral sentiment that expresses itself here. What is expressed is a certain reverence for life, and also a fear and horror at its loss, as in wars; but the moral condemnation of a particular deed is far in the background, if not entirely absent. Indeed, if we recall my six stories, it is clear that most of the consequences of the actions described are quite insignificant. All are things that happen normally, all the time; and, yet, the moral judgment is identical, except for degree, in the first three examples and identical again in the rest. In one set of cases an insect dies, a cat dies, and an old man and an infant die, all things that happen pretty regularly. Now one might want, with good reason, to insist that the death of two human beings is hardly trivial, but the thing to note is that even if it were known that these two would have died soon of starvation, had they not been discovered, this would not in the least reduce the moral repugnance of their murders. The moral revulsion arises not from their deaths, but how they died and, in particular, from what was in the hearts of their murderers. And in the second set of stories we find that some pigeons live, to rejoin the millions of them already on earth, a man receives less of a beating than appeared imminent, and another, who had just narrowly escaped death in battle, does not die after all. These are hardly consequences that change the direction of man's destiny. From the standpoint of the good of the world as a whole, they are almost devoid of significance. Yet, one stands in a certain awe of them all, as soon as he sees what lies behind them: it is a compassionate heart that manages to overcome fear, hatred, and the sense of duty itself. However little it has won the praise of moralists and theologians, however little it may deck itself out with the ornamentation of intellect and reason, however strange and mysterious it may seem to the mind, it is still the fugitive and unpredictable thing that alone quickens moral esteem and stamps its possessor as a man who, although fallible and ignorant and capable of much evil, is nevertheless a man of deep goodness and virtue.

STUDY QUESTIONS

1. Taylor believes that a morality not founded in compassion is inadequate. Do you agree?

2. Taylor observes that much suffering and death (for example, from natural disasters) in not connected with morality. What sort of suffering *is* relevant to morality?

3. Is Taylor underestimating the role of reason in guiding and conditioning our sympathies? How would he account for the fact that otherwise decent people enjoy the spectacle of animal misery (for example, bullfights) or, in an earlier era, the spectacle of victims in a Roman Circus? Does this not suggest that our sympathies come into play only after we intellectually dispel prejudices against certain classes of beings?

4. Imagine a class of rational but emotionless beings. Can such rational beings have a moral system? What would Taylor say?

The Moral Insight

JOSIAH ROYCE

Josiah Royce (1855–1916), a professor of philosophy at Harvard University, was a colleague of William James and a teacher of George Santayana during what are known as the "golden years" of Harvard philosophy. Royce wrote in almost every area of philosophy, but is principally known as a proponent of idealism. His best known work in ethics is *The Philosophy of Loyalty* (1908).

For Royce the key to moral understanding lies in the realization that our neighbor is a center of experience and desire just as we are. Royce asks that we look upon that neighbor in much the same way we look upon our *future* selves—as a distant and somewhat unreal center of experience, but nevertheless of great concern. Sympathy and pity for another are not enough: Fellow feeling must also bring us to the point of what Royce calls the moral insight: "Such as that is for me, so is it for him, nothing less."

. . . [The following] is our reflective account of the process that, in some form, must come to every one under the proper conditions. In this process we see the beginning of the real knowledge of duty to others. The process is one that any child can and does, under proper guidance, occasionally accomplish. It is the process

THE MORAL INSIGHT From *The Religious Aspects of Philosophy* (Boston: Houghton Mifflin Co., 1885).

by which we all are accustomed to try to teach humane behavior in concrete cases. We try to get people to realize what they are doing when they injure others. But to distinguish this process from the mere tender emotion of sympathy, with all its illusions, is what moralists have not carefully enough done. Our exposition [tries] to take this universally recognized process, to distinguish it from sympathy as such, and to set it up before the gates of ethical doctrine as the great producer of insight.

But when we say that to this insight common sense must come, under the given conditions, we do not mean to say: "So the man, once having attained insight, must act thenceforth." The realization of one's neighbor, in the full sense of the word realization, is indeed the resolution to treat him as if he were real, that is, to treat him unselfishly. But this resolution expresses and belongs to the moment of insight. Passion may cloud the insight in the very next moment. It always does cloud the insight after no very long time. It is as impossible for us to avoid the illusion of selfishness in our daily lives, as to escape seeing through the illusion at the moment of insight. We see the reality of our neighbor, that is, we determine to treat him as we do ourselves. But then we go back to daily action, and we feel the heat of hereditary passions, and we straightway forget what we have seen. Our neighbor becomes obscured. He is once more a foreign power. He is unreal. We are again deluded and selfish. This conflict goes on and will go on as long as we live after the manner of men. Moments of insight, with their accompanying resolutions; long stretches of delusion and selfishness: That is our life.

To bring home this view . . . to the reader, we ask him to consider carefully just what experience he has when he tries to realize his neighbor in the full sense that we have insisted upon. Not pity as such is what we desire him to feel. For whether or not pity happens to work in him as selfishly and blindly as we have found that it often does work, still not the emotion, but its consequences, must in the most favorable case give us what we seek. All the forms of sympathy are mere impulses. It is the insight to which they bring us that has moral value. And again, the realization of our neighbor's existence is not at all the discovery that he is more or less useful to us personally. All that would contribute to selfishness. In an entirely different way we must realize his existence, if we are to be really altruistic. What then is our neighbor?

We find that out by treating him in thought just as we do ourselves. What art thou? Thou art now just a present state, with its experiences, thoughts, and desires. But what is thy future Self? Simply future states, future experiences, future thoughts and desires, that, although not now existing for thee, are postulated by thee as certain to come, and as in some real relation to thy present Self. What then is thy neighbor? He too is a mass of states, of experiences, thoughts, and desires, just as real as thou art, no more but yet no less present to thy experience now than is thy future Self. He is not that face that frowns or smiles at thee, although often thou thinkest of him as only that. He is not the arm that strikes or defends thee, not the voice that speaks to thee, not that machine that gives thee what thou desirest when thou movest it with the offer of money. To be sure, thou dost often think of him as if he were that automaton yonder, that answers thee when thou speakest to it. But no, thy neighbor is as actual, as concrete, as thou art. Just as thy future is real, though not now thine, so thy neighbor is real, though his thoughts never are thy thoughts. Dost thou believe this? Art thou sure what it means? This is for thee the turning-point of thy whole conduct towards him. What we now ask of thee is no sentiment, no gush of pity, no tremulous weakness of sympathy, but a calm, clear insight. . . .

If he is real like thee, then is his life as bright a light, as warm a fire, to him, as thine to thee; his will is as full of struggling desires, of hard problems, of fateful decisions; his pains are as hateful, his joys as dear. Take whatever thou knowest of desire and of striving, of burning love and of fierce hatred, realize as fully as thou canst what that means, and then with clear certainty add: *Such as that is for me, so is it for him, nothing less.* If thou dost that, can he remain to thee what he has been, a picture, a plaything, a comedy, or a tragedy, in brief a mere Show? Behind all that show thou hast indeed dimly felt that there is something. Know that truth thoroughly. Thou hast regarded his thought, his feeling, as somehow different in sort from thine. Thou hast said: "A pain in him is not like a pain in me, but something far easier to bear." Thou hast made of him a ghost, as the imprudent man makes of his future self a ghost. Even when thou hast feared his scorn, his hate, his contempt, thou hast not fully made him for thee as real as thyself. His laughter at thee has made thy face feel hot, his frowns and clenched fists have cowed thee, his sneers have made thy throat feel choked. But that was only the social instinct in thee. It was not a full sense of his reality. Even so the little baby smiles back at one that smiles at it, but not because it realizes the approving joy of the other, only because it by instinct enjoys a smiling face; and even so the baby is frightened at harsh speech, but not because it realizes the other's anger. So, dimly and by instinct, thou has lived with thy neighbor, and hast known him not, being blind. Thou hast even desired his pain, but thou hast not fully realized the pain that thou gavest. It has been to thee, not pain in itself, but the sight of his submission, of his tears, or of his pale terror. Of thy neighbor thou hast made a thing, no Self at all.

When thou hast loved, hast pitied, or hast reverenced thy neighbor, then thy feeling has possibly raised for a moment the veil of illusion. Then thou hast known what he truly is, a Self like thy present Self. But thy selfish feeling is too strong for thee. Thou hast forgotten soon again what thou hadst seen, and hast made even of thy beloved one only the instrument of thy own pleasure. Even out of thy power to pity thou hast made an object of thy vainglory. Thy reverence has turned again to pride. Thou hast accepted the illusion once more. No wonder that in his darkness thou findest selfishness the only rule of any meaning for thy conduct. Thou forgottest that without realization of thy future and as yet unreal self, even selfishness means nothing. Thou forgottest that if thou gavest thy present thought even so to the task of realizing thy neighbor's life, selfishness would seem no more plain to thee than the love of thy neighbor.

Have done then with this illusion that thy Self is all in all. Intuition tells thee no more about thy future Self than it tells thee about thy neighbors. Desire, bred in thee by generations of struggle for existence, emphasizes the expectation of thy own bodily future, the love for thy own bodily welfare, and makes thy body's life seem alone real. But simply try to know the truth. The truth is that all this world of life about thee is as real as thou art. All conscious life is conscious in its own measure. Pain is pain, joy is joy, everywhere even as in thee. The result of thy insight will be inevitable. The illusion vanishing, the glorious prospect opens before thy vision. Seeing the oneness of this life everywhere, the equal reality of all its moments, thou wilt be ready to treat it all with the reverence that prudence would have thee show to thy own little bit of future life. What prudence in its narrow respectability counseled, thou wilt be ready to do universally. As the prudent man, seeing the reality of his future self, inevitably works for it; so the enlightened man, seeing the reality of all conscious life, realizing that it is no shadow, but fact, at once and inevitably desires, if only for that one moment of insight, to enter into the service of the whole of it. . . .Lift up thy eyes, behold that life, and then turn away and forget it as thou canst; but if thou hast known that, thou hast begun to know thy duty.

STUDY QUESTIONS

1. Some people call Royce's "Moral Insight" a description of the moral point of view. Do you agree?
2. Is Royce's Insight really another version of the Golden Rule?
3. Royce recommends that we look upon our neighbor in the same way we look upon our future selves. Are you morally considerate of your future self? Should this be a basic moral precept: Do unto others as you would do unto your future self?

The Tragedy of King Lear

LIONEL TRILLING

Lionel Trilling (1905–1975) was a professor of English at Columbia University and a renowned critic and writer. He is the author of several books, including *The Liberal Imagination* (1940), *Beyond Culture* (1965), and *Sincerity and Authenticity* (1972). In 1967, he published a college textbook anthology in which he introduced each of the literary selections with a short critical commentary. Trilling's fifty-two introductions have come to be considered small critical classics and have been published independently in *Prefaces to the Experience of Literature*. "The Tragedy of King Lear" is an excerpt from Trilling's introduction to *King Lear*.

King Lear, regarded by many as Shakespeare's greatest play, takes place in ancient Britain and opens in the palace of King Lear. Now an old man, Lear has decided to divide his kingdom among his three daughters: Whoever professes the greatest love for him will receive the largest share. Regan and Goneril, being greedy and corrupt, lavish praise on their old father; Cordelia, Lear's youngest and most beloved daughter, refuses to take part in this love test. Her refusal so enrages him that he disinherits her and divides his kingdom between Goneril and Regan. Lear arranges to spend half his time with Regan and half with Goneril, but very soon his

THE TRAGEDY OF KING LEAR Abridged from the "The Tragedy of King Lear" in *Prefaces to the Experience of Literature*, copyright © 1967 by Lionel Trilling. Reprinted by permission of Harcourt Brace Jovanovich, Inc.

presence annoys them and they begin to mistreat him. When Lear finally realizes that he has put himself at the mercy of these treacherous and cruel daughters ("unnatural hags"), he is driven half mad and runs out into a raging storm. He is eventually rescued and reunited with Cordelia. They are both taken prisoner by Goneril and Regan, but Lear is content to be with Cordelia and does not care. Regan, Goneril, and their cohorts are soon defeated, but one of their henchmen manages to carry out an order to kill Cordelia. In the final scene, Lear appears carrying his dead daughter in his arms. He dies of a broken heart.

Trilling observes in his preface that, in *King Lear,* Shakespeare gives us some ground for thinking that human existence is absurd, that it appears at times to be in the grips of an inimical power the more terrible because "no purpose can be ascribed to its enmity." But the play also shows that human beings themselves cause human suffering whenever they disturb the natural social order. Lear does so when, out of foolish pride, he divides his kingdom and disinherits his youngest daughter. The tragedy could have been averted. By showing that Lear is himself the author of the untoward events depicted in the play, says Trilling, Shakespeare takes for granted a rational and moralized universe that human beings all too often disturb at their own peril.

Of the supreme achievements of the creative mind with which *King Lear* is usually compared, it is perhaps the only one that seems to issue in hopelessness. Our conception of greatness in art inclines to set special store by the tragic vision, and our highest admiration most readily goes to those works that have some large element of darkness and dread. But when we bring to mind the masterpieces of art, and not only of literary art, with which *King Lear* is commonly ranked—the *Iliad, Oedipus Rex, The Divine Comedy,* Michelangelo's *Last Judgment,* Bach's *B-Minor Mass,* Beethoven's *Fifth Symphony*—we perceive that in all of them the dark elements are countered by strong affirmative emotions and attitudes. If in any of these works hope is not fully ascendant, it at least holds in balance the elements that might make for despair.

We do not necessarily feel this of *King Lear.* Here is a preeminently great work in which the positive expectations of life are considerably outweighed by the horrifying circumstances that are put before us. It is true that at the end of the play the evil-doers have been destroyed, the good are in control of the kingdom, and order and justice are soon to be restored. But the concluding scene speaks less of peace, let alone of hope, than of an ultimate weariness. Again and again in the course of the play the goodness and meaningfulness of life have been brought into question, and now, as life is about to resume its normal course, it can show little of the energy that might dispel the doubts that have been raised. In his last speech Kent refuses Albany's invitation to share the rule of the realm, giving as his reason that his death, which he desires, is near at hand. And Edgar's concluding words seem so charged with fatigue that they can scarcely get themselves uttered:

> The weight of this sad time we must obey;
> Speak what we feel, not what we ought to say.
> The oldest hath borne most; we that are young
> Shall never see so much, nor live so long.

No other of Shakespeare's tragedies ends on anything like the note of exhaustion sounded by these gray monosyllables. The closing speeches of *Hamlet, Macbeth,* and *Antony and Cleopatra* move to a music that summons the future into being. . . .

There can be no doubt that *King Lear* gives us ground for thinking the universe absurd. Again and again it proposes the idea of some ineluctable contradiction between the universe and man. Man's existence proceeds in circumstances so painful that we may well think of them as arranged by a hostile power which is the more terrible because no purpose can be ascribed to its enmity nor any order discerned in its behavior. Against this irrational animus there is no defence—all that men can do is endure. And the despair that King Lear embodies is concentrated in the line in which Edgar says what it is that they must endure, their "going hence, even as their coming hither"—it is surely a despairing imagination that proposes the bitterness of dying in terms of the bitterness of being born. The phrase that follows, "Ripeness is all," does not qualify the sentiment, for "ripeness" here does not mean richness or fulness of life but readiness for death, the only escape from absurdity.

But the incompatibility between rational man and an absurd

universe is only one of the two explanations of human suffering suggested in *King Lear*. The other holds man himself accountable for his pain, either through his self-deception or through the cruelty of other members of the race. The play makes no hard and fast distinction between the two explanations. Nevertheless we can scarcely doubt that it requires us to see that the immediate cause of any man's suffering is his fellow man: the cruel will of nonhuman powers is put into execution by evil men. The intensity of the suffering is such and the bitterness over man's destiny of suffering is such that they can find adequate expression only by crying out to heaven. But at the quiet heart of the whirling speculations about the universe or the absolute there lies the idea of human justice and human mercy. When it is said that Lear is "regenerated" and "redeemed," the change that is being remarked upon in the aged king is his new consciousness of man's inhumanity to man, of the general failure of justice: his mind becomes obsessed with justice, he is filled with disgust at those human traits that stand in the way of its being done—greed, lust, pride, and the hypocrisy that masks them. And with the new consciousness of justice goes a new sense of the need for *caritas*, which is not "charity" in our usual modern sense, but "caring," the solicitude of loving-kindness:

> Poor naked wretches, wheresoe'er you are,
> That bide the pelting of this pitiless storm,
> How shall your houseless heads and unfed sides,
> Your loop'd and window'd raggedness, defend you
> From seasons such as these? O, I have ta'en
> Too little care of this! Take physic, pomp;
> Expose thyself to feel what wretches feel,
> That thou mayst shake the superflux to them,
> And show the heavens more just.

Although Lear does touch upon the cruelty of the universe, this is far less the object of his new consciousness than the failure of man's governance of himself, his falling short of what is required of him in doing justice and in loving mercy.

If we speak of a "failure" and a "falling short," we suggest not merely a thing to be desired, but also a standard or norm. I have said that we never know just how to understand the word "nature" as it is used in *King Lear*. But we cannot fail to recognize that among its several meanings is that of a normative principle. And one element of the human norm it implies, one term of the definition of man, is a certain degree of moral virtue, or at least the propensity for conduct which, if it departs from virtue, does not do so beyond a certain point. The play offers abundant evidence that human beings are capable of going well beyond that point. Yet the supposition that man's nature is to be defined in moral terms is not thereby denied.

Our commitment to the idea of the normative virtue of man is apparent in our language, as in our use of the word "humanity" to mean kindness or at least compunction in dealing with other members of the race, or with animals. Burns's famous lines, "Man's inhumanity to man/Makes countless thousands mourn," which everyone understands, would be nonsense were we not to take normative virtue for granted, for what could it possibly mean to speak of human beings acting in an inhuman fashion unless the *idea* of being human implied a degree of goodness, whatever the *actuality* of being human may mean? Bradley has remarked on the frequency with which the idea of monstrosity appears in *King Lear;* the play, he says, is replete with "beings, actions, states of mind, which appear not only abnormal but absolutely contrary to nature." In the degree to which people are good, they are felt to be natural, Kent and Cordelia being obvious cases in point: we are aware of their naturalness as a positive quality of their being, expressing itself in their manner and mode of speech. But Goneril and Regan are said by Lear to be "unnatural hags." Cornwall's blinding of Gloucester is an unnatural act, and an especially moving moment of the play represents the natural response to the monstrosity of this deed: one of Cornwall's servants cannot endure it and, knowing that he risks his life, draws his sword to prevent it. To Shakespeare's contemporary audience, this action must have been even more momentous that it is to us, for to the Elizabethans the idea of a servant confronting his master with a show of force would have been shocking, even unnatural. The Elizabethan judgment is underscored by Cornwall's crying out amazed, "My villian!" (using the word in its old sense of farm servant), and by Regan's exclamation, "A peasant stand up thus!" To the feudal lord and lady it was as much a shattering of the natural order for their servant to defy them as Lear felt it to be when his daughters rejected him. Shakespeare quite shared the opinion of his time; he believed that the deference given to superiors was in the order of nature. But in this instance his sympathy is given to the peasant who flares into hopeless rebellion at the hideous deed, who, though he break the "natural" bonds of society, does so because he recognizes a claim yet *more* natural, that of his humanity, of justice and mercy.

An awareness of the Elizabethan feeling about the naturalness of the social order will lead us to a more accurate judgment of the act out of which all the horrors and misfortunes arose, Lear's division of his kingdom. To this no Elizabethan, and surely not Shakespeare himself, would have responded with indifference. Again and again in his plays, Shakespeare speaks in praise of unity, of the organic interrelation of the parts of a polity. To divide a kingdom, to treat a realm as if it were not a living organism, was worse than imprudent, it was unnatural. It may have been unavoidable in view of Lear's failing strength and the lack of a male heir, but still it went against nature; its consequences could only be bad.

In short, *King Lear* raises moral, social, and even political considerations that mark out an area in which human life is not wholly determined by nonhuman forces, in which the absurdity of the universe is not wholly decisive. Although this area is not coextensive with man's existence, it is of very large extent. One hesitates to speak of it as an area of freedom, if only because any one individual is so little likely to be free within it. Yet it is the precinct in which mankind as a whole, with due regard to the well-being of its individual members, has the possibility of freedom. To be aware of this possibility will scarcely dispel all the dark thoughts that the play induces. But it does qualify the view that human suffering is to be referred only to an absurd dispensation.

Some large part of the human condition is, however, imposed upon man and makes a fate that is as grotesque as it is inescapable. Lear must grow old, his powers of body and mind must wane and fail. Nothing can save him from this destined end. Yet this in itself is not the root of his suffering as the play represents it. What maddens the old man is the loss of what might sustain him in his decline, the honor and dignity he has assumed to be his inalienable right. To grow old is a hard destiny. But to grow old in honor and dignity is not unendurable, while to grow old shorn of respect is a nightmare, the very essence of the grotesque. Respect is sometimes regarded as a sort of social fiction because it is expressed through signs and outward forms, such as the manner and tone in which the respected person is addressed, or the appurtenances of life that are bestowed upon him. Lear himself defines the symbolic nature of respect in his great reply to Regan's statement that he has no "need" of his train of knights:

> O, reason not the need! Our basest beggars
> Are in the poorest thing superfluous.
> Allow not nature more than nature needs,
> Man's life is cheap as beast's. Thou art a lady;
> If only to go warm were gorgeous,
> Why, nature needs not what thou gorgeous wear'st,
> Which scarcely keeps thee warm.

He says in effect that man creates his own needs—and that these are even more imperative than those of biology. The meanings and "values" that social man invents for himself are presented as of transcendent importance not only in this speech of Lear's but throughout the play, most notably in all that Kent and Cordelia say to the old man and all they do for him, in the one short time when they have him in their loving charge, to assure him that he has been restored to his kingliness and to the respect that befits it.

Of all that is implied by the play's intense awareness of that area of life in which human conceptions and conduct are prepotent, Professor Kott takes no account in his effort to demonstrate the nihilism of *King Lear.* "The theme of *King Lear,*" he says, "is the decay and fall of the world." And so in part it is, but in part only—the full theme of *King Lear* is the decay and fall of the world as a consequence of a decay and fall of the human soul. It is indeed true that the vitality of the meanings and values created by man depends to some extent on a belief in a transcendent reason, and that to doubt the existence of such reason puts all in doubt. This would seem to be the animating idea of the theatre of the absurd in which Professor Kott finds such strong affinities with *King Lear.* But the dramatist of the theatre of the absurd takes for granted a metaphysical negation which has the effect of destroying the old human meanings and of making human life grotesque, whereas such a causal sequence was not conceived by Shakespeare. He took for granted a rational and moralized universe but proposed the idea that this universal order might be reduced to chaos by human evil.

Speaking in praise of *King Lear,* the English novelist Iris Murdoch said, "Only the very greatest art invigorates without consoling. . . ." That *King Lear* does not console is plain enough. If we ask how, in the face of its dire report of life, this play can be said to invigorate, the answer is that it does us the honor of supposing that we will make every possible effort of mind to withstand the force of its despair and to understand the complexity of what it tells us about the nature of human existence: it draws us into more activity than we had thought ourselves capable of.

STUDY QUESTIONS

1. According to Trilling, what two explanations of human suffering are suggested in *King Lear*?
2. What does Trilling mean by the "symbolic nature of respect"?
3. Do you agree with (what seems to be) Shakespeare's view that being fully human implies a degree of goodness?
4. Many critics read *King Lear* as unrelieved tragedy and attribute to Shakespeare a wholly despairing and pessimistic viewpoint. Unlike these critics, Trilling defends a more optimistic interpretation of the play. Does he make his case?
5. Assuming, for the sake of argument, that Trilling's interpretation of *King Lear* is wrong, is he also wrong to suggest that human beings can achieve dignity and create the conditions for a rational and "moralized" world?

SUGGESTED READINGS

Arendt, Hannah. *Eichmann in Jerusalem: A Report on the Banality of Evil*. New York: Viking Press, 1965.

Douglass, Frederick. *Life and Times of Frederick Douglass: Written by Himself.* New York: Collier Press, 1962.

Hallie, Philip. *Lest Innocent Blood Be Shed*. New York: Harper and Row, 1979.

———. *The Paradox of Cruelty*. Middletown, Conn.: Wesleyan University, 1979.

Shakespeare, William. *King Lear.*

Taylor, Richard. *Good and Evil*. Buffalo, N.Y.: Prometheus Press, 1970.

Twain, Mark. *Huckleberry Finn.*

Chapter

2

THEORIES OF
MORAL CONDUCT

In this section we begin by presenting several sacred texts of the Judeo-Christian tradition that are central to the moral heritage of the Western world. The Ten Commandments, the Psalms, the Sermon on the Mount, and the parable of the good Samaritan have inspired and guided people for centuries. The view that our moral obligations come directly from God is known as the Divine Command theory of morality. A number of philosophers have sought alternative accounts of morality: Some are atheists and therefore reject out of hand any theory that presupposes a deity; others, though believers, look for an account of right and wrong that does not rely on revelation. Plato, in his dialogue the *Euthyphro*, first asked a question that often arises in connection with the Divine Command theory: Are the actions that God decrees good only because God approves of them, or does He approve of them because they are good? Might God just as easily decree that we be cruel and refrain from kindness, or do the divine decrees conform to independently valid criteria of good and evil? Perhaps the majority of moral philosophers believe that morality is independently valid. And some theologians go between the horns of the dilemma, maintaining that God's will and objective good are coincident. Much of moral philosophy since Plato consists of attempts to formulate objective criteria for what is right and good.

Two of the most influential alternatives to the Divine Command theory are utilitarianism and Kantianism. Utilitarianism was developed by the British philosophers Jeremy Bentham (1748–1832) and John Stuart Mill (1806–1873). For the utilitarian, morally good actions are actions that increase the happiness of conscious beings. According to Mill's Greatest Happiness Principle, "actions are right in proportion as they tend to promote happiness, wrong as they tend to produce the reverse of happiness." (And, says Mill, God's decrees are good precisely because obedience to them increases happiness; that is *why* God decreed them.) Mill and Bentham thought of the principle of utility as a moral yardstick. Just as two people who disagree over the height of a ceiling can settle the matter with a ruler, so two people who disagree over the rightness of an action need only subject it to the test of utility: Will it increase or diminish happiness?

Though many contemporary philosophers favor utilitarianism over other moral theories (indeed, one philosopher recently remarked that utilitarians constitute a silent majority among professional philosophers), they generally acknowledge it to be seriously flawed. Suppose we could greatly increase human happiness and diminish misery by occasionally, and perhaps secretly, abducting derelicts from city streets for use in fatal but urgent medical experiments. If utilitarian considerations were decisive, this practice might well be justifiable, even desirable. Yet it is surely wrong. Such a case suggests that we cannot always explain good and bad simply in terms of increasing or decreasing overall happiness.

Many philosophers reject utilitarianism in favor of Kantianism. The eighteenth-century philosopher Immanuel Kant (1724–1804) sought the foundations of morality in the human capacity to act rationally. A rational being is free to act out of principle and to refrain from acting from mere impulse or the desire for pleasure. According to Kant, the proper exercise of reason reveals to us our moral duties. It is not, he says, the *consequences* of an action (its "utility" as Mill claims) that determine its moral character, but the principle on which the action is based. As rational creatures we must be consistent and objective. So, says Kant, we must always ask ourselves whether or not we base an action on a principle (Kant calls it a "maxim") that we consistently want to see adopted as a universal law governing the behavior of all rational beings. A utilitarian might justify an occasional lie that has pleasant consequences. For Kant this is unacceptable: Reason dictates honesty as a *universal* principle. Any deception, however one might try to justify it, is for Kant an affront to the dignity of the deceived. Principled behavior invariably respects oneself and others; it brooks no exceptions.

Kantianism is attractive for its emphasis on conscientiousness and human dignity, but, like utilitarianism, it faces difficulties. Acting on principle without regard for the consequences does not always seem right. According to Kant, if a murderer comes to your door demanding to know the whereabouts of an intended victim who is hiding in your house, you must not lie to him no matter what the consequences. Utilitarians criticize Kantians for their readiness to sacrifice human happiness for the sake of principles; on their side, the Kantians object to utilitarianism for failing to give duty a proper place in its moral theory.

Because Kant and Mill differ in very important ways, their fundamental similarities are easy to ignore. Both hold that morality is the same for everyone everywhere; thus both Mill and Kant are prepared to judge exotic practices in other cultures by the same standards they judge the practices of their own society. In particular, both would condemn the practice that Mary Midgley cites in her essay "Trying Out One's New Sword" in which a Samurai warrior determines the effectiveness of his sword by seeing how cleanly it can slice an unsuspecting passerby in two. And both theories are in keeping with the spirit of the sacred texts that begin this chapter. Indeed, both Kant and Mill claim that their theories are little more than an elaborate working out of the Golden Rule.

The moral theories of Kant and Mill are designed to provide a theoretical foundation for the Judeo-Christian ethic. Not all moral theories aim to do this. Ethical egoism is a theory that gives no privileged status to any traditional set of moral precepts. Its central teaching: Act in such a way as to increase *your* happiness and advance *your* interests. In the selection "Egoism and Moral Skepticism," James Rachels exposes some of the logical errors in the doctrine, but he also criticizes it for being morally perverse. As he notes, the ethical egoist who likes watching fires can consistently hold that burning down a department store full of people is "right for him."

Finally, we must consider the influential views of the ethical relativist, who claims that there are no objective criteria or standards for determining right and wrong: Each society has its own ethic, just as it has its own rules of etiquette and style of dress. Ethical relativism became popular in the nineteenth century when social scientists traveled to distant corners of the globe and discovered the wide variety of moral practices. According to the ethical relativist, the moral precepts found in the Bible are no more or less correct than the quite different moral precepts found in the sacred texts of other societies. The anthropologist Ruth Benedict (1887–1948) presents the consequences in "A Defense of Moral Relativism." Her experiences as a field anthropologist convinced her that morals, like rules of etiquette, are just a matter of group practice. Says Benedict, "Mankind has always preferred to say, 'It is morally good,' rather than 'It is habitual,' . . . But historically the two phrases are synonymous."

Ethical relativism is a tempting doctrine because it appeals to our desire to be tolerant of other societies. But it has not found much favor among professional philosophers. W. T. Stace's article, "Ethical Relativism: A Critique," presents many of the objections that can be raised against it. Mary Midgley makes the interesting point, in "Trying Out One's New Sword," that if each society is a distinct unit and not to be judged except on its own terms, then not only are we unable to criticize another society for practices we as outsiders find morally objectionable; we are, by the same token, unable to praise that society for those things that we find admirable.

A number of philosophers point out that those who adopt ethical relativism because they wish to be respectful of other cultures cannot be selective in what they choose to tolerate. For example, they must not only tolerate the Aztecs, who practice human sacrifice in their religious service, but also the mercenaries and colonialists whose moral code permits them to exterminate or enslave such "heathens." Tolerance of exotic practices is double-edged in another respect as well. On one hand, it is a manifestation of a sophisticated appreciation of difference; on the other hand, our tolerance of violence or cruelty in other cultures verges on callousness toward the sufferings of the unfortunate victims. And, generally, as long as the perpetrator of what we look upon as a crime can point out that his behavior is acceptable and customary on "his own island," we cannot clearly say that an honest and consistent ethical relativist has grounds to condemn him.

The Judeo-Christian Tradition

The Ten Commandments (Exodus 20:1–17) and the First, Fifteenth, and Twenty-third Psalms are from the Old Testament. The Sermon on the Mount (Luke 6:17–49) and the parable of the good Samaritan (Luke 10: 25–37) are from the New Testament. The two testaments comprehend 1,000 years of Judeo-Christian history. They do not constitute a single ethical system. But they powerfully express moral ideals of incalculable authority and influence.

The Ten Commandments

Then God delivered all these commandments:

"I, the LORD, am your God, who brought you out of the land of Egypt, that place of slavery. You shall not have other gods besides me. You shall not carve idols for yourselves in the shape of anything in the sky above or on the earth below or in the waters beneath the earth; you shall not bow down before them or worship them. For I, the LORD, your God, am a jealous God, inflicting punishment for their fathers' wickedness on the children of those who hate me, down to the third and fourth generation; but bestowing mercy down to the thousandth generation, on the children of those who love me and keep my commandments.

"You shall not take the name of the Lord, your God, in vain. For the Lord will not leave unpunished him who takes his name in vain.

"Remember to keep holy the sabbath day. Six days you may labor and do all your work, but the seventh day is the sabbath of the Lord, your God. No work may be done then either by you, or your son or daughter, or your male or female slave, or your beast, or by the alien who lives with you. In six days the Lord made the heavens and the earth, the sea and all that is in them; but on the seventh day he rested. That is why the Lord has blessed the sabbath day and made it holy.

"Honor your father and your mother, that you may have a long life in the land which the Lord, your God, is giving you.

"You shall not kill.

"You shall not commit adultery.

"You shall not steal.

"You shall not bear false witness against your neighbor.

"You shall not covet your neighbor's house. You shall not covet your neighbor's wife, nor his male or female slave, nor his ox or ass, nor anything else that belongs to him."

Psalm 1

True Happiness

I

Happy the man who follows not
   the counsel of the wicked
Nor walks in the way of sinners,
   nor sits in the company of the
     insolent,
But delights in the law of the Lord
   and meditates on his law day and
     night.
He is like a tree
   planted near running water,

That yields its fruit in due season,
    and whose leaves never fade.
    [Whatever he does, prospers.]

II

Not so the wicked, not so;
    they are like chaff which the wind
        drives away.
Therefore in judgment the wicked
    shall not stand,
    nor shall sinners, in the assembly of
        the just.
For the LORD watches over the way
    of the just,
    but the way of the wicked vanishes.

Psalm 15

The Guest of God

A psalm of David.

I

O LORD, who shall sojourn in your
    tent?
Who shall dwell on your holy
    mountain?

II

He who walks blamelessly and does
    justice;
    who thinks the truth in his heart
    and slanders not with his tongue;
Who harms not his fellow man,
    nor takes up a reproach against his
        neighbor;
By whom the reprobate is despised,
    while he honors those who fear the
        LORD;

Who, though it be to his loss, changes
    not his pledged word;
  who lends not his money at usury
  and accepts not bribe against the
    innocent.

Psalm 23

The Lord, Shepherd and Host

A psalm of David.

I

The LORD is my shepherd; I shall not
    want
  In verdant pastures he gives me
    repose;
Beside restful waters he leads me;
  he refreshes my soul.
He guides me in right paths
  for his name's sake.
Even though I walk in the dark valley
  I fear no evil; for you are at my
    side
With your rod and your staff
  that give me courage.

II

You spread the table before me
  in the sight of my foes;
You anoint my head with oil;
  my cup overflows.
Only goodness and kindness follow
    me
  all the days of my life;
And I shall dwell in the house of the
    LORD
  for years to come.

The Sermon on the Mount

Coming down the mountain with them, he stopped at a level stretch where there were many of his disciples; a large crowd of people was with them from all Judea and Jerusalem and the coast of Tyre and Sidon, people who came to hear him and be healed of their diseases. Those who were troubled with unclean spirits were cured; indeed, the whole crowd was trying to touch him because power went out from him which cured all.

Then, raising his eyes to his disciples, he said:

> "Blest are you poor; the reign of God is yours.
> Blest are you who hunger; you shall be filled.
> Blest are you who are weeping; you shall laugh.

Blest shall you be when men hate you, when they ostracize you and insult you and proscribe your name as evil because of the Son of Man. On the day they do so, rejoice and exult, for your reward shall be great in heaven. Thus it was that their fathers treated the prophets.

> "But woe to you rich, for your consolation is now.
> Woe to you who are full; you shall go hungry.
> Woe to you who laugh now; you shall weep in your grief.

"Woe to you when all speak well of you. Their fathers treated the false prophets in just this way.

Love of One's Enemy

"To you who hear me, I say: Love your enemies, do good to those who hate you; bless those who curse you and pray for those who maltreat you. When someone slaps you on one cheek, turn and give him the other; when someone takes your coat, let him have your shirt as well. Give to all who beg from you. When a man takes what is yours, do not demand it back. Do to others what you would have them do to you. If you love those who love you, what credit is that to you? Even sinners love those who love them. If you do good to those who do good to you, how can you claim any credit? Sinners do as much. If you lend to those from whom you expect repayment, what merit is there in it for you? Even sinners lend to sinners, expecting to be repaid in full.

"Love your enemy and do good; lend without expecting repay-

75

ment. Then will your recompense be great. You will rightly be called sons of the Most High, since he himself is good to the ungrateful and the wicked.

"Be compassionate, as your Father is compassionate. Do not judge, and you will not be judged. Do not condemn, and you will not be condemned. Pardon, and you shall be pardoned. Give, and it shall be given to you. Good measure pressed down, shaken together, running over, will they pour into the fold of your garment. For the measure you measure with will be measured back to you."

He also used images in speaking to them: "Can a blind man act as guide to a blind man? Will they not both fall into a ditch? A student is not above his teacher; but every student when he has finished his studies will be on a par with his teacher.

"Why look at the speck in your brother's eye when you miss the plank in your own? How can you say to your brother, 'Brother, let me remove the speck from your eye,' yet fail yourself to see the plank lodged in your own? Hypocrite, remove the plank from your own eye first; then you will see clearly enough to remove the speck from your brother's eye.

"A good tree does not produce decayed fruit any more than a decayed tree produces good fruit. Each tree is known by its yield. Figs are not taken from thornbushes, nor grapes picked from brambles. A good man produces goodness from the good in his heart; an evil man produces evil out of his store of evil. Each man speaks from his heart's abundance. Why do you call me 'Lord, Lord,' and not put into practice what I teach you? Any man who desires to come to me will hear my words and put them into practice. I will show you with whom he is to be compared. He may be likened to the man who, in building a house, dug deeply and laid the foundation on a rock. When the floods came the torrent rushed in on that house, but failed to shake it because of its solid foundation. On the other hand, anyone who has heard my words but not put them into practice is like the man who built his house on the ground without any foundation. When the torrent rushed upon it, it immediately fell in and was completely destroyed."

The Good Samaritan

On one occasion a lawyer stood up to pose him this problem: "Teacher, what must I do to inherit everlasting life?"

Jesus answered him: "What is written in the law? How do you read it?" He replied:

"You shall love the Lord your God
with all your heart,
with all your soul,
with all your strength,
and with all your mind;
and your neighbor as yourself."

Jesus said, "You have answered correctly. Do this and you shall live." But because he wished to justify himself he said to Jesus, "And who is my neighbor?" Jesus replied: "There was a man going down from Jerusalem to Jericho who fell prey to robbers. They stripped him, beat him, and then went off leaving him half-dead. A priest happened to be going down the same road; he saw him but continued on. Likewise there was a Levite who came the same way; he saw him and went on. But a Samaritan who was journeying along came on him and was moved to pity at the sight. He approached him and dressed his wounds, pouring in oil and wine. He then hoisted him on his own beast and brought him to an inn, where he cared for him. The next day he took out two silver pieces and gave them to the innkeeper with the request: 'Look after him, and if there is any further expense I will repay you on my way back.'

"Which of these three, in your opinion, was neighbor to the man who fell in with the robbers?" The answer came. "The one who treated him with compassion." Jesus said to him, "Then go and do the same."

STUDY QUESTIONS

1. Several of the Ten Commandments are theological. What, in your opinion, is the relationship between a belief in God and divine law and a belief in moral laws such as prohibition of theft and murder? What are the advantages or disadvantages of a moral theory not founded on religious beliefs?
2. Draw up and justify a list of commandments that have no theological content. Be succinct.
3. What moral ideals does Psalm 1 express? What rewards adhere

77

to them? Do you believe that the descriptions of the contrasting lives of just and unjust individuals are substantially correct?

4. What principles of personal morality are prominent in the Fifteenth Psalm? Do you believe the principles are binding on yourself or would you wish to revise them? Explain and justify.

5. A sermon often contains hyperbole. Do you believe that the ideal of loving one's enemy and doing good to those who hate us is seriously and literally intended? If it is not literal but rhetorical, what was the point of stating it?

6. The Sermon on the Mount exhorts us to be compassionate "as your Father is compassionate." We also find this theme of *imitatio dei* in the Old Testament. This suggests that one approach to the moral life is to conceive of ourselves as striving to imitate a perfect and divine being. Do you think that this is a helpful way of thinking about the moral life?

7. The moral teachings of Jesus are sometimes criticized for setting too high a standard for human behavior. Do you think the criticism is justified?

Utilitarianism

JOHN STUART MILL

John Stuart Mill (1806–1873) was one of the greatest philosophers of the nineteenth century. Though he wrote in many different areas in philosophy, he is best known for his defense of utilitarianism. Mill was an active political reformer; while a member of Parliament, he introduced a bill to give the vote to women. His best known works are *On Liberty* (1859), *Utilitarianism* (1863), and *The Subjection of Women* (1869).

Mill defines happiness as pleasure and the absence of pain, and asserts the general principle (elsewhere called the principle of utility) that "actions are right in proportion as they tend to promote happiness, wrong as they tend to produce the reverse of happiness."

Some opponents of utilitarianism charge that the pursuit of pleasure is an unworthy ideal ("a doctrine worthy of swine"). Mill defends his principle by distinguishing higher and lower pleasures. One pleasure is higher than another if people who have experienced both usually prefer the former. In fact, most human beings prefer the higher pleasures, choosing an existence that employs their higher faculties (their ability to enjoy good music) over an existence that employs the lower faculties they share with swine. "Few human creatures would consent to be changed into any of the lower animals, for a promise of the fullest allowance of a beast's pleasures. . . ." The actions enjoined by the principle of utility tend to produce the greatest happi-

UTILITARIANISM From *Utilitarianism* by John Stuart Mill (1863).

ness altogether; the principle is not restricted to an agent's own happiness. In considering their own happiness and that of others, good utilitarians are strictly impartial. This is Mill's version of the Golden Rule: "to do as you would be done by, and to love your neighbour as yourself."

What Utilitarianism Is

. . . [T]he Greatest Happiness Principle, holds that actions are right in proportion as they tend to promote happiness, wrong as they tend to produce the reverse of happiness. By happiness is intended pleasure, and the absence of pain; by unhappiness, pain, and the privation of pleasure. To give a clear view of the moral standard set up by the theory, much more requires to be said; in particular, what things it includes in the ideas of pain and pleasure; and to what extent this is left an open question. But these supplementary explanations do not affect the theory of life on which this theory of morality is grounded—namely, that pleasure, and freedom from pain, are the only things desirable as ends; and that all desirable things (which are as numerous in the utilitarian as in any other scheme) are desirable either for the pleasure inherent in themselves, or as means to the promotion of pleasure and the prevention of pain.

Now, such a theory of life excites in many minds, and among them in some of the most estimable in feeling and purpose, inveterate dislike. To suppose that life has (as they express it) no higher end than pleasure—no better and nobler object of desire and pursuit—they designate as utterly mean and grovelling; as a doctrine worthy only of swine, to whom the followers of Epicurus were, at a very early period, contemptuously likened; and modern holders of the doctrine are occasionally made the subject of equally polite comparisons by its German, French, and English assailants.

When thus attacked, the Epicureans have always answered, that it is not they, but their accusers, who represent human nature in a degrading light; since the accusation supposes human beings to be capable of no pleasures except those of which swine are capable. If this supposition were true, the charge could not be gainsaid, but would then be no longer an imputation; for if the sources of pleasure were precisely the same to human beings and to swine, the rule of life which is good enough for the one would be good enough for the other. The comparison of the Epicurean life to that of beasts is felt as degrading, precisely because a beast's pleasures do not satisfy a human being's conceptions of happiness. Human beings have faculties more elevated than the animal appetites, and when once made conscious of them, do not regard anything as happiness which does not include their gratification. I do not, indeed, consider the Epicureans to have been by any means faultless in drawing out their scheme of consequences from the utilitarian principle. To do this in any sufficient manner, many Stoic, as well as Christian elements require to be included. But there is no known Epicurean theory of life which does not assign to the pleasures of the intellect, of the feelings and imagination, and of the moral sentiments, a much higher value as pleasures than to those of mere sensation. It must be admitted, however, that utilitarian writers in general have placed the superiority of mental over bodily pleasures chiefly in the greater permanency, safety, uncostliness, etc., of the former—that is, in their circumstantial advantages rather than in their intrinsic nature. And on all these points utilitarians have fully proved their case; but they might have taken the other, and, as it may be called, higher ground, with entire consistency. It is quite compatible with the principle of utility to recognise the fact, that some *kinds* of pleasure are more desirable and more valuable than others. It would be absurd that while, in estimating all other things, quality is considered as well as quantity, the estimation of pleasures should be supposed to depend on quantity alone.

If I am asked, what I mean by difference of quality in pleasures, or what makes one pleasure more valuable than another, merely as a pleasure, except its being greater in amount, there is but one possible answer. Of two pleasures, if there be one to which all or almost all who have experience of both give a decided preference, irrespective of any feeling of moral obligation to prefer it, that is the more desirable pleasure. If one of the two is, by those who are competently acquainted with both, placed so far above the other that they prefer it, even though knowing it to be attended with a greater amount of discontent, and would not resign it for any quantity of the other pleasure which their nature is capable of, we are justified in ascribing to the preferred enjoyment a superiority in quality, so far outweighing quantity as to render it, in comparison, of small account.

81

Now it is an unquestionable fact that those who are equally acquainted with, and equally capable of appreciating and enjoying, both, do give a most marked preference to the manner of existence which employs their higher facilities. Few human creatures would consent to be changed into any of the lower animals, for a promise of the fullest allowance of a beast's pleasures; no intelligent human being would consent to be a fool, no instructed person would be an ignoramus, no person of feeling and conscience would be selfish and base, even though they should be persuaded that the fool, the dunce, or the rascal is better satisfied with his lot than they are with theirs. They would not resign what they possess more than he for the most complete satisfaction of all the desires which they have in common with him. If they ever fancy they would, it is only in cases of unhappiness so extreme, that to escape from it they would exchange their lot for almost any other, however undesirable in their own eyes. A being of higher faculties requires more to make him happy, is capable probably of more acute suffering, and certainly accessible to it at more points, than one of an inferior type; but in spite of these liabilities, he can never really wish to sink into what he feels to be a lower grade of existence. We may give what explanation we please of this unwillingness; we may attribute it to pride, a name which is given indiscriminately to some of the most and to some of the least estimable feelings of which mankind are capable: we may refer it to the love of liberty and personal independence, an appeal to which was with the Stoics one of the most effective means for the inculcation of it; to the love of power, or to the love of excitement, both of which do really enter into and contribute to it: but its most appropriate appellation is a sense of dignity, which all human beings possess in one form or other, and in some, though by no means in exact, proportion to their higher faculties, and which is so essential a part of the happiness of those in whom it is strong, that nothing which conflicts with it could be, otherwise than momentarily, an object of desire to them. Whoever supposes that this preference takes place at a sacrifice of happiness—that the superior being, in anything like equal circumstances, is not happier than the inferior—confounds the two very different ideas, of happiness, and content. It is indisputable that the being whose capacities of enjoyment are low, has the greatest chance of having them fully satisfied; and a highly endowed being will always feel that any happiness which he can look for, as the world is constituted, is imperfect. But he can learn to bear its imperfections, if they are at all bearable; and they will not make him envy the being who is indeed unconscious of the imperfections, but only because he feels not at all the good which those imperfections qualify. It is better to be a human being dissatisfied than a pig satisfied; better to be Socrates dissatisfied than a fool satisfied. And if the fool, or the pig, are of a different opinion, it is because they only know their own side of the question. The other party to the comparison knows both sides.

It may be objected, that many who are capable of the higher pleasures, occasionally, under the influence of temptation, postpone them to the lower. But this is quite compatible with a full appreciation of the intrinsic superiority of the higher. Men often, from infirmity of character, make their election for the nearer good, though they know it to be the less valuable; and this no less when the choice is between two bodily pleasures, than when it is between bodily and mental. They pursue sensual indulgences to the injury of health, though perfectly aware that health is the greater good. It may be further objected, that many who begin with youthful enthusiasm for everything noble, as they advance in years sink into indolence and selfishness. But I do not believe that those who undergo this very common change, voluntarily choose the lower description of pleasures in preference to the higher. I believe that before they devote themselves exclusively to the one, they have already become incapable of the other. Capacity for the nobler feelings is in most natures a very tender plant, easily killed, not only by hostile influences, but by mere want of substance; and in the majority of young persons it speedily dies away if the occupations to which their position in life has devoted them, and the society into which it has thrown them, are not favourable to keeping that higher capacity in exercise. Men lose their high aspirations as they lose their intellectual tastes, because they have not time or opportunity for indulging them; and they addict themselves to inferior pleasures, not because they deliberately prefer them, but because they are either the only ones to which they have access, or the only ones which they are any longer capable of enjoying. It may be questioned whether any one who has remained equally susceptible to both classes of pleasures, ever knowingly and calmly preferred the lower; though many, in all ages, have broken down in an ineffectual attempt to combine both.

From this verdict of the only competent judges, I apprehend there can be no appeal. On a question which is the best worth having of two pleasures, or which of two modes of existence is the most grateful to the feelings, apart from its moral attributes and from its consequences, the judgment of those who are qualified by knowledge of both, or, if they differ, that of the majority among them, must be admitted as final. And there needs be the less hesitation to accept this judgment respecting the quality of pleasures, since there is no other tribunal to be referred to even on the question of quantity. What means are there of determining which is the acutest of two pains, or the intensest of two pleasurable sensations, except the general suffrage of those who are familiar with both? Neither pains nor pleasures are homogeneous, and pain is always heterogeneous with pleasure. What is there to decide whether a particular pleasure is worth purchasing at the cost of a particular pain, except the feelings and judgment of the experienced? When, therefore, those feelings and judgment declare the pleasures derived from the higher faculties to be preferable *in kind,* apart from the question of intensity, to those of which the animal nature, disjoined from the higher faculties, is suspectible, they are entitled on this subject to the same regard.

I have dwelt on this point, as being a necessary part of a perfectly just conception of Utility or Happiness, considered as the directive rule of human conduct. But it is by no means an indispensable condition to the acceptance of the utilitarian standard; for that standard is not the agent's own greatest happiness, but the greatest amount of happiness altogether; and if it may possibly be doubted whether a nobel character is always the happier for its nobleness, there can be no doubt that it makes other people happier, and that the world in general is immensely a gainer by it. Utilitarianism, therefore, could only attain its end by the general cultivation of nobleness of character, even if each individual were only benefited by the nobleness of others, and his own, so far as happiness is concerned, were a sheer deduction from the benefit. But the bare enunciation of such an absurdity as this last, renders refutation superfluous.

According to the Greatest Happiness Principle, as above explained, the ultimate end, with reference to and for the sake of which all other things are desirable (whether we are considering our own good or that of other people), is an existence exempt as far as possible from pain, and as rich as possible in enjoyments, both in point of quantity and quality; the test of quality, and the rule for measuring it against quantity, being the preference felt by those who in their opportunities of experience, to which must be added their habits of self-consciousness and self-observation, are best furnished with the means of comparison. This, being, according to the utilitarian opinion, the end of human action, is necessarily also the standard of morality; which may accordingly be defined, the rules and precepts for human conduct, by the observance of which an existence such as has been described might be, to the greatest extent possible, secured to all mankind; and not to them only, but, so far as the nature of things admits, to the whole sentient creation. . . .

. . . I must again repeat, what the assailants of utilitarianism seldom have the justice to acknowledge, that the happiness which forms the utilitarian standard of what is right in conduct, is not the agent's own happiness, but that of all concerned. As between his own happiness and that of others, utilitarianism requires him to be as strictly impartial as a disinterested and benevolent spectator. In the golden rule of Jesus of Nazareth, we read the complete spirit of the ethics of utility. To do as you would be done by, and to love your neighbour as yourself, constitute the ideal perfection of utilitarian morality.

STUDY QUESTIONS

1. Mill defines happiness in terms of pleasure. Can you think of a more natural definition?
2. What charge is made against the Epicureans and how does Mill defend them?
3. What does Mill mean by the quality of a pleasure? Presumably the quality of pleasure in listening to Mozart is higher than the quality of pleasure in listening to a television commercial jingle. How would Mill show that this is so?
4. Examine Mill's remarks about the capacity for nobler feelings. Do you agree with him? Do his views suggest that the primary function of education must be the development of a sensibility for the nobler pleasures? How could this be implemented?
5. Do you agree with critics who say that utilitarianism demands too much of people?

Good Will, Duty, and the Categorical Imperative

IMMANUEL KANT

TRANSLATED BY T. K. ABBOTT

Immanuel Kant (1724–1804) is considered to be one of the greatest philosophers of all time. He lived in Königsberg, in East Prussia, and was a professor at the University there. Kant made significant and highly original contributions to esthetics, jurisprudence, and the philosophy of religion as well as to ethics and epistemology. His best known works are the *Critique of Pure Reason* (1781) and the *Foundations of the Metaphysics of Morals* (1785).

Human beings have desires and appetites. They are also rational, capable of knowing what is right and capable of willing to do it. They can therefore exercise their wills in the rational control of desire for the purpose of right action. This is what persons of moral worth do. According to Kant, to possess moral worth is more important than to possess intelligence, humor, strength, or any other talent of the mind or body. These talents are valuable but moral worth has *absolute* value, commanding not mere admiration but reverence and respect. Human beings who do right merely because it pleases them are not yet intrinsically moral. For had it

GOOD WILL, DUTY, AND THE CATEGORICAL IMPERATIVE From *Fundamental Principles of the Metaphysics of Morals*, by Immanuel Kant. Translated by T. K. Abbott (1898).

pleased them they would have done wrong. To act morally is to act from no other motive than the motive of doing what is right. This kind of motive has nothing to do with anything as subjective as pleasure. To do right out of principle is to recognize an objective right that poses an obligation on any rational being. Moral persons act in such a way that they could will that the principles of their actions should be universal laws for everyone else as well. This is one test of a moral act: Is it the kind of act that everyone should perform? Kant illustrates how this test can be applied to determine whether a given principle is moral and objective or merely subjective. For example, I may wish to break a promise, but that cannot be moral since I cannot will that promise-breaking be a universal practice.

Universal principles impose *categorical* imperatives. An imperative is a demand that I act in a certain fashion. For example, if I want to buy a house, it is imperative that I learn something about houses. But "Learn about houses!" is a *hypothetical* imperative since it is *conditional* on my wanting to buy a house. A *categorical* imperative is unconditional. An example is "Keep your promises." Thus an imperative is not preceded by any condition such as "if you want a good reputation." Hypothetical imperatives are "prudential": "If you want security, buy theft insurance." Categorical imperatives are moral: "Do not lie!" Kant argues that the categorical imperative presupposes the absolute worth of all rational beings as ends in themselves. Thus another formulation of the categorical imperative is, "So act as to treat humanity . . . as an end withal, never as a means only." Kant calls the domain of beings that are to be treated in this way the "kingdom of ends."

Nothing can possibly be conceived in the world, or even out of it, which can be called good, without qualification, except a Good Will. Intelligence, wit, judgment, and the other *talents* of the mind, however they may be named, or courage, resolution, perseverance, as qualities of temperament, are undoubtedly good and desirable in many respects; but these gifts of nature may also become extremely bad and mischievous if the will which is to make use of them, and which, therefore, constitutes what is called *character,* is not good. It is the same with the *gifts of fortune.* Power, riches, honour, even health, and the general well-being and contentment with one's condition which is called *happiness,* inspire pride, and often presumption, if there is not a good will to correct the influence of these on the mind, and with this also to rectify the whole principle of acting, and adapt it to its end. The sight of a being who is not adorned with a single feature of a pure and good will, enjoying unbroken prosperity, can never give pleasure to an impartial rational spectator. Thus a good will appears to constitute the indispensable condition even of being worthy of happiness.

There are even some qualities which are of service to this good will itself, and may facilitate its action, yet which have no intrinsic unconditional value, but always presuppose a good will, and this qualifies the esteem that we justly have for them, and does not permit us to regard them as absolutely good. Moderation in the affections and passions, self-control, and calm deliberation are not only good in many respects, but even seem to constitute part of the intrinsic worth of the person; but they are far from deserving to be called good without qualification, although they have been so unconditionally praised by the ancients. For without the principles of a good will, they may become extremely bad; and the coolness of a villain not only makes him far more dangerous, but also directly makes him more abominable in our eyes than he would have been without it.

A good will is good not because of what it performs or effects, not by it aptness for the attainment of some proposed end, but simply by virtue of the volition, that is, it is good in itself, and considered by itself is to be esteemed much higher than all that can be brought about by it in favour of any inclination, nay, even of the sum-total of all inclinations. Even if it should happen that, owing to special disfavour of fortune, or the niggardly provision of a step-motherly nature, this will should wholly lack power to accomplish its purpose, if with its greatest efforts it should yet achieve nothing, and there should remain only the good will (not, to be sure, a mere wish, but the summoning of all means in our power), then, like a jewel, it would still shine by its own light, as a thing which has its whole value in itself. Its usefulness or fruitlessness can neither add to nor take away anything from this value.

Thus the moral worth of an action does not lie in the effect expected from it, nor in any principle of action which requires to borrow its motive from this expected effect. For all these effects—agreeableness of one's condition, and even the promotion of the happiness of others—could have been also brought about by other causes, so that for this there would have been no need of the will of a rational being; whereas it is in this alone that the supreme and unconditional good can be found. The pre-eminent good which we call moral can therefore consist in nothing else than *the conception of law* in itself, *which certainly is only possible in a rational being,* in so far as this conception, and not the expected effect, determines the will. This is a good which is already present in the person who acts accordingly, and we have not to wait for it to appear first in the result.

But what sort of law can that be, the conception of which must determine the will, even without paying any regard to the effect expected from it, in order that this will may be called good absolutely and without qualification? As I have deprived the will of every impulse which could arise to it from obedience to any law, there remains nothing but the universal conformity of its actions to law in general, which alone is to serve the will as a principle, *i.e.* I am never to act otherwise than *so that I could also will that my maxim should become a universal law.* Here, now, it is the simple conformity to law in general, without assuming any particular law applicable to certain actions, that serves the will as its principle, and must so serve it, if duty is not to be a vain delusion and a chimerical notion. The common reason of men in its practical judgments perfectly coincides with this and always has in view the principle here suggested. Let the question be, for example: May I when in distress make a promise with the intention not to keep it? I readily distinguish here between the two significations which the question may have: Whether it is prudent, or whether it is right, to make a false promise? The former may undoubtedly often be the case. I see clearly indeed that it is not enough to extricate myself from a present difficulty by means of this subterfuge, but it must be well considered whether there may not hereafter spring from this lie much greater inconvenience than that from which I now free myself, and as, with all my supposed *cunning,* the consequences cannot be so easily foreseen but that credit once lost may be much more injurious to me than any mischief which I seek to avoid at present, it should be considered whether it would not be more *prudent* to act herein according to a universal maxim, and to make it a habit to promise nothing except with the intention of keeping it. But it is soon clear to me that such a maxim will still only be based on the fear of consequences. Now it is a wholly different thing to be truthful from duty, and to be so from apprehension of injurious consequences. In the first case, the very notion of the action already implies a law for me; in the second case, I must first look about elsewhere to see what results may be combined with it which would affect myself. For to deviate from the principle of duty is beyond all doubt wicked; but to be unfaithful to my maxim of prudence may often be very advantageous to me, although to abide by it is certainly safer. The shortest way, however, and an unerring one, to discover the answer to this question whether a lying promise is consistent with duty, is to ask myself, Should I be content that my maxim (to extricate myself from difficulty by a false promise) should hold good as a universal law, for myself as well as for others? and should I be able to say to myself, "Every one may make a deceitful promise when he finds himself in a difficulty from which he cannot otherwise extricate himself"? Then I presently become aware that while I can will the lie, I can by no means will that lying should be a universal law. For with such a law there would be no promises at all, since it would be in vain to allege my intention in regard to my future actions to those who would not believe this allegation, or if they over-hastily did so, would pay me back in my own coin. Hence my maxim, as soon as it should be made a universal law, would necessarily destroy itself.

I do not, therefore, need any far-reaching penetration to discern what I have to do in order that my will be morally good. Inexperienced in the course of the world, incapable of being prepared for all its contingencies, I only ask myself: Canst thou also will that thy maxim should be a universal law? If not, then it must be rejected, and that not because of a disadvantage accruing from it to myself or even to others, but because it cannot enter as a principle into a possible universal legislation, and reason extorts from me immediate respect for such legislation. I do not indeed as yet *discern* on what this respect is based (this the philosopher may inquire), but at least I understand this, that it is an estimation of the worth which far outweighs all worth of what is recommended by inclination, and that the necessity of acting from *pure* respect for the practical law is what constitutes duty, to which every other motive must give place, because it is the condition of a will being good *in itself,* and the worth of such a will is above everything. . . .

. . . Everything in nature works according to laws. Rational beings alone have the faculty of acting according *to the conception* of laws, that is according to principles, *i.e.* have a *will.* Since the deduction of actions from principles requires *reason,* the will is nothing but practical reason. If reason infallibly determines the will, then the actions of such a being which are recognized as objectively necessary are subjectively necessary also, *i.e.* the will is a faculty to choose *that only* which reason independent on inclination recognizes as practically necessary, *i.e.* as good. But if reason of itself does not sufficiently determine the will, if the latter is subject also to subjective conditions (particular impulses) which do not always coincide with the objective conditions; in a word, if the will does not *in itself* completely accord with reason (which is actually the case with men), then the actions which objectively are recognized as necessary are subjectively contingent, and the determination of such a will according to objective laws is *obligation,* that is to say, the relation of the objective laws to a will that is not thoroughly good is conceived as the determination of the will of a rational being by principles of reason, but which the will from its nature does not of necessity follow.

The conception of an objective principle, in so far as it is obligatory for a will, is called a command (of reason), and the formula of the command is called an Imperative. . . .

Now all *imperatives* command either *hypothetically* or *categorically.* The former represent the practical necessity of a possible action as means to something else that is willed (or at least which one might possibly will). The categorical imperative would be that which represented an action as necessary of itself without reference to another end, *i.e.* as objectively necessary.

Since every practical law represents a possible action as good, and on this account, for a subject who is practically determinable by reason, necessary, all imperatives are formulae determining an action which is necessary according to the principle of a will good in some respects. If now the action is good only as a means *to something else,* then the imperative is *hypothetical;* if it is conceived as good *in itself* and consequently as being necessarily the principle of a will which of itself conforms to reason, then it is *categorical.* . . .

When I conceive a hypothetical imperative, in general I do not know beforehand what it will contain until I am given the condition. But when I conceive a categorical imperative, I know at once what it contains. For as the imperative contains besides the law only the necessity that the maxims shall conform to this law, while the law contains no conditions restricting it, there remains nothing but the general statement that the maxim of the action should conform to a universal law, and it is this conformity alone that the imperative properly represents as necessary.

There is . . . but one categorical imperative, namely, this: *Act only on that maxim whereby thou canst at the same time will that it should become a universal law.*

Now if all imperatives of duty can be deduced from this one imperative as from their principle, then, although it should remain undecided whether what is called duty is not merely a vain notion, yet at least we shall be able to show what we understand by it and what this notion means.

Since the universality of the law according to which effects are produced constitutes what is properly called *nature* in the most general sense (as to form), that is the existence of things so far as it is determined by general laws, the imperative of duty may be expressed thus: *Act as if the maxim of thy action were to become by thy will a universal law of nature.*

We will now enumerate a few duties, adopting the usual division of them into duties to ourselves and to others, and into perfect and imperfect duties.

1. A man reduced to despair by a series of misfortunes feels wearied of life, but is still so far in possession of his reason that he can ask himself whether it would not be contrary to his duty to himself to take his own life. Now he inquires whether the maxim of his action could become a universal law of nature. His maxim is: From self-love I adopt it as a principle to shorten my life when its longer duration is likely to bring more evil than satisfaction. It is asked then simply whether this principle founded on self-love can become a universal law of nature. Now we see at once that a system of nature of which it should be a law to destroy life by means of the very feeling whose special nature it is to impel to the improvement

of life would contradict itself, and therefore could not exist as a system of nature; hence that maxim cannot possibly exist as a universal law of nature, and consequently would be wholly inconsistent with the supreme principle of all duty.

2. Another finds himself forced by necessity to borrow money. He knows that he will not be able to repay it, but sees also that nothing will be lent to him, unless he promises stoutly to repay it in a definite time. He desires to make this promise, but he has still so much conscience as to ask himself: Is it not unlawful and inconsistent with duty to get out of a difficulty in this way? Suppose, however, that he resolves to do so, then the maxim of his action would be expressed thus: When I think myself in want of money, I will borrow money and promise to repay it, although I know that I never can do so. Now this principle of self-love or of one's own advantage may perhaps be consistent with my whole future welfare; but the question now is, Is it right? I change then the suggestion of self-love into a universal law, and state the question thus: How would it be if my maxim were a universal law? Then I see at once that it could never hold as a universal law of nature, but would necessarily contradict itself. For supposing it to be a universal law that everyone when he thinks himself in a difficulty should be able to promise whatever he pleases, with the purpose of not keeping his promise, the promise itself would become impossible, as well as the end that one might have in view in it, since no one would consider that anything was promised to him, but would ridicule all such statements as vain pretences.

3. A third finds in himself a talent which with the help of some culture might make him a useful man in many respects. But he finds himself in comfortable circumstances, and prefers to indulge in pleasure rather than to take pains in enlarging and improving his happy natural capacities. He asks, however, whether his maxim of neglect of his natural gifts, besides agreeing with his inclination to indulgence, agrees also with what is called duty. He sees then that a system of nature could indeed subsist with such a universal law although men (like the South Sea islanders) should let their talents rest, and resolve to devote their lives merely to idleness, amusement, and propagation of their species—in a word, to enjoyment; but he cannot possibly *will* that this should be a universal law of nature, or be implanted in us as such by a natural instinct. For, as a

rational being, he necessarily wills that his faculties be developed, since they serve him, and have been given him, for all sorts of possible purposes.

4. A fourth, who is in prosperity, while he sees that others have to contend with great wretchedness and that he could help them, thinks: What concern is it of mine? Let everyone be as happy as Heaven pleases, or as he can make himself; I will take nothing from him nor even envy him, only I do not wish to contribute anything to his welfare or to his assistance in distress! Now no doubt if such a mode of thinking were a universal law, the human race might very well subsist, and doubtless even better than in a state in which everyone talks of sympathy and good-will, or even takes care occasionally to put it into practice, but, on the other side, also cheats when he can, betrays the rights of men, or otherwise violates them. But although it is possible that a univeral law of nature might exist in accordance with that maxim, it is impossible to *will* that such a principle should have the universal validity of a law of nature. For a will which resolved this would contradict itself, inasmuch as many cases might occur in which one would have need of the love and sympathy of others, and in which, by such a law of nature, sprung from his own will, he would deprive himself of all hope of the aid he desires. . . .

We have thus established at least this much, that if duty is a conception which is to have any import and real legislative authority for our actions, it can only be expressed in categorical, and not at all in hypothetical imperatives. We have also, which is of great importance, exhibited clearly and definitely for every practical application the content of the categorical imperative, which must contain the principle of all duty if there is such a thing at all. We have not yet, however, advanced so far as to prove *à priori* that there actually is such an imperative, that there is a practical law which commands absolutely of itself, and without any other impulse, and that the following of this law is duty . . . .

Now I say: man and generally any rational being *exists* as an end in himself, *not merely as a means* to be arbitrarily used by this or that will, but in all his actions, whether they concern himself or other rational beings, must be always regarded at the same time as an end. All objects of the inclinations have only a conditional worth; for if the inclinations and the wants founded on them did not exist, then their object would be without value. But the inclinations themselves being sources of want are so far from having an absolute worth for which they should be desired, that, on the contrary, it must be the universal wish of every rational being to be wholly free from them. Thus the worth of any object which is *to be acquired* by our action is always conditional. Beings whose existence depends not on our will but on nature's, have nevertheless, if they are rational beings, only a relative value as means, and are therefore called *things;* rational beings, on the contrary, are called *persons,* because their very nature points them out as ends in themselves, that is as something which must not be used merely as means, and so far therefore restricts freedom of action (and is an object of respect). These, therefore, are not merely subjective ends whose existence has a worth *for us* as an effort of our action, but *objective ends,* that is things whose existence is an end in itself: an end moreover for which no other can be substituted, which they should subserve *merely* as means, for otherwise nothing whatever would possess *absolute worth;* but if all worth were conditioned and therefore contingent, then there would be no supreme practical principle of reason whatever.

If then there is a supreme practical principle or, in respect of the human will, a categorical imperative, it must be one which, being drawn from the conception of that which is necessarily an end for everyone because it is an *an end in itself,* constitutes an *objective* principle of will, and can therefore serve as a universal practical law. The foundation of this principle is: *rational nature exists as an end in itself.* Man necessarily conceives his own existence as being so: so far then this is a *subjective* principle of human actions. But every other rational being regards its existence similarly, just on the same rational principle, that holds for me: so that it is at the same time an objective principle, from which as a supreme practical law all laws of the will must be capable of being deduced. Accordingly the practical imperative will be as follows: *So act as to treat humanity, whether in thine own person or in that of any other, in every case as an end withal, never as means only.* . . .

The conception of every rational being as one which must consider itself as giving all the maxims of its will universal laws, so as to judge itself and its actions from this point of view—this conception leads to another which depends on it and is very fruitful, namely, that of a *kingdom of ends.*

By a *kingdom* I understand the union of different rational beings in a system by common laws. Now since it is by laws that ends are determined as regards their universal validity, hence, if we abstract from the personal differences of rational beings, and likewise from all the content of their private ends, we shall be able to conceive all ends combined in a systematic whole (including both rational beings as ends in themselves, and also the special ends which each may propose to himself), that is to say, we can conceive a kingdom of ends, which on the preceding principles is possible.

For all rational beings come under the *law* that each of them must treat itself and all others *never merely as means,* but in every case *at the same time as ends in themselves.* Hence results a systematic union of rational beings by common objective laws, *i.e.* a kingdom which may be called a kingdom of ends, . . .

STUDY QUESTIONS

1. Why does Kant say that the good will is good without qualification?
2. What relationship does duty have to appetite? Duty to reason?
3. What does Kant mean by saying that certain beings have intrinsic value as ends in themselves? What obligations do such
   beings impose on moral agents?
4. For Kant, animals are not ends in themselves because they
   cannot reason. So, says Kant, they have no moral rights. Does
   this seem right to you?
5. How does Kant distinguish between hypothetical and categorical imperatives? What kind of imperatives do "prudential"
   concerns enjoin?
6. In World War II, the British deciphered the German military
   intelligence code, thereby saving countless lives. Learning from
   messages that certain intelligence officers were going to be
   captured and tortured, they nevertheless sent them back to the
   Continent to preserve the secret that the code had been cracked.
   Evaluate this case from the standpoint of (a) a utilitarian, (b) a
   Kantian, (c) yourself.

Egoism and Moral Skepticism

JAMES RACHELS

James Rachels (1941) is the Dean of the School of Humanities at the University of Alabama. He is the editor of several books, including *Moral Problems: A Collection of Philosophical Essays* (1979) and *Understanding Moral Philosophy* (1976).

Psychological egoism is the view that human beings always act from a single motive: self-love. Ethical egoism is the moral theory that says we *ought* to act only from self-love. Rachels tries to expose the logical and moral weaknesses of both theories. For example, he challenges the view often proffered by defenders of psychological egoism: We are selfish because we *always do what we want to do*. One person *wants* to visit and cheer up a lonely elderly neighbor; another wants to rob and terrorize his neighbor. Both do what they want; both are selfish. Rachels points out that what makes an act selfish is its *object*, not that you want to do it. If the object of most of your actions is to please yourself, then you are selfish; if you often want to please your neighbors, you are kind. If you want to harm them, you are malicious. Rachels also argues that both psychological and ethical egoisms rest upon a distorted view of human

EGOISM AND MORAL SKEPTICISM By James Rachels (pp. 423–434) from *A New Introduction to Philosophy*, edited by Steven M. Cahn. Copyright © 1971 by Steven M. Cahn. Reprinted by permission the author and Harper & Row, Publishers, Inc.

nature. Most of us are sympathetic and care about the well-being of others. The reason we do not burn down a department store is not because it might not be in our long-range best interest to do so, but because "people might be burned to death."

I

Our ordinary thinking about morality is full of assumptions that we almost never question. We assume, for example, that we have an obligation to consider the welfare of other people when we decide what actions to perform or what rules to obey; we think that we must refrain from acting in ways harmful to others, and that we must respect their rights and interests as well as our own. We also assume that people are in fact capable of being motivated by such considerations, that is, that people are not wholly selfish and that they do sometimes act in the interests of others.

Both of these assumptions have come under attack by moral skeptics, as long ago as by Glaucon in Book II of Plato's *Republic*. Glaucon recalls the legend of Gyges, a shepherd who was said to have found a magic ring in a fissure opened by an earthquake. The ring would make its wearer invisible and thus would enable him to go anywhere and do anything undetected. Gyges used the power of the ring to gain entry to the Royal Palace where he seduced the Queen, murdered the King, and subsequently seized the throne. Now Glaucon asks us to determine that there are two such rings, one given to a man of virtue and one given to a rogue. The rogue, of course, will use his ring unscrupulously and do anything necessary to increase his own wealth and power. He will recognize no moral constraints on his conduct, and, since the cloak of invisibility will protect him from discovery, he can do anything he pleases without fear of reprisal. So there will be no end to the mischief he will do. But how will the so-called virtuous man behave? Glaucon suggests that he will behave no better than the rogue: "No one, it is commonly believed, would have such iron strength of mind as to stand fast in doing right or keep his hands off other men's goods, when he could go to the market-place and fearlessly help himself to anything he wanted, enter houses and sleep with any woman he chose, set prisoners free and kill men at his pleasure, and in a word go about among men with the powers of a god. He would behave no better than the other; both would take the same course."[1] Moreover, why shouldn't he? Once he is freed from the fear of reprisal, why shouldn't a man simply do what he pleases, or what he thinks is best for himself? What reason is there for him to continue being "moral" when it is clearly not to his own advantage to do so?

These skeptical views suggested by Glaucon have come to be known as *psychological egoism* and *ethical egoism* respectively. Psychological egoism is the view that all men are selfish in everything that they do, that is, that the only motive from which anyone ever acts is self-interest. On this view, even when men are acting in ways apparently calculated to benefit others, they are actually motivated by the belief that acting in this way is to their own advantage, and if they did not believe this, they would not be doing that action. Ethical egoism is, by contrast, a normative view about how men *ought* to act. It is the view that, regardless of how men do in fact behave, they have no obligation to do anything except what is in their own interests. According to the ethical egoist, a person is always justified in doing whatever is in his own interest, regardless of the effect on others.

Clearly, if either of these views is correct, then "the moral institution of life" (to use Butler's well-turned phrase) is very different than what we normally think. The majority of mankind is grossly deceived about what is, or ought to be, the case, where morals are concerned.

II

Psychological egoism seems to fly in the face of the facts. We are tempted to say, "Of course people act unselfishly all the time. For example, Smith gives up a trip to the country, which he would have enjoyed very much, in order to stay behind and help a friend with his studies, which is a miserable way to pass the time. This is a perfectly clear case of unselfish behavior, and if the psychological egoist thinks that such cases do not occur, then he is just mistaken."

---

[1] *The Republic of Plato*, trans. F. M. Cornford (Oxford, 1941), p. 45.

Given such obvious instances of "unselfish behavior," what reply can the egoist make? There are two general arguments by which he might try to show that all actions, including those such as the one just outlined, are in fact motivated by self-interest. Let us examine these in turn:

A. The first argument goes as follows. If we describe one person's action as selfish, and another person's action as unselfish, we are overlooking the crucial fact that in both cases, assuming that the action is done voluntarily, *the agent is merely doing what he most wants to do*. If Smith stays behind to help his friend, that only shows that he wanted to help his friend more than he wanted to go to the country. And why should he be praised for his "unselfishness" when he is only doing what he wants to do, he cannot be said to be acting unselfishly.

This argument is so bad that it would not deserve to be taken seriously except for the fact that so many otherwise intelligent people have been taken in by it. First, the argument rests on the premise that people never voluntarily do anything except what they want to do. But this is patently false; there are at least two classes of actions that are exceptions to this generalization. One is the set of actions which we may not want to do, but which we do anyway as a means to an end which we want to achieve; for example, going to the dentist in order to stop a toothache, or going to work every day in order to be able to draw our pay at the end of the month. These cases may be regarded as consistent with the spirit of the egoist argument, however, since the ends mentioned are wanted by the agent. But the other set of actions are those which we do, not because we want to, nor even because there is an end which we want to achieve, but because we feel ourselves *under an obligation* to do them. For example, someone may do something because he has promised to do it, and thus feels obligated, even though he does not want to do it. It is sometimes suggested that in such cases we do the action, because, after all, we want to keep our promises; so, even here, we are doing what we want. However, this dodge will not work: If I have promised to do something, and if I do not want to do it, then it is simply false to say that I want to keep my promise. In such cases we feel a conflict precisely because we do not want to do what we feel obligated to do. It is reasonable to think that Smith's action falls roughly into this second category:

He might stay behind, not because he wants to, but because he feels that his friend needs help.

But suppose we were to concede, for the sake of the argument, that all voluntary action is motivated by the agent's wants, or at least that Smith is so motivated. Even if these were granted, it would not follow that Smith is acting selfishly or from self-interest. For if Smith wants to do something that will help his friend, even when it means forgoing his own enjoyments, that is precisely what makes him *unselfish*. What else could unselfishness be, if not wanting to help others? Another way to put the same point is to say that it is the *object* of a want that determines whether it is selfish or not. The mere fact that I am acting on *my* wants does not mean that I am acting selfishly; that depends on *what it is* that I want. If I want only my own good, and care nothing for others, then I am selfish; but if I also want other people to be well-off and happy, and if I act on *that* desire, then my action is not selfish. So much for this argument.

B.   The second argument for psychological egoism is this. Since so-called unselfish actions always produce a sense of self-satisfaction in the agent,[2] and since this sense of satisfaction is a pleasant state of consciousness, it follows that the point of the action is really to achieve a pleasant state of consciousness, rather than bring about any good for others. Therefore, the action is "unselfish" only at a superficial level of analysis. Smith will feel much better with himself for having stayed to help his friend—if he had gone to the country, he would have felt terrible about it—and that is the real point of the action. According to a well-known story, this argument was once expressed by Abraham Lincoln:

> Mr. Lincoln once remarked to a fellow-passenger on an old-time mud-coach that all men were prompted by selfishness in doing good. His fellow-passenger was antagonizing this position when they were passing over a corduroy bridge that spanned a slough. As they crossed this bridge they espied an old razor-backed sow on the bank making a terrible noise because her pigs had got into the slough and were in danger of drowning. As the old coach began to climb the hill, Mr. Lincoln called out, "Driver, can't you stop just a

---

[2]Or, as it is sometimes said, "It gives him a clear conscience," or "He couldn't sleep at night if he had done otherwise," or "He would have been ashamed of himself for not doing it," and so on.

moment?" Then Mr. Lincoln jumped out, ran back, and lifted the little pigs out of the mud and water and placed them on the bank. When he returned, his companion remarked: "Now, Abe, where does selfishness come in on this little episode?" "Why, bless your soul, Ed, that was the very essence of selfishness. I should have had no peace of mind all day had I gone on and left that suffering old sow worrying over those pigs. I did it to get peace of mind, don't you see?"[3]

This argument suffers from defects similar to the previous one. Why should we think that merely because someone derives satisfaction from helping others this makes him selfish? Isn't the unselfish man precisely the one who *does* derive satisfaction from helping others, while the selfish man does not? If Lincoln "got peace of mind" from rescuing the piglets, does this show him to be selfish, or, on the contrary, doesn't it show him to be compassionate and good-hearted? (If a man were truly selfish, why should it bother his conscience that *others* suffer—much less pigs?) Similarly, it is nothing more than shabby sophistry to say, because Smith takes satisfaction in helping his friend, that he is behaving selfishly. If we say this rapidly, while thinking about something else, perhaps it will sound all right; but if we speak slowly, and pay attention to what we are saying, it sounds plain silly.

Moreover, suppose we ask *why* Smith derives satisfaction from helping his friend. The answer will be, it is because Smith cares for him and wants him to succeed. If Smith did not have these concerns, then he would take no pleasure in assisting him; and these concerns, as we have already seen, are the marks of unselfishness, not selfishness. To put the point more generally: If we have a positive attitude toward the attainment of some goal, then we may derive satisfaction from attaining that goal. But the *object* of our attitude is *the attainment of that goal;* and we must want to attain the goal *before* we can find any satisfaction in it. We do not, in other words, desire some sort of "pleasurable consciousness" and then try to figure out how to achieve it; rather, we desire all sorts of different things—money, a new fishing-boat, to be a better chess-player, to get a promotion in our work, etc.—and because we desire these things, we derive satisfaction from attaining them. And

---

[3]Frank C. Sharp, *Ethics* (New York, 1928), pp. 74–75. Quoted from the Springfield (Ill.) *Monitor* in the *Outlook*, vol. 56, p. 1059.

so, if someone desires the welfare and happiness of another person, he will derive satisfaction from that; but this does not mean that this satisfaction is the object of his desire, or that he is in any way selfish on account of it.

It is a measure of the weakness of psychological egoism that these insupportable arguments are the ones most often advanced in its favor. Why, then, should anyone ever have thought it a true view? Perhaps because of a desire for theoretical simplicity: In thinking about human conduct, it would be nice if there were some simple formula that would unite the diverse phenomena of human behavior under a single explanatory principle, just as simple formulae in physics bring together a great many apparently different phenomena. And since it is obvious that self-regard is an overwhelmingly important factor in motivation, it is only natural to wonder whether all motivation might not be explained in these terms. But the answer is clearly No; while a great many human actions are motivated entirely or in part by self-interest, only by a deliberate distortion of the facts can we say that all conduct is so motivated. This will be clear, I think, if we correct three confusions which are commonplace. The exposure of these confusions will remove the last traces of plausibility from the psychological egoist thesis.

The first is the confusion of selfishness with self-interest. The two are clearly not the same. If I see a physician when I am feeling poorly, I am acting in my own interest but no one would think of calling me "selfish" on account of it. Similarly, brushing my teeth, working hard at my job, and obeying the law are all in my self-interest but none of these are examples of selfish conduct. This is because selfish behavior is behavior that ignores the interests of others, in circumstances in which their interests ought not to be ignored. This concept has a definite evaluative flavor; to call someone "selfish" is not just to describe his action but to condemn it. Thus, you would not call me selfish for eating a normal meal in normal circumstances (although it may surely be in my self-interest); but you would call me selfish for hoarding food while others about are starving.

The second confusion is the assumption that every action is done *either* from self-interest or from other-regarding motives. Thus, the egoist concludes that if there is no such thing as genuine altruism then all actions must be done from self-interest. But this is certainly a false dichotomy. The man who continues to smoke cigarettes, even after learning about the connection between smoking and cancer, is surely not acting from self-interest, not even by his own standards—self-interest would dictate that he quit smoking at once—and he is not acting altruistically either. He *is*, no doubt, smoking for the pleasure of it, but all that this shows is that undisciplined pleasure-seeking and acting from self-interest are very different. This is what led Butler to remark that "The thing to be lamented is, not that men have so great regard to their own good or interest in the present world, for they have not enough."[4]

The last two paragraphs show (*a*) that it is false that all actions are selfish, and (*b*) that it is false that all actions are done out of self-interest. And it should be noted that these two points can be made, and were, without any appeal to putative examples of altruism.

The third confusion is the common but false assumption that a concern for one's own welfare is incompatible with any genuine concern for the welfare of others. Thus, since it is obvious that everyone (or very nearly everyone) does desire his own well-being, it might be thought that no one can really be concerned with others. But again, this is false. There is no consistency in desiring that everyone, including oneself *and* others, be well-off and happy. To be sure, it may happen on occasion that our own interests conflict with the interests of others, and in these cases we will have to make hard choices. But even in these cases we might sometimes opt for the interests of others, especially when the others involved are our family or friends. But more importantly, not all cases are like this: Sometimes we are able to promote the welfare of others when our own interests are not involved at all. In these cases not even the strongest self-regard need prevent us from acting considerately toward others.

Once these confusions are cleared away, it seems to me obvious enough that there is no reason whatever to accept psychological egoism. On the contrary, if we simply observe people's behavior with an open mind, we may find that a great deal of it is motivated by self-regard, but by no means all of it; and that there is no reason to deny that "the moral institution of life" can include a place for the virtue of beneficence.[5]

---

[4] *The Works of Joseph Butler*, ed. W. E. Gladstone (Oxford, 1896), vol. 2, p. 26.

[5] The capacity for altruistic behavior is not unique to human beings. Some interesting experiments with rhesus monkeys have shown that these animals will refrain from

III

The ethical egoist would say at this point, "Of course it is possible for people to act altruistically, and perhaps many people do act that way—but there is no reason why they *should* do so. A person is under no obligation to do anything except what is in his own interests."[6] This is really quite a radical doctrine. Suppose I have an urge to set fire to some public building (say, a department store) just for the fascination of watching the spectacular blaze: According to this view, the fact that several people might be burned to death provides no reason whatever why I should not do it. After all, this only concerns *their* welfare, not my own, and according to the ethical egoist the only person I need think of is myself.

Some might deny that ethical egoism has any such monstrous consequences. They would point out that it is really to my own advantage not to set the fire—for, if I do that I may be caught and put into prison (unlike Gyges, I have no magic ring for protection). Moreover, even if I could avoid being caught it is still to my advantage to respect the rights and interests of others, for it is to my advantage to live in a society in which people's rights and interests are respected. Only in such a society can I live a happy and secure life; so, in acting kindly toward others, I would merely be doing my part to create and maintain the sort of society which it is to my advantage to have.[7] Therefore, it is said, the egoist would not be such a bad man; he would be as kindly and considerate as anyone else, because he would see that it is to his own advantage to be kindly and considerate.

This is a seductive line of thought, but it seems to me mistaken. Certainly it is to everyone's advantage (including the egoist's) to preserve a stable society where people's interests are generally protected. But there is no reason for the egoist to think that merely because *he* will not honor the rules of the social game, decent society will collapse. For the vast majority of people are not egoists, and there is no reason to think that they will be converted by

---

operating a device for securing food if this causes other animals to suffer pain. See Masserman, Wechkin, and Terris, " 'Altruistic Behavior in Rhesus Monkeys," *The American Journal of Psychiatry*, vol. 121 (1964), 584–585.

[6]I take this to be the view of Ayn Rand, insofar as I understand her confusing doctrine.

[7]Cf. Thomas Hobbes, *Leviathan* (London, 1651), chap. 17.

his example—especially if he is discreet and does not unduly flaunt his style of life. What this line of reasoning shows is not that the egoist himself must act benevolently, but that he must encourage *others* to do so. He must take care to conceal from public view his own self-centered method of decision-making, and urge others to act on precepts very different from those on which he is willing to act.

The rational egoist, then, cannot advocate that egoism be universally adopted by everyone. For he wants a world in which is own interests are maximized; and if other people adopted the egoistic policy of pursuing their own interests to the exclusion of his interest, as he pursues his interest to the exclusion of theirs, then such a world would be impossible. So he himself will be egoist, but he will want others to be altruists.

This brings us to what is perhaps the most popular "refutation" of ethical egoism current among philosophical writers—the argument that ethical egoism is at bottom inconsistent because it cannot be universalized.[8] The argument goes like this:

To say that any action or policy of action is *right* (or that it *ought* to be adopted) entails that it is right for *anyone* in the same sort of circumstances. I cannot, for example, say that it is right for me to lie to you, and yet object when you lie to me (provided, of course, that the circumstances are the same). I cannot hold that it is all right for me to drink your beer and then complain when you drink mine. This is just the requirement that we be consistent in our evaluations; it is a requirement of logic. Now it is said that ethical egoism cannot meet this requirement because, as we have already seen, the egoist would not want others to act in the same way that he acts. Moreover, suppose he *did* advocate the universal adoption of egoistic policies: he would be saying to Peter, "You ought to pursue your own interests even if it means destroying Paul"; and he would be saying to Paul, "You ought to pursue your own interests even if it means destroying Peter." The attitudes expressed in these two recommendations seem clearly inconsistent—he is urging the advancement of Peter's interest at one moment, and countenancing their defeat at the next. Therefore, the argument goes, there is no

---

[8]See, for example, Brian Medlin, "Ultimate Principles and Ethical Egoism," *Australasian Journal of Philosophy*, vol. 35 (1957), 111–118; and D. H. Monro, *Empiricism and Ethics* (Cambridge, 1967), chap. 16.

way to maintain the doctrine of ethical egoism as a consistent view about how we ought to act. We will fall into inconsistency whenever we try.

What are we to make of this argument? Are we to conclude that ethical egoism has been refuted? Such a conclusion, I think, would be unwarranted; for I think that we can show, contrary to this argument, how ethical egoism can be maintained consistently. We need only to interpret the egoist's position in a sympathetic way: We should say that he has in mind a certain kind of world which he would prefer over all others; it would be a world in which his own interests were maximized, regardless of the effects on other people. The egoist's primary policy of action, then, would be to act in such a way as to bring about, as nearly as possible, this sort of world. Regardless of however morally reprehensible we might find it, there is nothing *inconsistent* in someone's adopting this as his ideal and acting in a way calculated to bring it about. And if someone did adopt this as his ideal, then he would advocate universal egoism; as we have already seen, he would want other people to be altruists. So if he advocates any principles of conduct for the general public, they will be altruistic principles. This would not be inconsistent; on the contrary, it would be perfectly consistent with his goal of creating a world in which his own interests are maximized. To be sure, he would have to be deceitful; in order to secure the good will of others, and a favorable hearing for his exhortations to altruism, he would have to pretend that he was himself prepared to accept altruistic principles. But again, that would be all right; from the egoist's point of view, this would merely be a matter of adopting the necessary means to the achievement of his goal—and while we might not approve of this, there is nothing inconsistent about it. Again, it might be said, "He advocates one thing, but does another. Surely *that's* inconsistent." But it is not; for what he advocates and what he does are both calculated as means to an end (the *same* end, we might note); and as such, he is doing what is rationally required in each case. Therefore, contrary to the previous argument, there is nothing inconsistent in the ethical egoist's view. He cannot be refuted by the claim that he contradicts himself.

Is there, then, no way to refute the ethical egoist? If by "refute" we mean show that he has made some *logical* error, the answer is that there is not. However, there is something more than can be said. The egoist challenge to our ordinary moral convictions amounts to a demand for an explanation of why we should adopt certain policies of action, namely policies in which the good of others is given importance. We can give an answer to this demand, albeit an indirect one. The reason one ought not to do actions that would hurt other people is: Other people would be hurt. The reason one ought to do actions that would benefit other people is: Other people would be benefited. This may at first seem like a piece of philosophical sleight-of-hand, but it is not. The point is that the welfare of human beings is something that most of us value *for its own sake,* and not merely for the sake of something else. Therefore, when *further* reasons are demanded for valuing the welfare of human beings, we cannot point to anything further to satisfy this demand. It is not that we have no reason for pursuing these policies, but that our reason *is* that these policies are for the good of human beings.

So if we are asked, "Why shouldn't I set fire to this department store?" one answer would be, "Because if you do, people may be burned to death." This is a complete, sufficient reason which does not require qualification or supplementation of any sort. If someone seriously wants to know why this action shouldn't be done, that's the reason. If we are pressed further and asked the skeptical question, "But why shouldn't I do actions that will harm others?" we may not know what to say—but this is because the questioner has included in his question the very answer we would like to give: "Why shouldn't you do actions that will harm others? Because doing those actions would harm others." The egoist, no doubt, will not be happy with this. He will protest that *we* may accept this as a reason, but *he* does not. And here the argument stops: There are limits to what can be accomplished by argument, and if the egoist really doesn't care about other people—if he honestly doesn't care whether they are helped or hurt by his actions—then we have reached those limits. If we want to persuade him to act decently toward his fellow humans, we will have to make our appeal to such other attitudes as he does possess, by threats, bribes, or other cajolery. That is all that we can do.

Though some may find this situation distressing (we would like to be able to show that the egoist is just *wrong*), it holds no embarrassment for common morality. What we have come up against is simply a fundamental requirement of rational action, namely, that the existence of reasons for action always depends on the prior existence of certain attitudes in the agent. For example, the fact that a certain course of action would make the agent a lot of money is a reason for doing it only if the agent wants to make money; the fact that practicing at chess makes one a better player is a reason for practicing only if one wants to be a better player; and so on. Similarly, the fact that a certain action would help the agent is a reason for doing the action only if the agent cares about his own welfare, and the fact that an action would help others is a reason for doing it only if the agent cares about others. In this respect ethical egoism and what we might call ethical altruism are in exactly the same fix: Both require that the agent *care* about himself, or other people, before they can get started.

So a nonegoist will accept "It would harm another person" as a reason not to do an action simply because he cares about what happens to that other person. When the egoist says that he does *not* accept that as a reason, he is saying something quite extraordinary. He is saying that he has no affection for friends or family, that he never feels pity or compassion, that he is the sort of person who can look on scenes of human misery with complete indifference, so long as he is not the one suffering. Genuine egoists, people who really don't care at all about anyone than themselves, are rare. It is important to keep this in mind when thinking about ethical egoism; it is easy to forget just how fundamental to human psychological makeup the feeling of sympathy is. Indeed, a man without any sympathy at all would scarcely be recognizable as a man; and that is what makes ethical egoism such a disturbing doctrine in the first place.

IV

There are, of course, many different ways in which the skeptic might challenge the assumptions underlying our moral practice. In this essay I have discussed only two of them, the two put forward by Glaucon in the passage that I cited from Plato's *Republic*. It is important that the assumptions underlying our moral practice should not be confused with particular judgments made within that practice. To defend one is not to defend the other. We may assume—quite properly, if my analysis has been correct—that the virtue of beneficence does, and indeed should, occupy an important place in "the moral institution of life"; and yet we may make constant and miserable errors when it comes to judging when and in what ways this virtue is to be exercised. Even worse, we may often be able to make accurate moral judgments, and know what we ought to do, but not do it. For these ills, philosophy alone is not the cure.

STUDY QUESTIONS

1. The great Renaissance philosopher Thomas Hobbes was a proponent of psychological egoism. Someone once saw him giving money to a beggar and asked if this kindly gesture did not prove that psychological egoism was wrong. Hobbes replied that his action was indeed self-interested because helping beggars made him feel good. Evaluate Hobbes's riposte in light of Rachel's discussion.
2. If you found the Ring of Gyges and no longer needed to appear to abide by moral rules, do you think you would behave as Gyges did? Do you think that other controls would prevent you from becoming amoral?
3. What is Rachel's strongest argument against psychological egoism? Against ethical egoism? Are Rachel's arguments persuasive?
4. The psychological egoist says that self-love motivates all human action. A number of philosophers have argues that self-hate, altruism, and malice also motivate human beings. Who do you think is right?

A Defense of Moral Relativism

RUTH BENEDICT

Ruth Benedict (1887–1948) was one of America's foremost anthropologists. Her *Patterns of Culture* (1935) is considered a classic of comparative anthropology.

Morality, says Benedict, is a convenient term for socially approved customs (mores). What one society approves may be disgraceful and unacceptable to another. Moral rules, like rules of etiquette or styles of dress, vary from society to society. Morality is culturally relative. Values are shaped by culture. As Benedict points out, trances are highly regarded in India, so in India many people have trances. Some ancient societies praised homosexual love, so there homosexuality was a norm; where material possessions are highly valued, people amass property. "Most individuals are plastic to the moulding force of the society into which they are born."

Modern social anthropology has become more and more a study of the varieties and common elements of cultural environment and the consequences of these in human behavior. For such a study of diverse social orders primitive peoples fortunately provide a laboratory not yet entirely vitiated by the spread of a standardized worldwide civilization. Dyaks and Hopis, Fijians and Yakuts are signi-

A DEFENSE OF MORAL RELATIVISM From "Anthropology and the Abnormal," by Ruth Benedict, in *The Journal of General Psychology* 10 (1934): 59–82. Reprinted by permission of Clark University Press.

ficant for psychological and sociological study because only among these simpler peoples has there been sufficient isolation to give opportunity for the development of localized social forms. In the higher cultures the standardization of custom and belief over a couple of continents has given a false sense of the inevitability of the particular forms that have gained currency, and we need to turn to a wider survey in order to check the conclusions we hastily base upon this near-universality of familiar customs. Most of the simpler cultures did not gain the wide currency of the one which, out of our experience, we identify with human nature, but this was for various historical reasons, and certainly not for any that gives us as its carriers a monopoly of social good or of social sanity. Modern civilization, from this point of view, becomes not a necessary pinnacle of human achievement but one entry in a long series of possible adjustments.

These adjustments, whether they are in mannerisms like the ways of showing anger, or joy, or grief in any society, or in major human drives like those of sex, prove to be far more variable than experience in any one culture would suggest. In certain fields, such as that of religion or of formal marriage arrangements, these wide limits of variability are well known and can be fairly described. In others it is not yet possible to give a generalized account, but that does not absolve us of the task of indicating the significance of the work that has been done and of the problems that have arisen.

One of these problems relates to the customary modern normal-abnormal categories and our conclusions regarding them. In how far are such categories culturally determined, or in how far can we with assurance regard them as absolute? In how far can we regard inability to function socially as diagnostic of abnormality, or in how far is it necessary to regard this as a function of the culture?

As a matter of fact, one of the most striking facts that emerge from a study of widely varying cultures is the ease with which our abnormals function in other cultures. It does not matter what kind of "abnormality" we choose for illustration, those which indicate extreme instability, or those which are more in the nature of character traits like sadism or delusions of grandeur or of persecution, there are well-described cultures in which these abnormals function at ease and with honor, and apparently without danger or difficulty to the society.

The most notorious of these is trance and catalepsy. Even a very mild mystic is aberrant in our culture. But most peoples have regarded even extreme psychic manifestations not only as normal and desirable, but even as characteristic of highly valued and gifted individuals. This was true even in our own cultural background in that period when Catholicism made the ecstatic experience the mark of sainthood. It is hard for us, born and brought up in a culture that makes no use of the experience, to realize how important a role it may play and how many individuals are capable of it, once it has been given an honorable place in any society. . . .

Cataleptic and trance phenomena are, of course, only one illustration of the fact that those whom we regard as abnormals may function adequately in other cultures. Many of our culturally discarded traits are selected for elaboration in different societies. Homosexuality is an excellent example, for in this case our attention is not constantly diverted, as in the consideration of trance, to the interruption of routine activity which it implies. Homosexuality poses the problem very simply. A tendency toward this trait in our culture exposes an individual to all the conflicts to which all aberrants are always exposed, and we tend to identify the consequences of this conflict with homosexuality. But these consequences are obviously local and cultural. Homosexuals in many societies are not incompetent, but they may be such if the culture asks adjustments of them that would strain any man's vitality. Wherever homosexuality has been given an honorable place in any society, those to whom it is congenial have filled adequately the honorable roles society assigns to them. Plato's *Republic* is, of course, the most convincing statement of such a reading of homosexuality. It is presented as one of the major means to the good life, and it was generally so regarded in Greece at that time.

The cultural attitude toward homosexuals has not always been on such a high ethical plane, but it has been very varied. Among many American Indian tribes there exists the institution of the berdache, as the French called them. These men-women were men who at puberty or thereafter took the dress and the occupations of women. Sometimes they married other men and lived with them. Sometimes they were men with no inversion, persons of weak sexual endowment who chose this rôle to avoid the jeers of the women. The berdaches were never regarded as of first-rate supernatural power, as similar men-women were in Siberia, but rather as leaders in women's occupations, good healers in certain diseases, or, among certain tribes, as the genial organizers of social affairs. In any case, they were socially placed. They were not left exposed to the conflicts that visit the deviant who is excluded from participation in the recognized patterns of his society.

The most spectacular illustrations of the extent to which normality may be culturally defined are those cultures where an abnormality of our culture is the cornerstone of their social structure. It is not possible to do justice to these possibilities in a short discussion. A recent study of an island of northwest Melanesia by Fortune describes a society built upon traits which we regard as beyond the border of paranoia. In this tribe the exogamic groups look upon each other as prime manipulators of black magic, so that one marries always into an enemy group which remains for life one's deadly and unappeasable foes. They look upon a good garden crop as a confession of theft, for everyone is engaged in making magic to induce into his garden the productiveness of his neighbors'; therefore no secrecy in the island is so rigidly insisted upon as the secrecy of a man's harvesting of his yams. Their polite phrase at the acceptance of a gift is, "And if you now poison me, how shall I repay you this present?" Their preoccupation with poisoning is constant; no woman ever leaves her cooking pot for a moment untended. Even the great affinal economic exchanges that are characteristic of this Melanesian culture area are quite altered in Dobu since they are incompatible with this fear and distrust that pervades the culture. They go farther and people the whole world outside their own quarters with such malignant spirits that all-night feasts and ceremonials simply do not occur here. They have even rigorous religiously enforced customs that forbid the sharing of seed even in one family group. Anyone else's food is deadly poison to you, so that communality of stores is out of the question. For some months before harvest the whole society is on the verge of starvation, but if one falls to the temptation and eats up one's seed yams, one is an outcast and a beachcomber for life. There is no coming back. It involves, as a matter of course, divorce and the breaking of all social ties.

Now in this society where no one may work with another and no one may share with another, Fortune describes the individual who was regarded by all his fellows as crazy. He was not one of those who periodically ran amok and, beside himself and frothing at the mouth, fell with a knife upon anyone he could reach. Such behavior they did not regard as putting anyone outside the pale. They did not even put the individuals who were known to be liable to these attacks under any kind of control. They merely fled when they saw the attack coming on and kept out of the way. "He would be all right tomorrow." But there was one man of sunny, kindly disposition who liked work and liked to be helpful. The compulsion was too strong for him to repress it in favor of the opposite tendencies of his culture. Men and women never spoke of him without laughing; he was silly and simple and definitely crazy. Nevertheless, to the ethnologist used to a culture that has, in Christianity, made his type the model of all virtue, he seemed a pleasant fellow. . . .

. . . Among the Kwakiutl it did not matter whether a relative had died in bed of disease, or by the hand of an enemy, in either case death was an affront to be wiped out by the death of another person. The fact that one had been caused to mourn was proof that one had been put upon. A chief's sister and her daughter had gone up to Victoria, and either because they drank bad whiskey or because their boat capsized they never came back. The chief called together his warriors. "Now I ask you, tribes, who shall wail? Shall I do it or shall another?" The spokesman answered, of course, "Not you, Chief. Let some other of the tribes." Immediately they set up the war pole to announce their intention of wiping out the injury, and gathered a war party. They set out, and found seven men and two children asleep and killed them. "Then they felt good when they arrived at Sebaa in the evening."

The point which is of interest to us is that in our society those who on that occasion would feel good when they arrived at Sebaa that evening would be the definitely abnormal. There would be some, even in our society, but it is not a recognized and approved mood under the circumstances. On the Northwest Coast those are favored and fortunate to whom that mood under those circumstances is congenial, and those to whom it is repugnant are unlucky. This latter minority can register in their own culture only by doing violence to their congenial responses and acquiring others that are difficult for them. The person, for instance, who, like a Plains Indian whose wife has been taken from him, is too proud to fight, can deal with the Northwest Coast civilization only by ignoring its strongest bents. If he cannot achieve it, he is the deviant in that culture, their instance of abnormality.

115

This head-hunting that takes place on the Northwest Coast after a death is no matter of blood revenge or of organized vengeance. There is no effort to tie up the subsequent killing with any responsibility on the part of the victim for the death of the person who is being mourned. A chief whose son has died goes visiting wherever his fancy dictates, and he says to his host, "My prince has died today, and you go with him." Then he kills him. In this, according to their interpretation, he acts nobly because he has not been downed. He has thrust back in return. The whole procedure is meaningless without the fundamental paranoid reading of bereavement. Death, like all the other untoward accidents of existence, confounds man's pride and can only be handled in the category of insults.

Behavior honored upon the Northwest Coast is one which is recognized as abnormal in our civilization, and yet it is sufficiently close to the attitudes of our own culture to be intelligible to us and to have a definite vocabulary with which we may discuss it. The megalomaniac paranoid trend is a definite danger in our society. It is encouraged by some of our major preoccupations, and it confronts us with a choice of two possible attitudes. One is to brand it as abnormal and reprehensible, and is the attitude we have chosen in our civilization. The other is to make it an essential attribute we have chosen in our civilization. The other is to make it an essential attribute of ideal man, and this is the solution in the culture of the Northwest Coast.

These illustrations, which it has been possible to indicate only in the briefest manner, force upon us the fact that normality is culturally defined. An adult shaped to the drives and standards of either of these cultures, if he were transported into our civilization, would fall into our categories of abnormality. He would be faced with the psychic dilemmas of the socially unavailable. In his own culture, however, he is the pillar of society, the end result of socially inculcated mores, and the problem of personal instability in his case simply does not arise.

No one civilization can possibly utilize in its mores the whole potential range of human behavior. Just as there are great numbers of possible phonetic articulations, and the possibility of language depends on a selection and standardization of a few of these in order that speech communication may be possible at all, so the possibility of organized behavior of every sort, from the fashions of local dress and houses to the dicta of a people's ethics and religion, depends upon a similar selection among the possible behavior traits. In the field of recognized economic obligations or sex tabus this selection is as nonrational and subconscious a process as it is in the field of phonetics. It is a process which goes on in the group for long periods of time and is historically conditioned by innumerable accidents of isolation or of contact of peoples. In any comprehensive study of psychology, the selection that different cultures have made in the course of history within the great circumference of potential behavior is of great significance.

Every society, beginning with some slight inclination in one direction or another, carries its preference farther and farther, integrating itself more and more completely upon its chosen basis, and discarding those types of behavior that are uncongenial. Most of those organizations of personality that seem to us most uncontrovertibly abnormal have been used by different civilizations in the very foundations of their institutional life. Conversely the most valued traits of normal individuals have been looked on in differently organized cultures as aberrant. Normality, in short, within a very wide range, is culturally defined. It is primarily a term for the socially elaborated segment of human behavior in any culture; and abnormality, a term for the segment that that particular civilization does not use. The very eyes with which we see the problem are conditioned by the long traditional habits of our own society.

It is a point that has been made more often in relation to ethics than in relation to psychiatry. We do not any longer make the mistake of deriving the morality of our locality and decade directly from the inevitable constitution of human nature. We do not elevate it to the dignity of a first principle. We recognize that morality differs in every society, and is a convenient term for socially approved habits. Mankind has always preferred to say, "It is morally good," rather than "It is habitual," and the fact of this preference is matter enough for a critical science of ethics. But historically the two phrases are synonymous.

The concept of the normal is properly a variant of the concept of the good. It is that which society has approved. A normal action is one which falls well within the limits of expected behavior for a particular society. Its variability among different peoples is essentially a function of the variability of the behavior patterns that different societies have created for themselves, and can never be wholly divorced from a consideration of culturally institutionalized types of behavior.

Each culture is a more or less elaborate working-out of the potentialities of the segment it has chosen. In so far as a civilization is well integrated and consistent within itself, it will tend to carry farther and farther, according to its nature, its initial impulse toward a particular type of action, and from the point of view of any other culture those elaborations will include more and more extreme and aberrant traits.

Each of these traits, in proportion as it reinforces the chosen behavior patterns of that culture, is for that culture normal. Those individuals to whom it is congenial either congenitally, or as the result of childhood sets, are accorded prestige in that culture, and are not visited with the social contempt or disapproval which their traits would call down upon them in a society that was differently organized. On the other hand, those individuals whose characteristics are not congenial to the selected type of human behavior in that community are the deviants, no matter how valued their personality traits may be in a contrasted civilization.

The Dobuan who is not easily susceptible to fear of treachery, who enjoys work and likes to be helpful, is their neurotic and regarded as silly. On the Northwest Coast the person who finds it difficult to read life in terms of an insult contest will be the person upon whom fall all the difficulties of the culturally unprovided for. The person who does not find it easy to humiliate a neighbor, nor to see humiliation in his own experience, who is genial and loving, may, of course, find some unstandardized way of achieving satisfactions in his society, but not in the major patterned responses that his culture requires of him. If he is born to play an important rôle in a family with many hereditary privileges, he can succeed only by doing violence to his whole personality. If he does not succeed, he has betrayed his culture; that is, he is abnormal.

I have spoken of individuals as having sets toward certain types of behavior, and of these sets as running sometimes counter to the types of behavior which are institutionalized in the culture to which they belong. From all that we know of contrasting cultures it seems clear that differences of temperament occur in every society. The matter has never been made the subject of investigation, but from the available material it would appear that these temperament types are very likely of universal recurrence. That is, there is an ascertainable range of human behavior that is found wherever a sufficiently large series of individuals is observed. But the proportion in which behavior types stand to one another in different societies is not universal. The vast majority of the individuals in any group are shaped to the fashion of that culture. In other words, most individuals are plastic to the moulding force of the society into which they are born. In a society that values trance, as in India, they will have supernormal experience. In a society that institutionalizes homosexuality, they will be homosexual. In a society that sets the gathering of possessions as the chief human objective, they will amass property. The deviants, whatever the type of behavior the culture has institutionalized, will remain few in number, and there seems no more difficulty in moulding that vast malleable majority to the "normality" of what we consider an aberrant trait, such as delusions of reference, than to the normality of such accepted behavior patterns as acquisitiveness. The small proportion of the number of the deviants in any culture is not a function of the sure instinct with which that society has built itself upon the fundamental sanities, but of the universal fact that, happily, the majority of mankind quite readily take any shape that is presented to them. . . .

STUDY QUESTIONS

1. Do you think that the fact of cultural diversity is itself an argument for ethical relativism?
2. If Benedict's defense of ethical relativism is correct, then the correct way to resolve a personal dilemma might be to take a survey or poll to see what the majority in your society thinks is right. If the majority favors capital punishment and opposes abortion, for example, then capital punishment is right and abortion is wrong. Can you defend Benedict against this odd consequence?
3. Do you think that certain types of behavior (for example, executing children or beating animals to death) are wrong wherever they occur, despite attitudes prevailing in the societies that practice them? What makes these acts wrong?
4. How could Benedict account for notions of moral enlightenment and moral progress?

Ethical Relativism: A Critique

W. T. STACE

Walter Terence Stace (1886–1967) was a professor of philosophy at Princeton University. He is the author of a number of highly acclaimed books in philosophy of religion, metaphysics, and ethics.

The ethical relativist claims that there are no objective moral standards: Right and wrong vary from culture to culture. Stace criticizes this ethical relativism and tries to defend the opposite view: ethical absolutism. According to ethical absolutism, all people everywhere are accountable to certain universal moral standards. The fact that not all societies are aware of them just shows that such a thing as moral ignorance exists. Stace criticizes ethical relativism for making it impossible to compare societies as morally better or worse. The same is true of the same society at an earlier and a later time, and renders the whole notion of moral progress meaningless. He also points out the difficulties of determining what constitutes a cultural group. (Does the American nation constitute a group having a single moral standard?) Rejecting all religious solutions, Stace acknowledges the difficulties moral philosophers face in trying to prove that there is a universal morality. But he is

ETHICAL RELATIVISM: A CRITIQUE Reprinted with permission of Macmillan Publishing Company from *The Concept of Morals* by Walter T. Stace. Copyright 1937 by Macmillan Publishing Company, renewed 1965 by Walter T. Stace.

hopeful that philosophers will work it out. Meanwhile, he advises against the tempting but incoherent and demoralizing doctrine of ethical relativism.

I

Any ethical position which denies that there is a single moral standard which is equally applicable to all men at all times may fairly be called a species of ethical relativity. There is not, the relativist asserts, merely one moral law, one code, one standard. There are many moral laws, codes, standards. What morality ordains in one place or age may be quite different from what morality ordains in another place or age. The moral code of Chinamen is quite different from that of Europeans, that of African savages quite different from both. Any morality, therefore, is relative to the age, the place, and the circumstances in which it is found. It is in no sense absolute.

This does not mean merely—as one might at first sight be inclined to suppose—that the very same kind of action which is *thought* right in one country and period may be *thought* wrong in another. This would be a mere platitude, the truth of which everyone would have to admit. Even the absolutist would admit this— would even wish to emphasize it—since he is well aware that different people have different sets of moral ideas, and his whole point is that some of these sets of ideas are false. What the relativist means to assert is, not this platitude, but that the very same kind of action which *is* right in one country and period may *be* wrong in another. And this, far from being a platitude, is a very startling assertion.

It is very important to grasp thoroughly the difference between the two ideas. For there is a reason to think that many minds tend to find ethical relativity attractive because they fail to keep them clearly apart. It is so very obvious that moral ideas differ from country to country and from age to age. And it is so very easy, if you are mentally lazy, to suppose that to say this means the same as to say that no universal moral standard exists—or in other words that it implies ethical relativity. We fail to see that the word "standard" is used in two different senses. It is perfectly true that, in one sense, there are many variable moral standards. We speak of judging a man by the standard of his time. And this implies that different times have different standards. And this, of course, is quite true. But when the word "standard" is used in this sense it means simply the set of moral ideas current during the period in question. It means what people *think* right, whether as a matter of fact it *is* right or not. On the other hand when the absolutist asserts that there exists a single universal moral "standard," he is not using the word in this sense at all. He means by "standard" what *is* right as distinct from what people merely think right. His point is that although what people think right varies in different countries and periods, yet what actually is right is everywhere and always the same. And it follows that when the ethical relativist disputes the position of the absolutist and denies that any universal moral standard exists, he too means by "standard" what actually is right. But it is exceedingly easy, if we are not careful, to slip loosely from using the word in the first sense to using it in the second sense, and to suppose that the variability of moral beliefs is the same thing as the variability of what really is moral. And unless we keep the two senses of the word "standard" distinct, we are likely to think the creed of ethical relativity much more plausible than it actually is.

The genuine relativist, then, does not merely mean that Chinamen may think right what Frenchmen think wrong. He means that what *is* wrong for the Frenchman may *be* right for the Chinaman. And if one inquires how, in those circumstances, one is to know what actually is right in China or in France, the answer comes quite glibly. What is right in China is the same as what people think right in China; and what is right in France is the same as what people think right in France. So that if you want to know what is moral in any particular country or age, all you have to do is to ascertain what are the moral ideas current in that age or country. Those ideas are, *for that age or country,* right. Thus what is morally right is identified with what is thought to be morally right, and the distinction which we made above between these two is simply denied. To put the same thing in another way, it is denied that there can be or ought to be any distinction between the two senses of the word "standard." There is only one kind of standard of right and wrong, namely, the moral ideas current in any particular age or country.

Moral right *means* what people think morally right. It has no other meaning. What Frenchmen think right is, therefore, right *for Frenchmen*. And evidently one must conclude—though I am not aware that relativists are anxious to draw one's attention to such unsavory but yet absolutely necessary conclusions from their creed—that cannibalism is right for people who believe in it, that human sacrifice is right for those races which practice it, and that burning widows alive was right for Hindus until the British stepped in and compelled the Hindus to behave immorally by allowing their widows to remain alive.

When it is said that, according to the ethical relativist, what is thought right in any social group is right for that group, one must be careful not to misinterpret this. The relativist does not, of course, mean that there actually is an objective moral standard in France and a different objective standard in England, and that French and British opinions respectively give us correct information about these different standards. His point is rather that there are not objectively true moral standards at all. There is no single universal objective standard. Nor are there a variety of local objective standards. All standards are subjective. People's subjective feelings about morality are the only standards which exist.

To sum up: The ethical relativist consistently denies, it would seem, whatever the ethical absolutist asserts. For the absolutist there is a single universal moral standard. For the relativist there is no such standard. There are only local, ephemeral, and variable standards. For the absolutist there are two senses of the word "standard." Standards in the sense of sets of current moral ideas are relative and changeable. But the standard in the sense of what is actually morally right is absolute and unchanging. For the relativist no such distinction can be made. There is only one meaning of the word standard, namely, that which refers to local and variable sets of moral ideas. Or if it is insisted that the word must be allowed two meanings, then the relativist will say that there is at any rate no actual example of a standard in the absolute sense, and that the word as thus used is an empty name to which nothing in reality corresponds; so that the distinction between the two meanings becomes empty and useless. Finally—though this is merely saying the same thing in another way—the absolutist makes a distinction between what actually is right and what is thought right. The relativist rejects this distinction and identifies what is moral with what is thought moral by certain human beings or groups of human beings. . . .

II

I shall now proceed to consider, first, the main arguments which can be urged in favor of ethical relativity; and secondly, the arguments which can be urged against it. . . . The first [in favor] is that which relies upon the actual varieties of moral "standards" found in the world. It was easy enough to believe in a single absolute morality in older times when there was no anthropology, when all humanity was divided clearly into two groups, Christian peoples and the "heathen." Christian peoples knew and possessed the one true morality. The rest were savages whose moral ideas could be ignored. But all this is changed. Greater knowledge has brought greater tolerance. We can no longer exalt our own morality as alone true, while dismissing all other moralities as false or inferior. The investigations of anthropologists have shown that there exist side by side in the world a bewildering variety of moral codes. On this topic endless volumes have been written, masses of evidence piled up. Anthropologists have ransacked the Melanesian Islands, the jungles of New Guinea, the steppes of Siberia, the deserts of Australia, the forests of central Africa, and have brought back with them countless examples of weird, extravagant, and fantastic "moral" customs with which to confound us. We learn that all kinds of horrible practices are, in this, that, or the other place, regarded as essential to virtue. We find that there is nothing, or next to nothing, which has always and everywhere been regarded as morally good by all men. Where, then, is our universal morality? Can we, in face of all this evidence, deny that it is nothing but an empty dream?

This argument, taken by itself, is a very weak one. It relies upon a single set of facts—the variable moral customs of the world. But this variability of moral ideas is admitted by both parties to the dispute, and is capable of ready explanation upon the hypothesis of either party. The relativist says that the facts are to be explained by the nonexistence of any absolute moral standard. The absolutist says that they are to be explained by human ignorance of what the absolute moral standard is. And he can truly point out that men have differed widely in their opinions about all manner of topics—including the subject-matters of the physical sciences—just as much as they differ about morals. And if the various different opinions which men have held about the shape of the earth do not prove that it has no one real shape, neither do the various opinions which they have held about morality prove that there is no one true morality.

Thus the facts can be explained equally plausibly on either hypothesis. There is nothing in the facts themselves which compels us to prefer the relativistic hypothesis to that of the absolutist. And therefore the argument fails to prove the relativist conclusion. If that conclusion is to be established, it must be by means of other considerations.

This is the essential point. But I will add some supplementary remarks. The works of the anthropologists, upon which ethical relativists seem to rely so heavily, has as a matter of fact added absolutely nothing *in principle* to what has always been known about the variability of moral ideas. Educated people have known all along that the Greeks tolerated sodomy, which in modern times has been regarded in some countries as an abominable crime; that the Hindus thought it a sacred duty to burn their widows; that trickery, now thought despicable, was once believed to be a virtue; that terrible torture was thought by our own ancestors only a few centuries ago to be a justifiable weapon of justice; that it was only yesterday that western peoples came to believe that slavery is immoral. Even the ancients knew very well that moral customs and ideas vary—witness the writings of Herodotus. Thus the principle of the variability of moral ideas was well understood long before modern anthropology was ever heard of. Anthropology has added nothing to the knowledge of this principle except a mass of new and extreme examples of it drawn from very remote sources. But to multiply examples of a principle already well known and universally admitted adds nothing to the argument which is built upon that principle. The discoveries of the anthropologists have no doubt been of the highest importance in their own sphere. But in any considered opinion they have thrown no new light upon the special problems of the moral philosopher.

Although the multiplication of examples has no logical bearing on the argument, it does have an immense *psychological* effect upon people's minds. These masses of anthropological learning are impressive. They are propounded in the sacred name of "science." If they are quoted in support of ethical relativity—as they often are—people *think* that they must prove something important. They bewilder and over-awe the simple-minded, batter down their resistance, make them ready to receive humbly the doctrine of ethical relativity from those who have acquired a reputation by their immense learning and their claims to be "scientific." Perhaps this is why so much ado is made by ethical relativists regarding the anthropological evidence. But we must refuse to be impressed. We must discount all this mass of evidence about the extraordinary moral customs of remote peoples. Once we have admitted—as everyone who is instructed must have admitted these last two thousand years without any anthropology at all—the principle that moral ideas vary, all this new evidence adds nothing to the argument. And the argument itself proves nothing for the reasons already given. . . .

The second argument in favor of ethical relativity . . . does not suffer from the disadvantage that it is dependent upon the acceptance of any particular philosophy such as radical empiricism. It makes its appeal to considerations of a quite general character. It consists in alleging that no one has ever been able to discover upon what foundation an absolute morality could rest, or from what source a universally binding moral code could derive its authority.

If, for example, it is an absolute and unalterable moral rule that all men ought to be unselfish, from whence does this *command* issue? For a command it certainly is, phrase it how you please. There is no difference in meaning between the sentence "You ought to be unselfish" and the sentence "Be unselfish." Now a command implies a commander. An obligation implies some authority which obliges. Who is this commander, what this authority? Thus the vastly difficult question is raised of *the basis of moral obligation*. Now the argument of the relativist would be that it is impossible to find any basis for a universally binding moral law; but that it is quite easy to discover a basis for morality if moral codes are admitted to be variable, ephemeral, and relative to time, place, and circumstance.

In this paper I am assuming that it is no longer possible to solve this difficulty by saying naïvely that the universal moral law is based upon the uniform commands of God to all men. There will be many, no doubt, who will dispute this. But I am not writing for them. I am writing for those who feel the necessity of finding for morality a basis independent of particular religious dogmas. And I shall therefore make no attempt to argue the matter.

The problem which the absolutist has to face, then, is this. The religious basis of the one absolute morality having disappeared, can there be found for it any other, any secular, basis? If not, then it would seem that we cannot any longer believe in absolutism. We shall have to fall back upon belief in a variety of perhaps mutually inconsistent moral codes operating over restricted areas and limited periods. No one of these will be better, or more true, than any other. Each will be good and true for those living in those areas and periods. We shall have to fall back, in a word, on ethical relativity.

For there is not great difficulty in discovering the foundations of morality, or rather of moralities, if we adopt the relativistic hypothesis. Even if we cannot be quite certain *precisely* what these foundations are—and relativists themselves are not entirely agreed about them—we can at least see in a general way the *sort* of foundations they must have. We can see that the question on this basis is not in principle impossible of answer—although the details may be obscure; while, if we adopt the absolutist hypothesis—so the argument runs—no kind of answer is conceivable at all. . . .

This argument is undoubtedly very strong. It *is* absolutely essential to solve the problem of the basis of moral obligation if we are to believe in any kind of moral standards other than those provided by mere custom or by irrational emotions. It is idle to talk about a universal morality unless we can point to the source of its authority—or at least to do so is to indulge in a faith which is without rational ground. To cherish a blind faith in morality may be, for the average man whose business is primarily to live right and not to theorize, sufficient. Perhaps it is his wisest course. But it will not do for the philosopher. His function, or at least one of his functions, is precisely to discover the rational grounds of our every day beliefs—if they have any. Philosophically and intellectually, then, we cannot accept belief in a universally binding morality unless we can discover upon what foundation its obligatory character rests.

But in spite of the strength of the argument thus posed in favor of ethical relativity, it is not impregnable. For it leaves open one loophole. It is always possible that some theory, not yet examined, may provide a basis for a universal moral obligation. The argument rests upon the [universal] negative proposition that *there is no theory which can provide a basis for a universal morality*. But it is notoriously difficult to prove a negative. How can you prove that there are no green swans? All you can show is that none have been found so far. And then it is always possible that one will be found tomorrow. . . .

III

It is time that we turned our attention from the case in favor of ethical relativity to the case against it. Now the case against it consists, to a very large extent, in urging that, if taken seriously and pressed to its logical conclusion, ethical relativity can only end in destroying the conception of morality altogether, in undermining its practical efficacy, in rendering meaningless many almost universally accepted truths about human affairs, in robbing human beings of any incentive to strive for a better world, in taking the life-blood out of every ideal and every aspiration which has ever ennobled the life of man. . . .

First of all, then, ethical relativity, in asserting that the moral standards of particular social groups are the only standards which exist, renders meaningless all propositions which attempt to compare these standards with one another in respect of their moral worth. And this is a very serious matter indeed. We are accustomed to think that the moral ideas of one nation or social group may be "higher" or "lower" than those of another. We believe, for example, that Christian ethical ideals are nobler than those of the savage races of central Africa. Probably most of us would think that the Chinese moral standards are higher than those of the inhabitants of New Guinea. In short we habitually compare one civilization with another and judge the sets of ethical ideas to be found in them to be some better, some worse. The fact that such judgments are very difficult to make with any justice, and that they are frequently made on very superficial and prejudiced grounds, has no bearing on the question now at issue. The question is whether such judgments have any *meaning*. We habitually assume that they have.

But on the basis of ethical relativity they can have none whatever. For the relativist must hold that there is no *common* standard which can be applied to the various civilizations judged. Any such comparison of moral standards implies the existence of some superior standard which is applicable to both. And the existence of any such standard is precisely what the relativist denies. According to him the Christian standard is applicable only to Christians, the Chinese standard only to Chinese, the New Guinea standard only to the inhabitants of New Guinea.

What is true of comparisons between the moral standards of different races will also be true of comparisons between those of different ages. It is not unusual to ask such questions as whether the standard of our own day is superior to that which existed among our ancestors five hundred years ago. And when we remember that our ancestors employed slaves, practiced barbaric physical tortures, and burned people alive, we may be inclined to think that it is. At any rate we assume that the question is one which has meaning and is capable of rational discussion. But if the ethical relativist is right, whatever we assert on this subject must be totally meaningless. For here again there is no common standard which could form the basis of any such judgments.

This in its turn implies that the whole notion of moral *progress* is a sheer delusion. Progress means an advance from lower to higher, from worse to better. But on the basis of ethical relativity it has no meaning to say that the standards of this age are better (or worse) than those of a previous age. For there is no common standard by which both can be measured. Thus it is nonsense to say that the morality of the New Testament is higher than that of the Old. And Jesus Christ, if he imagined that he was introducing into the world a higher ethical standard than existed before his time, was merely deluded. . . .

I come now to a second point. Up to the present I have allowed it to be taken tacitly for granted that, though judgments comparing different races and ages in respect of the worth of their moral codes are impossible for the ethical relativist, yet judgments of comparison between individuals living within the same social group would be quite possible. For individuals living within the same social group would presumably be subject to the same moral code, that of their group, and this would therefore constitute, as between these individuals, a common standard by which they could both be measured. We have not here, as we had in the other case, the difficulty of the absence of any common standard of comparison. It should therefore be possible for the ethical relativist to say quite meaningfully that President Lincoln was a better man than some criminal or moral imbecile of his own time and country, or that Jesus was a better man than Judas Iscariot.

But is even this minimum of moral judgment really possible on relativist grounds? It seems to me that it is not. For when once the whole of humanity is abandoned as the area covered by a single moral standard, what smaller areas are to be adopted as the *loci* of different standards? Where are we to draw the lines of demarcation? We can split up humanity, perhaps—though the procedure will be very arbitrary—into races, races into nations, nations into tribes, tribes into families, families into individuals. Where are we going to draw the *moral* boundaries? Does the *locus* of a particular moral standard reside in a race, a nation, a tribe, a family, or an individual? Perhaps the blessed phrase "social group" will be dragged in to save the situation. Each such group, we shall be told, has its own moral code which is, for it, right. But what *is* a "group"? Can any one define it or give it boundaries? This is the seat of that ambiguity in the theory of ethical relativity to which reference was made on an earlier page.

The difficulty is not, as might be thought, merely an academic difficulty of logical definition. If that were all, I should not press the point. But the ambiguity has practical consequences which are disastrous for morality. No one is likely to say that moral codes are confined within the arbitrary limits of the geographical divisions of countries. Nor are the notions of race, nation, or political state likely to help us. To bring out the essentially practical character of the difficulty let us put it in the form of concrete questions. Does the American nation constitute a "group" having a single moral standard? Or does the standard of what I ought to do change continuously as I cross the continent in a railway train? Do different States of the Union have different moral codes? Perhaps every town and village has its own peculiar standard. This may at first sight seem reasonable enough. "In Rome do as Rome does" may seem as good a rule in morals as it is in etiquette. But can we stop there? Within the village are numerous cliques each having its own set of ideas. Why should not each of these claim to be bound only by its own special and peculiar moral standards? And if it comes to that, why should not the gangsters of Chicago claim to constitute a group having its own morality, so that its murders and debaucheries must be viewed as "right" by the only standard which can legitimately be applied to it? And if it be answered that the nation will not tolerate this, that may be so. But this is to put the foundation of right simply in the superior force of the majority. In that case whoever is stronger will be right, however monstrous his ideas and actions. And if we cannot deny to any set of people the right to have its own morality, is it not clear that, in the end, we cannot even deny this right to the individual? Every individual man and woman can put up, on this view, an irrefutable claim to be judged by no standard except his or her own.

If these arguments are valid, the ethical relativist cannot really maintain that there is anywhere to be found a moral standard binding upon anybody against his will. And he cannot maintain that, even within the social group, there is a common standard as between individuals. And if that is so, then even judgments to the effect that one man is morally better than another become meaningless. All moral valuation thus vanishes. There is nothing to prevent each man from being a rule unto himself. The result will be moral chaos and the collapse of all effective standards. . . .

But even if we assume that the difficulty about defining moral groups has been surmounted, a further difficulty presents itself. Suppose that we have now definitely decided what are the exact boundaries of the social group within which a moral standard is to be operative. And we will assume—as is invariably done by relativists themselves—that this group is to be some actually existing social community such as a tribe or nation. How are we to know, even then, what actually is the moral standard within that group? How is anyone to know? How is even a member of the group to know? For there are certain to be within the group—at least this will be true among advanced peoples—wide differences of opinion as to what is right, what wrong. Whose opinion, then, is to be taken as representing *the* moral standard of the group? Either we must take the opinion of the majority within the group, or the opinion of some minority. If we rely upon the ideas of the majority, the results will be disastrous. Wherever there is found among a people a small band of select spririts, or perhaps one man, working for the establishment of higher and nobler ideas than those com-

131

monly accepted by the group, we shall be compelled to hold that, for that people at that time, the majority are right, and that the reformers are wrong and are preaching what is immoral. We shall have to maintain, for example, that Jesus was preaching immoral doctrines to the Jews. Moral goodness will have to be equated always with the mediocre and sometimes with the definitely base and ignoble. If on the other hand we said that the moral standard of the group is to be identified with the moral opinions of some minority, then what minority is this to be? We cannot answer that it is to be the minority composed of the best and most enlightened individuals of the group. This would involve us in a palpably vicious circle. For by what standard are these individuals to be judged the best and the most enlightened? There is no principle by which we could collect the right minority. And therefore we should have to consider every minority as good as every other. And this means that we should have no logical right whatever to resist the claim of the gangsters of Chicago—if such a claim were made—that their practices represent the highest standards of American morality. It means in the end that every individual is to be bound by no standard save his own.

The ethical relativists are great empiricists. *What* is the actual moral standard of any group can only be discovered, they tell us, by an examination on the ground of the moral opinions and customs of that group. But will they tell us how they propose to decide, when they get to the ground, which of the many moral opinions they are sure to find there is *the* right one in that group? To some extent they will be able to do this for the Melanesian Islanders—from whom apparently all lessons in the nature of morality are in future to be taken. But it is certain that they cannot do it for advanced peoples whose members have learned to think for themselves and to entertain among themselves a wide variety of opinions. They cannot do it unless they accept the calamitous view that the ethical opinion of the majority is always right. We are left therefore once more with the conclusion that, even within a particular social group, anybody's moral opinion is as good as anybody else's, and that every man is entitled to be judged by his own standards.

Finally, not only is ethical relativity disastrous in its consequences for moral theory. It cannot be doubted that it must end to be equally disastrous in its impact upon practical conduct. If men come really to believe that one moral standard is as good as another, they will conclude that their own moral standard has nothing special to recommend it. They might as well then slip down to some lower and easier standard. It is true that, for a time, it may be possible to hold one view in theory and to act practically upon another. But ideas, even philosophical ideas, are not so ineffectual that they can remain for ever idle in the upper chambers of the intellect. In the end they seep down to the level of practice. They get themselves acted on.

STUDY QUESTIONS

1. How does Stace criticize the argument that the variety of moral customs in the world proves that we cannot have a single correct moral standard?
2. Do you agree with Stace that ethical relativism undermines the notion of moral progress?
3. If ethical relativism is true, were moral rebels like Gandhi and Martin Luther King immoral?
4. How does Stace reply to the relativist claim that finding any basis for a universally binding moral law is impossible? Do you think his reply is satisfactory?
5. Why does Stace believe that widespread acceptance of ethical relativism could lead to moral chaos? Do you agree?

Trying Out One's New Sword

MARY MIDGLEY

Mary Midgley is a senior Lecturer at the University of Newcastle-upon-Tyne, England. She is the author of *Beast and Man* (1978) and *Heart and Mind* (1981).

Midgley criticizes "moral isolationalists" who disapprove of those who morally judge other cultures. She notes that moral isolationists disapprove less when someone from another culture passes moral judgment on *our* culture. Also, moral isolationists are inconsistent: They do not oppose *praising* an exotic culture. Moral judgment, says Midgley, is a human necessity: Why ban it interculturally? She points out that such a ban would not permit us to express disapproval of the Samurai custom of trying out a new sword by cleanly slicing an innocent passerby in two.

All of us are, more or less, in trouble today about trying to understand cultures strange to us. We hear constantly of alien customs. We see changes in our lifetime which would have astonished our parents. I want to discuss here one very short way of dealing with this difficulty, a drastic way which many people now theoretically favour. It consists in simply denying that we can ever understand any culture except our own well enough to make judgments about it. Those who recommend this hold that the

TRYING OUT ONE'S NEW SWORD   From *Heart and Mind* by Mary Midgley. © by M. Midgley, to be used with permission from St. Martin's Press, Inc.

world is sharply divided into separate societies, sealed units, each with its own system of thought. They feel that the respect and tolerance due from one system to another forbids us ever to take up a critical position to any other culture. Moral judgment, they suggest, is a kind of coinage valid only in its country of origin.

I shall call this position 'moral isolationism'. I shall suggest that it is certainly not forced upon us, and indeed that it makes no sense at all. People usually take it up because they think it is a respectful attitude to other cultures. In fact, however, it is not respectful. Nobody can respect what is entirely unintelligible to them. To respect someone, we have to know enough about him to make a *favorable* judgment, however general and tentative. And we do understand people in other cultures to this extent. Otherwise a great mass of our most valuable thinking would be paralysed.

To show this, I shall take a remote example, because we shall probably find it easier to think calmly about it than we should with a contemporary one, such as female circumcision in Africa or the Chinese Cultural Revolution. The principles involved will still be the same. My example is this. There is, it seems, a verb in classical Japanese which means 'to try out one's new sword on a chance wayfarer'. (The world is *tsujigiri,* literally 'crossroads-cut'.) A samurai sword had to be tried out because, if it was to work properly, it had to slice through someone at a single blow, from the shoulder to the opposite flank. Otherwise, the warrior bungled his stroke. This could injure his honour, offend his ancestors, and even let down his emperor. So tests were needed, and wayfarers had to be expended. Any wayfarer would do—provided, of course, that he was not another Samurai. Scientists will recognize a familiar problem about the rights of experimental subjects.

Now when we hear of a custom like this, we may well reflect that we simply do not understand it; and therefore are not qualified to criticize it at all, because we are not members of that culture. But we are not members of any other culture either, except our own. So we extend the principle to cover all extraneous cultures, and we seem therefore to be moral isolationists. But this is, as we shall see, an impossible position. Let us ask what it would involve.

We must ask first: Does the isolating barrier work both ways? Are people in other cultures equally unable to criticize *us*? This question struck me sharply when I read a remark in *The Guardian* by an anthropologist about a South American Indian who had been taken into a Brazilian town for an operation, which saved his life. When he came back to his village, he made several highly critical remarks about the white Brazilians' way of life. They may very well have been justified. But the interesting point was that the anthropologist called these remarks 'a damning indictment of Western civilization'. Now the Indian had been in that town about two weeks. Was he in a position to deliver a damning indictment? Would we ourselves be qualified to deliver such an indictment on the Samurai, provided we could spend two weeks in ancient Japan? What do we really think about this?

My own impression is that we believe that outsiders can, in principle, deliver perfectly good indictments—only, it usually takes more than two weeks to make them damning. Understanding has degrees. It is not a slapdash yes-or-no matter. Intelligent outsiders can progress in it, and in some ways will be at an advantage over the locals. But if this is so, it must clearly apply to ourselves as much as anybody else.

Our next question is this: Does the isolating barrier between cultures block praise as well as blame? If I want to say that the Samurai culture has many virtues, or to praise the South American Indians, am I prevented from doing *that* by my outside status? Now, we certainly do need to praise other societies in this way. But it is hardly possible that we could praise them effectively if we could not, in principle, criticize them. Our praise would be worthless if it rested on on definite grounds, if it did not flow from some understanding. Certainly we may need to praise things which we do not *fully* understand. We say 'there's something very good here, but I can't quite make out what it is yet'. This happens when we want to learn from strangers. And we can learn from strangers. But to do this we have to distinguish between those strangers who are worth learning from and those who are not. Can we then judge which is which?

This brings us to our third question: What is involved in judging? Now plainly there is no question here of sitting on a bench in a red robe and sentencing people. Judging simply means forming an opinion, and expressing it if it is called for. Is there anything wrong about this? Naturally, we ought to avoid forming—and expressing—*crude* opinions, like that of a simple-minded missionary, who might dismiss the whole Samurai culture as entirely bad, because non-Christian. But this is a different objection. The trouble with crude opinions is that they are crude, whoever forms them, not that they are formed by the wrong people. Anthropologists, after all, are outsiders quite as much as missionaries. Moral isolationism forbids us to form *any* opinions on these matters. Its ground for doing so is that we don't understand them. But there is much that we don't understand in our own culture too. This brings us to our last question: If we can't judge other cultures, can we really judge our own? Our efforts to do so will be much damaged if we are really deprived of our opinions about other societies, because these provide the range of comparison, the spectrum of alternatives against which we set what we want to understand. We would have to stop using the mirror which anthropology so helpfully holds up to us.

In short, moral isolationism would lay down a general ban on moral reasoning. Essentially, this is the programme of immoralism, and it carries a distressing logical difficulty. Immoralists like Nietzsche are actually just a rather specialized sect of moralists. They can no more afford to put moralizing out of business than smugglers can afford to abolish customs regulations. The power of moral judgment is, in fact, not a luxury, not a perverse indulgence of the self-righteous. It is a necessity. When we judge something to be bad or good, better or worse than something else, we are taking it as an example to aim at or avoid. Without opinions of this sort, we would have no framework of comparison for our own policy, no chance of profiting by other people's insights or mistakes. In this vacuum, we could form no judgments on our own actions.

Now it would be odd if Homo sapiens had really got himself into a position as bad as this—a position where his main evolutionary asset, his brain, was so little use to him. None of us is going to accept this sceptical diagnosis. We cannot do so, because our involvement in moral isolationism does not flow from apathy, but from a rather acute concern about human hypocrisy and other forms of wickedness. But we polarize that concern around a few selected moral truths. We are rightly angry with those who despise, oppress or steamroll other cultures. We think that doing these things is actually *wrong*. But this is itself a moral judgment. We could not condemn oppression and insolence if we thought that all our condemnations were just a trivial local quirk of our own culture. We could still less do it if we tried to stop judging altogether.

Real moral scepticism, in fact, could lead only to inaction, to our losing all interest in moral questions, most of all in those which concern other societies. When we discuss these things, it becomes instantly clear how far we are from doing this. Suppose, for instance, that I criticize the bisecting Samurai, that I say his behaviour is brutal. What will usually happen next is that someone will protest, will say that I have no right to make criticisms like that of another culture. But it is most unlikely that he will use this move to end the discussion of the subject. Instead, he will justify the Samurai. He will try to fill in the background, to make me understand the custom, by explaining the exalted ideals of discipline and devotion which produced it. He will probably talk of the lower value which the ancient Japanese placed on individual life generally. He may well suggest that this is a healthier attitude than our own obsession with security. He may add, too, that the wayfarers did not seriously mind being bisected, that in principle they accepted the whole arrangement.

Now an objector who talks like this is implying that it *is* possible to understand alien customs. That is just what he is trying to make me do. And he implies, too, that if I do succeed in understanding them, I shall do something better than giving up judging them. He expects me to change my present judgment to a truer one—namely, one that is favourable. And the standards I must use to do this cannot just be Samurai standards. They have to be ones current in my own culture. Ideals like discipline and devotion will not move anybody unless he himself accepts them. As it happens, neither discipline nor devotion is very popular in the West at present. Anyone who appeals to them may well have to do some more arguing to make *them* acceptable, before he can use them to explain the Samurai. But if he does succeed here, he will have persuaded us, not just that there was something to be said for them in ancient Japan, but that there would be here as well.

Isolating barriers simply cannot arise here. If we accept something as a serious moral truth about one culture, we can't refuse to apply it—in however different an outward form—to other cultures as well, wherever circumstance admit it. If we refuse to do this, we just are not taking the other culture seriously. This becomes clear if we look at the last argument used by my objector—that of justification by consent of the victim. It is suggested that sudden bisection is quite in order, *provided* that it takes place between consenting adults. I cannot now discuss how conclusive this justification is. What I am pointing out is simply that it can only work if we believe that *consent* can make such a transaction respectable—and this is a thoroughly modern and Western idea. It would probably never occur to a Samurai; if it did, it would surprise him very much. It is *our* standard. In applying it, too, we are likely to make another typically Western demand. We shall ask for good factual evidence that the wayfarers actually do have this rather surprising taste—that they are really willing to be bisected. In applying Western standards in this way, we are not being confused or irrelevant. We are asking the questions which arise *from where we stand*, questions which we can see the sense of. We do this because asking questions which you can't see the sense of is humbug. Certainly we can extend our questioning by imaginative effort. We can come to understand other societies better. By doing so, we may make their questions our own, or we may see that they are really forms of the questions which we are asking already. This is not impossible. It is just very hard work. The obstacles which often prevent it are simply those of ordinary ignorance, laziness and prejudice.

If there were really an isolating barrier, of course, our own culture could never have been formed. It is no sealed box, but a fertile jungle of different influences—Greek, Jewish, Roman, Norse, Celtic and so forth, into which further influences are still pouring—American, Indian, Japanese, Jamaican, you name it. The moral isolationist's picture of separate, unmixable cultures is quite unreal. People who talk about British history usually stress the value of this fertilizing mix, no doubt rightly. But this is not just an odd fact about Britain. Except for the very smallest and most remote, all cultures are formed out of many streams. All have the problem of digesting and assimilating things which, at the start, they do not understand. All have the choice of learning something from this challenge, or, alternatively, of refusing to learn, and fighting it mindlessly instead.

This universal predicament has been obscured by the fact that anthropologists used to concentrate largely on very small and remote cultures, which did not seem to have this problem. These tiny societies, which had often forgotten their own history, made neat, self-contained subjects for study. No doubt it was valuable to emphasize their remoteness, their extreme strangeness, their independence of our cultural tradition. This emphasis was, I think, the root of moral isolationism. But, as the tribal studies themselves showed, even there the anthropologists were able to interpret what they saw and make judgments—often favourable—about the tribesmen. And the tribesmen, too, were quite equal to making judgments about the anthropologists—and about the tourists and Coca-Cola salesmen who followed them. Both sets of judgments, no doubt, were somewhat hasty, both have been refined in the light of further experience. A similar transaction between us and the Samurai might take even longer. But that is no reason at all for deeming it impossible. Morally as well as physically, there is only one world, and we all have to live in it.

STUDY QUESTIONS

1. How would a philosophical Samurai defend the practice of trying out a new sword? Does this defense have any merit? Explain your answer.
2. The word "mores" usually connotes a variety of social practices. Yet Midgley says, "Morally as well as physically, there is only one world." If you believe she is right about this, then defend her view that we can judge the social practices and traditions of exotic cultures. If you disagree, show where she goes wrong.
3. Someone else might call Midgley's "moral isolationism" a "sophisticated tolerance of cultural difference." Argue the case against Midgley and for "tolerance" to see whether you end up convincing yourself that she is wrong.

SUGGESTED READINGS

Baier, Kurt. *The Moral Point of View.* Ithaca, N.Y.: Cornell University Press, 1958.

Benedict, Ruth. *Patterns of Culture.* Boston: Houghton Mifflin Co., 1934.

Butler, Joseph. *Fifteen Sermons Upon Human Nature.* 1726.

Frankera, William. *Ethics.* Englewood Cliffs, N.J.: Prentice-Hall, 1973.

Gert, Bernard. *The Moral Rules: A New Rational Foundation for Morality.* New York: Harper and Row, 1970.

Harman, Gilbert. *The Nature of Morality: An Introduction to Ethics.* New York: Oxford University Press, 1977.

Hospers, John. *Human Conduct.* New York: Harcourt, Brace and World, 1961.

Ladd, John, ed. *Ethical Relativism.* Belmont, Calif.: Wadsworth, Books, 1973.

Mackie, J. L. *Ethics: Inventing Right and Wrong.* New York: Penguin Books, 1977.

Midgley, Mary. *Heart and Mind.* New York: St. Martin's Press, 1981.

Singer, Marcus. *Generalization in Ethics.* New York: Alfred A. Knopf, 1961.

Smart, J. J. C., and Bernard Williams. *Utilitarianism: For and Against.* Cambridge: Cambridge University Press, 1973.

Chapter

3

VIRTUE

Several acorns fall from a tree. One is eaten by a squirrel. Another decays on the ground. A third grows into an oak tree. We say that the third acorn's fate is appropriate to it, that it succeeds where the other two fail. In our view, the acorn's goal or purpose is to become an oak tree, as if its self-fulfillment depends on achieving this goal. Yet we are aware that to speak of a goal here is grossly anthropomorphic. The acorn is not a conscious being trying to achieve the happy outcome of development. Nor do we feel that this happy outcome is really more natural than the outcome of rotting or being eaten. Indeed, since only a tiny minority of acorns become oak trees, the unhappy outcomes are more natural than the happy one.

All the same, our intuition that becoming an oak tree is the appropriate career for an acorn is sound. Any organic matter, a leaf, for example, can rot on the ground, and nuts can serve as squirrel fodder. But only the acorn can grow into an oak tree. The Greeks defined the function or natural purpose of a thing as an activity that is specific to it, an activity that it alone performs or one that it performs better than anything else can. In this sense, we think that the third acorn's career is the "happy" or proper one. The metaphor of a happy outcome for the acorn leans heavily on the Greek meaning of happiness (*eudaimonia*) as well-functioning, self-fulfilling activity.

A biologist could tell us quite a bit about the special characteristics that enable the acorn to perform its function. The Greeks called such characteristics "excellences" or "virtues." In the broad sense a virtue is any trait or capacity that enables an object to perform its appropriate function. More commonly, "virtue" refers to a special kind of excellence that only human beings possess or lack. In this narrow sense, the virtues are *moral* excellences contributing to a life of human fulfillment. And in this sense we speak of the virtues in contrast to vices. A question now arises: What goal is appropriate for human beings? There are, in fact, rival conceptions of human fulfillment; some of them are represented by the selections in this chapter. We shall discuss this presently. Our immediate concern is with the virtues themselves.

No one is born virtuous; the virtues are in part distinguished from other excellences by being subject to conscious development. But this alone does not distinguish them. As Philippa Foot points out in "Virtues and Vices," health is an excellence we quite often consciously develop, but we do not consider it to be a moral excellence. The moral philosopher who investigates virtue confronts the task of distinguishing moral excellences from other kinds of excellences. For example, we have little doubt that many traits contribute to self-preservation and are necessary for any well-functioning human being. One such trait, sometimes called a virtue, is prudence. Yet we do not usually think of prudence as a moral quality. W. D. Falk's discussion, "Prudence and Courage," is a fine example of the way a philosopher studies a particular trait and analyzes it to see if it possesses the features that make it a virtue.

Several articles presented here give a good idea of the sort of investigation the contemporary philosopher of virtue pursues. In his article on generosity, James D. Wallace distinguishes economic generosity from generous-mindedness. Wallace formulates characteristics of generosity, one of which is that the generous person gives more than duty requires. Here we touch on an important difference between a morality of duty and a morality of virtue. Fred Berger, in his study of gratitude, observes that the notion of having a *duty* to show gratitude is problematical. Berger proposes that a moral education must not only teach us about what we ought to do or not do; it must also teach that certain feelings (such as gratitude) are appropriate to certain situations and "in some sense ought to be had" in those situations. For the philosopher of virtue, being moral means being a certain kind of person (compassionate, generous, capable of gratitude, just, and brave) as much as it means doing the right thing. Not surprisingly, some philosophers of virtue openly oppose Kantianism and utilitarianism, two doctrines that have dominated modern moral theory. They see both theories as primarily concerned with the question, What is the moral thing to do? Kant answers that one must follow the universal laws that constitute one's duty. Mill tells us to act to maximize utility. Neither directly addresses another equally fundamental moral question: What kind of person must I be?

Part of the reason that virtue-based ethics has declined is that philosophers of recent times are skeptical about the possibility of formulating an acceptable description of human fulfillment. We need a clear conception of this fulfillment in order to explain the virtues in the teleological manner of classical philosophy, as excellences that enable a person to live the good life. But what kind of life is appropriate to human beings? Some of the philosophers in this chapter give significantly different answers. Others avoid the question altogether. Of course, the answer one gives determines what one counts as virtues and how one ranks the contribution various virtues make to the good life.

The Greeks confronted this question with their characteristic simplicity and boldness. Human beings, says Aristotle, are rational animals. They are also social animals. They naturally fulfill themselves in functioning as rational and social beings. Given such a conception of human purpose, virtues such as temperance, magnanimity, and courage come to the fore as traits that allow people to lead graceful lives in a political community.

Saint Augustine conceives of the life appropriate to a human being rather differently. Human beings are rational and social beings, but that they are creatures of God is even more important: Human purpose and happiness are found in following God. While the Greeks, with their secular conception of the good life, primarily emphasize such "cardinal virtues" as wisdom, courage, and temperance, Augustine, with his Christian conception of the good life, gives priority to other virtues, such as charity, humility, and faith.

In "The Virtues in Heroic Societies," Alasdair MacIntyre describes yet another conception of human fulfillment. A society such as Homer describes in the *Iliad* exclusively emphasizes human social character. Focusing on social role and social obligation, the heroic ideal gives priority to such virtues as courage, honor, and fidelity. MacIntyre concludes from his study of the heroic societies that social context and tradition are always crucial in defining human virtue. "There is no way to possess the virtues except as part of a tradition in which we inherit them. . . ."

Many modern philosophers believe that no one universally acceptable conception of human fulfillment exists and have largely dropped the effort to formulate one. They do not do so because they generally disagree with Aristotle's conception of humans as rational and social beings. That conception is, after all, a truism. But philosophers by now recognize it as a very general truism from which they cannot deduce an interesting set of particular virtues. In fact, they can argue that Aristotle himself does not proceed in a teleological way when he analyzes the particular virtues. But in any case, most current philosophers of virtue proceed without conceiving of human happiness as neatly tied to certain moral traits that contribute to the good life. Reading Philippa Foot, we see a careful attempt to clarify the virtues by isolating the features that distinguish them from other excellences. She does not justify the virtues by some teleological deduction, although in a general way we recognize that they are beneficial to their possessor. The contemporary philosopher's hardest work comes in understanding the virtues not through the contribution they make to human happiness, but as qualities, in themselves, of a good and decent person. In effect, the virtues themselves define the good life. (And again, Aristotle also defines happiness as activity in accordance with the virtues.) Foot finds a common denominator of the virtues in the will. Mayo thinks of virtue-based ethics as "the philosophy of moral character."

One question students of moral philosophy often ask is, "Why should I be moral?" The question seems critical for the philosophy of virtue, especially in light of philosophers being unable to see precisely how the virtues contribute to the good life. J. L. Mackie outlines an answer for a virtue-based ethic. According to Mackie, humans who possess the virtues are better equipped for living than those who lack them. Not only will they live better with their consciences (and most of us do have consciences) but they will live better with others. Persons who (abnormally) lack virtue may often face situations that require "instinctual" courage or generosity. Failure to act courageously or generously puts them at a disadvantage. For clearly a disposition to behave virtuously can be beneficial or even profitable. Mackie's argument is reminiscent of Bertrand Russell's account of how many Quaker shopkeepers in the eighteenth century became rich. According to Russell, they felt dishonest quoting customers a price that was higher than the lowest price they were willing to accept. After a while, people learned of this and flocked to the Quakers' stores. Thus the disposition to honesty here turned out to be a good policy. So whatever one thinks of the intrinsic value of the virtues, plausible arguments can be made for the thesis that having them is a very good thing all around, and not only for business.

The Moral Virtues

ARISTOTLE

TRANSLATED BY J. A. K. THOMSON

Aristotle (384–322 B.C.) is one of the greatest philosophers of all time. He was the son of a Macedonian physician, the personal tutor of Alexander the Great, and a student of Plato. He wrote on a wide range of subjects, including logic (which he founded as a science), metaphysics, biology, ethics, politics, and literature. During the Middle Ages, the authority of his teachings in all matters of secular philosophy was undisputed. It would be difficult to exaggerate his influence on the development of Western culture.

Aristotle defines happiness as functioning well. The function of a thing is its special kind of activity, what it can do better than anything else. Thus, the function of human beings is the exercise of their capacity to reason. A capacity that enables a thing or a being to function well is a virtue. Aristotle defines happiness (well-functioning) as an activity in accordance with virtue. Reason plays a part in all of the specified human virtues. Courageous persons, for example, use reason to control fear; temperate persons use it to control their appetites. Properly employed, reason directs us to a course of moderation between extremes (for example, between the excesses of fear and folly, or gluttony and abstemiousness). Aristotle gives some general rules for pur-

THE MORAL VIRTUES From The *Ethics of Aristotle*. Translated by J. A. K. Thomson. Reprinted with permission of George Allen & Unwin (Publishers) Ltd.

suing the course of virtuous moderation: (i) avoid the extreme that more strongly opposes the virtue, (ii) guard against excessive hedonism, and (iii) attend to your characteristic faults. These are not hard and fast rules, but rough and ready guides.

No doubt people will say, 'To call happiness the highest good is a truism. We want a more distinct account of what it is.' We might arrive at this if we could grasp what is meant by the 'function' of a human being. If we take a flautist or a sculptor or any craftsman—in fact any class of men at all who have some special job or profession—we find that his special talent and excellence comes out in that job, and this is his function. The same thing will be true of man simply as man—that is of course if 'man' does have a function. But is it likely that joiners and shoemakers have certain functions or specialized activities, while man as such has none but has been left by Nature a functionless being? Seeing that eye and hand and foot and every one of our members has some obvious function, must we not believe that in like manner a human being has a function over and above these particular functions? Then what exactly is it? The mere act of living is not peculiar to man—we find it even in the vegetable kingdom—and what we are looking for is something peculiar to him. We must therefore exclude from our definition the life that manifests itself in mere nurture and growth. A step higher should come the life that is confined to experiencing sensations. But that we see is shared by horses, cows, and the brute creation as a whole. We are left, then, with a life concerning which we can make two statements. First, it belongs to the rational part of man. Secondly, it finds expression in actions. The rational part may be either active or passive: passive in so far as it follows the dictates of reason, active in so far as it possesses and exercises the power of reasoning. A similar distinction can be drawn within the rational life; that is to say, the reasonable element in it may be active or passive. Let us take it that what we are concerned with here is the reasoning power in action, for it will be generally allowed that when we speak of 'reasoning' we really mean *exercising* our reasoning faculties. (This seems the more correct use of the word). Now

let us assume for the moment the truth of the following propositions. (*a*) The function of a man is the exercise of his non-corporeal
faculties or 'soul' in accordance with, or at least not divorced from,
a rational principle. (*b*) The function of an individual and of a *good*
individual in the same class—a harp player, for example, and a
good harp player, and so through the classes—is generically the
same, except that we must add superiority in accomplishment to
the function, the function of the harp player being merely to play
on the harp, while the function of the good harp player is to play on
it well. (*c*) The function of man is a certain form of life, namely an
activity of the soul exercised in combination with a rational principle or reasonable ground of action. (*d*) The function of a good man
is to exert such activity well. (*e*) A function is performed well when
performed in accordance with the excellence proper to it.—If these
assumptions are granted, we conclude that the good for man is 'an
activity of soul in accordance with goodness' or (on the supposition
that there may be more than one form of goodness) 'in accordance
with the best and most complete form of goodness.'

. . . Let us begin, then, with this proposition. Excellence of
whatever kind affects that of which it is the excellence in two ways.
(1) It produces a good state in it. (2) It enables it to perform its
function well. Take eyesight. The goodness of your eye is not only
that which makes your eye good, it is also that which makes it
function well. Or take the case of a horse. The goodness of a horse
makes him a good horse, but it also makes him good at running,
carrying a rider, and facing the enemy. Our proposition, then,
seems to be true, and it enables us to say that virtue in a man will be
the disposition which (*a*) makes him a good man, (*b*) enables him to
perform his function well. We have already touched on this point,
but more light will be thrown upon it if we consider what is the
specific nature of virtue.

Every form, then, of applied knowledge, when it performs its
function well, looks to the mean and works to the standard set by
that. It is because people feel this that they apply the *cliché*, 'You
couldn't add anything to it or take anything from it' to an artistic
masterpiece, the implication being that too much and too little alike
destroy perfection, while the mean preserves it. Now if this be so,
and if it be true, as we say, that good craftsmen work to the
standard of the mean, then, since goodness like Nature is more
exact and of a higher character than any art, it follows that good-

ness is the quality that hits the mean. By 'goodness' I mean goodness of moral character, since it is moral goodness that deals with feelings and actions, and it is in them that we find excess, deficiency, and a mean. It is possible, for example, to experience fear, boldness, desire, anger, pity, and pleasures and pains generally, too much or too little or to the right amount. If we feel them too much or too little, we are wrong. But to have these feelings at the right times on the right occasions towards the right people for the right motive and in the right way is to have them in the right measure, that is, somewhere between the extremes; and this is what characterizes goodness. The same may be said of the mean and extremes in actions. Now it is in the field of actions and feelings that goodness operates; in them we find excess, deficiency, and, between them, the mean, the first two being wrong, the mean right and praised as such. Goodness, then, is a mean condition in the sense that it aims at hits the mean.

Consider, too, that it is possible to go wrong in more ways than one. (In Pythagorean terminology evil is a form of the Unlimited, good of the Limited.) But there is only one way of being right. That is why going wrong is easy, and going right is difficult; it is easy to miss the bull's-eye and difficult to hit it. Here, then, is another explanation of why the too much and the too little are connected with evil and the mean with good. As the poet says,

Goodness is one, evil is multiform.

We may now define virtue as a disposition of the soul in which, when it has to choose among actions and feelings, it observes the mean relative to us, this being determined by such a rule or principle as would take shape in the mind of a man of sense or practical wisdom. We call it a mean condition as lying between two forms of badness, one being excess and the other deficiency; and also for this reason, that, whereas badness either falls short of or exceeds the right measure in feelings and actions, virtue discovers the mean and deliberately chooses it. Thus, looked at from the point of view of its essence as embodied in its definition, virtue no doubt is a mean; judged by the standard of what is right and best, it is an extreme.

Aristotle enters a caution. Though we have said that virtue observes the mean in actions and passions, we do not say this of all acts and all feelings.

Some are essentially evil and, when these are involved, our rule of applying the mean cannot be brought into operation.[1]

But choice of a mean is not possible in every action or every feeling. The very names of some have an immediate connotation of evil. Such are malice, shamelessness, envy among feelings, and among actions adultery, theft, murder. All these and more like them have a ban name as being evil in themselves; it is not merely the excess or deficiency of them that we censure. In their case, then, it is impossible to act rightly; whatever we do is wrong. Nor do circumstances make any difference in the rightness or wrongness of them. When a man commits adultery there is no point in asking whether it is with the right woman or at the right time or in the right way, for to do anything like that is simply wrong. It would amount to claiming that there is a mean and excess and defect in unjust or cowardly or intemperate actions. If such a thing were possible, we should find ourselves with a mean quantity of excess, a mean of deficiency, an excess of excess and a deficiency of deficiency. But just as in temperance and justice there can be no mean or excess or deficiency, because the mean in a sense *is* an extreme, so there can be no mean or excess or deficiency in those vicious actions—however done, they are wrong. Putting the matter into general language, we may say that there is no mean in the extremes, and no extreme in the mean, to be observed by anybody.

After the definition comes its application to the particular virtues. In these it is always possible to discover a mean—at which the virtue aims— between an excess and a deficiency. Here Aristotle found that a table or diagram of the virtues between their corresponding vices would be useful, and we are to imagine him referring to this in the course of his lectures.

But a generalization of this kind is not enough; we must show that our definition fits particular cases. When we are discussing actions particular statements come nearer the heart of the matter, though general statements cover a wider field. The reason is that human behaviour consists in the performance of particular acts, and our theories must be brought into harmony with them.

---

[1] The italicized interpolations in this selection are the translator's.

You see here a diagram of the virtues. Let us take our particular instances from that. In the section confined to the feelings inspired by danger you will observe that the mean state is 'courage'. Of those who go to extremes in one direction or the other the man who shows an excess of fearlessness has no name to describe him, the man who exceeds in confidence or daring is called 'rash' or 'foolhardy', the man who shows an excess of fear and a deficiency of confidence is called a 'coward'. In the pleasures and pains— though not all pleasures and pains, especially pains—the virtue which observes the mean is 'temperance', the excess is the vice of 'intemperance'. Persons defective in the power to enjoy pleasures are a somewhat rare class, and so have not had a name assigned to them: suppose we call them 'unimpressionable'. Coming to the giving and acquiring of money, we find that the mean is 'liberality', the excess 'prodigality', the deficiency 'meanness'. But here we meet a complication. The prodigal man and the mean man exceed and fall short in opposite ways. The prodigal exceeds in giving and falls short in getting money, whereas the mean man exceeds in getting and falls short in giving it away. Of course this is but a summary account of the matter—a bare outline. But it meets our immediate requirements. Later on these types of character will be more accurately delineated.

But there are other dispositions which declare themselves in the way they deal with money. One is 'lordliness' or 'magnificence', which differs from liberality in that the lordly man deals in large sums, the liberal man is small. Magnificence is the mean state here, the excess is 'bad taste' or 'vulgarity', the defect is 'shabbiness'. These are not the same as the excess and defect on either side of liberality. How they differ is a point which will be discussed later. In the matter of honour the mean is 'proper pride', the excess 'vanity', the defect 'poor-spiritedness'. And just as liberality differs, as I said, from magnificence in being concerned with small sums of money, so there is a state related to proper pride in the same way, being concerned with small honours, while pride is concerned with great. For it is possible to aspire to small honours in the right way, or to a greater or less extent than is right. The man who has this aspiration to excess is called 'ambitious'; if he does not cherish it enough, he is 'unambitious'; but the man who has it to the right extent—that is, strikes the mean—has no special designation. This is true also of corresponding dispositions with one exception, that of the ambitious man, which is called 'ambitiousness'. This will explain why each of the extreme characters stakes out a claim in the middle region. Indeed we ourselves call the character between the extremes sometimes 'ambitious' and sometimes 'unambitious'. That is proved by our sometimes praising a man for being ambitious and sometimes for being unambitious. The reason will appear later. In the meantime let us continue our discussion of the remaining virtues and vices, following the method already laid down.

Let us next take anger. Here too we find excess, deficiency, and the mean. Hardly one of the states of mind involved has a special name; but, since we call the man who attains the mean in this sphere 'gentle', we may call his disposition 'gentleness'. Of the extremes the man who is angry over-much may be called 'irascible', and his vice 'irascibility'; while the man who reacts too feebly to anger may be called 'poor-spirited' and his disposition 'poor-spiritedness'.

. . . As regards veracity, the character who aims at the mean may be called 'truthful' and what he aims at 'truthfulness'. Pretending, when it goes too far, is 'boastfulness' and the man who shows it is a 'boaster' or 'braggart'. If it takes the form of understatement, the pretence is called 'irony' and the man who shows it 'ironical'. In agreeableness in social amusement the man who hits the mean is 'witty' and what characterizes him is 'wittiness'. The excess is 'buffoonery' and the man who exhibits that is a 'buffoon'. The opposite of the buffoon is the 'boor' and his characteristic is 'boorishness'. In the other sphere of the agreeable—the general business of life—the person who is agreeable in the right way is 'friendly' and his disposition 'friendliness'. The man who makes himself too agreeable, supposing him to have no ulterior object, is 'obsequious'; if he has such an object, he is a 'flatterer'. The man who is deficient in this quality and takes every opportunity of making himself disagreeable may be called 'peevish' or 'sulky' or 'surly'.

But it is not only in settled dispositions that a mean may be observed in passing states of emotion.

Even when feelings and emotional states are involved one notes that mean conditions exist. And here also, it would be agreed, we may find one man observing the mean and another going beyond

154

it, for instance, the 'shamefaced' man, who is put out of countenance by anything. Or a man may fall short here of the due mean. Thus any one who is deficient in a sense of shame, or has none at all, is called 'shameless'. The man who avoids both extremes is 'modest', and him we praise. For, while modesty is not a form of goodness, it is praised; it and the modest man. Then there is 'righteous indignation'. This is felt by any one who strikes the mean between 'envy' and 'malice', by which last word I mean a pleased feeling at the misfortunes of other people. These are emotions concerned with the pains and pleasures we feel at the fortunes of our neighbours. The man who feels righteous indignation is pained by undeserved good fortune; but the envious man goes beyond that and is pained at anybody's success. The malicious man, on the other hand, is so far from being pained by the misfortunes of another that he is actually tickled by them.

However, a fitting opportunity of discussing these matters will present itself in another place. And after that we shall treat of justice. In that connexion we shall have to distinguish between the various kinds of justice—for the word is used in more senses than one—and show in what way each of them is a mean.

But after all, proceeds Aristotle, the true determinant of the mean is not the geometer's rod but the guiding principle in the good man's soul. The diagram of the virtues and vices, then, is just an arrangement and, as Aristotle goes on to show, an unimportant one at that.

Thus there are three dispositions, two of them taking a vicious form (one in the direction of excess, the other of defect) and one a good form, namely, the observance of the mean. They are all opposed to one another, though not all in the same way. The extreme states are opposed both to the mean and one another, and the mean is opposed to both extremes. For just as the equal is greater compared with the less, and less compared with the greater, so the mean states (whether in feelings or actions) are in excess if compared with the deficient, and deficient if compared with the excessive, states. Thus a brave man appears rash when set beside a coward, and cowardly when set beside a rash man; a temperate man appears intemperate beside a man of dull sensibilities, and dull if contrasted with an intemperate man. This is the reason why each extreme character tries to push the mean nearer the other. The

155

coward calls the brave man rash, the rash man calls him a coward.
And so in the other cases. But, while all the dispositions are
opposed to one another in this way, the greatest degree of opposition is that which is found between the two extremes. For they are
separated by a greater interval from one another than from the
mean, as the great is more widely removed from the small, and the
small from the great, than either from the equal. It may be added
that sometimes an extreme bears a certain resemblance to a mean.
For example, rashness resembles courage, and prodigality resembles liberality. But between the extremes there is always the maximum dissimilarity. Now opposites are by definition things as far
removed as possible from one another. Hence the farther apart
things are, the more opposite they will be. Sometimes it is the
deficiency, in other instances it is the excess, that is more directly
opposed to the mean. Thus cowardice, a deficiency, is more
opposed to courage than is rashness, an excess. And it is not
insensibility, the deficiency, that is more opposed to temperance
but intemperance, the excess. This arises from one or other of two
causes. One lies in the nature of the thing itself and may be
explained as follows. When one extreme is nearer to the mean and
resembles it more, it is not that extreme but the other which we
tend to oppose to the mean. For instance, since rashness is held to
be nearer and liker to courage than is cowardice, it is cowardice
which we tend to oppose to courage on the principle that the
extremes which are remoter from the mean strike us as more
opposite to it. The other cause lies in ourselves. It is the things to
which we are naturally inclined that appear to us more opposed to
the mean. For example, we have a natural inclination to pleasure,
which makes us prone to fall into intemperance. Accordingly we
tend to describe as opposite to the mean those things towards
which we have an instinctive inclination. For this reason intemperance, the excess, is more opposed to temperance than is insensibility to pleasure, the deficiency.

I have said enough to show that moral excellence is a mean, and I
have shown in what sense it is so. It is, namely, a mean between
two forms of badness, one of excess and the other of defect, and is
so described because it aims at hitting the mean point in feelings
and in actions. This makes virtue hard of achievement, because
finding the middle point is never easy. It is not everybody, for
instance, who can find the centre of a circle—that calls for a

geometrician. Thus, too, it is easy to fly into a passion—anybody can do that—but to be angry with the right person and to the right extent and at the right time and with the right object and in the right way—that is not easy, and it is not everyone who can do it. This is equally true of giving or spending money. Hence we infer that to do these things properly is rare, laudable and fine.

Aristotle now suggests some rules for our guidance.

In view of this we shall find it useful when aiming at the mean to observe these rules. (1) *Keep away from that extreme which is the more opposed to the mean.* It is Calypso's advice:

> Swing around the ship clear of this surf and surge.

For one of the extremes is always a more dangerous error than the other; and—since it is hard to hit the bull's-eye—we must take the next best course and choose the least of the evils. And it will be easiest for us to do this if we follow the rule I have suggested. (2) *Note the errors into which we personally are most liable to fall.* (Each of us has his natural bias in one direction or another.) We shall find out what ours are by noting what gives us pleasure and pain. After that we must drag ourselves in the opposite direction. For our best way of reaching the middle is by giving a wide berth to our darling sin. It is the method used by a carpenter when he is straightening a warped board. (3) *Always be particularly on your guard against pleasure and pleasant things.* When Pleasure is at the bar the jury is not impartial. So it will be best for us if we feel towards her as the Trojan elders felt towards Helen, and regularly apply their words to her. If we are for packing her off, as they were with Helen, we shall be the less likely to go wrong.

To sum up. These are the rules by observation of which we have the best chance of hitting the mean. But of course difficulties spring up, especially when we are confronted with an exceptional case. For example, it is not easy to say precisely what is the right way to be angry and with whom and on what grounds and for how long. In fact, we are inconsistent on this point, sometimes praising people who are deficient in the capacity for anger and calling them 'gentle', sometimes praising the choleric and calling them 'stout fellows'. To be sure we are not hard on a man who goes off the straight path in the direction of too much or too little, if he goes off only a little way. We reserve our censure for the man who swerves widely from the course, because then we are bound to notice it. Yet it is not easy to find a formula by which we may determine how far and up to what point a man may go wrong before he incurs blame. But this difficulty of definition is inherent in every object of perception; such questions of degree are bound up with the circumstances of the individual case, where our only criterion *is* the perception.

So much, then, has become clear. In all our conduct it is the mean state that is to be praised. But one should lean sometimes in the direction of the more, sometimes in that of the less, because that is the readiest way of attaining to goodness and the mean.

STUDY QUESTIONS

1. How, according to Aristotle, does reason determine right action? How does this connect with the general principle that virtuous action is a mean between extremes?
2. In Aristotle's view, what is happiness and how does it relate to virtue?
3. Of two extremes, one is usually worse, being "more opposed to the mean." Aristotle proposes that we take special care to avoid that extreme. Give an example (not found in Aristotle) of a person in a situation that falls under Aristotle's rule. Be concrete in showing how to apply the rule.
4. In the typical situation where we must choose an action guided by Aristotle's principles, do we have several choices, all falling within the range of the mean between two extremes, or does the principle of the mean uniquely determine a particular course of action? Answer this question, supplying a concrete example of your own.

Of the Morals of the Catholic Church

SAINT AUGUSTINE

Saint Augustine (354–420 A.D.), born in North Africa, is recognized as one of the very greatest Christian philosophers. His best known works are his *Confessions* (400 A.D.) and *The City of God* (427 A.D.)

Augustine defines happiness as the enjoyment of the highest good. The highest good is not something that can be lost by accident or misfortune, for then we cannot enjoy it confidently. Such a good must therefore be of the soul and not the body. Augustine concludes that the chief good is the possession of virtue. The virtuous Christian follows God, avoiding sin and obeying His will.

Happiness is in the enjoyment of man's chief good. Two conditions of the chief good: 1st, Nothing is better than it; 2d, it cannot be lost against the will.

How then, according to reason, ought man to live? We all certainly desire to live happily; and there is no human being but assents to this statement almost before it is made. But the title happy cannot, in my opinion, belong either to him who has not what he loves, whatever it may be, or to him who has what he loves if it is hurtful, or to him who does not love what he has, although it is good in

OF THE MORALS OF THE CATHOLIC CHURCH From *The Works of Aurelius Augustine*. Edited by M. Dods (T. & T. Clark, Edinburgh, 1892). Reprinted with permission from T. & T. Clark Ltd., Edinburgh, Scotland.

perfection. For one who seeks what he cannot obtain suffers torture, and one who has got what is not desirable is cheated, and one who does not seek for what is worth seeking for is diseased. Now in all these cases the mind cannot but be unhappy, and happiness and unhappiness cannot reside at the same time in one man; so in none of these cases can the man be happy. I find, then, a fourth case, where the happy life exists,—when that which is man's chief good is both loved and possessed. For what do we call enjoyment but having at hand the object of love? And no one can be happy who does not enjoy what is man's chief good, nor is there any one who enjoys this who is not happy. We must then have at hand our chief good, if we think of living happily.

We must now inquire what is man's chief good, which of course cannot be anything inferior to man himself. For whoever follows after what is inferior to himself, becomes himself inferior. But every man is bound to follow what is best. Wherefore man's chief good is not inferior to man. Is it then something similar to man himself? It must be so, if there is nothing above man which he is capable of enjoying. But if we find something which is both superior to man, and can be possessed by the man who loves it, who can doubt that in seeking for happiness man should endeavour to reach that which is more excellent than the being who makes the endeavour? For if happiness consists in the enjoyment of a good than which there is nothing better, which we call the chief good, how can a man be properly called happy who has not yet attained to his chief good? or how can that be the chief good beyond which something better remains for us to arrive at? Such, then, being the chief good, it must be something which cannot be lost against the will. For no one can feel confident regarding a good which he knows can be taken from him, although he wishes to keep and cherish it. But if a man feels no confidence regarding the good which he enjoys, how can he be happy while in such fear of losing it?

Man—what?

Let us then see what is better than man. This must necessarily be hard to find, unless we first ask and examine what man is. I am not now called upon to give a definition of man. The question here seems to me to be,—since almost all agree, or at least, which is enough, those I have now to do with are of the same opinion with me, that we are made up of soul and body,—What is man? Is he both of these? or is he the body only, or the soul only? For although the things are two, soul and body, and although neither without the other could be called man (for the body would not be man without the soul, nor again would the soul be man if there were not a body animated by it), still it is possible that one of these may be held to be man, and may be called so. What then do we call man? Is he soul and body, as in a double harness, or like a centaur? Or do we mean the body only, as being in the service of the soul which rules it, as the word lamp denotes not the light and the case together, but only the case, though on account of the light? Or do we mean only mind, and that on account of the body which it rules, as horseman means not the man and the horse, but the man only, and that as employed in ruling the horse? This dispute is not easy to settle; or, if the proof is plain, the statement requires time. This is an expenditure of time and strength which we need not incur. For whether the name man belongs to both, or only to the soul, the chief good of man is not the chief good of the body; but what is the chief good either of both soul and body, or of the soul only, that is man's chief good.

Man's chief good is not the chief good of the body only, but the chief good of the soul.

Now if we ask what is the chief good of the body, reason obliges us to admit that it is that by means of which the body comes to be in its best state. But of all the things which invigorate the body, there is nothing better or greater than the soul. The chief good of the body, then, is not bodily pleasure, not absence of pain, not strength, not beauty, not swiftness, or whatever else is usually reckoned among the goods of the body, but simply the soul. For all the things mentioned the soul supplies to the body by its presence, and, what is above them all, life. Hence I conclude that the soul is not the chief good of man, whether we give the name of man to soul and body together, or to the soul alone. For as, according to reason, the chief good of the body is that which is better than the body, and from which the body receives vigour and life, so whether the soul itself is man, or soul and body both, we must discover whether there is anything which goes before the soul

161

itself, in following which the soul comes to the perfection of good of which it is capable in its own kind. If such a thing can be found, all uncertainty must be at an end, and we must pronounce this to be really and truly the chief good of man.

If, again, the body is man, it must be admitted that the soul is the chief good of man. But clearly, when we treat of morals,—when we inquire what manner of life must be held in order to obtain happiness,—it is not the body to which the precepts are addressed, it is not bodily discipline which we discuss. In short, the observance of good customs belongs to that part of us which inquires and learns, which are the prerogatives of the soul; so, when we speak of attaining to virtue, the question does not regard the body. But if it follows, as it does, that the body which is ruled over by a soul possessed of virtue is ruled both better and more honourably, and is in its greatest perfection in consequence of the perfection of the soul which rightfully governs it, that which gives perfection to the soul will be man's chief good, though we call the body man. For if my coachman, in obedience to me, feeds and drives the horses he has charge of in the most satisfactory manner, himself enjoying the more of my bounty in proportion to his good conduct, can any one deny that the good condition of the horses, as well as that of the coachman, is due to me? So the question seems to me to be not, whether soul and body is man, or the soul only, or body only, but what gives perfection to the soul; for when this is obtained, a man cannot but be either perfect, or at least much better than in the absence of this one thing.

Virtue gives perfection to the soul; the soul obtains virtue by following God; following God is the happy life.

No one will question that virtue gives perfection to the soul. But it is a very proper subject of inquiry whether this virtue can exist by itself or only in the soul. Here again arises a profound discussion, needing lengthy treatment; but perhaps my summary will serve the purpose. God will, I trust, assist me, so that, notwithstanding our feebleness, we may give instruction on these great matters briefly as well as intelligibly. In either case, whether virtue can exist by itself without the soul, or can exist only in the soul, undoubtedly in the pursuit of virtue the soul follows after something, and this must be either the soul itself, or virtue, or something else. But if the soul follows after itself in the pursuit of virtue, it follows after a foolish thing; for before obtaining virtue it is foolish. Now the height of a follower's desire is to reach that which he follows after. So the soul must either not wish to reach what it follows after, which is utterly absurd and unreasonable, or, in following after itself while foolish, it reaches the folly which it flees from. But if it follows after virtue in the desire to reach it, how can it follow what does not exist? or how can it desire to reach what it already possesses? Either, therefore, virtue exists beyond the soul, or if we are not allowed to give the name of virtue except to the habit and disposition of the wise soul, which can exist only in the soul, we must allow that the soul follows after something else in order that virtue may be produced in itself; for neither by following after nothing, nor by following after folly, can the soul, according to my reasoning, attain to wisdom.

This something else, then, by following after which the soul becomes possessed of virtue and wisdom, is either a wise man or God. But we have said already that it must be something that we cannot lose against our will. No one can think it necessary to ask whether a wise man, supposing we are content to follow after him, can be taken from us in spite of our unwillingness or our persistence. God then remains, in following after whom we live well, and in reaching whom we live both well and happily.

STUDY QUESTIONS

1. What does Augustine mean by happiness? How does this conception of happiness differ from others with which you are acquainted?
2. What does Augustine mean by "following God"? How does he argue that happiness consists in following God?
3. What does the idea of virtue as primarily theological imply for morality in general?

The Virtues in Heroic Societies

ALASDAIR MACINTYRE

Alasdair MacIntyre (b. 1929) is a professor of philosophy at Vanderbilt University. He is the author of many books, including *A Short History of Ethics* (1966) and *After Virtue* (1981).

Today, the concept of virtue found in the heroic society of the Homeric poem is somewhat alien to us. Its foremost virtue is courage, a quality needed to sustain households and communities. Friendship and personal fidelity are also primary virtues in heroic societies; here, too, social roles and social obligations determine the rules governing conduct. Honor is conferred by peers on the basis of fulfillment of social roles. Morality is essentially bound up with honor, and the idea of a morality apart from social roles does not apply. We do not find the idea of a Self independent of social role and duties in heroic society. "Identity involves accountability": Without honor a person is worthless and lacks a sense of identity.

The virtues in heroic societies tie in to tribal, local traditions that determine particular duties. MacIntyre maintains that a traditional conception of honor is important for the cohesiveness of *any* society. And he

THE VIRTUES IN HEROIC SOCIETIES From *After Virtue* by Alasdair MacIntyre. Copyright 1981, *After Virtue*, University of Notre Dame Press, Notre Dame, Indiana 46556.

suggests that the current "morality of modernity" that pretends to a universality freed from tradition is an illusion.

The word *aretê*, which later comes to be translated as 'virtue', is in the Homeric poems used for excellence of any kind; a fast runner displays the *aretê* of his feet (*Iliad* 20.411) and a son excels in his father in every kind of *aretê*—as athlete, as soldier and in mind (*Iliad* 15. 642) This concept of virtue or excellence is more alien to us than we are apt at first to recognise. It is not difficult for us to recognise the central place that strength will have in such a conception of human excellence or the way in which courage will be one of the central virtues, perhaps the central virtue. What is alien to our conception of virtue is the intimate connection in heroic society between the concept of courage and its allied virtues on the other hand and the concepts of friendship, fate and death on the other.

Courage is important, not simply as a quality of individuals, but as the quality necessary to sustain a household and a community. *Kudos*, glory, belongs to the individual who excels in battle or in contest as a mark of recognition by his household and his community. Other qualities linked to courage also merit public recognition because of the part they play in sustaining the public order. In the Homeric poems cunning is such a quality because cunning may have its achievements where courage is lacking or courage fails. In the Icelandic sagas a wry sense of humour is closely bound up with courage. In the saga account of the battle of Clontarf in 1014, where Brian Boru defeated a Viking army, one of the norsemen, Thorstein, did not flee when the rest of his army broke and ran, but remained where he was, tying his shoestring. An Irish leader, Kerthialfad, asked him why he was not running. 'I couldn't get home tonight,' said Thorstein. 'I live in Iceland.' Because of the joke, Kerthialfad spared his life.

To be courageous is to be someone on whom reliance can be placed. Hence courage is an important ingredient in friendship. The bonds of friendship in heroic societies are modelled on those of kinship. Sometimes friendship is formally vowed, so that by the vow the duties of brothers are mutually incurred. Who my friends are and who my enemies, is as clearly defined as who my kinsmen are. The other ingredient of friendship is fidelity. My friend's courage assures me of his power to aid me and my household; my friend's fidelity assures me of his will. My household's fidelity is the basic guarantee of its unity. So in women, who constitute the crucial relationships within the household, fidelity is the key virtue. Andromache and Hector, Penelope and Odysseus are friends (*philos*) as much as are Achilles and Patroclus.

What I hope this account makes clear already is the way in which any adequate account of the virtues in heroic society would be impossible which divorced them from their context in its social structure, just as no adequate account of the social structure of heroic society would be possible which did not include an account of the heroic virtues. But to put it in this way is to understate the crucial point: morality and social structure are in fact one and the same in heroic society. There is only one set of social bonds. Morality as something distinct does not yet exist. Evaluative questions *are* questions of social fact. It is for this reason that Homer speaks always of *knowledge* of what to do and how to judge. Nor are such questions difficult to answer, except in exceptional cases. For the given rules which assign men their place in the social order and with it their identity also prescribe what they owe and what is owed to them and how they are to be treated and regarded if they fail and how they are to treat and regard others if those others fail.

Without such a place in the social order, a man would not only be incapable of receiving recognition and response from others; not only would others not know, but he would not himself know who he was. It is precisely because of this that heroic societies commonly have a well-defined status to which any stranger who arrives in the society from outside can be assigned. In Greek the word for 'alien' and the word for 'guest' are the same word. A stranger has to be received with hospitality, limited but well-defined. When Odysseus encounters the Cyclopes the question as to whether they possess *themis* (the Homeric concept of *themis* is the concept of customary law shared by all civilised peoples) is to be answered by discovering how they treat strangers. In fact they eat them—that is, for them strangers have no recognised human identity.

We might thus expect to find in heroic societies an emphasis upon the contrast between the expectations of the man who not

only possesses courage and its allied virtues, but who also has
kinsmen and friends on the one hand and the man lacking all these
on the other. Yet one central theme of heroic societies is also that
death waits for both alike. Life is fragile, men are vulnerable and it
is of the essence of the human situation that they are such. For in
heroic societies life is the standard of value. If someone kills you,
my friend or brother, I owe you their death and when I have paid
my debt to you their friend or brother owes them my death. The
more extended my system of kinsmen and friends, the more liabilities I shall incur of a kind that may end in my death.

Moreover there are powers in the world which no one can
control. Human life is invaded by passions which appear sometimes as impersonal forces, sometimes as gods. Achilles' wrath
disrupts Achilles as well as his relationship to the other Greeks.
These forces and the rules of kinship and friendship together constitute patterns of an ineluctable kind. Neither willing nor cunning
will enable anyone to evade them. Fate is a social reality and the
descrying of fate an important social role. It is no accident that the
prophet or the seer flourishes equally in Homeric Greece, in saga
Iceland and in pagan Ireland.

The man therefore who does what he ought moves steadily
towards his fate and his death. It is defeat and not victory that lies at
the end. To understand this is itself a virtue; indeed it is a necessary
part of courage to understand this. But what is involved in such
understanding? What would have been understood if the connections between courage, friendship, fidelity, the household, fate and
death had been grasped? Surely that human life has a determinate
form, the form of a certain kind of story. It is not just that poems
and sagas narrate what happens to men and women, but that in
their narrative form poems and sagas capture a form that was
already present in the lives which they relate.

'What is character but the determination of incident?' wrote
Henry James. 'What is incident but the illustration of character?'
But in heroic society character of the relevant kind can only be
exhibited in a succession of incidents and the succession itself must
exemplify certain patterns. Where heroic society agrees with James
is that character and incident cannot be characterised independently
of each other. So to understand courage as a virtue is not just to
understand how it may be exhibited in character, but also what

place it can have in a certain kind of enacted story. For courage in heroic society is a capacity not just to face particular harms and dangers but to face a particular kind of pattern of harms and dangers, a pattern in which individual lives find their place and which such lives in turn exemplify.

What epic and saga then portray is a society which already embodies the form of epic or saga. Its poetry articulates its form of individual and social life. To say this is still to leave open the question of whether there ever were such societies; but it does suggest that if there were such societies they could only be adequately understood through their poetry. Yet epic and saga are certainly not simple mirror images of the society they profess to portray. For it is quite clear that the poet or the saga writer claims for himself a kind of understanding which is denied to the characters about whom he writes. The poet does not suffer from the limitations which define the essential condition of his characters. Consider especially the *Iliad*.

As I said earlier of heroic society in general, the heroes in the *Iliad* do not find it difficult to know what they owe one another; they feel *aidôs* —a proper sense of shame—when confronted with the possibility of wrongdoing, and if that is not sufficient, other people are always at hand to drive home the accepted view. Honour is conferred by one's peers and without honour a man is without worth. There is indeed in the vocabulary available to Homer's characters no way for them to view their own culture and society as if from the outside. The evaluative expressions which they employ are mutually interdefined and each has to be explained in terms of the others.

Let me use a dangerous, but illuminating analogy. The rules which govern both action and evaluative judgment in the *Iliad* resemble the rules and the precepts of a game such as chess. It is a question of fact whether a man is a good chess player, whether he is good at devising end-game strategies, whether a move is the right move to make in a particular situation. The game of chess presupposes, indeed is partially constituted by, agreement on how to play chess. Within the vocabulary of chess it makes no sense to say 'That was the one and only move which would achieve checkmate, but was it the right move to make?' And therefore someone who said this and understood what he was saying would have to be employing some notion of 'right' which receives its definition from outside chess, as someone might ask this whose purpose in playing chess was to amuse a small child rather than to win.

One reason why the analogy is dangerous is that we do play games such as chess for a variety of purposes. But there is nothing to be made of the question: for what purpose do the characters in the *Iliad* observe the rules that they observe and honour the precepts which they honour? It is rather the case that it is only within their framework of rules and precepts that they are able to frame purposes at all; and just because of this the analogy breaks down in another way, too. All questions of choice arise within the framework; the framework itself therefore cannot be chosen.

There is thus the sharpest of contrasts between the emotivist self of modernity and the self of the heroic age. The self of the heroic age lacks precisely that characteristic which we have already seen that some modern moral philosophers take to be an essential characteristic of human selfhood: the capacity to detach oneself from any particular standpoint or point of view, to step backwards, as it were, and view and judge that standpoint or point of view from the outside. In heroic society there is no 'outside' except that of the stranger. A man who tried to withdraw himself from his given position in heroic society would be engaged in the enterprise of trying to make himself disappear.

Identity in heroic society involves particularity and accountability. I am answerable for doing or failing to do what anyone who occupies my role owes to others and this accountability terminates only with death. I have until my death to do what I have to do. Moreover this accountability is particular. It is to, for and with specific individuals that I must do what I ought, and it is to these same and other individuals, members of the same local community, that I am accountable. The heroic self does not itself aspire to universality even although in retrospect we may recognise universal worth in the achievements of that self.

The exercise of the heroic virtues thus requires both a particular kind of human being and a particular kind of social structure. Just because this is so, an inspection of the heroic virtues may at first sight appear irrelevant to any general enquiry into moral theory and practice. If the heroic virtues require for their exercise the presence of a kind of social structure which is now irrevocably lost—as they do—what relevance can they possess for us? Nobody now can be a Hector or a Gisli. The answer is that perhaps what we have to learn from heroic societies is twofold: first that all morality is always to some degree tied to the socially local and particular and that the aspirations of the morality of modernity to a universality freed from all particularity is an illusion; and secondly that there is no way to possess the virtues except as part of a tradition in which we inherit them and our understanding of them from a series of predecessors in which series heroic societies hold first place. . . .

STUDY QUESTIONS

1. How does MacIntyre relate personal identity to social role? Do you think that what you are as a person is partly determined by your social position and by what you believe your duty to be?
2. What virtues came to the fore in the "heroic society"? What gives the heroic virtues their special character?
3. Why does MacIntyre say that members of a heroic society cannot view themselves from the outside? By implication, this is possible for us today. In what sense is it possible?
4. MacIntyre suggests that the ideal of a universal human being freed from particularity is an illusion. What are his grounds? Do you agree with him?

Virtue or Duty?

BERNARD MAYO

Bernard Mayo (b. 1920) is an English philosopher. He is the author of *Ethics and the Modern Life* (1958).

Mayo points out that the classical philosophers did not lay down principles of moral behavior but concentrated instead on the character of the moral person. He claims that classical moral theory is superior to a modern (Kantian) ethics of duty. "The basic moral question, for Aristotle, is not, What shall I do? but, What shall I be?" The morality of "doing" is logically simple: We determine what we ought to do by seeing whether it maximizes happiness (utilitarianism) or is universalizable (Kantianism). The morality of "being" has another kind of simplicity, which Mayo calls the unity of character. Persons of character, heroes or saints, do not merely give us principles to follow; more importantly, they provide an example for us to follow. An ethics of character is more flexible than an ethics of rules. We can find more than one good way to follow a good personal example.

The philosophy of moral principles, which is characteristic of Kant and the post-Kantian era, is something of which hardly a trace exists in Plato. . . . Plato says nothing about rules or principles or laws, except when he is talking politics. Instead he talks about

VIRTUE OR DUTY? From *Ethics and the Moral Life* by Bernard Mayo. Reprinted by permission of Macmillan Accounts and Administration Ltd., London and Basingstoke.

virtues and vices, and about certain types of human character. The key word in Platonic ethics is Virtue; the key word in Kantian ethics is Duty. And modern ethics is a set of footnotes, not to Plato, but to Kant. . . .

Attention to the novelists can be a welcome correction to a tendency of philosophical ethics of the last generation or two to lose contact with the ordinary life of man which is just what the novelists, in their own way, are concerned with. Of course there are writers who can be called in to illustrate problems about Duty (Graham Greene is a good example). But there are more who perhaps never mention the words duty, obligation or principle. Yet they are all concerned—Jane Austen, for instance, entirely and absolutely—with the moral qualities or defects of their heroes and heroines and other characters. This points to a radical one-sidedness in the philosophers' account of morality in terms of principles: it takes little or no account of qualities, of what people *are*. It is just here that the old-fashioned word Virtue used to have a place; and it is just here that the work of Plato and Aristotle can be instructive. Justice, for Plato, though it is closely connected with acting according to law, does not *mean* acting according to law: it is a quality of character, and a just action is one such as a just man would do. Telling the truth, for Aristotle, is not, as it was for Kant, fulfilling an obligation; again it is a quality of character, or, rather, a whole range of qualities of character, some of which may actually be defects, such as tactlessness, boastfulness, and so on—a point which can be brought out, in terms of principles, only with the greatest complexity and artificiality, but quite simply and naturally in terms of character.

If we wish to enquire about Aristotle's moral views, it is no use looking for a set of principles. Of course we can find *some* principles to which he must have subscribed—for instance, that one ought not to commit adultery. But what we find much more prominently is a set of character-traits, a list of certain types of person—the courageous man, the niggardly man, the boaster, the lavish spender and so on. The basic moral question, for Aristotle, is not, What shall I do? but, What shall I be?

These contrasts between doing and being, negative and positive, and modern as against Greek morality were noted by John Stuart Mill; I quote from the *Essay on Liberty:*

Christian morality (so-called) has all the characters of a reaction; it is, in great part, a protest against Paganism. Its ideal is negative rather than positive, passive rather than active; Innocence rather than Nobleness; Abstinence from Evil, rather than energetic Pursuit of the Good; in its precepts (as has been well said) "Thou shalt not" predominates unduly over "Thou shalt . . ." Whatever exists of magnanimity, highmindedness, personal dignity, even the sense of honour, is derived from the purely human, not the religious part of our education, and never could have grown out of a standard of ethics in which the only worth, professedly recognised, is that of obedience.

Of course, there are connections between being and doing. It is obvious that a man cannot just *be*; he can only be what he is by doing what he does; his moral qualities are ascribed to him because of his actions, which are said to manifest those qualities. But the point is that an ethics of Being must include this obvious fact, that Being involves Doing; whereas an ethics of Doing, such as I have been examining, may easily overlook it. As I have suggested, a morality of principles is concerned only with what people do or fail to do, since that is what rules are for. And as far as this sort of ethics goes, people might well have no moral qualities at all except the possession of principles and the will (and capacity) to act accordingly.

When we speak of a moral quality such as courage, and say that a certain action was courageous, we are not merely saying something about the action. We are referring, not so much to what is done, as to the kind of person by whom we take it to have been done. We connect, by means of imputed motives and intentions, with the character of the agent as courageous. This explains, incidentally, why both Kantians and Utilitarians encounter, in their different ways, such difficulties in dealing with motives, which their principles, on the face of it, have no room for. A Utilitarian, for example, can only praise a courageous action in some such way as this: the action is of a sort such as a person of courage is likely to perform, and courage is a quality of character the cultivation of which is likely to increase rather than diminish the sum total of human happiness. But Aristotelians have no need of such circumlocution. For them a courageous action just is one which proceeds from and manifests a certain type of character, and is praised because such a character trait is good, or better than others, or is a virtue. An evaluative criterion is sufficient: there is no need to look for an imperative criterion as well, or rather instead, according to which it is not the character which is good, but the cultivation of the character which is right. . . .

No doubt the fundamental moral question is just "What ought I to do?" And according to the philosophy of moral principles, the answer (which must be an imperative "Do this") must be derived from a conjunction of premises consisting (in the simplest case) firstly of a rule, or universal imperative, enjoining (or forbidding) all actions of a certain type in situations of a certain type, and, secondly, a statement to the effect that this is a situation of that type, falling under that rule. In practice the emphasis may be on supplying only one of these premises, the other being assumed or taken for granted: one may answer the question "What ought I to do?" either by quoting a rule which I am to adopt, or by showing that my case is legislated for by a rule which I do adopt. To take a previous example of moral perplexity, if I am in doubt whether to tell the truth about his condition to a dying man, my doubt may be resolved by showing that the case comes under a rule about the avoidance of unnecessary suffering, which I am assumed to accept. But if the case is without precedent in my moral career, my problem may be soluble only by adopting a new principle about what I am to do now and in the future about cases of this kind.

This second possibility offers a connection with moral ideas. Suppose my perplexity is not merely an unprecedented situation which I could cope with by adopting a new rule. Suppose the new rule is thoroughly inconsistent with my existing moral code. This may happen, for instance, if the moral code is one to which I only pay lip-service; if . . . its authority is not yet internalised, or if it has ceased to be so; it is ready for rejection, but its final rejection awaits a moral crisis such as we are assuming to occur. What I now need is not a rule for deciding how to act in this situation and others of its kind. I need a whole set of rules, a complete morality, new principles to live by.

Now according to the philosophy of moral character, there is another way of answering the fundamental question "What ought I to do?" Instead of quoting a rule, we quote a quality of character, a virtue: we say "Be brave," or "Be patient" or "Be lenient." We may even say "Be a man": if I am in doubt, say, whether to take a risk, and someone says "Be a man," meaning a morally sound man, in this case a man of sufficient courage. (Compare the very different ideal invoked in "Be a gentleman." I shall not discuss whether this is a *moral* ideal.) Here, too, we have the extreme cases, where a man's moral perplexity extends not merely to a particular situation but to his whole way of living. And now the question "What ought I to do?" turns into the question "What ought I to be?"—as, indeed, it was treated in the first place. ("Be brave.") It is answered, not by quoting a rule or a set of rules, but by describing a quality of character or a type of person. And here the ethics of character gains a practical simplicity which offsets the greater logical simplicity of the ethics of principles. We do not have to give a list of characteristics or virtues, as we might list a set of principles. We can give a unity to our answer.

Of course we can in theory give a unity to our principles: this is implied by speaking of a *set* of principles. But if such a set is to be a system and not merely aggregate, the unity we are looking for is a logical one, namely the possibility that some principles are deductible from others, and ultimately from one. But the attempt to construct a deductive moral system is notoriously difficult, and in any case ill-founded. Why should we expect that all rules of conduct should be ultimately reducible to a few?

Saints and Heroes

But when we are asked "What shall I be?" we can readily give a unity to our answer, though not a logical unity. It is the unity of character. A person's character is not merely a list of dispositions; it has the organic unity of something that is more than the sum of its parts. And we can say, in answer to our morally perplexed questioner, not only "Be this" and "Be that," but also "Be like So-and-So"—where So-and-So is either an ideal type of character, or else an actual person taken as representative of the ideal, an exemplar. Examples of the first are Plato's "just man" in the Republic; Aristotle's man of practical wisdom, in the Nicomachean Ethics; Augustine's citizen of the City of God; the good Communist; the American way of life (which is a collective expression for a type of character). Examples of the second kind, the exemplar, are Socrates, Christ, Buddha, St. Francis, the heroes of epic writers and of novelists. Indeed the idea of the Hero, as well as the idea of the Saint, are very much the expression of this attitude to morality.

Heroes and saints are not merely people who did things. They are people whom we are expected, and expect ourselves, to imitate. And imitating them means not merely doing what they did; it means being like them. Their status is not in the least like that of legislators whose laws we admire; for the character of a legislator is irrelevant to our judgment about his legislation. The heroes and saints did not merely give us principles to live by (though some of them did that as well): they gave us examples to follow.

Kant, as we should expect, emphatically rejects this attitude as "fatal to morality." According to him, examples serve only to render *visible* an instance of the moral principle, and thereby to demonstrate its practical feasibility. But every exemplar, such as Christ himself, must be judged by the independent criterion of the moral law, before we are entitled to recognize him as worthy of imitation. I am not suggesting that the subordination of exemplars to principles is incorrect, but that it is one-sided and fails to do justice to a large area of moral experience.

Imitation can be more or less successful. And this suggests another defect of the ethics of principles. It has no room for ideals, except the ideal of a perfect set of principles (which, as a matter of fact, is intelligible only in terms of an ideal character or way of life), and the ideal of perfect conscientiousness (which is itself a charac-ter-trait). This results, of course, from the "black-or-white" nature of moral verdicts based on rules. There are no degrees by which we approach or recede from the attainment of a certain quality or virtue; if there were not, the word "ideal" would have no mean-ing. Heroes and saints are not people whom we try to be *just* like, since we know that is impossible. It is precisely because it is impossible for ordinary human beings to achieve the same qualities as the saints, and in the same degree, that we do set them apart from the rest of humanity. It is enough if we try to be a little like them. . . .

STUDY QUESTIONS

1. Morality, says Mayo, involves "being" as well as "doing." What does he mean by "being" and "doing" in this context? What sort of moral theory concentrates on doing? On being?

2. Philosophers of virtue or moral character tell us how to develop

ourselves as moral persons. They answer the question "What ought I to do?" by telling us what to be. How does that work?
3. Mayo says that the moral content of literature emphasizes character and virtue more than duty and obligation. Is he right about this? If he is, then is a moral philosophy of duty necessarily inadequate?

Virtues and Vices

PHILIPPA FOOT

Philippa Foot (b. 1920) is a Senior Research Fellow of Somerville College, Oxford. She also teaches at the University of California at Los Angeles. She is the author of *Theories of Ethics* (1967) and *Virtues and Vices* (1978).

Foot distinguishes the virtues from other beneficial human traits such as health or good memory. These latter are not virtues since they do not engage a person's will and character. A generous or courageous person is virtuous in wanting the good fortune or safety of others and in having the strength of character to act. Wisdom presents a difficulty: How can knowledge or wisdom be a matter of intention or desire? Foot replies that a wise person values (wants) the proper ends; such valuation engages the will. The virtues are also "corrective" in inhibiting the tendency to yield to temptation. Foot addresses a special problem: Can anyone with evil purpose exercise a virtue, for example, show courage in murdering someone? Her answer is no.

VIRTUES AND VICES From *Virtues and Vices* by Philippa Foot. Reprinted by permission of the publisher, University of California Press.

. . . It seems clear that virtues are, in some general way, beneficial. Human beings do not get on well without them. Nobody can get on well if he lacks courage, and does not have some measure of temperance and wisdom, while communities where justice and charity are lacking are apt to be wretched places to live, as Russia was under the Stalinist terror, or Sicily under the Mafia. But now we must ask to whom the benefit goes, whether to the man who has the virtue or rather to those who have to do with him? In the case of some of the virtues the answer seems clear. Courage, temperance and wisdom benefit both the man who has these dispositions and other people as well; and moral failings such as pride, vanity, worldliness, and avarice harm both their possessor and others, though chiefly perhaps the former. But what about the virtues of charity and justice? These are directly concerned with the welfare of others, and with what is owed to them; and since each may require sacrifice of interest on the part of the virtuous man both may seem to be deleterious to their possessor and beneficial to others. Whether in fact it is so has, of course, been a matter of controversy since Plato's time or earlier. It is a reasonable opinion that on the whole man is better off for being charitable and just, but this is not to say that circumstances may not arise in which he will have to sacrifice everything for charity or justice.

Nor is this the only problem about the relation between virtue and human good. For one very difficult question concerns the relation between justice and the common good. Justice, in the wide sense in which it is understood in discussions of the cardinal virtues, and in this paper, has to do with that to which someone has a right—that which he is owed in respect of non-interference and positive service—and rights may stand in the way of the pursuit of the common good. Or so at least it seems to those who reject utilitarian doctrines. This dispute cannot be settled here, but I shall treat justice as a virtue independent of charity, and standing as a possible limit on the scope of that virtue.

Let us say then, leaving unsolved problems behind us, that virtues are in general beneficial characteristics, and indeed ones that a human being needs to have, for his own sake and that of his fellows. This will not, however, take us far towards a definition of a virtue, since there are many other qualities of a man that may be similarly beneficial, as for instance bodily characteristics such as health and physical strength, and mental powers such as those of memory and concentration. What is it, we must ask, that differentiates virtues from such things?

As a first approximation to an answer we might say that while health and strength are excellences of the body, and memory and concentration of the mind, it is the will that is good in a man of virtue. But this suggestion is worth only as much as the explanation that follows it. What might we mean by saying that virtue belongs to the will?

In the first place we observe that it is primarily by his intentions that a man's moral dispositions are judged. If he does something unintentionally this is usually irrelevant to our estimate of his virtue. But of course this thesis must be qualified, because failures in performance rather than intention may show a lack of virtue. This will be so when, for instance, one man brings harm to another without realising he is doing it, but where his ignorance is itself culpable. Sometimes in such cases there will be a previous act or omission to which we can point as the source of the ignorance. Charity requires that we take care to find out how to render assistance where we are likely to be called on to do so, and thus, for example, it is contrary to charity to fail to find out about elementary first aid. But in an interesting class of cases in which it seems again to be performance rather than intention that counts in judging a man's virtue there is no possibility of shifting the judgment to previous intentions. For sometimes one man succeeds where another fails not because there is some specific difference in their previous conduct but rather because his heart lies in a different place; and the disposition of the heart is part of virtue.

Thus it seems right to attribute a kind of moral failing to some deeply discouraging and debilitating people who say, without lying, that they mean to be helpful; and on the other side to see virtue *par excellence* in one who is prompt and resourceful in doing good. In his novel *A Single Pebble* John Hersey describes such a man, speaking of a rescue in a swift flowing river.

> It was the head tracker's marvellous swift response that captured my admiration at first, his split second solicitousness when he heard a cry of pain, his finding in mid-air, as it were, the only way to save the injured boy. But there was more to it than that. His action,

which could not have been mulled over in his mind, showed a deep, instinctive love of life, a compassion, an optimism, which made me feel very good . . .

What this suggests is that a man's virtue may be judged by his innermost desires as well as by his intentions; and this fits with our idea that a virtue such as generosity lies as much in someone's attitudes as in his actions. Pleasure in the good fortune of others is, one thinks, the sign of a generous spirit; and small reactions of pleasure and displeasure often the surest signs of a man's moral disposition.

None of this shows that it is wrong to think of virtues as belonging to the will; what it does show is that 'will' must here be understood in its widest sense, to cover what is wished for as well as what is sought.

A different set of considerations will, however, force us to give up any simple statement about the relation between virtue and will, and these considerations have to do with the virtue of wisdom. Practical wisdom, we said, was counted by Aristotle among the intellectual virtues, and while our *wisdom* is not quite the same as *phronēsis* or *prudentia* it too might seem to belong to the intellect rather than the will. Is not wisdom a matter of knowledge, and how can knowledge be a matter of intention or desire? The answer is that it isn't, so that there is good reason for thinking of wisdom as an intellectual virtue. But on the other hand wisdom has special connexions with the will, meeting it at more than one point.

In order to get this rather complex picture in focus we must pause for a little and ask what it is that we ourselves understand by wisdom: what the wise man knows and what he does. Wisdom, as I see it, has two parts. In the first place the wise man knows the means to certain good ends; and secondly he knows how much particular ends are worth. Wisdom in its first part is relatively easy to understand. It seems that there are some ends belonging to human life in general rather than to particular skills such as medicine or boatbuilding, ends having to do with such matters as friendship, marriage, the bringing up of children, or the choice of ways of life; and it seems that knowledge of how to act well in these matters belongs to some people but not to others. We call those who have this knowledge wise, while those who do not have it are seen as lacking wisdom. So, as both Aristotle and Aquinas insisted, wisdom is to be contrasted with cleverness because cleverness is the ability to take the right steps to any end, whereas wisdom is related only to good ends, and to human life in general rather than to the ends of particular arts.

Moreover, we should add, there belongs to wisdom only that part of knowledge which is within the reach of any ordinary adult human being: knowledge that can be acquired only by someone who is clever or who has access to special training is not counted as part of wisdom, and would not be so counted even if it could serve the ends that wisdom serves. It is therefore quite wrong to suggest that wisdom cannot be a moral virtue because virtue must be within the reach of anyone who really wants it and some people are too stupid to be anything but ignorant even about the most fundamental matters of human life. Some people are wise without being at all clever or well informed: they make good decisions and they know, as we say, 'what's what'.

In short wisdom, in what we called its first part, is connected with the will in the following ways. To begin with it presupposes good ends: the man who is wise does not merely know *how* to do good things such as looking after his children well, or strengthening someone in trouble, but must also want to do them. And then wisdom, in so far as it consists of knowledge which anyone can gain in the course of an ordinary life, is available to anyone who really wants it. As Aquinas put it, it belongs 'to a power under the direction of the will'.[1]

The second part of wisdom, which has to do with values, is much harder to describe, because here we meet ideas which are curiously elusive, such as the thought that some pursuits are more worthwhile than others, and some matters trivial and some important in human life. Since it makes good sense to say that most men waste a lot of their lives in ardent pursuit of what is trivial and unimportant it is not possible to explain the important and the trivial in terms of the amount of attention given to different subjects by the average man. But I have never seen, or been able to think out, a true account of this matter, and I believe that a complete account of wisdom, and of certain other virtues and vices must wait until this gap can be filled. What we can see is that one of the things a wise man knows and a foolish man does not is that such

---

[1] Aquinas, *Summa Theologica*, 1a2ae Q.56 a.3.

things as social position, and wealth, and the good opinion of the world, are too dearly bought at the cost of health or friendship or family ties. So we may say that a man who lacks wisdom 'has false values', and that vices such as vanity and worldliness and avarice are contrary to wisdom in a special way. There is always an element of false judgment about these vices, since the man who is vain for instance sees admiration as more important than it is, while the worldly man is apt to see the good life as one of wealth and power. Adapting Aristotle's distinction between the weak-willed man (the akratēs) who follows pleasure though he knows, in some sense, that he should not, and the licentious man (the akolastos) who sees the life of pleasure as the good life,[2] we may say that moral failings such as these are never purely 'akratic'. It is true that a man may criticise himself for his worldliness or vanity or love of money, but then it is his values that are the subject of his criticism.

Wisdom in this second part is, therefore, partly to be described in terms of apprehension, and even judgment, but since it has to do with a man's attachments it also characterises his will.

The idea that virtues belong to the will, and that this helps to distinguish them from such things as bodily strength or intellectual ability has, then, survived the consideration of the virtue of wisdom, albeit in a fairly complex and slightly attenuated form. And we shall find this idea useful again if we turn to another important distinction that must be made, namely that between virtues and other practical excellences such as arts and skills.

Aristotle has sometimes been accused, for instance by von Wright, of failing to see how different virtues are from arts or skills,[3] but in fact one finds, among the many things that Aristotle and Aquinas say about this difference, the observation that seems to go the heart of the matter. In the matter of arts and skills, they say, voluntary error is preferable to involuntary error, while in the matter of virtues (what we call virtues) it is the reverse.[4] The last part of the thesis is actually rather hard to interpret, because it is not clear what is meant by the idea of involuntary viciousness. But we can leave this aside and still have all we need in order to distinguish

---

[2]Aristotle, *Nicomachean Ethics*, especially bk. VII.

[3]G. H. von Wright, *The Varieties of Goodness* (London, 1963), chapter VIII.

[4]Aristotle op. cit. 1140 b. 22–25. Aquinas op. cit. 1a2ae Q.57 a.4.

arts or skills from virtues. If we think, for instance, of someone who deliberately makes a spelling mistake (perhaps when writing on the blackboard in order to explain this particular point) we see that this does not in any way count against his skill as a speller: 'I did it deliberately' rebuts an accusation of this kind. And what we can say without running into any difficulties is that there is no comparable rebuttal in the case of an accusation relating to lack of virtue. If a man acts unjustly or uncharitably, or in a cowardly or intemperate manner, 'I did it deliberately' cannot on any interpretation lead to exculpation. So, we may say, a virtue is not, like a skill or an art, a mere capacity: it must actually engage the will.

II

I shall now turn to another thesis about the virtues, which I might express by saying that they are *corrective,* each one standing at a point at which there is some temptation to be resisted or deficiency of motivation to be made good. As Aristotle put it, virtues are about what is difficult for men, and I want to see in what sense this is true, and then to consider a problem in Kant's moral philsophy in the light of what has been said.

Let us first think about coverage and temperance. Aristotle and Aquinas contrasted these virtues with justice in the following respect. Justice was concerned with operations and courage and temperance with passions.[5] What they meant by this seems to have been, primarily, that the man of courage does not fear immoderately nor the man of temperance have immoderate desires for pleasure, and that there was no corresponding moderation of a passion implied in the idea of justice. This particular account of courage and temperance might be disputed on the ground that a man's courage is measured by his action and not by anything as uncontrollable as fear; and similarly that the temperate man who must on occasion refuse pleasures need not *desire* them any less than the intemperate man. Be that as it may (and something will be said about it later) it is obviously true that courage and temperance have to do with particular springs of action as justice does not. Almost

[5]Aristotle op. cit. 1106 b. 15 and 1129 a.4 have this implication; but Aquinas is more explicit in op.cit. 1a2ae Q.60 a.2.

any desire can lead a man to act unjustly, not even excluding the desire to help a friend or to save a life, whereas a cowardly act must be motivated by fear or a desire for safety, and an act of intemperance by a desire for pleasure, perhaps even for a particular range of pleasures such as those of eating or drinking or sex. And now, going back to the idea of virtues as correctives one may say that it is only because fear and the desire for pleasure often operate as temptations that courage and temperance exist as virtues at all. As things are we often want to run away not only where that is the right thing to do but also where we should stand firm; and we want pleasure not only where we should seek pleasure but also where we should not. If human nature had been different there would have been no need of a corrective disposition in either place, as fear and pleasure would have been good guides to conduct throughout life. So Aquinas says, about the passions,

> They may incite us to something against reason, and so we need a curb, which we name *temperance*. Or they may make us shirk a course of action dictated by reason, through fear of dangers or hardships. Then a person needs to be steadfast and not run away from what is right; and for this *courage* is named.[6]

As with courage and temperance so with many other virtues: there is, for instance, a virtue of industriousness only because idleness is a temptation; and of humility only because men tend to think too well of themselves. Hope is a virtue because despair too is a temptation; it might have been that no one cried that all was lost except where he could really see it to be so, and in this case there would have been no virtue of hope.

With virtues such as justice and charity it is a little different, because they correspond not to any particular desire or tendency that has to be kept in check but rather to a deficiency of motivation; and it is this that they must make good. If people were as much attached to the good of others as they are to their own good there would no more be a general virtue of benevolence than there is a general virtue of self-love. And if people cared about the rights of others as they care about their own rights no virtue of justice would be needed to look after the matter, and rules about such things as

---

[6]Aquinas op. cit. 1a2ae Q.61 a.3.

contracts and promises would only need to be made public, like the rules of a game that everyone was eager to play.

On this view of the virtues and vices everything is seen to depend on what human nature is like, and the traditional catalogue of the two kinds of dispositions is not hard to understand. Nevertheless it may be defective, and anyone who accepts the thesis that I am putting forward will feel free to ask himself where the temptations and deficiencies that need correcting are really to be found. It is possible, for example, that the theory of human nature lying behind the traditional list of virtues and vices puts too much emphasis on hedonistic and sensual impulses, and does not sufficiently take account of less straightforward inclinations such as the desire to be put upon and dissatisfied, or the unwillingness to accept good things as they come along.

It should now be clear why I said that virtues should be seen as correctives; and part of what is meant by saying that virtue is about things that are difficult for men should also have appeared. The further application of this idea is, however, controversial, and the following difficulty presents itself: that we both are and are not inclined to think that the harder a man finds it to act virtuously the more virtue is needed where it is particularly hard to act virtuously; yet on the other it could be argued that difficulty in acting virtuously shows that the agent is imperfect in virtue: according to Aristotle, to take pleasure in virtuous action is the mark of true virtue, with the self-mastery of the one who finds virtue difficult only a second best. How then is this conflict to be decided? Who shows most courage, the one who wants to run away but does not, or the one who does not even want to run away? Who shows most charity, the one who finds it easy to make the good of others his object, or the one who finds it hard?

What is certain is that the thought that virtues are corrective does not constrain us to relate virtue to difficulty in each individual man. Since men in general find it hard to face great dangers or evils, and even small ones, we may count as courageous those few who without blindness or indifference are nevertheless fearless even in terrible circumstances. And when someone has a natural charity or generosity it is, at least part of the virtue that he has; if natural virtue cannot be the whole of virtue this is because a kindly or fearless disposition could be disastrous without justice and wisdom, and these virtues have to be learned, not because natural virtue is too easily acquired. I have argued that the virtues can be seen as correctives in relation to human nature in general but not that each virtue must present a difficulty to each and every man.

Nevertheless many people feel strongly inclined to say that it is for moral effort that moral praise is to be bestowed, and that in proportion as a man finds it easy to be virtuous so much the less is he to be morally admired for his good actions. The dilemma can be resolved only when we stop talking about difficulties standing in the way of virtuous action as if they were of only one kind. The fact is that some kinds of difficulties do indeed provide an occasion for much virtue, but that others rather show that virtue is incomplete.

To illustrate this point I shall first consider an example of honest action. We may suppose for instance that a man has an opportunity to steal, in circumstances where stealing is not morally permissible, but that he refrains. And now let us ask our old question. For one man it is hard to refrain from stealing and for another man it is not: which shows the greater virtue in acting as he should? It is not difficult to see in this case that it makes all the difference whether the difficulty comes from circumstances, as that a man is poor, or that his theft is unlikely to be detected, or whether it comes from something that belongs to his own character. The fact that a man is *tempted* to steal is something about him that shows a certain lack of honesty: of the thoroughly honest man we say that it 'never entered his head', meaning that it was never a real possibility for him. But the fact that he is poor is something that makes the occasion more *tempting*, and difficulties of this kind make honest action all the more virtuous.

A similar distinction can be made between different obstacles standing in the way of charitable action. Some circumstances, as that great sacrifice is needed, or that the one to be helped is a rival, give an occasion on which a man's charity is severely tested. Yet in given circumstances of this kind it is the man who acts easily rather than the one who finds it hard who shows the most charity. Charity is a virtue of attachment, and that sympathy for others which makes it easier to help them is part of the virtue itself.

These are fairly simple cases, but I am not supposing that it is always easy to say where the relevant distinction is to be drawn. What, for instance, should we say about the emotion of fear as an obstacle to action? Is a man more courageous if he fears much and nevertheless acts, or if he is relatively fearless? Several things must be said about this. In the first place it seems that the emotion of fear is not a necessary condtion for the display of courage; in face of a great evil such as death or injury a man may show courage even if he does not tremble. On the other hand even irrational fears may give an occasion for courage: if someone suffers from claustrophobia or a dread of heights he may require courage to do that which would not be a courageous action for others. But not all fears belong from this point of view to the circumstances rather than to a man's character. For while we do not think of claustrophobia or a dread of heights as features of character, a general timorousness may be. Thus, although pathological fears are not the result of a man's choices and values some fears may be. The fears that count against a man's courage are those that we think he could overcome, and among them, in a special class, those that reflect the fact that he values safety too much.

In spite of problems such as these, which have certainly not all been solved, both the distinction between different kinds of obstacles to virtuous action, and the general idea that virtues are correctives, will be useful in resolving a difficulty in Kant's moral philosophy closely related to the issues discussed in the preceding paragraphs. In a passage in the first section of the *Groundwork of the Metaphysics of Morals* Kant notoriously tied himself into a knot in trying to give an account of those actions which have as he put it 'positive moral worth'. Arguing that only actions done out of a sense of duty have this worth he contrasts a philanthropist who 'takes pleasure in spreading happiness around him' with one who acts out of respect for duty, saying that the actions of the latter but not the former have moral worth. Much scorn has been poured on Kant for this curious doctrine, and indeed it does seem that something has gone wrong, but perhaps we are not in a position to scoff unless we can give our own account of the idea on which Kant is working. After all it does seem that he is right in saying that some actions are in accordance with duty, and even required by duty, without being the subjects of moral praise, like those of the honest trader who deals honestly in a situation in which it is in his interest to do so.

It was this kind of example that drove Kant to his strange conclusion. He added another example, however, in discussing acts of self-preservation; these he said, while they normally have no positive moral worth, any have it when a man preserves his life not from inclination but without inclination and from a sense of duty. Is he not right in saying that acts of self-preservation normally have no moral significance but that they may have it, and how do we ourselves explain this fact?

To anyone who approaches this topic from a consideration of the virtues the solution readily suggests itself. Some actions are in accordance with virtue without requiring virtue for their performance, whereas others are both in accordance with virtue and such as to show possession of a virtue. So Kant's trader was dealing honestly in a situation in which the virtue of honesty is not required for honest dealing, and it is for this reason that his action did not have 'positive moral worth'. Similarly, the care that one ordinarily takes for one's life, as for instance on some ordinary morning in eating one's breakfast and keeping out of the way of a car on the road, is something for which no virtue is required. As we said earlier there is no general virtue of self-love as there is a virtue of benevolence or charity, because men are generally attached sufficiently to their own good. Nevertheless in special circumstances virtues such as temperance, courage, fortitude, and hope may be needed if someone is to preserve his life. Are these circumstances in which the preservation of one's own life is a duty? Sometimes it is so, for sometimes it is what is owed to others that should keep a man from destroying himself, and then he may act out of a sense of duty. But not all cases in which acts of self-preservation show virtue are like this. For a man may display each of the virtues just listed even where he does not do any harm to others if he kills himself or fails to preserve his life. And it is this that explains why there may be a moral aspect to suicide which does not depend on possible injury to other people. It is not that suicide is 'always wrong', whatever that would mean, but that suicide is *sometimes* contrary to virtues such as courage and hope.

Let us now return to Kant's philanthropists, with the thought that it is action that is in accordance with virtue and also displays a virtue that has moral worth. We see at once that Kant's difficulties are avoided, and the happy philanthropist reinstated in the position which belongs to him. For charity is, as we said, a virtue of attachment as well as action, and the sympathy that makes it easier to act with charity is part of the virtue. The man who acts charitably out of a sense of duty is not to be undervalued, but it is the other who most shows virtue and therefore to the other that most moral worth is attributed. Only a detail of Kant's presentation of the case of the dutiful philanthropist tells on the other side. For what he actually said was that this man felt no sympathy and took no pleasure in the good of others because 'his mind was clouded by some sorrow of his own', and this is the kind of circumstance that increases the virtue that is needed if a man is to act well.

III

It was suggested above that an action with 'positive moral worth', or as we might say a positively good action, was to be seen as one which was in accordance with virtue, by which I mean contrary to no virtue, and moreover one for which a virtue was required. Nothing has so far been said about another case, excluded by the formula, in which it might seem that an act displaying one virtue was nevertheless contrary to another. In giving this last description I am thinking not of two virtues with competing claims, as if what were required by justice could nevertheless be demanded by charity, or something of that kind, but rather of the possibility that a virtue such as courage or temperance or industry which overcomes a special temptation, might be displayed in an act of folly or villainy. Is this something that we must allow for, or is it only good or innocent actions which can be acts of these virtues? Aquinas, in his definition of virtue, said that virtues can produce only good actions, and that they are dispositions 'of which no one can make bad use',[7] except when they are treated as objects, as in being the subject of hatred or pride. The common opinion nowadays is, however, quite different. With the notable exception of Peter Geach hardly anyone sees any difficulty in the thought that virtues may sometimes be displayed in bad actions. Von Wright, for instance, speaks of the courage of the villain as if this were a quite unproblematic idea, and most people take it for granted that the virtues of courage and temperance may aid a bad man in his evil work. It is also supposed that charity may lead a man to act badly, as when someone does what he has no right to do, but does it for the sake of a friend.

There are, however, reasons for thinking that the matter is not as

---

[7] Aquinas op. cit. 1a2ae Q.56 a.5.

simple as this. If a man who is willing to do an act of injustice to help a friend, or for the common good, is supposed to act out of charity, and he so acts where a just man will not, it should be said that the unjust man has more charity than the just man. But do we not think that someone not ready to act unjustly may yet be perfect in charity, the virtue having done its whole work in prompting a man to do the acts that are permissible? And is there not more difficulty than might appear in the idea of an act of injustice which is nevertheless an act of courage? Suppose for instance that a sordid murder were in question, say a murder done for gain or to get an inconvenient person out of the way, but that this murder had to be done in alarming circumstances or in the face of real danger; should we be happy to say that such an action was an act of courage or a courageous act? Did the murderer, who certainly acted boldly, or with intrepidity, if he did the murder, also act courageously? Some people insist that they are ready to say this, but I have noticed that they like to move over to a murder for the sake of conscience, or to some other act done in the course of a villainous enterprise but whose immediate end is innocent or positively good. On their hypothesis, which is that bad acts can easily be seen as courageous acts or acts of courage, my original example should be just as good.

What are we to say about this difficult matter? There is no doubt that the murderer who murdered for gain was *not a coward*: he did not have a second moral defect which another villain might have had. There is no difficulty about this because it is clear that one defect may neutralise another. As Aquinas remarked, it is better for a blind horse if it is slow.[8] It does not follow, however, that an act of villainy can be courageous; we are inclined to say that it 'took courage', and yet it seems wrong to think of courage as equally connected with good actions and bad.

One way out of this difficulty might be to say that the man who is ready to pursue bad ends does indeed have courage, and shows courage in his action, but that in him courage is not a virtue. Later I shall consider some cases in which this might be the right thing to say, but in this instance it does not seem to be. For unless the murderer consistently pursues bad ends his courage will often

---

[8]Aquinas op. cit. 1a2ae Q.58 a.4.

result in good; it may enable him to do many innocent or positively good things for himself or for his family and friends. On the strength of an individual bad action we can hardly say that in him courage is not a virtue. Nevertheless there is something to be said even about the individual action to distinguish it from one that would readily be called an act of courage or a courageous act. Perhaps the following analogy may help us to see what it is. We might think of words such as 'courage' as naming characteristics of human beings in respect of a certain power, as words such as 'poison' and 'solvent' and 'corrosive' so name the properties of physical things. The power to which virtue-words are so related is the power of producing good action, and good desires. But just as poisons, solvents and corrosives do not always operate characteristically, so it could be with virtues. If P (say arsenic) is a poison it does not follow that P acts as a poison wherever it is found. It is quite natural to say on occasion 'P does not act as a poison here' though P is a poison and it is P that is acting here. Similarly courage is not operating as a virtue when the murderer turns his courage, which is a virtue to bad ends. Not surprisingly the resistance that some of us registered was not to the expression 'the courage of the murderer' or to the assertion that what he did 'took courage' but rather to the description of that action as an act of courage or a courageous act. It is not that the action *could* not be so described, but that the fact that courage does not here have its characteristic operation is a reason for finding the description strange.

In this example we were considering an action in which courage was not operating as a virtue, without suggesting that in that agent it generally failed to do so. But the latter is also a possibility. If someone is both wicked and foolhardy this may be the case with courage, and it is even easier to find examples of a general connexion with evil rather than good in the case of some other virtues. Suppose, for instance, that we think of someone who is over-industrious, or too ready to refuse pleasure, and this is characteristic of him rather than something we find on one particular occasion. In this case the virtue of industry, or the virtue of temperance, has a systematic connexion with defective action rather than good action; and it might be said in either case that the virtue did not operate as a virtue in this man. Just as we might say in a certain setting 'P is not a poison here' though P is a poison and P is here, so we might say that industriousness, or temperance, is not a virtue in some. Similarly in a man habitually given to wishful thinking, who clings to false hopes, hope does not operate as a virtue and we may say that it is not a virtue in him.

The thought developed in the last paragraph, to the effect that not every man who has a virtue has something that is a virtue in him, may help to explain a certain discomfort that one may feel when discussing the virtues. It is not easy to put one's finger on what is wrong, but it has something to do with a disparity between the moral ideas that may seem to be implied in our talk about the virtues, and the moral judgments that we actually make. Someone reading the foregoing pages might, for instance, think that the author of this paper always admired most those people who had all the virtues, being wise and temperate as well as courageous, chari-table, and just. And indeed it is sometimes so. There are some people who do possess all these virtues and who are loved and admired by all the world, as Pope John XXIII was loved and admired. Yet the fact is that many of us look up to some people whose chaotic lives contain rather little of wisdom or temperance, rather than to some others who possess these virtues. And while it may be that this is just romantic nonsense I suspect that it is not. For while wisdom always operates as a virtue, its close relation prudence does not, and it is prudence rather than wisdom that inspires many a careful life. Prudence is not a virtue in everyone, any more than industriousness is, for in some it is rather an over-anxious concern for safety and propriety, and a determination to keep away from people or situations which are apt to bring trouble with them; and by such defensiveness much good is lost. It is the same with temperance. Intemperance can be an appalling thing, as it was with Henry VIII of whom Wolsey remarked that

> rather than he will either miss or want any part of his will or appetite, he will put the loss of one half of his realm in danger.

Nevertheless in some people temperance is not a virtue, but is rather connected with timidity or with a grudging attitude to the acceptance of good things. Of course what is best is to live boldly yet without imprudence or intemperance, but the fact is that rather few can manage that.

STUDY QUESTIONS

1. What does Foot mean by saying "Virtue belongs to the will"?
2. How do the virtues benefit their possessors? What special features must a beneficial trait possess to be counted as a virtue?
3. What is wisdom's relation to the will? To all of the other virtues?
4. Foot argues that what appears to be courage in a murder really is not. Do you agree with her?
5. Do you agree with Foot that wise persons know the means to good ends *and* want those ends? Can wise persons not desire the ends they judge to be worthwhile?
6. In what sense are the virtues "corrective"? What significance does Foot give to this feature of virtue?

Gratitude

FRED R. BERGER

Fred R. Berger (b. 1937) is a professor of philosophy at the University of California at Davis. He is the author of *Happiness, Justice and Freedom: Central Themes in the Moral and Political Philosophy of John Stuart Mill* (1983).

Berger notes that moral philosophers do not often explore gratitude, taking its virtuous character for granted. We owe gratitude whenever we benefit because someone has acted to help us (and not by inadvertence, or merely to fulfill a contract). In showing gratitude we

---

I should like to record some of my own acknowledgments of aid: I first discussed some of these matters a number of years ago with H. L. A. Hart, from whom I gained important insights; I also benefited greatly from discussion of these matters with Torstein Eckhoff, of the University of Oslo Law School.

GRATITUDE Reprinted from *Ethics* 85:4 (July, 1975), pp. 298–309, by permission of The University of Chicago Press.

show feelings. We respond to others' concern for us. Sometimes words are not enough and we must respond in other ways. Because much of parental benevolence is an expression of concern, we own gratitude to our parents. Demonstrations of gratitude strengthen family and communal bonds. Yet the idea that we have a duty to express our grateful feelings seems odd. We cannot be forced to show certain feelings—and what if we actually lack them? Does this mean that gratitude is not a moral virtue? This difficulty suggests that a duty-based ethic that concentrates simply on what we ought to do, to the relative neglect of the kind of person we ought to be, is insufficient. Ingratitude is a character defect. A proper account of gratitude (and related topics such as trust, resentment, and compassion) needs a broader basis than the concept of duty supplies. This broader ethic will give the notion of character its due importance.

Gratitude is not a subject much discussed in the philosophical literature, though hardly a book or article is published without some expression of gratitude by the author for the help of others. From the literature, one would have to conclude that gratitude plays a role in our moral life which, with only a few exceptions, philosophers have not seen fit to explore. Later I shall have a few suggestions as to why this is so. I cannot help but speculate now, however, that one source for this neglect has been the view that gratitude does not play an important role in morality and thus does not deserve extended treatment. I want to show in this essay that the study of gratitude is indeed fruitful, in that it reveals important aspects of our moral life. Gratitude may or may not itself be important to our morality; it is, however, intertwined with an aspect of our moral relations which I believe has been unjustly neglected and on which the analysis of gratitude sheds light.

The paper is divided into three sections. In the first, I shall explore important aspects of the duty to *show* gratitude: under what conditions that duty does or does not hold, precisely to what gratitude is a response, and ways in which this duty differs from other principles involving reciprocation. Using these results, I shall then, in the second section, turn to an analysis of the "internal" aspects of gratitude—that is, to an analysis of what it is that is shown or expressed in demonstration of gratitude. In the concluding section, I shall attempt to show what the analysis reveals concerning the nature of morality. In particular, I shall hold that the analysis of gratitude shows that our feelings and attitudes (as well as our actions) play a role in our moral life which has been insufficiently acknowledged and stressed. Thus, I believe, we have not understood very well the morality of interpersonal relations.

In this section I shall concentrate on the duty to show gratitude. I shall assume there is (at least in our culture) a general duty to show gratitude under certain conditions, though it is, to be sure, a somewhat unusual "duty." I shall not seek to elucidate the *sense* in which we recognize a duty to show gratitude; in a final section, though, I shall try to deal with some of the anomalies the notion of a duty to show gratitude presents.

The first point I want to make about the duty to show gratitude is that a show of gratitude is not simply a response to other persons having done things which benefit us. That this is so can be seen by exploring the questions of the conditions under which gratitude is due and what factors affect the issue of what is required in the way of specific performance.

Two such factors suggest themselves immediately: the value of the benefit to the recipient and the degree of sacrifice or concession made by the grantor. There are other important factors, however. Suppose someone does something involving a sacrifice on his part which benefits us, but he was forced by threats to do it. In such a case, gratitude is not due; the appropriate response may be to return the gift, if possible, or to make sufficient restitution or replacement of it. The voluntariness with which the benefits are produced for us is thus a factor in determining if gratitude is appropriate when others benefit us.

Suppose further that someone did something which benefited us, but he was utterly unaware of this fact. That we are benefited is a fortuitous and unforeseen consequence of something he has done without any intention on his part to help us. Where it is clear that such intention was lacking, gratitude is not due. Insofar as he did not choose to do something to give us benefits (which he could not do if he had no foresight of the consequences), he did not *grant* them to us. Similarly, if the person knew he was creating benefits for us, but engaged in the behavior only because it also brought

195

him benefits, gratitude is not due; the benefits were a mere by-product of acts done for self-gain. We may be glad for the benefits, but no gratitude is owed. Of course, in actual cases, motivation may not be entirely clear, or singlefactored, and perhaps we owe one another the benefit of the doubt; but in the clear sense, gratitude is not involved.

These facets of our practice with respect to gratitude reveal something important. The kinds of considerations cited are indices that the act was or was not done *in order to help us*. If the act was done only because the actor chose the lesser of two evils or sacrifices to himself, or without any knowledge or thought that it would benefit us, or solely because it would bring him benefits, there is no debt of gratitude, because nothing was done in order to help us. Gratitude, then, does not consist in the requital of benefits but in a response to *benevolence*; it is a response to a grant of benefits (or the attempt to benefit us) which was motivated by a desire to help us.

This fact about gratitude can be used to decide difficult cases in ways which seem plausible. For example, we might want to know if we owe gratitude for benefits which are *owed* us, that is, in which those providing them are fulfilling their duties to us. The answer is complicated by cases which incline us toward divergent answers. We owe gratitude to our parents for the sacrifices involved in their caring for us and giving us a decent upbringing, though it is their duty to provide this to the best of their ability. On the other hand, with regard to most contractual transactions, we do not usually feel we owe gratitude to the other contracting party when he fulfills his part of the deal. Of course, we owe him the performance of our part of the bargain, but that is not, in itself, a show of gratitude. All this becomes easily dealt with once we see gratitude as the requital of benevolence. Though our parents are under a duty to give us a decent upbringing and to care for us, it is almost never solely for this reason that parents make the sacrifices requisite for proper care and rearing. These sacrifices are normally made because our parents care for us and love us and want us to have the benefits of a good upbringing. On the other hand, many a contemporary novel has made capital out of the justified lack of gratitude in situations in which parents have given children the outward manifestations of a good rearing in our society (e.g., clothes, good schools, etc.) but solely for selfish reasons such as keeping up the family name or social standing. Indeed, to the extent that a *really* good rearing cannot be given without love as its base, it is something which by its nature deserves gratitude. In contrast to this, contractual arrangements are usually thought to be means for advancing the interests of both parties and hence tend not to be cases of benefits granted in order to help another, and gratitude would be out of place. This is not to say, however, that one cannot enter into a contract to help another. People quite often accept unfavorable terms of a contract in order to help the other party. When this happens, we *do* think there is an obligation to show gratitude. These features of our moral practices are readily understood once we perceive gratitude as a response to benevolence.

Even more subtle features of the duty to show gratitude are explicable in these terms. While we have no hesitation in saying there is an obligation to show gratitude for help or for a gift, we do not feel at ease in saying it is something owed the grantor in the sense that he has a right to demand it.[1] Such a demand shows the help or gift to be something less than a show of benevolence; it appears to be something done in order to gain favor, and to the extent we feel this to be case, the duty to show gratitude is diminished.

The analysis of gratitude as a response to benevolence is also important because it forms part of the basis on which the duty to show gratitude is to be distinguished from other duties involving reciprocity. Consider a principle dubbed by H. L. A. Hart "mutuality of restrictions": "When a number of persons conduct any joint enterprises according to rules . . . those who have submitted to these restrictions when required have a right to a similar submission from those who have benefited by their submission."[2]

This principle, underlying cooperation, differs from gratitude in a crucial respect. Cooperation does not imply benevolence; it is compatible with complete, but enlightened, self-interest. Selfish

---

[1] *Other* parties may rightly criticize the failure to discharge it, and even the person to whom it is owed may be entitled to complain of the *insult* such a failure represents.

[2] H. L. A. Hart, "Are There Any Natural Rights?" *Philosophical Review* 64 (1955): 185. This principle should be compared with one called by John Rawls "the duty of fair play." He has discussed it in numerous places. See, for example, "Legal Obligation and the Duty of Fair Play," in *Law and Philosophy*, ed. Sidney Hook (New York: New York University Press, 1964), pp. 3–18. No doubt Hart's statement of his principle requires important qualifications to be acceptable.

motivation on the part of the participants in no way diminishes the obligation to reciprocate with the requisite behavior when one has enjoyed the benefits of the practice. The point of such an activity is to produce *mutual* benefits. One who has enjoyed the benefits of a cooperative scheme would not present an adequate justification for his refusal to cooperate if he merely pointed out that the others restricted their behavior in order to obtain the benefits of the practice. Unlike gratitude, such a fact is not a rebuttal to the claim that a duty of reciprocation is owed. In fact, it is part of the ground on which the duty to do one's share in the production of the benefits is based. The benefits were *not* a gift to him.

Thus we are led to our first major conclusion: showing gratitude is a response to the benevolence of others. I want now to turn to the question of what it is that is shown or expressed in gratitude.

II

Thus far we have dealt only with the external aspects of gratitude— the duty to show or express gratitude. What *is* it that we show or express? And why can we distinguish "sincere" from "insincere" expressions? Moreover, we speak of "feeling" grateful and of having "feelings" of gratitude. All this suggests that when we express gratitude we simply show or give vent to certain internal states. Even if this were correct, it would not go very far toward explaining why we regard gratitude as part of our moral relations—why ingratitude has been regarded by philosophers as a vice.[3] Nor would it explain why gratitude should be proportionate in the ways it is expressed, rather than in relation to the intensity of one's feelings. And it would not explain why sometimes mere *verbal* expression of one's feelings is not enough to constitute a sincere demonstration of gratitude. In what follows in this section, I want to attempt an account which goes some way toward dealing with these issues.

We should begin by noting that an act of benevolence evinces certain things about the actor. If I am the recipient of another's benevolence, his action indicates he cares about me, he values me, he respects me.[4] This is especially the case where any measure of

---

[3]See Immanuel Kant, *Lectures on Ethics*, ed. Lewis White Beck (New York: Harper & Row, 1963), p. 218, in which ingratitude is described as one of the three vices which "are the essence of vileness and wickedness."

[4]There is an important ambiguity in this which I shall ignore in this paper. Benevo-

sacrifice or concession or consideration is shown; he has been willing to incur a sacrifice of his own convenience or welfare to assist me. This shows that my welfare is valued by him in addition to his own.[5] *I* am an object of his concern.

When we show gratitude, then, it is this display of the other's attitude toward us to which we are responding. Note that in each of the cases in the last section in which we said gratitude is *not* due, no such indication of concern or valuing of the recipient was involved. A sincere expression of gratitude thus involves at least the recognition of the other's having done something which indicates he values us. Clearly, more than just this is involved, however. It seems to me that all of the following are accomplished by sincere, adequate expressions of gratitude: (*a*) the recipient shows he recognizes the value of the donor's act—that is, that it was an act benefiting him and done *in order to* benefit him; (*b*) the recipient shows that he does not regard the *actor* as having value only as an instrument of his own welfare; and (*c*) a relationship of moral community is established, maintained, or recognized, consisting of mutual respect and regard. Reciprocation makes the relationship two-way.

If this account is right, then expressions of gratitude are demonstrations of a complex of beliefs, feelings, and attitudes. By showing gratitude for the benevolence of others, we express our beliefs that they acted with our interests in mind and that we benefited; we show that we are glad for the benefit and the others' concern—we appreciate what was done; we indicate that we also have an attitude of regard for them, at least in the respect that we do not look on them as objects in the world whose movements have happened to

---

lence can take a *general* and a *specific* form. Someone who cares about humanity (supposing this to be possible) may be motivated to act because he wishes to help people. *I* just happen to be the object of his largess by virtue of my humanity. On the other hand, it may be *me* he cares about, independently of any concern for humanity. In some contexts, this might be an important distinction. There is also some discussion of the issue by C. D. Broad in his treatment of Butler's ethics, as sometimes Butler seems to have supposed benevolence to be a concern for humanity and at other times a concern for the well-being of particular persons. See C. D. Broad, *Five Types of Ethical Theory* (Paterson, N.J.: Littlefield, Adams & Co., 1959), pp. 70 ff. But also see the discussion of Butler in T. A. Robert's *The Concept of Benevolence* (London: Macmillan Co., 1973).

[5] We sometimes distinguish ordinary men, great-hearted men, and saints according to how much they value the welfare of others in relation to their own. (Of course, we assume that they do not hate themselves.)

bring us benefits (for then no response would be necessary). And we show that we do not regard their sacrifices and concessions as mere instruments of our welfare. The donor has shown his valuing of the recipient; the donee shows the relationship is mutual by some form of reciprocation, and each has demonstrated attitudes appropriate to members of a moral community.

It is important to note two features of our actual practice which this account is meant to tie in with. First, while some form of reciprocation is requisite, this need not be, and often *ought not to be*, the giving of the same or an equivalent benefit to the grantor. Not only is this not always possible, but sometimes it would destroy the force of the original gift. When someone grants us a benefit because of his concern for us, or because he wishes to make us happy, it can be an insult to return it or to show that we feel obligated to make a like return. The grant was made with no strings attached, with no desire to obligate us. To show that we feel we *are* obligated demonstrates that the gift misfired to a certain extent or, at worst, gives reason to think the donee misread the intentions of the grantor. It is one thing to show that we think we owe a sign of appreciation; it is quite another thing to show we think we owe a gift in return. Sometimes the most adequate display of gratitude is a loving hug or a warm handshake, and anything more would be inappropriate in some degree.

On the other hand, there are times when a mere "thank you" or warm handshake will not do, when an adequate showing of gratitude requires putting ourselves out in some way, at least a little. The sort of continual sacrifice and caring involved in a decent upbringing is not reciprocated to parents by a warm handshake at the legal age of independence. While the notion of gratitude to one's parents can easily be overdone, it is clear enough that an adequate showing of gratitude to them cannot be made with mere verbal expressions.

The explanation of gratitude I have provided can give a partial explanation to these features of our practices. First of all, on the account given, a crucial aspect of the practices associated with gratitude is the showing of one's recognition of the value of the donor's act. But, if one scrupulously attends to reciprocating in kind, that may undercut this showing, since part of the value of the act is constituted by its being given with no objective of a return. Furthermore, it is not only a set of beliefs and feelings which are involved in gratitude but attitudes as well: appreciation for the gift and the actor's caring, along with mutual respect for him as a person of value in himself. But having an attitude or expressing an attitude is not merely a matter of saying some words. Attitudes are expressed through behavior also, and *certain* behaviors are the appropriate, concomitant expressions of attitudes. One does not take or have that attitude without some appropriate behavior. One cannot claim truly to care for someone and never act in certain appropriate ways. Indeed, gratitude is not so much the *expression* of our appreciation and respect as it is the *demonstration* of these attitudes. Sometimes we can demonstrate those attitudes by expressing them verbally; sometimes more is required for the demonstration to be adequate to the situation. Thus an adequate demonstration of our appreciation and concern for our parents could never be a mere handshake. A kiss on the cheek might suffice for a particular birthday present, but it is not an adequate demonstration of appreciation for years of care, inconvenience, and, perhaps, sacrifice. It is very hard to say just what is appropriate, and it may be that there can be no answer in the abstract, that it will depend on the nature of the particular family and the nature of the particular relationships within it. It is clear, however, that a handshake or kiss on the cheek normally will not do. The account of gratitude I have provided can explain, in part, why not.[6]

I have acknowledged that gratitude to one's parents can be overstressed, and that one's response to others' benevolence can be overdone in various ways. These points indicate that the practices associated with gratitude may take what I shall call "pathological" forms. By considering some of these, I believe we can bring into sharper focus the features of gratitude and will be better able to see its role in our normal life.

The first kind of pathology I wish to pick out takes the form of the man who does favors for others in order to place them in his

---

[6]The question of the "appropriateness" of a response is complicated by cases in which only *part* of the complex of beliefs, feelings, and attitudes involved in being grateful are present, e.g., when we resent the other's benevolence because we personally dislike him and do not wish to be indebted to him, or where we do not desire the benefit sufficiently to warrant the sacrifice made, or a commensurate response. Here, the duties to be sincere and to show gratitude are in conflict. My account can help to explain this, though, of course, it does not show how to resolve it.

debt. Where it is clear that something is expected in return, of course, there need be nothing wrong. But the debt, then, will not be one of gratitude. On the other hand, the act may be one in which the actor plays on, and takes advantage of, the conventional practices associated with gratitude and the recipent's inclination to be grateful for favors and to demonstrate his gratitude. Such an act involves deception (at least with respect to motivation) and is pathological in that respect. But it is also pathological in the deeper sense that the practices involved in gratitude presuppose that the agents are manifesting their mutual valuing of one another as ends in themselves, whereas *this* act treats the recipient as an instrument of the donor's welfare and thus as having instrumental value only.

A second form of the pathological practice of gratitude involves the tendency to overemphasize it and to ritualize it, so that every act under the sun which benefits someone else is viewed as requiring gratitude, and the constant display of gratitude is insisted on. In its mildest form, this consists in reducing giftgiving and returning to the level of matters of etiquette of no greater moral importance than simple social amenities. There are, however, more trenchant forms. In Western cultures with a strong family life, it is a familiar story for young people to be in rebellion at the constant insistence that they behave in traditional ways, or assume certain roles, or take up certain religious practices, in order to show gratitude to their parents for the sacrifices made in bringing them up. Any act of disobedience is viewed by the parents as ingratitude, and everything done for the children is viewed as deserving gratitude. The combination of these two beliefs, of course, makes it impossible for the children ever to be properly grateful, unless they are willing to cater to every wish of the parents.[7] Such situations, when carried to extremes, are pathological in a number of respects. Even loving parents cannot claim that everything done for their children springs from their concern. Moreover, if truly done from love, these deeds would not be viewed as giving the right to make incessant demands on the children's life styles. The constant expectation of concessions as a sign of gratitude can be an oppression; and departure is a

---

[7]For a case history, see Philip Roth, *Portnoy's Complaint* (N.Y.: Random House, 1969).

source of guilt, and the relations with the parents become clouded with feelings of resentment. All of this destroys love. In addition, this is a pathological misuse of the practices involved in gratitude, because it undercuts the moral relations presupposed by those practices (at least this is the case when the children have reached a certain age). To treat someone as a person in his own right entails granting him the right to work out the plan of his life as he sees fit. To use the fact of one's past aid in order to control another's life is to deny him the independence befitting a moral agent. A set of practices which function to demonstrate mutual regard is employed by one party to impose behavior on another as the price of his past regard and to demand the signs of regard, irrespective of the party's own judgment as to the appropriateness of those particular expressions. If we really have a concern with the well-being of someone, there are some aspects of his life which we ought not to seek to control and which we cannot obligate him to let us control.

To summarize my main points briefly: (*a*) being grateful to someone involves having a set of beliefs, feelings, and attitudes which are manifested when we show gratitude; (*b*) but showing gratitude involves a *demonstration* of those beliefs and attitudes and, thus, may require forms of behavior in addition to verbal expression; (*c*) such a demonstration of gratitude is a response to another's (perceived) benevolence; (*d*) as such, it involves the mutual demonstration of respect and regard—the indication that neither treats the other, or the sacrifices of the other, as a mere means to his own welfare; (*e*) thus the practices associated with gratitude are a manifestation of, and serve to strengthen, the bonds of moral community—the sharing of a common moral life based on respect for each person as having value in himself.

Much more needs to be said about gratitude before we can be content that we have a very full understanding of it, even if the account I have given is correct. It would be important to know, for example, to what extent gratitude is conventional, whether there could be a community having a shared morality which did not incorporate gratitude in some recognizable form, the role of spontaneity in gratitude, the necessary and sufficient conditions of sincerity, etc. Without seeking to explore these issues further, I shall turn in the concluding section to speculate on the significance for moral philosophy of the points already made.

III

What I find most significant about gratitude, as I have analyzed it, is that it involves in a crucial way our feelings and attitudes toward people. Requisite behavior is involved primarily as a demonstration of those feelings and attitudes or as natural concomitants of them. This suggests the ancient view, held by Aristotle, that the moral life of a creature of a composite nature—having both rational and affective aspects—involves the right ordering of both elements. The moral virtues, then, involve not merely acting in certain ways but also having appropriate attitudes and feelings toward others.[8] Certain actions have value, then, *as* expressions of attitudes.

The recent history of moral philosophy shows great emphasis on such concepts as "right," "wrong," and "duty." These are notions applicable primarily to actions. Goodness tends to be treated either as something it is our duty to act to produce or as a property of actions themselves. Moreover, the notion of one's having a *duty* to have certain feelings and attitudes is problematical, at the least. There seems no room left for the affective life in our moral world; it is entirely ancillary or incidental, helping or hindering us from performing our duties, possibly the basis for excuses, but forming no essential part of the basic concepts of morality. Even in views which emphasize a good will or proper motivation as basic to morality, the subjective factor emphasized is that of intention, and it is the intention to *act* in particular ways which is involved. Missing almost completely in the literature is the idea of certain attitudes as underlying a common moral life and actions as being natural or conventional expressions and demonstrations of those attitudes.

It is for such reasons as these, as well as others, that gratitude is not much dealt with in the literature. Consider that we do not, generally, *punish* people for failing to show gratitude; there is rarely a *particular* act which *must* be done if we are to show gratitude; there

---

[8]Aristotle stated his view in this way: "I mean moral virtue; for it is this that is concerned with passions and actions, and in these there is excess, defect, and the intermediate. For instance, both fear and confidence and appetite and anger and pity and in general pleasure and pain may be felt both too much and too little, and in both cases not well; but to feel them at the right times, with reference to the right objects, toward the right people, with the right motive, and in the right way, is what is both intermediate and best, and this is characteristic of virtue" (*Nicomachean Ethics* 1106b25)

are no acts which the benevolent person may *demand* as a grateful return for his largess; and, though we sometimes speak of an act as entailing a *debt* of gratitude, it is a debt which differs in important ways from others, and there seem to be no acts which it is our duty to perform in order to discharge the debt, even though a range of acts may be sufficient.

Far from showing that gratitude has nothing to do with morality, I think such facts show that the traditional ways of talking about morality, in which the concepts of "right," "wrong," "duty," "punishment," etc., are central, has led to an insufficient picture of what it is to have a morality. The sorts of feelings and attitudes involved in gratitude *do* play an important role in our moral life. Though we do not punish ingratitude, and though it *may* be logically impossible to make the having of certain feelings and attitudes (and thus their sincere display) a matter of duty, we nonetheless do not ignore gratitude in moral training. We teach that certain feelings and attitudes are appropriate and in *some* sense *ought* to be had in certain situations. Moreover, a statement like "You should be glad for his gift," while not a demand that one should be glad, *is* a criticism of moral character and does play a role in moral education. We do not blame people for character defects, but blame is not the only form of criticism and not the only impetus to reform; and we certainly do *praise* those who display exemplary character. We can, to be sure, encourage and develop in people certain feelings and attitudes and the sort of characters in which these are appropriately displayed. We do this through example, exhortation, being pleased when those feelings and attitudes spontaneously show through, etc. In any particular culture, many kinds of affective and attitudinal responses become appropriate in certain situations, and a well-developed moral personality is expected, as a matter of course, to display these. In Western cultures, worried concern is appropriate to the difficulties faced by friends and associates (would one *be* a friend if he did not have a concern for our tribulations?); distress is appropriate to the ill fare of loved ones, joy or gladness is appropriate to great gains made by those close to us, anger is appropriate to situations in which an individual does great harm to another.[9] Not only do we strive to develop the affective life

[9] One writer who *has* stressed the idea that attitudes are appropriate to take and express to certain situations is J. N. Findlay. See his important article. "The Justification of Attitudes," *Mind* 63 (1954): 145–61.

in certain ways rather than others, expressing appropriate approval or disapproval at proper or improper displays of attitudes, but we regard the failure to have the requisite responses as a defect of character. Consider the judgment one would make of one who finds the pain of others humorous, or who is incapable of pitying the unfortunate, or who does not feel pride in the accomplishments of his offspring, or feels no genuine gratitude for the sacrifices made for him by others. There is something lacking in these cases in relations held with others, and the atttitudes of the individual are deficient. These lackings are not punishable *offenses* (nor, by themselves, do they seem grounds for saying the persons are *immoral*), but they are not mere personality defects, either, in the way that, say, being boring is merely a defect of personality. Ingratitude, in particular, may rightly prompt castigation and reproval—the marks of a moral defect.

In addition, gratitude shows the role of the affective life in morality in an especially cogent way. If my account is correct, among the feelings and attitudes expressed in gratitude are those of appreciation of the other person and one's attitude of respect for the other person as someone of value in himself, and not merely as the source of one's own welfare. Having this kind of regard, taking these attitudes toward others is essentially involved in having a morality. Those with whom we share moral relations are not merely creatures whose behavior exhibits certain patterns but whose behavior manifests attitudes of valuing, respect, and concern.

It may be that these points, though important in themselves, can readily enough be accounted for on traditional conceptions of morality, even that of the utilitarian tradition. For example, John Stuart Mill often emphasized the importance of the development of moral character, and that this involves the cultivation of appropriate feelings and desires. Indeed, he criticized Bentham and the utilitarian tradition for ignoring this aspect of morality.[10] Mill's reason for stressing the development of the affective aspects of man was that these have consequences for our actions.[11] We must get men to feel and desire properly in order to get them to act properly. Indeed, he advocated inculcating in people desires for things other

---

[10]John Stuart Mill, "Remarks on Bentham's Philosophy,' in *Collected Works*, vol. 10, ed. J. M. Robson (Toronto: University of Toronto Press, 1969), pp. 7–8.

[11]Ibid.

than the general welfare, for the reason that by acting from such desires they will, in fact, produce the general welfare more perfectly than if they always and solely acted from the desire to maximize the general welfare.[12]

There is no question that the practices associated with gratitude and the feelings and attitudes which comprise it are useful in these ways. An amateur sociologist would have little trouble pointing out the ways in which such displays reinforce dispositions to gift-giving and enlarge the degree of concession and concern people show one another. This, however, seems to me an unsatisfactory account of why reflective people seek to maintain the conventions of gratitude. Quite without regard to any further consequences, we care how people feel toward us and how they regard us. It is not enough that our friend does the right things in our interrelationship; it is equally important that he does them (at least in part) because he *likes* and *cares* for us. We are not satisfied if a friend does a favor for us if we think he begrudges it to us for some reason. Gratitude plays a role in our interrelationships precisely because it involves the demonstration of our feelings toward another. Thus it has value quite without regard to any further contribution to the good of society, quite without regard to any further actions it tends to produce. Our conception of our status with respect to others involves our view of how they *feel* toward us, what their *attitudes* are toward us, how they *regard* us.[13] Our idea of how we are valued, how we are thought of by others, and, thus, our view of the basis of our moral relations with them, is bound up with these perceptions. We can put this point another way: having regard for someone as of value, as deserving respect and concern, involves having certain feelings and attitudes; thus when we display these, we exhibit what their moral status is in our eyes.

---

[12]See "Utilitarianism," in *Collected Works*, 10:238–39. Also, the later editions of Mill's *A System of Logic* contain a passage at the very end which makes this point.

[13]I would be remiss were I not to mention an important article by Peter Strawson, in which he stresses the great importance to us of others' attitudes and feelings toward us. And he interprets gratitude, as I have, in terms of what he calls "reactive attitudes" toward another's benevolence. Of "reactive attitudes," he writes: "What I have called the participant reactive attitudes are essentially natural human reactions to the good or ill will of others towards us, as displayed in *their* attitudes and actions" (P. F. Strawson, "Freedom and Resentment," in *Studies in the Philosophy of Thought and Action*, ed. P. F. Strawson [London: Oxford University Press, 1968], p. 80).

Still, it may seem, even these points can be accommodated within the utilitarian framework. It may be thought that what this shows is that our *happiness* requires that we perceive that others have certain feelings and attitudes toward us. Thus the practices involved in gratitude have value, since they produce an essential element of happiness directly. Mill, it seems to me, regarded our sense of our own dignity as human beings to be an essential element of human happiness, and so may well have found a view such as this acceptable.[14] I do not wish to speculate further as to whether happiness can be properly viewed this way, or whether some further aspect of gratitude resists utilitarian treatment or can be brought within the rubrics of traditional philosophical concepts. For my purposes, it will suffice to have shown that demonstrations of our feelings and attitudes and the proper ordering of our affective lives are importantly involved in morality, whether or not there is a way of dealing with these points in traditional terms.

I shall close by pointing out that, if the present analysis is correct, a number of similar topics bear serious philosophical treatment, as there are large patterns of our moral relations which involve elements of the kinds I have isolated in gratitude. Among such related topics are: friendship, trust, loyalty, fidelity, pity, charity, digust, resentment, hatred, etc. These and other such notions are importantly involved in the morality of our interpersonal relationships, and some of them can be more important for us to understand in our daily lives than, say, the logic of promising or even the principles of justice.

STUDY QUESTIONS

1. Berger says we owe gratitude to our parents. On what grounds? What qualification does he place on this?
2. What, according to Berger, is the role of feelings and attitudes in the moral life?
3. What is odd about having a duty to show gratitude? How does Berger explain that, all the same, we *owe* gratitude to our benefactors?

---

[14]See especially "Utilitarianism," p. 212. I should note, however, that on this view it would appear that there is no moral difference between an insincere show of gratitude, in which the insincerity is completely concealed, and a sincere display.

Prudence and Courage

W. D. FALK

W. D. Falk (b. 1906) taught philosophy in England, Scotland, and Australia. He is now at the University of North Carolina.

Falk examines and rejects the commonly held view that self-interested actions are *ipso facto* not morally praiseworthy. He distinguishes types of self-interested actions and finds that they are not always prudential. An example of a nonprudential action is taking a high risk for gain. This may be recommended despite its imprudence. A courageous act may be imprudent and self-interested, and morally right as well. Sometimes a person acts in a socially useful manner hoping to better his lot. To call such conduct morally indifferent or "merely expedient" is a mistake. Generally, joint concern for our own good and that of society motivates our social virtues, but they are nonetheless virtues for all that. Falk criticizes recent academic morality for thinking that virtue must be disinterested, and attacks Hobbes for thinking that selfish considerations motivate all action. He recommends the common sense attitude of earlier philosophers who counted some self-interested dispositions among the virtues.

Whenever one remarks that clearly there are things which one ought to avoid or do if only for one's own sake, someone is sure to

PRUDENCE AND COURAGE From *Morality and the Language of Conduct*, Hector-Neri Castaneda and George Naknikian, eds., by permission of the Wayne State University Press.

say, "No doubt; but any such ought is only a precept of prudence or expediency." It is a textbook cliché against Hobbes that his account of morality comes to just this. And this is said as if it were an obvious truth and enough to discredit all such precepts in one go. This assumes a great deal and settles nothing.

What it assumes is this: that everything that one ever does for one's own sake, one does as a matter of prudence *or* expediency; that there is no difference between these two; that morality always differs from prudence as a scent differs from a bad smell; and that everyone knows how so and why.

None of this will do.

In the first place, not everything done for oneself is done for reasons of prudence. That one ought to insure one's house, save for one's old age, not put all one's money into one venture, are precepts of prudence. But it is not a precept of prudence, though it may be a good precept, that someone ought to undergo a dangerous operation as a long shot to restoring his health rather than linger under a disability forever after.

The point is that prudence is only one way of looking after oneself. To act prudently is to play safe, for near-certain gains at small risks. But some good things one cannot get in this way. To get them at all one has to gamble, taking the risk of not getting them even so, or of coming to harm in the process. If one values them enough, one will do better by oneself to throw prudence to the winds, to play for high stakes, knowing full well the risk and the price of failure. Explorers, artists, scientists, mountaineers are types who may serve themselves better by this course. So will most people at some juncture. Thus, if someone values security, then that he ought to save in order to be secure is a precept of prudence. But that someone ought to stick to his vocation when his heart is in it enough to make it worth risking security or health or life itself is not a precept of *prudence*, but of *courage*.

One says sometimes, "I ought to save, as I *want* to be prudent," but sometimes "as I *ought* to be prudent." One may also decide that in one's own best interests one ought to be prudent rather than daring, or daring rather than prudent, as the case may be. Now, that one ought to do something as it would be prudent is a dictate of prudence. But that one really ought to be prudent, in one's own best interests, would not be a dictate of prudence again. One then ought to play safe in order to serve oneself *best* and not in order to serve oneself *safely*.

A dictate of prudence where one wants to be prudent but ought to be courageous in one's own best interests is a dictate of timidity. A dictate of courage, where one feels reckless but ought to be prudent, is a dictate of foolhardiness. Both will then plainly be morally imperfect precepts. But there is nothing obviously imperfect about a dictate of prudence where one ought to be daring. Such precepts seem near-moral enough to allow one to call the habit of acting on them a virtue. The Ancients considered both prudence and courage as moral virtues. Oddly enough, in our time, one is more ready to view courage on one's own behalf as a moral virtue than prudence. It needs the reminder that precepts of self-protection may be precepts of courage as well as of prudence for one to see that any precept of self-protection may have a moral flavor. I think that the dim view which we take of prudence corresponds to a belief that to be daring is harder than to be level-headed, a belief most likely justified within our own insurance-minded culture. But such belief would have seemed strange to Bishop Butler and the fashionable eighteenth-century gentlemen to whom he addressed himself. Prudence in Butler's time, as throughout the ancient world, was not yet the cheap commodity which it is with us; and the price of virtue varies with the market.

There are other precepts of self-protection which are not "just a matter of prudence" either. That one ought not to take to drugs or drink, indulge oneself in one's sorrows, waste one's talents, commit suicide just in the despair of the moment, are precepts made of sterner stuff. One wants to say, "Surely, it is more than just a matter of prudence that one ought to avoid these things." And rightly so. The effect on oneself of taking to drugs or drink, or of any of the others, is not conjectural, but quite certain. To avoid them is therefore more than a matter of *taking no risks*. Sometimes, when one looks down a precipice, one feels drawn to jump. If one refrains, it will hardly be said of one, "How prudent he is, he takes no chances." The avoidance of excesses of all kinds in one's own best interests is in this class. The habit of avoiding them the Greeks called temperance, a virtue distinct from prudence.

Another error is to equate the prudent with the expedient, and, again, the expedient with everything that is for one's own good. To save may be prudent; but whether it is expedient or convenient to start now is another matter. With a lot of money to spare at the moment it will be expedient; otherwise it will not. But it may be prudent all the same. Again, one marries in the hope of finding happiness; but marriage in this hope is not a marriage of convenience. The point is that reasons of expediency are reasons of a special sort: reasons for doing something on the ground that it is incidentally at hand to serve one's purpose, or because it serves a purpose quite incidental to the purpose for which one would normally be doing this thing. One marries for reasons of expediency when one marries for money, but not when in hope of finding happiness. Hobbes said that "men never act except with a view to some good to themselves." This would be quite different from saying that "they never act except with a view to what is expedient."

There is also this difference between the prudent and the expedient: one can speak of "rules of prudence," but less well of "rules of expediency." The expedient is what happens to serve. It is not therefore easily bottled in rules.

The word "prudence" is used too freely in still one more context. When one wishes to justify the social virtues to people, a traditional and inviting move is to refer them, among other things at least, to their own good. "You ought to hold the peace, be honest, share with others." "Why?" "Because an order in which such practices were universal is of vital concern to you; and your one hope of helping to make such an order is in doing your share." The classical formulation of this standard move is Hooker's, quoted with approval by Locke: "If I cannot but wish to receive good . . . how should I look to have any part of my desire herein satisfied, unless I myself be careful to satisfy the like desire: my desire therefore to be loved of my equals in nature, as much as possible may be, imposes upon me a *natural duty* of bearing to themward fully the like affection."

Now, it is said again, "So defended, the social duties come to no more than precepts of prudence"; and this goes with the veiled suggestion that it is morally improper to use this defense. But, even if so defended, the social duties are not necessarily reduced purely to precepts of prudence. For they may be recommended in this way either as mere *rules* or as *principles* of self-protection; and as principles they would be misdescribed as mere precepts of prudence. The distinction is this: When one says, "People ought to practice the social virtues, if only for their own benefit," one may be saying, "They ought to practice them for this reason as a *rule*, i.e., normally, as much as each time this is likely to be for their own good." Or one may be saying, "They ought to practice them for this reason not merely as a rule but as a *matter of principle*, i.e., every time, whether at that time this is likely to be for their good or not." And one might defend the adoption of this *principle* by saying, "Because your best, even if slim, hope of contributing to a society fit for you to live in lies in adding to the number of principled people who will do their share each time, without special regard for their good at that time."

Now this seems to me a precept of courage rather than one of prudence. The game of attempting by one's actions to make society a place fit for one to live in is a gamble worth the risk only because of the known price of not attempting it. This gamble is a root condition of social living. One is sure to give hostages to fortune, but again, what other hope has one got? Hence, if a man practiced the social virtues, thinking that he ought to as a matter of principle, and on these grounds, one will praise him for his *wisdom*, his firm grasp of vital issues, his steadfastness, his courage. But one will not necessarily congratulate him on his prudence. For many times the prudent course might have been otherwise. It may be wise to persist in being honest with cheats, or forbearing with the aggressive, or helpful to those slow to requite helpfulness; but it might have been more prudent to persist for no longer than there was requital, or not even to start before requital was assured.

Now would it be a moral precept or not that, if only out of proper care for oneself, one ought to act on principles of wisdom and courage? That one ought to risk life in order to gain it? And, assuming a society of men acting fixedly on these principles but no others, would it or would it not contain men of moral virtue? One might as well ask, "Is a ski an article of footwear?" There is no more of a straight answer here than there. One may say, "Not quite"; and the point of saying this needs going into. But it would be more misleading to say, "Not at all." For it is part of the meaning of "moral precept" that it prescribes what a man would do in his wisdom—if he were to consider things widely, looking past the immediate concerns of self and giving essentials due weight before incidentals. As it is also part of what is meant by one's moral capacities that one can live by such considerations, it becomes fruitless after a time to press the point whether such precepts are properly called moral.

There are then varieties of the personal ought, differing in the considerations on which they are based and the qualities needed to follow them; and they all seem at least akin to a "moral" ought in their action-guiding force and function. But I grant that one does not want to speak of more than a kinship, and the point of this needs considering. One's hesitancy derives from various sources which have to be traced one by one.

Some of the hesitancy comes from contexts where one can say disparagingly, "He did this *only* for reasons of prudence, *only* for reasons of expediency, *only* for himself." This plainly applies sometimes, but it does not apply always. One would hardly say of someone without dependents, "He thought that he ought to save, but *only* for reasons of prudence"; or of someone, "He thought that he ought to have the carpenter in along with the plumber, but *only* for reasons of expediency or convenience"; or "He thought that he ought to become a doctor, but *only* because the career would suit him." "Only" has no point here. Why else should a man without dependents save, except to be prudent? Why else should anyone have the carpenter in along with the plumber, except for convenience? What better reason is there normally for choosing a career than that it will suit one? On the other hand, there is point in saying, "He held the peace only because it was prudent," "He saved only because it was convenient," "He practices the social virtues only for self-protection." It is plain why "only" applies here and is disparaging. One says "only" because something is done for the wrong or for not quite the right reason—done for *one* reason where there is *another* and nearer reason for doing it anyway. Personal reasons are often in this position, and then they are disparaged as inferior. One saves "only" because it is expedient, if one ought to have saved anyway for reasons of prudence. One holds the peace "only" because it was prudent when one ought to have done so anyway as a matter of principle and even it if had not been prudent. And one practices the social virtues "only" for self-protection when one does not *also* practice them for the general good.

The last case is different from the others. Plainly, one ought to practice the social virtues as principles of general good. But on none but perhaps pure Christian principles would it hold, or neces-

sarily hold, that one ought to practice them on this ground unconditionally, however great the provocation to oneself. The case for
the social virtues is weakened when the social environment becomes hostile and intractable by peaceable means; it is correspondingly strengthened where they can also be justified as wise principles of self-protection. That someone practices forbearance "only"
as a wise principle of self-protection is not therefore to say that he
practices it for a reason which is neither here nor there; but rather
for a reason which falls short of all the reason there is. This was, in
effect, the view of the old Natural Law moralists—Hooker, Grotius, Puffendorf: the social virtues derive joint support from our
natural concern for our own good and for that of society. Hobbes
streamlined this account by denying the second, which provoked
subsequent moralists to deny the first. Both Hobbes's sophistical
toughness and the well-bread innocence of the academic moralists
since are distorted visions which are less convincing than the un-
squeamish common sense of the philosophers and divines of earlier
times.

STUDY QUESTIONS

1. What is Falk's attitude toward prudence? Is prudence a virtue?
   Why?
2. What distinguishes prudence from expedience? Can an expedient act have moral worth?
3. How does Falk argue that some self-interested actions have
   moral worth?
4. How do the social virtues relate to self-interestedness? What
   does Falk mean by saying that the social vitures derive from
   "our natural concern with ourselves"?

Generosity

JAMES D. WALLACE

James D. Wallace (b. 1937) is a professor of philosophy at the University of Illinois in Urbana. He is the author of *Virtues and Vices* (1978).

Generosity is a virtue concerned with giving. Wallace distinguishes between economic generosity, where the object one gives has a market value, and generosity of the heart or mind, where one gives intangible things such as kindness or encouragement. In primary generosity, agents directly concern themselves with the good of others rather than being inadvertently helpful. Normally, generosity exceeds what is expected or required by custom. The distinguishing features of economic generosity are (1) giving with the intention to benefit, (2) giving what has market value, and (3) giving more than is normally required. In the case of generous-mindedness, what one gives has no market value but the other criteria apply. The virtue of generosity illustrates that morality is sometimes a matter of acting beyond the call of duty.

Economic Generosity

Generosity is concerned with giving, and different kinds of generosity can be distinguished according to the kind of things given. Aristotle said that generosity (*eleutheriotēs*) has to do with giving

GENEROSITY From *Virtues and Vices* by James D. Wallace. Reprinted by permission of the author and Cornell University Press.

and taking of things whose value is measured in money.[1] There is a virtue called generosity, the actions fully characteristic of which are meritorious, which has to do with freely giving things that have a *market value*—freely giving goods and services of a type that normally are exchanged on the open market. This sort of generosity I call "economic generosity" to distinguish it from other varieties. One can be generous in the judgments one makes about the merits and demerits of others, and one can be generous in forgiving those who trespass against one. "Generous-mindedness" and "generous-heartedness," as these other kinds of generosity might be called, do not involve being generous with things whose value is measured in money. These are like economic generosity in certain ways, but they also differ in important respects, as I shall try subsequently to show. Unless otherwise indicated, however, by generosity I mean economic generosity.

A generous person is one who has a certain attitude toward his own things, the value of which is measured in money, and who also has a certain attitude toward other people. Generosity, like other forms of benevolence, in its primary occurrence, involves as one of its constitutents a concern for the happiness and well-being of others. The actions fully characteristic of generosity have as their goal promoting someone else's well-being, comfort, happiness, or pleasure—someone else's good. In *primary generosity*, the agent is concerned directly about the good of another. Thus, an action fully characteristic of generosity might be done to please someone or to help someone, with no further end in view beyond pleasing or helping. "I just wanted to do something nice for them" or "I just wanted her to have it" are typical explanations of generous acts.

That an act fully characteristic of *the virtue*, generosity, is motivated in this way by a direct concern for the good of another is not immediately obvious, because we sometimes call giving "generous" and mean only that the giver is giving more than someone in his situation normally gives. Thus, the host is being generous with the mashed potatoes when he unthinkingly heaps unusually large portions on the plates. Or perhaps he does not do it unthinkingly. It might be that he is giving such generous portions because he wants to use up all the potatoes to prevent them from spoiling. Being

---

[1]*Nicomachean Ethics*, IV, 1, 1119b21–27.

generous in this way—giving a lot for reasons such as these—would not tend to show that the host is a *generous person*, even if he did so frequently. If we restrict ourselves to the kind of generous action that is fully characteristic of a generous person, then in every case, the agent's giving will be motivated by a direct concern for the good (in the broad sense) of another. I shall say in such cases that the agent intends to *benefit* the recipient.

There is a further complication. The virtue generosity, in its *primary occurrence*, I have said, involves a sort of direct concern for the good of others, as do other forms of benevolence. Someone who is deficient in such concern or who lacks it altogether might admire generous people for their generosity and want as far as he can to be like them. He might then want to do in certain situations what a generous person would do. Acting as a generous person would act because one regards generosity as a virtue, and wants, therefore, to emulate the generous person is meritorious, and it reflects credit upon the agent. It is, however, a secondary sort of generosity. It depends, for its merit, upon the fact that primary generosity *is* a virtue and is thus a worthy ideal at which to aim. I will concentrate, therefore, upon primary generosity, which does involve a direct concern for the good of another. An account of why this is a virtue is easily extended to explain why a generous person is worthy of emulation.

A certain sort of attitude on the part of the agent toward what he gives is also a feature of actions fully characteristic of the virtue generosity. In acting generously, one must give something that one values—something that one, therefore, has some reason to keep rather than discard or abandon. If, for example, one is about to throw away an article of clothing, and on the way to the trash barrel one meets someone who would like to have it, it would not be *generous* of one to give it to him. What disqualifies such giving from being generous is neither the giver's motive nor the nature of what is given but rather the fact that the giver himself does not value the object enough. Similarly, when we do favors for one another, giving matches or coins for parking meters, often what is given is too insignificant for the giving of it to be generous. One may be being kind in giving things that one does not particularly value, but for the giving to be generous, one must value the thing given for some reason. I may have acquired a particularly repulsive piece of primitive art that I have no desire to keep. Still, I might gnerously give it to a museum if it were a valuable piece—one I could sell or exchange for something I really want. How *generous* one is being in giving something generally depends upon how much one values the thing given, how much one is giving up.

Usually, the giver must give in excess of what he is required to give by morality or custom, if his giving is to be generous. Where there exists a generally recognized moral obligation to give, or where giving is customary, then normally one's giving is not generous even though it is prompted by a direct concern for the good of the recipient. If one were certain of a more than ample and continuing supply of food, so that it would clearly be wrong not to give some food to a neighbor who would otherwise go hungry, giving the neighbor a portion of food would not be generous. Similarly, to give a person a gift when one is expected to do so, because it is customary to exchange gifts (for example birthdays, Christmas, weddings, etc.), is normally not a matter of generosity, even though one aims to please the recipient. If one gives *more* than what is expected in such cases, then the giving might be generous. A generous person is one who exceeds normal expectations in giving, and one who gives no more than what is generally expected in the circumstances is not apt to be cited for generosity.

A special problem arises in cases of the following sort. Although it would clearly be wrong for a certain person *not* to give, he does not see this. Nevertheless, he does give on a generous impulse. Suppose, for example, that a certain person is a social Darwinist, convinced that it is wrong to give the necessities of life to people in need, because this enables the weak to survive, thus weakening the species. She encounters a starving family, and touched by their plight, she provides food for them, though not without a twinge of social Darwinist guilt. Assuming that what she gives is not insignificant to her, but that it is no more than what the family needs to keep them alive, is her giving generous? On the one hand, she is really doing no more than the minimum required of her by the duty to help people in distress, and this makes one hesitate to say that she is being generous. On the other hand, *she* does not recognize any moral obligation here, and it is the kind and generous side of her nature that overcomes her cruel principles and leads her to give. This seems to support the view that she is being generous.

An act fully characteristic of generosity will normally have the following features.

(1) The agent, because of his direct concern for the good of the recipient, gives something with the intention of benefiting the recipient.

(2) The agent gives up something of his that has a market value and that he has some reason to value and, therefore, to keep.

(3) The agent gives more than one is generally expected, because of moral requirements or custom, to give in such circumstances.

In normal cases, an act that meets these three conditions will be a generous act, and a generous act will have these three features. There are, however, abnormal cases—cases in which the agent has, concerning the circumstances mentioned in the three conditions, a false belief or an unusual or eccentric attitude. The case of the social Darwinist is such a case. She thinks she is morally required *not* to give, when in fact she is required to give. If one accepts *her* view of the situation, her act is generous. In fact, however, the third condition is not satisfied. In another sort of abnormal case, the agent values what he gives, but in fact the gift is utterly worthless—it is literally trash. Here it is not clear that the second condition is fulfilled, but from the agent's odd point of view, the act is generous. The very rich often give to charity sums of money that are large in comparison with what others give, and their gifts seem generous. These sums, however, which are substantial, may be relatively insignificant to the donors, and one may wonder whether condition (2) is satisfied in such a case. Does the donor, who has so much, in fact have reason to value and keep what he gives, or is his "gift" analogous to an ordinary person's giving away a book of matches? In a rather different sort of case, someone might be convinced that he is morally required to give away nearly all he has to the poor. For this reason, he divests himself of a substantial fortune. In such cases, it may be that condition (1) is not satisfied. The agent believes, in effect, that condition (3) is not satisfied, since he believes that he is required to do this. These circumstances will make one hesitate to call his giving generous, although other features of the case incline one toward the view that he is being generous.

In these cases involving unusual beliefs or attitudes, one is pulled simultaneously in two different directions. The way the agent sees the situation and the way one expects him to see the situation diverge. Crucial conditions are satisfied from one way of regarding the case and unsatisfied from the other. It is not surprising that one is reluctant to say simply that the act is (or is not) fully characteristic of the virtue generosity. Any such statement must be qualified, and the actual consequences of the qualification may or may not be important, depending upon the case. Normally, of course, the agent's beliefs about the features in (1)–(3) will not be grossly mistaken nor will his attitudes toward those things be unusual or eccentric. In such cases, if the three conditions are satisfied, the act is unqualifiedly generous, and vice versa.

A generous person is one who has a tendency to perform actions that meet these conditions. The stronger the tendency, the more generous the person.

Generous-Mindedness

The conditions in the preceding section are meant as an account of actions that are fully characteristic of *economic generosity*—generosity that involves giving things whose value is measured in money. Another kind of generosity, however, has to do with making judgments about the merits and failings of other people. This too is a virtue, which sometimes is called *generous-mindedness*.[2] I will try briefly to indicate some similarities and differences between this virtue and economic generosity.

Generous-mindedness is shown by seeing someone else's merit (technical, moral, etc.) in cases where it is difficult to see because the facts of the case admit of other, not unreasonable interpretations, or because the situation is complex and the merit is not immediately apparent. Generous-mindedness is also shown by seeing that a derogatory judgment is not called for in cases where the facts might not unreasonably be taken to indicate a derogatory judgment. Many of us actually dislike to find that others are as good or better than we are, so that we have some desire to find grounds for derogatory judgments. It is plausible to think that

---

[2] I am indebted to David Shwayder for bringing this topic to my attention.

people of otherwise fair judgment are sometimes led to think less of others than they should because they do not want to think well of them or because they want to think ill of them. They do not purposely close their eyes to merit; rather because they do not wish to find it, they do not try hard enough to find it. This may involve a certain amount of self-deception, but I suspect that in many cases the matter is more straightforward. If someone wants to find another inferior to himself in some respect, then where he sees some (prima facie) grounds for such a judgment, he is apt to be quick to seize upon it and regard the matter as settled. A generous-minded person is one who wants to think well of other people, so that in such cases he will look and find the merit that might otherwise go overlooked. Of course, it is possible to be too generous-minded—to overlook demerit because one does not want to find it.

If someone exhibits generous-mindedness in his judgment on a particular occasion, his act of judgment will not fulfill the conditions for an act of economic generosity. It will have features, however, that can be seen as analogous to the features characteristics of economic generosity. If an individual is well-disposed toward other people, then besides wanting to benefit them by giving them things, he will wish them well. He will tend to want their undertakings to succeed and to reflect well on them. If he wants to think well of others, he will be apt to look harder for merit, and he will, therefore, be more likely to find it. Generous-mindedness seems properly regarded as a manifestation of good will toward others that shows a direct concern for the well-being of others.

Economic generosity generally involves giving more than is required or customary, and there is a counterpart to this in generous-mindedness. The generous-minded person sees merit where a competent evaluator might miss it, where it would be reasonable (though incorrect) to find that there is no such merit. In this way, one might say that generous-mindedness leads a person to go beyond what is required of an evaluator. . . .

For generous-mindedness not to distort one's judgment—for it not to lead one to incorrect evaluations—an individual must be a competent evaluator and be conscientious about reaching a correct judgment. Also, it does seem that if one has sufficiently good judgment and is sufficiently concerned to make the right judgment, then this by itself should lead one to see merit when it is present just as well as would the desire *to find merit*. The strong desire to make favorable judgments, moreover, *may* distort one's judgment. It may lead one to overlook defects and to find merit where it is not. A strong desire to make *the correct evaluation* cannot distort one's judgment in this way. Generous-mindedness should not be regarded as a primary virtue of evaluators. It can counteract an inclination to build oneself up by tearing others down, but so too can a strong desire to evaluate correctly. Generous-mindedness is a manifestation of the sort of concern for others that is characteristic of all forms of benevolence. It derives the greatest part of its merit from this concern. . . .

STUDY QUESTIONS

1. How would you measure the extent of generosity when (a) the person is mean-spirited but forces himself to give out of a sense of moral obligation; or (b) the person is innately kind and gives effortlessly?
2. What does Wallace mean by generous-mindedness? Do you believe that a stingy person who lacks economic generosity can be generous-minded? Conversely, can a mean-spirited person be economically generous?
3. Do we have a duty to be generous? Would not that be like having a duty to do more than our duty?

Virtue

JOHN MACKIE

John Mackie (1917–1982) was a Fellow of University College, Oxford. Among his published works are *Truth, Probability and Paradox* (1973), *The Cement of the University* (1974), and *Ethics: Inventing Right and Wrong* (1977).

Mackie concisely describes the Aristotelian theory of virtue. He points out that the Aristotelian virtues do not specify a particular life as good, but allow for many different types of good lives within a range. Mackie defines the virtues as dispositions we have developed that help us choose within an acceptable range. To the question "Why be virtuous?" he answers that a developed disposition to, say, courage or generosity enhances a person's life. Also, the virtuous person has a good conscience and is internally more serene.

I

Aristotle tells us that the well-being or *eudaimonia* which is the good for man is an activity in accordance with virtue; each virtue is a disposition for making (right) choices, and one that is trained or developed by experience rather than inborn; with most virtues, the right sort of choice which it enables its possessor to make is somehow intermediate between two wrong sorts of choice; one can do or show too little or too much of something, one can go too far

VIRTUE From *Ethics* by J. L. Mackie (Penguin Books, 1977), pp. 186–192. Copyright © J. L. Mackie, 1977. Reprinted by permission of Penguin Books Ltd.

or not far enough; what constitutes the right amount, the virtuous choice, is determined as the man of practical widsom would determine it; and he is the man who is good at choosing the means to the end of *eudaimonia*.

As guidance about what is the good life, what precisely one ought to do, or even by what standard one should try to decide what one ought to do, this is too circular to be very helpful. And though Aristotle's account is filled out with detailed descriptions of many of the virtues, moral as well as intellectual, the air of indeterminacy persists. We learn the names of the pairs of contrary vices that contrast with each of the virtues, but very little about where or how to draw the dividing lines, where or how to fix the mean. As Sidgwick says, he 'only indicates the whereabouts of virtue'. We must, then, take this mainly as a formal sketch of the structure of the good life, which leaves the specific content still to be filled in. To fill in this specific content, to mark off each virtue from the contrasting excesses and defects, we can draw on three sources. One will be the ways of behaving that are, at a particular place and time, conventionally admired; another will be one's own conception of the good. The third is at once more objective and less often noticed. When Hume maintained that reason alone can never be a motive for or against any action, that it can neither oppose nor support any passion or preferences, he was right in so far as he was stressing the logical independence of preferences on the one hand and factual information and valid inferences on the other. Yet we must also admit that in practice some degrees of emotion, some states of feeling and spirit, harmonize with seeing things as they are, and some do not. The man who 'thinks with his blood' cannot think with his mind at the same time on the same subject. Yet it is not being completely 'dispassionate' or detached, a total absence of feeling, that fits in best with seeing things as they are. It is rather a certain degree of enterprise and involvement that goes along with understanding. Also, some states of feeling can, and others cannot, survive an honest scrutiny and clear-sighted realization of their causes. As Spinoza says, 'An emotion which is a passion ceases to be a passion as soon as we form a clear and distinct idea of it.' This gives us a possible ground of distinction between a virtue and the contrasting vices of excess and defect: a virtue is a disposition which harmonizes with understanding, with seeing things as they are, while a vice is one which distorts appreciation of the qualities of the relevant situation, which needs such distortion in order to maintain itself, and which is manifested by states of mind which cannot stand honest reflection on the ways in which they have themselves arisen. This approach would define courage, for example, as a disposition for choice in relation to danger which neither cultivates nor depends upon either the exaggerating or the minimizing of those dangers, and which is compatible with self-awareness. We may compare this with, for example, Locke's definition of courage as 'For a man to be undisturbed in danger [which he perceives], sedately to consider what is fittest to be done, and to execute it steadily.' Other traditional virtues could be defined in systematically analogous ways. Though there is a lot of sophistry in the details of the argument by which Plato, in the *Protagoras*, tries to establish the unity of the virtues by assimilating them all to knowledge or wisdom, there is considerable force in the general suggestion that the virtues can be identified as dispositions that harmonize with knowledge. It must be conceded, however, that this approach would not narrowly determine the sort of choice to which a virtue would lead: it equates each virtue (or rather the corresponding choices) with a broad band rather than with a particular point on some scale; it leaves room, therefore, for reference to one's own conception of the good or to what is conventionally admired (or to both) to help to determine just how much of this or that can go into what is to count as an action in accordance with virtue.

But however this specific content is to be filled in, there is merit in Aristotle's formal sketch taken simply as such. The good life will consist in activities that manifest and realize developed dispositions for choice. To say this is to avoid two contrary errors. These activities will manifest *dispositions*; that is, the good life is not just a collection of separate choices (either separately calculated or arbitrary) or of equally separate pleasures and satisfactions, or of both. But on the other hand these are dispositions *for choice*—preferential choice—not just instincts or habits.

Though dispositions can change and develop, they are fairly persistent. They cannot be switched on and off at will. Also, though dispositions can be discriminating, there are practical limits to the fineness of the discriminations they can make. A disposition for choice can express itself in differential choices only if the agent not only judges but also feels the cases to be significantly different.

One can have a complex disposition, say of being honest with friends and deceitful towards enemies. It is more difficult to be deceitful on a particular occasion towards someone who is normally a friend but who has now taken on the role of an enemy. On the other hand being poker-faced is itself a disposition that can be cultivated. One can treat a special class of persons, or persons in some special setting, as opponents towards whom one is not honest by disposition, but to whom one offers a judicious mixture of truth and falsehood without betraying which is which.

The part that virtues play in the good life depends crucially on the fact that they are dispositions of this sort: fairly persistent and not too finely discriminating. The virtues that go with a particular conception of the good will be dispositions which, given that conception, it is advantageous for their possessor to have. But not every choice in which they are manifested will be advantageous considered on its own.

For example, courage—in a fairly conventional sense which is included in but more narrowly defined than that given by the above-mentioned third approach—is a kind of strength. It makes its possessor more likely to achieve whatever he sets out to do, whereas the foolhardy man is likely to destroy himself or his enterprise or both, and the timid man is too easily turned aside. Besides, most worthwhile enterprises involve risks of some kind, and the courageous man can enjoy the activity, risks and all, whereas the coward cannot. Again, both vice and virtue in this area are hard to conceal, and the brave man will be a more acceptable partner for others than either the foolhardy man or the coward. There can be no doubt that such courage is in general advantageous to its possessor—more advantageous than a tendency to calculate advantage too nicely. In so far as one can choose one's dispositions—say by cultivating them—this is one which it would be rational, even on purely egoistic grounds, to choose. Admittedly there will be particular occasions when rashness would be rewarded, and others when only the coward would survive. But it is hard to calculate which these are, and almost impossible to switch the dispositions on and off accordingly. To be a coward on the one occasion when courage is fatal one would have had to be a coward on many other occasions when it was much better to be courageous. The real alternatives are the various persisting dispositions, courage and those that contrast with it, and it is clear which of these the rational egoist would prefer. A far from negligible part of discretion is valour.

II The Motive for Morality

It is easy to brush aside the question 'Why should I be moral?' by pointing out that if the 'should' is a moral one, 'You should be moral' is tautological, and if it is anything else, say a prudential one, this statement is sometimes false, so that our question either answers itself or, having a false presupposition, admits of no answer. But this reply is superficial and evasive. The real question is whether there is, as Sidgwick, for example, thought, an unresolvable tension between moral reason and rationality of self-interest, between any recommendations that we could defend as moral and the advice that anyone could be given about his own well-being. . . .

I have argued [elsewhere] that egoism is not immoral, but forms a considerable part of any viable moral system. I have also given abundant reasons why almost everyone should, in his own interest, welcome the fact that there is, and hope that there will continue to be, some system of morality, and why, even if the existing system does not suit him, his aim should be to modify it, at least locally, rather than to destroy it. But this does not completely resolve the tension. It leaves unanswered the question 'Why should I not at the same time profit from the moral system but evade it? Why should I not encourage others to be moral and take advantage of the fact that they are, but myself avoid fulfilling moral requirements if I can in so far as they go beyond rational egoism and conflict with it?' It is not an adequate answer to this question to point out that one is not likely to be able to get away with such evasions for long. There will be at least some occasions when one can do so with impunity and even without detection. Then why not? To this no complete answer of the kind that is wanted can be given. In the choice of actions moral reasons and prudential ones will not always coincide. Rather, the point of morality, and particularly of that branch of it which I have called morality in the narrow sense, is that it is necessary for the well-being of people in general that they should act to some extent in ways that they cannot see to be (egoistically) prudential and also in ways that in fact are not prudential. Morality has the function of checking what would be the natural result of prudence alone.

When Plato raises this question in the *Republic*, the answer that he puts into the mouth of Socrates is that the just man is happy because his soul is harmoniously ordered, because, as we would say, he has an integrated personality, whereas the unjust man's personality is disintegrated, and the man who represents the extreme of injustice is psychotic, his soul is a chaos of internal strife. This is a forceful argument against the extreme of injustice; but perhaps injustice in moderation will do no harm. However, though Plato is wrong in suggesting that there is only one sort of leading motive around which a personality can be integrated, we can concede that one who, in the pursuit of apparent self-interest, evades on special occasions a morality which he not only professes and encourages but allows ordinarily to control his conduct will probably be incurring costs in the form of psychological discomfort which he may not have taken adequately into account when calculating his self-interest. But we must not make too much of this. A completely harmonious soul, a fully integrated personality, is in any case an unattainable ideal, and in the post-Freudian era we know that an appearance of harmony is likely to be achieved only by pushing the conflicts out of sight. In particular the man who, commendably, develops and retains moral ideals which are at variance with those currently dominant in the society in which he lives will also thereby incur psychological costs which a merely conventionally well-behaved person does not. . . .

. . . We can, then, fall back on the comparable fact that nearly all of us do have moral feelings and do tend to think in characteristically moral ways, and that these help to determine our real interests and well-being. Why we are like this is in the first place a psychological question, to be answered, perhaps, as Hutcheson, Hume, and Adam Smith suggested, by reference to 'sympathy'; but more fundamentally it is a sociological and biological question to be answered, as I have said, by an evolutionary explanation. If someone, from whatever causes, has at least fairly strong moral tendencies, the prudential course, for him, will almost certainly coincide with what he sees as the moral one, simply because he will have to live with his conscience. What *is* prudent is then not the same as what would be prudent if he did not have moral feelings.

But if someone else has only very weak moral tendencies—or, if that is possible none at all—then it may be prudent for him to act immorally.

About the choice of actions there may be no more to be said. But as both Plato and Aristotle remind us, behind the choice of actions lies the choice of dispositions, of characters, of overall patterns of life. If it is asked what action will be the most prudent or the most egoistically rational, we must answer that that depends partly on what sort of person you are, and consequentially on what sort of person you want to be. And what was said at the end of the last section about courage applies also to other virtues, including those that are not as purely self-regarding as courage can be: dispositions cannot be switched on and off in deference to the calculation of likely consequences on particular occasions, and there are limits to the fineness of the discriminations they can incorporate. The practical choice will be between one fairly persistent disposition and others, equally persistent, that contrast with it. If we then ask what sort of person it is in one's own interest to be, what dispositions it is advantageous to have, there is little doubt that it will be ones that can be seen as virtues, as determined at least in the way emphasized in Section I as dispositions that harmonize with knowledge, but also more specifically in the light of some conception of the good and with some respect for the way of life of the society in which one lives.

STUDY QUESTIONS

1. What does Mackie mean when he says, "The virtues can be identified as dispositions that harmonize with knowledge"?

2. According to Mackie (and according to Mackie's interpretation of Aristotle), "the part that virtues play in the good life depends crucially on the fact that [as dispositions for actions] they are . . . not too finely discriminating." Why does he think that this is crucial if the virtues are to be advantageous for the good life?

3. What, according to Mackie, are some of the advantages of being virtuous? Has Mackie made a persuasive case? In this connection, comment on his quip that "A far from negligible part of discretion is valour."

SUGGESTED READINGS

Aristotle. *Nicomachean Ethics.*

Aquinas, Saint Thomas. *Treatise on the Virtues.* Translated and edited by John Oesterle. Englewood Cliffs, N.J.: Prentice-Hall, 1966.

Cooper, John M. *Reason and the Human Good in Aristotle.* Cambridge: Harvard University Press, 1975.

Feinberg, Joel. *Moral Concepts.* Oxford: Oxford University Press, 1969.

Fried, Charles. *Right and Wrong.* Cambridge, Mass.: Harvard University Press, 1978.

Geach, Peter. *The Virtues.* Cambridge: Cambridge University Press, 1977.

MacIntyre, Alisdair. *After Virtue.* Notre Dame, Ind.: University of Notre Dame Press, 1981.

Mayo, Bernard. *Ethics and the Moral Life.* New York: Saint Martin's Press, 1958.

Plato. *The Republic.*

Slote, Michael. *Goods and Virtues.* Oxford: Oxford University Press, 1983.

Von Wright, G. H. *The Varieties of Goodness.* London: Humanities Press, 1963.

Wallace, J. D. *Virtues and Vices.* Ithaca, N.Y.: Cornell University Press, 1978.

Warnock, G. J. *The Object of Morality.* Princeton, N.J.: Princeton University Press, 1969.

Chapter

4

VICE

What is vice? The question has both Christian and pagan answers. The philosophers of antiquity, from Plato to Plutarch, saw vice as a defect that we may overcome by education and discipline, including self-discipline. Virtuous persons are free of vice; their lives are ordered and rational. Plutarch's analysis of vice and virtue is fairly representative of the views of most educated thinkers in the pre-Christian era. Base persons are not controlled by reason; they are prone to impulse, discontented, ridden with anxiety. Plutarch was influenced as much by the Stoic and Epicurean philosophers as he was by Plato and Aristotle. The popular connotations of the word "epicurean" distort the doctrine; the Epicureans were far more concerned with the problem of avoiding pain and frustration than with the pursuit of pleasure and satisfaction. For both Stoics and Epicureans, contentment and inner tranquility, not pleasure, is the essence of the good life. Conversely, a vice is a character defect that promotes inner tensions and chaos as well as outer deeds that are base or ignoble.

Why are some people so susceptible to vice? The pagans attribute vice to improper development. Aristotle and Plato, in somewhat different ways, stress the *learned* character of the virtues. Virtue is a product of an education that includes self-discipline as well as discipline by parents and teachers. Persons of vice, then, have failed to shape a better character for themselves and are responsible for what they are.

The great pagan philosophers thought of virtue as the disposition to do what is right and the developed disinclination to do what is wrong. The Christian philosophers did not disagree with this, but their conception of vice is more highly seasoned. For Augustine and Abelard, to do wrong is to *sin*, to rebel against God: The sinner defies God by transgressing His law. Augustine argues that the impulse to sin is not simply a drive to satisfy desires. As he sees it, sin needs no motive beyond the perverse desire to sin. The desire to do evil is an endowment of Adam and Eve, the original sinners: Since the Fall, man has loved sin for its own sake; sin is, as it were, its own reward. According to Augustine, the pagan view that humans are fully able to control vice and develop the virtues by education and self-discipline is unduly optimistic. He maintains that we cannot achieve salvation or happiness without God's grace.

The question of human perfectability is important whether or not one views it in theological terms. Is it altogether utopian to hope for a day when cruelty and gratuitous malice are things of the past? If Augustine is right, this change will take a miracle.

Sin construed as defiance and rebellion against the powers of good is a more dramatic affair than character defect due to improper education. Augustine and Abelard locate the moment of sin at the moment one consents to do wrong. The act itself is anticlimactic. If, for example, I decide to murder someone, then the moment I *intend* to do this is the moment of sin. Even if I subsequently fail to carry out my intention, my sin is already complete. Kant's deontological ethic of the good will ("nothing is absolutely good except the good will") is a later variant of the Christian doctrine that locates the moment of doing right or wrong in the consent rather than in the act itself.

We should note that Abelard's view of sin is somewhat more complimentary to humanity than Augustine's. Abelard does not emphasize perversity, stressing instead the natural pleasure we achieve by sinning. The inclination to sin is natural and not blameworthy, but we are obligated to resist temptation; in failing to resist we "consent" to wrong and sin. Thus Christian philosophers differ on the nature of vice: Are we vicious because we

234

succumb to natural desire (Abelard), or are we somewhat diabolical (Augustine)?

Recognizing a strong tendency to evil in humans, the Christian philosophers consider persons who have base desires to be virtuous provided they do not "consent" to those desires. The pagan philosophers would have found this odd. Philippa Foot echoes their view (see her "Virtues and Vices" in Chapter 3) when she points out that we feel something is not quite right about the idea of a virtuous person beset by base desires and constantly overcoming them. Both viewpoints have strengths. Surely the pagans were not realistic in thinking of virtue as freedom from even the temptation to do wrong. And surely, as Abelard says, the very merit of doing what is right is due at least in part to the existence of a temptation to do what is wrong, a temptation we resist. If the temptation to vice is absent altogether, we are less praiseworthy for remaining virtuous. On the other hand, we do think of people as virtuous if they are not even tempted to do what is base. The two intuitions conflict, yet each is persuasive. This usually shows that more analysis is needed. The interested reader may wish to go back to Foot's article and proceed from there.

Modern philosophers tend to reject the Augustinian thesis that something in man is ineradicably corrupt. Kant and Butler do so explicitly. Butler argues that all vice is due to self-deception stemming from a false regard for oneself. He denies that anyone loves sin.

> Vice in general consists in having an unreasonable and too great regard for ourselves, in comparison of others. Robbery and murder is never from the love of injustice or cruelty, but to gratify some other passion, to gain some supposed advantage: and it is false selfishness alone, whether cool or passionate, which makes a man resolutely pursue that end, be it ever so much to the injury of another.

Kant, too, denies the existence of any impulse to evil that is not connected with a desire to satisfy oneself in some way. "We have . . . no direct inclination towards evil as evil, but only an indirect one." If Kant and Butler are right, the evil we do is always inadvertent: It is not what we are after.

Most traditional philosophers agree that we need a uniform account of vice and virtue. We have already seen that Augustine and Abelard find the common denominator of the vices in the consent to wrongdoing in defiance of God. Butler finds it in the element of self-deception that permits people to do what they want without admitting to themselves that an action is wrong and self-debasing. Kant, we saw, finds the unity of virtue in the will. The very first philosopher to propose a unified theory of the virtues and vices was Plato, who identified virtue with knowledge and vice with ignorance. Ever since then, philosophers have been hard at work trying to give meaningful substance to what seems right about these identifications.

Several of the selections represented here belong to the kind of writing called "phenomenological description." The philosopher takes a particular vice and carefully describes it and its effects on the person who possesses it. Pure phenomenological description is free of theory or the attempt to explain what is being described. In that respect, all of the selections fall short of being purely phenomenological. But some, such as Dante's "Hypocrites," Samuel Johnson's "On Self-Deception," and Theroux's "Revenge," are pretty nearly that. And Kant's description of jealousy, envy, and spite is very straightforward with many an acute insight into these vices.

Though contemporary philosophers (and some novelists) are still in the business of praising virtue and condemning vice, the atmosphere in which this is done has changed. Nowadays writers on virtue will take pains to show that what they are praising really is a virtue and beneficial, or, if they are condemning a particular vice, will be at some pains to show that it really is a vice and harmful. For example, while the Christian philosophers simply assumed that greed or promiscuity is immoral, modern philosophers argue the pros and cons of thinking of them as immoral. In "The Evil of Lying," Charles Fried tries to give *reasons* for our belief that the liar is indeed a bad character. And Alexander Theroux shows how revenge harms the person who seeks it. Peter Singer takes on the task of justifying virtue and condemning vice in a wholesale way when he tries to show that *having* a moral sense is essential to happiness. For example, some people seem to lack any sense of right and wrong. Such persons, the "psychopaths" or "sociopaths" of psychological literature, can commit the most outrageous acts without apparent remorse. Singer argues that these amoral types lead dreary and meaningless lives and are desperately bored. Such is the price of radical vice.

Vice

PLUTARCH

TRANSLATED BY FRANK COLE BABBITT

Plutarch (46–120 A.D.) was a Greek moralist and biog-
raher. His *Lives* is a classic in the genre of short biography. Plutarch's philosophy was neo-Platonic and he was
a sharp critic of Epicureanism.

Plutarch contrasts persons of virtue with persons of
vice, claiming that the former can achieve equanimity
even in poverty. He depicts the latter as ill and peevish,
incapable of truly enjoying even the external things they
covet. Plutarch points out that we cannot rid ourselves
of vice the way we rid ourselves of bad company.
Vicious persons must live in constant proximity to their
unpleasant selves.

1. Clothes are supposed to make a man warm, not of course by
warming him themselves in the sense of adding their warmth to
him, because each garment by itself is cold, and for this reason very
often persons who feel hot and feverish keep changing from one set
of clothes to another; but the warmth which a man gives off from
his own person the clothing, closely applied to the body, confines
and enwraps, and does not allow it, when thus imprisoned in the
body, to be dissipated again. Now the same condition existing in

VICE Reprinted by permission of the publishers and the Loeb Classical Library from Plutarch's
Moralia, trans. by Frank Cole Babbitt, Cambridge, Mass.: Harvard University Press, 1928,
1956, 1962.

human affairs deceives most people, who think that, if they surround themselves with vast houses, and get together a mass of
slaves and money, they shall live pleasantly. But a pleasant and
happy life comes not from external things, but, on the contrary,
man draws on his own character as a source from which to add the
element of pleasure and joy to the things which surround him.

Bright with a blazing fire a house looks far more cheerful,

and wealth is pleasanter, and repute and power more resplendent, if
with them goes the gladness which springs from the heart; and so
too men bear poverty, exile, and old age lightly and gently in
proportion to the serenity and mildness of their character.

2. As perfumes make coarse and ragged garments fragrant, but
the body of Anchises gave off a noisome exudation,

Damping the linen robe adown his back,

so every occupation and manner of life, if attended by virtue, is
untroubled and delightful, while, on the other hand, any admixture
of vice renders those things which to others seem splendid, precious, and imposing, only troublesome, sickening, and unwelcome
to their possessors.

This man is happy deemed 'mid public throng,
But when he opes his door he's thrice a wretch;
His wife controls, commands, and always fights.

Yet it is not difficult for any man to get rid of a bad wife if he be a
real man and not a slave; but against his own vice it is not possible
to draw up a writing of divorcement and forthwith to be rid of
troubles and to be at peace, having arranged to be by himself. No,
his vice, a settled tenant of his very vitals always, both at night and
by day,

Burns, but without e'er a brand, and consigns to an eld all untimely.

For in travelling vice is a troublesome companion because of arrogance, at dinner an expensive companion owing to gluttony, and a
distressing bedfellow, since by anxieties, cares and jealousies it
drives out and destroys sleep. For what slumber there may be is a
sleep and repose for the body only, but for the soul terrors, dreams,
and agitations, because of superstition.

> When grief o'ertakes me as I close my eyes,
> I'm murdered by my dreams.

says one man. In such a state do envy, fear, temper, and licentiousness put a man. For by day vice, looking outside of itself and
conforming its attitude to others, is abashed and veils its emotions,
and does not give itself up completely to its impulses, but oftentimes resists them and struggles against them; but in the hours of
slumber, when it has escaped from opinion and law, and got away
as far as possible from feeling fear or shame, it sets every desire
stirring, and awakens its depravity and licentiousness. It "attempts
incest," as Plato says, partakes of forbidden meats, abstains from
nothing which it wishes to do, but revels in lawlessness so far as it
can, with images and visions which end in no pleasure or accomplishment of desire, but have only the power to stir to fierce
activity the emotional and morbid propensities.

3. Where, then, is the pleasure in vice, if in no part of it is to be
found freedom from care and grief, or contentment or tranquillity
or calm? For a well-balanced and healthy condition of the body
gives room for engendering the pleasures of the flesh; but in the
soul lasting joy and gladness cannot possibly be engendered, unless
it provide itself first with cheerfulness, fearlessness, and coura-
geousness as a basis to rest upon, or as a calm tranquillity that no
billows disturb; otherwise, even though some hope or delectation
lure us with a smile, anxiety suddenly breaks forth, like a hidden
rock appearing in fair weather, and the soul is overwhelmed and
confounded.

4. Heap up gold, amass silver, build stately promenades, fill
your hourse with slaves and the city with your debtors; unless you
lay level the emotions of your soul, put a stop to your insatiate
desires, and quit yourself of fears and anxieties, you are but decant-
ing wine for a man in a fever, offering honey to a bilious man, and
preparing tid-bits and dainties for sufferers from colic or dysentery,
who cannot retain them or be strengthened by them, but are only
brought nearer to death thereby. Does not your observation of sick
persons teach you that they dislike and reject and decline the finest
and costliest viands which their attendants offer and try to force
upon them; and then later, when their whole condition has
changed, and good breathing, wholesome blood, and normal
temperature have returned to their bodies, they get up and have joy

and satisfaction in eating plain bread with cheese and cress? It is such a condition that reason creates in the soul. You will be contented with your lot if you learn what the honourable and good is. You will be luxurious in poverty, and live like a king, and you will find no less satisfaction in the care-free life of a private citizen than in the life connected with high military or civic office. If you become a philosopher, you will live not unpleasantly, but you will learn to subsist pleasantly anywhere and with any resources. Wealth will give your gladness for the good you will do to many, poverty for your freedom from many cares, repute for the honours you will enjoy, and obscurity for the certainty that you shall not be envied.

STUDY QUESTIONS

1. Plutarch seems to deny that vice contains any real pleasure or satisfaction. Do you agree?
2. Do you agree with his claim that persons given over to vice are "poor company" for everyone, including themselves?
3. Plutarch associates vice with a troubled nature, and virtue with a contented, serene nature. Are these correlations realistic?
4. Plutarch claims that the person of vice is subject to the ills of poverty, while the person of virtue transcends them. Does this claim have merit? In your opinion, what effect does economic circumstance have on a virtuous or a vicious nature?

The Depths of Vice

SAINT AUGUSTINE

TRANSLATED BY JOHN K. RYAN

A biographical sketch of Saint Augustine is found on page 159.

Augustine, writing about his sixteenth year, describes the time he and his friends stole some pears for which they had no use. He ponders the motive and concludes that the perverse desire to defy God's will, an expression of man's corrupted nature, was itself the motive. Augustine is now disgusted with his past self, but confesses that he was once ready to sin whenever someone urged, "Let's go! Let's do it!"

I wish to bring back to mind my past foulness and the carnal corruptions of my soul. This is not because I love them, but that I may love you, my God. Out of love for your love I do this. In the bitterness of my remembrance, I tread again my most evil ways, so that you may grow sweet to me, O sweetness that never fails, O sweetness happy and enduring, whichs gathers me together again from that disordered state in which I lay in shattered pieces, wherein, turned away from you, the one, I spent myself upon the many. For in my youth, I burned to get my fill of hellish things. I dared to run wild in different darksome ways of love. My comeliness wasted away. I stank in your eyes, but I was pleasing to myself and I desired to be pleasing to the eyes of men. . . .

The Stolen Fruit

Surely, Lord, your law punishes theft, as does that law written on the hearts of men, which not even iniquity itself blots out. What thief puts up with another thief with a calm mind? Not even a rich thief will pardon one who steals from him because of want. But I willed to commit theft, and I did so, not because I was driven to it by any need, unless it were by poverty of justice, and dislike of it, and by a glut of evildoing. For I stole a thing of which I had plenty of my own and of much better quality. Nor did I wish to enjoy that thing which I desired to gain by theft, but rather to enjoy the actual theft and the sin of theft.

In a garden nearby to our vineyard there was a pear tree, loaded with fruit that was desirable neither in appearance nor in taste. Late one night—to which hour, according to our pestilential custom, we had kept our street games—a group of very bad youngsters set out to shake down and rob this tree. We took great loads of fruit from it, not for our own eating, but rather to throw it to the pigs; even if we did eat a little of it, we did this to do what pleased us for the reason that it was forbidden. . . .

When there is discussion concerning a crime and why it was committed, it is usually held that there appeared possibility that the appetites would obtain some of these goods, which we have termed lower, or there was fear of losing them. These things are beautiful and fitting, but in comparison with the higher goods, which bring happiness, they are mean and base. A man commits murder: why did he do so? He coveted his victim's wife or his property; or he wanted to rob him to get money to live on; or he feared to be deprived of some such thing by the other; or he had been injured, and burned for revenge. Would anyone commit murder without reason and out of delight in murder itself? Who can believe such a thing? Of a certain senseless and utterly cruel man it was said that he was evil and cruel without reason. Nevertheless, a reason has been given, for he himself said, "I don't want to let my hand or will get out of practice through disuse." Why did he want that? Why so? It was to the end that after he had seized the city by the practice of crime, he would attain to honors, power, and wealth, and be free from fear of the law and from trouble due to lack of wealth or from a guilty conscience. Therefore, not even Catiline himself loved his crimes, but something else, for sake of which he committed them.

The Anatomy of Evil

What was it that I, a wretch, loved in you, my act of theft, my deed of crime done by night, done in the sixteenth year of my age? You were not beautiful, for you were but an act of thievery. In truth, are you anything at all, that I may speak to you? The fruit we stole was beautiful, for it was your creation, O most beautiful of all beings, creator of all things, God the good, God the supreme good and my true good. Beautiful was the fruit, but it was not what my unhappy soul desired. I had an abundance of better pears, but those pears I gathered solely that I might steal. The fruit I gathered I threw away, devouring in it only iniquity, and that I rejoiced to enjoy. For if I put any of that fruit into my mouth, my sin was its seasoning. But now, O Lord my God, I seek out what was in that theft to give me delight, and lo, there is no loveliness in it. I do not say such loveliness as there is in justice and prudence, or in man's mind, and memory, and senses, and vigorous life, nor that with which the stars are beautiful and glorious in their courses, or the land and the sea filled with their living kinds, which by new births replace those that die, nor even that flawed and shadowy beauty found in the vices that deceive us.

For pride imitates loftiness of mind, while you are the one God, highest above all things. What does ambition seek, except honor and glory, while you alone are to be honored above all else and are glorious forever? The cruelty of the mighty desires to be feared: but who is to be feared except the one God, and from his power what can be seized and stolen away, and when, or where, or how, or by whom? The caresses of the wanton call for love; but there is naught more caressing than your charity, nor is anything to be loved more wholesomely than your truth, which is beautiful and bright above all things. Curiosity pretends to be a desire for knowledge, while you know all things in the highest degree. Ignorance itself and folly are cloaked over the names of simplicity and innocence, because nothing more simple than you can be found. What is more innocent than you, whereas to evil men their own works are hostile? Sloth seeks rest as it were, but what sure rest is there apart from the Lord? Luxury of life desires to be called plenty and abundance; you are the fullness and the unfailing plenty of incorruptible pleasure. Prodigality casts but the shadow of liberality, while you are the most affluent giver of all good things. Avarice desires to possess many things, and you possess all things. Envy contends for excellence: what is more excellent than you? Anger seeks vengeance: who takes vengeance with more justice than you? Fear shrinks back at sudden and unusual things threatening what it loves, and is on watch for its own safety. But for you what is unusual or what is sudden? Or who can separate you from what you love? Where, except with you, is there firm security? Sadness wastes away over things now lost in which desire once took delight. It did not want this to happen, whereas from you nothing can be taken away.

Thus the soul commits fornication when it is turned away from you and, apart from you, seeks such pure, clean things as it does not find except when it returns to you. In a perverse way, all men imitate you who put themselves far from you, and rise up in rebellion against you. Even by such imitation of you they prove that you are the creator of all nature, and that therefore there is no place where they can depart entirely from you.

What, therefore did I love in that theft of mine, in what manner did I perversely or viciously imitate my Lord? Did it please me to go against your law, at least by trickery, for I could not do so with might? Did it please me that as a captive I should imitate a deformed liberty, by doing with impunity things illicit bearing a shadowy likeness of your omnipotence? Behold, your servant flees from his Lord and follows after a shadow! O rottenness! O monstrous life and deepest death! Could a thing give pleasure which could not be done lawfully, and which was done for no other reason but because it was unlawful? . . .

Evil Communications

What was my state of mind? Truly and clearly, it was most base, and woe was it to me who had it. Yet, what was it? Who understands his sins? It was like a thing of laughter, which reached down as it were into our hearts, that we were tricking those who did not know what we were doing and would most strenuously resent it. Why, then, did even the fact that I did not do it alone give me pleasure? Is it because no one can laugh readily when he is alone? No one indeed does laugh readily when alone. However, individual men, when alone and when no one else is about, are sometimes overcome by laughter if something very funny affects their senses or strikes their mind. But that deed I would not have done alone; alone I would never have done it.

Behold, the living record of my soul lies before you, my God. By myself I would not have committed that theft in which what pleased me was not what I stole but the fact that I stole. This would have pleased me not at all if I had done it alone; nor by myself would I have done it at all. O friendship too unfriendly! Unfathomable seducer of the mind, greed to do harm for fun and sport, desire for another's injury, arising not from desire for my own gain or for vengeance, but merely when someone says, "Let's go! Let's do it!" and it is shameful not to be shameless!

A Soul in Waste

Who can untie this most twisted and intricate mass of knots? It is a filthy thing: I do not wish to think about it; I do not wish to look upon it. I desire you, O justice and innocence, beautiful and comely to all virtuous eyes, and I desire this unto a satiety that can never be satiated. With you there is true rest and life untroubled. He who enters into you enters into the joy of his Lord, and he shall have no fear, and he shall possess his soul most happily in him who is the supreme good. I fell away from you, my God, and I went astray, too far astray from you, the support of my youth, and I became to myself a land of want.

STUDY QUESTIONS

1. Do you agree with Augustine that we often pursue vice for its own sake?
2. Explain what Augustine means when he says that, "in a perverse way, all men imitate [God] who put themselves far from [Him], and rise up in rebellion against [Him]."
3. Do you agree with Augustine's implicit claim that a crime such as theft is worse when committed for the thrill of it rather than for personal material gain?
4. People sometimes say that evil will be greatly mitigated when human nature changes for the better. Do you believe that human beings have evolved morally? Can we reasonably expect that they may become significantly more moral than they now are? What would Augustine say?

Desire and Sin

PETER ABELARD

TRANSLATED BY R. McCALLUM

Peter Abelard (1079–1142) was the foremost logician of his age and one of the greatest philosophers of the Middle Ages. He is best known, however, for his tragic love affair with Heloise. He wrote influential treatises on theology, metaphysics, logic, and ethics.

Abelard distinguishes moral defects from other "defects of the mind" such as poor memory or dullwittedness. Moral defects dispose us to bad actions; morally defective individuals have characters that lead them or allow them to do the evil they want to do. In actually sinning they consent to an evil impulse: Instead of resisting it, they will it and act on it. Abelard denies that the truly virtuous person is free of evil impulses. To be virtuous is precisely to have the capacity or disposition to control the evil impulses that even the good person possesses, by not consenting to act on those impulses. By emphasizing the active will to do right in the face of a natural desire to do wrong, Abelard is a forerunner of Kant.

Prologue

In the study of morals we deal with the defects or qualities of the mind which dispose us to bad or good actions. Defects and qualities are not only mental, but also physical. There is bodily weakness;

DESIRE AND SIN From *Abelard's Ethics*. Translated by R. McCallum. Reprinted by permission of the publisher, Basil Blackwell Publisher Limited.

there is also the endurance which we call strength. There is slug-
gishness or speed; blindness or sight. When we now speak of
defects, therefore, we pre-suppose defects of the mind, so as to
distinguish them from the physical ones. The defects of the mind
are opposed to the qualities; injustice to justice; cowardice to con-
stancy; intemperance to temperance.

Chapter I. The Defect of Mind Bearing upon Conduct

Certain defects or merits of mind have no connection with morals.
They do not make human life a matter of praise or blame. Such are
dull wits or quick insight; a good or a bad memory; ignorance or
knowledge. Each of these features is found in good and bad alike.
They have nothing to do with the system of morals, nor with
making life base or honourable. To exclude these we safeguarded
above the phrase 'defects of mind' by adding 'which dispose to bad
actions,' that is, those defects which incline the will to what least of
all either should be done or should be left undone.

Chapter II. How Does Sin Differ from a Disposition to Evil?

Defect of this mental kind is not the same thing as sin. Sin, too, is not
the same as a bad action. For example, to be irascible, that is, prone or
easily roused to the agitation of anger is a defect and moves the mind to
unpleasantly impetuous and irrational action. This defect, however,
is in the mind so that the mind is liable to wrath, even when it is not
actually roused to it. Similarly, lameness, by reason of which a man is
said to be lame, is in the man himself even when he does not walk and
reveal his lameness. For the defect is there though action be lacking.
So, also, nature or constitution renders many liable to luxury. Yet
they do not sin because they are like this, but from this very fact they
have the material of a struggle whereby they may, in the virtue of
temperance, triumph over themselves and win the crown. As Solomon says: 'Better a patient than a strong man; and the Lord of his soul
than he that taketh a city.' (Prov. xvi, 32.) For religion does not think it
degrading to be beaten by man; but it is degrading to be beaten by
one's lower self. The former defeat has been the fate of good men. But,
in the latter, we fall below ourselves. The Apostle commends victory
of this sort; 'No one shall be crowned who has not truly striven.' (2
Tim. ii, 5.) This striving, I repeat, means standing less against men
than against myself, so that defects may not lure me into base consent.

Though men cease to oppose us, our defects do not cease. The fight with them is the more dangerous because of its repetition. And as it is the more difficult, so victory is the more glorious. Men, however much they prevail over us, do not force baseness upon us, unless by their practice of vice they turn us also to it and overcome us through our own wretched consent. They may dominate our body; but while our mind is free, there is no danger to true freedom. We run no risk of base servitude. Subservience to vice, not to man, is degradation. It is the overlordship of defects and not physical serfdom which debases the soul.

Chapter III. Definition of 'Defect' and of Sin

Defect, then, is that whereby we are disposed to sin. We are, that is, inclined to consent to what we ought not to do, or to leave undone what we ought to do. Consent of this kind we rightly call sin. Here is the reproach of the soul meriting damnation or being declared guilty by God. What is that consent but to despise God and to violate His laws? God cannot be set at enmity by injury, but by contempt. He is the highest power, and is not diminished by any injury, but He avenges contempt of Himself. Our sin, therefore, is contempt of the Creator. To sin is to despise the Creator; that is, not to do for Him what we believe we should do for Him, or, not to renounce what we think should be renounced on His behalf. We have defined sin negatively by saying that it means not doing or not renouncing what we ought to do or renounce. Clearly, then, we have shown that sin has no reality. It exists rather in *not being* than in *being*. Similarly we could define shadows by saying: The absence of light where light usually is.

Perhaps you object that sin is the desire or will to do an evil deed, and that this will or desire condemns us before God in the same way as the will to do a good deed justifies us. There is as much quality, you suggest, in the good will as there is sin in the evil will; and it is no less 'in being' in the latter than in the former. By willing to do what we believe to be pleasing to God we please Him. Equally, by willing to do what we believe to be displeasing to God, we displease Him and seem either to violate or despise His nature.

But diligent attention will show that we must think far otherwise of this point. We frequently err, and from no evil will at all. Indeed, the evil will itself, when restrained, though it may not be quenched, procures the palm-wreath for those who resist it. It provides, not merely the materials for combat, but also the crown of glory. It should be spoken of rather as a certain inevitable weakness than as sin. Take, for example, the case of an innocent servant whose harsh master is moved with fury against him. He pursues the servant, drawing his sword with intent to kill him. For a while the servant flies and avoids death as best he can. At last, forced all unwillingly to it, he kills his master so as not to be killed by him. Let anyone say what sort of evil will there was in this deed. His will was only to flee from death and preserve his own life. Was this an evil will? You reply: 'I do not think this was an evil will. But the will that he had to kill the master who was pursuing him was evil.' Your answer would be admirable and acute if you could show that the servant really willed what you say that he did. But, as I insisted, he was unwillingly forced to his deed. He protracted his master's life as long as he could, knowing that danger also threatened his own life from such a crime. How, then was a deed done voluntarily by which he incurred danger to his own life? . . .

Sin, therefore, is sometimes committed without an evil will. Thus sin cannot be defined as 'will.' True, you will say, when we sin under constraint, but not when we sin willingly, for instance, when we will to do something which we know ought not to be done by us. There the evil will and sin seem to be the same thing. For example a man sees a woman; his concupiscence is aroused; his mind is enticed by fleshly lust and stirred to base desire. This wish, this lascivious longing, what else can it be, you say, than sin?

I reply: What if that wish may be bridled by the power of temperance? What if its nature is never to be entirely extinguished but to persist in struggle and not fully fail even in defeat? For where is the battle if the antagonist is away? Whence the great reward without grave endurance? When the fight is over nothing remains but to reap the reward. Here we strive in contest in order elsewhere to obtain as victors a crown. Now, for a contest, an opponent is needed who will resist, not one who simply submits. This opponent is our evil will over which we triumph when we subjugate it to the divine will. But we do not entirely destroy it. For we needs must ever expect to encounter our enemy. What achievement before God is it if we undergo nothing contrary to our own will, but merely practice what we please? Who will be grateful to us if in what we say we do for him we merely satisfy our own fancy?

You will say, what merit have we with God in acting willingly or unwillingly? Certainly none: I reply. He weighs the intention rather than the deed in his recompense. Nor does the deed, whether it proceed from a good or an evil will, add anything to the merit, as we shall show shortly. But when we set His will before our own so as to follow His and not ours, our merit with God is magnified, in accordance with that perfect word of Truth: 'I came not to do mine own will, but the will of Him that sent me." (John vi, 38.) To this end He exhorts us: 'If anyone comes to me, and does not hate father, and mother . . . yea his own soul also, he is not worthy of me.' (Luke xiv, 26.) That is to say, 'unless a man renounces his parents' influence and his own will and submits himself to my teaching, he is not worthy of me.' Thus we are bidden to hate our father, not to destroy him. Similarly with our own will. We must not be led by it; at the same time, we are not asked to root it out altogether.

When the Scripture says: 'Go not after your own desires' (Eccles. xviii, 30) . . . I think that it is plain that no natural physical delight can be set down as sin, nor can it be called guilt for men to delight in what, when it is done, must involve the feeling of delight.

For example, if anyone obliged a monk, bound in chains, to lie among women, and the monk by the softness of the couch and by contact with his fair flatterers is allured into delight, though not into consent, who shall presume to designate guilt the delight which is naturally awakened?

You may urge, with some thinkers, that the carnal pleasure, even in lawful intercourse, involves sin. Thus David says: 'Behold in sin was I conceived.' (Ps. 1, 7.) And the Apostle, when he had said: 'Ye return to it again' (I Cor. vii, 5), adds nevertheless, 'This I say by way of concession, not of command.' (ibid., v, 6.) Yet authority rather than reason, seems to dictate the view that we should allow simple physical delight to be sin. For, assuredly, David was conceived not in fornication, but in matrimony: and concession, that is forgiveness, does not, as this standpoint avers, condone when there is no guilt to forgive. As for what David meant when he says that he had been conceived 'in iniquity' or 'in sin' and does not say 'whose' sin, he referred to the general curse of original sin, wherein from the guilt of our first parents each is subject to damnation, as it is elsewhere stated: 'None are pure of stain, not the infant a day old, if he has life on this earth.' As the blessed Jerome reminds us and as manifest reason teaches, the soul of a young child is without sin. If, then, it is pure of sin, how is it also impure by sinful corruption? We must understand the infant's purity from sin in reference to its personal guilt. But its contact with sinful corruption, its 'stain,' is in reference to penalty owed by mankind because of Adam's sin. He who has not yet perceived by reason what he ought to do cannot be guilty of contempt of God. Yet he is not free from the contamination of the sin of his first parents, from which he contracts the penalty, though not the guilt, and bears in penalty what they committed in guilt. When, therefore, David says that he was conceived in iniquity or sin, he sees himself subject to the general sentence of damnation from the guilt of his racial parents, and he assigns the sins, not to his father and mother but to his first parents. . . .

We come, then, to this conclusion, that no one who sets out to assert that all fleshly desire is sin may say that the sin itself is increased by the doing of it. For this would mean extending the consent of the soul into the exercise of the action. In short, one would be stained not only by consent to baseness, but also by the mire of the deed, as if what happens externally in the body could possibly soil the soul. Sin is not, therefore, increased by the doing of an action: and nothing mars the soul except what is of its own nature, namely consent. This we affirmed was alone sin, preceding action in will, or subsequent to the performance of action. Although we wish for, or do, what is unseemly, we do not therefore sin. For such deeds not uncommonly occur without there being any sin. On the other hand, there may be consent without the external effects, as we have indicated. There was wish without consent in the case of the man who was attracted by a woman whom he caught sight of, or who was tempted by his neighbour's fruit, but who was not enticed into consent. There was evil consent without evil desire in the servant who unwillingly killed his master.

Certain acts which ought not to be done often are done, and without any sin, when, for instance, they are committed under force or ignorance. No one, I think, ignores this fact. A woman under constraint of violence, lies with another's husband. A man, taken by some trick, sleeps with one whom he supposed to be his wife, or kills a man, in the belief that he himself has the right to be both judge and executioner. Thus to desire the wife of another or actually to lie with her is not sin. But to consent to that desire or to that action is sin. This consent to covetousness the law calls covetousness in saying: 'Thou shalt not covet.' (Deut. v, 21.) Yet that which we cannot avoid ought not to be forbidden, nor that wherein, as we said, we do not sin. But we should be cautioned about the consent to covetousness. So, too, the saying of the Lord must be understood: 'Whosoever shall look upon a woman to desire her.' (Matt. v, 28.) That is, whosoever shall so look upon her as a slip into consent to covetousness, 'has already committed adultery with her in his heart' (Matt. v, 28), even though he may not have committed adultery in deed. He is guilty of sin, though there be no sequel to his intention. . . .

Blessed Augustine, in his careful view of this question, reduces every sin or command to terms of charity and covetousness, and not to works. 'The law,' he says, 'inculcates nothing but charity, and forbids nothing but covetousness.' The Apostle, also, asserts: 'All the law is contained in one word: thou shalt love thy neighbour as thyself,' (Rom. xiii, 8, 10), and again, 'Love is the fulfilling of the law.' (ibid.)

Whether you actually give alms to a needy person, or charity makes you ready to give, makes no difference to the merit of the deed. The will may be there when the opportunity is not. Nor does it rest entirely with you to deal with every case of need which you encounter. Actions which are right and actions which are far from right are done by good and bad men alike. The intention alone separates the two classes of men. . . .

Briefly to summarize the above argument: Four things were postulated which must be carefully distinguished from one another.

1. Imperfection of soul, making us liable to sin.
2. Sin itself, which we decided is consent to evil or contempt of God.
3. The will or desire of evil.
4. The evil deed.

To wish is not the same thing as to fulfil a wish. Equally, to sin is not the same as to carry out a sin. In the first case, we sin by consent of the soul: the second is a matter of the external effect of an action, namely, when we fulfil in deed that whereunto we have previously consented. When, therefore, temptation is said to proceed through three stages, suggestion, delight, consent, it must be understood that, like our first parents, we are frequently led along these three paths to the commission of sin. The devil's persuasion comes *first* promising from the taste of the forbidden fruit immortality. Delight follows. When the woman sees the beautiful tree, and perceives that the fruit is good, her appetite is whetted by the anticipated pleasure of tasting. This desire she ought to have repressed, so as to obey God's command. But in consenting to it, she was drawn *secondly* into sin. By penitence she should have put right this fault, and obtained pardon. Instead, she *thirdly* consummated the sin by the deed. Eve thus passed through the three stages to the commission of sin.

By the same avenues we also arrive not at sin, but at the action of sin, namely, the doing of an unseemly deed through the suggestion or prompting of something within us. If we already know that such a deed will be pleasant, our imagination is held by anticipatory delight and we are tempted thereby in thought. So long as we give consent to such delight, we sin. Lastly, we pass to the third stage, and actually commit the sin.

It is agreed by some thinkers that carnal suggestion, even though the person causing the suggestion be not present, should be included under sinful suggestion. For example, a man having seen a woman falls into a sensual desire of her. But it seems that this kind of suggestion should simply be called delight. This delight, and other delights of the like kind, arise naturally and, as we said above, they are not sinful. The Apostle calls them 'human temptations.' No temptation has taken you yet which was not common to men. God is faithful, and will not suffer you to be tempted above what you are able; but will, with the temptation make a way of escape, that you may be able to bear it.' By temptation is meant, in general, any movement of the soul to do something unseemly, whether in wish or consent. We speak of human temptation without which it is hardly or never possible for human weakness to exist. Such are sexual desire, or the pleasures of the table. From these the Psalmist asks to be delivered when he says: 'Deliver me from my wants, O Lord' (Ps. xxiv, 17); that is, from the temptations of natural and necessary appetites that they may not influence him into sinful consent. Or, he may mean: 'When this life is over, grant me to be without those temptations of which life has been full.'

When the Apostle says: 'No temptation has taken you but what is human,' his statement amounts to this: Even if the soul be stirred by that delight which is, as we said, human temptation, yet God would not lead the soul into that consent wherein sin consists. Someone may object: But by what power of our own are we able to resist those desires? We may reply: 'God is faithful, who will not allow you to resist those desires? We may reply: 'God is faithful, who will not allow you to be tempted,' as the Scripture says. In other words: We should rather trust him than rely upon ourselves. He promises help, and is true to his promises. He is faithful, so that we should have complete faith in him. Out of pity God diminishes the degree of human temptation, does not suffer us to be tempted above what we are able, in order that it may not drive us to sin at a pace we cannot endure, when, that is, we strive to resist it. Then, too, God turns the temptation to our advantage: for He trains us thereby so that the recurrence of temptation causes us less care, and we fear less the onset of a foe over whom we have already triumphed, and whom we know how to meet. . . .

STUDY QUESTIONS

1. Abelard maintains that persons who will to murder others but are externally prevented from carrying out their purpose have sinned as completely as those who actually murder. Do you agree? What are the implications of this for moral philosophy?
2. The moral report card has one grade for accomplishment and another for effort. Which grade counts more for Abelard? How does he argue for giving it more weight?
3. What does Abelard mean by "consent to baseness"? How does "consent" differ from "desire"? Can consent to baseness occur without base desire?
4. How does Abelard's Christian conception of vice differ from one that is not grounded in a religious doctrine? Is the difference significant?

The Hypocrites

DANTE ALIGHIERI

TRANSLATED BY JOHN CIARDI

Dante Alighieri (1265–1321) is the Florentine author of the *Divine Comedy*, which is regarded as one of the supreme literary works of all time. It recounts the poet's journey through Hell (the *Inferno*), Purgatory (the *Purgatorio*), and finally Heaven (the *Paradiso*), and describes the fate of human souls after death.

Dante intended the *Divine Comedy* as an allegory. In a letter to his patron he wrote, "[I]ts subject is: 'Man, as by good or ill deserts, in the exercise of his free choice, becomes liable to rewarding or punishing justice.' " The *Inferno* is also meant as an allegorical description of the state of sinners' souls while they are still alive. Thus, hypocrites, even while alive, may appear to be "all dazzle, golden and fair," but on the inside they are heavy, leaden, and tormented. For Dante, the internal effects of sin are as punishing as the torments of Hell.

About us now in the depth of the pit we found
  a painted people, weary and defeated.
  Slowly, in pain, they paced it round and round.

All wore great cloaks cut to as ample a size
  as those worn by the Benedictines of Cluny.[1]
  The enormous hoods were drawn over their eyes.

THE HYPOCRITES From the *Inferno* by Dante Alighieri. Translated by John Ciardi. Copyright 1954, 1982 by John Ciardi. Reprinted by arrangement with the New American Library.

The outside is all dazzle, golden and fair;
   the inside, lead, so heavy that Frederick's capes,[2]
   compared to these, would seem as light as air.

O weary mantle for eternity!
   We turned to the left again along their course,
   listening to their moans of misery,

but they moved so slowly down that barren strip,
   tired by their burden, that our company
   was changed at every movement of the hip.[3]

And walking thus, I said: "As we go on,
   may it please you to look about among these people
   for any whose name or history may be known."

And one who understood Tuscan cried to us there
   as we hurried past: "I pray you check your speed,
   you who run so fast through the sick air:

it may be I am one who will fit your case."
   And at his words my Master turned and said:
   "Wait now, then go with him at his own pace."

I waited there, and saw along that track
   two souls who seemed in haste to be with me;
   but the narrow way and their burden held them back.

When they had reached me down that narrow way
   they stared at me in silence and amazement,
   then turned to one another. I heard one say:

---

[1] *the Benedictines of Cluny*: The habit of these monks was especially ample and elegant. St. Bernard once wrote ironically to a nephew who had entered this monastery: "If length of sleeves and amplitude of hood made for holiness, what could hold me back from following [your lead]."

[2] *Frederick's capes*: Frederick II executed persons found guilty of treason by fastening them into a sort of leaden shell. The doomed man was then placed in a cauldron over a fire and the lead was melted around him.

[3] *our company was changed, etc.*: Another tremendous Dantean figure. Sense: "They moved so slowly that at every step (movement of the hip) we found ourselves beside new sinners."

"This one seems, by the motion of his throat,
    to be alive; and if they are dead, how is it
    they are allowed to shed the leaden coat?"

And then to me "O Tuscan, come so far
    to the college of the sorry hypocrites,
    do not disdain to tell us who you are."

And I: "I was born and raised a Florentine
    on the green and lovely banks of Arno's waters,
    I go with the body that was always mine.

But who are *you*, who sighing as you go
    distill in floods of tears that drown your cheeks?
    What punishment is this that glitters so?"

"These burnished robes are of thick lead," said one,
    "and are hung on us like counterweights, so heavy
    that we, their weary fulcrums, creak and groan.

Jovial Friars and Bolognese were we.[4]
    We were chosen jointly by your Florentines[5]
    to keep the peace, an office usually

held by a single man; near the Gardingo[6]
    one still may see the sort of peace we kept.
    I was called Catalono, he, Loderingo."

---

[4]*Jovial Friars*: A nickname given to the military monks of the order of the Glorious Virgin Mary founded at Bologna in 1261. Their original aim was to serve as peacemakers, enforcers of order, and protectors of the weak, but their observance of their rules became so scandalously lax, and their management of worldly affairs so self-seeking, that the order was disbanded by Papal decree.

[5]*We were chosen jointly . . . to keep the peace*: Catalano del Malavolti (c. 1210–1285), a Guelph, and Loderingo degli Andolo (c. 1210–1293), a Ghibelline, were both Bolognese and, as brothers of the Jovial Friars, both had served as *podestà* (the chief officer charged with keeping the peace) of many cities for varying terms. In 1266 they were jointly appointed to the office of *podestà* of Florence on the theory that a bipartisan administration by men of God would bring peace to the city. Their tenure of office was marked by great violence, however; and they were forced to leave in a matter of months. Modern scholarship has established the fact that they served as instruments of Clement IV's policy in Florence, working at his orders to overthrow the Ghibellines under the guise of an impartial administration.

[6]*Gardingo*: The site of the palace of the Ghibelline family degli Uberti. In the riots resulting from the maladministration of the two Jovial Friars, the Ghibellines were forced out of the city and the Uberti palace was razed.

I began: "O Friars, your evil . . ."—and then I saw
    a figure crucified upon the ground[7]
    by three great stakes, and I fell still in awe.

When he saw me there, he began to puff great sighs
    into his beard, convulsing all his body;
    and Friar Catalano, following my eyes,

said to me: "That one nailed across the road
    counselled the Pharisees that it was fitting
    one man be tortured for the public good.

Naked he lies fixed there, as you see,
    in the path of all who pass; there he must feel
    the weight of all through all eternity.

His father–in–law and the others of the Council[8]
    which was a seed of wrath to all the Jews,
    are similarly staked for the same evil."

Then I saw Virgil marvel for a while[9]
    over that soul so ignominiously
    stretched on the cross in Hell's eternal exile.

Then, turning, he asked the Friar: "If your law permit,
    can you tell us if somewhere along the right
    there is some gap in the stone wall of the pit

through which we two may climb to the next brink
    without the need of summoning the Black Angels
    and forcing them to raise us from this sink?"

He: "Nearer than you hope, there is a bridge
    that runs from the great circle of the scarp
    and crosses every ditch from ridge to ridge,

---

[7] *a figure crucified upon the ground*: Caiaphas. His words were: "It is expedient that one man shall die for the people and that the whole nation perish not." (*John* xi, 50).

[8] *his father-in-law and the others*: Annas, father-in-law of Caiaphas, was the first before whom Jesus was led upon his arrest. (*John* xviii, 13). He had Jesus bound and delivered to Caiaphas.

[9] *I saw Virgil marvel*: Caiaphas had not been there on Virgil's first descent into Hell.

except that in this it is broken; but with care
    you can mount the ruins which lie along the slope
    and make a heap on the bottom." My Guide stood
                            there

motionless for a while with a dark look.
    At last he said: "He lied about this business,
    who spears the sinners yonder with his hook."[10]

And the Friar: "Once at Bologna I heard the wise
    discussing the Devil's sins; among them I heard
    that he is a liar and the father of lies."

When the sinner had finished speaking, I saw the face
    of my sweet Master darken a bit with anger:[11]
    he set off at a great stride from that place,

and I turned from that weighted hypocrite
    to follow in the prints of his dear feet.

STUDY QUESTIONS

1. Why is hypocrisy a vice?
2. What forms of hypocrisy are most damaging?
3. Do hypocrites deceive themselves as well as others?
4. Is Dante right about the psychological and spiritual effects of hypocrisy? Does hypocrisy weigh people down and make them "weary and defeated"?
5. Can a hypocrite be happy?

---

[10]*he lied . . . who spears the sinners yonder*: Malacoda.

[11]*darken a bit*: The original is *turbato un poco d'ira*. A bit of anger befits the righteous indignation of Human Reason, but immoderate anger would be out of character. One of the sublimities of Dante's writing is the way in which even the smallest details reinforce the great concepts.

Self-deception

SAMUEL JOHNSON

Samuel Johnson (1709–1784), immortalized by his famous biographer, Boswell, was one of the most prominent figures of eighteenth-century English intellectual life. He wrote essays, novels, biographies, political tracts, a dictionary, and poetry, all in a scintillating style.

Johnson examines the devices of self-deceivers. One device they use is to congratulate themselves on a single act of generosity, thereby conferring on themselves the attribute "compassionate" or "generous," even though the vast majority of their actions are mean and self-serving. Or they may praise goodness verbally, and thereby deceive themselves into thinking they are good. Still another device is to appear virtuous by dwelling on the evils of others. Self-deceivers will try to keep their distance from people who truly know what they are like, preferring the company of those who won't expose them to themselves. And they avoid "self-communion."

One sophism by which men persuade themselves that they have those virtues which they really want, is formed by the substitution of single acts for habits. A miser who once relieved a friend from the danger of a prison, suffers his imagination to dwell for ever upon his own heroick generosity; he yields his heart up to indignation at those who are blind to merit, or insensible to misery, and who can please themselves with the enjoyment of that wealth, which they never permit others to partake. From any censures of the world, or reproaches of his conscience, he has an appeal to action and to knowledge; and though his whole life is a course of rapacity and avarice, he concludes himself to be tender and liberal, because he has once performed an act of liberality and tenderness.

As a glass which magnifies objects by the approach of one end to the eye, lessens them by the application of the other, so vices are extenuated by the inversion of that fallacy, by which virtues are augmented. Those faults which we cannot conceal from our own notice, are considered, however frequent, not as habitual corruptions, or settled practices, but as casual failures, and single lapses. A man who has, from year to year, set his country to sale, either for the gratification of his ambition or resentment, confesses that the heat of party now and then betrays the severest virtue to measures that cannot be seriously defended. He that spends his days and nights in riot and debauchery, owns that his passions oftentimes overpower his resolution. But each comforts himself that his faults are not without precedent, for the best and the wisest men have given way to the violence of sudden temptations.

There are men who always confound the praise of goodness with the practice, and who believe themselves mild and moderate, charitable and faithful, because they have exerted their eloquence in commendation of mildness, fidelity, and other virtues. This is an error almost universal among those that converse much with dependents, with such whose fear or interest disposes them to a seeming reverence for any declamation, however enthusiastick, and submission to any boast, however arrogant. Having none to recall their attention to their lives, they rate themselves by the goodness of their opinions, and forget how much more easily men may shew their virtue in their talk than in their actions.

The tribe is likewise very numerous of those who regulate their lives, not by the standard of religion, but the measure of other men's virtue; who lull their own remorse with the remembrance of crimes more atrocious than their own, and seem to believe that they are not bad while another can be found worse.

For escaping these and a thousand other deceits, many expedients have been proposed. Some have recommended the frequent consultation of a wise friend, admitted to intimacy, and encouraged to sincerity. But this appears a remedy by no means adapted to general use: for in order to secure the virtue of one, it presupposes more virtue in two than will generally be found. In the first, such a desire of rectitude and amendment, as may incline him to hear his own accusation from the mouth of him whom he esteems, and by whom, therefore, he will always hope that his faults are not discovered; and in the second such zeal and honesty, as will make him content for his friend's advantage to lose his kindness.

A long life may be passed without finding a friend in whose understanding and virtue we can equally confide, and whose opinion we can value at once for its justness and sincerity. A weak man, however honest, is not qualified to judge. A man of the world, however penetrating, is not fit to counsel. Friends are often chosen for similitude of manners, and therefore each palliates the other's failings, because they are his own. Friends are tender and unwilling to give pain, or they are interested, and fearful to offend.

These objections have inclined others to advise, that he who would know himself, should consult his enemies, remember the reproaches that are vented to his face, and listen for the censures that are uttered in private. For his great business is to know his faults, and those malignity will discover, and resentment will reveal. But this precept may be often frustrated; for it seldom happens that rivals or opponents are suffered to come near enough to know our conduct with so much exactness as that conscience should allow and reflect the accusation. The charge of an enemy is often totally false, and commonly so mingled with falsehood, that the mind takes advantage from the failure of one part to discredit the rest, and never suffers any disturbance afterward from such partial reports.

Yet it seems that enemies have been always found by experience the most faithful monitors; for adversity has ever been considered as the state in which a man most easily becomes acquainted with himself, and this effect it must produce by withdrawing flatterers, whose business it is to hide our weaknesses from us, or by giving loose to malice, and licence to reproach; or at least by cutting off those pleasures which called us away from meditation on our conduct, and repressing that pride which too easily persuades us, that we merit whatever we enjoy.

Part of these benefits it is in every man's power to procure himself, by assigning proper portions of his life to the examination of the rest, and by putting himself frequently in such a situation by retirement and abstraction, as may weaken the influence of external objects. By this practice he may obtain the solitude of adversity without its melancholy, its instructions without its censures, and its sensibility without its perturbations.

The necessity of setting the world at a distance from us, when we are to take a survey of ourselves, has sent many from high stations to the severities of a monastick life; and indeed, every man deeply engaged in business, if all regard to another state be not extinguished, must have the conviction, tho', perhaps, not the resolution of Valdesso, who, when he solicited Charles the Fifth to dismiss him, being asked, whether he retired upon disgust, answered that he laid down his commission, for no other reason but because "there ought to be some time for sober reflection between the life of a soldier and his death."

There are few conditions which do not entangle us with sublunary hopes and fears, from which it is necessary to be at intervals disencumbered, that we may place ourselves in his presence who views effects in their causes, and actions in their motives; that we may, as Chillingworth expresses it, consider things as if there were no other beings in the world but God and ourselves; or, to use language yet more awful, "may commune with our own hearts, and be still."

STUDY QUESTIONS

1. Self-deceivers are sometimes virtuous. How, in Johnson's opinion, does this aid in self-deception?
2. What part does self-deception play in our choice of friends?
3. Why does Johnson say that we should consult not our friends but our enemies if we want to learn about ourselves? Do you think he is right?
4. What techniques of self-deception does Johnson mention? Can you think of others?

Upon Self-deceit

BISHOP BUTLER

Joseph Butler (1692–1752) was an English moral philosopher and theologian. In 1738, he was made a bishop of the Church of England. Butler's *Fifteen Sermons*, from which the present selection is taken, are still admired for their style, acumen, and good sense.

Butler cites the example of King David to show how easily even good persons can deceive themselves. King David committed an injustice without condemning himself, but was morally outraged on hearing that someone else had done a similar thing. Butler points out the difficulty of living by the ancient dictum "Know thyself." Self-deception often works in the service of self-regard. We want something and make ourselves believe we do right in acquiring it when, in fact, we do wrong. Moreover, we retain a good opinion of ourselves by avoiding the company of those who would condemn us. Self-deceit is especially prevalent in the undefined areas of moral behavior where moral duties are not *explicit*. There self-deceivers can be ungenerous and spiteful, and still remain within the letter of the law, comfortably at peace with their conscience. Butler argues that self-deception is a very grave moral defect because it enables us to do evil in a self-righteous manner. Self-deception "undermines the whole principle of good" and so is worse than open, unhypocritical wickedness.

UPON SELF-DECEIT From *Fifteen Sermons upon Human Nature* by Joseph Butler (1726).

Nathan charges the self-complacent David.

These words are the application of Nathan's parable to David, upon occasion of his adultery with Bathsheba, and the murder of Uriah her husband. The parable, which is related in the most beautiful simplicity, is this: *There were two men in one city; the one rich, and the other poor. The rich man had exceeding many flocks and herds: but the poor man had nothing, save one little ewe lamb, which he had bought and nourished up: and it grew up together with him, and with his children: it did eat of his own meat, and drank of his own cup, and lay in his bosom, and was unto him as a daughter. And there came a traveller unto the rich man, and he spared to take of his own flock and of his own herd, to dress for the wayfaring man that was come unto him; but took the poor man's lamb, and dressed it for the man that was come to him. And David's anger was greatly kindled against the man; and he said to Nathan, As the Lord liveth, the man that hath done this thing shall surely die: and he shall restore the lamb fourfold, because he did this thing, and because he had not pity.* David passes sentence, not only that there should be a fourfold restitution made; but he proceeds to the rigour of justice, *the man that hath done this thing shall die:* and this judgment is pronounced with the utmost indignation against such an act of inhumanity; *As the Lord liveth, he shall surely die: and his anger was greatly kindled against the man.* And the Prophet answered, *Thou art the man.* He had been guilty of much greater inhumanity, with the utmost deliberation, thought, and contrivance. Near a year must have passed, between the time of the commission of his crimes, and the time of the Prophet's coming to him; and it does not appear from the story, that he had in all this while the least remorse or contrition.

Nothing is more strange than our self-partiality.

There is not any thing, relating to men and characters, more surprising and unaccountable, than this partiality to themselves, which is observable in many; as there is nothing of more melancholy reflection, respecting morality, virtue, and religion. Hence it is that many men seem perfect strangers to their own characters. They think, and reason, and judge quite differently upon any matter relating to themselves, from what they do in cases of others where they are not interested. Hence it is one hears people exposing follies, which they themselves are eminent for; and talking with great severity against particular vices, which, if all the world be not mistaken, they themselves are notoriously guilty of. This self-ignorance and self-partiality may be in all different degrees. It is a lower degree of it which David himself refers to in these words, *Who can tell how oft he offendeth? O cleanse thou me from my secret faults.* This is the ground of that advice of Elihu to Job: *Surely it is meet to be said unto God,—That which I see not, teach thou me; if I have done iniquity, I will do no more.* And Solomon saw this thing in a very strong light, when he said, *He that trusteth his own heart is a fool.*

Hence the 'Know thyself' of the ancients.

This likewise was the reason why that precept, *Know thyself,* was so frequently inculcated by the philosophers of old. For if it were not for that partial and fond regard to ourselves, it would certainly be no great difficulty to know our own character, what passes within, the bent and bias of our mind; much less would there be any difficulty in judging rightly of our own actions. But from this partiality it frequently comes to pass, that the observation of many men's being themselves last of all acquainted with what falls out in their own families, may be applied to a nearer home, to what passes within their own breasts.

Usual temper: (a) absence of mistrust: (b) assumption that all is right: (c) disregard of precept, when against ourselves.

There is plainly, in the generality of mankind, an absence of doubt or distrust, in a very great measure, as to their moral character and behaviour; and likewise a disposition to take for granted, that all is right and well with them in these respects. The former is owing to their not reflecting, not exercising their judgment upon themselves; the latter, to self-love. I am not speaking of that extravagance, which is sometimes to be met with; instances of persons declaring in words at length, that they never were in the wrong, nor had ever any diffidence to the justness of their conduct, in their whole lives. No, these people are too far gone to have anything said to them. The thing before us is indeed of this kind, but in a lower degree, and confined to the moral character; somewhat of which we almost all of us have, without reflecting upon it. Now consider how long, and how grossly, a person of the best understanding might be imposed upon by one of whom he had not any suspicion, and in whom he placed an entire confidence; especially if there were friendship and real kindness in the case: surely this holds even stronger with respect to that self we are all so fond of. Hence arises in men a disregard of reproof and instruction, rules of conduct and moral discipline, which occasionally come in their way: a disregard, I say, of these; not in every respect, but in this single one, namely, as what may be of service to them in particular towards mending their own hearts and tempers, and making them better men. It never in earnest comes into their thoughts, whether such admonitions may not relate, and be of service to themselves; and this quite distinct from a positive persuasion to the contrary, a persuasion from reflection that they are innocent and blameless in those respects. Thus we may invert the observation which is somewhere made upon Brutus, that he never read, but in order to make himself a better man. It scarce comes into the thoughts of the generality of mankind, that this use is to be made of moral reflections which they meet with; that this use, I say, is to be made of them by themselves, for every body observes and wonders that it is not done by others.

Also exclusive self-interest.

Further, there are instances of persons having so fixed and steady an eye upon their own interest, whatever they place it in, and the interest of those whom they consider as themselves, as in a manner to regard nothing else; their views are almost confined to this alone. Now we cannot be acquainted with, or in any propriety of speech be said to know any thing, but what we attend to. If therefore they attend only to one side, they really will not, cannot see or know what is to be alleged on the other. Though a man hath the best eyes in the world, he cannot see any way but that which he turns them. Thus these persons, without passing over the least, the most minute thing, which can possibly be urged in favour of themselves, shall overlook entirely the plainest and most obvious things on the other side.

They inquire only to justify.

And whilst they are under the power of this temper, thought and consideration upon the matter before them has scarce any tendency to set them right: because they are engaged; and their deliberation concerning an action to be done, or reflection upon it afterwards, is not to see whether it be right, but to find out reasons to justify or palliate it; palliate it, not to others, but to themselves.

With self–ignorance, perhaps, only in the favourite propensity.

In some there is to be observed a general ignorance of themselves, and wrong way of thinking and judging in every thing relating to themselves; their fortune, reputation, every thing in which self can come in: and this perhaps attended with the rightest judgment in all other matters. In others this partiality is not so general, has not taken hold of the whole man, but is confined to some particular favourite passion, interest, or pursuit; suppose ambition, covetousness, or any other. And these persons may probably judge and determine what is perfectly just and proper, even in things in which they themselves are concerned, if these things have no relation to their particular favourite passion or pursuit. Hence arises that amazing incongruity, and seeming inconsistency of character, from whence slight observers take it for granted, that the whole is hypocritical and false; not being able otherwise to reconcile the several parts: whereas in truth there is real honesty, so far as it goes. There is such a thing as men's being honest to such a degree, and in such respects, but no further. And this, as it is true, so it is absolutely necessary to be taken notice of, and allowed them; such general and undistinguishing censure of their whole character, as designing and false, being one main thing which confirms them in their self–deceit. They know that the whole censure is not true; and so take for granted that no part of it is.

The judgment is perverted through the passions.

But to go on with the explanation of the thing itself: Vice in general consists in having an unreasonable and too great regard to ourselves, in comparison of others. Robbery and murder is never from the love of injustice or cruelty, but to gratify some other passion, to gain some supposed advantage: and it is false selfishness alone, whether cool or passionate, which makes a man resolutely pursue that end, be it ever so much to the injury of another. But whereas, in common and ordinary wickedness, this unreasonable-ness, this partiality and selfishness, relates only, or chiefly, to the temper and passions in the characters we are now considering, it reaches to the understanding, and influences the very judgment. And, besides that general want of distrust and diffidence concerning our own character, there are, you see, two things, which may thus prejudice and darken the understanding itself: that overfondness for ourselves, which we are all so liable to; and also being under the power of any particular passion or appetite, or engaged in any particular pursuit. And these, especially the last of the two, may be in so great a degree, as to influence our judgment, even of other persons and their behavior. Thus a man, whose temper is former to ambition or covetousness, shall even approve of them sometimes in others. . . .

Frequent difficulty of defining: enhanced by vice.

It is to be observed then, that as there are express determinate acts of wickedness, such as murder, adultery, theft: so, on the other hand, there are numberless cases in which the vice and wickedness cannot be exactly defined; but consists in a certain general temper and course of action, or in the neglect of some duty, suppose charity or any other, whose bounds and degrees are not fixed. This is the very province of self-deceit and self-partiality: here it governs without check or control. 'For what commandment is there broken? Is there a transgression where there is no law? a vice which cannot be defined?'

Whoever will consider the whole commerce of human life, will see that a great part, perhaps the greatest part, of the intercourse amongst mankind, cannot be reduced to fixed determinate rules. Yet in these cases there is a right and a wrong: a merciful, a liberal, a kind and compassionate behaviour, which surely is our duty; and an unmerciful contracted spirit, an hard and oppressive course of behaviour, which is most certainly immoral and vicious. But who can define precisely, wherein that contracted spirit and hard usage of others consist, as murder and theft may be defined? there is not a word in our language, which expresses more detestable wickedness than *oppression*: yet the nature of this vice cannot be so exactly stated, nor the bounds of it so determinately marked, as that we shall be able to say in all instances, where rigid right and justice ends, and oppression begins. In these cases there is great latitude left, for every one to determine for, and consequently to deceive himself. It is chiefly in these cases that self-deceit comes in; as every one must see that there is much larger scope for it here, than in express, single, determinate acts of wickedness. . . .

It is safer to be wicked in the ordinary way, than from this corruption lying at the root.

Upon the whole it is manifest, that there is such a thing as this self-partiality and self-deceit: that in some persons it is to a degree which would be thought incredible, were not the instances before our eyes; of which the behaviour of David is perhaps the highest possible one, in a single particular case; for there is not the least appearance, that it reached his general character: that we are almost all of us influenced by it in some degree, and in some respects: that therefore every one ought to have an eye to and beware of it. And all that I have further to add upon this subject is, that either there is a difference between right and wrong, or there is not: religion is true, or it is not. If it be not, there is no reason for any concern about it: but if it be true, it requires real fairness of mind and honesty of heart. And, if people will be wicked, they had better of the two be so from the common vicious passions without such refinements, than from this deep and calm source of delusion; which undermines the whole principle of good; darkens that light, that *candle of the Lord within*, which is to direct our steps; and corrupts conscience, which is the guide of life.

STUDY QUESTIONS

1. What does Butler mean when he says that many people are strangers to their own character? How far is he right in believing that we succeed in deceiving ourselves? Is there not a part of us that knows the truth?
2. Do you agree that the injunction "Know thyself" should be a fundamental moral rule?
3. According to Butler, vice results from having an unreasonably high regard for ourselves in comparison with others. Do you think he is right?
4. What does Butler mean when he tells us that being wicked in "ordinary ways" is safer than being deeply self-deluded?

Jealousy, Envy, and Spite

IMMANUEL KANT

TRANSLATED BY LOUIS ENFIELD

A biographical sketch of Immanuel Kant is found on page 86.

In this selection, excerpted from his lectures on ethics, Kant gives readers an account of the vices of jealousy. envy, spite, ingratitude, and malice. When we compare ourselves with others who are morally or materially better than us, we may become jealous of what they possess; then we may either attempt to depreciate that possession or try to emulate them by acquiring those same moral qualities or material objects. *Grudge* is the displeasure we feel when someone else has what we lack. Grudge becomes *envy* when we begrudge others their happiness. If we possess a good we do not need, but take pleasure in refusing to give it to someone who needs it, then we are *spiteful*. Another vice, *ingratitude*, has its origin in the resentment of another's superiority. In the extreme, ungrateful persons hate their benefactors. Kant calls the extremes of envy and ingratitude "devilish vices." A third devilish vice is *malice*—the gratuitous desire to see others fail. Malicious persons

JEALOUSY, ENVY, AND SPITE From "Jealousy, Envy, and Grudge" from *Lectures on Ethics* by Immanuel Kant. Translated by Louis Enfield (Harper & Row, 1963). Reprinted by permission of Methuen and Company Ltd.

enjoy the misery of others. Kant denies that people are directly inclined to be "devilish." In this respect he differs from Augustine.

There are two methods by which men arrive at an opinion of their worth: by comparing themselves with the idea of perfection and by comparing themselves with others. The first of these methods is sound; the second is not, and it frequently even leads to a result diametrically opposed to the first. The Idea of perfection is a proper standard, and if we measure our worth by it, we find that we fall short of it and feel that we must exert ourselves to come nearer to it; but if we compare ourselves with others, much depends upon who those others are and how they are constituted, and we can easily believe ourselves to be of great worth if those with whom we set up comparison are rogues. Men love to compare themselves with others, for by that method they can always arrive at a result favourable to themselves. They choose as a rule the worst and not the best of the class with which they set up comparison; in this way their own excellence shines out. If they choose those of greater worth the result of the comparison is, of course, unfavourable to them.

When I compare myself with another who is better than I, there are but two ways by which I can bridge the gap between us. I can either do my best to attain to his perfections, or else I can seek to depreciate his good qualities. I either increase my own worth, or else I diminish his so that I can always regard myself as superior to him. It is easier to depreciate another than to emulate him, and men prefer the easier course. They adopt it, and this is the origin of jealousy. When a man compares himself with another and finds that the other has many more good points, he becomes jealous of each and every good point he discovers in the other, and tries to depreciate it so that his own good points may stand out. This kind of jealousy may be called grudging. The other species of the genus jealousy, which makes us try to add to our good points so as to compare well with another, may be called emulating jealousy. The jealousy of emulation is, as we have stated, more difficult than the jealousy of grudge and so is much the less frequent of the two.

Parents ought not, therefore, when teaching their children to be good, to urge them to model themselves on other children and try to emulate them, for by so doing they simply make them jealous. If I tell my son, 'Look, how good and industrious John is', the result will be that my son will bear John a grudge. He will think to himself that, but for John, he himself would be the best, because there would be no comparison. By setting up John as a pattern for imitation I anger my son, make him feel a grudge against this so-called paragon, and I instil jealousy in him. My son might, of course, try to emulate John, but not finding it easy, he will bear John ill-will. Besides, just as I can say to my son, 'Look, how good John is', so can he reply: 'Yes, he is better than I, but are there not many who are far worse? Why do you compare me with those who are better? Why not with those who are worse than I?' Goodness must, therefore, be commended to children in and for itself. Whether other children are better or worse has no bearing on the point. If the comparison were in the child's favour, he would lose all ground of impulse to improve his own conduct. To ask our children to model themselves on others is to adopt a faulty method of upbringing, and as time goes on the fault will strike its roots deep. It is jealousy that parents are training and presupposing in their children when they set other children before them as patterns. Otherwise, the children would be quite indifferent to the qualities of others. They will find it easier to belittle the good qualities of their patterns than to emulate them, so they will choose the easier path and learn to show a grudging disposition. It is true that jealousy is natural, but that is no excuse for cultivating it. It is only a motive, a reserve in case of need. While the maxims of reason are still undeveloped in us, the proper course is to use reason to keep it within bounds. For jealousy is only one of the many motives, such as ambition, which are implanted in us because we are designed for a life of activity. But so soon as reason is enthroned, we must cease to seek perfection in emulation of others and must covet it in and for itself. Motives must abdicate and let reason bear rule in their place.

Persons of the same station and occupation in life are particularly prone to be jealous of each other. Many business-men are jealous of each other; so are many scholars, particularly in the same line of scholarship; and women are liable to be jealous of each other regarding men.

Grudge is the displeasure we feel when another has an advantage; his advantage makes us feel unduly small and we grudge it him. But to grudge a man his share of happiness is envy. To be envious is to desire the failure and unhappiness of another not for the purpose of advancing our own success and happiness but because we might then ourselves be perfect and happy as we are. An envious man is not happy unless all around him are unhappy; his aim is to stand alone in the enjoyment of his happiness. Such is envy, and we shall learn below that it is satanic. Grudge, although it too should not be countenanced, is natural. Even a good-natured person may at times be grudging. Such a one may, for instance, begrudge those around him their jollity when he himself happens to be sorrowful; for it is hard to bear one's sorrow when all around are joyful. When I see everybody enjoying a good meal and I alone must content myself with inferior fare, it upsets me and I feel a grudge; but if we are all in the same boat I am content. We find the thought of death bearable, because we know that all must die; but if everybody were immortal and I alone had to die, I should feel aggrieved. It is not things themselves that affect us, but things in their relation to ourselves. We are grudging because others are happier than we. But when a good-natured man feels happy and cheerful, he wishes that every one else in the world were as happy as he and shared his joy; he begrudges no one his happiness.

When a man would not grant to another even that for which he himself has no need, he is spiteful. Spite is a maliciousness of spirit which is not the same thing as envy. I may not feel inclined to give to another something which belongs to me, even though I myself have no use for it, but it does not follow that I grudge him his own possessions, that I want to be the only one who has anything and wish him to have nothing at all. There is a deal of grudge in human nature which could develop into envy but which is not itself envy. We feel pleasure in gossiping about the minor misadventures of other people; we are not averse, although we may express no pleasure thereat, to hearing of the fall of some rich man; we may enjoy in stormy weather, when comfortably seated in our warm, cosy parlour, speaking of those at sea, for it heightens our own feeling of comfort and happiness; there is grudge in all this, but it is not envy.

The three vices which are the essence of vileness and wickedness are ingratitude, envy, and malice. When these reach their full degree they are devilish.

Men are shamed by favours. If I receive a favour, I am placed under an obligation to the giver; he has a call upon me because I am indebted to him. We all blush to be obliged. Noble-minded men accordingly refuse to accept favours in order not to put themselves under an obligation. But this attitude predisposes the mind to ingratitude. If the man who adopts it is noble-minded, well and good; but if he be proud and selfish and has perchance received a favour, the feeling that he is beholden to his benefactor hurts his pride and, being selfish, he cannot accomodate himself to the idea that he owes his benefactor anything. He becomes defiant and ungrateful. His ingratitude might even conceivably assume such dimensions that he cannot bear his benefactor and becomes his enemy. Such ingratitude is of the devil; it is out of all keeping with human nature. It is inhuman to hate and persecute one from whom we have reaped a benefit, and if such conduct were the rule it would cause untold harm. Men would then be afraid to do good to anyone lest they should receive evil in return for their good. They would become misanthropic.

The second devilish vice is envy. Envy is in the highest degree detestable. The envious man does not merely want to be happy; he wants to be the only happy person in the world; he is really contented only when he sees nothing but misery around him. Such an intolerable creature would gladly destroy every source of of joy and happiness in the world.

Malice is the third kind of viciousness which is of the devil. It consists in taking a direct pleasure in the misfortunes of others. Men prone to this vice will seek, for instance, to make mischief between husband and wife, or between friends, and then enjoy the misery they have produced. In these matters we should make it a rule never to repeat to a person anything that we may have heard to his disadvantage from another, unless our silence would injure him. Otherwise we start an enmity and disturb his peace of mind, which our silence would have avoided, and in addition we break faith with our informant. The defence against such mischief-makers is upright conduct. Not by words but by our lives we should confute them. As Socrates said: We ought so to conduct ourselves that people will not credit anything spoken in disparagement of us.

These three vices—ingratitude (*ingratitudo qualificata*), envy, and malice—are devilish because they imply a direct inclination to evil. There are in man certain indirect tendencies to wickedness which are human and not unnatural. The miser wants everything for himself, but it is no satisfaction to him to see that his neighbour is destitute. The evilness of a vice may thus be either direct or indirect. In these three vices it is direct.

We may ask whether there is in the human mind an immediate inclination to wickedness, an inclination to the devilish vices. Heaven stands for the acme of happiness, hell for all that is bad, and the earth stands midway between these two extremes; and just as goodness which transcends anything which might be expected of a human being is spoken of as being angelic, so also do we speak of devilish wickedness when the wickedness oversteps the limits of human nature and becomes inhuman. We may take it for granted that the human mind has no immediate inclination to wickedness, but is only indirectly wicked. Man cannot be so ungrateful that he simply must hate his neighbour; he may be too proud to show his gratitude and so avoid him, but he wishes him well. Again, our pleasure in the misfortune of another is not direct. We may rejoice, for example, in a man's misfortunes, because he was haughty, rich and selfish; for man loves to preserve equality. We have thus no direct inclination towards evil as evil, but only an indirect one. But how are we to explain the fact that even young children have the spirit of mischief strongly developed? For a joke, a boy will stick a pin in an unsuspecting playmate, but it is only for fun. He has no thought of the pain the other must feel on all such occasions. In the same spirit he will torture animals; twisting the cat's tail or the dog's. Such tendencies must be nipped in the bud, for it is easy to see where they will lead. They are, in fact, something animal, something of the beast of prey which is in us all, which we cannot overcome, and the source of which we cannot explain. There certainly are in human nature characteristics for which we can assign no reason. There are animals too who steal anything that comes their way, though it is quite useless to them; and it seems as if man had retained this animal tendency in his nature.

Ingratitude calls for some further observations here. To help a man in distress is charity; to help him in less urgent needs is benevolence; to help him in the amenities of life is courtesy. We may be the recipients of a charity which has not cost the giver much and our gratitude is commensurate with the degree of good-will which moved him to the action. We are grateful not only for what we have received but also for the good intention which prompted it, and the greater the effort it has cost our benefactor, the greater our gratitude.

Gratitude may be either from duty or from inclination. If an act of kindness does not greatly move us, but if we nevertheless feel that it is right and proper that we should show gratitude, our gratitude is merely prompted by a sense of duty. Our heart is not grateful, but we have principles of gratitude. If, however, our heart goes out to our benefactor, we are grateful from inclination. There is a weakness of the understanding which we often have cause to recognize. It consists in taking the conditions of our understanding as conditions of the thing understood. We can estimate force only in terms of the obstacles it overcomes. Similarly, we can only estimate the degree of good-will in terms of the obstacles it has to surmount. In consequence we cannot comprehend the love and goodwill of a being for whom there are no obstacles. If God has been good to me, I am liable to think that after all it has cost God no trouble, and that gratitude to God would be mere fawning on my part. Such thoughts are not at all unnatural. It is easy to fear God, but not nearly so easy to love God from inclination because of our consciousness that God is a being whose goodness is unbounded but to whom it is no trouble to shower kindness upon us. This is not to say that such should be our mental attitude; merely that when we examine our hearts, we find that this is how we actually think. It also explains why to many races God appeared to be a jealous God, seeing that it cost Him nothing to be more bountiful with His goodness; it explains why many nations thought that their gods were sparing of their benefits and that they required propitiating with prayers and sacrifices. This is the attitude of man's heart; but when we call reason to our aid we see that God's goodness must be of a high order if He is to be good to a being so unworthy of His goodness. This solves our difficulty. The gratitude we owe to God is not gratitude from inclination, but from duty, for God is not a creature like ourselves, and can be no object of our inclinations.

We ought not to accept favours unless we are either forced to do so by dire necessity or have implicit confidence in our benefactor (for he ceases to be our friend and becomes our benefactor) that he will not regard it as placing us under an obligation to him. To accept favours indiscriminately and to be constantly seeking them is ignoble and the sign of a mean soul which does not mind placing itself under obligations. Unless we are driven by such dire necessity that it compels us to sacrifice our own worth, or unless we are convinced that our benefactor will not account it to us as a debt, we ought rather to suffer deprivation than accept favours, for a favour is a debt which can never be extinguished. For even if I repay my benefactor tenfold, I am still not even with him, because he has done me a kindness which he did not owe. He was the first in the field, and even if I return his gift tenfold I do so only as repayment. He will always be the one who was the first to show kindness and I can never be beforehand with him.

The man who bestows favours can do so either in order to make the recipient indebted to him or as an expression of his duty. If he makes the recipient feel a sense of indebtedness, he wounds his pride and diminishes his sense of gratitude. If he wishes to avoid this he must regard the favours he bestows as the discharge of a duty he owes to mankind, and he must not give the recipient the impression that it is a debt to be repaid. On the other hand, the recipient of the favour must still consider himself under an obligation to his benefactor and must be grateful to him. Under these conditions there can be benefactors and beneficiaries. A right-thinking man will not accept kindnesses, let alone favours. A grateful disposition is a touching thing and brings tears to our eyes on the stage, but a generous disposition is lovelier still. Ingratitude we detest to a surprising degree; even though we are not ourselves the victims of it, it angers us to such an extent that we feel inclined to intervene. But this is due to the fact that ingratitude decreases generosity.

Envy does not consist in wishing to be more happy than others—that is grudge—but in wishing to be the only one to be happy. It is this feeling which makes envy so evil. Why should not others be happy along with me? Envy shows itself also in relation to thing which are scarce. Thus the Dutch, who as a nation are rather envious, once valued tulips at several hundreds of florins apiece. A rich merchant, who had one of the finest and rarest specimens, heard that another had a similar specimen. He thereupon bought it from him for 2,000 florins and trampled it underfoot, saying that he had no use for it, as he already possessed a specimen, and that he only wished that no one else should share that distinction with him. So it is also in the matter of happiness.

Malice is different. A malicious man is pleased when others suffer, he can laugh when others weep. An act which wilfully brings unhappiness is cruel; when it produces physical pain it is bloodthirsty. Inhumanity is all these together, just as humanity consists in sympathy and pity, since these differentiate man from the beasts. It is difficult to explain what gives rise to a cruel disposition. It may arise when a man considers another so evilly disposed that he hates him. A man who believes himself hated by another, hates him in return, although the former may have good reason to hate him. For if a man is hated because he is selfish and has other vices, and he knows that he is hated for these reasons, he hates those who hate him although these latter do him no injustice. Thus kings who know that they are hated by their subjects become even more cruel. Equally, when a man has done a good deed to another, he knows that the other loves him, and so he loves him in return, knowing that he himself is loved. Just as love is reciprocated, so also is hate. We must for our own sakes guard against being hated by others lest we be affected by that hatred and reciprocate it. The hater is more disturbed by his hatred than is the hated.

STUDY QUESTIONS

1. How does Kant distinguish spite from envy? Why is the extreme of envy "devilish"?
2. We sometimes say to a friend, "I envy you." Can we envy people without begrudging their happiness? How does Kant view this?
3. Why does Kant advise us to compare ourselves with the ideal of perfection? What vices are associated with comparing ourselves with others?
4. What are the three devilish vices and what is devilish about them? Does Kant believe that the devilish vices are natural? What is their origin in people?
5. What does Kant think is wrong about accepting favors? Do you think Kant demands too much of the average person? Is his doctrine too austere?

Revenge

ALEXANDER THEROUX

Alexander Theroux is a novelist. His most recent work
is *Darconville's Cat* (1981).

Theroux describes the effects that desire for revenge has
on those who seek it; it transfigures them, poisons their
lives, and turns them into monsters. Persons who give
themselves over to revenge consent to their own destruction. Theroux recommends foregiveness, the contrary of revenge.

I remember—forgive the paradox—an unmemorable girlfriend of
mine who in leaving me for someone else left me as well with a
previously unfelt and inadmissible emotion, it being for a moment
impossible to face the truth, never mind tell it; but as surprise ebbed
another urge flowed. My immediate thought was a simple and
uncomplicated one: I wanted to kill her.

Revenge, exactly what I felt, is forgiveness's other face. It is an
emotion, discounting mercy, neat to the taste and born of a desperate need to rectify a wrong by inflicting harm in return for an
injury, a slight, or an insult and to exact satisfaction for that which,
at least in the sufferer's eye, blind and stupid fate (never, of course,
without its specific agent) not only has allowed but in a way has
cruelly fostered. The sole desire in retribution is to equalize: "I'll
get even with you!" To revenge is, in fact, to avenge. Simply put, it
seeks—it demands—justice.

A popular legend has it that the Italian composer Antonio Salieri, overshadowed by his rival Mozart's glory but, worse, nursing a deep wound at the cosmic inequality of things-as-distributed, at the first-night performance of *Don Giovanni*, alone of all the others, hissed and stormed out of the theater—and then when opportunity arose poisoned his enemy. Caesar was stabbed by senators, Socrates was murdered by judges, and Christ was slapped by lackeys. So envy is always involved in revenge, but that is only the beginning, for the overwhelming and monomaniacal conviction superseding it is the thought on the revenger's part that without his personal intervention, correcting happenstance, the galling want of fairness will forever prevail and the suddenly—and often reasonlessly—despised will go scot-free. It will be remembered that while Salieri toiled desperately over his own mediocre compositions, feeling ever unrewarded, Mozart's work reputedly came easy and fame followed. Salieri couldn't abide this. In *Mozart and Salieri* (1830), Pushkin gives us his complaint:

> Where, where is justice, when the sacred gift,
> When deathless genius comes not to reward
> Perfervid love and utter self-denial,
> And toils and strivings and beseeching prayers,
> But puts her halo round a lack-wit's skull,
> A frivolous idler's brow? . . . O Mozart, Mozart!

Revenge transfigures you. It boils and concocts into poisonous nourishment all the facts and fictions it compounds from the lives of its enemies, and fuels the delight it abhors, for your grief has found the one thing in this life that *causes* it. Alive, it is your plague, instigates against you, throttles all you are. The vigorous if irrational idea is that you alone of all others on earth are left to correct what otherwise must go forever uncorrected. And in spite of the fact that in the process you become a cauldron of pure pain—owned, in fact, by that which you would sell, and are diminished by ("The murderer," writes Nabokov, "is always the victim's inferior")—there is often a crazy comfort in the obsession with whatever must be vindicated by whomever must be abused or punished or killed.

Revenge, like hemorrhoids, seems to have been created to locate in one particular place one particular pain to absolve the body in all other places of all other pains.

Do we fear the Gorgon or simply create it to locate our fears? The retributive aspect of revenge, in any case, whether logical or not—to put things right—is nevertheless its primal scream, what indeed gives it its most commonly applied epithet: "sweet."

Revenge! Where hasn't this shadow reached? It is a poem by Tennyson, the name of Sir Richard Grenville's famous ship, and a tragedy by Edward Young. There is an Iranian drink so named. Fairy tales virtually have no other plot. It is as old as the first murder ("And Cain was very wroth and his countenance fell") and as recent as the summer of 1982, when the Israelis invaded Lebanon and announced that this was in retaliation for the shooting of a diplomat in London. It is the central theme of Elizabethan and Jacobean tragedy, animates every discussion of capital punishment, and is even implied in the Virginia state motto: *Sic semper tyrannis*— Booth, avenging the lost Civil War, shot Lincoln howling those very words. I'd suggest that along with love and war, with which themes, let us say, it has more than passing acquaintance, revenge is the single most informing element of great world literature. And George Orwell, in his essay "Why I Write" (1947), cites it as the first motive for many taking up the profession ("the desire . . . to get your own back on grownups who snubbed you in childhood, etc."). The revengeful personality—it is more often than not an intellectual's, of which Hamlet, a thinker, not a "rash and splenetic" type, is only one example—very often has the power, in fact, to give a significant penetrating quality to literary expression; one thinks of Juvenal on Roman decadence, Luther on papistical excesses, Milton on Charles I, and Hitler on the Treaty of Versailles. But for the pure, unadulterated masterpiece of contumely very little surpasses Alexander Pope's almost gibbering attack, in his "Epistle to Dr. Arbuthnot" (1735), on the effeminate Lord Hervey ("Sporus"), who had been collaborating with Lady Mary Wortley Montagu on scurrilities against him and so met with this response:

> Let Sporus tremble—"What? that Thing of silk,
> Sporus, that mere white Curd of Ass's milk?
> Satire or sense alas! Can Sporus feel?
> Who breaks a Butterfly upon a Wheel?"
> Yet let me flap this Bug with gilded wings,
> This painted Child of Dirt that stinks and stings . . .
> Whether in florid Impotence he speaks

And, as the Prompter breathes, the Puppet squeaks;
Or at the Ear of Eve, familiar Toad,
Half Froth, half Venom, spits himself abroad . . .

While black, there is something splendid, almost mythological, in such ramping revenge, the wicked ebullience, the *folie de grandeur* mounted to frame a prose so determined to collaborate with anger, disappointment, and fury. The beating heart of revenge is its excessiveness, and its excesses—the pathological lengths to which it will go—are astonishing. The misandrous Delia Bacon, part critic, part crank, spent her entire life trying to besmirch William Shakespeare. Rufus W. Griswolda, who secretly hated Poe but was made his literary executor by wheedling it out of Mrs. Clemm, maliciously proceeded upon Poe's death to blacken his reputation through hundreds of lies and falsifications. Revenge is a feral branch of hatred. The anticlerical historian of philosophy Will Durant (educated by the Jesuits) dismisses all of medieval philosophy in one sentence: "A baffling circuit from faith to reason and back to faith again."

There is something intriguing here worth another word. Another sort of pathos seems involved. There is a certain hopeless kind of revenge, never far from insanity, that insists on mounting itself against the abstract, the too vast, the uncircumscribable, a few examples of which might be Nietzsche's opposition to Christianity, Frederick Rolfe's position against the Anglicans, Hitler's vindictiveness toward the Jews. Otto Weininger, riding his hobbyhorse, wrote the dense neo-Kantian *Sex and Character* to prove women had no souls! Such mountainous fury can only consume, wear away, and rot the antagonist, but it is a type on intransigence, even if in a negative way, that in its uncompromising madness approaches genius. The person given over to revenge is never an ordinary man. The New York Yankees played so poorly in a doubleheader against Chicago on the night of August 3, 1982, dropping both games, that owner George Steinbrenner, rancid with fury, publicly declared as a humiliation to his team—"they weren't worth even watching"—that all 34,000 fans attending that night could attend another game free!

It is the lot of such people, if to be opposed, then also to be invigorated by opposition, beholding their enemies in an eternal vigil, like the lifeless cobra in whose eye the murderer's image is forever embedded, and they actually crave to hate that constant hallucination of face—whether smirking through the attack it signals or the absolution it seeks—which becomes, in fact, almost a badge of those enemies, for one attributes to them not that state of normal human happiness, shot through with the common moods of mankind, that should move us to entertain for them a feeling of kindly sympathy, but a species of arrogant delight that merely pours oil on the furnace of our rage. One thinks of Richard Nixon and the press, imagined leaks, the enemies list.

In its usual form, revenge is the change in behavior that is classic reaction—a response to a stimulus. For instance, Mr. Ahme Tariki, the radical Saudi Arabian founder of OPEC (currently living in exile), organized the oil-exporting states specifically to strike a blow at the United States, where, because of the treatment he received during six years' engineering study in Texas in the late 1950s—the "Jim Crow" years, when he was considered black and treated vilely—he became embittered for life. The not-to-be-disowned John Hinckley was shown in his trial for shooting President Reagan to be nursing a deep grudge against authority figures (his wealthy father, advised by a psychiatrist, had sent him packing with only $100), who in his confused mind seemed fully unimpressed with his young, impossibly high, certainly megalomaniacal ambitions to be a successful rock star and boyfriend of a famous movie star. And then Peter Sutcliffe, the "Yorkshire Ripper," was a pathetic and cowardly little boy who, bullied at school, grew to take up body-building and was soon snarling at the weak himself. He adored his mother, who, however, had an affair that desolated him, and within months of his marriage (he both hated and feared his wife, Sonia) he began attacking and killing women—prostitutes—who, queerly, were an essential part of both his despair and his marriage. There is something in the dark soul of the mass murderer—J. B. Troppmann, who did away with a woman and her five children, Henri Desiré Landru, the French Bluebeard, and Theodore Bundy come immediately to mind—that is never far from revenge, its weird little posture giving destruction added motive in early failure, grievous disappointment, remembered scorn.

The revenger is, by definition, a victim. He is solitary, often in exile, forgoing communion with the society he terrifies. "What dog," asks George Eliot in *Silas Marner*, "likes a figure bent under a heavy bag?" The world has done badly by him. A formula of rupture has taken place; suddenly his consciousness is heightened, for he has spied (a word he'd favor) what he immediately can neither countenance nor forgive, and he fixes upon that one thing that the reductionist mind madly isolates as the only solution to the world's woes. Every former excellence of his enemy becomes every conceivable fault, every promise—expected, if not actually made—an impervestigable lie, and every memory a viper eating through the bowels of his benefits, all to set in motion such a fell and deadly hate that through a sea of sins he'd wade to his revenge. Human feeling curdles. Lenin, visiting Maxim Gorky, once demanded that he shut off a phonograph playing Beethoven's "Appassionata" lest it weaken his anticzarist resolve with feelings of sentiment. Oliver Cromwell sent his soldiers back to Drogheda to slaughter the Irish children they thought to spare, with the remark "Nits will be lice." There are many passions that we are condemned to feel only in a reduced form: never revenge. With it you have come under the shadow. You would countenance black magic. And yet how little is achieved, though other problems be solved! How *mistakenly* can a person have wanted what, taken away, repudiates the meaning of life itself?

Revenge is a restless desire precisely for the *ideal*. The tormented soul, hobbled by denial, by prohibition, sees himself betrayed and so, paradoxically, tries to recover by an act of supreme alienation and anger that which has been taken from him and which, constantly fleering at and ridiculing him by the very nature of its existence, mocks the mind to murder. "I want satisfaction!" cried the duelist in his humiliation. And yet what most generates, most often animates, revenge? Disappointed love, perfidy, dissolved friendship. And why so? The revenger is a person, usually, who has expected eternal unflinching fidelity from family and from friendship, and often in a quite ungainsayable way, but having lost it—he literally suffers a reverse—then employs the most effective and rigorous means of correction and so goes through life fixed on delirious hope in order to pledge allegiance to an inverted form of the same ideal. "Oh," cries Ahab, "now I feel my topmost greatness lies in my topmost grief."

The smoldering aspect of revenge is often in direct proportion to the degree in which the person's right to exist as a human being has been taken away. In his illness—he is literally infected—he has been handed, so to speak, a writ of non exeat. He must be cured. The cure is freedom. Whoever will set the revenger free—and the cry for release is the sine qua non of his gnawing vindictiveness—can be the only one, in fact, able to do so, and so ironically remains, as the singular agent of deliverance, also the sole abettor of his own destruction. It is a marriage, pledged until death do them part. A man in the grip of revenge has not so much lost the ideal as he has transferred the whole concept of one ideal to the furthest extreme of another, and challenging in the process the necessity of injustice that exists—often as the emanation of a punitive or arbitrary God—he writes in his own bitter soul not just a complaint but an entire destructive theology.

Revenge, indeed, has curiously theological implications. The law of talion—an eye for an eye, a tooth for a tooth—cries out to its cognate, "Retaliate!" Blood revenge is actually sanctioned in the Old Testament, the returning of evil for evil, blood for blood, a "justifying"—in the printer's phrase—of an unbalanced line. In Melville's *Moby-Dick*, the rankling Captain Ahab, named after the Old Testament ruler who "did more to provoke the Lord God of Israel to anger than all the Kings of Israel that were before him," becomes the embodiment of revenge itself. He has been wounded ("unmanned") by the whale, inexplicably, and the dismemberment has driven him to such a pitch of anguish—homicidal, suicidal, and deicidal, all at once—that in maniacal pursuit of his nemesis ("the incarnation of all those malicious agencies which some deep men feel eating in them . . .") he has to be confined at times to a straitjacket in which, mad, he "swung to the rockings of the gales."

Ahab's intellect is enslaved but yet also concentrated by his madness, and, as happens in the matter of revenge, he has lost his humanity in the very act of vindicating it—the essential paradox of revenge—and has become the very image of the thing he hates, a statue of penalty cast in a single mold, a fireman of punishment and egotism. "I'd strike the sun if it insulted me!" he shrieks. Every dilemma has two horns. For Ahab has made himself not just a proud, self-appointed judge like Prometheus, Faust, Manfred, and Lucifer but also, like them, revenge's plaintiff, a tragic scapegoat. He is both victim and executioner—revenge always involves both—who in his compulsion for seeking equality has also elected to accept vengeance as the sole law of existence (the opposite was his intention), and so transmogrifies virtue into vice.

The greater the punishment each revenger feels merited by his action, the greater the value the agent of revenge attributes to the burden of his having to do so. Each constructs his revenge more or less according to the only logic available to him in a world that, however, illogically presents itself, for since he is forced to accept the fact that a positive, lost, is evil, the alternative of a negative, found, must perforce be the only good at hand to address it—and so the breach actually becomes the observance in a desperate attempt to settle a matter of contradiction by means of conflicting evidence. There is no better poacher than an ex-gamekeeper. We have here inversion, a topsyturvification of moral values that in revenge becomes its canon law. The condition is found in, among others, the autobiographer as avenger, the rejected lover, the disaffiliated child who grows up to settle the score.

Shakespeare's *Hamlet*, which takes its cue from Kyd's *The Spanish Tragedy* (1587), the father of all revenge plays, simply cannot be understood except in its theological context. It is, characteristically, not just the case of an eye for an eye, for the jaw must be taken, along with the tongue and ears—and the victim must, after exquisite torments of both body and mind, go straight to hell. Revenge, to the Elizabethans and Jacobeans, demanded hellfire and everlasting torment.

Excess is all. Extremism in the pursuit of justice—the revenger's conundrum—is no vice. And it's to be taken as a matter of breviary, this supernatural backdrop before which revenge is enacted—heaven, hell, and purgatory—that only with so much at stake can this terrible emotion be comprehended or, in fact, taken to have in it something akin to the slow grinding of the mills of divine vengeance—slow, yes, for often extreme patience is required.

Revenge is not always blister upon heat. It loiters, it bides its time, it grows. It perhaps alone gives full *meaning* to the full measure of the injury suffered. Months, years, decades may wear away, but not the corrosive and intolerable recollection of an injustice burning a hole in your sleep, if ever sleep there is. The nightmare that prevents, however, eventually *corrects* sleep. The wheel of fortune turns. It is the gift opportunity hands to adversity, a reward crowning pursuit and throwing up the exact set of circumstances that only time can give when, for the victim, it is most inopportune—he has moved away, say, remarried, grown older, changed his name, and, perhaps best of all, *forgotten*—but when, for the executioner, irony is made iron in the delirious turnabout that literally defines serendipity and without which, it may be argued, revenge can never be sufficiently *raffiné*. The revenger is a sinner with patience, a saint without forbearance, a master of what Borges calls the art of the *cachada* (to grab, to take somebody unawares). Delay is in fact only a kind of subtlety. The infernal deity Nemesis, goddess of vengeance—her statue in Rome was in the Capitol—is the daughter of Nox, and under the carapace of night one waits, waits, until all is ready. Revenge a hundred years old still has milk teeth.

Edmond Dantès, left to rot for fourteen years as a prisoner in the gloomy Château d'If in Dumas's *The Count of Monte Cristo*, finally escapes ("Enough of this prison, let me now seek the anti-dote . . .") masterfully—and premeditatively—to wreak vengeance on each of his persecutors. "They'll remember my carbuncles," said Karl Marx from obscurity, writing *Das Kapital* in ill health, poverty, and the exile forced on him, as on others, by a corrupt economic system.

This is what's called "revenge in lavender"—revenge reserved—hanging fire, truly, as the years lope over the hill. But the cancer has metastasized. And that's just when the fun begins. "I'm back!" cries the revenger, demanding remembrance. "Look at me! Pay attention!" I read in the papers a few years ago of a man whose son had been hazed to death during an initiation by several fraternity boys, and the aggrieved father chose to take his revenge only after ten long years had passed when, *pro re nata*, he methodically hunted down each of their sons and killed them in kind. "Thus," says Shakespeare in *Twelfth Night*, "the whirligig of time brings in his revenges." Revenge, as the proverb says, is a dish best served up cold.

There is finally—and importantly—a penalty in revenge that can never be disregarded, the calm willingness to slay the self in the attempt to free it by those who, in daring personally to mete out justice, even if as only they see it, must also take the medicine they dispense. There was, for example, an uprising in the Sixties on Pulau Senang Prison Island, off the coast of Singapore. The prisoners could have fled. But they lingered to mutilate their guards—they castrated them, put out their eyes, etc.—and because the revenge was such time-consuming cruelty they were quickly caught and hanged, sixty-six of them, six at a time, on the Singapore gallows.

It is a sensibility, the revenger's, that, if open to the asperity of insult and keen to redress it, is also one equally arranged to feel all the while the criminal denial of true justice his very act contravenes. The tragedy is that he can't do otherwise. Forgiveness to him is the absence of justice, and so he "commits" justice, so to speak, in order to abolish crime—even as he perpetuates it. The crime is the punishment. It's as if he reasons: I am pleased with defeat in what I do because secretly for what I do I know I am guilty and only punishment can redeem me. Revenge has something about it oddly propitiative, an act often spitefully but inexorably united to contrition. Let heaven exist, he seems to say, even though my dwelling place is hell.

Of penalties there are many. There's often an unconscious wish for revenge in alcoholism, an indirect aggression born of anger and resentment against either oneself or others, and the same might be said of impotence and frigidity—a disposition, often, involving a subconscious impulse to thwart—and I have no doubt that this might also apply to failure in school or gluttony or bedwetting.

There's suicide. The Chinese and Chuvashes often hanged themselves on the doors of their enemies. In Hugo's *Les Misérables*, the crafty, inexorable, and ubiquitous Inspector Javert dogs Jean Valjean for forty years (for stealing a loaf of bread to feed his sister's starving children) and then, robbed of his chance for retribution, commits suicide. His absolute fixation on revenge—*and in the name of law*—alone has given meaning to his sterile life. He has known only one emotion. Crazed with that detail, he cannot understand the whole. Or can he? Perversely, dreadfully, he comes to win *admiration* for the thief he's so long hated and pursued—a galley slave, a convict, who illogically, cruelly, returns pardon for hatred, good for evil! His nemesis in his forgiveness becomes his benefactor. An entire order of unexpected facts, fragmenting all certainty, arises to subjugate him, a moral sun rising only to blind him like an owl. All the axioms that had been the supports of his existence suddenly crumble:

> He saw before him two roads, both equally straight; but he saw two; and that terrified him—him who had never in his life known but one straight line. And, bitter anguish, these two roads were contradictory. One of these two straight lines excluded the other.

Which of the two was the true one? His condition was inexpressible
. . . what should he do? Give up Jean Valjean, that was wrong; leave
Jean Valjean, that was wrong . . . what then! Such enormities should
happen and nobody should be punished?

But someone must be punished. That is just the *point* of revenge,
that which for so long has given to it the battle cry "Somebody's
going to pay for this!"

But who? Compelled to recognize all of a sudden the existence of
forgiveness, Javert can only conclude—a horror of himself almost
as if he had lost his faith (which, in fact, he has)—that *he* has
become depraved, and so what should he then do? Call for Pontius
Pilate's basin and wash his claws? That is ontologically impossible
for him, precisely what the revengeful man is unable to do, for, as
we've seen, this emotion—"so durable and obstinate," according
to La Bruyère, "that reconciliation on a sickbed is the greatest sign
of death"—is fed by the law of balance, equality, and a mania for
justice that, even if it turns on itself, must be satsified. And so, like
the pygmy rattlesnake that bites and poisons itself in the convul-
sions of its fury, the empty Javert—"getting even"—revenges
himself on himself and plunges headlong in suicidal despair from a
parapet into the murky Seine. This is not victory, but if it is not
victory it is yet revenge, and that is perhaps its most terrifying side,
that, meeting nothing else, it becomes an end in itself. Who fights
with monsters may thereby become one. Let Ahab beware Ahab. It
is always ourselves we must fear first.

STUDY QUESTIONS

1. Do you agree with Theroux that the vengeful person is always
   envious?
2. If Theroux is right, why is revenge said to be sweet?
3. In *The Brothers Karamazov*, Feodor Dostoevski describes how a
   nobleman punishes a child who has thrown a stone at the paw
   of one of the man's favorite hounds. The child is forced to run
   naked through the woods and, before his mother's eyes, is torn
   apart by hounds. Ivan Karamazov asks his saintly brother
   Alyosha what he would do with the nobleman. Alyosha replies, "Shoot him." Could Theroux agree with Alyosha here? If

so, how could he explain this in light of his condemnation of revenge?

4. Is vengefulness a vice? Is revenge always wrong?
5. Do you believe that the evil of revenge is the same for society as it is for individuals? Does society have the right to avenge itself by punishing criminals? Or is punishment more a matter of reform or constraint against further criminal action?

The Evil of Lying

CHARLES FRIED

Charles Fried (b. 1935) is a professor of law at the Harvard University School of Law. He has written several books and articles in the area of ethics; his most recent books are *Right and Wrong* (1978) and *Contract as Promise: A Theory of Contractual Obligation* (1981).

Fried distinguishes between acts that are merely bad and acts that are wrong. He cites Bentham's belief that lying is not wrong and not always bad. He discusses the views of Kant and Augustine, who hold that lying is wrong even when the effects are good. We lie, says Fried, when we intentionally induce a false belief. He asks, If that effect is not bad, how can lying be wrong? He answers that lying is wrong because the effect of lying is *always* bad; lies tamper with the judgment of the persons lied to, thereby interfering with them in a fundamentally disrespectful way. If you could intentionally induce a false belief in yourself, that too would be wrong.

Lying is wrong because it violates the integrity of another's mind, and because it violates trust. In break-

THE EVIL OF LYING Reprinted by permission of the author and publisher from *Right and Wrong* by Charles Fried, Cambridge, Mass.: Harvard University Press, Copyright © 1978 by the President and Fellows of Harvard College.

ing that trust—here Fried quotes Kant—one does
wrong to men in general, not only to the gullible victims. Fried compares lying to passing a counterfeit bill.

The evil of lying is as hard to pin down as it is strongly felt. Is
lying wrong or is it merely something bad? If it is bad, why is it
bad—is it bad in itself or because of some tendency associated with
it? Compare lying to physical harm. Harm is a state of the world
and so it can only be classified as bad; the wrong I argued for was
the *intentional doing* of harm. Lying, on the other hand, can be
wrong, since it is an action. But the fact that lying is an action does
not mean that it *must* be wrong rather than bad. It might be that the
action of lying should be judged as just another state of the world—
a time-extended state, to be sure, but there is no problem about
that—and as such it would count as a negative element in any set of
circumstances in which it occurred. Furthermore, if lying is judged
to be bad it can be bad in itself, like something ugly or painful, or it
can be bad only because of its tendency to produce results that are
bad in themselves.

If lying were bad, not wrong, this would mean only that, other
things being equal, we should avoid lies. And if lying were bad not
in itself but merely because of its tendencies, we would have to
avoid lies only when those tendencies were in fact likely to be
realized. In either case lying would be permissible to produce a net
benefit, including the prevention of more or worse lies. By contrast
the categorical norm "Do not lie" does not evaluate states of affairs
but is addressed to moral agents, forbidding lies. Now if lying is
wrong it is also bad in itself, for the category of the intrinsically bad
is weaker and more inclusive than the category of the wrong. And
accordingly, many states of the world are intrinsically bad (such as
destruction of valuable property) but intentional acts bringing them
about are not necessarily wrong.

Bentham plainly believed that lying is neither wrong nor even
intrinsically bad: "Falsehood, take it by itself, consider it as not
being accompanied by any other material circumstances, nor therefore productive of any material effects, can never, upon the principle of utility, constitute any offense at all" (*An Introduction to the
Principles of Morals and Legislation*, ch. 16, sec. 24). By contrast,
Kant and Augustine argued at length that lying is wrong. Indeed,

they held that lying is not only wrong *unless* excused or justified in defined ways (which is my view) but that lying is always wrong. Augustine sees lying as a kind of defilement, the liar being tainted by the lie, quite apart from any consequences of the lie. Kant's views are more complex. He argues at one point that lying undermines confidence and trust among men generally: "Although by making a false statement I do no wrong to him who unjustly compels me to speak, yet I do wrong to men in general . . . I cause that declarations in general find no credit, and hence all rights founded on contract should lose their force; and this is a wrong to mankind" ("On a Supposed Right to Tell Lies from Benevolent Motives," in *Kant's Critique of Practical Reason and Other Works*, translated by T. K. Abbott [London: Longmans, Green, 1973]). This would seem to be a consequentialist argument, according to which lying is bad only insofar as it produces these bad results. But elsewhere he makes plain that he believes these bad consequences to be necessarily, perhaps even conceptually linked to lying. In this more rigoristic vein, he asserts that lying is a perversion of one's uniquely human capacities irrespective of any consequences of the lie, and thus lying is not only intrinsically bad but wrong.[1]

---

[1] "The greatest violation of man's duty to himself merely as a moral being (to humanity in his own person) is . . . the lie. In the doctrine of Law an intentional wrong is called a lie only if it infringes on another's right. But . . . in ethics . . . every deliberate untruth deserves this harsh name. By a lie a man makes himself contemptible . . . and violates the dignity of humanity in his own person. And so, since the harm that can come to others from it is not the characteristic property of this vice (for if it were, the vice would consist only in violating one's duty to others), we do not take this harm into account here . . . By a lie a man throws away and, as it were, annihilates his dignity as a man. A man [who lies] . . . has even less worth than if he were a mere thing. For a thing, as something real and given, has the property of being serviceable . . . But the man who communicates his thoughts to someone in words which yet (intentionally) contain the contrary of what he thinks on the subject has a purpose directly opposed to the natural purposiveness of the power of communicating one's thoughts and therefore renounces his personality and makes himself a mere deceptive appearance of man, not man himself.

"A lie (in the ethical sense of the term), as an intentional untruth as such, need not be harmful to others in order to be pronounced reprehensible; for then it would be a violation of the rights of others . . . A lie requires a second person whom one intends to deceive, and intentionally to deceive oneself seems to contain a contradiction.

"Man as a moral being (*homo noumenon*), cannot use his natural being (*homo phaenomenon*) as a mere means (a speaking machine), as if it were not bound to its intrinsic end (the communication of thought)." (*Tugendlehre* [428–430], translated by Mary J. Gregor, *The Doctrine of Virtue*, Philadelphia: University of Pennsylvania Press, 1964.)

Finally, a number of writers have taken what looks like an intermediate position: the evil of lying is indeed identified with its consequences, but the connection between lying and those consequences, while not a necessary connection, is close and persistent, and the consequences themselves are pervasive and profound. Consider this passage from a recent work by G. F. Warnock:

> I do not necessarily do you any harm at all by deed or word if I induce you to believe what is not in fact the case; I may even do you good, possibly by way, for example, of consolation or flattery. Nevertheless, though deception is not thus necessarily directly damaging it is easy to see how crucially important it is that the natural inclination to have recourse to it should be counteracted. It is, one might say, not the implanting of false beliefs that is damaging, but rather the generation of the suspicion that they may be being implanted. For this undermines trust; and, to the extent that trust is undermined, all cooperative undertakings, in which what one person can do or has reason to do is dependent on what others have done, are doing, or are going to do, must tend to break down. . . . There is no sense in my asking you for your opinion on some point, if I do not suppose that your answer will actually express your opinion (verbal communication is doubtless the most important of all our co-operative undertakings). (*The Object of Morality* [London: Methuen, 1971], p. 84.)

Warnock does not quite say that truth-telling is good in itself or that lying is wrong, yet the moral quality of truth-telling and lying is not so simply instrumental as it is, for instance, for Bentham. Rather, truth-telling seems to bear a fundamental, pervasive relation to the human enterprise, just as lying appears to be fundamentally subversive of that enterprise. What exactly is the nature of this relation? How does truth-telling bear to human goods a relation which is more than instrumental but less than necessary?

The very definition of lying makes plain that consequences are crucial, for lying is intentional and the intent is an intent to produce a consequence: false belief. But how can I then resist the consequentialist analysis of lying? Lying is an attempt to produce a certain effect on another, and if that effect (consequence) is not bad, how can lying be wrong? I shall have to argue, therefore, that to lie is to intend to produce an effect which always has something bad about it, an effect moreover of the special sort that it is wrong to produce it intentionally. To lay that groundwork for my argument about lying, I must consider first the moral value of truth.

Truth and Rationality

A statement is true when the world is the way the statement says it is.[2] Utilitarians insist (as in the quotation from Bentham above) that truth, like everything else, has value just exactly as it produces value—pleasure, pain, the satisfaction or frustration of desire. And of course it is easy to show that truth (like keeping faith, not harming the innocent, respecting rights) does not always lead to the net satisfactions of desire, to the production of utility. It may *tend* to do so, but that tendency explains only why we should discriminate between occasions when truth does and when it does not have value—an old story. It is an old story, for truth—like justice, respect, and self-respect—has a value which consequentialist analyses (utilitarian or any other) do not capture. Truth, like respect, is a foundational value.

The morality of right and wrong does not count the satisfaction of desire as the overriding value. Rather, the integrity of persons, as agents and as the objects of the intentional agency of others, has priority over the attainment of the goals which agents choose to attain. I have sought to show how respect for physical integrity is related to respect for the person. The person, I argued, is not just a locus of potential pleasure and pain but an entity with determinate characteristics. The person is, among other things, necessarily an incorporated, a physical, not an abstract entity. In relation to truth we touch another necessary aspect of moral personality: the capacity for judgment, and thus for choice. It is that aspect which Kant used to ground his moral theory, arguing that freedom and

---

[2]This definition is derived from Alfred Tarski via Donald Davidson, "Meaning and Truth," in Jay F. Rosenberg and Charles Travis, eds., *Reading in the Philosophy of Language* (Englewood Cliffs, N.J.: Prentice-Hall, 1971). See also Gottlob Frege, "The Thought: A Logical Inquiry," and Michael Dummett, "Truth," both in Peter Strawson, ed., *Philosophical Logic* (Oxford: Oxford University Press, 1967). The difficulties in arriving at a satisfactory conception of truth do not touch the moral issues that I discuss in this chapter. Indeed, I suppose that any of a large class of definitions might be substituted for the one I used in the text and my substantive argument would go through without a hitch.

rationality are the basis for moral personality. John Rawls makes the same point, arguing that "moral personality and not the capacity for pleasure and pain . . . [is] the fundamental aspect of the self . . . The essential unity of the self is . . . provided by the concept of right" (*A Theory of Justice* [Cambridge, Mass.: Harvard University Press, 1971], p. 563). The concept of the self is prior to the goods which the self chooses, and these goods gather their moral significance from the fact that they have been chosen by moral beings— beings capable of understanding and acting on moral principles.

In this view freedom and rationality are complementary capacities, or aspects of the same capacity, which is moral capacity. A man is free insofar as he is able to act on a judgment because he perceives it to be correct; he is free insofar as he may be moved to action by the judgments his reason offers to him. This is the very opposite of the Humean conception of reason as the slave of the passions. There is no slavery here. The man who follows the steps of a mathematical argument to its conclusion because he judges them to be correct is free indeed. To the extent that we choose our ends we are free; and as to objectively valuable ends which we choose because we see their value, we are still free.

Now, rational judgment is true judgment, and so the moral capacity for rational choice implies the capacity to recognize the matter on which choice is to act and to recognize the kind of result our choices will produce. This applies to judgments about other selves and to judgments in which one locates himself as a person among persons, a self among selves. These judgments are not just arbitrary suppositions: *they are judged to be true of the world.* For consider what the self would be like if these judgments were not supposed to be true. Maybe one might be content to be happy in the manner of the fool of Athens who believed all the ships in the harbor to be his. But what of our perceptions of other people? Would we be content to have those whom we love and trust the mere figments of our imaginations? The foundational values of freedom and rationality imply the foundational value of truth, for the rational man is the one who judges aright, that is, truly. Truth is not the same as judgment, as rationality; it is rather the proper subject of judgment. If we did not seek to judge truly, and if we did not believe we could judge truly, the act of judgment would not be what we know it to be at all.

Judgment and thus truth are *part* of a structure which as a whole makes up the concept of self. A person's relation to his body and the fact of being an incorporated self are another part of that structure. These two parts are related. The bodily senses provide matter for judgments of truth, and the body includes the physical organs of judgment.

The Wrong of Lying

So our capacity for judgment is foundational and truth is the proper object of that capacity, but how do we get to the badness of lying, much less its categorical wrongness? The crucial step to be supplied has to do not with the value of truth but with the evil of lying. We must show that to lie to someone is to injure him in a way that particularly touches his moral personality. From that, the passage is indeed easy to the conclusion that to inflict such injury intentionally (remember that all lying is by hypothesis intentional) is not only bad but wrong. It is this first, crucial step which is difficult. After all, a person's capacity for true judgment is not necessarily impaired by inducing in him a particular false belief. Nor would it seem that a person suffers a greater injury in respect to that capacity when he is induced to believe a falsity than when we intentionally prevent him from discovering the truth, yet only in the first case do we lie. Do we really do injury to a person's moral personality when we persuade him falsely that it rained yesterday in Bangkok—a fact in which he has no interest? And do we do him more injury than when we fail to answer his request for yesterday's football scores, in which he is mildly interested? Must we not calculate the injury by the *other* harm it does: disappointed expectations, lost property, missed opportunities, physical harm? In this view, lying would be a way of injuring a person in his various substantive interests—a way of stealing from him, hurting his feelings, perhaps poisoning him—but then the evil of lying would be purely instrumental, not wrong at all.

All truth, however irrelevant or trivial, has value, even though we may cheerfully ignore most truths, forget them, erase them as encumbrances from our memories. The value of every truth is shown just in the judgment that the only thing we must not do is falsify truth. Truths are like other people's property, which we can care nothing about but may not use for our own purposes. It is as if the truth were not ours (even truth we have discovered and which is known only to us), and so we may not exercise an unlimited dominion over it. Our relations to other people have a similar structure: we may perhaps have no duty to them, we may be free to put them out of our minds to make room for others whom we care about more, but we may not harm them. And so we may not falsify truth. But enough of metaphors—what does it mean to say that the truth is not ours?

The capacity for true judgment is the capacity to arrive at judgments which are in fact true of the world as it exists apart from our desires, our choices, our values. It is the world presented to us by true judgments—including true judgments about ourselves—which we then make the subject of our choices, our valuation. Now, if we treat the truth as our own, it must be according to desire or valuation. But for rational beings these activities are supposed to depend on truth; we are supposed to desire and choose according to the world as it is. To choose that something not be the case when it is in fact the case is very nearly self-contradictory—for choice is not *of* truth but *on the basis of* truth. To deliberate about whether to believe a truth (not whether it is indeed true—another story altogether) is like deciding whether to cheat at solitaire. All this is obvious. In fact I suppose one cannot even coherently talk about choosing to believe something one believes to be false. And this holds equally for all truths—big and little, useful, useless, and downright inconvenient. But we do and must calculate *about* (and not just *with*) truths all the time as we decide what truths to acquire, what to forget. We decide all the time not to pursue some inquiry because it is not worth it. Such calculations surely must go forward on the basis of what truths are useful, given one's plans and desires. Even when we pursue truth for its own sake, we distinguish between interesting and boring truths.

Considering what truth to acquire or retain differs, however, from deliberately acquiring false beliefs. All truths are acquired as propositions correctly (truly) corresponding to the world, and in this respect, all truths are equal. A lie, however, has the form and occupies the role of truth in that it too purports to be a proposition about the world; only the world does not correspond to it. So the choice of a lie is not like a choice among truths, for the choice of a lie is a choice to affirm as the basis for judgment a proposition which does not correspond to the world. So, when I say that truth is foundational, that truth precedes choice, what I mean is *not* that this or that truth is foundational but that judging according to the facts is foundational to judging at all. A scientist may deliberate about which subject to study and, having chosen his subject, about the data worth acquiring, but he cannot even deliberate as a scientist about whether to acquire false data. Clearly, then, there is something funny (wrong?) about lying to oneself, but how do we go from there to the proposition that it is wrong to lie to someone else? After all, much of the peculiarity about lying to oneself consists in the fact that it seems not so much bad as downright self-contradictory, logically impossible, but that does not support the judgment that it is wrong to lie to another. I cannot marry myself, but that hardly makes it wrong to marry someone else.

Let us imagine a case in which you come as close as you can to lying to yourself: You arrange some operation, some fiddling with your brain that has no effect other than to cause you to believe a proposition you know to be false and also to forget entirely the prior history of how you came to believe that proposition. It seems to me that you do indeed harm yourself in such an operation. This is because a free and rational person wishes to have a certain relation to reality: as nearly perfect as possible. He wishes to build his conception of himself and the world and his conception of the good on the basis of truth. Now if he affirms that the truth is available for fiddling in order to accommodate either his picture of the world or his conception of the good, then this affirms that reality is dependent on what one wants, rather than what one wants being fundamentally constrained by what there is. Rationality is the respect for this fundamental constraint of truth. This is just another way of saying that the truth is prior to our plans and prospects and must be respected whatever our plans might be. What if the truth we "destroy" by this operation is a very trivial and irrelevant truth—the state of the weather in Bangkok on some particular day? There is still an injury to self, because the fiddler must have some purpose in his fiddling. If it is a substantive purpose, then the truth is in fact relevant to that purpose, and my argument holds. If it is just to show it can be done, then he is only trying to show he can do violence to his rationality—a kind of moral blasphemy. Well, what if it is a very *little* truth? Why, then, it is a very little injury he does himself—but that does not undermine my point.[3]

Now, when I lie to you, I do to you what you cannot actually do to yourself—brain-fiddling being only an approximation. The nature of the injury I would do to myself, if I could, explains why lying to you is to do you harm, indeed why it is wrong. The lie is an injury because it produces an effect (or seeks to) which a person as a moral agent should not wish to have produced in him, and thus it is as much an injury as any other effect which a moral agent would not wish to have produced upon his person. To be sure, some people may want to be lied to. That is a special problem; they are like people who want to suffer (not just are willing to risk) physical injury. In general, then, I do not want you to lie to me in the same way that as a rational man I would not lie to myself if I could. But why does this make lying wrong and not merely bad?[4]

Lying is wrong because when I lie I set up a relation which is essentially exploitative. It violates the principle of respect, for I must affirm that the mind of another person is available to me in a way in which I cannot agree my mind would be available to him—for if I do so agree, then I would not expect my lie to be believed. When I lie, I am like a counterfeiter: I do not want the market flooded with counterfeit currency; I do not want to get back my own counterfeit bill. Moreover, in lying to you, I affirm such an unfairly unilateral principle in respect to an interest and capacity which is crucial, as crucial as physical integrity: your freedom and your rationality. When I do intentional physical harm, I say that your body, your person, is available for my purposes. When I lie, I lay claim to your mind.

Lying violates respect and is wrong, as is any breach of trust. Every lie is a broken promise, and the only reason this seems

---

[3]Distinguish from this the frequent and important instances where one refuses to receive certain truths: the man of honor who will not read scandalous accusations about another's private life, the judge who will not receive unauthorized information about a matter before him. These do not involve deliberate espousals of falsity. There is, after all, a proper domain of secret, private truths and of things which are none of our business.

[4]It may be the case that every instance of any intentional injury to another person constitutes a wrongful relation (is wrong), but I am not prepared to argue that. I would rather examine the circumstances of this one kind of injury, lying, and show how that is wrong.

strained is that in lying the promise is made and broken at the same moment. Every lie necessarily implies—as does every assertion—an assurance, a warranty of its truth. The fact that the breach accompanies the making should, however, only strengthen the conclusion that this is wrong. If promise-breaking is wrong, then a lie must be wrong, since there cannot be the supervening factor of changed circumstances which may excuse breaches of promises to perform in the future.

The final one of the convergent strands that make up the wrong of lying is the shared, communal nature of language. This is what I think Kant had in mind when he argued that a lie does wrong "to men in general." If whether people stood behind their statements depended wholly on the particular circumstances of the utterance, then the whole point of communication would be undermined. For every utterance would simply be the occasion for an analysis of the total circumstances (speaker's and hearer's) in order to determine what, if anything, to make of the utterance. And though we do often wonder and calculate whether a person is telling the truth, we do so from a baseline, a presumption that people do stand behind their statements. After all, the speaker surely depends on such a baseline. He wants us to think that he is telling the truth. Speech is a paradigm of communication, and all human relations are based on some form of communication. Our very ability to think, to conceptualize, is related to speech. Speech allows the social to penetrate the intimately personal. Perhaps that is why Kant's dicta seem to vacillate between two positions: lying as a social offense, and lying as an offense against oneself; the requirement of an intent to deceive another, and the insistence that the essence of the wrong is not injury to another but to humanity. Every lie violates the basic commitment to truth which stands behind the social fact of language.

I have already argued that bodily integrity bears a necessary relation to moral integrity, so that an attack upon bodily integrity is wrong, not just bad. The intimate *and* social nature of truth make the argument about lying stronger. For not only is the target aspect of the victim crucial to him as a moral agent but, by lying, we attack that target by a means which itself offends his moral nature; the means of attack are social means which can be said to belong as much to the victim as to his assailant. There is not only the attack at his moral vitals, but an attack with a weapon which belongs to him. Lying is, thus, a kind of treachery. (*Kind of* treachery? Why not treachery pure

301

and simple?) It is as if we not only robbed a man of his treasure but in doing so used his own servants or family as our agents. That speech is our *common* property, that it belongs to the liar, his victim and all of us makes the matter if anything far worse.

So this is why lying is not only bad (a hurt), but wrong, why lying is wrong apart from or in addition to any other injury it does, and why lying seems at once an offense against the victim and against mankind in general, an offense against the liar himself, and against the abstract entity, truth. Whom do you injure when you pass a counterfeit bill?

What about little pointless lies? Do I really mean they are wrong? Well, yes, even a little lie is wrong, *if* it is a true piece of communication, an assertion of its own truth and not just a conventional way of asserting nothing at all or something else (as in the case of polite or diplomatic formulas). A little lie is a little wrong, but it is still something you must not do.

STUDY QUESTIONS

1. Why does Fried think that lying is both wrong and bad?
2. What does Fried mean when he says, "Truth, like respect, is a foundational value." What does this imply for the nature of lying?
3. Lying must be deliberate. Can you lie to yourself? Could that be wrong? What is Fried's view?
4. What, precisely, is the effect of a lie on the person lied to? What is wrong with this effect? Give your own arguments in defense of the view that a serious lie is sometimes (never) justified.

Without Virtue

PETER SINGER

Peter Singer (b. 1946) teaches philosophy at La Trobe University in Victoria, Australia. His books include *Animal Liberation* (1975), *Practical Ethics* (1979), and *The Expanding Circle* (1981).

Singer examines the link between vice and unhappiness from a utilitarian standpoint. Psychopaths have a character type that enables them to pursue pleasure with indifference to the suffering they cause others. The existence of psychopaths untroubled by conscience and apparently enjoying themselves seems to count against the thesis that a lack of virtue leads to unhappiness. Singer counters this by arguing that psychopaths and others who completely lack such virtues as benevolence and compassion are unable to do more than pursue short-range objectives. All they can do is continue their selfish pursuit of more pleasure. But their satisfactions are short lived and their capacity for enjoyment soon becomes jaded. Even prudent egoists whose selfish goals are long range end up desperately bored and without the resources to relieve that boredom. If Singer is right, the utilitarian, too, can consistently maintain that a virtuous character is needed for an interesting and meaningful life.

WITHOUT VIRTUE From *Practical Ethics* by Peter Singer. Reprinted by permission of the publisher, Cambridge University Press.

It might be said that since philosophers are not empirical scientists, discussion of the connection between acting ethically and living a fulfilled and happy life should be left to psychologists, sociologists and other appropriate experts. The question is not, however, dealt with by any other single discipline and its relevance to practical ethics is reason enough for our looking into it.

What facts about human nature could show that ethics and self-interest coincide? One theory is that we all have benevolent or sympathetic inclinations which make us concerned about the welfare of others. Another relies on a natural conscience which gives rise to guilt feelings when we do what we know to be wrong. But how strong are these benevolent desires or feelings of guilt? Is it possible to suppress them? If so, isn't it possible that in a world in which humans and other animals are suffering in great numbers, suppressing one's conscience and sympathy for others is the surest way to happiness?

To meet this objection those who would link ethics and happiness must assert that we cannot be happy if these elements of our nature are suppressed. Benevolence and sympathy, they might argue, are tied up with the capacity to take part in friendly or loving relations with others, and there can be no real happiness without such relationships. For the same reason it is necessary to take at least some ethical standards seriously, and to be open and honest in living by them—for a life of deception and dishonesty is a furtive life, in which the possibility of discovery always clouds the horizon. Genuine acceptance of ethical standards is likely to mean that we feel some guilt—or at least that we are less pleased with ourselves than we otherwise would be—when we do not live up to them.

These claims about the connection between our character and our prospects of happiness are no more than hypotheses. Attempts to confirm them by detailed research are sparse and inadequate. A. H. Maslow, an American psychologist, asserts that human beings have a need for self-actualization, which involves growing towards courage, kindness, knowledge, love, honesty, and unselfishness. When we fulfil this need we feel serene, joyful, filled with zest, sometimes euphoric, and generally happy. When we act contrary to our need for self-actualization we experience anxiety, despair, boredom, shame, emptiness and are generally unable to enjoy ourselves. It would be nice if Maslow should turn out to be right; unfortunately the data Maslow produces in support of his theory consist of very limited studies of selected people. The theory must await confirmation or falsification from larger, more rigorous and more representative studies.

Human nature is so diverse that one may doubt if any generalization about the kind of character that leads to happiness could hold for all human beings. What, for instance, of those we call 'psychopaths'? Psychiatrists use this term as a label for a person who is asocial, impulsive, egocentric, unemotional, lacking in feelings of remorse, shame or guilt, and apparently unable to form deep and enduring personal relationships. Psychopaths are certainly abnormal, but whether it is proper to say that they are mentally ill is another matter. At least on the surface, they do not *suffer* from their condition, and it is not obvious that it is in their interest to be 'cured'. Hervey Cleckley, the author of a classic study of psychopathy entitled *The Mask of Sanity*, notes that since his book was first published he has received countless letters from people desperate for help—but they are from the parents, spouses and other relatives of psychopaths, almost never from the psychopaths themselves. This is not surprising, for while psychopaths are asocial and indifferent to the welfare of others, they seem to enjoy life. Psychopaths often appear to be charming, intelligent people, with no delusions or other signs of irrational thinking. When interviewed they say things like:

> A lot has happened to me, a lot more will happen. But I enjoy living and I am always looking forward to each day. I like laughing and I've done a lot. I am essentially a clown at heart—but a happy one. I always take the bad with the good.

There is no effective therapy for psychopathy, which may be explained by the fact that psychopaths see nothing wrong with their behaviour and often find it extremely rewarding, at least in the short term. Of course their impulsive nature and lack of a sense of shame or guilt means that some psychopaths end up in prison, though it is hard to tell how many do not, since those who avoid prison are also more likely to avoid contact with psychiatrists. Studies have shown that a surprisingly large number of psychopaths are able to avoid prison despite grossly antisocial behaviour, probably because of their well-known ability to convince others that they are truly repentant, that it will never happen again, that they deserve another chance, etc., etc.

The existence of psychopathic people counts against the contention that benevolence, sympathy and feelings of guilt are present in everyone. It also appears to count against attempts to link happiness with the possession of these inclinations. But let us pause before we accept this latter conclusion. Must we accept psychopaths' own evaluations of their happiness? They are, after all, notoriously persuasive liars. Moreover even if they are telling the truth as they see it, are they qualified to say that they are really happy, when they seem unable to experience the emotional states that play such a large part in the happiness and fulfilment of more normal people? Admittedly, a psychopath could use the same argument against us: how can we say that we are truly happy when we have not experienced the excitement and freedom that comes from complete irresponsibility? Since we cannot enter into the subjective states of psychopathic people, nor they into ours, the dispute is not easy to resolve.

Cleckley suggests that the psychopaths' behaviour can be explained as a response to the meaninglessness of their lives. It is characteristic of psychopaths to work for a while at a job and then just when their ability and charm have taken them to the crest of success, commit some petty and easily detectable crime. A similar pattern occurs in their personal relationships. (There is support to be found here for Thomas Nagel's account of imprudence as rational only if one fails to see oneself as a person existing over time, with the present merely one among other times one will live through. Certainly psychopathic people live largely in the present and lack any coherent life plan.)

Cleckley explains this erratic and to us inadequately motivated behaviour by likening the psychopath's life to that of children forced to sit through a performance of *King Lear*. Children are restless and misbehave under these conditions because they cannot enjoy the play as adults do. They act to relieve boredom. Similarly, Cleckley says, psychopaths are bored because their emotional poverty means that they cannot take interest in, or gain satisfaction from, what for others are the most important things in life: love, family, success in business or professional life, etc. These things simply do not matter to them. Their unpredictable and anti-social behaviour is an attempt to relieve what would otherwise be a tedious existence.

These claims are speculative and Cleckley admits that they may not be possible to establish scientifically. They do suggest, however, an aspect of the psychopath's life that undermines the otherwise attractive nature of the psychopath's free-wheeling life. Most reflective people, at some time or other, want their life to have some kind of meaning. Few of us could deliberately choose a way of life which we regarded as utterly meaningless. For this reason most of us would not choose to live a psychopathic life, however enjoyable it might be.

Yet there is something paradoxical about criticizing the psychopath's life for its meaninglessness. Don't we have to accept, in the absence of religious belief, that life really is meaningless, not just for the psychopath but for all of us? And if this is so, why should we not choose—if it were in our powers to choose our personality—the life of a psychopath? But is it true that, religion aside, life is meaningless? Now our pursuit of reasons for acting morally has led us to what is often regarded as the ultimate philosophical question.

Has Life a Meaning?

In what sense does rejection of belief in a god imply rejection of the view that life has any meaning? If this world had been created by some divine being with a particular goal in mind, it could be said to have a meaning, at least for that divine being. If we could know what the divine being's purpose in creating us was, we could then know what the meaning of our life was for our creator. If we accepted our creator's purpose (though why we should do that would need to be explained) we could claim to know the meaning of life.

When we reject belief in a god we must give up the idea that life on this planet has some preordained meaning. Life *as a whole* has no meaning. Life began, as the best available theories tell us, in a chance combination of gases; it then evolved through random mutations and natural selection. All this just happened; it did not happen for any overall purpose. Now that it has resulted in the existence of beings who prefer some states of affairs to others, however, it may be possible for particular lives to be meaningful. In this sense atheists can find meaning in life.

Let us return to the comparison between the life of a psychopath and that of a more normal person. Why should the psychopath's life not be meaningful? We have seen that psychopaths are egocentric to an extreme: neither other people, nor worldly success, nor anything else really matters to them. But why is their own enjoyment of life not sufficient to give meaning to their lives?

Most of us would not be able to find happiness by deliberately setting out to enjoy ourselves without caring about anyone or anything else. The pleasures we obtained in that way would seem empty, and soon pall. We seek a meaning for our lives beyond our own pleasures, and find fulfilment and happiness in doing what we see to be meaningful. If our life has no meaning other than our own happiness, we are likely to find that when we have obtained what we think we need to be happy, happiness itself still eludes us.

That those who aim at happiness for happiness's sake often fail to find it, while others find happiness in pursuing altogether different goals, has been called 'the paradox of hedonism'. It is not, of course, a logical paradox but a claim about the way in which we come to be happy. Like other generalizations on this subject it lacks empirical confirmation. Yet it matches our everyday observations, and is consistent with our nature as evolved, purposive beings. Human beings survive and reproduce themselves through purposive action. We obtain happiness and fulfilment by working towards and achieving our goals. In evolutionary terms we could say that happiness functions as an internal reward for our achievements. Subjectively, we regard achieving the goal (or progressing towards it) as a reason for happiness. Our own happiness, therefore, is a by-product of aiming at something else, and not to be obtained by setting our sights on happiness alone.

The psychopath's life can now be seen to be meaningless in a way that a normal life is not. It is meaningless because it looks inward to the pleasures of the present moment and not outward to anything more long-term or far-reaching. More normal lives have meaning because they are lived to some larger purpose.

All this is speculative. You may accept or reject it to the extent that it agrees with your own observation and introspection. My next—and final—suggestion is more speculative still. It is that to find an enduring meaning in our lives it is not enough to go beyond psychopaths who have no long-term commitments or life-plans; we must also go beyond more prudent egoists who have long-term plans concerned only with their own interests. The prudent egoists may find meaning in their lives for a time, for they have the purpose of furthering their own interests; but what, in the end, does that amount to? When everything in our interests has been achieved, do we just sit back and be happy? Could we be happy in this way? Or would we decide that we had still not quite reached our target, that there was something else we needed before we could sit back and enjoy it all? Most materially successful egoists take the latter route, thus escaping the necessity of admitting that they cannot find happiness in permanent holidaying. People who slaved to establish small businesses, telling themselves they would do it only until they had made enough to live comfortably, keep working long after they have passed their original target. Their material 'needs' expand just fast enough to keep ahead of their income. Retirement is a problem for many because they cannot enjoy themselves without a purpose in life. The recommended solution is, of course, to find a new purpose, whether it be stamp collecting or voluntary work for a charity.

Now we begin to see where ethics comes into the problem of living a meaningful life. If we are looking for a purpose broader than our own interests, something which will allow us to see our lives as possessing significance beyond the narrow confines of our own conscious states, one obvious solution is to take up the ethical point of view. The ethical point of view does, as we have seen, require us to go beyond a personal point of view to the standpoint of an impartial spectator. Thus looking at things ethically is a way of transcending our inward-looking concerns and identifying ourselves with the most objective point of view possible—with, as Sidgwick put it, 'the point of view of the universe'.

The point of view of the universe is a lofty standpoint. In the rarefied air that surrounds it we may get carried away into talking, as Kant does, of the moral point of view 'inevitably' humbling all who compare their own limited nature with it. I do not want to suggest anything as sweeping as this. Earlier in this chapter, in rejecting Thomas Nagel's argument for the rationality of altruism, I said that there is nothing irrational about being concerned with the quality of one's own existence in a way that one is not concerned with the quality of existence of other individuals. Without going back on this, I am now suggesting that rationality, in the broad sense which includes self-awareness and reflection on the nature and point of our own existence, may push us towards concerns broader than the quality of our own existence; but the process is not a necessary one and those who do not take part in it—or, in taking part, do not follow it all the way to the ethical point of view—are not irrational or in error. Psychopaths, for all I know, may simply be unable to obtain as much happiness through caring about others as they obtain by antisocial acts. Other people find collecting stamps an entirely adequate way of giving purpose to their lives. There is nothing irrational about that; but others again grow out of stamp collecting as they become more aware of their situation in the world and more reflective about their purposes. To this third group the ethical point of view offers a meaning and purpose in life that one does not grow out of.

(At least, one cannot grow out of the ethical point of view until all ethical tasks have been accomplished. If that utopia were ever achieved, our purposive nature might well leave us dissatisfied, much as the egoist is dissatisfied when he has everything he needs to be happy. There is nothing paradoxical about this, for we should not expect evolution to have equipped us, in advance, with the ability to enjoy a situation that has never previously occurred. Nor is this going to be a practical problem in the near future.)

'Why act morally?' cannot be given an answer that will provide everyone with overwhelming reasons for acting morally. Ethically indefensible behaviour is not always irrational. We will probably always need the sanctions of the law and social pressure to provide additional reasons against serious violations of ethical standards. On the other hand, those reflective enough to ask the question we have been discussing in this chapter are also those most likely to appreciate the reasons that can be offered for taking the ethical point of view.

STUDY QUESTIONS

1. Do you think ethics and self-interest coincide? Compare Singer's defense of this general proposition with that of some classical philosophers who also believe that the virtuous person is happy.

2. Should we accept the psychopaths' claim that they are actually happy when they appear to be enjoying themselves?
3. Singer believes that the lives of psychopaths and rational egoists are meaningless and boring, perhaps even despairingly so. Has he made a persuasive case for this conclusion?
4. What does Singer mean by the ethical point of view and why does he recommend it to us?

SUGGESTED READINGS

Alighieri, Dante. *Inferno*.

Bloomfield, Morton. *The Seven Deadly Sins*. East Lansing, Mich.: Michigan State University Press, 1967.

Burton, Robert. *The Anatomy of Melancholy* (originally published 1621). New York: Vintage Press, 1977.

Freud, Sigmund. *Civilization and Its Discontents*. Edited and translated by James Strachey. New York: W. W. Norton and Co. 1962.

Jacoby, Susan. *Wild Justice: The Evolution of Revenge*. New York: Harper and Row, 1983.

Ross, Edward Alsworth. *Sin and Society: An Analysis of Latter Day Iniquity*. (originally published 1907). New York: Harper Torchbooks, 1973.

Chapter

5

FREEDOM AND RESPONSIBILITY

The philosopher Sidney Hook tells the story of one Waldemar Debbler, who, in 1935, was found guilty of burglary and sentenced to two years in prison. Upon hearing his sentence, he rose and addressed the court:

> Gentlemen, you see in me the victim of an unwavering destiny. So-called freedom of decision does not exist. Every human action in this world is determined. The causes are given by the circumstances and the results inevitable. By my inclinations of character, for which I am not responsible, since they were born in me, by my upbringing, my experiences, I was predetermined to become what I am. If you, gentlemen, had a heredity similar to mine and had been subjected to the same influence as I, you would also have committed the burglary in this particular situation. With this theory I am in good company. I refer you to Spinoza and Leibnitz. Even St. Augustine and, later, Calvin attributed all human actions to the immutable decree of destiny. As I have only done what I had to do, you have no moral right to punish me, and I therefore plead for my acquittal.

313

The judge replied:

> We have followed the prisoner's reasoning with attention. Whatever happens is the necessary and immutable sequel of preceding causes which, once given, could not be other than it is. Consequently the prisoner, by reason of his character and experience, was destined to commit the burglary. On the other hand, destiny also decrees that the court, as a result of the submitted testimony, must judge the prisoner guilty of burglary. The causes—the deed, the law, the nature of the judge—being given, the sentence of guilty and punishment follows as a natural consequence.

When asked his reaction to his sentence, the defendant declared:

> Destiny demands that I appeal!

And the judge replied:

> That may be. However, destiny will see to it that your appeal is rejected.

Hook will not vouch for the authenticity of the story and he correctly points out that it confuses determinism, the view that all human decisions and actions are causally determined, with fatalism, the view, popular in fairy tales, that whatever happens is fated to happen and cannot be prevented no matter what anyone does. All the same, the defendant Debbler touches on a real philosophical problem: Are human beings responsible for what they do? Do we freely choose vice over virtue or do our heredity and environment always determine our choices for us? Are we mistaken when we think of ourselves as free moral agents?

One basic assumption of common-sense morality is that we often act freely and may be held responsible for what we do. We praise the virtuous and blame the vicious because we believe they freely choose their actions. And, conversely, we do not praise or blame people for actions completely beyond their control. The assumption of personal responsibility underlies our legal institutions. We find it somewhat bizarre that, in the Middle Ages, farm animals that misbehaved were put on trial and ritually executed for their "crimes." Human beings, so we believe, are different: Much of what we do is freely done. Many of our actions are "up to us," and for them we may be morally responsible.

The position of common sense embodied in the legal traditions of most modern societies maintains the following propositions:

(1) much of what people do is an expression of their character, and human character is shaped by heredity and environment; and

(2) human beings often choose freely and act freely and are morally responsible for their choices.

Each proposition seems true but we cannot easily see how both can be true together. The first proposition asserts determinism; the second, freedom and responsibility. But if determinism is correct, then we are unfree and should not be held responsible. "Hard" determinists, such as Robert Blatchford, Clarence Darrow, and John Hospers, deny that these two propositions are compatible. Being forced to choose between them, hard determinists choose (1) and declare that (2) is false. For Blatchford, our sense of freedom is a delusion. Hospers claims that almost all the actions and choices we think are freely made are subconsciously determined. According to Darrow, we are "victims of nature" and are not morally responsible for our choices.

In 1924, the reknowned trial lawyer Clarence Darrow defended two teenagers, Nathan Leopold and Richard Loeb, who had kidnapped and murdered Loeb's cousin, fourteen-year-old Bobby Franks. Both boys were child prodigies and sons of millionaires. Darrow claimed that their extraordinary intelligence, the emotional poverty of their homes, and their early fascination with detective stories led them to become obsessed with the idea of committing the "perfect crime." Capital punishment was then the norm, but Darrow's philosophical defense of determinism was so moving and effective that, after he finished, the judge was in tears and Leopold and Loeb received life sentences. Darrow pleaded before the judge:

> But, Your Honor, . . . [n]ature is strong and she is pitiless. She works in her own mysterious way, and we are her victims . . . In the words of old Omar Khayyan, we are only: "But helpless pieces in the game He plays/Upon this checkerboard of night and days; . . ."

Defenders of the common-sense view must show that both (1) and (2) can hold without contradiction. Two lines of defense have been used. The first, called "libertarianism," concentrates on inter-

315

preting (1) to make it consistent with (2). Denying that human beings are ever fully shaped by heredity and environment, libertarians call attention to the role a person's "inner self" or "consciousness" plays. Consider a very virtuous and thoroughly reliable man named Jones, who is, as we say, incapable of hurting a fly, telling a lie, or looking the other way when he can help someone in need, even at risk to himself. Given Jones's character, many of his actions are easy to predict. In his personal relations, Jones is kind and considerate. If he gives his word, you can predict he will make every effort to keep it. Common sense finds Jones's decency and courage altogether praiseworthy. And common sense is not impressed by the determinist argument that, given Jones's character, he cannot help *but* behave as he does. According to the libertarian, common sense is right. Jones is praiseworthy because what Jones is like now results partly from what he has made of himself over the years. According to libertarians such as Jean-Paul Sartre and C. A. Campbell, heredity and environment do *not* exhaustively determine one's character; rather, the Self enters at crucial points in choosing certain lines of development. Although character often determines conduct, we praise or blame the conduct so determined. For we hold people responsible for being virtuous or vicious. "Man," says Sartre, "is nothing else but what he makes of himself."

Moreover, the libertarian claims that even the character for which one is responsible does not fully determine conduct. Consider Jones's opposite number, Smith. Smith is a selfish person who never allows the misfortunes of others to interfere with his plans. One day he is driving and sees, alongside the road, an elderly man who needs help with a flat tire. Smith, being the man he is, is strongly tempted to drive on and spare himself a tedious episode. Anyone who knows Smith might well predict that he will not stop. Yet Smith *might* stop. That is not out of the question. For even now Smith is free to remake himself. Campbell sees this as an example of how our conscience, or our "higher self," can sometimes override even the dispositions of our developed character. Of course, Campbell admits that character usually wins out (this is why so much human action is, in fact, predictable). Nevertheless, a person's character is a product of an ongoing process of self-determination: Character is not destiny. Waldemar Debbler is acting in "bad faith" (to use Sartre's well-known phrase) when he claims he is a victim of his own character. For he treats himself not as a free "consciousness" but as an object whose nature is causally determined.

Sartre's version of libertarianism is "existentialist" but we do not need to be existentialists to believe in a self that determines itself. Thus, Immanuel Kant, who is not an existentialist, holds that heredity and environment do not determine a rational being's will. Since will enters into the determination of character, Kant holds that people are responsible for their character. Campbell's strong libertarian position is likewise free of the more radical doctrines associated with Sartrean existentialism. Indeed, the doctrine that people choose to be what they are can be found in Plato.

Another major defense of the common-sense position concentrates on showing how the *second* common-sense thesis (human beings choose and act freely) is compatible with the first (character is shaped by heredity and environment). This approach, known as "compatibilism" or "soft determinism" is represented in this chapter by W. T. Stace. The compatibilist has been characterized as holding that, though we can sometimes do as we please, we can never please as we please. We "cannot please as we please" because heredity and environment determine all our choices. In this respect the compatibilists' form of determinism is "hard." But they differ from hard determinists by maintaining, as the common sense theory does, that people can act freely and are morally responsible for acts freely done. To avoid the charge of inconsistency, compatibilists never use "free" to mean "undetermined" or "uncaused," but only to mean "unconstrained" or "uncompelled." If you are in jail, you are under constraint and so not free. If you act while someone holds a gun to your head, you do not act freely. Thus all our choices are determined, but some determined choices are made freely in the narrow sense that we do not make them under compulsion or threat. The compatibilist may therefore agree with the second common-sense thesis that human beings are sometimes free and morally responsible. Jones freely helps his friends; Smith freely chooses to drive on. The thesis that the characters, choices, and actions of Jones and Smith are causally determined is wholly compatible with the thesis that some of the choices they make, some of the actions they perform, are unconstrained and free in the narrow sense of "free" that soft determinists favor.

Soft determinism has attracted a distinguished following:

Thomas Hobbes (1588–1679), David Hume (1711–1776), and John Stuart Mill (1806–1873) are among its proponents. But neither libertarians nor hard determinists are impressed by the compatibilist claim that freedom from external constraint can bear the whole weight of moral responsibility. In some circumstances, we are disinclined to hold people morally responsible even though all their actions are free in the sense of being externally unconstrained. Suppose someone, a hypnotist or a mad scientist, for example, gained control of your inner states. Your actions would be "free" in the soft determinist sense of the word, but we could not consider you responsible for them. If soft determinists object by saying that a person whose desires are manipulated by outside forces is not free, then they would seem to lose ground to hard determinists such as Hospers. For hard determinists claim that we are all "hypnotized" and controlled, if not by hypnotists and mad scientists, then unconsciously by genetic forces, parents, grandparents, teachers, friends, and other determinants.

Much of the controversy over free will revolves around the conception of the Self to which we attribute freedom. We are not likely to resolve the controversy over freedom until philosophers and scientists answer some fundamental questions about the nature of consciousness and subjectivity. Meanwhile we may say this much: Lacking a clear conception of the Self, it is certainly too early to insist that what we are is wholly determined by our parents and the environment we are born into. In any case, the very strongly held common-sensical conviction that we are, at times, free and morally responsible is itself one of the salient points that any adequate theory of the Self must explain.

Leopold and Loeb: The Crime of Compulsion

CLARENCE DARROW

Clarence Darrow (1857–1938) was one of America's best known trial lawyers. His most famous cases were the Scopes evolution trial in Tennessee and the Leopold and Loeb murder trial. He was an outspoken agnostic and a proponent of prison reform.

In 1924, Clarence Darrow defended two teenagers, Nathan Leopold and Richard Loeb, who had murdered Loeb's fourteen-year-old cousin, Bobby Franks, just for the thrill of committing "the perfect crime." Both boys were child prodigies, sons of millionaires, and avid readers of crime stories. In summing up his defense of Richard Loeb, Darrow appeals to determinism, claiming that the "seed of corruption" was planted before Loeb ever committed his crime. The responsibility for Loeb's crime lay somewhere in the infinite number of his ancestors or in his surroundings or in both. Darrow depicts Loeb as having been overwhelmed by advantage, pushed too far in his studies, and influenced at an early age by books on crime that led him "naturally" to think of the perfect crime. The crime is therefore traceable to heredity and environment.

LEOPOLD AND LOEB: THE CRIME OF COMPULSION From *Attorney for the Damned.* Edited by Arthur Weinberg. Copyright © 1957 by Arthur Weinberg. Reprinted by permission of Simon and Schuster, Inc.

I have tried to study the lives of these two most unfortunate boys. Three months ago, if their friends and the friends of the family had been asked to pick out the most promising lads of their acquaintance, they probably would have picked these two boys. With every opportunity, with plenty of wealth, they would have said that those two would succeed.

In a day, by an act of madness, all this is destroyed, until the best they can hope for now is a life of silence and pain, continuing to the end of their years.

How did it happen?

Let us take Dickie Loeb first.

I do not claim to know how it happened; I have sought to find out. I know that something, or some combinations of things, is responsible for this mad act. I know that there are no accidents in nature. I know that effect follows cause. I know that, if I were wise enough, and knew enough about this case, I could lay my finger on the cause. I will do the best I can, but it is largely speculation.

The child, of course, is born without knowledge.

Impressions are made upon its mind as it goes along. Dickie Loeb was a child of wealth and opportunity. Over and over in this court Your Honor has been asked, and other courts have been asked, to consider boys who have no chance; they have been asked to consider the poor, whose home had been the street, with no education and no opportunity in life, and they have done it, and done it rightfully.

But, Your Honor, it is just as often a great misfortune to be the child of the rich as it is to be the child of the poor. Wealth has its misfortunes. Too much, too great opportunity and advantage, given to a child has its misfortunes, and I am asking Your Honor to consider the rich as well as the poor (and nothing else). Can I find what was wrong? I think I can. Here was a boy at a tender age, placed in the hands of a governess, intellectual, vigorous, devoted, with a strong ambition for the welfare of this boy. He was pushed in his studies, as plants are forced in hothouses. He had no pleasures, such as a boy should have, except as they were gained by lying and cheating.

Now, I am not criticizing the nurse. I suggest that some day Your Honor look at her picture. It explains her fully. Forceful, brooking no interference, she loved the boy, and her ambition was that he should reach the highest perfection. No time to pause, no time to stop from one book to another, no time to have those pleasures which a boy ought to have to create a normal life. And what happened? Your Honor, what would happen? Nothing strange or unusual. This nurse was with him all the time, except when he stole out at night, from two to fourteen years of age. He, scheming and planning as healthy boys would do, to get out from under her restraint; she, putting before him the best books, which children generally do not want; and he, when she was not looking, reading detective stories, which he devoured, story after story, in his young life. Of all this there can be no question.

What is the result? Every story he read was a story of crime. We have a statute in this state, passed only last year, if I recall it, which forbids minors reading stories of crime. Why? There is only one reason. Because the legislature in its wisdom felt that it would produce criminal tendencies in the boys who read them. The legislature of this state has given its opinion, and forbidden boys to read these books. He read them day after day. He never stopped. While he was passing through college at Ann Arbor he was still reading them. When he was a senior he read them, and almost nothing else.

Now, these facts are beyond dispute. He early developed the tendency to mix with crime, to be a detective; as a little boy shadowing people on the street; as a little child going out with his fantasy of being the head of a band of criminals and directing them on the street. How did this grow and develop in him? Let us see. It seems to be as natural as the day following the night. Every detective story is a story of a sleuth getting the best of it: trailing some unfortunate individual through devious ways until his victim is finally landed in jail or stands on the gallows. They all show how smart the detective is, and where the criminal himself falls down.

This boy early in his life conceived the idea that there could be a perfect crime, one that nobody could ever detect; that there could be one where the detective did not land his game—a perfect crime. He had been interested in the story of Charley Ross, who was kidnapped. He was interested in these things all his life. He believed in his childish way that a crime could be so carefully planned that there would be no detection, and his idea was to plan and accomplish a perfect crime. It would involve kidnapping and involve murder.

There had been growing in Dickie's brain, dwarfed and twisted—

as every act in this case shows it to have been dwarfed and twisted—there had been growing this scheme, not due to any wickedness of Dickie Loeb, for he is a child. It grew as he grew; it grew from those around him; it grew from the lack of the proper training until it possessed him. He believed he could beat the police. He believed he could plan the perfect crime. He had thought of it and talked of it for years—had talked of it as a child, had worked at it as a child—this sorry act of his, utterly irrational and motiveless, a plan to commit a perfect crime which must contain kidnapping, and there must be ransom, or else it could not be perfect, and they must get the money. . . .

The law knows and has recognized childhood for many and many a long year. What do we know about childhood? The brain of the child is the home of dreams, of castles, of visions, of illusions and of delusions. In fact, there could be no childhood without delusions, for delusions are always more alluring than facts. Delusions, dreams and hallucinations are a part of the warp and woof of childhood. You know it and I know it. I remember, when I was a child, the men seemed as tall as the trees, the trees as tall as the mountains. I can remember very well when, as a little boy, I swam the deepest spot in the river for the first time. I swam breathlessly and landed with as much sense of glory and triumph as Julius Caesar felt when he led his army across the Rubicon. I have been back since, and I can almost step across the same place, but it seemed an ocean then. And those men whom I thought so wonderful were dead and left nothing behind. I had lived in a dream. I had never known the real world which I met, to my discomfort and despair, and that dispelled the illusions of my youth.

The whole life of childhood is a dream and an illusion, and whether they take one shape or another shape depends not upon the dreamy boy but on what surrounds him. As well might I have dreamed of burglars and wished to be one as to dream of policemen and wished to be one. Perhaps I was lucky, too, that I had no money. We have grown to think that the misfortune is in not having it. The great misfortune in this terrible case is the money. That has destroyed their lives. That has fostered these illusions. That has promoted this mad act. And, if Your Honor shall doom them to die, it will be because they are the sons of the rich. . . .

I know where my life has been molded by books, amongst other things. We all know where our lives have been influenced by books. The nurse, strict and jealous and watchful, gave him one kind of book; by night he would steal off and read the other.

Which, think you, shaped the life of Dickie Loeb? Is there any kind of question about it? A child. Was it pure maliciousness? Was a boy of five or six or seven to blame for it? Where did he get it? He got it where we all get our ideas, and these books became a part of his dreams and a part of his life, and as he grew up his visions grew to hallucinations.

He went out on the street and fantastically directed his companions, who were not there, in their various moves to complete the perfect crime. Can there be any sort of question about it?

Suppose, Your Honor, that instead of this boy being here in this court, under the plea of the State that Your Honor shall pronounce a sentence to hang him by the neck until dead, he had been taken to a pathological hospital to be analyzed, and the physicians had inquired into his case. What would they have said? There is only one thing that they could possibly have said. They would have traced everything back to the gradual growth of the child.

That is not all there is about it. Youth is hard enough. The only good thing about youth is that it has no thought and no care; and how blindly we can do things when we are young!

Where is the man who has not been guilty of delinquencies in youth? Let us be honest with ourselves. Let us look into our own hearts. How many men are there today—lawyers and congressmen and judges, and even state's attorneys—who have not been guilty of some mad act in youth? And if they did not get caught, or the consequences were trivial, it was their good fortune.

We might as well be honest with ourselves, Your Honor. Before I would tie a noose around the neck of a boy I would try to call back into my mind the emotions of youth. I would try to remember what the world looked like to me when I was a child. I would try to remember how strong were these instinctive, persistent emotions that moved my life. I would try to remember how weak and inefficient was youth in the presence of the surging, controlling feelings of the child. One that honestly remembers and asks himself the question and tries to unlock the door that he thinks is closed, and calls back the boy, can understand the boy.

But, Your Honor, that is not all there is to boyhood. Nature is strong and she is pitiless. She works in her own mysterious way, and we are her victims. We have not much to do with it ourselves.

Nature takes this job in hand, and we play our parts. In the words of old Omar Khayyam, we are only:

> But helpless pieces in the game He plays
> Upon this checkerboard of nights and days;
> Hither and thither moves, and checks, and slays,
> And one by one back in the closet lays.

What had this boy to do with it? He was not his own father; he was not his own mother; he was not his own grandparents. All of this was handed to him. He did not surround himself with governesses and wealth. He did not make himself. And yet he is to be compelled to pay.

There was a time in England, running down as late as the beginning of the last century, when judges used to convene court and call juries to try a horse, a dog, a pig, for crime. I have in my library a story of a judge and jury and lawyers trying and convicting an old sow for lying down on her ten pigs and killing them.

What does it mean? Animals were tried. Do you mean to tell me that Dickie Loeb had any more to do with his making than any other product of heredity that is born upon the earth? . . .

For God's sake, are we crazy? In the face of history, of every line of philosophy, against the teaching of every religionist and seer and prophet the world has ever given us, we are still doing what our barbaric ancestors did when they came out of the caves and the woods.

From the age of fifteen to the age of twenty or twenty-one, the child has the burden of adolescence, of puberty and sex thrust upon him. Girls are kept at home and carefully watched. Boys without instruction are left to work the period out for themselves. It may lead to excess. It may lead to disgrace. It may lead to perversion. Who is to blame? Who did it? Did Dickie Loeb do it?

Your Honor, I am almost ashamed to talk about it. I can hardly imagine that we are in the twentieth century. And yet there are men who seriously say that for what nature has done, for what life has done, for what training has done, you should hang these boys.

Now, there is no mystery about this case, Your Honor. I seem to be criticizing their parents. They had parents who were kind and good and wise in their way. But I say to you seriously that the parents are more responsible than these boys. And yet few boys had better parents.

Your Honor, it is the easiest thing in the world to be a parent. We talk of motherhood, and yet every woman can be a mother. We talk of fatherhood, and yet every man can be a father. Nature takes care of that. It is easy to be a parent. But to be wise and farseeing enough to understand the boy is another thing; only a very few are so wise and so farseeing as that. When I think of the light way nature has of picking our parents and populating the earth, having them born and die, I cannot hold human beings to the same degree of responsibility that young lawyers hold them when they are enthusiastic in a prosecution. I know what it means.

I know there are no better citizens in Chicago than the fathers of these poor boys. I know there were no better women than their mothers. But I am going to be honest with this court, if it is at the expense of both. I know that one of two things happened to Richard Loeb: that this terrible crime was inherent in his organism, and came from some ancestor; or that it came through his education and his training after he was born. Do I need to prove it? Judge Crowe said at one point in this case, when some witness spoke about their wealth, that "probably that was responsible."

To believe that any boy is responsible for himself or his early training is an absurdity that no lawyer or judge should be guilty of today. Somewhere this came to the boy. If his failing came from his heredity, I do not know where or how. None of us are bred perfect and pure; and the color of our hair, the color of our eyes, our stature, the weight and fineness of our brain, and everything about us could, with full knowledge, be traced with absolute certainty to somewhere. If we had the pedigree it could be traced just the same in a boy as it could in a dog, a horse or a cow.

I do not know what remote ancestors may have sent down the seed that corrupted him, and I do not know through how many ancestors it may have passed until it reached Dickie Loeb.

All I know is that it is true, and there is not a biologist in the world who will not say that I am right.

If it did not come that way, then I know that if he was normal, if he had been understood, if he had been trained as he should have been it would not have happened. Not that anybody may not slip, but I know it and Your Honor knows it, and every schoolhouse and every church in the land is an evidence of it. Else why build them?

Every effort to protect society is an effort toward training the youth to keep the path. Every bit of training in the world proves it, and it likewise proves that it sometimes fails. I know that if this boy had been understood and properly trained—properly for him—and the training that he got might have been the very best for someone; but if it had been the proper training for him he would not be in this courtroom today with the noose above his head. If there is responsibility anywhere, it is back of him; somewhere in the infinite number of his ancestors, or in his surroundings, or in both. And I submit, Your Honor, that under every principle of natural justice, under every principle of conscience, of right, and of law, he should not be made responsible for the acts of someone else. . . .

It is when these dreams of boyhood, these fantasies of youth still linger, and the growing boy is still a child—a child in emotion, a child in feeling, a child in hallucinations—that you can say that it is the dreams and the hallucinations of childhood that are responsible for his conduct. There is not an act in all this horrible tragedy that was not the act of a child, the act of a child wandering around in the morning of life, moved by the new feelings of a boy, moved by the uncontrolled impulses which his teaching was not strong enough to take care of, moved by the dreams and the hallucinations which haunt the brain of a child. I say, Your Honor, that it would be the height of cruelty, of injustice, of wrong and barbarism to visit the penalty upon this poor boy.

STUDY QUESTIONS

1. Does the case Darrow makes for Loeb apply to everyone? If so, what happens to the idea of personal responsibility? If not, what makes Loeb special?
2. Darrow cites an Illinois statute forbidding minors to read crime stories. Is he suggesting that we need this sort of statute to prevent crime? What are the implications of his position for the issue of violence and the media?
3. Do you believe that in some cases a person's history makes criminality inevitable? Give arguments to support your position.
4. If you had served on Loeb's jury, would Darrow's plea have moved you to vote for a lighter sentence?
5. Can we use Darrow's defense as an argument for aquittal?

The Delusion of Free Will

ROBERT BLATCHFORD

Robert Blatchford (1851–1943) was an English social reformer well known for his defense of socialism, agnosticism, and determinism.

Blatchford is a hard determinist. For him, heredity and environment determine all our decisions, and the belief that we are sometimes free is a delusion. Our wishes, choices, and preferences, even when "moral," are all determined. If Jones decides to do A and Smith decides to do B, they could not have decided to do otherwise. To reverse their decisions, "we should have to reverse their heredities and environment." Blatchford asserts that he has "disposed of the claim that man is responsible because his will is free."

The free will delusion has been a stumbling block in the way of human thought for thousands of years. Let us try whether common sense and common knowledge cannot remove it.

Free will is a subject of great importance to us in this case; and it is one we must come to with our eyes wide open and our wits wide awake; not because it is very difficult, but because it has been tied and twisted into a tangle of Gordian knots by twenty centuries full of wordy but unsuccessful philosophers.

THE DELUSION OF FREE WILL From *Not Guilty* by Robert Blatchford. Reprinted by permission of the publisher, Vanguard Press, Inc. Copyright © 1927.

The free will party claim that man is responsible for his acts, because his will is free to choose between right and wrong. . . .

When a man says his will is free, he means that it is free of all control or interference: that it can overrule heredity and environment.

We reply that the will is ruled by heredity and environment.

The cause of all the confusion on this subject may be shown in a few words.

When the free will party say that man has a free will, they mean that he is free to act as he chooses to act.

There is no need to deny that. *But what causes him to choose?*

That is the pivot upon which the whole discussion turns.

The free will party seem to think of the will as something independent of the man, as something outside him. They seem to think that the will decides without the control of the man's reason.

If that were so, it would not prove the man responsible. "The will" would be responsible, and not the man. It would be as foolish to blame a man for the act of a "free" will as to blame a horse for the action of its rider.

But I am going to prove to my readers, by appeals to their common sense and common knowledge, that the will is not free; and that it is ruled by heredity and environment.

To begin with, the average man will be against me. He knows that he chooses between two courses every hour, and often every minute, and he thinks his choice is free. But that is a delusion: His choice is not free. He can choose, and does choose. But he can only choose as his heredity and his environment cause him to choose. He never did choose and never will choose except as his heredity and his enviroment—his temperament and his training—cause him to choose. And his heredity and his environment have fixed his choice before he makes it.

The average man says, "I know that I can act as I wish to act." But what causes him to wish?

The free will party say, "We know that a man can and does choose between two acts." But what settles the choice?

There is a cause for every wish, a cause for every choice; and every cause of every wish and choice arises from heredity, or from environment.

For a man acts always from temperament, which is heredity, or from training, which is environment.

And in cases where a man hesitates in his choice between two acts, the hesitation is due to a conflict between his temperament and his training, or, as some would express it, "between his desire and his conscience."

A man is practicing at a target with a gun, when a rabbit crosses his line of fire. The man has his eye and his sights on the rabbit, and his finger on the trigger. The man's will is free. If he presses the trigger the rabbit will be killed.

Now, how does the man decide whether or not he shall fire? He decides by feeling, and by reason.

He would like to fire, just to make sure that he could hit the mark. He would like to fire, because he would like to have the rabbit for supper. He would like to fire, because there is in him the old, old hunting instinct, to kill.

But the rabbit does not belong to him. He is not sure that he will not get into trouble if he kills it. Perhaps—if he is a very uncommon kind of man—he feels that it would be cruel and cowardly to shoot a helpless rabbit.

Well. The man's will is free. He can fire if he likes; he can let the rabbit go if he likes. How will he decide? On what does his decision depend?

His decision depends upon the relative strength of his desire to kill the rabbit, and of his scruples about cruelty, and the law.

Not only that, but, if we knew the man fairly well, we could guess how his free will would act before it acted. The average sporting Briton would kill the rabbit. But we know that there are men who would on no account shoot any harmless wild creature.

Broadly put, we may say that the sportsman would will to fire, and that the humanitarian would not will to fire.

Now, as both their wills are free, it must be something outside the wills that makes the difference.

Well. The sportsman will kill, because he is a sportsman; the humanitarian will not kill, because he is a humanitarian.

And what makes one man a sportsman and another a humanitarian? Heredity and environment; temperament and training.

One man is merciful, another cruel, by nature; or one is thoughtful and the other thoughtless, by nature. That is a difference of heredity.

One may have been taught all his life that to kill wild things is "sport"; the other may have been taught that it is inhuman and wrong: That is a difference of environment.

Now, the man by nature cruel or thoughtless, who has been trained to think of killing animals as sport, becomes what we call a sportsman, because heredity and environment have made him a sportsman.

The other man's heredity and environment have made him a humanitarian.

The sportsman kills the rabbit because he is a sportsman, and he is a sportsman because heredity and environment have made him one.

That is to say the "free will" is really controlled by heredity and environment.

Allow me to give a case in point. A man who had never done any fishing was taken out by a fisherman. He liked the sport, and for some months followed it eagerly. But one day an accident brought home to his mind the cruelty of catching fish with a hook, and he instantly laid down his rod, and never fished again.

Before the change he was always eager to go fishing if invited; after the change he could not be persuaded to touch a line. His will was free all the while. How was it that his will to fish changed to his will not to fish? It was the result of environment. He had learned that fishing was cruel. This knowledge controlled his will.

But, it may be asked, how do you account for a man doing the thing he does not wish to do?

No man ever did a thing he did not wish to do. When there are two wishes the stronger rules.

Let us suppose a case. A young woman gets two letters by the same post; one is an invitation to go with her lover to a concert, the other is a request that she will visit a sick child in the slums. The girl is very fond of music, and is rather afraid of the slums. She wishes to go to the concert, and to be with her lover; she dreads the foul street and the dirty home, and shrinks from the risk of measles or fever. But she goes to the sick child, and she foregoes the concert. Why?

Because her sense of duty is stronger than her self-love.

Now, her sense of duty is partly due to her nature—that is, to her heredity—but it is chiefly due to environment. Like all of us, this girl was born without any kind of knowledge, and with only the rudiments of a conscience. But she has been well taught, and the teaching is part of her environment.

We may say that the girl is free to act as she chooses, but she *does* act as she has been *taught* that she *ought* to act. This teaching, which is part of her environment, controls her will.

We may say that a man is free to act as he chooses. He is free to act as *he* chooses, but *he* will choose as heredity and environment cause *him* to choose. For heredity and environment have made him that which he is.

A man is said to be free to decide between two courses. But really he is only free to decide in accordance with his temperament and training. . . .

How, then, can we believe that free will is outside and superior to heredity and environment? . . .

"What! Cannot a man be honest if he choose?" Yes, if he choose. But that is only another way of saying that he can be honest if his nature and his training lead him to choose honesty.

"What! Cannot I please myself whether I drink or refrain from drinking?" Yes. But that is only to say you will not drink because it pleases *you* to be sober. But it pleases another man to drink, because his desire for drink is strong, or because his self-respect is weak.

And you decide as you decide, and he decides as he decides, because you are *you* and he is *he*; and heredity and environment made you both that which you are.

And the sober man may fall upon evil days, and may lose his self-respect, of find the burden of his trouble greater than he can bear, and may fly to drink for comfort, or oblivion, and may become a drunkard. Has it not been often so?

And the drunkard may, by some shock, or some disaster, or some passion, or some persuasion, regain his self-respect, and may renounce drink, and lead a sober and useful life. Has it not been often so?

An in both cases the freedom of the will is untouched: It is the change in the environment that lifts the fallen up, and beats the upright down.

We might say that a woman's will is free, and that she could, if she wished, jump off a bridge and drown herself. But she cannot *wish*. She is happy, and loves life, and dreads the cold and crawling river. And yet, by some cruel turn of fortune's wheel, she may become destitute and miserable; so miserable that she hates life and longs for death, and *then* she can jump into the dreadful river and die.

Her will was free at one time as at another. It is the environment

331

that has wrought the change. Once she could not wish to die; now she cannot wish to live.

The apostles of free will believe that all men's wills are free. But a man can only will that which he is able to will. And one man is able to will that which another man is unable to will. To deny this is to deny the commonest and most obvious facts of life. . . .

We all know that we can foretell the action of certain men in certain cases, because we know the men.

We know that under the same conditions Jack Sheppard would steal and Cardinal Manning would not steal. We know that under the same conditions the sailor would flirt with the waitress, and the priest would not; that the drunkard would get drunk, and the abstainer would remain sober. We know that Wellington would refuse a bribe, that Nelson would not run away, that Buonaparte would grasp at power, that Abraham Lincoln would be loyal to his country, that Torquemada would not spare a heretic. Why? If the will is free, how can we be sure, before a test arises, how the will must act?

Simply because we know that heredity and environment have so formed and molded men and women that under certain circumstances the action of their wills is certain.

Heredity and environment having made a man a thief, he will steal. Heredity and environment having made a man honest, he will not steal.

That is to say, heredity and environment have decided the action of the will, before the time has come for the will to act.

This being so—and we all know that it is so—what becomes of the sovereignty of the will?

Let any man that believes that he can "do as he likes" ask himself *why* he *likes*, and he will see the error of the theory and of free will, and will understand why the will is the servant and not the master of the man: For the man is the product of heredity and environment, and these control the will.

As we want to get this subject as clear as we can, let us take one or two familiar examples of the action of the will.

Jones and Robinson meet and have a glass of whiskey. Jones asks Robinson to have another. Robinson says, "No thank you, one is enough." Jones says, "All right: Have another cigarette." Robinson takes the cigarette. Now, here we have a case where a man refuses a second drink but takes a second smoke. Is it because he would like another cigarette but would not like another glass of whiskey? No. It is because he knows that it is *safer* not to take another glass of whiskey.

How does he know that whiskey is dangerous? He has learned it—from his environment.

"But he *could* have taken another glass if he wished."

But he could not wish to take another, because there was something he wished more strongly—to be safe.

And why did he want to be safe? Because he had learned—from his environment—that it was unhealthy, unprofitable, and shameful to get drunk. Because he had learned—from his environment—that it is easier to avoid forming a bad habit than to break a bad habit when formed. Because he valued the good opinion of his neighbors, and also his position and prospects.

These feelings and this knowledge ruled his will, and caused him to refuse the second glass.

But there was no sense of danger, no well-learned lesson of risk to check his will to smoke another cigarette. Heredity and environment did not warn him against that. So, to please his friend and himself, he accepted.

Now suppose Smith asks Williams to have another glass. Williams takes it, takes several, finally goes home—as he often goes home. Why?

Largely because drinking is a habit with him. And not only does the mind instinctively repeat an action but, in the case of drink, a physical craving is set up and the brain is weakened. It is easier to refuse the first glass than the second; it is easier to refuse the second than the third; and it is very much harder for a man to keep sober who has frequently gotten drunk.

So when poor Will has to make his choice, he has habit against him, he has a physical craving against him, and he has a weakened brain to think with.

"But Williams could have refused the first glass."

No. Because in his case the desire to drink, or to please a friend, was stronger than his fear of the danger. Or he may not have been so conscious of the danger as Robinson was. He may not have been so well taught, or he may not have been so sensible, or he may not have been so cautious. So that his heredity and environment, his temperament and training, led him to take the drink, as surely as Robinson's heredity and environment led him to refuse it.

And now it is my turn to ask a question. If the will is "free," if conscience is a sure guide, how is it that the free will and the conscience of Robinson caused him to keep sober, while the free will and conscience of Williams caused him to get drunk?

Robinson's will was curbed by certain feelings which failed to curb the will of Williams. Because in the case of Williams the feelings were stronger on the other side.

It was nature and the training of Robinson which made him refuse the second glass, and it was the nature and the training of Williams which made him drink the second glass.

What had free will to do with it?

We are told that *every* man has a free will, and a conscience.

Now, if Williams had been Robinson, that is to say if his heredity and his environment had been exactly like Robinson's, he would have done exactly as Robinson did.

It was because his heredity and environment were not the same that his act was not the same.

Both men had free wills. What made one do what the other refused to do?

Heredity and environment. To reverse their conduct we should have to reverse their heredity and environment. . . .

Two boys work at a hard and disagreeable trade. One leaves it, finds other work, "gets on," is praised for getting on. The other stays at the trade all his life, works hard all his life, is poor all his life, and is respected as an honest and humble working man; that is to say he is regarded by society as Mr. Dorgan was regarded by Mr. Dooley—"He is a fine man and I despise him."

What causes these two free wills to will so differently? One boy knew more than the other boy. He "knew better." All knowledge is environment. Both boys had free wills. It was in knowledge they differed: environment!

Those who exalt the power of the will, and belittle the power of environment, belie their words by their deeds.

For they would not send their children among bad companions or allow them to read bad books. They would not say the children have free will and therefore have power to take the good and leave the bad.

They know very well that evil environment has power to pervert the will, and that good environment has power to direct it properly.

334

They know that children may be made good or bad by good or evil training, and that the will follows the training.

That being so, they must also admit that the children of other people may be good or bad by training.

And if a child gets bad training, how can free will save it? Or how can it be blamed for being bad? It never had a chance to be good. That they know this is proved by their carefulness in providing their own children with better environment.

As I have said before, every church, every school, every moral lesson is a proof that preachers and teachers trust to good environment, and not to free will, to make children good.

In this, as in so many other matters, actions speak louder than words.

That, I hope, disentangles the many knots into which thousands of learned men have tied the simple subject of free will; and disposes of the claim that man is responsible because his will is free.

STUDY QUESTIONS

1. Blatchford appeals to common sense in his argument against free will. Yet common sense holds that we have free will. Does Blatchford successfully use common sense to subvert the common-sense belief in free will?
2. What are the consequences of Blatchford's views for the notion of moral responsibility?

A Defense of Compatibilism

W. T. STACE

A biographical sketch of W. T. Stace is found on page 120.

Stace denies that freedom means indeterminism, pointing out that, in common-sense usage, the contrary of freedom is compulsion or constraint. Doing something freely means doing it without being forced by circumstances beyond your control. Acts freely done, according to Stace, are caused by the psychological states of the agents themselves and agents are responsible even though the acts are psychologically caused. Moral responsibility is therefore consistent with a determinism of inner states. Moreover, responsibility presupposes determinism. For example, we hold criminals responsible and punish them, expecting that the punishment will bring about (that is, determine) a reformed mode of behavior.

A great problem which the rise of scientific naturalism has created for the modern mind concerns the foundations of morality. The old religious foundations have largely crumbled away, and it may well be thought that the edifice built upon them by generations of men is in danger of collapse. A total collapse of moral behavior is . . .

A DEFENSE OF COMPATIBILISM Abridged from Chapter 11 (pp. 279–291, under the title "A Defense of Compatibilism") in *Religion and the Modern Mind* by W. T. Stace (J. B. Lippincott). Copyright, 1952, by W. T. Stace. Reprinted by permission of Harper & Row, Publishers, Inc.

very unlikely. For a society in which this occurred could not survive. Nevertheless the danger to moral standards inherent in the virtual disappearance of their old religious foundations is not illusory.

I shall first discuss the problem of free will, for it is certain that if there is not free will there can be no morality. Morality is concerned with what men ought and ought not do. But if a man has not freedom to choose what he will do, if whatever he does is done under compulsion, then it does not make sense to tell him that he ought not to have done what he did and that he ought to do something different. All moral precepts would in such case be meaningless. Also if he acts always under compulsion, how can he be held morally responsible for his actions? How can he, for example, be punished for what he could not help doing?

It is to be observed that those learned professors of philosophy or psychology who deny the existence of free will do so only in their professional moments and in their studies and lecture rooms. For when it comes to doing anything practical, even of the most trivial kind, they invariably behave as if they and others were free. They inquire from you at dinner whether you will choose this dish or that dish. They will ask a child why he told a lie, and will punish him for not having chosen the way of truthfulness. All of which is inconsistent with a disbelief in free will. This should cause us to suspect that the problem is not a real one; and this, I believe, is the case. The dispute is merely verbal, and is due to nothing but a confusion about the meanings of words. It is what is now fashionably called a semantic problem.

How does a verbal dispute arise? Let us consider a case which, although it is absurd in the sense that no one would ever make the mistake which is involved in it, yet illustrates the principle which we shall have to use in the solution of the problem. Suppose that someone believed that the word "man" means a certain sort of five-legged animal; in short that "five-legged animal" is the correct *definition* of man. He might then look around the world, and rightly observing that there are no five-legged animals in it, he might proceed to deny the existence of men. This preposterous conclusion would have been reached because he was using an incorrect definition of "man." All you would have to do to show him his mistake would be to give him the correct definition, or at least to show him that his definition was wrong. Both the problem and its solution would, of course, be entirely verbal. The problem of free will, and its solution, I shall maintain, is verbal in exactly the same way. The problem has been created by the fact that learned men, especially philosophers, have assumed an incorrect definition of free will, and then finding that there is nothing in the world which answers to their definition have denied its existence. As far as logic is concerned, their conclusion is just as absurd as that of the man who denies the existence of men. The only difference is that the mistake in the latter case is obvious and crude, while the mistake which deniers of free will have made is rather subtle and difficult to detect.

Throughout the modern period, until quite recently, it was assumed, both by the philosophers who denied free will and by those who defended it, that *determinism is inconsistent with free will*. If a man's actions were wholly determined by chains of causes stretching back into the remote past, so that they could be predicted beforehand by a mind which knew all the causes, it was assumed that they could not in that case be free. This implies that a certain definition of actions done from free will was assumed, namely that they are actions *not* wholly determined by causes or predictable beforehand. Let us shorten this by saying that free will was defined as meaning indeterminism. This is the incorrect definition which has led to the denial of free will. As soon as we see what the true definition is we shall find that the question whether the world is deterministic, as Newtonian science implied, or in a measure indeterministic, as current physics teaches, is wholly irrelevant to the problem.

Of course there is a sense in which one can define a word arbitrarily in any way one pleases. But a definition may nevertheless be called correct or incorrect. It is correct if it accords with a *common usage* of the word defined. It is incorrect if it does not. And if you give an incorrect definition, absurd and untrue results are likely to follow. For instance, there is nothing to prevent you from arbitrarily defining a man as a five-legged animal, but it is incorrect in the sense that it does not accord with the ordinary meaning of the word. Also it has the absurd result of leading to a denial of the existence of men. This shows that *common usage is the criterion for deciding whether a definition is correct or not*. And this is the principle which I shall apply to free will. I shall show that indeterminism is not what is meant by the phrase "free will" *as it is commonly used.*

And I shall attempt to discover the correct definition by inquiring how the phrase is used in ordinary conversation.

Here are a few samples of how the phrase might be used in ordinary conversation. It will be noticed that they include cases in which the question whether a man acted with free will is asked in order to determine whether he was morally and legally responsible for his acts.

> *Jones* I once went without food for a week.
> *Smith* Did you do that of your own free will?
> *Jones* No. I did it because I was lost in a desert and could find no food.

But suppose that the man who had fasted was Mahatma Gandhi. The conversation might then have gone:

> *Gandhi* I once fasted for a week.
> *Smith* Did you do that of your own free will?
> *Gandhi* Yes. I did it because I wanted to compel the British Government to give India its independence.

Take another case. Suppose that I had stolen some bread, but that I was as truthful as George Washington. Then, if I were charged with the crime in court, some exchange of the following sort might take place:

> *Judge* Did you steal the bread of your own free will?
> *Stace* Yes. I stole it because I was hungry.

Or in different circumstances the conversation might run:

> *Judge* Did you steal of your own free will?
> *Stace* No. I stole because my employer threatened to beat me if I did not.

At a recent murder trial in Trenton some of the accused had signed confessions, but afterwards asserted that they had done so under police duress. The following exchange might have occurred:

> *Judge* Did you sign this confession of your own free will?
> *Prisoner* No. I signed it because the police beat me up.

Now suppose that a philosopher had been a member of the jury. We could imagine this conversation taking place in the jury room:

> *Foreman of the Jury*   The Prisoner says he signed the confession because he was beaten, and not of his own free will.
>
> *Philosopher*   This is quite irrelevant to the case. There is no such thing as free will.
>
> *Foreman*   Do you mean to say that it makes no difference whether he signed because his conscience made him want to tell the truth or because he was beaten?
>
> *Philosopher*   None at all. Whether he was caused to sign by a beating or by some desire of his own—the desire to tell the truth, for example—in either case his signing was causally determined, and therefore in neither case did he act of his own free will. Since there is no such thing as free will, the question whether he signed of his own free will ought not to be discussed by us.

The foreman and the rest of the jury would rightly conclude that the philosopher must be making some mistake. What sort of a mistake could it be? There is only one possible answer. The philosopher must be using the phrase "free will" in some peculiar way of his own which is not the way in which men usually use it when they wish to determine a question of moral responsibility. That is, he must be using an incorrect definition of it as implying action not determined by causes.

Suppose a man left his office at noon, and were questioned about it. Then we might hear this:

> *Jones*   Did you go out of your own free will?
>
> *Smith*   Yes. I went out to get my lunch.

But we might hear:

> *Jones*   Did you leave your office of your own free will?
>
> *Smith*   No. I was forcibly removed by the police.

We have now collected a number of cases of actions which, in the ordinary usage of the English language, would be called cases in which people have acted of their own free will. We should also say in all these cases that they *chose* to act as they did. We should also say that they could have acted otherwise, if they had chosen. For instance, Mahatma Gandhi was not compelled to fast; he chose to do so. He could have eaten if he had wanted to. When Smith went out to get his lunch, he chose to do so. He could have stayed and done some more work, if he had wanted to. We have also collected a number of cases of the opposite kind. They are cases in which men were not able to exercise their free will. They had no choice. They were compelled to do as they did. The man in the desert did not fast of his own free will. He had no choice in the matter. He was compelled to fast because there was nothing for him to eat. And so with the other cases. It ought to be quite easy, by an inspection of these cases, to tell what we ordinarily mean when we say that a man did or did not exercise free will. We ought therefore to be able to extract from them the proper definition of the term. Let us put the cases in a table:

Free Acts	Unfree Acts
Gandhi fasting because he wanted to free India.	The man fasting in the desert because there was no food.
Stealing bread because one is hungry.	Stealing because one's employer threatened to beat one.
Signing a confession because one wanted to tell the truth.	Signing because the police beat one.
Leaving the office because one wanted one's lunch.	Leaving because forcibly removed.

It is obvious that to find the correct definition of free acts we must discover what characteristic is common to all the acts in the left-hand column, and is, at the same time, absent from all the acts in the right-hand column. This characteristic which all free acts have, and which no unfree acts have, will be the defining characteristic of free will.

Is being uncaused, or not being determined by causes, the characteristic of which we are in search? It cannot be, because although it is true that all the acts in the right-hand column have causes, such as the beating by the police or the absence of food in the desert, so also do the acts in the left-hand column. Mr. Gandhi's fasting was caused by his desire to free India, the man leaving his office by his hunger, and so on. Moreover there is no reason to doubt that these causes of the free acts were in turn caused by prior conditions, and that these were again the results of causes, and so on back indefinitely into the past. Any physiologist can tell us the causes of hunger. What caused Mr. Gandhi's tremendously powerful desire to free India is no doubt more difficult to discover. But it must have had causes. Some of them may have lain in peculiarities of his glands or brain, others in his past experiences, others in his heredity, others in his education. Defenders of free will have usually tended to deny such facts. But to do so is plainly a case of special pleading, which is unsupported by any scrap of evidence. The only reasonable view is that all human actions, both those which are freely done and those which are not, are either wholly determined by causes, or at least as much determined as other events in nature. It may be true, as the physicists tell us, that nature is not as deterministic as was once thought. But whatever degree of determinism prevails in the world, human actions appear to be as much determined as anything else. And if this is so, it cannot be the case that what distinguishes actions freely chosen from those which are not free is that the latter are determined by causes while the former are not. Therefore, being uncaused or being undetermined by causes must be an incorrect definition of free will.

What, then, is the difference between acts which are freely done and those which are not? What is the characteristic which is present to all the acts in the left-hand column and absent from all those in the right-hand column? Is it not obvious that, although both sets of actions, have causes, the causes of those in the left-hand column are *of a different kind* from the causes of those in the right-hand column? The free acts are all caused by desires, or motives, or by some sort of internal psychological states of the agent's mind. The unfree acts, on the other hand, are all caused by physical forces or physical conditions outside the agent. Police arrest means physical force exerted from the outside; the absence of food in the desert is a physical condition of the outside world. We may therefore frame the following rough definitions. *Acts freely done are those whose immediate causes are psychological states in the agent. Acts not freely done are those whose immediate causes are states of affairs external to the agent.*

It is plain that if we define free will in this way, then free will certainly exists, and the philosopher's denial of its existence is seen to be what it is—nonsense. For it is obvious that all those actions of men which we should ordinarily attribute to the exercise of their free will, or of which we should say that they freely chose to do them, are in fact actions which have been caused by their own desires, wishes, thoughts, emotions, impulses, or other psychological states.

In applying our definition we shall find that it usually works well, but that there are some puzzling cases which it does not seem exactly to fit. These puzzles can always be solved by paying careful attention to the ways in which words are used, and remembering that they are not always used consistently. I have space for only one example. Suppose that a thug threatens to shoot you unless you give him your wallet, and suppose that you do so. Do you, in giving him your wallet, do so of your own free will or not? If we apply our definition, we find that you acted freely, since the immediate cause of the action was not an actual outside force but the fear of death, which is a psychological cause. Most people, however, would say that you did not act of your own free will but under compulsion. Does this show that our definition is wrong? I do not think so. Aristotle, who gave a solution of the problem of free will substantially the same as ours (though he did not use the term "free will"), admitted that there are what he called "mixed" or borderline cases in which it is difficult to know whether we ought to call the acts free or compelled. In the case under discussion, though no actual force was used, the gun at your forehead so nearly approximated to actual force that we tend to say the case was one of compulsion. It is a borderline case.

Here is what may seem like another kind of puzzle. According to our view an action may be free though it could have been predicted beforehand with certainty. But suppose you told a lie, and it was certain beforehand that you would tell it. How could one then say, "You could have told the truth"? The answer is that it is perfectly true that you could have told the truth *if* you had wanted to. In fact you would have done so, for in that case the causes producing your action, namely your desires, would have been different, and would therefore have produced different effects. It is a delusion that predictability and free will are incompatible. This agrees with common sense. For if, knowing your character, I predict that you will act honorably, no one would say when you do act honorably that this shows you did not do so of your own free will.

Since free will is a condition of moral responsibility, we must be sure that our theory of free will gives a sufficient basis for it. To be held morally responsible for one's actions means that one may be justly punished or rewarded, blamed or praised, for them. But it is not just to punish a man for what he cannot help doing. How can it be just to punish him for an action which it was certain beforehand that he would do? We have not attempted to decide whether, as a matter of fact, all events, including human actions, are completely determined. For that question is irrelevant to the problem of free will. But if we assume for the purposes of argument that complete determinism is true, but that we are nevertheless free, it may then be asked whether such a deterministic free will is compatible with moral responsibility. For it may seem unjust to punish a man for an action which it could have been predicted with certainty beforehand that he would do.

But that determinism is incompatible with moral responsibility is as much a delusion as that it is incompatible with free will. You do not excuse a man for doing a wrong act because, knowing his character, you felt certain beforehand that he would do it. Nor do you deprive a man of a reward or prize because, knowing his goodness or his capabilities, you felt certain beforehand that he would win it.

Volumes have been written on the justification of punishment. But so far as it affects the question of free will, the essential principles involved are quite simple. The punishment of a man for doing a wrong act is justified either on the ground that it will correct his own character or on the ground that it will deter other people from doing similar acts. The instrument of punishment has been in the past, and no doubt still is, often unwisely used; so that it may often have done more harm than good. But that is not relevant to our present problem. Punishment, if and when it is justified, is justified only on one or both of the grounds just mentioned. The question, then, is how, if we assume determinism, punishment can correct character or deter people from evil actions.

Suppose that your child develops a habit of telling lies. You give him a mild beating. Why? Because you believe that his personality is such that the usual motives for telling the truth do not cause him to do so. You therefore supply the missing cause, or motive, in the shape of pain and the fear of future pain if he repeats his untruthful behavior. And you hope that a few treatments of this kind will condition him to the habit of truth-telling, so that he will come to tell the truth without the infliction of pain. You assume that his actions are determined by causes, but that the usual causes of truth-telling do not in him produce their usual effects. You therefore supply him with an artificially injected motive, pain and fear, which you think will in the future cause him to speak truthfully.

The principle is exactly the same where you hope, by punishing one man, to deter others from wrong actions. You believe that the fear of punishment will cause those who might otherwise do evil to do well.

We act on the same principle with nonhuman, and even with inanimate, things, if they do not behave in the way we think they ought to behave. The rose bushes in the garden produce only small and poor blooms, whereas we want large and rich ones. We supply a cause which will produce large blooms, namely fertilizer. Our automobile does not go properly. We supply a cause which will make it go better, namely oil in the works. The punishment for the man, the fertilizer for the plant, and the oil for the car are all justified by the same principle and in the same way. The only difference is that different kinds of things require different kinds of causes to make them do what they should. Pain may be the appropriate remedy to apply, in certain cases, to human beings, and oil to the machine. It is, of course, of no use to inject motor oil into the boy or to beat the machine.

Thus we see that moral responsibility is not only consistent with determinism but requires it. The assumption on which punishment is based is that human behavior is causally determined. If pain could not be a cause of truth-telling there would be no justification at all for punishing lies. If human actions and volitions were uncaused, it would be useless either to punish or reward, or indeed to do anything else to correct people's bad behavior. For nothing that you could do would in any way influence them. Thus moral responsibility would entirely disappear. If there were no determinism of human beings at all, their actions would be completely unpredictable and capricious, and therefore irresponsible. And this is in itself a strong argument against the common view of philosophers that free will means being undetermined by causes.

STUDY QUESTIONS

1. What does Stace understand by freedom and why is it compatible with determinism? Do you agree that if we are free in the compatibilist sense we are fully responsible for our actions?
2. How does Stace attempt to show that "free" is the contrary of "constrained" and not the contrary of "determined"?
3. What is Stace's argument for the thesis that responsibility only makes sense if determinism is correct? Do you find Stace persuasive here?

Free Will and the Unconscious

JOHN HOSPERS

John Hospers (b. 1918) is the Director of the School of Philosophy at the University of Southern California. He has published a number of books, including *Libertarianism: A Political Philosophy for Tomorrow* (1971) and *Understanding the Arts* (1982).

Hospers gives a psychoanalytic account of human desire and action and finds that much of what people take to be spontaneous or free preference is unconsciously determined. In the past, we did not blame people for the color of their eyes. In the enlightened present, we extend this to withhold blame from kleptomaniacs and schizophrenics. In the enlightened future, we may extend this to all behavior, for we shall realize that our unconscious mind determines almost all we choose to do. Hospers asks, "Is there any room left for freedom?" Not much. But, theoretically, we may be free to the extent that we are psychically healthy.

I

It is extremely common for nonprofessional philosophers and iconoclasts to deny that human freedom exists, but at the same time to have no clear idea of what it is that they are denying to exist. The first thing that needs to be said about the free-will issue is that any

FREE WILL AND THE UNCONSCIOUS From *Philosophy and Phenomenological Research* 10, no. 3 (March 1950). Reprinted with permission of Brown University.

meaningful term must have a meaningful opposite: If it is meaningful to assert that people are not free, it must be equally meaningful
to assert that people *are* free, whether this latter assertion is in fact
true or not. Whether it is true, of course, will depend on the
meaning that is given to the weasel-word "free." For example, if
freedom is made dependent on indeterminism, it may well be that
human freedom is nonexistent. But there seem to be no good
grounds for asserting such a dependence, especially since lack of
causation is the furthest thing from people's minds when they call
an act free. Doubtless there are other senses that can be given to the
word "free"—such as "able to do anything we want to do"—in
which no human beings are free. But the first essential point about
which the denier of freedom must be clear is *what* it is that he is
denying. If one knows what it is like for people not to be free, one
must know what it *would* be like for them to *be* free.

Philosophers have advanced numerous senses of "free" in which
countless acts performed by human beings can truly be called free
acts. The most common conception of a free act is that according to
which an act is free if and only if it is a *voluntary* act. But the word
"voluntary" does not always carry the same meaning. Sometimes
to call an act voluntary means that we can do the act *if* we choose to
do it: In other words, that it is physically and psychologically
possible for us to do it, so that the occurrence of the act follows
upon the decision to do it. (One's decision to raise his arm is in fact
followed by the actual raising of his arm, unless he is a paralytic;
one's decision to pluck the moon from the sky is not followed by
the actual event.) Sometimes a voluntary act is conceived . . . as an
act which would not have occurred if, just beforehand, the agent
had chosen not to perform it. But these senses are different from
the sense in which a voluntary act is an act resulting from *deliberation*, or perhaps merely from *choice*. For example, there are many
acts which we could have avoided, if we had chosen to do so, but
which we nevertheless did not *choose* to perform, much less *deliberate* about them. The act of raising one's leg in the process of taking
a step while out for a walk is one which a person could have
avoided by choosing to, but which, after one has learned to walk,
takes place automatically or semi-automatically through habit, and
thus is not the result of choice. (One may have chosen to take the
walk, but not take this or that step while walking.) . . .

Now, no matter in which of the above ways we may come to

define "voluntary," there are still acts which are voluntary *but which we would be very unlikely to think of as free*. Thus, when a person submits to the command of an armed bandit, he may do so voluntarily in every one of the above senses: He may do so as a result of choice, even of deliberation, and he could have avoided doing it by willing not to—he could, instead, have refused and been shot. The man who reveals a state secret under torture does the same: He could have refused and endured more torture. Yet such acts, and persons in respect of such acts, are not generally called free. We said that they were performed *under compulsion*, and if an act is performed under compulsion we do not call if free. We say, "He wasn't free because he was forced to do as he did," though of course his act was voluntary.

This much departure from the identification of free acts with voluntary acts almost everyone would admit. Sometimes, however, it would be added that this is all the departure that can be admitted. According to Schlick, for example,

> Freedom means the opposite of compulsion; a man is *free* if he does not act under *compulsion*, and he is compelled or unfree when he is hindered from without in the realization of his natural desires. Hence he is unfree when he is locked up, or chained, or when someone forces him at the point of a gun to do what otherwise he would not do. This is quite clear, and everyone will admit that the everyday or legal notion of the lack of freedom is thus correctly interpreted, and that a man will be considered quite free . . . if no such external compulsion is exerted upon him.[1]

Schlick adds that the entire vexed free-will controversy in philosophy is so much wasted ink and paper, because compulsion has been confused with causality and necessity with uniformity. If the question is asked whether every event is caused, the answer is doubtless yes; but if it is whether every event is compelled, the answer is clearly no. Free acts are uncompelled acts, not uncaused acts. Again, when it is said that some state of affairs (such as water flowing downhill) is necessary, if "necessary" means "compelled," the answer is no; if it means merely that it always happens that way, the answer is yes: Universality of application is confused with

---

[1] *The Problems of Ethics*, Rynin translation, p. 150.

compulsion. And this, according to Schlick, is the end of the matter.

Schlick's analysis is indeed clarifying and helpful to those who have fallen victim to the confusions he exposes—and this probably includes most persons in their philosophical growing-pains. But *is* this the end of the matter? Is it true that all acts, though caused, are free as long as they are not compelled in the sense which he specifies? May it not be that, while the identification of "free" with "uncompelled" is acceptable, the area of compelled acts is vastly greater than he or most other philosophers have ever suspected? . . . We remember statements about human beings being pawns of their early environment, victims of conditions beyond their control, the result of causal influences stemming from their parents, and the like, and we ponder and ask, "Still, are we really free?" Is there not something in what generations of sages have said about man being fettered? Is there not perhaps something too facile, too sleight-of-hand, in Schlick's cutting of the Gordian knot? For example, when a metropolitan newspaper headlines an article with the words "Boy Killer Is Doomed Long Before He Is Born,"[2] and then goes on to describe how a twelve-year-old boy has been sentenced to prison for the murder of a girl, and how his parental background includes records of drunkenness, divorce, social maladjustment, and paresis, are we still to say that his act, though voluntary and assuredly *not* done at the point of a gun, is free? The boy has early displayed a tendency toward sadistic activity to hide an underlying masochism and "prove that he's a man"; being coddled by his mother only worsens this tendency until, spurned by a girl in his attempt on her, he kills her—not simply in a fit of anger, but calculatingly, deliberately. Is he free in respect of his criminal act, or for that matter in most of the acts of his life? Surely to ask this question is to answer it in the negative. Perhaps I have taken an extreme case; but it is only to show the superficiality of the Schlick analysis the more clearly. Though not everyone has criminotic tendencies, everyone has been molded by influences which in large measure at least determine his present behavior; he is literally the product of these influences, stemming from periods prior to his "years of discretion," giving him a host of character traits that he

---

[2] *New York Post*, Tuesday, May 18, 1948, p. 4.

cannot change now even if he would. So obviously does what a man is depend upon how a man comes to be, that it is small wonder that philosophers and sages have considered man far indeed from being the master of his fate. It is not as if man's will were standing high and serene above the flux of events that have molded him; it is itself caught up in this flux, itself carried along on the current. An act is free when it is determined by the man's character, say moralists; but what if the most decisive aspects of his character were already irrevocably acquired before he could do anything to mold them? What if even the degree of will power available to him in shaping his habits and disciplining himself now to overcome the influence of his early environment is a factor over which he has no control? What are we to say of this kind of "freedom"? Is it not rather like the freedom of the machine to stamp labels on cans when it has been devised for just that purpose? Some machines can do so more efficiently than others, but only because they have been better constructed.

II

It is not my purpose here to establish this thesis in general, but only in one specific respect which has received comparatively little attention, namely, the field referred to by psychiatrists as that of unconscious motivation. In what follows I shall restrict my attention to it because it illustrates as clearly as anything the point I wish to make.

Let me try to summarize very briefly the psychoanalytic doctrine on this point.[3] The conscious life of the human being, including the conscious decisions and volitions, is merely a mouthpiece for the unconscious—not directly for the enactment of unconscious drives, but of the compromise between unconscious drives and unconscious reproaches. There is a Big Three behind the scenes which the automaton called the conscious personality carries out:

---

[3] I am aware that the theory presented below is not accepted by all practicing psychoanalysts. Many non-Freudians would disagree with the conclusions presented below. But I do not believe that this fact affects my argument, as long as the concept of unconscious motivation is accepted. I am aware, too, that much of the language employed in the following descriptions is animistic and metaphorical; but as long as I am presenting a view I would prefer to "go the whole hog" and present it in its most dramatic form. The theory can in any case be made clearest by the use of such language, just as atomic theory can often be made clearest to students with the use of models.

The id, an "eternal gimme," presents its wish and demands its immediate satisfaction; the super-ego says no to the wish immediately upon presentation; and the unconscious ego, the mediator between the two, tries to keep peace by means of compromise.[4]

To go into examples of the functioning of these three "bosses" would be endless; psychoanalytic case books supply hundreds of them. The important point for us to see in the present context is that *it is the unconscious that determines what the conscious impulse and the conscious action shall be.* . . .

We have always been conscious of the fact that we are not masters of our fate in every respect—that there are many things which we cannot do, that nature is more powerful than we are, that we cannot disobey laws without danger of reprisals, etc. We have become "officially" conscious, too, though in our private lives we must long have been aware of it, that we are not free with respect to the emotions that we feel—whom we love or hate, what types we admire, and the like. More lately still we have been reminded that there are unconscious motivations for our basic attractions and repulsions, our compulsive actions or inabilities to act. But what is not welcome news is that our very acts of volition, and the entire train of deliberations leading up to them, are but façades for the expression of unconscious wishes, or rather, unconscious compromises and defenses.

A man is faced by a choice: Shall he kill another person or not? Moralists would say, "Here is a free choice—the result of deliberation, an action consciously entered into." And yet, though the agent himself does not know it, and has no awareness of the forces that are at work within him, his choice is already determined for him: His conscious will is only an instrument, a slave, in the hands of a deep unconscious motivation which determines his action. If he has a great deal of what the analyst calls "free-floating guilt," he will not; but if the guilt is such as to demand immediate absorption in the form of self-damaging behavior, this accumulated guilt will have to be discharged in some criminal action. The man himself does not know what the inner clockwork is; he is like the hands on the clock, thinking they move freely over the face of the clock.

---

[4]This view is very clearly developed in Edmund Bergler, *Divorce Won't Help*, especially Chapter I.

A woman has married and divorced several husbands. Now she is faced with a choice for the next marriage: shall she marry Mr. A, or Mr. B, or nobody at all? She may take considerable time to "decide" this question and her decision may appear as a final triumph of her free will. Let us assume that A is a normal, well-adjusted, kind and generous man while B is a leech, an impostor, one who will become entangled constantly in quarrels with her. If she belongs to a certain classifiable psychological type, she will inevitably choose B, and she will do so even if her previous husbands have resembled B, so that one would think that she "had learned from experience." Consciously, she will of course "give the matter due consideration," etc., etc. To the psychoanalyst all this is irrelevant chaff in the wind—only a camouflage for the inner workings about which she knows nothing consciously. If she is of a certain kind of masochistic strain, as exhibited in her previous set of symptoms, she *must* choose B: Her super-ego, always out to maximize the torment in the situation, seeing what dazzling possibilities for self-damaging behavior are promised by the choice of B, compels her to make the choice she does, and even to conceal the real basis of the choice behind an elaborate façade of rationalization. . . .

A man has wash-compulsion. He must be constantly washing his hands—he uses up perhaps 400 towels a day. Asked why he does this, he says, "I need to, my hands are dirty"; and if it is pointed out to him that they are not really dirty, he says, "They feel dirty anyway, I feel better when I wash them." So once again he washes them. He "freely decides" every time; he feels that he must wash them, he deliberates for a moment perhaps, but he always ends by washing them. What he does not see, of course, are the invisible wires inside him pulling him inevitably to do the thing he does: The infantile id-wish concerns preoccupation with dirt, the super-ego charges him with this, and the terrified ego must respond, "No, I don't like dirt, see how clean I like to be, look how I wash my hands!"

Let us see what further "free acts" the same patient engages in (this is an actual case history): He is taken to a concentration camp and given the worst of treatment by the Nazi guards. In the camp he no longer chooses to be clean, does not even try to be—on the contrary, his choice is now to wallow in filth as much as he can. All he is aware of now is a disinclination to be clean, and every time he must choose he chooses not to be. Behind the scenes, however, another drama is being enacted: The super-ego, perceiving that enough torment is being administered from the outside, can afford to cease pressing its charges in this quarter—the outside world is doing the torturing now, so the super-ego is relieved of the responsibility. Thus, the ego is relieved of the agony of constantly making terrified replies in the form of washing to prove that the super-ego is wrong. The defense no longer being needed, the person slides back into what is his natural predilection anyway, for filth. This becomes too much even for the Nazi guards: They take hold of him one day, sayings "We'll teach you how to be clean!" drag him into the snow, and pour bucket after bucket of icy water over him until he freezes to death. Such is the end-result of an original id-wish, caught in the machinations of a destroying super-ego.

Let us take, finally, a less colorful, more everyday example. A student at a university, possessing wealth, charm, and all that is usually considered essential to popularity, begins to develop the following personality-pattern: Although well taught in the graces of social conversation, he always makes a *faux pas* somewhere, and always in the worst possible situation; to his friends he makes cutting remarks which hurt deeply—and always apparently aimed in such a way as to hurt the most: A remark that would not hurt A but would hurt B he invariably makes to B rather than to A, and so on. None of this is conscious. Ordinarily he is considerate of people, but he contrives always (unconsciously) to impose on just those friends who would resent it most, and at just the times when he should know that he should not impose: At 3 o'clock in the morning, without forewarning, he phones a friend in a nearby city demanding to stay at his apartment for the weekend; naturally the friend is offended, but the person himself is not aware that he has provoked the grievance ("common sense" suffers a temporary eclipse when the neurotic pattern sets in, and one's intelligence, far from being of help in such a situation, is used in the interest of the neurosis), and when the friend is cool to him the next time they meet, he wonders why and feels unjustly treated. Aggressive behavior on his part invites resentment and aggression in turn, but all that he consciously sees is others' behavior toward him—and he considers himself the innocent victim of an unjustified "persecution."

Each of these acts is, from the moralist's point of view, free: He

353

chose to phone his friend at 3 a.m.; he chose to make the cutting remark that he did, etc. What he does not know is that an ineradicable masochistic pattern has set in. His unconscious is far more shrewd and clever than is his conscious intellect; it sees with uncanny accuracy just what kind of behavior will damage him most, and unerringly forces him into that behavior. Consciously, the student "doesn't know why he did it"—he gives different "reasons" at different times, but they are all, once again, rationalizations cloaking the unconscious mechanism which propels him willy-nilly into actions which his "common sense" eschews.

The more of this sort of thing one observes, the more he can see what the psychoanalyst means when he talks about *the illusion of freedom*. And the more of a psychiatrist one becomes, the more he is overcome with a sense of what an illusion this free-will can be. In some kinds of cases most of us can see it already: It takes no psychiatrist to look at the epileptic and sigh with sadness at the thought that soon this person before you will be as one possessed, not the same thoughtful intelligent person you knew. But people are not aware of this in other contexts, for example when they express surprise at how a person whom they have been so good to could treat them so badly. Let us suppose that you help a person financially or morally or in some other way, so that he is in your debt; suppose further that he is one of the many neurotics who unconsciously identify kindness with weakness and aggression with strength. Then he will unconsciously take your kindness to him as weakness and use it as the occasion for enacting some aggression against you. He can't help it, he may regret it himself later; still, he will be driven to do it. If we gain a little knowledge of psychiatry, we can look at him with pity, that a person otherwise so worthy should be so unreliable—but we will exercise realism too, and be aware that there are some types of people that you cannot be good to in "free" acts of their conscious volition; they will use your own goodness against you. . . .

We talk about free-will, and we say, for example, the person is free to do so-and-so if he can do so *if* he wants to—and we forget that his wanting to is itself caught up in the stream of determinism, that unconscious forces drive him into the wanting or not wanting to do the thing in question. The analogy of the puppet whose motions are manipulated from behind by invisible wires, or better still, by springs inside, is a telling one at almost every point.

And the glaring fact is that it all started so early, before we knew what was happening. The personality-structure is inelastic after the age of five, and comparatively so in most cases after the age of three. Whether one acquires a neurosis or not is determined by that age—and just as involuntarily as if it had been a curse of God. If, for example, a masochistic pattern was set up, under pressure of hyper-narcissism combined with real or fancied infantile deprivation, then the masochistic snowball was on its course downhill long before we or anybody else knew what was happening, and long before anyone could do anything about it. To speak of human beings as "puppets" in such a context is no idle metaphor, but a stark rendering of a literal fact: Only the psychiatrist knows what puppets people really are; and it is no wonder that the protestations of philosophers that "the act which is the result of a volition, a deliberation, a conscious decision, is free" leave these persons, to speak mildly, somewhat cold.

But, one may object, all the states thus far described have been abnormal, neurotic ones. The well-adjusted (normal) person at least is free.

Leaving aside the question of how clearly and on what grounds one can distinguish the neurotic from the normal, let me use an illustration of a proclivity that everyone would call normal, namely, the decision of a man to support his wife and possibly a family, and consider briefly its genesis, according to psychoanalytic accounts.[5]

Every baby comes into the world with a full-fledged case of megalomania—interested only in himself, acting as if believing that he is the center of the universe and that others are present only to fulfill his wishes, and furious when his own wants are not satisfied immediately no matter for what reason. Gratitude, even for all the time and worry and care expended on him by the mother, is an emotion entirely foreign to the infant, and as he grows older it is inculcated in him only with the greatest difficulty; his natural tendency is to assume that everything that happens to him is due to himself, except for denials and frustrations, which are due to the "cruel, denying" outer world, in particular the mother; and that he owes nothing to anyone, is dependent on no one. This omnipotence-complex, or illusion of nondependence, has been called the

---

[5] E.g., Edmund Bergler, *The Battle of the Conscience,* Chapter I.

"autarchic fiction." Such a conception of the world is actually fostered in the child by the conduct of adults, who automatically attempt to fulfill the infant's every wish concerning nourishment, sleep, and attention. The child misconceives causality and sees in these wish-fulfillments not the results of maternal kindness and love, but simply the result of his own omnipotence.

This fiction of omnipotence is gradually destroyed by experience, and its destruction is probably the deepest disappointment of the early years of life. First of all, the infant discovers that he is the victim of organic urges and necessities: hunger, defecation, urination. More important, he discovers that the maternal breast, which he has not previously distinguished from his own body (he has not needed to, since it was available when he wanted it), is not a part of himself after all, but of another creature upon whom he is dependent. He is forced to recognize this, e.g., when he wants nourishment and it is at the moment not present; even a small delay is most damaging to the "autarchic fiction." Most painful of all is the experience of weaning, probably the greatest tragedy in every baby's life, when his dependence is most cruelly emphasized; it is a frustrating experience because what he wants is no longer there at all; and if he has been able to some extent to preserve the illusion of nondependence heretofore, he is not able to do so now—it is plain that the source of his nourishment is not dependent on him, but he on it. The shattering of the autarchic fiction is a great disillusionment to every child, a tremendous blow to his ego which he will, in one way or another, spend the rest of his life trying to repair. How does he do this?

First of all, his reaction to frustration is anger and fury; and he responds by kicking, biting, etc., the only way he knows. But he is motorically helpless, and these measures are ineffective, and only serve to emphasize his dependence the more. Moreover, against such responses of the child the parental reaction is one of prohibition, often involving deprivation of attention and affection. Generally the child soon learns that this form of rebellion is profitless, and brings him more harm than good. He wants to respond to frustration with violent aggression, and at the same time learns that he will be punished for such aggression, and that in any case the latter is ineffectual. What face-saving solution does he find? Since he must "face facts," since he must in any case "conform" if he is to have any peace at all, he tries to make it seem as if he himself is the source of the commands and prohibitions: The *external* prohibitive force is *internalized*—and here we have the origin of conscience. By making the prohibitive agency seem to come from within himself, the child can "save face"—as if saying, "The prohibition comes from within me, not from outside, so I'm not subservient to external rule, I'm only obeying rules I've set up myself," and thus to some extent saving the autarchic fiction, and at the same time avoiding unpleasant consequences directed against himself by complying with parental commands.

Moreover, the boy[6] has unconsciously never forgiven the mother for his dependence on her in early life, for nourishment and all other things. It has upset his illusion of nondependence. These feelings have been repressed and are not remembered; but they are acted out in later life in many ways—e.g., in the constant deprecation man has for woman's duties such as cooking and housework of all sorts ("All she does is stay home and get together a few meals, and she calls that work"), and especially in the man's identification with the mother in his sex experiences with women. By identifying with someone one cancels out in effect the person with whom he identifies—replacing that person, unconsciously denying his existence, and the man, identifying with his early mother, playing the active rôle in "giving" to his wife as his mother has "given" to him, is in effect the denial of his mother's existence, a fact which is narcissistically embarrassing to his ego because it is chiefly responsible for shattering his autarchic fiction. In supporting his wife, he can unconsciously deny that his mother gave to him, and that he was dependent on her giving. Why is it that the husband plays the provider, and wants his wife to be dependent on no one else, although twenty years before he was nothing but a parasitic baby? This is a face-saving device on his part: He can act out the reasoning, "See, I'm not the parasitic baby, on the contrary I'm the provider, the giver." His playing the provider is a constant face-saving device, to deny his early dependence which is so embarras-

---

[6]The girl's development after this point is somewhat different. Society demands more aggressiveness of the adult male, and hence there are more super-ego strictures on tendencies toward passivity in the male; accordingly his defenses must be stronger.

357

sing to his ego. It is no wonder that men generally dislike to be reminded of their babyhood, when they were dependent on women.

Thus, we have here a perfectly normal adult reaction which is unconsciously motivated. The man "chooses" to support a family—and his choice is as unconsciously motivated as anything could be. (I have described here only the "normal" state of affairs, uncomplicated by the well-nigh infinite number of variations that occur in actual practice.)

III

Now, what of the notion of responsibility? What happens to it on our analysis?

Let us begin with an example, not a fictitious one. A woman and her two-year-old baby are riding on a train to Montreal in midwinter. The child is ill. The woman wants badly to get to her destination. She is, unknown to herself, the victim of a neurotic conflict whose nature is irrelevant here except for the fact that it forces her to behave aggressively toward the child, partly to spite her husband whom she despises and who loves the child, but chiefly to ward off super-ego charges of masochistic attachment. Consciously she loves the child, and when she says this she says it sincerely, but she must behave aggressively toward it nevertheless, just as many children love their mothers but are nasty to them most of the time in neurotic pseudo-aggression. The child becomes more ill as the train approaches Montreal; the heating system of the train is not working, and the conductor pleads with the woman to get off the train at the next town and get the child to a hospital at once. The woman refuses. Soon after, the child's condition worsens, and the mother does all she can to keep it alive, without, however, leaving the train, for she declares that it is absolutely necessary that she reach her destination. But before she gets there the child is dead. After that, of course, the mother grieves, blames herself, weeps hysterically, and joins the church to gain surcease from the guilt that constantly overwhelms her when she thinks of how her aggressive behavior has killed her child.

Was she responsible for her deed? In ordinary life, after making a mistake, we say, "Chalk it up to experience." Here we should say, "Chalk it up to neurosis." *She* could not help it if her neurosis forced her to act this way—she didn't even know what was going on behind the scenes; her conscious self merely acted out its assigned part. This is far more true than is generally realized: Criminal actions in general are not actions for which their agents are responsible; the agents are passive, not active—they are victims of a neurotic conflict. Their very hyper-activity is unconsciously determined.

To say this is, of course, not to say that we should not punish criminals. Clearly, for our own protection, we must remove them from our midst so that they can no longer molest and endanger organized society. And of course, if we use the word "responsible" in such a way that justly to hold someone responsible for a deed is by definition identical with being justified in punishing him, then we can and do hold people responsible. But this is like the sense of "free" in which free acts are voluntary ones. It does not go deep enough. In a deeper sense we cannot hold the person responsible: We can hold his neurosis responsible, but *he is not responsible for his neurosis*, particularly since the age at which its onset was inevitable was an age before he could even speak.

The neurosis is responsible—but isn't the neurosis a part of *him*? We have been speaking all the time as if the person and his unconscious were two separate beings; but isn't he one personality, including conscious and unconscious departments together?

I do not wish to deny this. But it hardly helps us here; for what people want when they talk about freedom, and what they hold to when they champion it, is the idea that the *conscious* will is the master of their destiny. "I am the master of my fate, I am the captain of my soul"—and they surely mean their conscious self, the self that they can recognize and search and introspect. Between an unconscious which willy-nilly determines your actions, and an external force which pushes you, there is little if anything to choose. The unconscious is just *as if* it were an outside force; and indeed, psychiatrists will assert that the inner Hitler (your superego) can torment you far more than any external Hitler can. Thus, the kind of freedom that people want, the only kind they will settle for, is precisely the kind that psychiatry says that they cannot have.

Heretofore it was pretty generally thought that, while we could not rightly blame a person for the color of his eyes or the morality of his parents, or even for what he did at the age of three, or to a large extent what impulses he had and whom he fell in love with, one *could* do so for other of his adult activities, particularly the acts

359

he performed voluntarily and with premeditation. Later this attitude was shaken. Many voluntary acts came to be recognized at least in some circles, as compelled by the unconscious. . . . The usual examples, such as the kleptomaniac and the schizophrenic, apparently satisfy most philosophers, and with these exceptions removed, the rest of mankind is permitted to wander in the vast and alluring fields of freedom and responsibility. So far, the inroads upon freedom left the vast majority of humanity untouched; they began to hit home when psychiatrists began to realize, though philosophers did not, that the domination of the conscious by the unconscious extended not merely to a few exceptional individuals, but to all human beings, that the "big three behind the scenes" are not respecters of persons, and dominate us all, even including that *sanctum sanctorum* of freedom, our conscious will. To be sure, the domination by the unconscious in the case of "normal" individuals is somewhat more benevolent than the tyranny and despotism exercised in neurotic cases, and therefore the former have evoked less comment; but the principle remains in all cases the same: The unconscious is the master of every fate and the captain of every soul.

We speak of a machine turning out good products most of the time but every once in a while turning out a "lemon." We do not, of course, hold the product responsible for this, but the machine, and via the machine, its maker. Is it silly to extend to inanimate objects the idea of responsibility? Of course, but is it any less so to employ the notion in speaking of human creatures? Are not the two kinds of cases analogous in countless important ways? Occasionally a child turns out badly too, even when his environment and training are the same as that of his brothers and sisters who turn out "all right." He is the "bad-penny." His acts of rebellion against parental discipline in adult life (such as the case of the gambler, already cited) are traceable to early experiences of real or fancied denial of infantile wishes. Sometimes the denial has been real, though many denials are absolutely necessary if the child is to grow up to observe the common decencies of civilized life; sometimes, if the child has an unusual quantity of narcissism, every event that occurs is interpreted by him as a denial of his wishes, and nothing a parent could do, even granting every humanly possible wish, would help. In any event, the later neurosis can be attributed to this. Can the person himself be held responsible? Hardly. If he engages in activities which are a menace to society, he must be put into prison, of course, but responsibility is another matter. The time when the events occurred which rendered his neurotic behavior inevitable was a time long before he was capable of thought and decision. As an adult, he is a victim of a world he never made—only this world is inside him.

What about the children who turn out "all right?" All we can say is that "it's just lucky for them" that what happened to their unfortunate brother didn't happen to them; *through no virtue of their own* they are not doomed to the life of unconscious guilt, expiation, conscious depression and terrified ego-gestures for the appeasement of a tyrannical super-ego that he is. The machine turned them out with a minimum of damage. But if the brother cannot be blamed for his evils, neither can they be praised for their good; unless, of course, we should blame people for what is not their fault, and praise them for lucky accidents.

We all agree that machines turn out "lemons," we all agree that nature turns out misfits in the realm of biology—the blind, the crippled, the diseased; but we hesitate to include the realm of the personality, for here, it seems, is the last retreat of our dignity as human beings. Our ego can endure anything but this; this island at least must remain above the encroaching flood. But may not precisely the same analysis be made here also? Nature turns out psychological "lemons" too, in far greater quantities than any other kind; and indeed all of us are "lemons" in some respect or other, the difference being one of degree. Some of us are lucky enough not to have a gambling-neurosis or criminotic tendencies or masochistic mother-attachment or overdimensional repetition-compulsion to make our lives miserable, but most of our actions, those usually considered the most important, are unconsciously dominated just the same. And, if a neurosis may be likened to a curse of God, let those of us, the elect, who are enabled to enjoy a measure of life's happiness without the hell-fire of neurotic guilt, take this not as our own achievement, but simply for what it is—a gift of God.

IV

Assuming the main conclusions of this paper to be true, is there any room left for freedom?

This, of course, all depends on what we mean by "freedom." In the senses suggested at the beginning of this paper, there are count-less free acts, and unfree ones as well. When "free" means "uncom-pelled," and only external compulsion is admitted, again there are countless free acts. But now we have extended the notion of compulsion to include determination by unconscious forces. With this sense in mind, our question is, "With the concept of compul-sion thus extended, and in the light of present psychoanalytic knowledge, is there any freedom left in human behavior?"

If practicing psychoanalysts were asked this question, there is little doubt that their answer would be along the following lines: They would say that they were not accustomed to using the term "free" at all, but that if they had to suggest a criterion for distin-guishing the free from the unfree, they would say that a person's freedom is present *in inverse proportion to his neuroticism*; in other words, the more his acts are determined by a *malevolent* uncon-scious, the less free he is. Thus, they would speak of *degrees* of freedom. They would say that as a person is cured of his neurosis, he becomes more free—free to realize capabilities that were blocked by the neurotic affliction. The psychologically well-adjusted individual is in this sense comparatively the most free. Indeed, those who are cured of mental disorders are sometimes said to have *regained their freedom*: They are freed from the tyranny of a malevolent unconscious which formerly exerted as much of a domination over them as if they had been the abject slaves of a cruel dictator.

But suppose one says that a person is free only to the extent that his acts are *not unconsciously determined at all*, be they unconsciously benevolent *or* malevolent? If this is the criterion, psychoanalysts would say, most human behavior cannot be called free at all: Our impulses and volitions having to do with our basic attitudes toward life, whether we are optimists or pessimists, tough-minded or tender-minded, whether our tempers are quick or slow, whether we are "naturally self-seeking" or "naturally benevolent" (and *all the acts consequent upon these things*), what things annoy us, whether we take to blondes or brunettes, old or young, whether we become philosophers or artists or businessmen—all this has its basis in the unconscious. If people generally call most acts free, it is not because they believe that compelled acts should be called free; it is rather through not knowing how large a proportion of our acts actually are compelled. Only the comparatively "vanilla-flavored" aspects of our lives—such as our behavior toward people who don't really matter to us—are exempted from this rule.

These, I think, are the two principal criteria for distinguishing freedom from the lack of it which we might set upon the basis of psychoanalytic knowledge. Conceivably we might set up others. In every case, of course, it remains trivially true that "it all depends on how we choose to use the word." The facts are what they are, regardless of what words we choose for labeling them. But if we choose to label them in a way which is not in accord with what human beings, however vaguely, have long had in mind in applying these labels, as we would be doing if we labeled as "free" many acts which we know as much about as we now do through modern psychoanalytic methods, then we shall only be manipulating words to mislead our fellow creatures.

STUDY QUESTIONS

1. What is Hospers's criticism of compatibilism?
2. What must a choice be like if it is to be free in the sense required for responsibility? Why does Hospers think that many of our choices are not free in the required sense?
3. In your opinion, does Hospers rely too much on psychiatry when he says that most of our preferences are unfree because they are "unconsciously determined"?
4. What is your impression of Hospers's general argument? Do you find that he leaves too little room for freedom and responsibility? Does his position square with common sense?

Free Will and the Self

C. A. CAMPBELL

C. A. Campbell (1897–1974) was a professor of philosophy at the University of Glasgow. He is the author of several books, including *On Selfhood and Godhood* (1957).

Campbell defends free will. At crucial moments in our lives we do decide whether to put forth or withhold the moral effort to resist temptation and rise to duty. We have no evidence for a determinism that rules out such moments. And both common sense and our inner experience support it.

It is something of a truism that in philosophic enquiry the exact formulation of a problem often takes one a long way on the road to its solution. In the case of the Free Will problem I think there is a rather special need of careful formulation. For there are many sorts of human freedom; and it can easily happen that one wastes a great deal of labour in proving or disproving a freedom which has almost nothing to do with the freedom which is at issue in the traditional problem of Free Will. The abortiveness of so much of the argument for and against Free Will in contemporary philosophical literature seems to me due in the main to insufficient pains being taken over the preliminary definition of the problem. . . .

Fortunately we can at least make a beginning with a certain amount of confidence. It is not seriously disputable that the kind of

FREE WILL AND THE SELF From *On Selfhood and Godhood* by C. A. Campbell. Reprinted by permission of the publisher, George Allen & Unwin (Publishers) Ltd.

freedom in question is the freedom which is commonly recognised to be in some sense a precondition of moral responsibility. Clearly, it is on account of this integral connection with moral responsibility that such exceptional importance has always been felt to attach to the Free Will problem. But in what precise sense is free will a pre-condition of moral responsibility, and thus a postulate of the moral life in general? This is an exceedingly troublesome question; but until we have satisfied ourselves about the answer to it, we are not in a position to state, let alone decide, the question whether "Free Will" in its traditional, ethical, significance is a reality . . . .

The first point to note is that the freedom at issue (as indeed the very name "Free *Will* Problem" indicates) pertains primarily not to overt acts but to inner acts. The nature of things has decreed that, save in the case of one's self, it is only overt acts which one can directly observe. But a very little reflection serves to show that in our moral judgments upon others their overt acts are regarded as significant only in so far as they are the expression of inner acts. We do not consider the acts of a robot to be morally responsible acts; nor do we consider the acts of a man to be so save in so far as they are distinguishable from those of a robot by reflecting an inner life of choice. Similarly, from the other side, if we are satisfied (as we may on occasion be, at least in the case of ourselves) that a person has definitely elected to follow a course which he believes to be wrong, but has been prevented by external circumstances from translating his inner choice into an overt act, we still regard him as morally blameworthy. Moral freedom, then, pertains to *inner* acts.

The next point seems at first sight equally obvious and uncontroversial; but, as we shall see, it has awkward implications if we are in real earnest with it (as almost nobody is). It is the simple point that the act must be one of which the person judged can be regarded as the *sole* author. It seems plain enough that if there are any *other* determinants of the act, external to the self, to that extent the act is not an act which the *self* determines, and to that extent not an act for which the self can be held morally responsible. The self is only part-author of the act, and his moral responsibility can logically extend only to those elements within the act (assuming for the moment that these can be isolated) of which he is the *sole* author. . . .

Thirdly we come to a point over which much recent controversy has raged. We may approach it by raising the following question.

Granted an act of which the agent is sole author, does this 'sole authorship' suffice to make the act a morally free act? We may be inclined to think that it does, until we contemplate the possibility than an act of which the agent is sole author might conceivably occur as a necessary expression of the agent's nature; the way in which, e.g. some philosophers have supposed the Divine act of creation to occur. This consideration excites a legitimate doubt; for it is far from easy to see how a person can be regarded as a proper subject for moral praise or blame in respect of an act which he *cannot help* performing—even if it be his own 'nature' which necessitates it. Must we not recognise it as a condition of the morally free act that the agent "could have acted otherwise" than he in fact did? It is true, indeed, that we sometimes praise or blame a man for an act about which we are prepared to say, in the light of our knowledge of his established character, that he "could no other." But I think that a little reflection shows that in such cases we are not praising or blaming the man strictly for what he does *now* (or at any rate we ought not to be), but rather for those past acts of his which have generated the firm habit of mind from which his *present* act follows 'necessarily.' In other words, our praise and blame, so far as justified, are really retrospective, being directed not to the agent *qua* performing *this* act, but to the agent *qua* performing those past acts which have built up his present character and in respect to which we presume that he *could* have acted otherwise, that there really *were* open possibilities before him. These cases, therefore, seem to me to constitute no valid exception to what I must take to be the rule, viz. than a man can be morally praised or blamed for an act only if he could have acted otherwise.

Now philosophers today are fairly well agreed that it is a postulate of the morally responsible act that the agent "could have acted otherwise" is *some* sense of that phrase. But sharp differences of opinion have arisen over the way in which the phrase ought to be interpreted. There is a strong disposition to water down its apparent meaning by insisting that it is not (as a postulate of moral responsibility) to be understood as a straightforward categorical proposition, but rather as a disguised hypothetical proposition. All that we really require to be assured of, in order to justify our holding X responsible for an act, is, we are told, that X could have acted otherwise *if* he had *chosen* otherwise (Moore, Stevenson); or perhaps that X could have acted otherwise *if* he had had a different character, or *if* he had been placed in different circumstances.

I think it is easy to understand, and even, in a measure, to sympathise with, the motives which induce philosophers to offer these counter-interpretations. It is not just the fact that "X could have acted otherwise," as a bald categorical statement, is incompatible with the universal sway of causal law—though this is, to some philosophers, a serious stone of stumbling. The more widespread objection is that it at least looks as though it were incompatible with that causal continuity of an agent's character with his conduct which is implied when we believe (surely with justice) that we can often tell the sort of thing a man will do from our knowledge of the sort of man he is.

We shall have to make our accounts with that particular difficulty later. At this stage I wish merely to show that neither of the hypothetical propositions suggested—and I think the same could be shown for *any* hypothetical alternative—is an acceptable substitute for the categorical proposition "X could have acted otherwise" as the presupposition of moral responsibility.

Let us look first at the earlier suggestion—"X could have acted otherwise *if* he had chosen otherwise." Now clearly there are a great many acts with regard to which we are entirely satisfied that the agent is thus situated. We are often perfectly sure that—for this is all it amounts to—if X had chosen otherwise, the circumstances presented no external obstacle to the translation of that choice into action. For example, we often have no doubt at all that X, who in point of fact told a lie, could have told the truth *if* he had so chosen. But does our confidence on this score allay all legitimate doubts about whether X is really blameworthy? Does it entail that X is free in the same sense required for moral responsibility? Surely not. The obvious question immediately arises: "But *could* X have *chosen* otherwise than he did?" It is doubt about the true answer to *that* question which leads most people to doubt the reality of moral responsibility. Yet on this crucial question the hypothetical proposition which is offered as a sufficient statement of the condition justifying the ascription of moral responsibility gives us no information whatsoever.

Indeed this hypothetical substitute for the categorical "X could have acted otherwise" seems to me to lack all plausibility unless one contrives to forget why it is, after all, that we ever come to feel fundamental doubts about man's moral responsibility. Such doubts are born, surely, when one becomes aware of certain reputable world views in religion or philosophy, or of certain reputable scientific beliefs, which in their several ways imply that man's actions are necessitated, and thus could not be otherwise than they in fact are. But clearly a doubt so based is not even touched by the recognition that man could very often act otherwise *if* he so chose. That proposition is entirely compatible with the necessitarian theories which generate our doubt: indeed it is this very compatibility that has recommended it to some philosophers, who are reluctant to give up either moral responsibility or Determinism. The proposition which we *must* be able to affirm if moral praise or blame of X is to be justified is the categorical proposition that X could have acted otherwise because—not if—he could have chosen otherwise; or, since it is essentially the inner side of the act that matters, the proposition simply that X could have chosen otherwise.

For the second of the alternative formulae suggested we cannot spare more than a few moments. But its inability to meet the demands it is required to meet is almost transparent. 'X could have acted otherwise', as a statement of a precondition of X's moral responsibility, really means (we are told) 'X could have acted otherwise *if* he were differently constituted, or *if* he had been placed in different circumstances'. It seems a sufficient reply to this to point out that the person whose moral responsibility is at issue is X; a specific individual, in a specific set of circumstances. It is totally irrelevant to X's moral responsibility that we should be able to say that some person differently constituted from X, or X in a different set of circumstances, could have done something different from what X did. . . .

That brings me to the second, and more constructive, part of this lecture. From now on I shall be considering whether it is reasonable to believe that man does in fact possess a free will of the kind specified in the first part of the lecture. If so, just how and where within the complex fabric of the volitional life are we to locate it?—for although free will must presumably belong (if anywhere) to the volitional side of human experience, it is pretty clear from the way in which we have been forced to define it that it does not pertain simply to volition as such; not even to all volitions that are commonly dignified with the name of 'choices'. It has been, I think, one of the more serious impediments to profitable discussion of the Free Will problem that Libertarians and Determinists alike have so often failed to appreciate the comparatively narrow area within which the free will that is necessary to 'save' morality is required to operate. It goes without saying that this failure has been gravely prejudicial to the case for Libertarianism. I attach a good deal of importance, therefore, to the problem of locating free will correctly within the volitional orbit. Its solution forestalls and annuls, I believe, some of the more tiresome clichés of Determinist criticism.

We saw earlier that Common Sense's practice of 'making allowances' in its moral judgments for the influence of heredity and environment indicates Common Sense's conviction, both that a just moral judgment must discount determinants of choice over which the agent has no control, and also (since it still accepts moral judgments as legitimate) that *something* of moral relevance survives which can be regarded as genuinely self-originated. We are now to try to discover what this 'something' is. And I think we may still usefully take Common Sense as our guide. Suppose one asks the ordinary intelligent citizen *why* he deems it proper to make allowances for X, whose heredity and/or environment are unfortunate. He will tend to reply, I think, in some such terms as these: that X has more and stronger temptations to deviate from what is right than Y or Z, who are normally circumstanced, so that he must put forth a *stronger moral effort* if he is to achieve the same level of external conduct. The intended implication seems to be that X is just as morally praiseworthy as Y or Z *if* he exerts an equivalent moral effort, even though he may not thereby achieve an equal success in conforming his will to the "concrete" demands of duty. And this implies, again, Common Sense's belief that *in moral effort* we have something for which a man is responsible *without qualification*, something that is *not* affected by heredity and environment but depends *solely* upon the self itself.

Now in my opinion Common Sense has here, in principle, hit upon the one and only defensible answer. Here, and here alone, so far as I can see, in the act of deciding whether to put forth or withhold the moral effort required to resist temptation and rise to duty, is to be found an act which is free in the sense required for moral responsibility; an act of which the self is sole author, and of which it is true to say that "it could be" (or, after the event, "could have been") "otherwise." Such is the thesis which we shall now try to establish.

The species of argument appropriate to the establishment of a thesis of this sort should fall, I think, into two phases. First, there should be a consideration of the evidence of the moral agent's own inner experience. What *is* the act of moral decision, and what does it imply, from the standpoint of the actual participant? Since there is no way of knowing the act of moral decision—or for that matter any other form of activity—except by actual participation in it, the evidence of the subject, or agent, is an issue of this kind of palmary importance. It can hardly, however, be taken as in itself conclusive. For even if that evidence should be overwhelmingly to the effect that moral decision does have the characteristics required by moral freedom, the question is bound to be raised—and in view of considerations from other quarters pointing in a contrary direction is *rightly* raised—Can we *trust* the evidence of inner experience? That brings us to what will be the second phase of the argument. We shall have to go on to show, if we are to make good our case, that the extraneous considerations so often supposed to be fatal to the belief in moral freedom are in fact innocuous to it. . . .

These arguments can, I think, be reduced in principle to no more than two: first, the argument from "predictability"; second, the argument from the alleged meaninglessness of an act supposed to be the self's act and yet no an expression of the self's character. Contemporary criticism of free will seems to me to consist almost exclusively on variations on these two themes. I shall deal with each in turn. . . .

Let us remind ourselves briefly of the setting within which, on our view, free will functions. There is X, the course which we believe we ought to follow, and Y, the course towards which we feel our desire is strongest. The freedom which we ascribe to the agent is the freedom to put forth, or refrain from putting forth the moral effort required to resist the pressure of desire and do what he thinks he ought to do.

But then there is surely an immense range of practical situations—covering by far the greater part of life—in which there is no question of a conflict within the self between what he most desires to do and what he thinks he ought to do? Indeed such conflict is a comparatively rare phenomenon for the majority of men. Yet over that whole vast range there is nothing whatever in our version of Libertarianism to prevent our agreeing that character determines conduct. In the absence, real or supposed, of any "moral" issue, what a man chooses will be simply that course which, after such reflection as seems called for, he deems most likely to bring him what he most strongly desires; and that is the same as to say the course to which his present character inclines him.

Over by far the greater area of human choices, then, our theory offers no more barrier to successful prediction on the basis of character than any other theory. For where there is no clash of strongest desire with duty, the free will we are defending has no business. There is just nothing for it to do.

But what about the situations—rare enough though they may be—in which there *is* this clash and in which free will does therefore operate? Does our theory entail that there at any rate, as the critic seems to suppose, "anything may happen"?

Not by any manner of means. In the first place, and by the very nature of the case, the range of the agent's possible choices is bounded by what he thinks he ought to do on the one hand, and what he most strongly desires on the other. The freedom claimed for him is a freedom of decision to make or withhold the effort required to do what he thinks he ought to do. There is no question of a freedom to act in some "wild" fashion, out of all relation to his characteristic beliefs and desires. This so-called "freedom of caprice," so often charged against the Libertarian, is, to put it bluntly, a sheer figment of the critic's imagination, with no *habitat* in serious Libertarian theory. Even in situations where free will does come into play it is perfectly possible, on a view like ours, given the appropriate knowledge of a man's character, to predict within certain limits how he will respond. . . .

I claim, therefore, that the view of free will I have been putting forward is consistent with predictability of conduct on the basis of character over a very wide field indeed. And I make the further claim that that field will cover all the situations in life concerning which there is any empirical evidence that successful prediction is possible.

Let us pass on to consider the second main line of criticism. This is, I think, much the more illuminating of the two, if only because it compels the Libertarian to make explicit certain concepts which are indispensable to him, but which, being desperately hard to state clearly, are apt not to be stated at all. The critic's fundamental point might be stated somewhat as follows:

"Free will as you describe it is completely unintelligible. On your own showing no *reason* can be given, because there just *is* no reason, why a man decides to exert rather than to withhold moral effort, or *vice versa*. But such an act—or more properly, such an 'occurrence'—it is nonsense to speak of as an act of a *self*. If there is nothing in the self's character to which it is, even in principle, in any way traceable, the self has nothing to do with it. Your so-called 'freedom,' therefore, so far from supporting the self's moral responsibility, destroys it as surely as the crudest Determinism could do."

If we are to discuss this criticism usefully, it is important, I think, to begin by getting clear about two different senses of the word "intelligible."

If, in the first place, we mean by an "intelligible" act one whose occurrence is in principle capable of being inferred, since it follows necessarily from something (though we may not know in fact from what), then it is certainly true that the Libertarian's free will is unintelligible. But that is only saying, is it not, that the Libertarian's "free" act is not an act which follows necessarily from something! This can hardly rank as a *criticism* of Libertarianism. It is just a description of it. That there can be nothing unintelligible in *this* sense is precisely what the Determinist has got to prove.

Yet it is surprising how often the critic of Libertarianism involves himself in this circular mode of argument. Repeatedly it is urged against the Libertarian, with a great air of triumph, that on his view he can't say *why* I now decide to rise to duty, or now decide to follow my strongest desire in defiance of duty. Of course he can't. If he could he wouldn't *be* a Libertarian. To "account for" a "free" act is a contradiction in terms. A free will is *ex hypothesi* the sort of thing of which the request for an *explanation* is absurd. The assumption that an explanation must be in principle possible for the act of moral decision deserves to rank as a classic example of the ancient fallacy of 'begging the question.'

But the critic usually has in mind another sense of the word "unintelligible." He is apt to take it for granted that an act which is unintelligible in the *above* sense (as the morally free act of the Libertarian undoubtedly is) is unintelligible in the *further* sense that we can attach no meaning to it. And this is an altogether more serious matter. If it could really be shown that the Libertarian's "free will" were unintelligible in this sense of being meaningless, that, for myself at any rate, would be the end of the affair. Libertarianism would have been conclusively refuted.

But it seems to me manifest that this can *not* be shown. The critic has allowed himself, I submit, to become the victim of a widely accepted but fundamentally vicious assumption. He has assumed that whatever is meaningful must exhibit its meaningfulness to those who view it from the standpoint of external observation. Now if one chooses thus to limit one's self to the role of external observer, it is, I think, perfectly true that one can attach no meaning to an act which is the act of something we call a 'self' and yet follows from nothing in that self's character. But then *why should we* so limit ourselves, when what is under consideration is a subjective activity? For the apprehension of subjective acts there is *another* standpoint available, that of *inner experience*, of the practical consciousness in its actual functioning. If our free will should turn out to be something to which we can attach a meaning from *this* standpoint, no more is required. And no more ought to be expected. For I must repeat that only from the inner standpoint of living experience *could* anything of the nature of 'activity' be directly grasped. Observation from without is in the nature of the case important to apprehend the active *qua* active. We can from without observe sequences of states. If into these we read activity (as we sometimes do), this can only be on the basis of what we discern in ourselves from the inner standpoint. It follows that if anyone insists upon taking his criterion of the meaningful simply from the standpoint of external observation, he is really deciding in advance of the evidence that the notion of activity, and *a fortiori* the notion of a free will, is "meaningless." He looks for the free act through a medium which is in the nature of the case incapable of revealing it, and then, because inevitably he doesn't find it, he declares that it doesn't exist!

But if, as we surely ought in this context, we adopt the inner standpoint, then (I am suggesting) things appear in a totally different light. From the inner standpoint, it seems to me plain, there is no difficulty whatever in attaching meaning to an act which is the self's act and which nevertheless does not follow from the self's character. So much I claim has been established by the phenemonological analysis, in this and the previous lecture, of the act of moral decision in face of moral temptation. It is thrown into particularly clear relief where the moral decision is to make the moral effort required to rise to duty. For the very function of moral effort, as it appears to the agent engaged in the act, is to enable the self to act against the line of least resistance, against the line to which his character as so far formed most strongly inclines him. But if the self is thus conscious here of *combating* his formed character, he surely cannot possibly suppose that the act, although his own act, *issues from* his formed character? I submit, therefore, that the self knows very well indeed—from the inner standpoint—what is meant by an act which is the *self's* act and which nevertheless does not follow from the self's *character*.

What this implies—and it seems to be an implication of cardinal importance for any theory of the self that aims at being more than superficial—is that the nature of the self is for itself something more than just its character as so far formed. The "nature" of the self and what we commonly call the "character" of the self are by no means the same thing, and it is utterly vital that they should not be confused. The "nature" of the self comprehends, but is not without remainder reducible to, its "character"; it must, if we are to be true to the testimony of our experience of it, be taken as including *also* the authentic creative power of fashioning and re-fashioning "character."

STUDY QUESTIONS

1. Why does Campbell confine freedom to inner acts?
2. Why does Campbell think that freedom is compatible with the fact that human behavior is very often predictable?
3. Does Campbell give convincing reasons for thinking that it is never too late for someone to change?
4. In what sense does Campbell think we are responsible for what we do? For what we are? For what we do because of what we are?
5. Does Campbell persuade you that we are, in fact, internally free? Is he right when he says that we ourselves must put forth the moral effort to resist the impulses and drives we possess?

6. Suppose a widower finds his wife's diary one year after her death. In it he discovers that she has made hundreds of detailed predictions about what he would be doing in the year following her death. Every single one of her predictions turns out to be true. Would this count against Campbell's argument for free will?

Existentialism and Freedom

JEAN-PAUL SARTRE

TRANSLATED BY BERNARD FRECHTMAN

Jean-Paul Sartre (1905–1980) was a French existentialist and is well known for his novels, plays, and philosophical works. With the outbreak of World War II he served in the French Army and became a leader in the French Resistance. He was awarded the Nobel Prize for literature in 1964, but refused it.

Sartre briefly explains existentialism as the doctrine that, in human beings, "existence precedes essence." An inanimate object—Sartre's example is a paper-cutter—is designed by someone who had in mind the object's purpose (essence) and then brought it into being (essence precedes existence). Human beings have no prior essence. We exist first and then determine what sort of beings we shall be (existence precedes essence). This is what Sartre means when he says that "man is nothing else but what he makes of himself." We are always faced

EXISTENTIALISM AND FREEDOM From *Existentialism* by Jean-Paul Sartre. Translated by Bernard Frechtman. Reprinted by permission of the publisher, The Philosophical Library.

with choices; in choosing we make ourselves what we are. Herein lies our dignity and our tragedy, for we can find no excuses for what we are. "The full responsibility of [our] existence rest[s] on [us]." In choosing a particular course of action as the right one to follow, we choose it as right for every other conscious being. With every act we "create an image of man as we think he ought to be." In this sense we create right and wrong. The responsibility is awesome; ethically we are alone and anguished. Sartre is an atheistic existentialist and recognizes no God-given rules. "That is the very starting point of existentialism": Human freedom is unqualified, and so is human responsibility.

What is meant by the term *existentialism*?

Most people who use the word would be rather embarrassed if they had to explain it, since, now that the word is all the rage, even the work of a musician or painter is being called existentialist. . . . It seems that for want of an advance-guard doctrine analogous to surrealism, the kind of people who are eager for scandal and flurry turn to this philosophy which in other respects does not at all serve their purposes in this sphere.

Actually, it is the least scandalous, the most austere of doctrines. It is intended strictly for specialists and philosophers. Yet it can be defined easily. What complicates matters is that there are two kinds of existentialists; first, those who are Christian, among whom I include Jaspers and Gabriel Marcel, both Catholic; and on the other hand, the atheistic existentialists, among whom I class Heidegger, and then the French existentialists and myself. What they have in common is that they think that existence precedes essence, or, if you prefer, that subjectivity must be the starting point.

Just what does that mean? Let us consider some object that is manufactured, for example, a book or a paper-cutter: here is an object which has been made by an artisan whose inspiration came from a concept. He referred to the concept of what a paper-cutter is and likewise to a known method of production, which is part of the concept, something which is, by and large, a routine. Thus, the paper-cutter is at once an object produced in a certain way and, on the other hand, one having a specific use; and one cannot postulate a man who produces a paper-cutter but does not know what it is used for. Therefore, let us say that, for the paper-cutter, essence—that is, the ensemble of both the production routines and the properties which enable it to be both produced and defined—precedes existence. Thus, the presence of the paper-cutter or book in front of me is determined. Therefore, we have here a technical view of the world whereby it can be said that production precedes existence.

When we conceive God as the Creator, He is generally thought of as a superior sort of artisan. Whatever doctrine we may be considering, whether one like that of Descartes or that of Leibnitz, we always grant that will more or less follows understanding or, at the very least, accompanies it, and that when God creates He knows exactly what He is creating. Thus, the concept of man in the mind of God is comparable to the concept of paper-cutter in the mind of the manufacturer, and, following certain techniques and a conception, God produces man, just as the artisan, following a definition and a technique, makes a paper-cutter. Thus, the individual man is the realization of a certain concept in the divine intelligence.

In the eighteenth century, the atheism of the *philosophes* discarded the idea of God, but not so much for the notion that essence precedes existence. To a certain extent, this idea is found everywhere; we find it in Diderot, in Voltaire, and even in Kant. Man has a human nature; this human nature, which is the concept of the human, is found in all men, which means that each man is a particular example of a universal concept, man. In Kant, the result of this universality is that the wild-man, the natural man, as well as the bourgeois, are circumscribed by the same definition and have the same basic qualities. Thus, here too the essence of man precedes the historical existence that we find in nature.

Atheistic existentialism, which I represent, is more coherent. It states that if God does not exist, there is at least one being in whom existence precedes essence, a being who exists before he can be defined by any concept, and that this being is man, or, as Heidegger says, human reality. What is meant here by saying that existence precedes essence? It means that, first of all, man exists, turns up, appears on the scene, and, only afterwards, defines himself. If man, as the existentialist conceives him, is indefinable, it is because at

377

first he is nothing. Only afterward will he be something, and he himself will have made what he will be. Thus, there is no human nature, since there is no God to conceive it. Not only is man what he conceives himself to be, but he is also only what he wills himself to be after this thrust toward existence.

Man is nothing else but what he makes of himself. Such is the first principle of existentialism. It is also what is called subjectivity, the name we are labeled with when charges are brought against us. But what do we mean by this, if not that man has a greater dignity than a stone or table? For we mean that man first exists, that is, that man first of all is the being in the future. Man is at the start a plan which is aware of itself, rather than a patch of moss, a piece of garbage, or a cauliflower; nothing exists prior to this plan; there is nothing in heaven; man will be what he will have planned to be. Not what he will want to be. Because by the word "will" we generally mean a conscious decision, which is subsequent to what we have already made of ourselves. I may want to belong to a political party, write a book, get married; but all that is only a manifestation of an earlier, more spontaneous choice that is called "will." But if existence really does precede essence, man is responsible for what he is. Thus, existentialism's first move is to make every man aware of what he is and to make the full responsibility of his existence rest on him. And when we say that a man is responsible for himself, we do not only mean that he is responsible for his own individuality, but that he is responsible for all men.

The word subjectivism has two meanings, and our opponents play on the two. Subjectivism means, on the one hand, that an individual chooses and makes himself; and, on the other, that it is impossible for man to transcend human subjectivity. The second of these is the essential meaning of existentialism. When we say that man chooses his own self, we mean that every one of us does likewise; but we also mean by that that in making this choice he also chooses all men. In fact, in creating the man that we want to be, there is not a single one of our acts which does not at the same time create an image of man as we think he ought to be. To choose to be this or that is to affirm at the same time the value of what we choose, because we can never choose evil. We always choose the good, and nothing can be good for us without being good for all.

If, on the other hand, existence precedes essence, and if we grant that we exist and fashion our image at one and the same time, the image is valid for everybody and for our whole age. Thus, our responsibility is much greater than we might have supposed, because it involves all mankind. If I am a workingman and choose to join a Christian trade-union rather than be a communist, and if by being a member I want to show that the best thing for man is resignation, that the kingdom of man is not of this world, I am not only involving my own case—I want to be resigned for everyone. As a result, my action has involved all humanity. To take a more individual matter, if I want to marry, to have children; even if this marriage depends solely on my own circumstances or passion or wish, I am involving all humanity in monogamy and not merely myself. Therefore, I am responsible for myself and for everyone else. I am creating a certain image of man of my own choosing. In choosing myself, I choose man.

This helps us understand what the actual content is of such rather grandiloquent words as anguish, forlornness, despair. As you will see, it's all quite simple.

First, what is meant by anguish? The existentialists say at once that man is anguish. What that means is this: the man who involves himself and who realizes that he is not only the person he chooses to be, but also a law-maker who is, at the same time, choosing all mankind as well as himself, cannot help escape the feeling of his total and deep responsibility. Of course, there are many people who are not anxious; but we claim that they are hiding their anxiety, that they are fleeing from it. Certainly, many people believe that when they do something, they themselves are the only ones involved, and when someone says to them, "What if everyone acted that way?" they shrug their shoulders and answer, "Everyone doesn't act that way." But really, one should always ask himself, "What would happen if everybody looked at things that way?" There is no escaping this disturbing thought except by a kind of double-dealing. A man who lies and makes excuses for himself by saying "not everybody does that," is someone with an uneasy conscience, because the act of lying implies that a universal value is conferred upon the lie.

Anguish is evident even when it conceals itself. This is the anguish that Kierkegaard called the anguish of Abraham. You know the story: an angel has ordered Abraham to sacrifice his son; if it really were an angel who has come and said, "You are Abraham, you shall sacrifice your son," everything would be all right.

379

But everyone might first wonder, "Is it really an angel, and am I really Abraham? What proof do I have?" . . .

Now, I'm not being singled out as an Abraham, and yet at every moment I'm obliged to perform exemplary acts. For every man, everything happens as if all mankind had its eyes fixed on him and were guiding itself by what he does. And every man ought to say to himself, "Am I really the kind of man who has the right to act in such a way that humanity might guide itself by my actions?" And if he does not say that to himself, he is masking his anguish.

There is no question here of the kind of anguish which would lead to quietism, to inaction. It is a matter of a simple sort of anguish that anybody who has had responsibilities is familiar with. For example, when a military officer takes the responsibility for an attack and sends a certain number of men to death, he chooses to do so, and in the main he alone makes the choice. Doubtless, orders come from above, but they are too broad; he interprets them, and on this interpretation depend the lives of ten or fourteen or twenty men. In making a decision he cannot help having a certain anguish. All leaders know this anguish. That doesn't keep them from acting; on the contrary, it is the very condition of their action. For it implies that they envisage a number of possibilities, and when they choose one, they realize that it has value only because it is chosen. We shall see that this kind of anguish, which is the kind that existentialism describes, is explained, in addition, by a direct responsibility to the other men whom it involves. It is not a curtain separating us from action, but is part of action itself.

When we speak of forlornness, a term Heidegger was fond of, we mean only that God does not exist and that we have to face all the consequences of this. The existentialist is strongly opposed to a certain kind of secular ethics which would like to abolish God with the least possible expense. About 1880, some French teachers tried to set up a secular ethics which went something like this: God is a useless and costly hypothesis; we are discarding it; but meanwhile, in order for there to be an ethics, a society, a civilization, it is essential that certain values be taken seriously and that they be considered as having an *a priori* existence. It must be obligatory, *a priori*, to be honest, not to lie, not to beat your wife, to have children, etc., etc. So we're going to try a little device which will make it possible to show that values exist all the same, inscribed in a heaven of ideas, though otherwise God does not exist. In other words—and this, I believe, is the tendency of everything called reformism in France—nothing will be changed if God does not exist. We shall find ourselves with the same norms of honesty, progress, and humanism, and we shall have made of God an outdated hypothesis which will peacefully die off by itself.

The existentialist, on the contrary, thinks it very distressing that God does not exist, because all possibility of finding values in a heaven of ideas disappears along with Him; there can be no longer an *a priori* Good, since there is no infinite and perfect consciousness to think it. Nowhere is it written that the Good exists, that we must be honest, that we must not lie; because the fact is we are on a plane where there are only men. Dostoievsky said, "If God didn't exist, everything would be possible." That is the very starting point of existentialism. Indeed, everything is permissible if God does not exist, and as a result man is forlorn, because neither within him nor without does he find anything to cling to. He can't start making excuses for himself.

If existence really does precede essence, there is no explaining things away by reference to a fixed and given human nature. In other words, there is no determinism, man is free, man is freedom. On the other hand, if God does not exist, we find no values or commands to turn to which legitimize our conduct. So, in the bright realm of values, we have no excuse behind us, no justification before us. We are alone, with no excuses.

That is the idea I shall try to convey when I say that man is condemned to be free. Condemned, because he did not create himself, yet, in other respects is free; because, once thrown into the world, he is responsible for everything he does. The existentialist does not believe in the power of passion. He will never agree that a sweeping passion is a ravaging torrent which fatally leads a man to certain acts and is therefore an excuse. He thinks that man is responsible for his passion.

The existentialist does not think that man is going to help himself by finding in the world some omen by which to orient himself. Because he thinks that man will interpret the omen to suit himself. Therefore, he thinks that man, with no support and no aid, is condemned every moment to invent man. Ponge, in a very fine article, has said, "Man is the future of man." That's exactly it. But if it is taken to mean that this future is recorded in heaven, that God sees it, then it is false, because it would really no longer be a future.

If it is taken to mean that, whatever a man may be, there is a future to be forged, a virgin future before him, then this remark is sound. But then we are forlorn.

To give you an example which will enable you to understand forlornness better, I shall cite the case of one of my students who came to see me under the following circumstances: his father was on bad terms with his mother, and, moreover, was inclined to be a collaborationist; his older brother had been killed in the German offensive of 1940, and the young man, with somewhat immature but generous feelings, wanted to avenge him. His mother lived alone with him, very much upset by the half-treason of her husband and the death of her older son; the boy was her only consolation.

The boy was faced with the choice of leaving for England and joining the Free French Forces—that is, leaving his mother behind—or remaining with his mother and helping her carry on. He was fully aware that the woman lived only for him and that his going-off—and perhaps his death—would plunge her into despair. He was also aware that every act that he did for his mother's sake was a sure thing, in the sense that it was helping her to carry on, whereas every effort he made toward going off and fighting was an uncertain move which might run aground and prove completely useless; for example, on his way to England he might, while passing through Spain, be detained indefinitely in a Spanish camp; he might reach England or Algiers and be stuck in an office at a desk job. As a result, he was faced with two very different kinds of action: one, concrete, immediate, but concerning only one individual; the other concerned an incomparably vaster group, a national collectivity, but for that very reason was dubious, and might be interrupted en route. And, at the same time, he was wavering between two kinds of ethics. On the one hand, an ethics of sympathy, of personal devotion; on the other, a broader ethics, but on whose efficacy was more dubious. He had to choose between the two.

Who could help him choose? Christian doctrine? No. Christian doctrine says, "Be charitable, love your neighbor, take the more rugged path, etc., etc." But which is the more rugged path? Whom should he love as a brother? The fighting man or his mother? Which does the greater good, the vague act of fighting in a group, or the concrete one of helping a particular human being to go on living? Who can decide *a priori*? Nobody. No book of ethics can tell him. The Kantian ethics says, "Never treat any person as a means, but as an end." Very well, if I stay with my mother, I'll treat her as an end and not as a means; but by virtue of this very fact, I'm running the risk of treating the people around me who are fighting, as means; and, conversely, if I go to join those who are fighting, I'll be treating them as an end, and, by doing that, I run the risk of treating my mother as a means.

If values are vague, and if they are always too broad for the concrete and specific case that we are considering, the only thing left for us is to trust our instincts. That's what this young man tried to do; and when I saw him, he said, "In the end, feeling is what counts. I ought to choose whichever pushes me in one direction. If I feel that I love my mother enough to sacrifice everything else for her—my desire for vengeance, for action, for adventure—then I'll stay with her. If, on the contrary, I feel that my love for my mother isn't enough, I'll leave."

But how is the value of a feeling determined. What gives his feeling for his mother value? Precisely the fact that he remained with her. I may say that I like so-and-so well enough to sacrifice a certain amount of money for him, but I may say so only if I've done it. I may say, "I love my mother well enough to remain with her" if I have remained with her. The only way to determine the value of this affection is, precisely, to perform an act which confirms and defines it. But, since I require this affection to justify my act, I find myself caught in a vicious circle. . . .

As for despair, the term has a very simple meaning. It means that we shall confine ourselves to reckoning only with what depends upon our will, or on the ensemble of probabilities which make our action possible. When we want something, we always have to reckon with probabilities. I may be counting on the arrival of a friend. The friend is coming by rail or street-car; this supposes that the train will arrive on schedule, or that the street-car will not jump the track. I am left in the realm of possibility; but possibilities are to be reckoned with only to the point where my action comports with the ensemble of these possibilities, and no further. The moment the possibilities I am considering are not rigorously involved by my action, I ought to disengage myself from them, because no God, no scheme, can adapt the world and its possibilities to my will. When Descartes said, "Conquer yourself rather than the world," he meant essentially the same thing.

383

The Marxists to whom I have spoken reply, "You can rely on the support of others in your action, which obviously has certain limits because you're not going to live forever. That means: rely on both what others are doing elsewhere to help you, in China, in Russia, and what they will do later on, after your death, to carry on the action and lead it to its fulfillment, which will be the revolution. You even *have* to rely upon that, otherwise you're immoral." I reply at once that I will always rely on fellow fighters insofar as these comrades are involved with me in a common struggle, in the unity of a party or a group in which I can more or less make my weight felt; that is, one whose ranks I am in as a fighter and whose movements I am aware of at every moment. In such a situation, relying on the unity and will of the party is exactly like counting on the fact that the train will arrive on time or that the car won't jump the track. But, given that man is free and that there is no human nature for me to depend on, I cannot count on men whom I do not know by relying on human goodness or man's concern for the good of society. I don't know what will become of the Russian revolution; I may make an example of it to the extent that at the present time it is apparent that the proletariat plays a part in Russia that it plays in no other nation. But I can't swear that this will inevitably lead to a triumph of the proletariat. I've got to limit myself to what I see.

Given that men are free, and that tomorrow they will freely decide what man will be, I cannot be sure that, after my death, fellow fighters will carry on my work to bring it to its maximum perfection. Tomorrow, after my death, some men may decide to set up Fascism, and the others may be cowardly and muddled enough to let them do it. Fascism will then be the human reality, so much the worse for us.

Actually, things will be as man will have decided they are to be. Does that mean that I should abandon myself to quietism? No. First, I should involve myself; then, act on the old saw, "Nothing ventured, nothing gained." Nor does it mean that I shouldn't belong to a party, but rather that I shall have no illusions and shall do what I can. For example, suppose I ask myself, "Will socialization, as such, ever come about?" I know nothing about it. All I know is that I'm going to do everything in my power to bring it about. Beyond that, I can't count on anything. Quietism is the attitude of people who say, "Let others do what I can't do." The doctrine I am presenting is the very opposite of quietism, since it declares, "There is no reality except in action." Moreover, it goes further, since it adds, "Man is nothing else than his plan; he exists only to the extent that he fulfills himself; he is, therefore, nothing else than the ensemble of his acts, nothing else than his life."

STUDY QUESTIONS

1. What does Sartre mean by saying that human beings are "condemned to be free"?
2. According to Sartre, we never decide solely on the basis of someone else's advice since we ourselves choose to seek that advice from that advisor. Do you think he is right?
3. Sartre says, in effect, "I am responsible for myself and for everyone else. I am creating a certain image of man of my own choosing. In choosing myself, I choose man." What do these assertions mean and how does Sartre argue for them?
4. Can an existentialist consistently adopt a demanding social ideology? From this standpoint, discuss the reservations Sartre expresses concerning Marxism and the Russian revolution.

SUGGESTED READINGS

Berofsky, B. *Determinism.* New York: Harper and Row, 1966.

Campbell, C. A. *On Selfhood and Godhood.* New York: MacMillan Co., 1957.

Dworkin, G., ed. *Determinism, Free Will and Moral Responsibility.* Englewood Cliffs, N.J.: Prentice-Hall, 1970.

Hook, Sidney, ed. *Determinism and Freedom.* New York: Collier Books, 1961.

Morgenhesser, S., and J. L. Walsh, eds. *Free Will.* Englewood Cliffs, N.J.: Prentice-Hall, 1962.

Van Inwagen, Peter. *An Essay on Free Will.* Oxford: Oxford University Press, 1983.

Chapter

6

SELF-RESPECT

A being capable of wronging another being is a moral agent. A being capable of being wronged by a moral agent is a moral patient. A moral agent has duties; a moral patient has rights. Robert Nozick aptly speaks of moral patients as exerting "ethical pull" on moral agents, who must treat them in a morally respectful manner.

Any person is at once a moral agent and a moral patient. Consider the notion of self-respect. Respect for oneself as a moral patient is one meaning of self-respect. So understood, to respect oneself is to fulfill the duties one owes to oneself. What does one owe to oneself? Christopher Lasch calls attention to the currently popular assumption—reflected in television commercials that urge us to indulge in certain expensive luxuries because "you owe it to yourself"—that we owe ourselves gratification and pleasure. Lasch is probably right to claim that many people today see self-indulgence as a *moral* duty. All the same, we recognize something slightly ludicrous about refusing to wear or eat something inferior "because I have too much respect for myself."

Contrast this narcissistic idea of self-respect with Kant's, that the primary self-duty is "the universal duty which devolves upon man of so ordering his life as to be fit for the performance of all moral duties." Kant is still talking of duties to one's ("patient") self. But he claims that morally we owe that self *not* happiness or gratification but self-development as a moral agent. This older ideal of self-obligation is entirely consistent with the conception of virtue-based ethics. The imperative is to become virtuous, to "build character." For Kant, as for the philosophers of virtue, human beings are, in the last analysis, responsible for the kind of person they are (selfish or kind, courageous or cowardly, temperate or self-indulgent). Since virtue is not given to us, we must develop it. Virtue-based ethics' answer to the question "What do we owe to ourselves?" thus (roughly) coincides with Kant's answer: We owe it to ourselves to develop ourselves as moral agents.

Respect for the self as moral patient is one aspect of self-respect. But the self has two aspects and "self-respect" has a second meaning: respect for oneself as moral agent. Persons who consistently behave in an honorable way (discharging their obligations to themselves and others) can justifiably view themselves as moral beings worthy of commendation. Their track record as moral agents is evidence of character, and, indeed, respect for one's "agent" self is respect for oneself as a "person of character." Conversely, persons of weak character necessarily lack this form of self-respect. In effect, persons who respect themselves and others as moral patients will also come to respect themselves as moral agents. Kant speaks of this as "noble pride" or "proper self-esteem."

Peter Berger's account of the concept of honor pertains to the self as morally obligated agent. Berger theorizes that honor concerns the duties that belong to people by virtue of their place and role in the social order. To fail in duties that define oneself in society is to become dishonorable. The loss of self-respect that comes from this kind of failure may be so severe that it endangers one's very sense of oneself as a person. In extreme cases, we feel the loss as an intolerable alienation.

Joan Didion's conception of self-respect is also agent oriented. To have self-respect is to be a person of character with a better than average record of acting in accordance with one's principles. Didion stresses that people with the strength of character to achieve this are also people who accept responsibility for their actions. Thus the tendency to find excuses for oneself indicates a lack of self-respect.

Anthony Quinton's article, a survey of the vicissitudes of virtue-based ethics in the past few centuries, offers a similar conception of self-respect and character. Quinton finds that the Victorian emphasis on strength of character is a thing of the past. The transformation Quinton describes can be characterized as a shift of emphasis from the self as an active moral agent to the patient self as a repository of rights, with a corresponding shift in the notion of self-respect. According to Quinton, persons of "character" are persons with the consistent strength of will to apply reason to achieve a long-range gain in situations where they are strongly tempted to forego that gain in favor of immediate satisfactions. Quinton's person of character is the very antithesis of the person whom Christopher Lasch calls "the new narcissist," a type Lasch finds alarmingly prevalent today.

Lasch, Berger, Didion, and Quinton all deal with the same general phenomenon: Morally speaking, modern men and women see themselves primarily as centers of needs and rights, and only secondarily as centers of obligations and duties. Lasch, Berger, and Quinton find that a weakening of tradition and social roles accompanies the shift of emphasis to the self as moral patient. Quinton recognizes character, honor, and self-abnegation as currently unfashionable. He believes that each of us must work to reverse this trend. For Berger and Lasch, the new narcissism is part of what Berger calls the "obsolescence" of honor. Berger is hopeful that character and honor will make a comeback. Lasch is rather more pessimistic.

Dignity and Self-respect

IMMANUEL KANT

TRANSLATED BY LOUIS ENFIELD

A biographical sketch of Immanuel Kant is found on page 86.

Moral persons do their duty to themselves as well as others; such persons deserve respect and will rightfully respect themselves. Self-respect is essential to self-worth. For example, says Kant, drunkards fail in their duty to themselves; the result is self-contempt. Similarly, weak persons who constantly find excuses for their moral lapses are contemptible in their own eyes as well as in the eyes of others. Suicide violates self-duty most seriously, since in suicide people use their own free will to destroy themselves as moral agents, thereby using themselves as a means (to avoid pain) and not as an end. Kant denies that we owe ourselves happiness: "Not self-favour but self-esteem" is the principle of self-duty. For Kant, self-respect comes to those who earn it by living a principled life.

I

By way of introduction it is to be noted that there is no question in moral philosophy which has received more defective treatment than that of the individual's duty towards himself. No one has

DIGNITY AND SELF-RESPECT From "Proper Self-respect," and "Duties to Oneself," from *Lectures on Ethics* by Immanuel Kant. Translated by Louis Enfield (Harper & Row, 1963). Reprinted by permission of Methuen and Company Ltd.

390

framed a proper concept of self-regarding duty. It has been regarded as a detail and considered by way of an afterthought, as an
appendix to moral philosophy, on the view that man should give a
thought to himself only after he has completely fulfilled his duty
towards others. . . . It was taken for granted that a man's duty
towards himself consisted . . . in promoting his own happiness. In
that case everything would depend on how an individual determined his own happiness; for our self-regarding duties would
consist in the universal rule to satisfy all our inclinations in order to
further our happiness. This would, however, militate seriously
against doing our duty towards others. In fact, the principle of
self-regarding duties is a very different one, which has no connexion with our well-being or earthly happiness. Far from ranking
lowest in the scale of precedence, our duties towards ourselves are
of primary importance and should have pride of place; for (deferring for the moment the definition of what constitutes this duty) it
is obvious that nothing can be expected from a man who dishon-
ours his own person. He who transgresses against himself loses his
manliness and becomes incapable of doing his duty towards his
fellows. A man who performed his duty to others badly, who
lacked generosity, kindness and sympathy, but who nevertheless
did his duty to himself by leading a proper life, might yet possess a
certain inner worth; but he who has transgressed his duty towards
himself, can have no inner worth whatever. Thus a man who fails
in his duty to himself loses worth absolutely; while a man who fails
in his duty to others loses worth only relatively. It follows that the
prior condition of our duty to others is our duty to ourselves; we
can fulfil the former only in so far as we first fulfil the latter. Let us
illustrate our meaning by a few examples of failure in one's duty to
oneself. A drunkard does no harm to another, and if he has a strong
constitution he does no harm to himself, yet he is an object of
contempt. We are not indifferent to cringing servility; man should
not cringe and fawn; by so doing he degrades his person and loses
his manhood. If a man for gain or profit submits to all indignities
and makes himself the plaything of another, he casts away the
worth of his manhood. Again, a lie is more a violation of one's
duty to oneself than of one's duty to others. A liar, even though by
his lies he does no harm to any one, yet becomes an object of
contempt, he throws away his personality; his behaviour is vile, he
has transgressed his duty towards himself. We can carry the argu-

ment further and say that to accept favours and benefits is also a breach of one's duty to oneself. If I accept favours, I contract debts which I can never repay, for I can never get on equal terms with him who has conferred the favours upon me; he has stolen a march upon me, and if I do him a favour I am only returning a *quid pro quo*; I shall always owe him a debt of gratitude, and who will accept such a debt? For to be indebted is to be subject to an unending constraint. I must for ever be courteous and flattering towards my benefactor, and if I fail to be so he will very soon make me conscious of my failure; I may even be forced to using subterfuge so as to avoid meeting him. But he who pays promptly for everything is under no constraint; he is free to act as he please; none will hinder him. Again, the faint-hearted who complain about their luck and sigh and weep about their misfortunes are despicable in our eyes; instead of sympathizing with them we do our best to keep away from them. But if a man shows a steadfast courage in his misfortune, and though greatly suffering, does not cringe and complain but puts a bold face upon things, to such a one our sympathy goes out. Moreover, if a man gives up his freedom and barters it away for money, he violates his manhood. Life itself ought not to be rated so highly as to warrant our being prepared, in order only not to lose it, to live otherwise than as a man should, i.e. not a life of ease, but so that we do not degrade our manhood. We must also be worthy of our manhood; whatsoever makes us unworthy of it makes us unfit for anything, and we cease to be men. Moreover, if a man offers his body for profit for the sport of others—if, for instance, he agrees in return for a few pints of beer to be knocked about—he throws himself away, and the perpetrators who pay him for it are acting as vilely as he. Neither can we without destroying our person abandon ourselves to others in order to satisfy their desires, even though it be done to save parents and friends from death; still less can this be done for money. If done in order to satisfy one's own desires, it is very immodest and immoral, but yet not so unnatural; but if it be done for money, or for some other reason, a person allows himself to be treated as a thing, and so throws away the worth of his manhood. It is the same with the vices of the flesh (*crimina carnis*), which for that reason are not spoken of. They do no damage to anyone, but dishonour and degrade a man's own person; they are an offence against the dignity of manhood in one's own person. The most serious offence against the duty one owes to oneself is suicide. But why should suicide be so abominable? It is no answer to say 'because God forbids it'. Suicide is not an abomination because God has forbidden it; it is forbidden by God because it is abominable. If it were the other way about, suicide would not be abominable if it were not forbidden; and I should not know why God had forbidden it, if it were not abominable in itself. The ground, therefore, for regarding suicide and other transgressions as abominable and punishable must not be found in the divine will, but in their inherent heinousness. Suicide is an abomination because it implies the abuse of man's freedom of action: he uses his freedom to destroy himself. His freedom should be employed to enable him to live as a man. He is free to dispose as he pleases of things appertaining to his person, but not of his person; he may not use his freedom against himself. For a man to recognize what his duty is towards himself in this respect is far from easy: because although man has indeed a natural horror of suicide, yet we can argue and quibble ourselves into believing that, in order to rid himself of trouble and misery, a man may destroy himself. The argument makes a strong appeal; and in terms of the rule of prudence suicide may often be the surest and best course; none the less suicide is in itself revolting. The rule of morality, which takes precedence of all rules of reflective prudence, commands apodeictically and categorically that we must observe our duties to ourselves; and in committing suicide and reducing himself to a carcase, man uses his powers and his liberty against himself. Man is free to dispose of his condition but not of his person; he himself is an end and not a means; all else in the world is of value only as a means, but man is a person and not a thing and therefore not a means. It is absurd that a reasonable being, an end for the sake of which all else is means, should use himself as a means. It is true that a person can serve as a means for others (e.g. by his work), but only in a way whereby he does not cease to be a person and an end. Whoever acts in such a way that he cannot be an end, uses himself as a means and treats his person as a thing. . . .

The duties we owe to ourselves do not depend on the relation of the action to the ends of happiness. If they did, they would depend on our inclinations and so be governed by rules of prudence. Such rules are not moral, since they indicate only the necessity of the means for the satisfaction of inclinations, and cannot therefore bind us. The basis of such obligation is not to be found in the advantages

393

we reap from doing our duty towards ourselves, but in the worth of manhood. This principle does not allow us an unlimited freedom in respect of our own persons. It insists that we must reverence humanity in our own person, because apart from this man becomes an object of contempt, worthless in the eyes of his fellows and worthless in himself. Such faultiness is absolute. Our duties towards ourselves constitute the supreme condition and the principle of all morality; for moral worth is the worth of the person as such; our capacities have a value only in regard to the circumstances in which we find ourselves. Socrates lived in a state of wretchedness; his circumstances were worthless; but though his circumstances were so ill-conditioned, yet he himself was of the highest value. Even though we sacrifice all life's amenities we can make up for their loss and sustain approval by maintaining the worth of our humanity. We may have lost everything else, and yet still retain our inherent worth. Only if our worth as human beings is intact can we perform our other duties; for it is the foundation stone of all other duties. A man who has destroyed and cast away his personality, has no intrinsic worth, and can no longer perform any manner of duty.

Let us next consider the basis of the principle of all self-regarding duties.

Freedom is, on the one hand, that faculty which gives unlimited usefulness to all other faculties. It is the highest order of life, which serves as the foundation of all perfections and is their necessary condition. All animals have the faculty of using their powers according to will. But this will is not free. It is necessitated through the incitement of *stimuli*, and the actions of animals involve a *bruta necessitas*. If the will of all beings were so bound to sensuous impulse, the world would possess no value. The inherent value of the world, the *summum bonum*, is freedom in accordance with a will which is not necessitated to action. Freedom is thus the inner value of the world. But on the other hand, freedom unrestrained by rules of its conditional employment is the most terrible of all things. The actions of animals are regular; they are performed in accordance with rules which necessitate them subjectively. Mankind apart, nature is not free; through it all there runs a subjectively necessitating principle in accordance with which everything happens regularly. Man alone is free; his actions are not regulated by any such subjectively necessitating principle; if they were, he would not be free. And what then? If the freedom of man were not kept within bounds by objective rules, the result would be the completest savage disorder. There could then be no certainty that man might not use his powers to destroy himself, his fellows, and the whole of nature. I can conceive freedom as the complete absence of orderliness, if it is not subject to an objective determination. The grounds of this objective determination must lie in the understanding, and constitute the restrictions to freedom. Therefore the proper use of freedom is the supreme rule. What then is the condition under which freedom is restricted? It is the law. The universal law is therefore as follows: Let thy procedure be such that in all thine actions regularity prevails. What does this restraint imply when applied to the individual? That he should not follow his inclinations. The fundamental rule, in terms of which I ought to restrain my freedom, is the conformity of free behaviour to the essential ends of humanity. I shall not then follow my inclinations, but bring them under a rule. He who subjects his person to his inclinations, acts contrary to the essential end of humanity; for as a free being he must not be subjected to inclinations, but ought to determine them in the exercise of his freedom; and being a free agent he must have a rule, which is the essential end of humanity. In the case of animals inclinations are already determined by subjectively compelling factors; in their case, therefore, disorderliness is impossible. But if man gives free rein to his inclinations, he sinks lower than an animal because he then lives in a state of disorder which does not exist among animals. A man is then in contradiction with the essential ends of humanity in his own person, and so with himself. All evil in the world springs from freedom. Animals, not being free, live according to rules. But free beings can only act regularly, if they restrict their freedom by rules. Let us reflect upon the actions of man which refer to himself, and consider freedom in them. These spring from impulse and inclinations or from maxims and principles. It is essential, therefore, that man should take his stand upon maxims and restrain by rules the free actions which relate to himself. These are the rules of his self-regarding duties. For if we consider man in respect of his inclinations and instincts, he is loosed from them and determined by neither. In all nature there is nothing to injure man in the satisfaction of his desires; all injurious things are his own invention, the outcome of his freedom. We need only instance strong drink and the many dishes concocted to tickle his palate. In the unregulated pursuit of an inclination of his own devising, man becomes an object of utter contempt, because his freedom makes it possible for him to turn nature inside out in order to satisfy himself. Let him devise what he pleases for satisfying his desires, so long as he regulates the use of his devices; if he does not, his freedom is his greatest misfortune. It must therefore be restricted, though not by other properties or faculties, but by itself. The supreme rule is that in all the actions which affect himself a man should so conduct himself that every exercise of his power is compatible with the fullest employment of them. Let us illustrate our meaning by examples. If I have drunk too much I am incapable of using my freedom and my powers. Again, if I kill myself, I use my powers to deprive myself of the faculty of using them. That freedom, the principle of the highest order of life, should annul itself and abrogate the use of itself conflicts with the fullest use of freedom. But freedom can only be in harmony with itself under certain conditions; otherwise it comes into collision with itself. If there were no established order in Nature, everything would come to an end, and so it is with unbridled freedom. Evils are to be found, no doubt, in Nature, but the true moral evil, vice, only in freedom. We pity the fortunate, but we hate the vicious and rejoice at their punishment. The conditions under which alone the fullest use of freedom is possible, and can be in harmony with itself, are the essential ends of humanity. It must conform with these. The principle of all duties is that the use of freedom must be in keeping with the essential ends of humanity. Thus, for instance, a human being is not entitled to sell his limbs for money, even if he were offered ten thousand thalers for a single finger. If he were so entitled, he could sell all his limbs. We can dispose of things which have no freedom but not of a being which has free will. A man who sells himself makes himself a thing and, as he has jettisoned his person, it is open to anyone to deal with him as he pleases. Another instance of this kind is where a human being makes himself a thing by making himself an object of enjoyment for some one's sexual desire. It degrades humanity, and that is why those guilty of it feel ashamed. We see, therefore, that just as freedom is the source of virtue which ennobles mankind, so is it also the root of the most dreadful vices—such as, for instance, a *crimen carnis contra naturam*, since it can devise all manner of means to satisfy its inclinations. Some crimes and vices, the result of freedom (e.g. suicide), make us shudder, others are nauseating; the mere mention of them is loathsome; we are ashamed of them because they degrade us below the level of beasts; they are grosser even than suicide, for the mention of suicide makes us shudder, but those other crimes and vices cannot be mentioned without producing nausea. Suicide is the most abominable of the vices which inspire dread and hate, but nausea and contempt indicate a lower level still.

Not self-favour but self-esteem should be the principle of our duties towards ourselves. This means that our actions must be in keeping with the worth of man. There are in us two grounds of action; inclinations, which belong to our animal nature, and humanity, to which the inclinations must be subjected. Our duties to ourselves are negative; they restrict our freedom in respect of our inclinations, which aim at our own welfare. Just as law restricts our freedom in our relations with other men, so do our duties to ourselves restrict our freedom in dealing with ourselves. All such duties are grounded in a certain love of honour consisting in self-esteem; man must not appear unworthy in his own eyes; his actions must be in keeping with humanity itself if he is to appear in his own eyes worthy of inner respect. . . .

II Proper Self-respect

Humility, on the one hand, and true, noble pride on the other, are elements of proper self-respect; shamelessness is its opposite. We have reason to have but a low opinion of ourselves as individuals, but as representatives of mankind we ought to hold ourselves in high esteem. In the light of the law of morality, which is holy and perfect, our defects stand out with glaring distinctness and on comparing ourselves with this standard of perfection we have sufficient cause to feel humble. But if we compare ourselves with others, there is no reason to have a low opinion of ourselves; we have a right to consider ourselves as valuable as another. This self-respect in comparison with others constitutes noble pride. A low opinion of oneself in relation to others is no humility; it is a sign of a little spirit and of a servile character. To flatter oneself that this is virtue is to mistake an imitation for the genuine article; it is monk's virtue and not at all natural; this form of humility is in fact a form of pride. There is nothing unjust or unreasonable in self-esteem; we do no harm to another if we consider ourselves equal to him in our estimation. But if we are to pass judgment upon ourselves we must draw a comparison between ourselves and the purity of the moral law, and we then have cause to feel humble. We should not compare ourselves with other righteous men who, like ourselves, model themselves on the moral law. The Gospel does not teach humility, but it makes us humble.

Our self-esteem may arise from self-love and then it is favour and partiality towards ourselves. This pragmatic self-respect in accordance with rules of prudence is reasonable and possible inasmuch as it keeps us in confidence. No one can demand of me that I should humiliate myself and value myself less than others; but we all have the right to demand of a man that he should not think himself superior. Moral self-esteem, however, which is grounded in the worth of humanity, should not be derived from comparison with others, but from comparison with the moral law. Men are greatly inclined to take others as the measure of their own moral worth, and if they find that there are some whom they surpass it gives them a feeling of moral pride; but it is much more than pride if a man believes himself perfect as measured by the standard of the moral law. I can consider myself better than some others; but it is not very much only to be better than the worst, and there is really not much moral pride in that. Moral humility, regarded as the curbing of our self-conceit in face of the moral law, can thus never rest upon a comparison of ourselves with others, but with the moral law. Humility is therefore the limitation of the high opinion we have of our moral worth by comparison of our actions with the moral law. The comparison of our actions with the moral law makes us humble. Man has reason to have but a low opinion of himself because his actions not only contravene the moral law but are also lacking in purity. His frailty causes him to transgress the law, and his weakness makes his actions fall short of its purity. If an individual takes a lenient view of the moral law, he may well have a high opinion of himself and be conceited, because he judges himself by a false standard. The conceptions which the ancients had of humility and all moral virtues were impure and not in keeping with the moral law. The Gospel first presented morality in its purity, and there is nothing in history to compare with it. But if this humility is wrongly construed, harm may result; for it does not bring courage, but the reverse. Conscious of his shortcomings, a man may feel that his actions can never attain to the level of the moral law and he may give up trying, and simply do nothing. Self-conceit and dejection are the two rocks on which man is wrecked if he deviates, in the one direction or the other, from the moral law. On the one hand, man should not despair, but should believe himself strong enough to follow the moral law, even though he himself is not conformable to it. On the other hand, he ought to avoid self-conceit and an exaggerated notion of his powers; the purity of the moral law should prevent him from falling into this pitfall, for no one who has the law explained to him in its absolute purity can be so foolish as to imagine that it is within his powers fully to comply with it. The existence of this safeguard makes the danger of self-conceit less than that of inertia grounded in faith. It is only the lazy, those who have no wish to do anything themselves but to leave it all to God, who interpret their religion thus. The remedy against such dejection and inertia is to be found in our being able to hope that our weakness and infirmity will be supplemented by the help of God if we but do the utmost that the consciousness of our capacity tells us we are able to do. This is the one and indispensable condition on which we can be worthy of God's help, and have a right to hope for it. In order to convince man of his weakness, make him humble and induce him to pray to God for help, some writers have tried to deny to man any good disposition. This can do no good. It is certainly right and proper that man should recognize how weak he is, but not by the sacrifice of his good dispositions, for if he is to receive God's help he must at least be worthy of it. If we depreciate the value of human virtues we do harm, because if we deny good intentions to the man who lives aright, where is the difference between him and the evil-doer? Each of us feels that at some time or other we have done a good action from a good disposition and that we are capable of doing so again. Though our actions are all very imperfect, and though we can never hope that they will attain to the standard of the moral law, yet they may approach ever nearer and nearer to it.

STUDY QUESTIONS

1. Do you agree with Kant that you have moral duties to yourself? If so, in your opinion, are they?
2. Do you find Kant's arguments against suicide convincing? Do you agree that suicide is "the most abominable of the vices"?

3. Kant says, "The duties we owe to ourselves do not depend on the relation of the action to the ends of happiness." Is our duty, then, to make *others* happy? No one happy? What does Kant see our duty to be?
4. A United States Congressman who was found guilty of accepting "Abscam" bribes pleaded before the judge, "Alcoholism made me lose my judgment." What would Kant say about this man's self-respect? In which ways, according to Kant, has this man failed in his duties to himself?
5. What does Kant mean by "worth"? By self-worth? Why does our human worth demand reverence? What follows when we lack a sense of self-worth?

Ethical Pull

ROBERT NOZICK

Robert Nozick (b. 1938), a professor at Harvard University, has published widely in many different areas of philosophy. His best known works are *Anarchy, State and Utopia* (1974) and *Philosophical Explanation* (1981).

What gives a being "ethical pull"? What characteristics must a being possess in order to be treated in a morally respectful manner? Nozick calls these characteristics "the moral basis" and attempts to specify what they are. He identifies three: "being an I," "being valued for being an I," and "being a seeker of value."

Ethical pull is the term we have used for the moral claim on us exerted by others so that, in virtue of what they are like, we ought to behave toward them in certain ways and not in others—or it

ETHICAL PULL Reprinted by permission of the author and the publishers from *Philosophical Explanations* by Robert Nozick, Cambridge, Mass.: The Belknap Press of Harvard University Press, Copyright © 1981 by the President and Fellows of Harvard College.

would be wrong to behave in certain ways, and so forth. The theory of ethical pull specifies and explains the moral oughts and constraints upon our behavior to which the existence or presence of others give rise.

Moral behavior is not owed to each and every thing, not to rocks or copies of newspapers; there is something about people, some characteristic or property of theirs, in virtue of which they are owed moral behavior. It will be useful to have a term to refer to the characteristic (or characteristics) of people, whatever it is, that plays this role of exerting the moral claim. Let us call it the moral basis, or the basic moral characteristic. This is the characteristic possessed by someone to whom moral behavior is owed. We must distinguish this from the characteristic in virtue of which someone owes moral behavior, the characteristic that makes someone a subject of moral judgment, as a tiger is not. (To be sure, some theory could maintain that it is one characteristic that plays both of these roles.)

The first task of the theory of the ethical pull is to specify the moral basis, the characteristic(s) in virtue of which ethics is called forth. I do not claim there is only one characteristic that exerts moral pull, only one moral threshold, so that there are no moral conditions on our behavior toward something lacking the most demanding basic moral characteristic. Perhaps animals do not have this characteristic, yet have another in virtue of which they are owed some moral behavior of a less stringent sort; there then would be multiple thresholds. Or perhaps the basic moral characteristic does not set a threshold but establishes a gradient over different types of beings, which calls for a matching gradient of behavior; having a status between people and stones, animals would have some intermediate claim.

The second task of the theory of ethical pull is to specify the moral conditions or constraints on the behavior of others given rise to by (someone's having) the basic moral characteristic. And the third task is to explain how and why this characteristic gives rise to those moral constraints or to any moral constraints on others at all. Even granting that it is that characteristic which does give rise to moral constraints, why does it do that, how is it possible that it does that? Why isn't the universe an ethical blank, containing beings with the characteristic but containing no moral conditions on any actions toward them?

The Moral Basis

The first task of the theory of ethical pull is to specify the moral basis, the characteristic in virtue of which ethical behavior is owed. What should we expect this characteristic to be like? Might it be some characteristic like 'having an elbow' or 'having a vestigial appendix' or 'walking upright', with it being a brute and ultimate fact that anything with that characteristic or part is owed moral behavior? The moral basis cannot be any old trivial characteristic; it itself must be something important, it must be something valuable.[1] To give rise to something as important as ethical pull, it must be important in itself.

Also, the moral basis must be a characteristic that is relevant to certain behavior by others, so that either we can specify the ways in which that behavior by others is appropriate to (the bearer of) that characteristic, or at least we can "see" that the behavior is a fitting response to the characteristic. Despite any inability to say what the linkage is between is and ought or fact and value, or even to say how there can be any linkage, the basic moral characteristic must at least appear to be relevantly linked to the called-for moral behavior. However much we are puzzled by is—ought questions, we would be puzzled even more to be told that the moral basis is 'having a vestigial appendix' and in virtue of that we ought not manipulate or use the person or cause him pain. Thus, we seek a characteristic that (at least) seems valuable and seems relevantly related to the behavior of others.

---

[1]Furthermore, I assume it must be something intrinsically valuable, or contribute directly to intrinsic value as a component or organizing principle. Thus are excluded theories which hold that people themselves are at best instrumentally valuable for some further extra-human effect, but they are to be treated in certain ways because of the characteristics that enable them to play this instrumental role.

Another possible view, worthy of more discussion, would be that people have no valuable characteristic but do have a characteristic in virtue of which certain behavior toward them (causally) produces disvalue (in them). This characteristic itself might be held to be (at least instrumentally) disvaluable, given its potential effects, yet certain behavior toward a bearer of this characteristic might be called for in order to avoid producing the disvalue. On this view, the moral basis that gives rise to the moral ought would not be anything valuable. One instance of such a view would hold that sentience is the moral basis, but that neither it nor any experiences are valuable, yet some painful ones are disvaluable, and so we must avoid producing them.

In assuming that the moral basis will be a valuable characteristic, I assume that such views cannot be the whole truth about moral pull.

We can round up the usual suspects: being rational, being an agent, being sentient, being conscious. I find that when I think about the matter, including thinking hypothetically of coming upon beings on other planets, the crucial characteristic in others that I feel gives rise to stringent moral claims upon me is "being an I", that is, having the special mode of reflexive consciousness of self which only an I, only a self, has. Something's being a self, now we can say someone's being one, seems to be crucial to our having to treat it in certain morally respectful ways.

This characteristic of "being an I" is a valuable one, as befits the moral basis. Selves, in virtue of being reflexively self-conscious, have a high degree of organic unity. The moral basis is not some superficial trait that its possessors themselves do not value or think important. Also, we can understand the distortion of the egoist, who instead of finding preciousness and a moral basis in "being an I", a property shared by others, finds it in "being myself".

It appears that the requisite moral basis, whatever it is, must satisfy two conditions. First, it must be a general characteristic, had by all other people (in the absence of special grave defects); other-wise, it will not provide the basis in virtue of which all people are owed ethical behavior. However, if the basic moral characteristic is shared by everyone, then it does not seem to have anything special to do with you. Your value would consist in being a bearer of this characteristic (for instance, rationality, ability to revere the moral law); you would not be valued for being yourself.[2] There then is the sense that any other bearer of the characteristic can equally well replace you, so that you are not valued or respected for being the particular person you are.

Let the second condition on the basic moral characteristic, then, be that the person who is valued (or behaved to in a certain way) in virtue of possessing that characteristic is valued for being himself.

---

[2]See Gregory Vlastos' discussion of whether, according to Plato's theory, it is a particular person who is loved, or instead it is the Form that is the primary object of love, where this love "spills over" to the Form's instances so that a person is loved merely as an instantiation of the Form ("The Individual as an Object of Love in Plato", in his *Platonic Studies*, Princeton University Press, Princeton, 1973, pp. 3–34). For a discussion of Kant's theory as (ultimately) valuing a person merely as a bearer of (what Kant holds to be) the basic moral characteristic, see Andreas Teuber, "Ideas of Equality" (unpublished doctoral dissertation, Harvard University, 1978), pp. 118–130.

This is in tension with the first condition, that the characteristic be one shared by all people; a general characteristic shared by everyone does not focus on any particular bearer. One type of characteristic, however, can satisfy both (apparently incompatible) conditions: a reflexive indexical characteristic. The characteristic "being an I" is had by every person, and so satisfies the first condition. Yet since its formulation contains the indexical reflexive term "I", this characteristic, unlike other general characteristics, does not draw the attention away from the particular bearer. The characteristic speaks of the bearer as a self, as a subjective particularity. Although the characteristic of being an I, being a reflexive self-aware being, is shared by all I's, it is a property I have in virtue of being myself. Thus, being myself, a property no one else has, is the ground of my value, as it brings along with it the general characteristic of being an I which others have. Still, this general characteristic leads not away from the I to others but back to the self in its reflexive particularity. Isn't to be valued for being a self tantamount to being valued for being yourself, or else doesn't it come as close as possession of a valuable general characteristic can bring one? Doesn't "being an I" resolve the tension between the two conditions on the basic moral characteristic? Perhaps not: although you are valued for being a self, some self or other, you are not thereby valued for being the particular self you are. We might say: you are valued for your self but not for yourself.

We can add, therefore, that the characteristic is not simply 'being an I' but 'being a unique, individualized I'. It is unclear to what extent such individuality, such distinctiveness, is essential to the nature of being a self. The self, we have seen, refers to itself reflexively, from the inside, but does that mean it must have an inside of subjective experience that constitutes its own perspective, a special slant on the world?[3] (It appears simpler to reach the consequence that a reflexively self-referring self, especially one that is self-synthesizing, will have a special slant on itself.) Even if such a perspective is held to be crucial to the nature of a self (yet does God have a special slant on the world?), must that perspective be unique

---

[3]The having of a slant, there being a way it is for the being, is discussed as an important component of the moral basis in Bernard Williams, "The Idea of Equality", in P. Laslett and W. G. Runciman eds., *Philosophy, Politics and Society* (2nd series, Blackwell, Oxford, 1962), pp. 110–131.

and individual? Surely we can imagine science fiction duplications (in a qualitatively indistinguishable environment) of all the nonreflexive characteristics of a self including the type of perspective or slant; this would be similar to Nietzsche's imagining such duplications under his doctrine of eternal recurrence. Yet these beings, all identical in perspective, would be selves. Thus, individuality and uniqueness is not guaranteed by the very nature of being a self; some may think such a nonunique self is less valuable, being less scarce.

Even if such individuality does not follow from the very nature of a self, we can build it into the characteristic that is to be the moral basis and exert the most pull. When the basic moral characteristic is being a unique and individual self, are you not then valued for being yourself, for being your unique and individual self? Not quite. You are valued for being *a* unique and individual self, and the only way to be that is to be some particular unique self, but you are not valued for being that particular self—any old unique and individual self would do just as well. There is a difference between valuing something for being unique, and valuing it for the (particular) uniqueness it has. This last is ambiguous between valuing it for having some feature which it happens to have uniquely, and valuing its having that feature uniquely, where (equal?) weight is given to each component: the content of the feature and its unique possession.

Let us list the possibilities here. First, that in general when each person is valued for being herself, each is valued for being a unique self, but not for being that one. Second, we value the particular uniqueness of each person; merely as a summary of this, we may say we value their being unique, but it is each unique unfolding that we value primarily. A third possibility, however, seems to me the most promising. We value being a unique self, and come therefore also to value the particular unique self someone is. Valuing that there is a unique self spills over to valuing, for itself, that unique self there is. (The path of spillover follows the logical principle of existential instantiation.)

The process of loving one's children exemplifies this spillover. One begins by loving one's child as a bearer of the characteristic 'being your child'. Any child that one believed had that characteristic would become the object of one's love; if the doctors in the maternity hospital told you another infant was your child (as sometimes happens when accidental "switches" are made), you would love that one. Sufficient for initiation of your love is bearing the characteristic 'being your child'. Over time, however, the love attaches to the child in its own individuality, not simply as a bearer of the initiating characteristic that could have applied to someone else; you come to love that child, nontransferably. The delight parents take in the particular behavior and accomplishments of their young children marks the transition to loving them in their particularity, no longer merely for being their child but for being *that* child. We all know parents who choose to celebrate this transition with public ceremony, telling all who will listen of the most recent cute or intelligent behavior of their young children. (Contrast our attitudes toward parents of older children; their similar tales are not discoveries of particularity but boasts.) It may be disconcerting for a child to realize its parents would love another child as much, had that other child been born in their place. However, that other equally great love would not be the same love, not the same particular love there exists for this particular person; and although if another child had been born, there would then have been another particular love for that particular person, still now the parent would not trade the particular love (or child) that exists for the other one, viewing each as equally good. The actual situation is valued above another possible one, even while realizing that had that other possibility been realized, *it* would have been valued then over this actuality—merely another possibility from its perspective then.[4]

In parallel to this process of parental love, I imagine that valuing others is based upon their possession of the characteristic of being a (unique) self, but then spills over and attaches to the particular self they are, the particular way they instantiate the possibilities of being human. Within this structure, we can value all people (in virtue of a general characteristic), yet value them for being themselves. This characteristic "being a unique I" and its attendant spillover can satisfy both of the apparently incompatible conditions on the basic moral characteristic.

---

[4]Compare the treatment of valuing someone for themselves, and of parents' love of their children, in Gregory Vlastos, "Justice and Equality", in R. Brandt, ed., *Social Justice* (Prentice-Hall, Englewood Cliffs, 1962), pp. 31–72.

People we do not know, however, we will value (only) as bearers of the general property "being a (unique) self". Even for some we know (or know of), we may find ourselves unable to value their particularity, to value that particularity, and so then too will value only their possession of the common general property. That we value someone's particularity may make it appropriate for us to aid him rather than another, even though we realize that if we knew and thereby valued the particularity of that other, we would differentially favor her. Some moral views hope to lift us above all such differential ties, whether to family or friends or one's people, so that we will consider ourselves and all others simply as members of humanity. As such, the others have claims on our moral behavior; however, these claims need not be as rich as those whose particularity is more closely intertwined with ours. A father may aid his own over other children, knowing that had the others been his, he would have loved and aided them. Some view all such particularistic ties to individuals or groups as parochial, something moral advance will eliminate. Others view these as derivatively justifiable, provided that the general interest is best advanced by all parents giving primary weight to taking care of their own children, or that a valuable variety—one everyone should value—is produced by ethnic differentiation and ties. Such views will countenance particularism on one level by deriving it from "universalistic" principles that hold at some deeper level. This misconstrues the moral weight of particularistic ties, it seems to me; it is a worthwhile task, one I cannot undertake explicitly here, to investigate the nature of a more consistently particularistic theory—particularistic all the way down the line.

Seeking Value

The characteristic we have considered as the moral basis, "being an I", is not unconnected with other usual candidates for this role. The process by which the I refers to itself involves the production of a token (or thought) with a certain intention, hence the I is an agent, and so forth. Still, this characteristic alone is not a sufficient basis for moral pull. Or so it seems to me.

In addition, the being, the self, must be a seeker after value, someone who searches for value and guides her behavior by value considerations. Neither trait alone—value seeking or self—is sufficient. A computer-like automaton tracking value, matching its behavior to value considerations but lacking any subjectivity and lacking a self, would be too slight to ground (the fullest) moral pull, as would a subjective I that was permanently indifferent to value, neither following nor seeking it. What is wanted is a self seeking value. Perhaps these two traits, being an I and seeking value, are not independent or easily separated. If so, that would give the ethical pull a more unified moral basis; however, I am not in a position to make the strong claim that one characteristic (necessarily) involves the other.[5]

With the addition of value seeking, we add to the mode of unification of reflexive self-consciousness the unity introduced by teleological value seeking. A value-seeking self, therefore, has some significant degree of organic unity and hence of intrinsic value in virtue of that (double) characteristic. I should emphasize that the characteristic of being a value-seeking I is a capacity or potentiality—infants and unconscious people have it. This capacity or potentiality can be destroyed or blocked, it can be impossible to exercise or exhibit. I leave aside here all the delicate questions about when the capacity first is present (in fetuses?), when it is destroyed (how severe the brain damage?), how individuals who lack that capacity which is characteristic of their species are to be treated, why the (unexercised) capacity is so important, and so forth.[6]

---

[5]For the view that value seeking is part of our nature, see Abraham Maslow, *The Farther Reaches of Human Nature* (Viking, New York, 1971), pp. 324–325. One might attempt to show that value seeking is intrinsic to (the nature of) a self, as follows. The self synthesizes itself and delineates its boundaries in accordance with a method of classification that classifies so as to maximize the organic unity of the resulting products; hence the self structures itself in accordance with the notion of organic unity and thereby both presupposes that organic unity is valuable and seeks this value in its most fundamental activity: self-synthesis. (Why otherwise doesn't it simply leave itself unsynthesized?)

However, many of these steps are shaky. Must it be organic unity that is built into the procedure of classification, must a self-synthesis in accordance with that notion presuppose that it is valuable, and so on?

Yet even if value seeking is not intrinsic to the notion of a self, one might think it intrinsic to one's (intuitive) notion of a person and reserve the latter term for the conjunction of the two characteristics. I would not want to treat this as anything more than a terminological point here.

[6]A recent discussion of these issues is Philip Devine, *The Ethics of Homicide* (Cornell University Press, Ithaca, 1978), pp. 94, 99–105.

STUDY QUESTIONS

1. What question does Nozick seek to answer in this article? Do you find his answer clear?
2. According to Nozick, where does the ethical egoist go wrong?
3. What does Nozick mean when he says that, morally speaking, "you are valued for your self but not for yourself"?
4. What is the "moral basis"? How does Nozick understand "being an I" and why does the explanation not suffice for the moral basis?
5. Does Nozick's account of ethical pull favor a special approach to moral philosophy, such as utilitarianism or Kantianism? Explain.

On Self-respect

JOAN DIDION

Joan Didion (b. 1934) is a well-known novelist and essayist. Her published works include novels such as *Play It as It Lays* (1971) and *A Book of Common Prayer* (1977), and collections of essays titled *Slouching Towards Bethlehem* (1970) and *The White Album* (1979).

What is self-respect and how does one develop it? For Didion, self-respecting persons are persons of character who accept responsibility for their lives and actions. Self-respect requires discipline, the ability to forego immediate gratification, and the ability to take risks and stick to plans. Persons who have these characteristics respect themselves. Persons who lack them live with a certain self-contempt and a contempt for those who uncritically admire them.

Once, in a dry season, I wrote in large letters across two pages of a notebook that innocence ends when one is stripped of the delusion that one likes oneself. Although now, some years later, I marvel that a mind on the outs with itself should have nonetheless made painstaking record of its every tremor, I recall with embarrassing clarity the flavor of those particular ashes. It was a matter of misplaced self-respect.

I had not been elected to Phi Beta Kappa. This failure could scarcely have been more predictable or less ambiguous (I simply did not have the grades), but I was unnerved by it; I had somehow thought myself a kind of academic Raskolnikov, curiously exempt from the cause-effect relationships which hampered others. Although even the humorless nineteen-year-old that I was must have recognized that the situation lacked real tragic stature, the day that I did not make Phi Beta Kappa nonetheless marked the end of something, and innocence may well be the word for it. I lost the conviction that lights would always turn green for me, the pleasant certainty that those rather passive virtues which had won me approval as a child automatically guaranteed me not only Phi Beta Kappa keys but happiness, honor, and the love of a good man; lost a certain touching faith in the totem power of good manners, clean hair, and proven competence on the Stanford-Binet scale. To such doubtful amulets had my self-respect been pinned, and I faced myself that day with the nonplused apprehension of someone who has come across a vampire and has no crucifix at hand.

Although to be driven back upon oneself is an uneasy affair at best, rather like trying to cross a border with borrowed credentials, it seems to me now the one condition necessary to the beginnings of real self-respect. Most of our platitudes notwithstanding, self-deception remains the most difficult deception. The tricks that work on others count for nothing in that very well-lit back alley where one keeps assignations with oneself: no winning smiles will do here, no prettily drawn lists of good intentions. One shuffles flashily but in vain through one's marked cards—the kindness done for the wrong reason, the apparent triumph which involved no real effort, the seemingly heroic act into which one had been shamed. The dismal fact is that self-respect has nothing to do with the approval of others—who are, after all, deceived easily enough; has nothing to do with reputation, which, as Rhett Butler told Scarlett O'Hara, is something people with courage can do without.

To do without self-respect, on the other hand, is to be an unwilling audience of one to an interminable documentary that details one's failings, both real and imagined, with fresh footage spliced in for every screening. *There's the glass you broke in anger, there's the hurt on X's face; watch now, this next scene, the night Y came back from Houston, see how you muff this one.* To live without self-respect is to lie awake some night, beyond the reach of warm milk, phenobarbital, and the sleeping hand on the coverlet, counting up the sins of commission and omission, the trusts betrayed, the promises subtly broken, the gifts irrevocably wasted through sloth or cowardice or carelessness. However long we postpone it, we eventually lie down alone in that notoriously uncomfortable bed, the one we make ourselves. Whether or not we sleep in it depends, of course, on whether or not we respect ourselves.

To protest that some fairly improbable people, some people who *could not possibly respect themselves*, seem to sleep easily enough is to miss the point entirely, as surely as those people miss it who think that self-respect has necessarily to do with not having safety pins in one's underwear. There is a common superstition that "self-respect" is a kind of charm against snakes, something that keeps those who have it locked in some unblighted Eden, out of strange beds, ambivalent conversations, and trouble in general. It does not at all. It has nothing to do with the face of things, but concerns instead a separate peace, a private reconciliation. Although the careless, suicidal Julian English in *Appointment in Samarra* and the careless, incurably dishonest Jordan Baker in *The Great Gatsby* seem equally improbable candidates for self-respect, Jordan Baker had it, Julian English did not. With that genius for accommodation more often seen in women than in men, Jordan took her own measure, made her own peace, avoided threats to that peace: "I hate careless people," she told Nick Carraway. "It takes two to make an accident."

Like Jordan Baker, people with self-respect have the courage of their mistakes. They know the price of things. If they choose to commit adultery, they do not then go running, in an access of bad conscience, to receive absolution from the wronged parties; nor do they complain unduly of the unfairness, the undeserved embarrassment, of being named co-respondent. In brief, people with self-respect exhibit a certain toughness, a kind of moral nerve; they display what was once called *character*, a quality which, although

411

approved in the abstract, sometimes loses ground to other, more instantly negotiable virtues. The measure of its slipping prestige is that one tends to think of it only in connection with homely children and United States senators who have been defeated, preferably in the primary, for reelection. Nonetheless, character—the willingness to accept responsibility for one's own life—is the source from which self-respect springs.

Self-respect is something that our grandparents, whether or not they had it, knew all about. They had instilled in them, young, a certain discipline, the sense that one lives by doing things one does not particularly want to do, by putting fears and doubts to one side, by weighing immediate comforts against the possibility of larger, even intangible, comforts. It seemed to the nineteenth century admirable, but not remarkable, that Chinese Gordon put on a clean white suit and held Khartoum against the Mahdi; it did not seem unjust that the way to free land in California involved death and difficulty and dirt. In a diary kept during the winter of 1846, an emigrating twelve-year-old named Narcissa Cornwall noted coolly: "Father was busy reading and did not notice that the house was being filled with strange Indians until Mother spoke about it." Even lacking any clue as to what Mother said, one can scarcely fail to be impressed by the entire incident: the father reading, the Indians filing in, the mother choosing the words that would not alarm, the child duly recording the event and noting further that those particular Indians were not, "fortunately for us," hostile. Indians were simply part of the *donnée*.

In one guise or another, Indians always are. Again, it is a question of recognizing that anything worth having has its price. People who respect themselves are willing to accept the risk that the Indians will be hostile, that the venture will go bankrupt, that the liaison may not turn out to be one in which *every day is a holiday because you're married to me*. They are willing to invest something of themselves; they may not play at all, but when they do play, they know the odds.

That kind of self-respect is a discipline, a habit of mind that can never be faked but can be developed, trained, coaxed forth. It was once suggested to me that, as an antidote to crying, I put my head in a paper bag. As it happens, there is a sound physiological reason, something to do with oxygen, for doing exactly that, but the psychological effect alone is incalculable: it is difficult in the extreme to continue fancying oneself Cathy in *Wuthering Heights* with one's head in a Food Fair bag. There is a similar case for all the small disciplines, unimportant in themselves; imagine maintaining any kind of swoon, commiserative or carnal, in a cold shower.

But those small disciplines are valuable only insofar as they represent larger ones. To say that Waterloo was won on the playing fields of Eton is not to say that Napoleon might have been saved by a crash program in cricket; to give formal dinners in the rain forest would be pointless did not the candlelight flickering on the liana call forth deeper, stronger disciplines, values instilled long before. It is a kind of ritual, helping us to remember who and what we are. In order to remember it, one must have known it.

To have that sense of one's intrinsic worth which constitutes self-respect is potentially to have everything: the ability to discriminate, to love and to remain indifferent. To lack it is to be locked within oneself, paradoxically incapable of either love or indifference. If we do not respect ourselves, we are on the one hand forced to despise those who have so few resources as to consort with us, so little perception as to remain blind to our fatal weaknesses. On the other, we are peculiarly in thrall to everyone we see, curiously determined to live out—since our self-image is untenable—their false notions of us. We flatter ourselves by thinking this compulsion to please others an attractive trait: a gist for imaginative empathy, evidence of our willingness to give. Of *course* I will play Francesca to your Paolo, Helen Keller to anyone's Annie Sullivan: no expectation is too misplaced, no role too ludicrous. At the mercy of those we cannot but hold in contempt, we play roles doomed to failure before they are begun, each defeat generating fresh despair at the urgency of divining and meeting the next demand made upon us.

It is the phenomenon sometimes called "alienation from self." In its advanced stages, we no longer answer the telephone, because someone might want something; that we could say *no* without drowning in self-reproach is an idea alien to this game. Every encounter demands too much, tears the nerves, drains the will, and the specter of something as small as an unanswered letter arouses such disproportionate guilt that answering it becomes out of the question. To assign unanswered letters their proper weight, to free us from the expectations of others, to give us back to ourselves—

413

there lies the great, the singular power of self-respect. Without it, one eventually discovers the final turn of the screw: one runs away to find oneself, and finds no one at home.

STUDY QUESTIONS

1. Do you agree with Didion's claim that self-respect has nothing to do with the approval of others?
2. Didion defines character as willingness to accept responsibility for your life. Can persons of character be self-righteous? Hypocritical? Self-excusers? Why does Didion think that being a self-excuser is inconsistent with having self-respect? Can you imagine people, ruthless criminals, for example, who accept responsibility for their actions, but can nevertheless be said to have no character or self-respect?
3. Didion says self-respect is a "discipline," or "a habit of mind that can never be faked, but can be developed [and] trained, . . ." How might someone develop more self-respect?
4. What, according to Didion, is the cost of living without self-respect?
5. Do you think most people are more concerned about their good reputation or their self-respect? Which is harder to live without?

On the Obsolescence of the Concept of Honor

PETER BERGER

Peter Berger (b. 1929) is a professor of sociology at Boston University. He is the author of several books, including *Pyramids of Scarcity* (1975) and *The Heretical Imperative* (1976).

Berger points out that honor is an ideological leftover from earlier days when people understood their stations and duties clearly. Honorable people had a set of well-defined obligations, as patriots, as husband or wives, as public officials. Failure to meet those obligations dishonored the trust of their positions. Berger contrasts honor with dignity. Dignity pertains to individuals as such, regardless of social role. The dignity of individuals is specified by their personal rights; their honor is specified by their social duties, by what is expected of them. Berger traces the "obsolescence" of honor and the new emphasis on individual rights from ancient Greece to modern times. Honor was in ascendance when people defined themselves by institutional roles. Dignity came to the fore when they saw themselves as independent of social roles. Honor links individuals to tradition and society, while dignity is ahistorical; modern individuals no longer define themselves as social prototypes, but as independent and "authentic" selves.

Berger views the obsolescence of honor with mixed

ON THE OBSOLESCENCE OF THE CONCEPT OF HONOR From the *Archives européennes de sociologie* XI (1970), 339–347. Reprinted with permission of the *Archives européennes de sociologie*.

feelings. He points out that the new emphasis on dignity is a great advance on earlier attitudes toward the self that ignored individuals' rights. On the other hand, he sees great danger in the decline of this honor that links individuals to social institutions of great value to civilization. The ideal would be a respect for the individual's role "experienced not as self-estranging tyranny but as a freely chosen vehicle of self-realization."

Honor occupies about the same place in contemporary usage as chastity. An individual asserting it hardly invites admiration, and one who claims to have lost it is an object of amusement rather than sympathy. Both concepts have an unambiguously outdated status in the *Weltanschauung* [world view] of modernity. Especially intellectuals, by definition in the vanguard of modernity, are about as likely to admit to honor as to be found out as chaste. At best, honor and chastity are seen as ideological leftovers in the consciousness of obsolete classes, such as military officers or ethnic grandmothers.

The obsolescence of the concept of honor is revealed very sharply in the inability of most contemporaries to understand insult, which in essense is an assault on honor. In this, at least in America, there is a close parallel between modern consciousness and modern law. Motives of honor have no standing in American law, and legal codes that still admit them, as in some countries of southern Europe, are perceived as archaic. In modern consciousness, as in American law (shaped more than any other by that prime force of modernization which is capitalism), insult in itself is not actionable, is not recognized as a real injury. The insulted party must be able to prove material damage. There are cases, indeed, where psychic harm may be the basis for a legal claim, but that too is a far cry from a notion of offense against honor. The *Weltanschauung* of everyday life closely conforms in this to the legal definitions of reality. If an individual is insulted and, as a result, is harmed in his career or his capacity to earn an income, he may not only have recourse to the courts but may count on the sympathy of his friends. His friends, and in some cases the courts, will come to his support if, say, the insult so unsettles him that he loses his self-esteem or has a nervous breakdown. If, however, neither kind of injury pertains, he will almost certainly be advised by lawyers and friends alike to just forget the whole thing. In other words, the *reality* of the offense will be denied. If the individual persists in maintaining it, he will be negatively categorized, most probably in psychiatric terms (as "neurotic," "overly sensitive," or the like), or if applicable in terms that refer to cultural lag (as "hopelessly European," perhaps, or as the victim of a "provincial mentality").

The contemporary denial of the reality of honor and of offenses against honor is so much part of a taken-for-granted world that a deliberate effort is required to even see it as a problem. The effort is worthwhile, for it can result in some, perhaps unexpected, new insights into the structure of modern consciousness.

The problem of the obsolescence of the concept of honor can be brought into better focus by comparing it with a most timely concept—that of dignity. Taken by itself, the demise of honor might be interpreted as part of a process of moral coarsening, of a lessening of respect for persons, even of dehumanization. Indeed, this is exactly how it looked to a conservative mind at the beginning of the modern era—for example, to the fifteenth-century French poet Eustache Deschamps: "Age of decline nigh to the end,/Time of horror which does all things falsely,/Lying age, full of pride and of envy,/ *Time without honour and without true judgment.*"[1] Yet it seems quite clear in retrospect that this pessimistic estimate was, to say the least, very one-sided. The age that saw the decline of honor also saw the rise of new moralities and of a new humanism, and most specifically of a historically unprecedented concern for the dignity and the rights of the individual. The same modern men who fail to understand an issue of honor are immediately disposed to concede the demands for dignity and for equal rights by almost every new group that makes them—racial or religious minorities, exploited classes, the poor, the deviant, and so on. Nor would it be just to question the genuineness of this disposition. A little thought, then, should make clear that the problem is not clarified by ethical pessimism. It is necessary to ask more fundamentally: What is honor? What is dignity? What can be learned about modern consciousness by the obsolescence of the one and the unique sway of the other?

---

[1] Cited in J. Huizinga, *The Waning of the Middle Ages* (N.Y.: Doubleday-Anchor, 1954), p. 33 [my italics].

Honor is commonly understood as an aristocratic concept, or at least associated with a hierarchical order of society. It is certainly true that Western notions of honor have been strongly influenced by the medieval codes of chivalry and that these were rooted in the social structures of feudalism. It is also true that concepts of honor have survived into the modern era best in groups retaining a hierarchical view of society, such as the nobility, the military, and traditional professions like law and medicine. In such groups honor is a direct expression of status, a source of solidarity among social equals and a demarcation line against social inferiors. Honor, indeed, also dictates certain standards of behavior in dealing with inferiors, but the full code of honor only applies among those who share the same status in the hierarcy. In a hierarchically ordered society the etiquette of everyday life consists of ongoing transactions of honor, and different groups relate differently to this process according to the principle of "To each his due." It would be a mistake, however, to understand honor *only* in terms of hierarchy and its delineations. To take the most obvious example, the honor of women in many traditional societies, while usually differentiated along class lines, may pertain in principle to women of *all* classes.

J. K. Campbell, in his study of contemporary rural culture in Greece,[2] makes this very clear. While the obligations of honor (*timi*) differ as between different categories of individuals, notably between men and women, everyone within the community exists within the same all-embracing system of honor. Those who have high status in the community have particular obligations of honor, but even the lowly are differentiated in terms of honor and dishonor. Men should exhibit manliness and women shame, but the failure of either implies dishonor for the individual, the family and, in some cases, the entire community. For all, the qualities enjoined by honor provide the link, not only between self and community, but between self and the idealized norms of the community: "Honour considered as the possession by men and women of these qualities is the attempt to relate existence to certain archetypal patterns of behaviour."[3] Conversely, dishonor is a fall from grace in the most comprehensive sense—loss of face in the community,

---

[2] J. K. Campbell, *Honour, Family and Patronage* (Oxford, 1964).
[3] Ibid., pp. 271 sq.

but also loss of self and separation from the basic norms that govern human life.

It is valid to view such a culture as essentially premodern, just as it is plausible to predict its disintegration under the impact of modernization. Historically, there are several stages in the latter process. The decline of medieval codes of honor did not lead directly to the contemporary situation in which honor is an all but meaningless concept. There took place first the *embourgeoisement* of honor, which has been defined by Norbert Elias as the process of "civilization," both a broadening and a mellowing process.[4] The contents had changed, but there was still a conception of honor in the age of the triumphant bourgeoisie. Yet it was with the rise of the bourgeoisie, particularly in the consciousness of its critical intellectuals, that not only the honor of the *ancien régime* and its hierarchical prototypes was debunked, but that an understanding of man and society emerged that would eventually liquidate *any* conception of honor.

Thus Cervantes' *Quixote* is the tragi-comedy of a particular obsolescence, that of the knight-errant in an age in which chivalry has become an empty rhetoric. The greatness of the *Quixote*, however, transcends this particular time-bound debunking job. It unmasks not only the "madness" of chivalry but, by extension, the folly of *any* identification of self with "archetypal patterns of behaviour." Put differently, Don Quixote's "enchanters" (whose task, paradoxically, is precisely what Max Weber had in mind as "*dis*enchantment") cannot be stopped so easily once they have started their terrible task. As Don Quixote tells Sancho in one of his innumerable homilies: "Is it possible that in the time you have been with me you have not yet found out that all the adventures of a knight-errant appear to be illusion, follies, and dreams, and turn out to be the reverse? Not because things are really so, but because in our midst there is a host of enchanters, forever changing, disguising and transforming our affairs as they please, according to whether they wish to favor or destroy us. So, what you call a barber's basin is to me Mambrino's helmet, and to another person it will appear to be something else."[5] These "enchanters," alas, have

---

[4] Norbert Elias, *Der Prozess der Zivilisation* (Bern: Francke, 1969).
[5] Cervantes, *Don Quixote*, trans. Walter Starkie (N.Y.: New American Library, 1964), I:25, p. 243.

not stopped with chivalry. Every human adventure, in which the self and its actions have been identified and endowed with the honor of collective prototypes has, finally, been debunked as "illusion, follies, and dreams." Modern man is Don Quixote on his deathbed, denuded of the multicolored banners that previously enveloped the self and revealed to be *nothing but a man*: "I was mad, but I am now in my senses; I was once Don Quixote of La Mancha, but I am now, as I said before, Alonso Quixano the Good."[6] The same self, deprived or, if one prefers, freed from the mystifications of honor is hailed in Falstaff's "catechism": "Honour is a mere scutcheon."[7] It is modern consciousness that unmasks it as such, that "enchants" or "disenchants" it (depending on one's point of view) until it is shown as nothing but a painted artifact. Behind the "mere scutcheon" is the face of modern man—man bereft of the consolation of prototypes, *man alone*.

It is important to understand that it is precisely this solitary self that modern consciousness has perceived as the bearer of human dignity and of inalienable human rights. The modern discovery of dignity took place precisely amid the wreckage of debunked conceptions of honor. Now, it would be a mistake to ascribe to modern consciousness alone the discovery of a fundamental dignity underlying all possible social disguises. The same discovery can be found in the Hebrew Bible, as in the confrontation between Nathan and David ("Thou art the man"); in Sophocles, in the confrontation between Antigone and Creon; and, in a different form, in Mencius' parable of a criminal stopping a child from falling into a well. The understanding that there is a humanity behind or beneath the roles and the norms imposed by society, and that this humanity has profound dignity, is not a modern prerogative. What is peculiarly modern is the manner in which the reality of this intrinsic humanity is related to the realities of society.

Dignity, as against honor, always relates to the intrinsic humanity divested of all socially imposed roles or norms. It pertains to the self as such, to the individual regardless of his position in society. This becomes very clear in the classic formulations of human rights, from the Preamble to the Declaration of Independence to

---

[6] Ibid., II:74.

[7] W. Shakespeare, *Henry IV*, Part I, V:I.

the Universal Declaration of Human Rights of the United Nations. These rights always pertain to the individual "irrespective of race, color or creed"—or, indeed, of sex, age, physical condition or any conceivable social status. There is an implicit sociology and an implicit anthropology here. The implicit sociology views all biological and historical differentiations among men as either downright unreal or essentially irrelevant. The implicit anthropology locates the real self over and beyond all these differentiations.

It should now be possible to see these two concepts somewhat more clearly. Both honor and dignity are concepts that bridge self and society. While either pertains to the individual in a very intimate way, it is in relations with others that both honor and dignity are attained, exchanged, preserved or threatened. Both require a deliberate effort of the will for their maintenance—one must *strive* for them, often against the malevolent opposition of others—thus honor and dignity become goals of moral enterprise. Their loss, always a possibility, has far-reaching consequences for the self. Finally, both honor and dignity have an infectious quality that extends beyond the moral person of the individual possessing them. The infection involves his body ("a dignified gait"), his material ambience (from clothing to the furnishings of his house) and other individuals closely associated with him ("He brought honor on his whole family"). What, then, is the difference between these two concepts of the social self? Or, substituting a more current term to avoid the metaphysical associations of "self," how do these two conceptions of identity differ?

The concept of honor implies that identity is essentially, or at least importantly, linked to institutional roles. The modern concept of dignity, by contrast, implies that identity is essentially independent of institutional roles. To return to Falstaff's image, in a world of honor the individual *is* the social symbols emblazoned on his escutcheon. The true self of the knight is revealed as he rides out to do battle in the full regalia of his role; by comparison, the naked man in bed with a woman represents a lesser reality of the self. In a world of dignity, in the modern sense, the social symbolism governing the interaction of men is a disguise. The escutcheons *hide* the true self. It is precisely the naked man, and even more specifically the naked man expressing his sexuality, who represents himself more truthfully. Consequently, the understanding of self-discovery and self-

421

mystification is reversed as between these two worlds. In a world of honor, the individual discovers his true identity in his roles, and to turn away from the roles is to turn away from himself—in "false consciousness," one is tempted to add. In a world of dignity, the individual can only discover his true identity by emancipating himself from his socially imposed roles—the latter are only masks, entangling him in illusion, "alienation" and "bad faith." It follows that the two worlds have a different relation to history. It is through the performance of institutional roles that the individual participates in history, not only the history of the particular institution but that of his society as a whole. It is precisely for this reason that modern consciousness, in its conception of the self, tends toward a curious ahistoricity. In a world of honor, identity is firmly linked to the past through the reiterated performance of prototypical acts. In a world of dignity, history is the succession of mystifications from which the individual must free himself to attain "authenticity."

It is important not to lose sight here of continuities in the constitution of man—of "anthropological constants," if one prefers. Modern man is not a total innovation or a mutation of the species. Thus he shares with any version of archaic man known to us both his intrinsic sociality and the reciprocal process with society through which his various identities are formed, maintained and changed. All the same, within the parameters set by his fundamental constitution, man has considerable leeway in constructing, dismantling and reassembling the worlds in which he lives. Inasmuch as identity is always part of a comprehensive world, and a humanly *constructed* world at that, there are far-reaching differences in the ways in which identity is conceived and, consequently, experienced. Definitions of identity vary with overall definitions of reality. Each such definition, however, has reality-generating power: Men not only define themselves, but they actualize these definitions in real experience—*they live them.*

No monocausal theory is likely to do justice to the transformation that has taken place. Very probably most of the factors commonly cited have in fact played a part in the process—technology and industrialization, bureaucracy, urbanization and population growth, the vast increase in communication between every conceivable human group, social mobility, the pluralization of social worlds and the profound metamorphosis in the social contexts in which children are reared. Be this as it may, the resultant situation has been aptly characterized by Arnold Gehlen with the terms "deinstitutionalization" and "subjectivization." The former term refers to a global weakening in the holding power of institutions over the individual. The institutional fabric, whose basic function has always been to provide meaning and stability for the individual, has become incohesive, fragmented and thus progressively deprived of plausibility. The institutions then confront the individual as fluid and unreliable, in the extreme case as unreal. Inevitably, the individual is thrown back upon himself, on his own subjectivity, from which he must dredge up the meaning and the stability that he requires to exist. Precisely because of man's intrinsic sociality, this is a very unsatisfactory condition. Stable identities (and this also means identities that will be subjectively plausible) can only emerge in reciprocity with stable social contexts (and this means contexts that are structured by stable institutions). Therefore, there is a deep uncertainty about contemporary identity. Put differently, there is a built-in identity crisis in the contemporary situation.

It is in this connection that one begins to understand the implicit sociology and the implicit anthropology mentioned above. Both are rooted in actual experience of the modern world. The literary, philosophical and even social-scientific formulations are ex post facto attempts to come to terms with this experience. Gehlen has shown this convincingly for the rise of the modern novel as the literary form most fully reflecting the new subjectivism. But the conceptualizations of man and society of, for instance, Marxism and existentialism are equally rooted in this experience. So is the perspective of modern social science, especially of sociology. Marx's "alienation" and "false consciousness," Heidegger's "authenticity" and Sartre's "bad faith," and such current sociological notions as David Reisman's "other-direction" or Erving Goffman's "impression management" could only arise and claim credibility in a situation in which the identity-defining power of institutions has been greatly weakened.

The obsolescence of the concept of honor may now be seen in a much more comprehensive perspective. The social location of honor lies in a world of relatively intact, stable institutions, a world in which individuals can with subjective certainty attach their iden-

423

tities to the institutional roles that society assigns to them. The disintegration of this world as a result of the forces of modernity has not only made honor an increasingly meaningless notion, but has served as the occasion for a redefinition of identity and its intrinsic dignity apart from and often *against* the institutional roles through which the individual expresses himself in society. The reciprocity between individual and society, between subjective identity and objective identification through roles, now comes to be experienced as a sort of struggle. Institutions cease to be the "home" of the self; instead they become oppressive realities that distort and estrange the self. Roles no longer actualize the self, but serve as a "veil of *maya*" hiding the self not only from others but from the individual's own consciousness. Only in the interstitial areas left vacant, as it were by the institutions (such as the so-called private sphere of social life) can the individual hope to discover or define himself. Identity ceases to be an objectively and subjectively given fact, and instead becomes the goal of an often devious and difficult quest. Modern man, almost inevitably it seems, is ever in search of himself. If this is understood, it will also be clear why both the sense of "alienation" and the concomitant identity crisis are most vehement among the young today. Indeed, "youth" itself, which is a matter of social definition rather than biological fact, will be seen as an interstitial area vacated or "left over" by the large institutional structures of modern society. For this reason it is, simultaneously, the locale of the most acute experiences of self-estrangement and of the most intensive quest for reliable identities.

A lot will depend, naturally, on one's basic assumptions about man whether one will bemoan or welcome these transformations. What to one will appear as a profound loss will be seen by another as the prelude to liberation. Among intellectuals today, of course, it is the latter viewpoint that prevails and that forms the implicit anthropological foundation for the generally "left" mood of the time. The threat of chaos, both social and psychic, which ever lurks behind the disintegration of institutions, will then be seen as a necessary stage that must precede the great "leap into freedom" that is to come. It is also possible, in a conservative perspective, to view the same process as precisely the root pathology of the modern era, as a disastrous loss of the very structures that enable men to be free and to be themselves. Such pessimism is expressed forcefully, if somewhat petulantly, in Gehlen's latest book, a conservative manifesto in which modernity appears as an all-engulfing pestilence.[8]

We could contend here that both perspectives—the liberation myth of the "left" and the nostalgia of the "right" for an intact world—fail to do justice to the anthropological and indeed the ethical dimensions of the problem. It seems clear to us that the unrestrained enthusiasm for total liberation of the self from the "repression" of institutions fails to take account of certain fundamental requirements of man, notably those of *order*—that institutional order of society without which both collectivities and individuals must descend into dehumanizing chaos. In other words, the demise of honor has been a very costly price to pay for whatever liberations modern man may have achieved. On the other hand, the unqualified denunciation of the contemporary constellation of institutions and identities fails to perceive the vast moral achievements made possible by just this constellation—the discovery of the autonomous individual, with a dignity deriving from his very being, over and above all and any social identifications. Anyone denouncing the modern world *tout court* should pause and question whether he wishes to include in that denunciation the specifically modern discoveries of human dignity and human rights. The conviction that even the weakest members of society have an inherent right to protection and dignity; the proscription of slavery in all its forms, of racial and ethnic oppression; the staggering discovery of the dignity and rights of the child; the new sensitivity to cruelty, from the abhorrence of torture to the codification of the crime of genocide—a sensitivity that has become politically significant in the outrage against the cruelties of the war in Vietnam; the new recognition of individual responsibility for all actions, even those assigned to the individual with specific institutional roles, a recognition that attained the force of law at Nuremberg—all these, and others, are moral achievements that would be unthinkable without the peculiar constellations of the modern world. To reject them is unthinkable ethically. By the same token, it is not possible to simply trace them to a false anthropology.

The task before us, rather, is to understand the empirical processes that have made modern man lose sight of honor at the expense

---

[8] Arnold Gehlen, *Moral and Hypermoral* (Frankfurt: Athenäum, 1969).

of dignity—and then to think through both the anthropological and the ethical implications of this. Obviously these remarks can do no more than point up some dimensions of the problem. It may be allowed, though, to speculate that a rediscovery of honor in the future development of modern society is both empirically plausible and morally desirable. Needless to say, this will hardly take the form of a regressive restoration of traditional codes. But the contemporary mood of anti-institutionalism is unlikely to last, as Anton Zijderveld implies.[9] Man's fundamental constitution is such that, just about inevitably, he will once more construct institutions to provide an ordered reality for himself. A return to institutions will ipso facto be a return to honor. It will then be possible again for individuals to identify themselves with the escutcheons of their institutional roles, experienced now not as self-estranging tyrannies but as freely chosen vehicles of self-realization. The ethical question, of course, is what these institutions will be like. Specifically, the ethical test of any future institutions, and of the codes of honor they will entail, will be whether they succeed in embodying and in stabilizing the discoveries of human dignity that are the principal achievements of modern man.

STUDY QUESTIONS

1. Do you agree with Berger that the concept of honor is out of date? Can you imagine yourself or one of your friends suffering over a loss of honor?
2. How does Berger distinguish honor from dignity? Why does he think they are both so important?
3. Do you think that most people in contemporary Western society do not have institutional roles?
4. Do you agree with people who see the disintegration of strong social institutions as liberating and progressive? Or do you side with those who see it as a disastrous loss of structures that are vital if people are to develop into mature, responsible citizens, parents, and friends? Defend your standpoint.

---

[9] Anton Zijderveld, *Abstract Society* (N.Y.: Doubleday, 1970).

The New Narcissism

CHRISTOPHER LASCH

Christopher Lasch (b. 1932) is a professor of history at the University of Rochester. He is the author of a number of books, including *Haven in a Heartless World* (1977) and *The Culture of Narcissism* (1979).

Christopher Lasch describes a new personal ideal that emphasizes living for the moment, and being for oneself. The "new narcissists" feel free to abandon their social roles (for example, as parent or citizen) for the higher purpose of self-fulfillment by self-gratification. The goal of these new individuals is "personal well-being, health, and psychic security." Seeking this goal is incompatible with a direct concern for politics. Nevertheless, Lasch observes that narcissists are sometimes radical politically when the risks give them a sense of well-being and importance. Lasch distinguishes between the nineteenth-century ideal of the rugged individualist and the new individualist ideal. The former were outwardly oriented; they saw the world as a "wilderness to be shaped by [their] own design." Contemporary individualists are self-absorbed; for them, "the world is a mirror." Lasch warns that the new narcissists cannot succeed since the psychic equilibrium of any individual requires "submission to the rules of

THE NEW NARCISSISM Reprinted from *The Culture of Narcissism: American Life in an Age of Diminishing Expectations*, by Christopher Lasch, by permission of W. W. Norton & Company, Inc. Copyright © 1979 by W. W. Norton & Company, Inc.

social intercourse." By denying themselves a social role, narcissists leave themselves open to a sense of inner emptiness. By their self-absorption they live a life of self-gratification in which love plays no part.

The Waning of the Sense of Historical Time

As the twentieth century approaches its end, the conviction grows that many other things are ending too. Storm warnings, portents, hints of catastrophe haunt our times. The "sense of an ending," which has given shape to so much of twentieth-century literature, now pervades the popular imagination as well. The Nazi holocaust, the threat of nuclear annihilation, the depletion of natural resources, well-founded predictions of ecological disaster have fulfilled poetic prophecy, giving concrete historical substance to the nightmare, or death wish, that avant-garde artists were the first to express. The question of whether the world will end in fire or in ice, with a bang or a whimper, no longer interests artists alone. Impending disaster has become an everyday concern, so commonplace and familiar that nobody any longer gives much thought to how disaster might be averted. People busy themselves instead with survival strategies, measures designed to prolong their own lives, or programs guaranteed to ensure good health and peace of mind.

Those who dig bomb shelters hope to survive by surrounding themselves with the latest products of modern technology. Communards in the country adhere to an opposite plan: to free themselves from dependence on technology and thus to outlive its destruction or collapse. A visitor to a commune in North Carolina writes: "Everyone seems to share this sense of imminent doomsday." Stewart Brand, editor of the *Whole Earth Catalogue*, reports that "sales of the *Survival Book* are booming; it's one of our fastest moving items." Both strategies reflect the growing despair of changing society, even of understanding it, which also underlies the cult of expanded consciousness, health, and personal "growth" so prevalent today.

After the political turmoil of the sixties, Americans have retreated to purely personal preoccupations. Having no hope of improving their lives in any of the ways that matter, people have convinced themselves that what matters is psychic self-improvement: getting in touch with their feelings, eating health food, taking lessons in ballet or belly-dancing, immersing themselves in the wisdom of the East, jogging, learning how to "relate," overcoming the "fear of pleasure." Harmless in themselves, these pursuits, elevated to a program and wrapped in the rhetoric of authenticity and awareness, signify a retreat from politics and a repudiation of the recent past. Indeed Americans seem to wish to forget not only the sixties, the riots, the new left, the disruptions on college campuses, Vietnam, Watergate, and the Nixon presidency, but their entire collective past, even in the antiseptic form in which it was celebrated during the Bicentennial. Woody Allen's movie *Sleeper*, issued in 1973, accurately caught the mood of the seventies. Appropriately cast in the form of a parody of futuristic science fiction, the film finds a great many ways to convey the message that "political solutions don't work," as Allen flatly announces at one point. When asked what he believes in, Allen, having ruled out politics, religion, and science, declares: "I believe in sex and death—two experiences that come once in a lifetime."

To live for the moment is the prevailing passion—to live for yourself, not for your predecessors or posterity. We are fast losing the sense of historical continuity, the sense of belonging to a succession of generations originating in the past and stretching into the future. It is the waning of the sense of historical time—in particular, the erosion of any strong concern for posterity—that distinguishes the spiritual crisis of the seventies from earlier outbreaks of millenarian religion, to which it bears a superficial resemblance. Many commentators have seized on this resemblance as a means of understanding the contemporary "cultural revolution," ignoring the features that distinguish it from the religions of the past. A few years ago, Leslie Fiedler proclaimed a "New Age of Faith." More recently, Tom Wolfe has interpreted the new narcissism as a "third great awakening," an outbreak of orgiastic, ecstatic religiosity. Jim Hougan, in a book that seems to present itself simultaneously as a critique and a celebration of contemporary decadence, compares the current mood to the millennialism of the waning Middle Ages. "The anxieties of the Middle Ages are not much different from those of the present," he writes. Then as now, social upheaval gave rise to "millenarian sects."

Both Hougan and Wolfe inadvertently provide evidence, however, that undermines a religious interpretation of the "consciousness movement." Hougan notes that survival has become the "catchword of the seventies" and "collective narcissism" the dominant disposition. Since "the society" has no future, it makes sense to live only for the moment, to fix our eyes on our own "private performance," to become connoisseurs of our own decadence, to cultivate a "transcendental self-attention." These are not the attitudes historically associated with millenarian outbreaks. Sixteenth-century Anabaptists awaited the apocalypse not with transcendental self-attention but with ill-concealed impatience for the golden age it was expected to inaugurate. Nor were they indifferent to the past. Ancient popular traditions of the "sleeping king"—the leader who will return to his people and restore a lost golden age—informed the millenarian movements of this period. The Revolutionary of the Upper Rhine, anonymous author of the *Book of a Hundred Chapters*, declared, "The Germans once held the whole world in their hands and they will do so again, and with more power than ever." He predicted that the resurrected Frederick II, "Emporer of the Last Days," would reinstate the primitive German religion, move the capital of Christendom from Rome to Trier, abolish private property, and level distinctions between rich and poor.

Such traditions, often associated with national resistance to foreign conquest, have flourished at many times and in many forms, including the Christian vision of the Last Judgment. Their egalitarian and pseudohistorical content suggests that even the most radically otherworldly religions of the past expressed a hope of social justice and a sense of continuity with earlier generations. The absence of these values characterizes the survivalist mentality of the seventies. The "world view emerging among us," writes Peter Marin, centers "solely on the self" and has "individual survival as its sole good." In an attempt to identify the peculiar features of contemporary religiosity, Tom Wolfe himself notes that "most people, historically, have *not* lived their lives as if thinking, 'I have only one life to live.' Instead they have lived as if they are living their ancestors' lives and their offspring's lives. . . ." These observations go very close to the heart of the matter, but they call into question his characterization of the new narcissism as a third great awakening.

The Therapeutic Sensibility

The contemporary climate is therapeutic, not religious. People today hunger not for personal salvation, let alone for the restoration of an earlier golden age, but for the feeling, the momentary illusion, of personal well-being, health, and psychic security. Even the radicalism of the sixties served, for many of those who embraced it for personal rather than political reasons, not as a substitute religion but as a form of therapy. Radical politics filled empty lives, provided a sense of meaning and purpose. In her memoir of the Weathermen, Susan Stern described their attraction in language that owes more to psychiatry and medicine than to religion. When she tried to evoke her state of mind during the 1968 demonstrations at the Democratic National Convention in Chicago, she wrote instead about the state of her health. "I felt good. I could feel my body supple and strong and slim, and ready to run miles, and my legs moving sure and swift under me." A few pages later, she says: "I felt real." Repeatedly she explains that association with important people made her feel important. "I felt I was part of a vast network of intense, exciting and brilliant people." When the leaders she idealized disappointed her, as they always did, she looked for new heroes to take their place, hoping to warm herself in their "brilliance" and to overcome her feeling of insignificance. In their presence, she occasionally felt "strong and solid"—only to find herself repelled, when disenchantment set in again, by the "arrogance" of those whom she had previously admired, by "their contempt for everyone around them."

Many of the details in Stern's account of the Weathermen would be familiar to students of the revolutionary mentality in earlier epochs: the fervor of her revolutionary commitment, the group's endless disputes about fine points of political dogma, the relentless "self-criticism" to which members of the sect were constantly exhorted, the attempt to remodel every facet of one's life in conformity with the revolutionary faith. But every revolutionary movement partakes of the culture of its time, and this one contained elements that immediately identified it as a product of American society in an age of diminishing expectations. The atmosphere in which the Weathermen lived—an atmosphere of violence, danger, drugs, sexual promiscuity, moral and psychic chaos—derived not so much from an older revolutionary tradition as from the turmoil and narcissistic anguish of contemporary America. Her preoccupation with the state of her psychic health, together with her dependence on others for a sense of selfhood, distinguish Susan Stern from the kind of religious seeker who turns to politics to find a secularized salvation. She needed to establish an identity, not to submerge her identity in a larger cause. The narcissist differs also, in the tenuous quality of his selfhood, from an earlier type of American individualist, the "American Adam" analyzed by R. W. B. Lewis, Quentin Anderson, Michael Rogin, and by nineteenth-century observers like Tocqueville. The contemporary narcissist bears a superficial resemblance, in his self-absorption and delusions of grandeur, to the "imperial self" so often celebrated in nineteenth-century American literature. The American Adam, like his descendants today, sought to free himself from the past and to establish what Emerson called "an original relation to the universe." Nineteenth-century writers and orators re-stated again and again, in a great variety of forms, Jefferson's doctrine that the earth belongs to the living. The break with Europe, the abolition of primogeniture, and the looseness of family ties gave substance to their belief (even if it was finally an illusion) that Americans, alone among the people of the world, could escape the entangling influence of the past. They imagined, according to Tocqueville, that "their whole destiny is in their own hands." Social conditions in the United States, Tocqueville wrote, severed the tie that formerly united one generation to another. "The woof of time is every instant broken and the track of generations effaced. Those who went before are soon forgotten; of those who will come after, no one has any idea: the interest of man is confined to those in close propinquity to himself."

Some critics have described the narcissism of the 1970s in similar language. The new therapies spawned by the human potential movement, according to Peter Marin, teach that "the individual will is all powerful and totally determines one's fate"; thus they intensify the "isolation of the self." This line of argument belongs to a well-established American tradition of social thought. Marin's plea for recognition of "the immense middle ground of human community" recalls Van Wyck Brooks, who criticized the New England transcendentalists for ignoring "the genial middle ground of human tradition." Brooks himself, when he formulated his own indictment of American culture, drew on such earlier critics as Santayana, Henry James, Orestes Brownson, and Tocqueville. The critical tradition they established still has much to tell us about the evils of untrammeled individualism, but it needs to be restated to take account of the differences between nineteenth-century Adamism and the narcissism of our own time. The critique of "privatism," though it helps to keep alive the need for community, has become more and more misleading as the possibility of genuine privacy recedes. The contemporary American may have failed, like his predecessors, to establish any sort of common life, but the integrating tendencies of modern industrial society have at the same time undermined his "isolation." Having surrendered most of his technical skills to the corporation, he can no longer provide for his material needs. As the family loses not only its productive functions but many of its reproductive functions as well, men and women no longer manage even to raise their children without the help of certified experts. The atrophy of older traditions of self-help has eroded everyday competence, in one area after another, and has made the individual dependent on the state, the corporation, and other bureaucracies.

Narcissism represents the psychological dimension of this dependence. Notwithstanding his occasional illusions of omnipotence, the narcissist depends on others to validate his self-esteem. He cannot live without an admiring audience. His apparent freedom from family ties and institutional constraints does not free him to stand alone or to glory in his individuality. On the contrary, it contributes to his insecurity, which he can overcome only by seeing his "grandiose self" reflected in the attentions of others, or by attaching himself to those who radiate celebrity, power, and charisma. For the narcissist, the world is a mirror, whereas the rugged individualist saw it as an empty wilderness to be shaped to his own design.

In the nineteenth-century American imagination, the vast continent stretching westward symbolized both the promise and the menace of an escape from the past. The West represented an opportunity to build a new society unencumbered by feudal inhibitions, but it also tempted men to throw off civilization and to revert to savagery. Through compulsive industry and relentless sexual repression, nineteenth-century Americans achieved a fragile triumph over the id. The violence they turned against the Indians and against nature originated not in unrestrained impulse but in the white Anglo-Saxon superego, which feared the wildness of the West because it objectified the wildness within each individual. While celebrating the romance of the frontier in their popular literature, in practice Americans imposed on the wilderness a new order designed to keep impulse in check while giving free rein to acquisitiveness. Capital accumulation in its own right sublimated appetite and subordinated the pursuit of self-interest to the service of future generations. In the heat of the struggle to win the West, the American pioneer gave full vent to his rapacity and murderous cruelty, but he always envisioned the result—not without misgivings, expressed in a nostalgic cult of lost innocence—as a peaceful, respectable, churchgoing community safe for his women and children. He imagined that his offspring, raised under the morally refining influence of feminine "culture," would grow up to be sober, law-abiding, domesticated American citizens, and the thought of the advantages they would inherit justified his toil and excused, he thought, his frequent lapses into brutality, sadism, and rape.

Today Americans are overcome not by the sense of endless possibility but by the banality of the social order they have erected against it. Having internalized the social restraints by means of which they formerly sought to keep possibility within civilized limits, they feel themselves overwhelmed by an annihilating boredom, like animals whose instincts have withered in captivity. A reversion to savagery threatens them so little that they long precisely for a more vigorous instinctual existence. People nowadays complain of an inability to feel. They cultivate more vivid experiences, seek to beat sluggish flesh to life, attempt to revive jaded appetites. They condemn the superego and exalt the lost life of the senses. Twentieth-century peoples have erected so many psychological barriers against strong emotion, and have invested those defenses with so much of the energy derived from forbidden impulse, that they can no longer remember what it feels like to be inundated by desire. They tend, rather, to be consumed with rage, which derives from defenses against desire and gives rise in turn to new defenses against rage itself. Outwardly bland, submissive, and sociable, they seethe with an inner anger for which a dense, over-populated, bureaucratic society can devise few legitimate outlets.

The growth of bureaucracy creates an intricate network of personal relations, puts a premium on social skills, and makes the unbridled egotism of the American Adam untenable. Yet at the same time it erodes all forms of patriarchal authority and thus weakens the social superego, formerly represented by fathers, teachers, and preachers. The decline of institutionalized authority in an ostensibly permissive society does not, however, lead to a "decline of the superego" in individuals. It encourages instead the development of a harsh, punitive superego that derives most of its psychic energy, in the absence of authoritative social prohibitions, from the destructive, aggressive impulses within the id. Unconscious, irrational elements in the superego come to dominate its operation. As authority figures in modern society lose their "credibility," the superego in individuals increasingly derives from the child's primitive fantasies about his parents—fantasies charged with sadistic rage—rather than from internalized ego ideals formed by later experience with loved and respected models of social conduct.

The struggle to maintain psychic equilibrium in a society that demands submission to the rules of social intercourse but refuses to ground those rules in a code of moral conduct encourages a form of self-absorption that has little in common with the primary narcissism of the imperial self. Archaic elements increasingly dominate personality structure, and "the self shrinks back," in the words of Morris Dickstein, "toward a passive and primeval state in which the world remains uncreated, unformed." The egomaniacal, experience-devouring, imperial self regresses into a grandiose, narcissistic, infantile, empty self: a "dark wet hole," as Rudolph Wurlitzer writes in *Nog*, "where everything finds its way sooner or later. I remain near the entrance, handling goods as they are shoved in, listening and nodding. I have been slowly dissolving into this cavity."

Plagued by anxiety, depression, vague discontents, sense of inner emptiness, the "psychological man" of the twentieth century seeks neither individual self-aggrandizement nor spiritual transcendence but peace of mind, under conditions that increasingly militate

435

against it. Therapists, not priests or popular preachers of self-help or models of success like the captains of industry, become his principal allies in the struggle for composure; he turns to them in the hope of achieving the modern equivalent of salvation, "mental health." Therapy has established itself as the successor both to rugged individualism and to religion; but this does not mean that the "triumph of the therapeutic" has become a new religion in its own right. Therapy constitutes an antireligion, not always to be sure because it adheres to rational explanation or scientific methods of healing, as its practitioners would have us believe, but because modern society "has no future" and therefore gives no thought to anything beyond its immediate needs. Even when therapists speak of the need for "meaning" and "love," they define love and meaning simply as the fulfillment of the patient's emotional requirements. It hardly occurs to them—nor is there any reason why it should, given the nature of the therapeutic enterprise—to encourage the subject to subordinate his needs and interests to those of others, to someone or some cause or tradition outside himself. "Love" as self-sacrifice or self-abasement, "meaning" as submission to a higher loyalty—these sublimations strike the therapeutic sensibility as intolerably oppressive, offensive to common sense and injurious to personal health and well-being. To liberate humanity from such out-moded ideas of love and duty has become the mission of the post-Freudian therapies and particularly of their converts and popularizers, for whom mental health means the overthrow of inhibitions and the immediate gratification of every impulse.

STUDY QUESTIONS

1. How does the narcissistic self differ from Kant's noble self, Quinton's person of character, or Didion's self-respecting individual?
2. In 1923, a study known as Middletown recorded the attitudes and practices of citizens in Muncie, Indiana. In 1977, researchers made another study in Muncie, called Middletown III, and were surprised to find that, despite more permissive views on

divorce, marijuana, and pornography, students at Muncie High
School answered a number of questions exactly the same way
their grandparents did in 1923. The majority in both groups,
for example, reported that they regarded the Bible as a "sufficient guide for modern life." Does this suggest that Lasch and
other pessimistic social critics may be exaggerating the changes
that have occurred in American society over the past two
decades?

3. What, for Lasch, is the importance of a sense of tradition and a
knowledge of history? What role does their presence or absence
play in moral development?

Character and Culture

ANTHONY QUINTON

Anthony Quinton (b. 1925) is President of Trinity College, Oxford. He is the author of a number of books
including *The Nature of Things* (1973), *Utilitarian Ethics*
(1973), and *Thoughts and Thinkers* (1982).

Quinton describes the decline of the concepts of character and will over the past hundred years. The person of
character "pursues purposes without being distracted by
passing impulses." Character and will are measured by
strength; thus, persons of very weak character are said
to have "no character." As Quinton understands it,
character is very much like self-control. He argues that
character is the essence of virtue in the classical sense,
since virtuous persons are those persons of reason who

CHARACTER AND CULTURE Reprinted by permission of The New Republic, © 1983, The New
Republic, Inc.

pursue their principled aims without letting passion interfere. Character in this sense was recently undermined, says Quinton, by several historical attacks. One came with the new sexual liberation espoused by some late Victorians and early twentieth-century rationalists (George Bernard Shaw and Bertrand Russell, for example). Another was initiated by estheticists such as Ruskin and Pater. The result is the current permissive morality in both its passive and ecstatic forms (the latter calling for active indulgence of instincts and drives). Both styles are hostile to character and will. The decline of religion is the third factor in the rise of the "characterless self." The religious impulse is transformed into "radical agitation in the interests of various species of underdog." Yet another concern is the current fear of total extinction that creates a climate of living for the moment, "for tomorrow we die." Quinton notes that the literature of modern moral philosophy has neglected character and will, paying far more attention to what people have a right to than to what sort of person they should be. Quinton calls on moral philosophy to redress the imbalance by attending once again to virtue.

In 1973, in "Art, Will and Necessity," Lionel Trilling wrote:

The concept of the will no longer figures significantly in the systematic psychology of our day. Those of us who are old enough to have been brought up in the shadow of the nineteenth century can recall how important the will was once thought to be in the conduct of the personal life, how confidently our parents and teachers pointed to the practical as well as the moral advantages of having a will of developed strength and discipline. Nothing could be more alien to the contemporary style of rearing and teaching the young. In the nineteenth century the will was a central and controlling topic in psychological and ethical theory—as how could it not be, given an economic system in which the unshakeable resolve of the industrial entrepreneur was of the essence, and given the temperaments of its great cultural figures?

I would like to reopen this question, to inquire what character and will actually are; and then, mindful of the fact that the word "ethics" means different things in the two main English-speaking countries—moral practice here, moral theory in England—I shall consider the declining presence of character and will in actual moral life and their distinctly marginal, even furtive, role in organized thinking about morality.

Character is different from personality. Personality is the style or form of a person's presentation of himself, typically in more or less short-lived encounters. It is, therefore, something that can be put on and taken off more or less at will, like clothing or makeup, the device which makes it possible to be all things to all men for those who want to be so. The derivation of the word from *persona*, a mask, is not evidence, but it is surely symptomatic. Character, by contrast, is something more deeply rooted, not innate or unalterable, but at least a fairly hard-won achievement; character is the reality of which personality is the appearance. I am treating personality here in the sense which it usually has in colloquial speech. Psychologists engaged in the study of what they call personality apply the word much more widely to cover the whole range of a person's dispositions, character and personality colloquially understood being among those dispositions but not exhausting them.

Character is essential or fundamental and not, like personality, a matter of the surface. It is modifiable by teaching and, in a way, by effort, unlike such innate and constitutional things as temperament, tastes, and intellectual power. It is comparatively unspecific, unlike abilities and skills. My main claim is that it is in essence resolution, determination, a matter of pursuing purposes without being distracted by passing impulses. It is something that is measured in terms of its strength. Its strength, indeed, is its existence, for the weaker it is the closer it comes to nonexistence. In that respect it is like the will, as we ordinarily conceive it. To have a will is to have a fairly strong one. To have a very weak will is the next best thing to having no will at all.

Is this a peculiar, idiosyncratic notion of character? It comprises, at any rate, three of the four virtues that Plato took to be most important: prudence, courage, moderation. Insofar as his fourth virtue, justice, is taken to be impartiality or fairness—the power, that is, to resist the promptings of immediate affection or favor—it is also a quality of character. The qualities of character I have mentioned are all dispositions to resist the immediate solicitations of impulse. Prudence is a settled resistance to whim, courage to fear, temperance to greed, justice or selfishness or particular affections. One could add industriousness as resistance to laziness, reliability as resistance to taking the easiest way. They are, generally speaking, ways of deferring gratification, of protecting the achievement of some valued object in the future from being underminded by the pull of lesser objects near at hand.

In the light of these considerations I propose that the idea of character is procedural rather than substantive. It is not a matter of having a particular set of desires alongside the instinctive, impulsive desires we share with other animals. It is the disposition or habit of controlling one's immediate, impulsive desires, so that we do not let them issue in action until we have considered the bearing of that action on the achievement of other, remoter objects of desire. Understood this way, character is much the same thing as self-control or strength of will. Like them it may be used for bad purposes. But one may suspect that only those of the most delightful innate temperament and preferences can achieve much morally without it, and then only if their circumstances are very safe and easy—that is, if all that is required of a moral agent is kindliness.

The cognitive distinguishing mark of the human species is its reasoning power, the ability that we have, conferred by language, to think about what is outside the immediate zone of perception and to work out what to do to produce or prevent future possibilities, contingent on our action, that we find attractive or repellent. Strength of character, by holding in check impulses excited by what is immediately present, allows the cognitive harvest of our reasoning powers to have an effect on what we do. To conceive character in this way is to give an acceptable sense to the idea that reason can and should control the passions.

In the English-speaking world we live and move amid the ruins of Victorian morality, in which character and will occupied an important place. Its central theme was one of strenuous self-discipline. It was itself a reaction against the consciously nonstrenuous morality of the eighteenth century which preceded it, and which was, in its turn, a reversal of the gloomy fanaticism of the seventeenth century and the epoch of the wars of religion. Character and strength of will were not repudiated by the secular good sense of the Augustans. Long-term aims were essential for the rational management of life and for morality, which was seen as an indispensable part of that code of rational living. But the aims now approved were secular and terrestrial, to be pursued by steady and prudent application, not with guilty fanatical enthusiasm. Hume's words for morally desirable qualities of character are representative: they are, he maintained, those that are "agreeable or useful," the properties, we might feel, more of an ideal weekend guest than of a collaborator in some risky and ambitious undertaking.

The morality of the eighteenth century was a relaxed and elegant version of the ideal of life of the Protestant commerical middle class, which had been progressively reconciled to life on this sinful earth by the worldly success that had accrued to its hard word and foresight. It was such sober and prudent people who established the first European settlement in North America, people of such moderate outlook as to be capable of using turkey for purposes of celebration. Acquiescing in their own good fortune, they found an emblem, after a century and a half, in Benjamin Franklin, a believer in only the most judicious and economical repression of instinct. By the middle of the nineteenth century an altogether more severe and ascetic ideal of life had replaced his genial accommodation of long-term goals and short-term needs.

The main ingredients of Victorianism are nearly all aspects of an ideal of self-reliance. At the top is industry, in which effort is accompanied by scrupulous workmanship. Honesty and fidelity to promises, so advantageous in the nineteeth-century business world of small enterprises, are seen as required in all people's activities. Waste is deplored, so that opportunity should not be let slip and so that provision is made against ill fortune. Sexuality is narrowly confined within the limits of monogamy. Benevolence is confined to the unfortunate; the merely pitiable do not as such deserve it, since they may be simply failures. Decorum must be maintained, serving as a kind of fireproof matting to keep down smoldering impulses to passion and extravagance.

This morality was overcome by two main lines of attack. The first of them is the rationalism of a group of late nineteenth- and early twentieth-century thinkers who sought to revive the Enlightenment, notably Samuel Butler, George Bernard Shaw, and Bertrand Russell. They attacked Victorian ideas about sex, property, the relations of men to women, and of adults to children; and, consequentially, the decorum that they saw as preserving the moral errors they attacked at one level and the religion they saw as sanctifying them at another. They hoped that a new, more rational morality would free people to perfect themselves. These late-Victorian and Edwardian moral reformers were themselves people of strong character, richly endowed with will. Shaw and Russell were very hard workers; Shaw was physically ascetic above and beyond the call of Victorianism, undefiled by drink, meat, or sexuality.

The other line of attack on Victorianism was, as far as England and no doubt the English-speaking world in general is concerned, an import from continental Europe, particularly France. What I have in mind is a sequence of hedonisms, by no means closely related or sympathetic to each other. To start with, there is the decadence of the 1890s, which, in its politer form, was aestheticism, the Paterian life of intense private sensation. After 1918 the sensations pursued become rougher and more primordial, but there is the same desire to shock and to ridicule older pieties. Vulgar Freudianism, the idea that all inhibition is bad, unhealthy, the cause of neurosis, helped to fill the sails of this pleasure-boat. Just as aestheticism had a kind of rural correlate in the sandal-wearing communities of admirers of Ruskin, given to free love or the drinking of fruit juice, so the rural arm of the hedonism of the 1920s was the instinctualism of D. H. Lawrence, who recruited Freud for his own special uses as did the heroines of Scott Fitzgerald and the early Evelyn Waugh.

In our time everyday morality, emancipated from Victorianism, takes two principal forms, corresponding in their rough and popular way to the two lines of moral reform I have described. The first is the negatively permissive morality whose ideal of life is one of passive consumption, of the more or less inert enjoyment of material and, one might say, recreational satisfactions. An important feature is the unloading onto someting called "society" of the duty of ensuring that the means of satisfaction are available at minimal cost and effort, and also of the responsibility for the failures and crimes of individuals. The quality most admired is amiability, a sort of uncritical endorsement of the wants and acts of others, free from all trace of censoriousness.

The second is the ecstatic morality that enjoins the unrestricted indulgence of instinct up to, and even beyond, the limits of ordinary self-preservation. It is less widespread than permissiveness, being largely confined to the young. On this view all frustration or inhibition is bad and unhealthy. Older ideas of the natural goodness of mankind are reanimated, often with the qualification that innocence can survive only in communities sequestered from the corrupting influences of the urban, industrial world. [In this system of thought the freaked-out adolescent takes over the role of Wordsworth's baby as "mighty prophet, seer blest."]

Both moral styles are, even at their best, hostile to character and will. For the permissive, strength of character is tiresome and embarrassing, a source of unnecessary trouble, spoiling things by its imposition of disagreeable restraints, souring the enjoyment of life with irrational guilt. For the ecstatic, strength of character is more like a disease, a neurotic deformation of personality fostered by individualism and to be helped by immersion in a collectivity in which selfhood is dismantled. From a point of view which neither would accept, both are juvenile: permissiveness in its idealization of the style of life of the pampered child, receiving presents and having fun; ecstaticism in its idealization of the wholly uncontrolled or runaway child, living wildly with a gang.

There is a great deal of social commentary and description in which the decline of character and will has been recorded, with and without implied attitudes of welcome or distaste. There is also a great deal of explanatory material to hand, ranging from the influence of theories at one extreme to that of new modes of social organization at the other. Of theories the most relevant are those that affirm the motivation of human conduct by forces that agents are not aware of, above all Freudian psychoanalysis. In particular, the Freudian account of the conscience or superego as the product of aggression turned by the individual against himself through fear of the withdrawal of parental love suggests that obedience to its commands is some sort of self-mutilation. Perhaps Freud did not intend his theory of the superego to have the comprehensively undermining effect that it has had. To argue that conscientiousness or a sense of guilt can be pathologically exaggerated need not show that conscientiousness in general is a sickness, let alone that character or strength of will is. Freud himself was the unashamed possessor of a will of great strength. There is an instructive aspect to his account of conscience in what he says about civilization. Although he sees it as having some the qualities of a collective neurosis, he takes the renunciation of instinct it requires to be preferable to the alternative of uncontrolled aggressiveness.

Another factor in the emergence of the characterless self is the decline of religion, or at least its transformation into radical agitation in the interests of various species of underdog. Other features of our times that might be cited in an explanatory way are the prospect of total extinction by nuclear war; the relapse to seventeenth-century levels of brutality in politics, intensified by improved technology; the general disappointment of enlightened liberal expectations as crime has increased at home and despotism abroad, particularly in those parts of the world that have secured political independence from the West. But more to the point, I believe, is the enlargement of the institutions in which people work or with which they are otherwise involved. In the first place, that instills feelings of powerlessness and dependence and so contracts the sphere of action of character and will. Secondly, conscientiousness diminishes when the actions to which it prompts us concern our relations to remote, impersonal organizations rather than concrete individuals.

Whatever the correct explanation may be, there can be no doubt of the fact that a large moral change has taken place in the Western, or at any rate English-speaking, world in the twentieth century. Many would see it as primarily a change in the content of morality, in our conceptions of what actions are right and wrong and of what states of affairs our actions should be morally applied to produce or prevent: specifically that hitherto dominant adult males are on the same footing with women and children, and that the supposed rights of those who earn and own should be subordinated to the claims of those who want and need.

What I am suggesting is that such an account of what has happened does not go far enough—that these changes of content or substance are less fundamental than changes of form which have accompanied them and have altered the whole conception of the moral agent. The liberal or progressive proposers of the changes in moral content that have taken place hoped they would provide conditions in which the dominated or unfortunate would be free to express their strength of character in achievement previously impossible for them. Instead we have witnessed the pervasive decline of character.

Character and will have been very much neglected in modern moral philosophy as well as in life. In fact, philosophers have neglected the subjects far longer—ever since philosophical reflection on morality began to be conducted in an independently rational manner, abstracted from, although not necessarily in conflict with, the morality of religion, in the seventeenth century. In the century that followed, Butler, Hume, and Kant all still concerned themselves with the topic of virtue, which is closely connected with character, since it is partly constitutive of it. But their prime interest was in rightness or duty, which is a property of actions, and only secondarily with the dispositions in agents from which right actions flow.

Since Hume and Kant the topic of virtue has been largely of marginal concern to moral philosophers. Their main concern has been with the question of whether the rightness of acts is intrinsic to them, as Kant and other rationalists like Samuel Clarke supposed, or is a function of the goodness of the consequences which actions of the kind in question can be reasonably expected to produce. Agreeing in general that virtue is the disposition to right action, they have divided into those who see as virtuous only the Kantian motive, which is more or less guaranteed to lead to right action, and those less rigorous thinkers who admit as virtuous any disposition of agents which tends to right action in most cases.

I used to be satisfied with the Humean view. What I now reject in it is the assimilation it makes of virtues in particular and, by implication, of qualities of character in general, to desires, conceived either as settled preferences or as qualities of temperament. Virtues and qualities of character are, I am now convinced, not just given

445

elements in an agent's appetitive constitution, but cultivated and disciplined modes of choice, by which passive appetites are held in check and so brought into contention with longer term purposes. The distinction can be conveniently illuminated by contrasting two ways in which the slightly archaic word "benevolence" can be taken. On the one hand it can be used to refer to a direct appetite or preference for the happiness of others or, again, to settled amiability of temperament. On the other, it can be taken as something more in the nature of a policy, or a principle of giving weight in one's decisions to others' happiness or well-being.

The emphasis was once very different in philosophical reflection on morality. In the classical world the notion of virtue was the primary or fundamental moral notion. The chief question for the moral philosopher, according to Plato and Aristotle, was not so much "what should I do?" asked at some specific juncture, but "how should I live?" or, more exactly, "what sort of person should I be?" Since the early modern period and the resecularization of philosophy the question has become "how am I to find out what I should do?" It is not that that question did not arise for the classical moral thinkers. But the Thrasymachus with whom Socrates argues in the early part of Plato's *Republic* is more a man who does not see that he has a motive for acting justly or rightly than one who is skeptical of conventional beliefs about what it is right or just to do.

Modern moral philosophy, like the rest of philosophy, is inveterately epistemological. And from that point of view, the picking out of certain human dispositions as virtues or morally good qualities of character is secondary. Both Hume and Kant determine the virtuousness of benevolence and fidelity in the one case and conscientiousness in the other by their relation to the independently established moral qualities of actions, that is by their rightness. Cognitively speaking, then, the moral quality of agents is derived from the moral quality of actions. For consequentialists the moral quality of actions is derived in its turn from the value of the states of affairs to which those actions can be reasonably expected to lead.

I have argued that the cognitive pre-occupations of moral philosophers in recent times have led them to ignore virtue, and character generally. It is as if they had seen their task as that of considering the activities of the moral agent in the thick of choice, of the moral critic hoping for some ratification of his critical authority, of the moral disputant involved in disagreement with someone who rejects his moral convictions. There is another perspective from which virtue and character bulk larger. This is the perspective of the moral educator. You have to have some confident idea about what is morally right before you can set about getting people to do it. But it is little use knowing what should be done unless you can get people to do it.

In general outline it seems clear enough that two factors operate in the moral development of the normally brought-up child. The first is simple imitation, the second that pursuit of parental approval which Freud painted in such funereal colors. The fact that virtue and character have such humble beginnings does not undermine or invalidate them. Since we start as minute savages it is inevitable that all our higher achievements should start in some more or less deplorable or undignified Yeatsian rag and bone shop. The fallacy involved in denying that is a curious survival of the pre-Darwinian superstition that the greater cannot come out of the lesser.

Not all development or improvement of character is externally induced. There is such an activity as self-examination; it was a habit for our pious forebears, but we are more likely to be pushed into it by some conspicuous occasion for disgust with ourselves. Morally mature human beings ordinarily acquire certain moral preferences, for courage over cowardice, for equability over petulance. There is no paradox in saying that one can be led by these preferences into the effort of seeking to improve one's character. The fact that in such self-improvement one will need to draw on qualities of character such as determination still does not generate the paradox of using a trait of character to bring itself into existence. The man who says to himself "I really must cultivate more resolution" is in a bit of a fix if he has none whatever. You cannot enter the game with nothing at all or develop the muscle in a missing limb.

There is a weird piece of argument in the ethics of Kant which I always used to ridicule. He said that if nature had intended men to make happiness their overriding end, they would have been fitted out with instincts that led them automatically to it. But, since we have reason, our proper purpose must be something different. I am not yet ready to swallow this whole, but I do now have some sympathy for it. Our instincts are not enough; evolution has orga-

447

nized and modified them, and provided us with a long infancy in which the formation of character can take place. If for no more dignified reason, we should hang on to character for self-defense, as the porcupine does to his prickles or the lobster to his shell.

STUDY QUESTIONS

1. Why does Quinton think of character as a hardwon achievement?
2. Character, says Quinton, is a disposition or habit of controlling one's immediate impulsive desires. Does this commit Quinton to the view that even a very immoral person may have a strong character? Do you see a difference between having a strong character and having a good character? Is having a strong character a necessary condition for being a morally good person?
3. What does Quinton mean when he calls the character a "procedural" rather than a "substantive" concept?
4. Quinton criticizes contemporary society for ignoring the traditional virtues by making a cardinal virtue of "amiability"—"a sort of uncritical endorsement of the wants and acts of others." Do you think his criticism is fair?
5. How and why, according to Quinton, has modern philosophy as a discipline neglected character and will?

SUGGESTED READINGS

Goffman, Erving. *The Presentation of Self in Everyday Life.* New York: Doubleday, 1979.

Kant, Immanuel. *Lectures on Ethics.* Translated by Louis Enfield. New York: The Century Company, 1930.

Lasch, Christopher. *The Culture of Narcissism.* New York: W. W. Norton and Co., 1979.

Sennett, Richard. *The Fall of Public Man.* New York: Alfred A. Knopf, 1977.

Rorty, Amelie. *The Identities of Persons*. Berkeley and Los Angeles: University of California Press, 1976.

Williams, Bernard. *Moral Luck*. Cambridge: Cambridge University Press, 1981.

Yankelovich, Daniel. *New Rules: Searching for Fulfillment in a World Turned Upside Down*. New York: Random House, 1981.

Chapter

7

MORALITY AND
THE FAMILY

What is happening to the family? We can find the answer by looking at the change in attitudes and practices regarding filial relations, parental authority, the status of women, sex, and divorce—changes that have destabilized traditional family ties.

Several authors in Chapter 7 see contemporary irreverence toward traditional family norms as socially pernicious. Rabbi Norman Lamm and Pope Paul VI are concerned with the family as an institution that guarantees the survival of moral and religious traditions. Pope Paul examines the effects of using artificial means of birth control, arguing that this widespread practice destroys family ties and ultimately harms the goal of a truly human civilization. Rebecca West discusses the effect of divorce on children of divorced parents and considers whether prohibiting divorce would be wise. Implicit in the articles of Lamm, Pope Paul, West, and Lin Yutang is the conviction of a need to preserve the family's integrity as a social institution of great value for civilization. Thus, they subordinate other moral considerations, such as the desirability of allowing family members a great deal of individual freedom, to the wider concern of preserving the family itself.

451

In contrast, Carl Cohen, Michael Slote, Jane English, and Sissela Bok aim to liberate individuals from family practices they view as oppressive. Slote and English challenge the related assumptions of parental authority and filial obligation. For Slote, parental authority over children is an illusion. (He compares it to many people's illusion that they are subordinate to the will of God.) The illusion is harmful because it engenders feelings of helplessness and inhibits growth and maturity. Slote finds it all to the good that modern society no longer encourages the illusion of parental authority. But he worries about its strength and fears that parental authority may make a comeback. Jane English covers some of the same ground as Slote. She provides an alternative account of duties to parents, one based not on filial obligation but on mutual friendship. According to English, we only owe our parents those duties we owe to good friends in general. No friendship, no obligations.

Lin Yutang, following Confucius and Mencius, would find the views that Slote and English express altogether unacceptable and inhumane. In the Chinese tradition, feelings of gratitude and respect for one's parents rank highly among the moral virtues. Lin Yutang points out that filial regard for parents and grandparents does not come naturally; it needs to be "taught by culture." Yutang finds Western society sadly lacking in the kind of acculturation that assures its members a dignified old age.

Edward Shils, in "Tradition and the Generations," is more generally concerned with contemporary Western culture's disrespect for tradition. According to Shils, life without respect for the past is blighted and the young suffer even more than the old from the erosion of tradition. This current disregard for tradition is socially and morally regressive, and, if Shils is right, the family is not the only threatened institution.

On Growing Old Gracefully

LIN YUTANG

Lin Yutang (1895–1976) was a novelist and a philosopher. He is the author of a number of books, including *The Importance of Living* (1937) and *The Wisdom of China and India* (1955).

Lin Yutang describes the Chinese family system's treatment of old people and contrasts it with Western norms and attitudes. He notes that we need strong cultural norms to assure respect for parents, grandparents, and older people in general. "A natural man loves his children, but a cultured man loves his parents." Chinese deference and respect for age contrasts sharply with Western attitudes, where we view growing old as almost disgraceful and expect old people not to "interfere" in the family's home life.

The Chinese family system, as I conceive it, is largely an arrangement of particular provision for the young and the old, for since childhood and youth and old age occupy half our life, it is important that the young and the old live a satisfactory life. It is true that the young are more helpless and can take less care of themselves, but on the other hand, they can get along better without material comforts than the old people. A child is often scarcely aware of material hardships, with the result that a poor child is often as

ON GROWING OLD GRACEFULLY From *The Importance of Living* by Lin Yutang (William Heinemann Ltd., 1931). Reprinted with the permission of Mrs. Lin Yutang.

happy as, if not happier than, a rich child. He may go barefooted, but that is a comfort, rather than a hardship to him, whereas going barefooted is often an intolerable hardship for old people. This comes from the child's greater vitality, the bounce of youth. He may have his temporary sorrows, but how easily he forgets them. He has no idea of money and no millionaire complex, as the old man has. At the worst, he collects only cigar coupons for buying a pop-gun, whereas the dowager collects Liberty Bonds. Between the fun of these two kinds of collection there is no comparison. The reason is the child is not yet intimidated by life as all grown-ups are. His personal habits are as yet unformed, and he is'not a slave to a particular brand of coffee, and he takes whatever comes along. He has very little racial prejudice and absolutely no religious prejudice. His thoughts and ideas have not fallen into certain ruts. Therefore, strange as it may seem, old people are even more dependent than the young because their fears are more definite and their desires are more delimited.

Something of this tenderness toward old age existed already in the primeval consciousness of the Chinese people, a feeling that I can compare only to the Western chivalry and feeling of tenderness toward women. If the early Chinese people had any chivalry, it was manifested not toward women and children, but toward the old people. That feeling of chivalry found clear expression in Mencius in some such saying as, "The people with grey hair should not be seen carrying burdens on the street," which was expressed as the final goal of a good government. Mencius also described the four classes of the world's most helpless people as: "The widows, widowers, orphans, and old people without children." Of these four classes, the first two were to be taken care of by a political economy that should be so arranged that there would be no unmarried men and women. What was to be done about the orphans Mencius did not say, so far as we know, although orphanages have always existed throughout the ages, as well as pensions for old people. Every one realizes, however, that orphanages and old age pensions are poor subsitutes for the home. The feeling is that the home alone can provide anything resembling a satisfactory arrangement for the old and the young. But for the young, it is to be taken for granted that not much need be said, since there is natural paternal affection. "Water flows downwards and not upwards," the Chinese always say, and therefore the affection for parents and grandparents is something that stands more in need of being taught by culture. A natural man loves his children, but a cultured man loves his parents. In the end, the teaching of love and respect for old people became a generally accepted principle, and if we are to believe some of the writers, the desire to have the privilege of serving their parents in their old age actually became a consuming passion. The greatest regret a Chinese gentleman could have was the eternally lost opportunity of serving his old parents with medicine and soup on their deathbed, or not to be present when they died. For a high official in his fifties or sixties not to be able to invite his parents to come from their native village and stay with his family at the capital, "seeing them to bed every night and greeting them every morning," was to commit a moral sin of which he should be ashamed and for which he had constantly to offer excuses and explanations to his friends and colleagues. This regret was expressed in two lines by a man who returned too late to his home, when his parents had already died:

> The tree desires repose, but the wind will not stop;
> The son desires to serve, but his parents are already gone.

It is to be assumed that if man were to live this life like a poem, he would be able to look upon the sunset of his life as his happiest period, and instead of trying to postpone the much feared old age, be able actually to look forward to it, and gradually build up to it as the best and happiest period of his existence. In my efforts to compare and contrast Eastern and Western life, I have found no differences that are absolute except in this matter of the attitude towards age, which is sharp and clearcut and permits of no intermediate positions. The differences in our attitude towards sex, toward women, and toward work, play, and achievement are all relative. The relationship between husband and wife in China is not essentially different from that in the West, nor even the relationship between parent and child. Not even the ideas of individual liberty and democracy and the relationship between the people and their ruler are, after all, so very different. But in the matter of our attitude toward age, the difference is absolute, and the East and West take exactly opposite points of view. This is clearest in the matter of asking about a person's age or telling one's own. In China, the first question a person asks the other on an official call, after asking about his name and surname is, "What is your glorious age?" If the person replies apologetically that he is twenty-three or twenty-eight, the other party generally comforts him by saying that he has still a glorious future, and that one day he may become old. But if the person replies that he is thirty-five or thirty-eight, the other party immediately exclaims with deep respect, "Good luck!"; enthusiasm grows in proportion as the gentleman is able to report a higher and higher age, and if the person is anywhere over fifty, the inquirer immediately drops his voice in humility and respect. That is why all old people, if they can, should go and live in China, where even a beggar with a white beard is treated with extra kindness. People in middle age actually look forward to the time when they can celebrate their fifty-first birthday, and in the case of successful merchants or officials, they would celebrate even their forty-first birthday with great pomp and glory. But the fifty-first birthday, or the half-century mark, is an occasion of rejoicing for people of all classes. The sixty-first is a happier and grander occasion than the fifty-first and the seventy-first is still happier and grander, while a man able to celebrate his eighty-first birthday is actually looked upon as one specially favored by heaven. The wearing of a beard becomes the special prerogative of those who have become grandparents, and a man doing so without the necessary qualifications, either of being a grandfather or being on the other side of fifty, stands in danger of being sneered at behind his back. The result is that young men try to pass themselves off as older than they are by imitating the pose and dignity and point of view of the old people, and I have known young Chinese writers graduated from the middle schools, anywhere between twenty-one and twenty-five, writing articles in the magazines to advise what "the young men ought and ought not to read," and discussing the pitfalls of youth with a fatherly condescension.

This desire to grow old and in any case to appear old is understandable when one understands the premium generally placed upon old age in China. In the first place, it is a privilege of the old people to talk, while the young must listen and hold their tongue. "A young man is supposed to have ears and no mouth," as a Chinese saying goes. Men of twenty are supposed to listen when people of thirty are talking, and these in turn are supposed to listen when men of forty are talking. As the desire to talk and to be listened to is almost universal, it is evident that the further along one gets in years, the better chance he has to talk and to be listened to when he goes about in society. It is a game of life in which no one is favored, for everyone has a chance of becoming old in his time. Thus a father lecturing his son is obliged to stop suddenly and change his demeanor the moment the grandmother opens her mouth. Of course he wishes to be in the grandmother's place. And it is quite fair, for what right have the young to open their mouth when the old men can say, "I have crossed more bridges than you have crossed streets!" What right have the young got to talk?

In spite of my acquaintance with Western life and the Western attitude toward age, I am still continually shocked by certain expressions for which I am totally unprepared. Fresh illustrations of this attitude come up on every side. I have heard an old lady remarking that she has had several grandchildren, but, "It was the first one that hurt." With the full knowledge that American people hate to be thought of as old, one still doesn't quite expect to have it put that way. . . .

I have no doubt that the fact that the old men of America still insist on being so busy and active can be directly traced to individualism carried to a foolish extent. It is their pride and their love of independence and their shame of being dependent upon their children. But among the many human rights the American people have provided for in the Constitution, they have strangely forgotten about the right to be fed by their children, for it is a right and an obligation growing out of service. How can any one deny that parents who have toiled for their children in their youth, have lost many a good night's sleep when they were ill, have washed their diapers long before they could talk and have spent about a quarter of a century bringing them up and fitting them for life, have the right to be fed by them and loved and respected when they are old? Can one not forget the individual and his pride of self in a general scheme of home life in which men are justly taken care of by their parents and, having in turn taken care of their children, are also justly taken care of by the latter? The Chinese have not got the sense of individual independence because the whole conception of life is based upon mutual help within the home; hence there is no shame attached to the circumstance of one's being served by his children in the sunset of one's life. Rather it is considered good luck to have children who can take care of one. One lives for nothing else in China.

In the West, the old people efface themselves and prefer to live

457

alone in some hotel with a restaurant on the ground floor, out of consideration for their children and an entirely unselfish desire not to interfere in their home life. But the old people have the right to interfere, and if interference is unpleasant, it is nevertheless natural, for all life, particularly the domestic life, is a lesson in restraint. Parents interfere with their children anyway when they are young, and the logic of noninterference is already seen in the results of Behaviorists, who think that all children should be taken away from their parents. If one cannot tolerate one's own parents when they are old and comparatively helpless, parents who have done so much for us, whom else can one tolerate in the home? One has to learn self-restraint anyway, or even marriage will go on the rocks. And how can the personal service and devotion and adoration of loving children ever be replaced by the best hotel waiters?

The Chinese idea supporting this personal service to old parents is expressly defended on the sole ground of gratitude. The debts to one's friends may be numbered, but the debts to one's parents are beyond number. Again and again, Chinese essays on filial piety mention the fact of washing diapers, which takes on significance when one becomes a parent himself. In return, therefore, is it not right that in their old age, the parents should be served with the best food and have their favorite dishes placed before them? The duties of a son serving his parents are pretty hard, but it is sacrilege to make a comparison between nursing one's own parents and nursing a stranger in a hospital. For instance, the following are some of the duties of the junior at home, as prescribed by Tu Hsishih and incorporated in a book of moral instruction very popular as a text in the old schools:

> In the summer months, one should, while attending to his parents, stand by their side and fan them, to drive away the heat and the flies and mosquitoes. In winter, he should see that the bed quilts are warm enough and the stove fire is hot enough, and see that it is just right by attending to it constantly. He should also see if there are holes or crevices in the doors and windows, that there may be no draft, to the end that his parents are comfortable and happy.

> A child above ten should get up before his parents in the morning, and after the toilet go to their bed and ask if they have had a good night. If his parents have already gotten up, he should first curtsy to them before inquiring after their health, and should retire with

another curtsy after the question. Before going to bed at night, he should prepare the bed, when the parents are going to sleep, and stand by until he sees that they have fallen off to sleep and then pull down the bed curtain and retire himself.

Who, therefore, wouldn't want to be an old man or an old father or grandfather in China?

This sort of thing is being very much laughed at by the proletarian writers of China as "feudalistic," but there is a charm to it which makes any old gentlemen inland cling to it and think that modern China is going to the dogs. The important point is that every man grows old in time, if he lives long enough, as he certainly desires to. If one forgets this foolish individualism which seems to assume that an individual can exist in the abstract and be literally independent, one must admit that we must so plan our pattern of life that the golden period lies ahead in old age and not behind us in youth and innocence. For if we take the reverse attitude, we are committed without our knowing to a race with the merciless course of time, forever afraid of what lies ahead of us—a race, it is hardly necessary to point out, which is quite hopeless and in which we are eventually all defeated. No one can really stop growing old; he can only cheat himself by not admitting that he is growing old. And since there is no use fighting against nature, one might just as well grow old gracefully. The symphony of life should end with a grand finale of peace and serenity and material comfort and spiritual contentment, and not with the crash of a broken drum or cracked cymbals.

STUDY QUESTIONS

1. Describe Lin Yutang's account of how the West and the East treat their elderly people.
2. Yutang asks, "How can any one deny that parents who have toiled for their children . . . have lost many a good night's sleep when they were ill, have washed their diapers . . . and have spent about a quarter of a century bringing them up . . . have the right to be fed by them and loved and respected when they are old?" Do you agree with him? Do you feel a moral obligation to care for your parents when they are old?

459

3. How does Yutang distinguish between debts of friendship and debts to parents? Do you see a fundamental difference between the two?
4. Does Yutang criticize Western mores fairly? Or does he fail to understand the kind of individualism that characterizes human relations in our society? Some say the price for deference to the aged is a feeling of obligation that may interfere with our sense of independence. Do you agree with this?

What Do Grown Children Owe Their Parents?

JANE ENGLISH

Jane English (1947–1978), who taught philosophy at the University of North Carolina, Chapel Hill, wrote several articles and edited a number of books in the area of practical ethics. She died tragically at 31 in an expedition on the Matterhorn.

Jane English argues that grown children have no filial obligations. She distinguishes between relations based on reciprocal favors and relationships of friendship. Both involve duties, but English argues that friendship and its duties ought to be the norm governing the relationship of grown children and parents. Filial obligation is not required per se; it is the result of friendship rather than a debt owed for services rendered. Thus obligations to parents exist "just so long as friendship exists."

WHAT DO GROWN CHILDREN OWE THEIR PARENTS © *Having Children: Philosophical and Legal Reflections on Parenthood*, edited by Onora O'Neill and William Ruddick. New York: Oxford University Press, 1979.

What do grown children owe their parents? I will contend that the answer is "nothing." Although I agree that there are many things that children *ought* to do for their parents, I will argue that it is inappropriate and misleading to describe them as things "owed." I will maintain that parents' voluntary sacrifices, rather than creating "debts" to be "repaid," tend to create love or "friendship." The duties of grown children are those of friends and result from love between them and their parents, rather than being things owed in repayment for the parents' earlier sacrifices. Thus, I will oppose those philosophers who use the word "owe" whenever a duty or obligation exists. Although the "debt" metaphor is appropriate in some moral circumstances, my argument is that a love relationship is not such a case.

Misunderstandings about the proper relationship between parents and their grown children have resulted from reliance on the "owing" terminology. For instance, we hear parents complain, "You owe it to us to write home (keep up your piano playing, not adopt a hippie lifestyle), because of all we sacrificed for you (paying for piano lessons, sending you to college)." The child is sometimes even heard to reply, "I didn't ask to be born (to be given piano lessons, to be sent to college)." This inappropriate idiom of ordinary language tends to be obscure, or even to undermine, the love that is the correct ground of filial obligation.

1. Favors Create Debts

There are some cases, other than literal debts, in which talk of "owing," though metaphorical, is apt. New to the neighborhood, Max barely knows his neighbor, Nina, but he asks her if she will take in his mail while he is gone for a month's vacation. She agrees. If, subsequently, Nina asks Max to do the same for her, it seems that Max has a moral obligation to agree (greater than the one he would have had if Nina had not done the same for him), unless for some reason it would be a burden far out of proportion to the one Nina bore for him. I will call this a *favor*: when A, at B's request, bears some burden for B, then B incurs an obligation to reciprocate. Here the metaphor of Max's "owing" Nina is appropriate. It is not literally a debt, of course, nor can Nina pass this IOU on to heirs, demand payment in the form of Max's taking out her garbage, or sue Max. Nonetheless, since Max ought to perform one act of similar nature and amount of sacrifice in return, the term is suggestive. Once he reciprocates, the debt is "discharged"—that is, their obligations revert to the condition they were in before Max's initial request.

Contrast a situation in which Max simply goes on vacation and, to his surprise, finds upon his return that his neighbor has mowed his grass twice weekly in his absence. This is a voluntary sacrifice rather than a favor, and Max has no duty to reciprocate. It would be nice for him to volunteer to do so, but this would be supererogatory on his part. Rather than a favor, Nina's action is a friendly gesture. As a result, she might expect Max to chat over the back fence, help her catch her straying dog, or something similar—she might expect the development of a friendship. But Max would be chatting (or whatever) out of friendship, rather than in repayment for mown grass. If he did not return her gesture, she might feel rebuffed or miffed, but not unjustly treated or indignant, since Max has not failed to perform a duty. Talk of "owing" would be out of place in this case.

It is sometimes difficult to distinguish between favors and non-favors, because friends tend to do favors for each other, and those who exchange favors tend to become friends. But one test is to ask how Max is motivated. Is it "to be nice to Nina" or "because she did x for me"? Favors are frequently performed by total strangers without any friendship developing. Nevertheless, a temporary obligation is created, even if the chance for repayment never arises. For instance, suppose that Oscar and Matilda, total strangers, are waiting in a long checkout line at the supermarket. Oscar, having forgotten the oregano, asks Matilda to watch his cart for a second. She does. If Matilda now asks Oscar to return the favor while she picks up some tomato sauce, he is obliged to agree. Even if she had not watched his cart, it would be inconsiderate of him to refuse, claiming he was too busy reading the magazines. He may have had a duty to help others, but he would not "owe" it to her. But if she had done the same for him, he incurs an additional obligation to help, and talk of "owing" is apt. It suggests an agreement to perform equal, reciprocal, canceling sacrifices.

2. The Duties of Friendship

The terms "owe" and "repay" are helpful in the case of favors, because the sameness of the amount of sacrifice on the two sides is important; the monetary metaphor suggests equal quantities of sacrifice. But friendship ought to be characterized by *mutuality* rather than reciprocity: friends offer what they can give and accept what they need, without regard for the total amounts of benefits exchanged. And friends are motivated by love rather than by the prospect of repayment. Hence, talk of "owing" is singularly out of place in friendship.

For example, suppose Alfred takes Beatrice out for an expensive dinner and a movie. Beatrice incurs no obligation to "repay" him with a goodnight kiss or a return engagement. If Alfred complains that she "owes" him something, he is operating under the assumption that she should repay a favor, but on the contrary his was a generous gesture done in the hopes of developing a friendship. We hope that he would not want her repayment in the form of sex or attention if this was done to discharge a debt rather than from friendship. Since, if Alfred is prone to reasoning in this way, Beatrice may well decline the invitation or request to pay for her own dinner, his attitude of expecting a "return" on his "investment" could hinder the development of a friendship. Beatrice should return the gesture only if she is motivated by friendship.

Another common misuse of the "owing" idiom occurs when the Smiths have dined at the Joneses' four times, but the Joneses at the Smiths' only once. People often say, "We owe them three dinners." This line of thinking may be appropriate between business acquaintances, but not between friends. After all, the Joneses invited the Smiths not in order to feed them or to be fed in turn, but because of the friendly contact presumably enjoyed by all on such occasions. If the Smiths do not feel friendship toward the Joneses, they can decline future invitations and not invite the Joneses; they owe them nothing. Of course, between friends of equal resources and needs, roughly equal sacrifices (though not necessarily roughly equal dinners) will typically occur. If the sacrifices are highly out of proportion to the resources, the relationship is closer to servility than to friendship.[1]

Another difference between favors and friendship is that after a friendship ends, the duties of friendship end. The party that has

---

[1] Cf. Thomas E. Hill, Jr., "Servility and Self-Respect," *Monist* 57 (1973). Thus, during childhood, most of the sacrifices will come from the parents, since they have most of the resources and the child has most of the needs. When children are grown, the situation is usually reversed.

sacrificed less owes the other nothing. For instance, suppose Elmer donated a pint of blood that his wife Doris needed during an operation. Years after their divorce, Elmer is in an accident and needs one pint of blood. His new wife, Cora, is also of the same blood type. It seems that Doris not only does not "owe" Elmer blood, but that she should actually refrain from coming forward if Cora has volunteered to donate. To insist on donating not only interferes with the newlyweds' friendship, but it belittles Doris and Elmer's former relationship by suggesting that Elmer gave blood in hopes of favors returned instead of simply out of love for Doris. It is one of the heart-rending features of divorce that it attends to quantity in a relationship previously characterized by mutuality. If Cora could not donate, Doris's obligation is the same as that for any former spouse in need of blood; it is not increased by the fact that Elmer similarly aided her. It *is* affected by the degree to which they are still friends, which in turn may (or may not) have been influenced by Elmer's donation.

In short, unlike the debts created by favors, the duties of friendship do not require equal quantities of sacrifice. Performing equal sacrifices does not cancel the duties of friendship, as it does the debts of favors. Unrequested sacrifices do not themselves create debts, but friends have duties regardless of whether they requested or initiated the friendship. Those who perform favors may be motivated by mutual gain, whereas friends should be motivated by affection. These characteristics of the friendship relation are distorted by talk of "owing."

3. Parents and Children

The relationship between children and their parents should be one of friendship characterized by mutuality rather than one of reciprocal favors. The quantity of parental sacrifice is not relevant in determining what duties the grown child has. The medical assistance grown children ought to offer their ill mothers in old age depends upon the mothers' need, not upon whether they endured a difficult pregnancy, for example. Nor do one's duties to one's parents cease once an equal quantity of sacrifice has been performed, as the phrase "discharging a debt" may lead us to think.

Rather, what children ought to do for their parents (and parents for children) depends upon (1) their respective needs, abilities, and resources and (2) the extent to which there is an ongoing friendship between them. Thus, regardless of the quantity of childhood sacrifices, an able, wealthy child has an obligation to help his needy parents more than does a needy child. To illustrate, suppose sisters Cecile and Dana are equally loved by their parents, even though Cecile was an easy child to care for, seldom ill, while Dana was often sick and caused some trouble as a juvenile delinquent. As adults, Dana is a struggling artist living far away, while Cecile is a wealthy lawyer living nearby. When the parents need visits and financial aid, Cecile has an obligation to bear a higher proportion of these burdens than her sister. This results from her abilities, rather than from the quantities of sacrifice made by the parents earlier.

Sacrifices have an important causal role in creating an ongoing friendship, which may lead us to assume incorrectly that it is the sacrifices that are the source of obligation. That the source is the friendship instead can be seen by examining cases in which the sacrifices occurred but the friendship, for some reason, did not develop or persist. For example, if a woman gives up her newborn child for adoption, and if no feelings of love ever develop on either side, it seems that the grown child does not have an obligation to "repay" her for her sacrifices in pregnancy. For that matter, if the adopted child has an unimpaired love relationship with the adoptive parents, he or she has the same obligations to help them as a natural child would have.

The filial obligations of grown children are a result of friendship, rather than owed for services rendered. Suppose that Vance married Lola despite his parents' strong wish that he marry within their religion, and that as a result, the parents refuse to speak to him again. As the years pass, the parents are unaware of Vance's problems, his accomplishments, the birth of his children. The love that once existed between them, let us suppose, has been completely destroyed by this event and thirty years of desuetude. At this point, it seems, Vance is under no obligation to pay his parents' medical bills in their old age, beyond his general duty to help those in need. An additional, filial obligation would only arise from whatever love he may still feel for them. It would be irrelevant for his parents to argue, "But look how much we sacrificed for you when you were young," for that sacrifice was not a favor but occurred as part of a friendship which existed at that time but is now, we have supposed, defunct. A more appropriate message would be, "We still love you, and we would like to renew our friendship."

I hope this helps to set the question of what children ought to do for their parents in a new light. The parental argument, "You ought to do x because we did y for you," should be replaced by, "We love you and you will be happier if you do x," or "We believe you love us, and anyone who loved us would do x." If the parents' sacrifice had been a favor, the child's reply, "I never asked you to do y for me," would have been relevant; to the revised parental remarks, this reply is clearly irrelevant. The child can either do x or dispute one of the parents' claims: by showing that a love relationship does not exist, or that love for someone does not motivate doing x, or that he or she will not be happier doing x.

Seen in this light, parental requests for children to write home, visit, and offer them a reasonable amount of emotional and financial support in life's crises are well founded, so long as a friendship still exists. Love for others does call for caring about and caring for them. Some other parental requests, such as for more sweeping changes in the child's lifestyle or life goals, can be seen to be insupportable, once we shift the justification from debts owed to love. The terminology of favors suggests the reasoning, "Since we paid for your college education, you owe it to us to make a career of engineering, rather than becoming a rock musician." This tends to alienate affection even further, since the tuition payments are depicted as investments for a return rather than done from love, as though the child's life goals could be "bought." Basing the argument on love leads to different reasoning patterns. The suppressed premise, "If A loves B, then A follows B's wishes as to A's lifelong career" is simply false. Love does not even dictate that the child adopt the parents' values as to the desirability of alternative life goals. So the parents' strongest available argument here is, "We love you, we are deeply concerned about your happiness, and in the long run you will be happier as an engineer." This makes it clear that an empirical claim is really the subject of the debate.

The function of these examples is to draw out our considered judgments as to the proper relation between parents and their grown children, and to show how poorly they fit the model of favors. What is relevant is the ongoing friendship that exists between parents and children. Although that relationship developed partly as a result of parental sacrifices for the child, the duties that grown children have to their parents result from the friendship rather than from the sacrifices. The idiom of owing favors to one's parents can actually be destructive if it undermines the role of mutuality and leads us to think in terms of quantitative reciprocal favors.

STUDY QUESTIONS

1. How does English distinguish between duties created by debts and duties created by friendship?
2. Do you agree with English that filial obligation is not owed for services rendered, but instead results from friendship? How would Lin Yutang react to this view?
3. In some states, law requires children of poor elderly people to contribute to their support. Do you think English would argue for or against this? Do you support legislation of this kind?
4. Can we criticize English for advocating a "minimalist ethic" (described by Daniel Callahan in Chapter 8) according to which no duties of self-sacrifice or altruism apply outside one's small circle of friends—all people, even family members, are moral strangers unless one voluntarily "contracts" an obligation?
5. How might English account for the moral duty many people feel to take care of not only their own elderly parents, but needy elderly people in general?

Traditional Jewish Family Values

NORMAN LAMM

Rabbi Norman Lamm (1927), president of Yeshiva University, is the author of *Faith and Doubt* (1971) and *The Good Society* (1974).

Lamm presents an idealized model of the traditional Jewish family and contrasts it with the average contemporary Jewish family. The traditional family is much more rigorously organized, its members' roles are strictly defined, and, consequently, the family itself is more important as an institution. This results in greater intimacy and a strong sense of mutual obligation, for example, to the elderly who are esteemed as authoritative. Members of the traditional family practice a great deal of restraint and forebearance, emphasizing duty, rather than rights. Finally, the family sees itself as part of a more general community of Jewish families that is, in turn, part of a continuous tradition and history. The traditional family is religious and committed to carrying on a Jewish tradition. This, says Lamm, gives it further cohesiveness.

Lamm argues for the importance of the "benevolent authority" that parents exercise, an authority all the more effective because the higher authority of God qualifies it. According to Lamm, a family that lacks a

TRADITIONAL JEWISH FAMILY VALUES From *Jewish Consciousness-raising*. Edited by Norman Linzer. © 1973 by the Board of Jewish Education of Greater New York. Reprinted by permission of the copyright holder.

central authority cannot be cohesive. The children of such families tend to be confused and disoriented. Lamm warns that we are losing our sense of commitment to tradition in a world without faith and cannot replace it simply by recognizing how badly we need it.

. . . I am going to set up a contrast between two arbitrarily designed models, one of a traditional and the other of a modern Jewish home. My excuse is that I am not aiming at sociological accuracy but at clarity of exposition. First, the idealized version of the traditional Jewish home is characterized by a high degree of intimacy, of love, of devotion, usually non-demonstrative. The husband normally is a monogamist and the wife is satisfied to be at home. As opposed to this, contemporary parents are more remote. They are encouraged to follow their own interests. The mother is told that she should not allow her life to be wrapped up entirely in her children and in her home, but should find outside interests. The father, when he comes back from the office, seeks out a peer group or other kinds of involvements. As a result, the parents seek their own particular levels of interest, or areas of interest, and are removed from the nexus of the home.

Second, in traditional Jewish homes there is a special esteem for age, which is cherished for its own sake. Of course, this goes back to the Biblical commandments of "Honor thy father and mother" and honor for the teacher and elder, but sociologically speaking, it is not so much a revealed norm as a lived value. The traditional home likely as not included an extended family larger than the nuclear family. Most Jewish children grew up in the presence of a grandfather or a grandmother, some kind of living relic of the past, and developed a natural respect and reverence for age not because of any specific function of the elderly, but because age itself was valued. Compare that now to the contemporary emphasis on youth and youthfulness, especially in America but all over the Western world as well. That the focus of our culture is the young is often revealed in some of the inanities of the Jewish community organizations and its press. We are so geared to the young that when we want to decide the great questions of the day, we send out a researcher to take a statistical analysis of what high school sophomores are thinking, because that represents "the wave of the future" which ought, by implication, to determine our stand, not only with regard to dress and speech but even with regard to policy, religion, etc. I am presenting a caricature, of course (although I have certain specific incidents in mind), but it does contain the kernel of a true reflection of the quality of life in America.

Third, in this idealized picture of the traditional Jewish home, there were more or less well defined roles for father and mother. Probably, this was not only true for the Jewish home: it was the case for general culture in which Jews found themselves in pre-modern or pre-contemporary times. A little boy knew what was expected of him when he became a big boy and a big man, and a little girl knew the role into which she was emerging and for which, therefore, she ought to be striving. This clear role definition is increasingly absent in the contemporary home, where there occurs a great deal of blurring and interchanging of roles, with consequent functional chaos when it comes to identifying the roles of father and mother as separate and distinct from each other.

Fourth, the traditional Jewish home emphasized the value of self-restraint, of renunciation, "Thou shalt not." The modern home, in our pop-culture, regards "Thou shalt not" as an excessive inhibition which can harm the emotions and mentality of the growing child. Morally, the modern home is characterized much more by permissiveness than by renunciation and restraint. Perhaps one can best describe the difference between the traditional Jewish home and the modern Jewish home by the polarity of duty and right. The traditional home emphasized duty. What am I supposed to do? What must I do? The modern Jewish home is more a matter of rights: the children's right, the wife's right, the mother's right, the father's right. Everyone has his or her rights, and in this competition of rights a balance has to be struck and a harmony established so that everyone gets his due. The emphasis is not on the contribution that I must make, but rather on what my fair share is, what my rights are.

Finally, in the traditional Jewish home there is understood and presupposed a commitment by all members of the family to a goal or a source that transcends the family. There is some kind of transcendent commitment which binds the members of the family. This transcendent commitment is usually some aspect of, or combination of aspects of, the Jewish tradition—the Jewish people, Jewish law, Jewish religion, God, Torah. The modern home lacks the axiological or ideological cohesiveness. If a religious or nationalistic commitment is present, it is not considered particularly important. It never really plays a central role in the life of the family. Again I ask you not to charge me with being unscientific. I am setting up models, and not insisting, of course, that every modern family follows one path or every traditional family the other.

The five elements, for the purpose of our discussion, may be reduced to three more basic issues: love, authority, and commitment.

Love

Let us begin with the first one, love. The traditional Jewish family structure is disintegrating. As time goes on and assimilation increases, you find that the whole pattern I have described as the paradigm of a Jewish family that we have inherited from the past, is falling apart. We are experiencing an accelerated decentralization of the family as a result of the various centrifugal forces which tend to pull the family apart. As it is wrenched out of the context of a stable, self-sufficient Jewish community life, the family begins to disintegrate at the edges. Eventually, the community as a whole follows suit. Furthermore, modern goals such as the desideratum of self-fulfillment and self-realization, which really are basic and important values for moderns, tend to polarize individuals in the family. They diminish the virtues of self-sacrifice, of loyalty, of restraint which had previously acted as centripetal forces in favor of the family unit. If I must seek my self-fulfillment and my self-realization, I will find that that often conflicts with what I might otherwise consider my specific duties to my parents, to my wife, to my children, to the family as a whole. . . .

Now, in the highly structured traditional Jewish family, especially the patriarchal one, where there is a clear source of authority (which we shall discuss in more detail later), the family enforces a practical conformity with its norms and its ideological commitment. Sometimes, however, the traditional Jewish family, in enforcing this ideological pattern, this whole routine of life for all its members, overuses its dicipline which overwhelms the element of love. In this model we have set up of the traditional Jewish family,

471

love and devotion were ever-present, but so was discipline, which guaranteed family cohesion. But sometimes it happened that the discipline was too strong, so that it became rigid, thus diminishing the element of love, warmth, spontaneity, and the sense of intimacy. That is why you find sometimes that within Orthodox families—especially in the modern or contemporary period—there is a rigidity and a defensiveness against the "outside world" that was not true when the entire community was more or less traditional. Often an Orthodox family in our days finds itself on the defensive as a cognitive minority and develops a kind of "man the ramparts" psychology, and even philosophy, that undergirds it. It is not always the healthiest thing for the development of a family's solidarity to feel that they are living in a beleagured fortress. Sometimes it helps, sometimes it doesn't. But because of it, parents in a truly Orthodox family will sometimes be harsh with children—overly harsh—neglecting, in this sense, some of the wisdom of their own tradition.

This wisdom can best be recapitulated in a famous story told of the founder of the Hasidic movement, the Besht (Rabbi Israel Baal Shem Tov.) A father once came to him to complain that his son was going off on the wrong path and leaving Jewish morality and Jewish religious practice. He said to the Rabbi, "What can I do? He is destroying my life, he is destroying everything I've stood for." The Besht answered in three words: *"Love him more."* Instead of bearing down on him, love him more. And with love you probably can achieve a great deal more than by cracking the whip. If you are overly harsh, if you are overly insistent upon conformity to standards that you have inherited which you cherish, then this kind of strictness can be counter-productive.

Authority

The center of gravity in the family makes it a family and not just a group of biologically related people who happen to live under the same roof. The father is usually the source of authority in the traditional Jewish family, but not always. Sometimes it is the mother. In a number of very pious families today in this country, as in the *shtetl*, a young husband will spend several years of intensive study in a *Kollel*, a school of advanced Talmudic research. If he was a great or at least a good scholar, he usually was the source of authority. It sometimes happened that the father who went off to study was not quite that competent and never amounted to much. In that case, the mother, who had much less education and was sometimes illiterate, often was, by virtue of her own gut wisdom, the real and effective head of the family. (One can cite similar instances of a secularized version of this pattern. There are young men in modern, non-religious families who go off to graduate school with their fellowships and scholarships to earn their degrees, while the working wife is the one who really is the "smart" one and runs the family.) However, as a rule it is the father who represented the patriarchal communal authority for his particular family. In the discussion that is now to follow, if I use the term "father", you may easily substitute "mother" if the particular family circumstances call for it. He or she is the one person who above all other represents authority for the entire family. . . .

This father in the traditional Jewish family is an *authority*. He is not a "pal" to his children. He does not run the family along the lines of a participatory democracy where every important problem is taken to a vote with children possessing one-man, one-vote rights equally with father and mother. In this family you do not find the contemporary penchant for an unconscious divination of the future by a reverential observation of the "younger set". Here, then, is no assumption that, since the future is always an improvement over the present, a higher point in inevitable "progress," therefore, children possess some intuitive wisdom to which parents must make obeisance. Not here do you find the phenomenon of treating children as the brokers of the peer group, who actually inform parents how to be "with it" and run things. Often, as you are well aware, the failure of parents to exercise discipline is not really a sign of their love for their children, but rather a disguise for their fundamental lack of concern. If I don't genuinely care for my child, the I will act like a "pal", let him do as he wishes, and delude myself into thinking that in this manner he will think better of me. But with such an attitude, the role of the authority in the family is eroded. This liberal posture, and in radical circles, this conscious and deliberate egalitarianism, represents a frontal attack on the structure of the family by gutting its source and focus of authority.

One must bear in mind that the authority of parents in traditional Judaism was never considered absolute, even in Biblical days. The father was not acknowledged as a kind of petty tyrant who could do with his family as he liked. He was, to follow the metaphor, a constitutional monarch. . . . The father was not the absolute sovereign of that family. This Biblical and Rabbinic teaching must be compared to the then contemporary or even later cultures. In the Grecian and Roman times, a father had the legal right to put a child to death for disobedience. In Greece, a child who was weak and therefore a drain on the family's finances could be taken up to a mountain and left to die. This was accepted as normal and legitimate practice by parents. Not so in Judaism, where *a* source of authority does not imply *absolute* authority. Only God is absolute authority. Parental direction had to be benevolent, and even loving, giving the family its reference point and its structure.

This description of the exercise of benevolent authority and discipline in the traditional Jewish family is, of course, idealized. It was not always so effective. There was apparently always present in Jewish life the phenomenon of Jewish overindulgence of children. Let me illustrate this with two interesting examples from Jewish literature and history. The universality of this proclivity for excessive forbearance by Jewish parents is given fascinating testimony in the following passage:

> There is yet one other evil disease regarding raising children that is not practiced by other people. A child sits at the table with his father and mother and he is the first to stretch forth his hand to partake of the food. He thus grows up arrogant, without fear or culture or refinement, acting as if his father and mother were friends or siblings. By the time he is 8 or 9 years old and his parents wish to correct their earlier mistakes, they no longer are able to, for his childish habits have already become second nature . . .

> Another bad and bitter practice: Parents take a child to school, and in front of the child, warn the teacher not to punish him. When the child hears this, he no longer pays attention to his school work and his disobedience grows worse. This was not the practice of our ancestors. In their days, if a child came crying to his father or mother and told of being punished by a teacher, they would send along the child a gift to the teacher and congratulate the teacher . . .

Modern though it sounds, this complaint comes from *Tzeror Hachayyim* by Rabbi Mosheh Hagiz, over 220 years ago. Two centuries ago, in the pre-modern period, Jewish parents were already indulgent, so this Jewish syndrome is older than the modern period.

Let us cite one more passage, this time advice by a German Jew on the desirable method of raising children.

> A man should begin to train his children in the service of God and in good character when they are yet very young. He must be careful not to permit his love for them to indulge them and permit them to do whatever they wish. . . . However, he must be very careful not to frighten them unnecessarily, lest the child be driven to harm himself. . . . Every parent must judge his child's individual personality and treat him accordingly. Also, if a parent is always angry, the child will come to despise him and pay no more attention to his approach than to a barking dog.

This frank and intelligent advice comes from *Yosef Ometz* of 350 years ago. It is worth listening to him closely. It summarizes, in a way, 3,000 years of cumulative Jewish experience. It is the frequent absence of this combined love and authority, which equals intelligent discipline, that bedevils so many families today.

Commitment

After love and authority, our third and final element for discussion is: commitment. The father in this idealized Jewish traditional family is not only the visible and present focus of authority for the children, but he is also a symbol, the representative and refractor of a Higher Authority. . . . The father effectively acts as the psychological focus for the child of an authority greater than the father himself. He is a surrogate, a broker, of a kind of authority that is beyond the family itself. The father as authority is not self-contained and, in traditional Judaism, he is not self-authenticating. There is a higher authority which legitimates the role of the father. The father is only the broker of this higher authority of God, Torah, Judaism, tradition. The father grounds his authority in the sanction of the Transcendent to which father and son and mother and daughter are all mutually committed. This sanction of the father's authority (or, if you will, the authority of his authority) is the cement of commitment that helped bind the family and make of it a cohesive, well-structured unit. The child knows: if I am angry at my father and I want to rebel, I may hate him; I may even have a death wish for him. But I know all along that there is something beyond father; he is not the ultimate ground of authority, and some day I will be the continuation of my own family because all of us are bound to something much higher.

The focus of the commitment must be beyond the father or whoever happens to be the authority in that family, in order for the family to be united by this commitment.

Thus, this religious commitment is a necessary but not sufficient condition for the reconstitution of family life. Most Jewish homes today are fundamentally non-Jewish. ("Ethnic Jewishness" is totally irrelevant in this respect.) Those Jewish values which do survive, however you want to describe them, are the fortuitous results of a cultural lag. When the fundamental commitment has spent itself, the accompanying phenomena tend to continue for a while: but you can't draw endlessly on that spent capital. Take a minor example: education. Most of us have or had parents whose formal education was less than the one that we possess. Why? The answer is: the Jewish drive for education. A Jewish boy and a Jewish girl must get an education. We, in turn, give this value to our children. But I don't know how much longer this is going to continue, not only because the counterculture makes a virtue a nonachievement rather than achievement, but because our whole impulse for education—to take this one Jewish value—derives from a religious commitment. It is not primarily a sociological phenomenon—the way for the immigrants to get out of the sweatshops. The original inclination comes from the *Mitzvah* of *Talmud Torah*, the religious commandment to study the Torah. This purely religious norm later became secularized, turning from "Torah" to "education," and that meant how to be a doctor or a lawyer or a professor. But when you cut off the major commitment—the religious commitment—all its derivative Jewish values can continue only by virtue of a cultural lag. Alone, these values have only limited endurance and must soon vanish.

Prescription

So much for analysis. Let us now turn to prescription. Unfortunately, I believe I have a much better grasp of what's wrong than I have any ability to prescribe for it. But since the theme assigned to me requires prescription as well, I shall try my hand and hope the medicine I offer you is at least somewhat effective. I feel that the best approach is the indirect one. Let me follow my outline with a slight change, and discuss authority first.

For a family to be cohesive, to be healthy, there has to be a source—a focus of authority. A totally shared authority is inadequate because it is unfocused; it means that no one really knows what's going on. Children under such conditions become confused, not knowing whom to turn to. . . . When I say authority, I hope I will not be misunderstood. I am not speaking of the petty tryant who pulls at his suspenders and says "I'm boss because I wear the pants in the family." I refer, rather, to an intelligent, enlightened attitude where there is, within rational psychological limits, a division of labor, a division of responsibility, and a division of authority, but where at least there is some kind of grouping around a center.

Of course, there are special problems with fatherless families. What does one do in a family made fatherless through death or divorce or separation or abandonment? Here I believe one ought to begin to search out a surrogate father. Either mother must learn how to assert authority or, if she is constitutionally unable to do so, there has to be some way for her children to find a father-model, whether it be a teacher or someone else who can firmly assert moral responsibility and moral authority. Granted, this is easier said than done.

Love. If it doesn't exist, the family situation seems almost hopeless, because of personal, psychological, and sociocultural reasons. Even the minimum effort that would be necessary to support it under such conditions appears to me to be heroic. The problem is complicated nowadays by the fact that the nuclear family in contemporary Jewish life is largely divorced from the extended family, and it is the extended family which tends to retain Judaism's social and moral norms longer than the solitary nuclear family. When a unit consisting of father and mother and children are pulled out of the context of the larger Jewish group, it will tend to lose any traditional values much more quickly than a continuing Jewish neighborhood will lose those same values even if they are already suffering the attrition of assimilation. The Jewish community as a whole has, of course, undergone assimilatory erosion, but I think that the great move to suburbia which came about during the '50s was the beginning of a precipitate abandonment of the whole

Jewish nexus, which was a core of the residue of Jewish values. In other words, upper social mobility spelled for us a very sudden downward trend in psychological stability and religious continuity.

Finally, let us turn to the theme of commitment. In the absence of any genuine inner religious commitment in a Jewish family, we must seek some external idea or cause which can attract and centralize the commitment of the individual members of the family. I am a great believer in the fact that the focus of family cohesiveness must be transcendent and not immanent. It cannot be the family for the family's sake. It just doesn't work in the kind of society in which we live, with all its centrifugal pulls. It has got to be something beyond the family to which all members, or most members of the family, are mutually committed.

Conclusions

. . . You say: what can we do? My answer is: we are facing a terribly messy situation. It is the universal condition of man to-day—of man without God, of man without faith, without an awareness of transcendence, man who feels terribly endangered by the gaping existential void within him, by the threat of meaninglessness which is aggravated by the ubiquitous awareness of death. You just cannot fill the transcendental void by values which we sit down and artificially create. There is no way out. To be honest, either we choose the real thing, or we are in despair. We cannot in one hour or in one lifetime ever hope to devise an adequate substitute for religious faith; in any event, according to my own commitments, substitutes are called—idols.

The Jewish family was strong not when it discussed values but when it lived them. It began to disintegrate when it substituted cocktails for *kiddush* and tuxedo for *tallit*. Traditional Jewish wholesomeness was grounded in a spiritual commitment, in a sublime web of ritual acts invested with both metaphysical significance and nostalgic and historic recollection, so that individuals were both synchronically and diachronically part of a people—a people called a *mishpachah* (family) at its very founding by Abraham. These are not just disembodied "values" or artificial "rituals," but part of a living organism, which gave life and vitality to the family and a sense of validity to its members, despite the ubiquitous domestic problems to which Jews, like all humans, are heir.

STUDY QUESTIONS

1. Lamm gives several criteria of family integrity. In your opinion, are these specific to the traditional Jewish family or are they more general? For example, would a cohesive Catholic or Protestant family satisfy *these* conditions or some others? Specify them.
2. According to Lamm, commitment to the authority of God is an important ingredient in the cohesive family. How, in your opinion, does such commitment contribute to a family's integrity? Is commitment to God an *essential* ingredient?
3. Assuming Lamm is right, how, if in any way, can we create the conditions necessary for stable families? Lamm himself points out that we cannot do this artificially. Are there natural ways?
4. If Lamm's criteria for the close-knit family are indeed too stringent for modern times, is the rapid decline of the family as an institution inevitable?

Obedience and Illusions

MICHAEL SLOTE

Michael Slote is a professor of philosophy at Trinity College in Dublin. He is the author of *Reason and Scepticism* (1970), *Metaphysics and Essence* (1974), and *Goods and Virtues* (1983).

Slote argues that children's obligation to obey parents cannot come from benefits (including life itself) bestowed by parents that children must now repay. In the main, children do not request such benefits and so they cannot be the ground of filial obedience. Parental authority, like divine authority, says Slote, is illusory.

OBEDIENCE AND ILLUSIONS © *Having Children: Philosophical and Legal Reflections on Parenthood,* edited by Onora O'Neill and William Ruddick. New York. Oxford University Press, 1979. Reprinted by permission of the author and editors.

479

The illusion is damaging because it inhibits the development of autonomy. Slote points out that modern culture no longer encourages a morality of filial obligation. He attributes this change to the growth of political democracy.

1. Obligations to Obey

Not long ago, the following reasoning would to many people have seem compelling, if not inescapable:

> We are all God's children. He has done for us what parents do for their children: created us and given us all we have. We owe Him a debt of gratitude of the kind children owe to (good) parents, and therefore owe Him the kind of obedience children owe to parents.

Today, most of us live in a world where reasoning like this has lost its power to persuade. Has the widespread loss of belief in God made the difference? In some measure, perhaps. But I think the change is also largely the result of the way our thoughts about childhood have matured. I shall spend much of this paper explaining the implications and significance of this last remark. I shall talk about authority and childhood, about divine authority and the important ways it resembles parental authority. Although I shall in no way be attacking religion or theism per se, I shall argue that both divine authority and parental authority are underlaid by illusions that must be shed in order to complete the process of growing up, and that the very knowledge that this is so is part of the ongoing maturation of our culture and ourselves.

The argument given at the beginning of the paper can be "stood on its head" in two different ways. First, it can be used to prove the very opposite of what it purports to prove. To many of us, it seems obvious that children have no *obligation* to obey their parents, any more than they have duties of *filial piety*. So any force there is to the analogy between God's creation and parental begetting can, for modern ways of seeing, tend to show that we have no duty to obey God, if He exists.

Moreover, one can reach this conclusion without necessarily holding that children have *no* obligations, owe *nothing*, to their parents. It may well be that good parents are owed a debt of gratitude—though the notion of "debt" here is probably somewhat loose and metaphorical, since it is difficult to believe that one has any moral *duty* to show gratitude for benefits one has not requested. Perhaps children also have a moral obligation to care for their parents when they become sick or infirm. But in neither case does anything seem to follow about debts or duties of obedience. If a stranger, unasked, gives me the money for a college education, I at most owe him a debt of gratitude, not of obedience. And why should it be any different with parents?

Furthermore, it seems entirely gratuitous to suppose that *very young children* have any moral obligations at all, even to their parents. Such obligations, it would seem, exist, if at all, only when moral concepts are firmly implanted. But, on the other hand, if we think of older children—say, adolescents—duties of obedience seem to vanish in another direction. Young children seem to be too young to have any *obligations* or *duties* of obedience or anything else. But older children, precisely because they are more mature, seem to possess a right to determine for themselves how they should live, and this seems to undermine any duty of *obedience* to parents. After reaching a certain age, children, e.g., on a family farm may have duties of cooperation; at least, they have no right to a share of the farm produce unless they cooperate. And such cooperation may entail doing what their more knowledgeable parents tell them to do. But it is unlikely that this constitutes any duty of obedience. Even if the child has a duty to cooperate, and cooperation, in a particular instance, requires doing what a more knowledgeable parent says to do, it does not follow that the child has any general obligation to follow parental instructions or any duty to *obey* his parents in the particular instance.

In addition, I have emphasized that the obligation to cooperate exists, if at all, only to the degree that the older child wants or demands some share in the goods produced by the family. There is, I think, no duty of fair play that requires him to stay with the family and share in its life and benefits because of his parents' past beneficence. The duty of fair play presumably exists only where benefits are voluntarily accepted within a cooperative scheme, and we can hardly suppose that a child has voluntarily accepted his role in (the cooperative scheme of) family life. The (older) child, then, may always opt out of his whole family situation, and we have, in all, found no reason to believe that any child has a duty to obey his parents.

The reasoning at the beginning of this paper needs to be stood on its head in another sense, because it implies an inverted picture of the nature and causality of parental and divine authority. It implies that our acknowledgment of or submission to parental (or divine) authority is (often) powered by our sense of the moral validity of such authority, and just the reverse seems to me to be the case. I believe that moral arguments for duties of obedience to authority are typically epiphenomena: secondary rationalizations of deeper feelings, habits, and (illusory) ideas connected with authority. People do not submit to authority because they recognize a duty to do so on the basis of abstract moral reasoning. Rather, they are, first, under the yoke of such authority—in certain matters feeling, for example, that they have no choice but to do what God or their parents tell them—and only then, or on that basis, make an intellectual accommodation with that authority.

I shall now argue that we are faced with (at least) two levels of illusion when we consider the nature of authority. Submission to authority, by its very nature, involves certain illusions about matters other than the nature of authority itself. However, such submission also typically gives rise to ideological support and reinforcement for the first illusions in the form of illusions *about what authority is*, and the illusion that parental authority (causally) derives from a moral sense of its legitimacy is a good example of such derivative "ideology of authority." We need to understand both these levels of illusion and their modes of interaction.

2. Illusions of Authority

Most parents have some legal authority over their children, but they almost always also have that "aura" of authority that makes their children accept most of their dictates unquestioningly. It is this sort of submission to parental authority that I mean to refer to when I speak hereafter of parental authority, and I believe that parental authority, in this sense, is closely related to the acceptance of divine authority by the devoutly religious.

When people submit to divine authority, they seem to think that they have no choice but to obey God. And I believe that when a devout person, confronted by what he takes to be God's will, thinks, "I have no choice in the matter," he represents himself as a mere object that lacks choice and will altogether—a mere instrument of divine purposes. No doubt, it will immediately be replied that in thinking this way, a devout person may simply be using a harmless metaphor and thus be under no illusion about what he is. But the devout person who thinks or says this sort of thing is typically not, at that moment, clear in his own mind about the merely metaphorical nature of his utterance. If my wife wants me to stay in bed in the morning, and I tell her, "I have no choice in the matter; I have to get to work," I speak in all *seriousness* and in order to *justify* my departure. I need to be *reminded* that what I am saying is not literally true, and am not, therefore, like someone who says that his wife has a heart of gold and never suffers any initial unclarity or confusion about the literal falsity of what he says. Similarly, I think someone who believes he has no choice once God has spoken is not, at least initially, as clear in his own mind about the literal falsity of what he says as is the person who says his wife has a heart of gold. And this gives us at least some reason to claim that religious people, at some point and at some level, actually imagine they lack choice and are mere instruments or things. I think, moreover, that having such illusory thoughts is part of what it is fully to accept God's authority. To see clearly that one has a choice—perhaps a coerced and threatened choice, but a choice, nonetheless—about whether to do as God asks is precisely *not* to submit to divine authority in the manner of the devout.

Important additional evidence for the existence of these illusions comes from the fact that someone who submits to divine authority invariably feels that the presence of God in the universe makes an automatic and total difference to his life and its meaning. The difference he supposes God to make does not seem to consist *merely* in the fact that if God exists, there is a totally wise and good being in the world from whom one can learn; nor can it simply involve God's ability to get us to do what He wants or to impose dire punishments if we do not. And it is very difficult to explain why so many religious people think God makes a total difference to life and its meaning. But we *can* explain this belief if we say that those who hold it are under the illusions we have discussed. For if we are choiceless things because of God's presence in the universe, then that presence clearly does make a total difference to one's life, since it in effect destroys human life and replaces it with the existence of a

483

mere thing. If, by virtue of the divine presence, we are mere instruments of God's purposes, then our lives have no meaning (of their own), and surely it makes a total difference to the meaning of a human life whether that life has or lacks meaning (of its own).[1]

What we have just said about submission to divine authority carries over, in great part, to the authority of parents. I think that children, like the devout, feel their submission to their parents as a loss of will. The child under effective parental authority feels that he has no choice or will of his own in certain matters where his parents have prescribed. And there is every reason to believe that if devout people are under illusions about whether they have choice and wills (or purposes) of their own, children who accept parental authority are under similar illusions. I shall now attempt to explain why children come to have such illusions of choicelessness and willlessness.

Many things can stand in the way of a child's development of autonomy. To learn to think and act for himself, he must also, along the way, rely heavily on his parents or parental substitutes; he must take some things for granted. The child is thus subject to a number of conflicting pressures. He seeks autonomy and is constantly tugging against parental bonds, and yet he needs his parents and has to depend on them for many things. And even as far as the drive for autonomy itself is concerned, parents represent both opportunity and threat. They themselves subject the child to conflicting pressures, wanting the child to grow up and mature, but

---

[1] Of course, in using this explanation, we assume that the belief that God can or does make an automatic total difference to our lives is as illusory as the beliefs that explain it. But I think it is impossible to specify a way in which God actually could make an automatic total difference to human life and its meaning; let the reader try for himself, if he will. So, I think the religious assumption that God can make such a difference is as illusory as the assumptions about choicelessness, etc., that are needed to explain it.

Perhaps the first philosopher to hold that submission to authority involves illusions was Sartre in *Being and Nothingness* and in his play "The Flies." But Sartre's conception of the content of those illusions differs considerably from what I have been saying here and is open to serious criticism. (On this, see my "Existentialism and the Fear of Dying," *American Philosophical Quarterly* 12 (1975), p. 27.) Most significantly of all, perhaps, Sartre does not see that the illusory religious belief that God can make a total difference provides some of the best evidence for the illusory character of submission to divine, or parental, authority. (In fact, in his essay "Existentialism Is a Humanism," Sartre comes close to *endorsing* the idea that God makes a total difference to human life.)

almost always also seeking to impose more intellectual, moral, and emotional baggage on the child than he needs to make his own way in the world.

But parents are not the only threat to a child's developing autonomy. Autonomy has its own risks, anxieties, and frustrations, and these can frighten a child and cause him to regress into dependency. Such a child may then desire to be taken care of again like an infant, to have others make his choices, to lose autonomy. Alternatively, if the parents themselves seek to block the child's autonomy with prohibitions, threats, or hostile accusations of ingratitude, the child may become panicky about the impending loss of his autonomy. And rather than fight his parents, who may seem practically omnipotent in his eyes, he may acquiesce in their domination. Faced with a losing battle, the child may try, defensively, to convince himself that he really didn't want to be autonomous in the first place. Or he may reason that he really has nothing to lose from his parents' domination because he has, in fact, no will of his own to be thwarted. He may welcome the loss of autonomy or imagine he never had any autonomy that could be taken away, in order to console himself for, or reconcile himself to, the loss he so greatly fears. That fear is not so much destroyed by these devices as kept out of direct awareness.

Such phenomena are not psychologically atypical or rare. It is, for example, a truism of psychiatry and a fact ordinary people are commonly aware of that an overwhelming anxiety in the face of impending death may give rise to the defensive thought-feeling that one doesn't really care if one dies, or even that one welcomes death. Similarly, when things take a dramatic turn *for the better*, people often say: I must be dreaming all this. And the explanation is fairly obvious. One tries to convince oneself that it is all a dream, and thus, that one has nothing to lose, in order to counteract and submerge one's fears of losing what one has suddenly gained and to soften the blow if one *does* lose it. And this is very close to what happens when a child who faces a loss of autonomy imagines he has no will of his own.

I think, then, that when children accept parental authority without question, even after they have arrived at a stage where they desire considerable autonomy for themselves, a kind of regression has occurred as a means of alleviating anxiety—anxiety at the frustrations of autonomy itself, anxiety over parental attempts to thwart the child's desires for autonomy, and perhaps other forms of anxiety as well. This regression involves an attempt to retreat to the stage of infancy where decisions were made for one and life was a blissful ease of dependency.[2] And to do this, one erects psychic structures of indifference to the loss of autonomy, either welcoming the loss one thinks will occur or denying that there is anything to lose. The acceptance of parental authority is such circumstances, then, is an easy retreat from threats and frustration, but it involves the illusion that one has no choice or will of one's own, a repudiation of one's real and persisting desires to be autonomous, and a certain amount of internal conflict as a result.

What I have just said, moreover, indicates that the threat power of parents lies behind, even if it is not the same as, their authority. It is their power to circumvent or coerce the child's will, their power to deprive it of the autonomy it seeks, that sends some children scurrying into the defenses and illusions that constitute submission to parental authority.[3] So, we must contrast living in fear of parental attempts to limit one's autonomy, which may involve no illusions at all, with submitting to those attempts, or to parental authority, which does. Since, in addition, the illusions involved in acquiescing in parental authority are part of the way children cope with and allay powerful anxieties, we should expect that they would resist exposure. To see that they were illusions would be to become partly free of them and thus no longer able to "use" them as part of one's psychological defenses. To protect the illusions involved in submission to authority, people often develop complicated and clever secondary rationalizations of such authority. This is the

---

[2] It is conventional psychiatric wisdom that if one's infancy was *not* very happy or tranquil, one will seek to regress to infancy when life is frustrating, in order to *make up for*, or *overcome*, that earlier lack of satisfaction.

[3] Submission to authority need not, I think, imply that there *is* an authority to whom one submits. However, it is not clear whether we should want to say that parents *lack* the authority that children attribute to them because they cannot take away their childrens' choice in the way children imagine; or whether we should not, instead, say that parents *have* authority over submissive children because to have authority is just to be in a position where others have certain habits and illusions. But whatever we decide to say about this question, we needn't conclude that there is any *validity* to parental authority of the kind we are focusing on. Authority cannot, I think, be valid when it *has to be* based on false beliefs or illusions. Cf. my "Morality and Ignorance," *Journal of Philosophy*, LXXIV (1977), pp. 745–767, for a lengthy elaboration of this and related themes.

derivative "ideology of authority" I mentioned earlier. The illusions of authority can be defended from discovery and preserved by means of a distorted intellectual picture of what submission to authority actually is. One will, for example, moralize about authority using the reasoning at the beginning of this paper. One will somehow be convinced that it is morality, and the rational acknowledgment of moral requirements, that powers one's submission to parental authority. So, the illusions intrinsic to authority naturally give rise to illusions *about* (submission to) authority— illusions that, in effect, deny the illusory character that submission to authority actually has. And these illusions about illusions serve to perpetuate the illusions they are about.[4]

3. Being Adult

What can we conclude from the fact that people so often seek an authority that involves illusions? To begin with, it may well be true that children in some measure *need* to submit to parental authority during childhood if they are later to have successful or satisfying adult lives. Perhaps the illusions of authority are "noble lies" of childhood, and it is good for children to believe such lies the way it is good for them to believe the fairy tales they hear.

But even if we need to have illusions about parental authority as children, it hardly seems likely that we are better off having such illusions when we become older. I have said that the child who submits to parental authority out of fear of parental threats to his autonomy is in a state of conflict. He retreats into dependence on his parents, yet never really loses his desire for autonomy; so, he both needs and resents his parents. He will not show that resentment for fear of retaliation, and if his parents continue to impose

---

[4] In many ways, my account of the desire for autonomy and of the ways we regress into dependency when it is threatened derives from Erich Fromm's *Escape from Freedom* (New York: Holt, 1941). But, more in the manner of Sartre, I have emphasized the illusions of authority. And Fromm not only ignores this aspect of authority but sometimes seems *himself* to fall under some of the illusions of authority I have described. He often says that when we submit to authority, we give up our freedom and individuality. And he speaks of both the annihilation and the loss of the self, in this connection. (See *Escape from Freedom*, pp. 140f., 154f., 185f., 206.) At the very least, he does not distinguish clearly enough between the *illusion* that we have no self or will of our own, an illusion involved in submitting to authority, and the (impossible) state of affairs that the illusion is *about*.

upon him well into adulthood, he may never get over his fearful submission to them. He will then frequently become the kind of parent his parents were to him—displaying to his children an aggression he could never vent against his parents. The "authoritarian personality" that often develops with submission to parental authority tends to perpetuate itself, generation after generation, and what is most clear about such continuing cycles of submission and domination is that *no one* has grown up completely. The dominating authoritarian parent acts as he does as a result of his own illusory and childish submissiveness to his parents. To become fully an adult, one has to cease submitting to the authority of one's parents—to become one's own parent, as it is said—and gain that autonomy that parents who seek to impose authority on a child may *seem to have* and that children themselves seek, but often permanently give away, before fully attaining it. If what I have been saying here is correct, the person who gains such automony will have to free himself from various illusions of authority, and from the inordinate fear of his parents that results in defensive submission to their authority and in internal conflicts between a desire for autonomy and a desire for dependence. That person will unequivocally accept his autonomy despite its risks and frustrations, and he fulfills (a great part of) my idea of what it is to be, morally speaking, an adult.[5]

Finally, I think that our culture has itself grown up to the degree that it has freed itself from various illusions of authority. There is evidence of this maturation, for example, in the present powerlessness of the argument with which we began. That we no longer see any need to believe in the child's moral obligation to obey his parents shows, it seems to me, that our culture no longer encourages as much submission to parental authority as it used to. Some of the illusions of parental authority are now harder to foster and maintain. Perhaps the development and spread of political democracy has aided the discovery of the illusions of parental and divine authority. When the authority of kings came into question, it perhaps became easier to recognize the illusions, rationalizations,

●

---

[5] To the degree, moreover, that submission to divine authority—as opposed to simple belief in or fear of God—involves similar illusions, resentments, and conflicts, adulthood may be incompatible with religious submissiveness of the sort I have been describing.

and conflicts inherent in other kinds of submission to authority. I hope, however, that I am under no illusions about the "progress" that has been made in discarding the illusions connected with authority. I do not doubt that the insights that have been developed are very frail reeds, pawns to future history and to the very needs and fears that so often give rise to submission to authority. I do not, then, believe that further progress in this area is inevitable, and sadly enough, it seems quite possible that our insight into the illusions of authority and our greater present freedom from submission to authority should someday, somehow, be lost.[6]

STUDY QUESTIONS

1. Do you agree with Slote that you have no moral duty to show gratitude for benefits you never requested?
2. Do you think children have a moral duty to obey their parents?
3. Does Slote's position entail that all authority is an illusion?
4. Throughout this article, Slote presumes a widespread decline in the number of people who believe in God. Yet studies show that, in the United States, almost 90% of the adult population profess that they do believe in God. Will Slote's arguments against authority convince the majority who believe in some form of divine authority?
5. Explain Slote's account of how children develop illusions of "choicelessness" and "will-lessness."
6. Sociologists distinguish between power and authority: Power is the ability to command, backed up by force (real or imagined); authority is competence or know-how based on experience and wisdom. Does Slote confuse authority with power?

---

[6] I am indebted to Arthur Fine, the editors of this book, and, especially, Hans Kleinschmidt and David Levin, for helpful criticisms and suggestions.

Lying to Children

SISSELA BOK

Sissela Bok, who teaches ethics at the Harvard Medical School, has written extensively in the area of applied ethics. Her published works include *Lying: Moral Choice in Public and Private Life* (1978) and *Secrets* (1983).

To act paternalistically is to guide or force people into a course of action *for their own good*. When parents make an unwilling child take vitamins or put on a coat before going outside, they act paternalistically. Lying to children is often justified by paternalism: Parents will lie to children to protect them from frightening news, or to keep them from hurting themselves. But Bok points out that parents' motives for lying to children are not always purely benevolent. They may lie to avoid an unpleasant confrontation, or for convenience. But they pay a serious price for such lies. If children discover that their parents have lied to them, the parents may lose the children's trust. Parents may also injure themselves by their lies, for keeping lies in good repair usually requires bolstering them with a few more lies. Bok advises parents to use lies very sparingly—only on occasions when force is justified (for example, to lure a child out of a burning house). Bok recommends a test for determining whether a particular lie is justified: The prospective liar should ask, Would the deceived, "if completely able to judge [their] own best interests," consent to being deceived? But she warns that this, too, can be morally risky.

Conquest, birth, and voluntary offer: by these three methods, said Hobbes, can one person become subjected to another.[1] So long as questions are not asked—as when power is thought divinely granted or ordained by nature—the right to coerce and manipulate is taken for granted. Only when this right is challenged does the need for justification arise. It becomes necessary to ask: When *can* authority be justly exercised—over a child for instance? And the answer given by paternalism is that such authority is at the very least justified when it is exercised over persons for their own good.

To act paternalistically is to guide and even coerce people in order to protect them and serve their best interests, as a father might his children. He must keep them out of harm's way, by force if necessary. If a small child wants to play with matches or drink ammonia, parents must intervene. Similarly, those who want to ride motorcycles are forced in many states to wear helmets for their own protection. And Odysseus asked to be tied to the mast of his ship when approaching the Sirens, who were "weaving a haunting song across the sea,"[2] bidding his sailors to take more turns of the rope to muffle him should he cry or beg to be untied. Paternalistic restraints may be brief and self-imposed, as in the case of Odysseus, or of much longer duration, and much less voluntary.[3]

Among the most thoroughgoing paternalistic proposals ever made were those of Johann Peter Frank, often called the Father of Public Health,[4] in eighteenth-century Germany. In his six-volume *System for a Complete Medical Policing* he proposed ways to "prevent

---

[1]Thomas Hobbes, *De Corpore Politico*, in *Body, Man, and Citizen: Selections from Thomas Hobbes*, ed. Richard Peters (New York: Collier Books, 1962), p. 330.

[2]Homer, *Odyssey* 12. 226.

[3]See John Stuart Mill, "On Liberty," in *The Philosophy of John Stuart Mill*, ed. Marshall Cohen, pp. 185–319, and Gerald Dworkin, "Paternalism," in R. Wasserstrom, ed., *Morality and the Law* (Belmont, Cal.: Wadsworth Publishing Company, 1971), pp. 107–126, for discussions of the problems of paternalism.

[4]See Leona Baumgartner and Elizabeth Mapelsden Ramsey, "Johann Peter Frank and His 'System einer vollständigen medizinischen Polizei,' " *Annals of Medical History* n.s. 5 (1933): 525–32, and n.s. 6: 69–90.

evils through wise ordinances." Laws should be passed, he argued, in every case where they might further the health of citizens. Sexual practices, marriages, and child rearing were to be regulated in the smallest detail; a law should be passed to prohibit the tight clothing women wore, if it interfered with their respiration; control of disease should be attempted in every village. Frank even suggested a law to require those who had been to a country dance to rest before leaving, lest the cool evening air give them a cold after their exertions.

The need for some paternalistic restraints is obvious. We survive only if protected from harm as children. Even as adults, we tolerate a number of regulations designed to reduce dangers such as those of infection or accidents. But it is equally obvious that the intention of guarding from harm has led, both through mistake and through abuse, to great suffering. The "protection" can suffocate; it can also exploit. Throughout history, men, women, and children have been compelled to accept degrading work, alien religious practices, institutionalization, and even wars alleged to "free" them, all in the name of what someone has declared to be their own best interest. And deception may well have outranked force as a means of subjection: duping people to conform, to embrace ideologies and cults—never more zealously perpetrated than by those who believe that the welfare of those deceived is at issue.

1. Paternalistic Deception

Deception among family members and friends is the form of paternalism in which most of us encounter the hardest choices between truthfulness and lying. We may never have to worry about whether to lie in court or as experimenters or journalists; but in our families, with our friends, with those whose well-being matters most to us, lies can sometimes seem the only way not to injure or disappoint.

Lies to protect these bonds carry a special sense of immediacy and appropriateness. Children are often deceived with the fewest qualms. They, more than all others, need care, support, protection. To shield them, not only from brutal speech and frightening news, but from apprehension and pain—to soften and embellish and disguise—is as natural as to shelter them from harsh weather. Because they are more vulnerable and more impressionable than adults, they cannot always cope with what they hear. Their efforts, however rudimentary, need encouragement and concern, rather than "objective" evaluation. Unvarnished facts, thoughtlessly or maliciously conveyed, can hurt them, even warp them, render them callous in self-defense.

But even apart from shielding and encouragement, strict accuracy is simply not very high on the list of essentials in speaking with children. With the youngest ones especially, the sharing of stories and fairy tales, of invention and play can suggest, in Erik Erikson's words,[5] at its best "some virgin chance conquered, some divine leeway shared"—leaving the conventionally "accurate" and "realistic" far behind.

A danger arises whenever those who deal with children fall into the familiar trap of confusing "truth" and "truthfulness." It may lead them to confuse fiction and jokes and all that departs from fact with lying. And so they may lose track of what it means to respect children enough to be honest with them. To lie to children then comes to seem much like telling stories to them or like sharing their leaps between fact and fancy. Such confusion fails to recognize the fact that fiction does not *intend* to mislead, that it calls for what Coleridge called a "willing suspension of disbelief," which is precisely what is absent in ordinary deception.

Equally destructive are those dour adults who draw the opposite conclusion from their confusion of fiction and deception and who try to eradicate both from the lives of their children. They fear what they take to be the unreality and falsity of fairy tales. They see lies and perversion in the stories children tell. They stifle every expression of imagination at crushing costs to their families and to themselves.[6]

Another reason for paternalistic deception stems from the very

---

[5]Erik Erikson, *Toys and Reasons* (New York: W. W. Norton & Co., 1977), p. 17.

For lying in childhood and children's views of lying, see Sigmund Freud, "Infantile Mental Life: Two Lies Told by Children." *Collected Papers*, ed. James Strachey (London: Hogarth Press, 1950), pp. 144–49; Jean Piaget, "Lying," *The Moral Judgment of the Child* (New York: Collier Books, 1962), pp. 139–96; Guy Durandin, *Les fondements du mensonge*, thesis, Faculté des Lettres et Sciences Humaines, Paris, 1970. For a developmental theory of the growth of moral judgment in children, see Lawrence Kohlberg, "The Development of Children's Orientations Toward a Moral Order: I. Sequence in the Development of Moral Thought," *Vita Humana* 6 (1963): 11–33, and subsequent writings.

[6]For a discussion of the role of fairy tales in child development, see Bruno Bettelheim, *The Uses of Enchantment* (New York: Alfred A. Knopf, 1976).

desire to *be* honest with children or those of limited understanding. In talking to them, one may hope to produce, for their own good, as adequate an idea of what is at stake as possible, so that they will be able to respond "appropriately"—neither too casually nor too intensely if it is a present danger, and without excessive worry if it is a future danger. The truth will then be bent precisely so as to convey what the speaker thinks is the right "picture"; it will compensate for the inexperience or the fears of the listener, much as raising one's voice helps in speaking to the hard of hearing and translation conveys one's meaning into another language.

Such "translation" into language the child can understand may seem very wide of the mark to bystanders, yet not be intended to deceive in the least, merely to evoke appropriate response. But it can, of course, be mixed with deception—to play down, for instance, dangers about which nothing can be done, or to create, conversely, some terror in the child to make sure he stays away from dangers he *can* do something to avoid. In this way, parents may tell a child that medicine won't taste bad, or that dressing a wound won't hurt. And they may exaggerate the troubles that befall those who don't eat the "right" foods. In each case, part of what the child learns is that grownups bend the truth when it suits them.

All these factors—the need for shielding and encouragement, the low priority on accuracy, and the desire to get meaningful information across in spite of difficulties of understanding or response—contribute to the ease with which children are deceived. Milton expressed the tolerance so commonly granted to misleading the young and the incapacitated:

> What man in his senses would deny that there are those whom we have the best grounds for considering that we ought to deceive—as boys, madmen, the sick, the intoxicated . . . ?[7]

---

[7]Milton's list of obvious targets for deception, as quoted by Cardinal John Henry Newman in *Apologia Pro Vita Sua: Being a History of His Religious Opinions* (London: Longmans Green & Co., 1880), p. 274, also included "enemies, men in error, and thieves." See also Erasmus, *Responsio ad Albertum Pium, Opera Omnia* vol. 9 (Leiden, 1706; reprinted Hildescheim, 1962), Hugo Grotius, *On the Law of War and Peace*, bk. 3, chap. 1, trans. Francis W. Kelsey (Indianapolis: Bobbs-Merrill Co., 1925); H. Sidgwick, *The Methods of Ethics*, p. 316, "nor do I perceive that any one shrinks from telling fictions to children on matters upon which it is thought well that they should not know the truth."

Following Grotius, many have taken the step of arguing that children can be deceived because they have no right to truthful information in the first place. Since children have no "liberty of judgment" with respect to what is said to them, one cannot wrong them or infringe on their liberty by lying to them.

Whatever we may conclude about the rightness of paternalistic lying at exceptional times, the argument that it is all right to lie to children and to the incompetent simply *because* they belong to these groups is clearly untenable. Someone who lied to harm a child would surely be more to blame, not less, because the victim could not fully understand the danger. Children can be wronged by lies as much as, or more than, others. And liars themselves can be as injured by lying to children as to all others. Finally, the lie to a child often turns out to affect his family as well, either because family members participate in the deceit or because they are themselves deceived.

But not only children and those in need of care are deceived on paternalistic grounds. We may weigh the same questions with respect to adults who are close to us or for whom we have some special responsibility—as teachers sometimes deceive their students in order not to hurt them, or as colleagues flatter failing judges that their acuteness is undiminished. We may express—falsely—assurance, approval, or love, to those who seek it so as not to let them down. This is especially likely in existing relationships, where a close bond is taken for granted—at work, for example, or between friends. To keep up appearances, to respect long-standing commitments, to refrain from wounding, lies are told which disguise and protect.

Even if an open rejection does not take place—as when an applicant is denied work, a request for money is turned down, an offer of marriage refused—paternalistic lies may be told to conceal the real reasons for the rejection, to retain the civility of the interaction, and to soften the blow to the self-respect of the rejected. It is easier to say that one cannot do something, or that the rules do not allow it, than that one does not want to do it; easier to say that there is no market for a writer's proposed book than that it is unreadable; or that there is no opening for the job seeker than that he lacks the necessary skills.

All such deceptive practices claim benevolence, concern for the deceived. Yet in looking at them, the discrepancy of perspectives stands out once again. We can share the desire to protect and to support that guides so many paternalistic lies; and recognize the importance of not using the truth as a weapon, even inadvertently. But from the perspective of the deceived, the power of paternalistic deception carries many dangers. Problems may go unexplored, as for the mother who was deceived about her suitability as a donor for the kidney her daughter so desperately needed. False hopes may be maintained, as for graduate students who have spent long years studying without ever being told that they could not hope to advance in their fields or even find employment. Unnecessary resentments may linger, as for the boy who was told that his sister was to blame for what an illness had caused. And eroded marriages and friendships may wear away further in the absence of an opportunity for the deceived to take stock of the situation.

One reason for the appeal of paternalistic lies is that they, unlike so much deception, are felt to be without bias and told in a disinterested wish to be helpful to fellow human beings in need. On closer examination, however, this objectivity and disinterest are often found to be spurious. The benevolent motives claimed by liars are then seen to be mixed with many others much less altruistic—the fear of confrontation which would accompany a more outspoken acknowledgement of the liar's feelings and intentions; the desire to avoid setting in motion great pressures to change, as where addiction or infidelity are no longer concealed; the urge to maintain the power that comes with duping others (never greater than when those lied to are defenseless or in need of care). These are motives of self-protection and of manipulation, of wanting to retain control over a situation and to remain a free agent. So long as the liar does not see them clearly, his judgment that his lies are altruistic and thus excused is itself biased and unreliable.

The perspective of the deceived, then, challenges the "helpfulness" of many paternalistic lies. It questions, moreover, even the benefits that are thought to accrue to the liar. The effects of deception on the liars themselves—the need to shore up lies, keeping them in good repair, the anxieties relating to possible discovery, the entanglements and threats to integrity—are greatest in a close relationship where it is rare that one lie will suffice. It can be very hard to maintain the deceit when one is in close contact with those one lies to. The price of "living a lie" often turns out not even to have been worth the gains for the liars themselves.

2. Justification?

Are there (other) ways to sort out the few justifiable paternalistic lies, if they exist, from the many abuses of paternalism? A first possibility is to take into account the frequent parallels between force and deception: Is lying for paternalistic reasons justified whenever force is?

In a crisis, to be sure, where an innocent life is threatened, and other alternatives have been exhausted, deception would certainly seem to be warranted to the extent that force is. Both might, for example, be justified in rescuing a child too frightened to leave a burning building. Carrying him out by force, or falsely saying there is no risk in running out, might both be justified. But the parallel is not complete. The very fact that paternalism so often thrives in families and in other relationships of closeness and dependence has a special effect on the choice between manipulation by force and by deception. These relationships require more trust than most others, and over a longer period of time. As a result, whereas in many crises such as that of a murderer seeking his victim, it may be as good or better to lie than to attempt force, the opposite may well be the case in family crises and wherever trust obtains.

Consider, for example, two parents trying to keep a small child from falling into a pond. They may try distraction or persuasion and resort to force if these do not succeed. But what if they choose instead to tell the child there are monsters in the pond? While such a tale might effectively avoid the danger of drowning and save the parents a certain amount of physical exertion, the strategy does not bode well for the family in the long run. (If, on the other hand, the parents were too far away, or unable to move to lift the child away, deception might be acceptable as a last resort.)

Not only does paternalistic concern for those to whom we are close not *add* a new excuse to those few [that may be acceptable] such as lies in crises, truly white lies, or lies where the deceived have given their consent. On the contrary, the very closeness of the bonds turns out to *limit* the justifiability even of lies in those narrow categories. Crises, as we have just seen, should call forth paternalistic deception only if persuasion and force are useless.[8] And

---

[8]Daniel Pekarski, in "Manipulation and Education" (Ph.D. diss., Harvard University, 1976), discusses such choices as they arise in education.

trivial lies mount up within families, among neighbors, close friends, and those who work together as they never can among more casual acquaintances. They can thus gather a momentum they would not otherwise have. For all such lies, there is the added harm to the relationship itself to be considered, and the fact that, as some of the lies come to be discovered, the liar will have to live with the resultant loss in trust at close hand.

Most problematic of all is the status of *consent* in paternalistic lying. It is rare that children, friends, or spouses will have consented in advance to being deceived for their own good. A variation of the requirement for consent is therefore sometimes brought forth: implied consent. Some day, this argument holds, those who are rightly deceived will be grateful for the restraints imposed upon them for their own good. And those who are wrongly deceived will not. This expectation of future gratitude is likened to the ordinary consent given in advance of an action in the following way: If those who are now being deceived for what is truly their own good were completely rational, sane, adult, or healthy, they would consent to what is being done for them.[9] If they were in the liar's position, they, too, would choose to lie out of this altruistic concern.

Can "implied consent" be used as a test of all the paternalistic lies told—in crises, under more trivial circumstances, to shelter or encourage or heal? It would then close the gap between the perspectives of liar and deceived; their aims—to benefit the deceived—would coincide. The way to tell rightful paternalistic lies from all the others would then be to ask whether the deceived, if completely able to judge his own best interests, would himself want to be duped. If he becomes rational enough to judge at a later time, one could then ask whether he gives his retroactive consent to the deceit—whether he is grateful he was lied to.

Sometimes the answer to such questions is clear. If someone asks in advance to be lied to or restrained, consent can often be assumed. Odysseus asked to be tied with ropes; some patients ask their doctors not to reveal an unhappy prognosis. At other times, there

---

[9]See Dworkin, "Paternalism," and John Rawls, *A Theory of Justice* (Cambridge, Mass.: Harvard University Press, Belknap Press, 1971), pp. 209, 249, for mentions of this form of implied consent in paternalistic contexts. See also Grotius, *On the Law of War and Peace.*

has been no prior consent, but every reasonable person would want to be thwarted, even lied to, for his own good. A temporarily deranged person who asks for a knife, or the child paralyzed with fear who has to be cajoled and lured out of a burning house, will not question the integrity of those who lied to them, once their good judgment has returned.

The questions work equally well to rule out cases where no one would give genuine consent to certain forms of coercion merely labeled paternalistic. To be incarcerated in mental hospitals in order to "help" one overcome political disagreement with a regime, for instance, is a fate for which there is no implied consent; and retroactive consent to such treatment is no longer free—it is the sign of a broken spirit.

But many times it is not so clear whether or not a rational person might at some future time give consent to having been deceived. Paternalistic lies are so often told in very private circumstances, where intricate webs of longstanding dissimulation make it hard to sort out what is a realistic alternative, whether the deceived is in fact not able to cope with the truth, what will benefit or harm, even what is a lie in the first place.

Should parents, for example, who have adopted a child, pretend to him that they are his biological parents?[10] Should a critically ill wife, afraid of her husband's inability to cope, lie to him about her condition? If one looks at the many lies which have been told—and lived—to conceal these matters, the consequences of telling the truth are not at all uniform. Most, if told the truth, might well agree that they prefer to know; but some would grieve, and wish that they had never been told.

Except in very clear cases, where all would *agree* to consent or to refuse consent, relying on implied consent is very different from having actual consent. Actual consent makes false statements no longer deceptive, as in a game to which the players have consented; the same cannot be said of implied consent. Whether or not one believes that such consent will be given, one must therefore still ask whether the lie is otherwise justified. The bond between liar and deceived does not in itself justify paternalistic lies, nor does the liar's belief in his good intentions, in the inability of the deceived to

---

[10] The current practice is to encourage parents to be open about this fact to an adopted child.

act reasonably if told the truth, and in the implied consent of the deceived. In assuming such consent, all the biases afflicting the liar's perspective are present in force.

If we assume the point of view of potential dupes, it becomes important to try not to fall into any predicament where others might believe that we ought to be deceived. It is possible to discuss in advance the degree of veracity that one can tolerate in a marriage, or friendship, or working relationship and to work out the ground rules well before there is much to conceal. With paternalistic lies, just as with white lies (and these often overlap), it may be difficult to eliminate from one's life all instances of duplicity; but there is no reason not to make the effort to reduce them to the extent possible, to be on the lookout for alternatives, to let it be known that one prefers to be dealt with openly. (Needless to say, however, it is as important here as with white lies not to imagine that abandoning deception must also bring with it the giving up of discretion and sensitivity.)

Such a working out of standards can succeed among spouses, friends, co-workers. But greater difficulties arise with respect to children and the retarded, who will not soon, perhaps never, reach the point where they will be able to discuss with others how honestly they want to be treated. Present consent to deceiving them is therefore difficult to obtain; and retroactive consent in the future either impossible or so distant as to be more unreliable than ever.

The difficulty for these groups is made greater still by the fact that the recourse to public debate has often worked especially poorly in protecting their interests. Eminently "reasonable" thinkers have supported the most brutal practices of manipulation and deception of the immature, the incompetent, and the irrational. Even John Stuart Mill, who spoke so powerfully for liberty, agreed that exceptions had to be made for children, those taken care of, and those "backward states in which the race itself may be considered in its nonage." He held that:

> Despotism is a legitimate mode of government in dealing with barbarians, provided the end of their improvement, and the means of justified by actually effecting that end.[11]

---

[11] Mill, "On Liberty," pp. 197–98.

The appeal to "reasonable persons" never has protected the interests of those considered outsiders, inferior, incompetent or immature. And they themselves have no way to distinguish between benevolent and malevolent motives for lying to them; nor would history give them many grounds for confidence that the benevolent motives predominate. Rather than accepting the common view, therefore, that it is somehow more justifiable to lie to children and to those the liars regard as being *like* children, special precautions are needed in order not to exploit them.

In summary, paternalistic lies, while they are easy to understand and to sympathize with at times, also carry very special risks: risks to the liar himself from having to lie more and more in order to keep up the appearance among people he lives with or sees often, and thus from the greater likelihood of discovery and loss of credibility; risks to the relationship in which the deception takes place; and risks of exploitation of every kind for the deceived.

STUDY QUESTIONS

1. When, according to Bok, is lying to children permissible? Do you find her position reasonable?
2. What would Bok say about the following cases of lying to children? Do you agree with her?
   (a) telling five-year-olds that Santa Claus exists
   (b) telling twelve-year-olds that cigarette smoking will stunt their growth
   (c) telling twelve-year-olds that they are not adopted when they are
   (d) telling nine-year-olds that you cannot stop at McDonald's because you have no money, though you do
   (e) telling twelve-year-olds that a dying parent is going to be fine
3. What significance does Bok attach to the notion of "implied consent" where lying is concerned?
4. Is lying to children acceptable in cases where you are quite sure they will be grateful to you someday for the lie? Can the same principle sometimes justify lying to adults?

Divorce

REBECCA WEST

Rebecca West (1892–1982) was one of the foremost figures in twentieth-century Anglo-American intellectual life. Her work, which includes fiction, criticism, biography, history, and travel reporting, is admired for its wit, eloquence, and intellectual power.

In her essay on divorce, Rebecca West assumes that the family is a vital institution. This raises a question: Should we preserve the family by outlawing divorce even at the cost of individual happiness? West's answer is a qualified no. She describes the harmful effects of divorce on children, effects of a "radiating kind, likely to travel down and down through the generations, such as few would care to have on their consciences." Conversely, she notes that, sometimes, remaining with a brutal parent can be even more harmful. West also argues in favor of the right to divorce because countries that do not allow it are often oppressive and sexually hypocritical.

The way one looks at divorce depends on the way one looks at a much broader question.

Is the mental state of humanity so low that it is best to lay down invariable rules for it which have been found to lead to the greatest

DIVORCE From *The London Daily Express*, 1930. Reprinted by permission of A. D. Peters & Co. Ltd.

happiness of the greatest number, and insist that everyone keep them in spite of the hardship necessarily inflicted on certain special cases, thus dragooning the majority into compulsory happiness? Or is it so high that it is safe to lay down rules which will admit of variation for different people in different circumstances, when it seems to them these variations can secure their happiness?

If one agrees with the first view, then one is bound to disapprove altogether of divorce. If one agrees with the second, then one is bound to approve of legislation which enables unhappily married persons to separate and remarry.

Though I have the kind of temperament that hates to own failure and would never wish to break a marriage I had made, I regard divorce laws as a necessary part of the arrangements in a civilized State. This is the result of my experience of life in countries where there is practically no divorce, and in countries where divorce is permissible on grounds of varying latitude.

Superficially the case against divorce is overwhelming: and indeed it should never be forgotten, least of all by those who approve of divorce as a possibility. Getting a divorce is nearly always as cheerful and useful an occupation as breaking very valuable china. The divorce of married people with children is nearly always an unspeakable calamity. It is only just being understood, in the light of modern psychological research, how much a child depends for its healthy growth on the presence in the home of both its parents. This is not a matter of its attitude to morals; if divorce did nothing more than make it accustomed to the idea of divorce, then no great harm would be done. The point is that if a child is deprived of either its father or its mother it feels that it has been cheated out of a right. It cannot be reasoned out of this attitude, for children are illogical, especially where their affections are concerned, to an even greater degree than ourselves. A child who suffers from this resentment suffers much more than grief: he is liable to an obscuring of his vision, to a warping of his character. He may turn against the parent to whom the courts have given him, and regard him or her as responsible for the expulsion of the other from the home. He may try to compensate himself for what he misses by snatching everything else he can get out of life, and become selfish and even thievish. He may, through yearning for the unattainable parent, get himself into a permanent mood of discontent, which will last his life long and make him waste every opportunity of love and happiness that comes to him later.

If either parent remarries, the child may feel agonies of jealousy. What is this intruder coming in and taking affection when already there is not as much as there ought to be? This is an emotion that is felt by children even in the case of fathers and mothers who have lost their partners by death: as witness the innumerable cases of children who come up before the Juvenile Courts and prove on examination to have committed their offences as acts of defiance against perfectly inoffensive and kindly step-parents. It is felt far more acutely in the case of parents whose relationships have been voluntarily severed, who have no excuse of widowhood or widowerhood to justify the introduction of a new partner. This, of course, need not always happen. One of the happiest homes I can think of is the second venture of a man and a woman who both divorced their first partners as a result of conduct that poisoned not only their lives but their children's: it is one of the most cheerful sights I know to see their combined family of four children realizing with joy and surprise that actually they can have a family life like other people. But that man and that woman are not only kindly people, they are clever people. They handle the children with extreme sensitiveness to the issues involved. More commonly the situation for the child is not completely salved.

In fact, people with children who divorce husbands or wives because they are troublesome are likely to find themselves saddled with rather more discontent than they hoped to escape. And the new trouble is of a radiating kind, likely to travel down and down through the generations, such as few would care to have on their consciences.

As for the divorce of childless married couples, there is of course a matter of infinitely less social significance. If it is regarded too lightly it cheats a lot of them out of their one chance of happiness. A man and woman marry each other because they represent to each other the types they have always found attractive and about which they have spun innumerable romantic dreams. They then grow disappointed with each other because they insist on being themselves, the human beings they happened to be born, instead of the dreamed-of types. If they stay together it may in time penetrate to each that the other may not have the qualities of the imagined one, but may have real and valuable virtues which are much more useful; and a very kindly feeling of attachment may develop. But if a couple break up during the first shock of disappointment they are certain to go off and immediately find other people who resemble the dreamed-of types, marry them, and go through the same process of disillusionment, ending in another separation. Thus a whole group of people will be involved in sterile and inharmonious excitements which will waste the very short time we are given to establish ourselves in fruitful and harmonious relationships

Against these considerations, of course, we have to reckon that although the consequences of being the child of divorced parents are heavy, they are sometimes not so heavy as the consequences of being a child brought up in close propinquity and at the mercy of a brutal and vicious parent. We have also to admit that in the case of a childless couple there may be reasons why a divorce may become as essential to a human being's continued existence as food or air. There is infidelity, there is drunkenness, there is, above all, cruelty, not only of the body but of the mind. No one who has not been through it can know the full horror of being tied to a man who craves war instead of peace, whose love is indistinguishable from hate. The day that is poisoned from its dawn by petty rages about nothing, by a deliberate destruction of everything pleasant: the night that is full of fear, because it is certain that no one can suffer all this without going mad, and if one goes mad there will be nobody to be kind; these are things to which no human being should have a life sentence.

But brutal and vicious parents are in a minority. Human nature is not so bad as all that. The opponents of divorce are therefore justified when they ask if it is not dangerous to give the victims of this minority the power to free themselves from these burdens that cannot be borne, when that power will inevitably be available to those who want to free themselves from burdens that they only think cannot be borne. For human beings are stupid; they do not know what is best for them, they certainly will not use that power wisely. If the majority is to suffer unnecessarily from these facilities for divorce, would it not be better to withdraw and let the minority fend for itself?

I do not think so. Because there is another element involved; and that is the general attitude of the community toward sex. That

505

seems to be invariably less sane where there is no divorce than where there is. What makes humanity stupid is that it will act on certain mad fairy-tales about life which it refuses to outgrow, and its attitude to sex determines all these mad fairy-tales.

The lack of divorce corrupts the community's attitude to sex for several reasons. First of all, it deprives marriage of all standards. If one cannot be penalized for failure in an activity, and the prizes for success in it are of a highly rarefied and spiritual nature, the baser man will regard it as a go-as-you-please affair. The man who knows that he can commit adultery without the slightest check from society will have to be a very high type if he does not come to the conclusion that, since society is so indifferent to it, adultery must be a trivial matter. But his natural jealousy will not permit him to think like that of his wife's adultery. That he will punish in all of the very extensive ways which are open to him through his economic power.

Thus there starts the fictitious system of morality which, instead of regarding sexual conduct as a means to an end, and that end the continuance of the species in the most harmonious conditions, places purely arbitrary values on different sexual entities and plays a game with them like Mah-Jong. Since a man's adultery does not matter and a woman's adultery does, it follows that a man's whole sexual life is without moral significance, and a woman's sexual life is portentous with it. Whenever you have no divorce laws you must have the double standard of morality. Consequently a large part of the male sex, as much as is not controlled by idealism, roves about the world trying with complete impunity to persuade the female sex to a course of action which, should the female comply, leads them to disaster. The seducer, it must be noted, has an enormous advantage in countries where there is no divorce. Even in England, we sometimes come across a Don Juan who has the luck to have a wife who will not divorce him, and note how useful he finds this in persuading ladies that he loves them. He can so safely say that he would marry them if he could, without danger that his bluff will be called. Every Don Juan enjoys this advantage in a country where there is no divorce. Illegitimate births follow which—because of the arbitrary distinction between the sexes—are not robbed of their sting as they are in the countries where divorce is possible by laws that guarantee the offspring its maintenance, but result in the persecution of mother and child.

In fact, sex is associated with cruelty in countries where there is no divorce, as it is in the institution of prostitution: this also flourishes wherever there is this double standard of morality. No illicit love affair, where both parties are exercising free choice, can possibly do the community as much harm as the traffic between the prostitute and her client. That a woman should be held in contempt for submitting to the same physical relationship that is the core of marriage degrades marriage, and all women, and all men; and the greater the contempt she is held in the more she becomes genuinely contemptible. For as she sinks lower she becomes more and more a source of disease, and more and more a brutalized machine. It is in countries where there is no divorce that the prostitute is most firmly established as the object of extra-marital adventures and is most deeply despised.

One can test this by its converse if one goes to a library and turns up old comic papers and plays, particularly farces. As the law and society began to sanction divorce, and impressed on the public a sense of moral obligation, this ceased to be the case.

It is one of the most important things in the world that people should have a sane and kindly outlook on sex; that it should not be associated with squalor and cruelty. Because divorce makes it clear to the ordinary man and woman that they must behave well in the married state or run the risk of losing its advantages, it does impress on them some rudiments of a sane attitude towards sex. It therefore lifts up the community to a level where happy marriages, in which the problem of our human disposition to cruelty and jealousy is satisfactorily solved, are much more likely to occur.

STUDY QUESTIONS

1. Rebecca West says that "people with children who divorce husbands or wives because they are troublesome are likely to find themselves saddled with rather more discontent than they hoped to escape. And the new trouble is of a radiating kind, likely to travel down and down through the generations, such as few would care to have on their consciences." Can West be consistent in permitting divorce, given her views on its ill effects?

2. Why does West believe that lack of divorce has a corrupting effect on a society? Do you agree that the human cost of permitting divorce is lower than the cost of outlawing it?
3. West notes that children suffer from the effects of divorce through several generations. If this is so, wouldn't prohibiting divorce be morally right in those cases where one or both parents do not brutalize the children? Why, after all, should parents be allowed to inflict a divorce on their innocent children?

Humanae Vitae

POPE PAUL VI

Pope Paul VI (1897–1978) was the 262nd Pontiff of the Roman Catholic Church. He served from 1963 to 1978.

In the *Humanae Vitae*, Pope Paul presents some of the traditional reasons for Catholic prohibition of contraception. The Church permits the act of conjugal love in the context of marriage. Pope Paul quotes the Vatican Council as saying, "Marriage and conjugal love are by their nature ordained toward the begetting and educating of children." Viewed in this light, the pope assigns two purposes to the "marriage act"; procreation and union of the partners. To intentionally render a conjugal act "infecund" violates the first purpose. On the other hand, the unitive purpose leaves room for conjugal acts during infertile periods. Pope Paul argues that use of artificial contraception increases the potential for marital infidelity and a "general lowering of morality" and may cause sexual partners to lose respect for one another. In its opposition to contraception, the pope argues that the Church defends "conjugal morality," thereby contribut-

HUMANAE VITAE NC News translation as published by The Catholic Free Press, Worcester, Mass.

ing to the establishment of a truly human civilization that assures the dignity of husband and wife and protects the family.

Conjugal Love

Conjugal love reveals its true nature and nobility, when it is considered in its supreme origin, God, who is love, "the Father, from whom every family in heaven and on earth is named."

Marriage is not, then, the effect of chance or the product of evolution of unconscious natural forces; it is the wise institution of the Creator to realize in mankind His design of love. By means of the reciprocal personal gift of self, proper and exclusive to them, husband and wife tend towards the communion of their beings in view of mutual personal perfection, to collaborate with God in the generation and education of new lives.

For baptized persons, moreover, marriage invests the dignity of a sacramental sign of grace, inasmuch as it represents the union of Christ and of the Church.

Its Characteristics

Under this light, there clearly appear the characteristic marks and demands of conjugal love, and it is of supreme importance to have an exact idea of these.

This love is first of all fully human, that is to say, of the senses and of the spirit at the same time. It is not, then, a simple transport of instinct and sentiment, but also, and principally, an act of the free will, intended to endure and to grow by means of the joys and sorrows of daily life, in such a way that husband and wife become only one heart and only one soul, and together attain their human perfection.

Then, this love is total, that is to say, it is a very special form of personal friendship, in which husband and wife generously share everything, without undue reservations or selfish calculations. Whoever truly loves his marriage partner loves not only for what he receives, but for the partner's self, rejoicing that he can enrich his partner with the gift of himself.

509

Again, this love is faithful and exclusive until death. Thus in fact, do bride and groom conceive it to be on the day when they freely and in full awareness assume the duty of the marriage bond. A fidelity, this, which can sometimes be difficult, but is always possible, always noble and meritorious, as no one can deny. The example of so many married persons down through the centuries shows, not only that fidelity is according to the nature of marriage, but also that it is a source of profound and lasting happiness and finally, this love is fecund for it is not exhausted by the communion between husband and wife, but is destined to continue, raising up new lives. "Marriage and conjugal love are by their nature ordained toward the begetting and educating of children. Children are really the supreme gift of marriage and contribute very substantially to the welfare of their parents.

Responsible Parenthood

Hence conjugal love requires in husband and wife an awareness of their mission of "responsible parenthood," which today is rightly much insisted upon, and which also must be exactly understood. Consequently it is to be considered under different aspects which are legitimate and connected with one another.

In relation to the biological processes, responsible parenthood means the knowledge and respect of their functions; human intellect discovers in the power of giving life biological laws which are part of the human person.

In relation to the tendencies of instinct or passion, responsible parenthood means that necessary dominion which reason and will must exercise over them.

In relation to physical, economic, psychological and social conditions, responsible parenthood is exercised, either by the deliberate and generous decision to raise a large family, or by the decision, made for grave motives and with due respect for the moral law, to avoid for the time being, or even for an indeterminate period, a new birth.

Responsible parenthood also and above all implies a more profound relationship to the objective moral order established by God, of which a right conscience is the faithful interpreter. The responsible exercise of parenthood implies, therefore, that husband and wife recognize fully their own duties towards God, towards themselves, towards the family and towards society, in a correct hierarchy of values.

In the task of transmitting life, therefore, they are not free to proceed completely at will, as if they could determine in a wholly autonomous way the honest path to follow; but they must conform their activity to the creative intention of God, expressed in the very nature of marriage and of its acts, and manifested by the constant teaching of the Church.

Respect for the Nature and Purpose of the Marriage Act

These acts, by which husband and wife are united in chaste intimacy, and by means of which human life is transmitted, are, as the council recalled, "noble and worthy," and they do not cease to be lawful if, for causes independent of the will of husband and wife, they are foreseen to be infecund, since they always remain ordained towards expressing and consolidating their union. In fact, as experience bears witness, not every conjugal act is followed by a new life. God has widely disposed natural laws and rhythms of fecundity which, of themselves, cause a separation in the succession of births. Nonetheless the Church, calling men back to the observance of the norms of the natural law, as interpreted by their constant doctrine, teaches that each and every marriage act (*quilibet matrimonii usus*) must remain open to the transmission of life.

Two Inseparable Aspects: Union and Procreation

That teaching, often set forth by the magisterium, is founded upon the inseparable connection, willed by God and unable to be broken by man on his own initiative, between the two meanings of the conjugal act: the unitive meaning and the procreative meaning. Indeed, by its intimate structure, the conjugal act, while most closely uniting husband and wife, empowers them to generate new lives, according to laws inscribed in the very being of man and of woman. By safeguarding both these essential aspects, unitive and procreative, the conjugal act preserves in its fullness the sense of true mutual love and its ordination towards man's most high

511

calling to parenthood. We believe that the men of our day are particularly capable of seizing the deeply reasonable and human character of this fundamental principle.

Faithfulness to God's Design

It is in fact justly observed that a conjugal act imposed upon one's partner without regard for his or her condition and lawful desires is not a true act of love, and therefore denies an exigency of right moral order in the relationships between huband and wife. Hence, one who reflects well must also recognize that a reciprocal act of love, which jeopardizes the responsibility to transmit life which God the Creator, according to particular laws, inserted therein is in contradiction with the design constitutive of marriage, and with the will of the Author of life. To use this divine gift destroying, even if only partially, its meaning and its purpose is to contradict the nature both of man and of woman and of their most intimate relationship, and therefore, it is to contradict also the plan of God and His will. On the other hand, to make use of the gift of conjugal love while respecting the laws of the generative process means to acknowledge oneself not to be the arbiter of the sources of human life, but rather the minister of the design established by the Creator. In fact, just as man does not have unlimited dominion over his body in general, so also, with particular reason, he has no such dominion over his generative faculties as such, because of their intrinsic ordination towards raising up life, of which God is the principle. "Human life is sacred," Pope John XXIII recalled; "from its very inception it reveals the creating hand of God."

Illicit Ways of Regulating Birth

In conformity with these landmarks in the human and Christian vision of marriage, we must once again declare that the direct interruption of the generative process already begun, and, above all, directly willed and procured abortion, even if for therapeutic reason, are to be absolutely excluded as licit means of regulating birth.

Equally to be excluded, as the teaching authority of the Church has frequently declared, is direct sterilization, whether perpetual or temporary, whether of the man or of the woman. Similarly excluded is every action which, either in anticipation of the conjugal act, or in its accomplishment, or in the development of its natural consequences, proposes, whether as an end or as a means, to render procreation impossible.

To justify conjugal acts made intentionally infecund, one cannot invoke as valid reasons the lesser evil, or the fact that such acts would constitute a whole together with the fecund acts already performed or to follow later, and hence would share in one and the same moral goodness. In truth, if it is sometimes licit to tolerate a lesser evil in order to avoid a greater evil or to promote a greater good it is not licit, even for the gravest reasons, to do evil so that good may follow therefrom, that is, to make into the object of a positive act of the will something which is intrinsically disordered, and hence unworthy of the human person, even when the intention is to safeguard or promote individual, family, or social well-being. Consequently it is an error to think that a conjugal act which is deliberately made infecund and so is intrinsically dishonest could be made honest and right by the ensemble of a fecund conjugal life.

The Church, on the contrary, does not at all consider illicit the use of those therapeutic means truly necessary to cure diseases of the organism, even if an impediment to procreation, which may be foreseen, should result therefrom, provided such impediment is not, for whatever motive, directly willed.

Licitness of Recourse to Infecund Periods

To this teaching of the Church on conjugal morals, the objection is made today, as we observed earlier, that it is the prerogative of the human intellect to dominate the energies offered by irrational nature and to orientate them towards an end conformable to the good of man. Now, some may ask: in the present case, is it not reasonable in many circumstances to have recourse to artificial birth control if, thereby, we secure the harmony and peace of the family, and better conditions for the education of the children already born? To this question it is necessary to reply with clarity: the Church is the first to praise and recommend the intervention of intelligence in a function which so closely associates the rational

513

creature with his Creator; but she affirms that this must be done with respect for the order established by God.

If, then, there are serious motives to space out births, which derive from the physical or psychological condition of husband and wife, or from external conditions, the Church teaches that it is then licit to take into account the natural rhythms immanent in the generative functions, for the use of marriage in the infecund periods only, and in this way to regulate birth without offending the moral principles which have been recalled earlier.

The Church is consistent with herself when she considers recourse to the infecund periods to be licit, while at the same time condemning, as being always illicit, the use of means directly contrary to fecundation, even if such use is inspired by reasons which may appear honest and serious. In reality, there are essential differences between the two cases; in the former, the married couple make legitimate use of a natural disposition; in the latter, they impede the development of natural processes. It is true that, in the one and the other case, the married couple are in agreement in the positive will of avoiding children for plausible reasons, seeking the certainty that offspring will not arrive; but it is also true that only in the former case are they able to renounce the use of marriage in the fecund periods when, for just motives, procreation is not desirable, while making use of it during infecund periods to manifest their affection and to safeguard their mutual fidelity. By so doing, they give proof of a truly and integrally honest love.

Grave Consequences of Methods of Artificial Birth Control

Upright men can even better convince themselves of the solid grounds on which the teaching of the Church in this field is based, if they care to reflect upon the consequences of methods of artificial birth control. Let them consider, first of all, how wide and easy a road would thus be opened up towards conjugal infidelity and the general lowering of morality. Not much experience is needed in order to know human weakness, and to understand that men—especially the young, who are so vulnerable on this point—have need of encouragement to be faithful to the moral law, so that they must not be offered some easy means of eluding its observance. It is also to be feared that the man, growing used to the employment of anticonceptive practices, may finally lose respect for the woman and, no longer caring for her physical and psychological equilibrium, may come to the point of considering her as a mere instrument of selfish enjoyment, and no longer as his respected and beloved companion.

Let it be considered also that a dangerous weapon would thus be placed in the hands of those public authorities who take no heed of moral exigencies. Who could blame a government for applying to the solution of the problems of the community those means acknowledged to be licit for married couples in the solution of a family problem? Who will stop rulers from favoring, from even imposing upon their peoples, if they were to consider it necessary, the method of contraception which they judge to be most efficacious? In such a way men, wishing to avoid individual, family, or social difficulties encountered in the observance of the divine law, would reach the point of placing at the mercy of the intervention of public authorities the most personal and most reserved sector of conjugal intimacy.

Consequently, if the mission of generating life is not to be exposed to the arbitrary will of men, one must necessarily recognize unsurmountable limits to the possibility of man's domination over his own body and its functions; limits which no man, whether a private individual or one invested with authority, may licitly surpass. And such limits cannot be determined otherwise than by the respect due to the integrity of the human organism and its functions, according to the principles recalled earlier, and also according to the correct understanding of the "principle of totality" illustrated by our predecessor Pope Pius XII.

The Church Guarantor of True Human Values

It can be foreseen that this teaching will perhaps not be easily received by all: Too numerous are those voices—amplified by the modern means of propaganda—which are contrary to the voice of the Church. To tell the truth, the Church is not surprised to be made, like her divine founder, a "sign of contradiction," yet she does not because of this cease to proclaim with humble firmness the entire moral law, both natural and evangelical. Of such laws the Church was not the author, nor consequently can she be their arbiter; she is only their depositary and their interpreter, without ever being able to declare to be licit that which is not so by reason of its intimate and unchangeable opposition to the true good of man.

In defending conjugal morals in their integral wholeness, the Church knows that she contributes towards the establishment of a truly human civilization; she engages man not to abdicate from his own responsibility in order to rely on technical means; by that very face she defends the dignity of man and wife. Faithful to both the teaching and the example of the Saviour, she shows herself to be the sincere and disinterested friend of men, whom she wishes to help, even during their earthly sojourn, "to share as sons in the life of the living God, the Father of all men."

STUDY QUESTIONS

1. Do you believe that constraints on sexual activity (for example, rules against adultery or homosexuality) can be defended on purely philosophical or universal grounds, or do you believe that all such constraints are grounded in adherence to a particular religious faith or cultural tradition?
2. The pope says that "the Church is consistent with herself" in permitting conjugal acts during infertile periods. In the pope's view, how does the Church avoid the charge of inconsistency, since it also maintains that an essential purpose of the conjugal act is procreation?
3. The pope asserts that use of contraception opens a "wide and easy . . . road . . . towards conjugal infidelity and the general lowering of morality." Do you agree that promiscuity and contraception are seriously connected?
4. What arguments can you give for or against the presumption that promiscuity is itself a moral evil?

A Reply to Pope Paul's Humanae Vitae

CARL COHEN

Carl Cohen (b. 1931) is a professor of philosophy at the University of Michigan. He has published extensively in legal and social ethics and is the author of *Civil Disobedience* (1972), *Democracy* (1973), and *Four Systems* (1983).

Carl Cohen examines and criticizes the papal encyclical prohibiting contraception and tries to show that its arguments are inconclusive even if one accepts the Church's general view of marriage. Marriage, in the eyes of the Church, provides a setting in which to beget and educate children and unify the husband and wife in love. The Church considers these two purposes, the "procreative" and "unitive," inseparable (the "inseparability premise"). When people use artificial means of birth control, they defeat the purpose. The inseparability premise entails the prohibition of birth control. Cohen devotes much of his article to showing that inseparability is a dogma that cannot be defended rationally. Moreover, says Cohen, prohibition of contraception means that couples will often qualify intercourse with the fear of unwanted pregnancy, which is inconsistent with the Church's assertion that sexual intercourse is an act of "love incarnate" in which partners unreservedly

A REPLY TO POPE PAUL'S *HUMANAE VITAE* Reprinted from "Sex, Birth Control, and Human Life," *Ethics* 79:4 (July 1969), 251–262 by Carl Cohen by permission of The University of Chicago Press.

and freely give to one another. Another inconsistency is that the Church does allow the natural rhythm method of birth control. Cohen argues that using it to prevent pregnancy does not square with the doctrine that the sexual act's purpose must be procreative. The encyclical, says Cohen, also distorts the sexual act by viewing it as "a tool for the accomplishment of something else," thereby implicitly denying the intrinsic worth of human passion. Cohen criticizes the pope's claim that artificial contraception fosters infidelity and promiscuity, arguing that the pope presents no evidence for this and that fidelity essentially depends on how marital partners relate to one another. Finally, Cohen points out that the encyclical ignores the wider consequences of denying artificial means of contraception to masses of people: If the use of the encyclical is enforced on a world scale, countries possess no effective way to prevent uncontrollable and disastrous population explosion.

The 1968 encyclical letter of Pope Paul VI, *Humanae Vitae*, has caused deep dismay both within and without the Roman Catholic Church. In reaffirming categorically its absolute prohibition of all devices for birth control, the Church creates with this document a new impediment to the slowing of the rate of population growth on earth. Some underdeveloped areas of the planet, where human crowding is now extreme and the need to limit population is already desperate, are greatly influenced by the teachings of the Catholic Church. Where its prohibitions are taken seriously by poverty-stricken masses, *Humanae Vitae* will have as its direct result the discouragement of effective birth control techniques, and therefore the creation of more new lives than can be decently fed or cared for—a greater number than would be the case if the encyclical had been more enlightened. Indirectly, its foreseeable results will be more of the suffering and misery that overpopulation necessarily imposes. It is an unhappy irony that the document whose name is "human life" will reap human death as its harvest.

My present aim is not to bemoan this encyclical further but to exhibit, through an examination of its argument, the internal weakness of the moral position it presents. The practical consequences of the conclusions of *Humanae Vitae* are simply awful; the argument it provides in defense of these conclusions is equally bad.

The argument begins by establishing a foundation of doctrinal principles of a very general sort regarding the nature of marriage and of conjugal love. These principles may well be doubted by one who does not accept the teachings of the Church, but they are not at issue here. Essentially they come to this: that marriage, love, and birth must be viewed not from any narrow perspective but in the light of an integral vision of man and his vocation, both natural and supernatural. Within this vision, conjugal love is understood to flow from God Who is Love, and marriage is the deliberate institution of the Creator realizing in mankind his design of love. Through marriage husband and wife collaborate with God in the generation of new lives. In this perspective, conjugal love is understood to possess certain essential characteristics: first, that it is fully human, love of the senses and of the spirit at the same time; second, that it is an act of free will, intended to endure and grow, and leading to greater human perfection; third, that it is total, in that in it husband and wife share everything without reservation or calculation; fourth, that it is faithful and exclusive until death; and, finally, that it is fecund, destined to raise up new lives. "In the task of transmitting life, therefore," the encyclical concludes, "they [husband and wife] are not free to proceed completely at will, as if they could determine in a wholly autonomous way the honest path to follow; but they must conform their activity to the creative intention of God, expressed in the very nature of marriage and of its acts." (All citations in this article are from the official English-language version of the encyclical letter.)

These are the doctrinal foundations. I now propose to show that the specific conclusions of the encyclical regarding birth control are not (as they purport to be) the logical consequences of these general principles. Even if one does accept the Church's general views on marriage, he is not obliged by reason to accept its dogmas on birth control. . . .

How does one get from the very general doctrine holding marriage to be a free, loving, and fecund relationship to the specific dogmas regarding birth control for which *Humanae Vitae* is so widely condemned? The argument requires certain additional premises; its completed form runs something like this:

The love of husband and wife has many aspects, natural and supernatural, physical and spiritual. The act of sexual intercourse between them is the physical manifestation of their spiritual union. The act itself, therefore, has two meanings, *unitive* and *procreative*, both of which inhere in it. Joining in sex as lovers one of another, and as the creators of new life one with another, are two aspects of the same sexual act. Men have the power to *distinguish* these two aspects of sex, but no human power can rightly separate them, because *the eternal conjunction of unitive and procreative functions is willed by God.* Therefore (it is held) "each and every marriage act must remain open to the transmission of life." Any single instance of sexual intercourse that does not remain open to the conception of life destroys the meaning and purpose of that intercourse, contradicts the nature of man and woman and their love, and serves, therefore, "to contradict the plan of God and His will." Birth control, as it is normally practiced, has just this consequence and must therefore be prohibited and condemned.

It will be seen that the crucial premise, upon which the entire argument of the encyclical depends, is the claim that sexual intercourse and procreation are *universally* and *indivisibly* conjoined. This proposition must be maintained literally and in its strongest form to support the conclusion drawn: that we must condemn "every action which, either in anticipation of the conjugal act, or in its accomplishment, or in the development of its natural consequences, proposes, whether as an end or as a means, to render procreation impossible." This is the fundamental premise which must be gravely questioned: that the unitive and procreative functions of sex are conjoined in such a way as to be totally inseparable in every case.

About this premise—let us call it the inseparability premise—several things need to be said. First, it is without good foundation. Second, it is false. Third, its denial is perfectly consistent with the larger doctrines of the Catholic Church regarding marriage. Fourth, it betrays an unwholesome, essentially instrumental view of sex. Fifth, it is a premise contradicted by the Church's own view of licit birth control. Elaboration upon these claims is called for.

How is the inseparability premise defended in *Humanae Vitae*? Rational argument based on the merits of the case is not even attempted. Scriptural authority (even if it were persuasive) cannot be offered, because it does not exist. The principle—that the procreative and unitive functions of sex must be invariably conjoined—is not encountered in any standard version of the natural law, nor in the consciences of most honest men within or without the Catholic Church. . . .

. . . Papal authority, however persuasive for some Catholics, cannot constitute proof for a moderately rational man. Too often have popes proclaimed as true and binding what has later been admitted (at a time too late to remedy the injury done) to be blatantly false. . . .

The inseparability premise is false. It is hard to reach certainty in matters of this sort, of course. But granting, *arguendo*, the twofold "meaning" of sexual intercourse, its procreative and unitive functions, such evidence as experience and reflection provide would strongly suggest that in many instances it is right for these functions to be separated. . . .

. . . Most men will allow that eating, in addition to its *nutritive* function, provides certain intrinsic satisfactions that we may call *gustatory*. A good meal will be rich in protein, carbohydrates, vitamins, and so on, but will also be agreeable to the palate. Eating may fulfill these functions concurrently, but is there any moral fault in eating with the intent to separate them? Sometimes, as when one is ill, we eat for the sake of nutrition, altogether without gusto. Often we eat with the deliberate intention of avoiding additional nutriment, yet relishing the taste of the dish. Many of the foods and flavors we prize are known to be without nutritive value— mushrooms, truffles, a cup of fine tea, for examples—but we do not think it wrong to eat them.

In the sphere of sex the case is essentially no different. The pleasures, emotional as well as physical, derived from the satisfaction of an appetite may be separated rationally and without wrong-doing from the fulfillment of organic functions also possible through the satisfaction of that appetite. Whether it is right, or wise, to satisfy an appetite repeatedly without ever fulfilling the organic functions of such satisfaction is a question that may remain moot here. But the force of this encyclical depends upon the claim that such separation is in *every* case immoral. That claim seems plainly false. . . .

Embedded in the argument of *Humanae Vitae* is a view of sex as an aspect of human life fundamentally unworthy in itself, because

521

essentially instrumental in character. The insistence that every coition be open to conception implicitly supposes that all sex, and every act of love sexually toned, is at bottom a tool for the accomplishment of something else. An uneasy distaste for fleshly things, partly disguised, is revealed in the refusal of the Church to approve of sexual intercourse for its own sake. The intrinsic worth of sexual passion is not precisely denied, but that denial is clearly suggested by insisting that, separated from procreation, the act is dishonest and contravenes God's will. A more generous conception of divine intentions might suppose sex to be a blessing that humans are peculiarly able to understand and appreciate. It might view sex as that animal function most essentially of a loving kind and its practice (whether fecund or not) the closest thing to the incarnation of the religious ideal of love. Such at least is a possible view, and with it sex might be conceived as an element of our condition having sometimes an instrumental role, sometimes a consummatory role, and often both. Even when not intended to produce new life it may serve to make tangible our union with another human creature. If it makes sense at all to infer the intentions of God, we may reasonably suppose that so rich and delightful a dimension of human life was designed by Him (if He is wise and loving) both as an instrument and as a satisfaction to be enjoyed mutually, for its own and each other's sake. To suppose narrowly that sexual intercourse must serve as an instrument in every circumstance is to demean its designer, if it has one. . . .

In approving the so-called rhythm method of birth control, the Church flatly contradicts its own dogmas in this sphere and shows clearly that in its more reflective moments it too denies the "inseparable connection" of sexual intercourse and procreation. *Humanae Vitae* says straightforwardly that it is entirely proper for the married couple to "take into account the natural rhythms immanent in the generative functions, for the use of marriage in the infecund periods only, and in this way to regulate birth without offending the moral principles." This form of birth regulation, the encyclical allows, remains licit *even though the married couple are engaging in sexual intercouse with the deliberate intention of avoiding the creation of new life.* . . .

The claim is that, with the rhythm method, the couple makes use of a "natural disposition"; with all other methods "they impede the development of natural processes." The encyclical supposes, but cannot demonstrate, that the use of timing only is a "legitimate use" of nature but that drugs or diaphragms are not legitimate. In what aspect of the latter cases does the claimed illegitimacy lie? All that can be said is that in the one case instruments are not used, in the other case they are. Surely civilization, and with it the Catholic Church, has passed the point where it was considered a disruption of God's plan to accomplish worthwhile objectives with the aid of rational and humane instruments. Is it legitimate to protect health with exercise but illegitimate to do so with vaccination? Is it legitimate to fight illness with nutrition but illegitimate to do so with medicines? Surely the notion that an act is illegitimate only because instruments are used is absurd. . . .

. . . By simply calling the rhythm method licit, and all other methods illicit, the encyclical begs the central question. Why is the one legitimate, the other not? The argument purports to exhibit a morally relevant difference, but never begins to do so.

This inconsistency is not just a minor slip; it is fatal to the entire position of *Humanae Vitae*. For that position depends utterly upon what has here been called the inseparability premise; and it is now clear that, even for the Church, where there are plausible reasons and honest love, a couple may indeed separate their desire for children from their desire for sex with each other. Both fecund and loving the marriage should be, perhaps, but even if true that principle gives no warrant for the prohibition of any humane method of birth control.

The leaders of the Catholic Church are far from callous men; they are fully aware of the human misery that flows from uncontrolled population growth, and they understand the grave need for the global control of human numbers. Hence their approval of the rhythm method. Still they argue that other forms of birth control, being instrinsically wrong, may not be practiced, because it is never permissible to do what is wrong even with a view to some larger good.

> [I]t is not licit, even for the gravest reasons, to do evil so that good may follow therefrom; that is, to make into the object of a positive act of the will something which is intrinsically disorder, and hence unworthy of the human person, even when the intention is to safeguard or promote individual, family, or social well-being. Con-

sequently it is an error to think that a conjugal act which is deliberately made infecund and so is intrinsically dishonest could be made honest and right by the ensemble of a fecund conjugal life.

This argument fails utterly; of its two premises, both are false. The major premise—that it is never right to do a minor evil in order that a greater good may come of it—will be denied by most reasonable men. But even granting that premise fully, the condemnation of birth control does not follow. In the first place, if all control of sexual intercourse with the deliberate intent of avoiding birth is dishonest and disorderly, it is so whatever the method employed to reach that end. The argument—protestation to the contrary notwithstanding—cuts as strongly against the rhythm method as against any other, since all birth control embodies the positive will to enjoy sex without procreation. More importantly, the argument depends also on the minor premise, that deliberate control of birth *is* intrinsically evil, dishonest, and disorderly. That premise *Humanae Vitae* does not and cannot establish. Even if one accepts the larger doctrinal principles of the Church regarding marriage and its essentially loving, total, faithful, and fecund character, family planning and the intelligent control of sexual intercourse to implement such planning may be approved and encouraged, not as instrumental evils but as acts wholly honest and right.

Finally, *Humanae Vitae* offers, in support of its prohibition of birth control, three arguments of a totally different sort, arguments aiming not to establish the wrongness of birth control in itself but to point out the evils alleged to flow from its employment. This emphasis upon consequences rather than intrinsic quality is not characteristic of the encyclical, not in harmony with its general spirit. Moreover, the arguments appear in abbreviated form, and not the slightest effort is made to show that the consequences alleged would in fact ensue. This pragmatic interlude does not play a major role in the document.

Still it is proper to give these arguments the little attention they deserve.

1. Birth control devices, it is claimed, offer "easy means of eluding" the observance of the moral law by leading to "conjugal infidelity and the general lowering of morality."

524

The argument is thrice bad:

a) There is no evidence to show that birth control would in fact increase the frequency of marital infidelity. Indeed, it is the Church's prohibition, in combination with a couple's inability to care properly for more children, which creates frustration, forces unnatural abstinence, and may lead to extramarital intercourse. This counterclaim is equally unproved, of course; but of the two positions it appears reasonable that the prohibition of birth control is at least as likely to encourage infidelity as its use would be, perhaps more likely to do so.

b) If the moral law is what the Church believes it to be, none of the consequences of the use of birth control, good or bad, are needed to enforce it, or able to do so. Obedience to it as a moral law is complete only when compliance is willing and free, not forced by the sanctions of disobedience. And those who deny the existence of that law, or wish to flout it, can as easily deny or flout the prohibition of birth control as well.

c) Even if the consequence—sexual intercourse more widely enjoyed—were evil, and even if the general use of birth control were shown to have that consequence, it is plainly unjust to force abstinence on faithful married couples, or compel them to rear more children than is good for them or the community, simply because the instrument that might avoid such hardship could be used improperly by others.

1. The argument is intolerable.

2. Birth control devices, it is claimed, give excessive power to public authorities, placing in their hands "a dangerous weapon" that may be easily abused. "Who will stop rulers from favoring, from even imposing upon their peoples, if they were to consider it necessary, the method of contraception which they deem to be most efficacious? In such a way men . . . would reach the point of placing at the mercy of the intervention of public authorities the most personal and most reserved sector of conjugal intimacy."

The scare of this argument is largely fictitious. What, precisely, is the grave danger being hinted at? That governments may play a more active role in stabilizing the size of human population? Such a development would be no bad thing. That governments might force individual couples to use contraceptive devices they do not wish to use? Considering the circumstances of most sexual intercourse, that would be quite a trick, even for Big Brother. That governments ("rulers," as the Pope perceives them) would use their power to encourage or oblige the use of contraceptives in ways contrary to the interests of citizens? There is that danger, of course, if government eludes the control of the people; but such dangers exist now, having been created by the very invention of the instruments in question. The general prohibition by the Church of all use of such instruments reduces that power not one iota. If it is the immoral use of power we fear, it is not precepts or the banning of instruments but the strengthened control of the people over their government that is called for.

3. The final argument is the most extraordinary of them all.

> It is also to be feared that the man, growing used to the employment of anti-conceptive practices, may finally lose respect for the woman and, no longer caring for her physical and psychological equilibrium, may come to the point of considering her as a mere instrument of selfish enjoyment, and no longer as his respected and beloved companion.

How in the world this consequence is drawn from the use of birth control is never rationally explained, nor could it be. The imagination is staggered by the picture of continuing sexual relations harbored in the minds of the authors of this passage; the males, blinded by lust and potent as satyrs—now freed by birth control— plunge relentlessly into the females who, in spite of their frailty, are reduced to instruments of carnal pleasure, then cast aside as useless when passion's spent. The speculation would be amusing if the circumstances were not deadly serious. Whoever supposes that sex is essentially a one-sided demand placed by men on women, and that sex separated from procreation leads inevitably to the selfish use of the woman by the man, tells us far more about himself and his sexual fantasies than about birth control in the real world. The complete failure to consider the woman's desire for sex and for the pleasure of it, the implicit distorted picture of what sexual intercourse for its own sake may be, reveal enough about the authors of this document to put their competence in this entire sphere, not to speak of their authority, in gravest doubt.

It is understandable that the encyclical does not rely in any serious way upon consequences to support its conclusions. For if consequences are relevant at all, the consequences of not using birth control devices must be weighed against the consequences of using them. And while the latter consequences are at worst controversial, and at best happy, the former—the results of population growth uncontrolled or controlled only by timing or abstinence—are famine, and sickness, and death for millions. Such suffering is already upon us; with the help of unenlightened dogmatism like that found in *Humanae Vitae*, far worse is yet in store.

The argument based on consequences the Church is obliged, for the security of its dogma on birth control, to skirt. The argument based on the intrinsic moral quality of the act itself the Church is unable, in behalf of this dogma, to defend. It is time for the dogma to be changed.

STUDY QUESTIONS

1. Cohen claims that the Church degrades sexual love by prohibiting it except for purposes of procreation. Examine Cohen's arguments for this and then give reasons for accepting or rejecting the proposition that prohibiting contraception depreciates sexual love.
2. The issue of contraception is part of the larger issue of whether or not any act that consenting adults engage in can be stigmatized as immoral. How do you view this larger question?
3. Cohen argues that, in permitting sex during infecund periods of the month, the Church is inconsistent. The encyclical itself states that the Church is "not inconsistent with herself." Re-examine the relevant passages on both sides. Do you find that one side has the better of the argument?
4. Cohen compares sexual activity to eating, stating that we may do both for their intrinsic pleasure as well as for their future benefits, such as health and children. Cohen objects that the Church ignores the intrinsic value of sex. Does this criticism fairly represent the Church's attitude as reflected in the papal encyclical?

Tradition and the Generations

EDWARD SHILS

Edward Shils (b. 1915) is a professor of sociology at the University of Chicago and an honorary fellow of Peterhouse, Cambridge. He is the editor of *Minerva: A Review of Science, Learning and Policy* and the author of several books, including *Tradition* (1981).

Shils is concerned with contemporary Western society's disrespect for tradition. He traces the history of this attitude and examines its effects on society. He sees the young, especially, as victims of an idea of the good life that fallaciously contrasts spontaneity, creativity, freedom, and gratification with tradition, discipline, and custom. Shils finds many young people in a state of normlessness, incapable of pursuing meaningful goals. For this he blames those who are supposedly the custodians of traditions: They fave failed to stand up to the pressures of the antitraditionalist forces. Among those who have failed are university teachers—themselves the product of antiestablishment youth cultures—some of whom Shils views as taking part in "a surreptitious offensive against traditional attitudes toward culture, authority, and society." Tradition, says Shils, is essential to human happiness: Human beings need to live in an ordered world. Thus, the extreme antitraditionalism of

TRADITION AND THE GENERATIONS Reprinted from *The American Scholar*, Volume 53, Number 1, Winter 1983/84. Copyright © 1983 by Edward Shils. By permission of the publisher, the United Chapters of Phi Beta Kappa, and the author.

contemporary society alarms him and he hopes for a reversal of this trend. We must act to strengthen the self-confidence of those who properly value tradition and culture. "In strengthening [them], we strengthen the hope for the future."

The present age is said to be a traditionless one, although some of its critics say that it is not sufficiently traditionless. It is, however, impossible for any age to be wholly traditionless. No society could exist if its members had not had the benefit of traditions. They could not have created their language; certainly they could not by themselves have created a language which resembles the language of their ancestors. And once they share that language, they share very widely many of its referents, the insights it affords, and its distinctions and overtones. The living members of any society could never have created all their governmental institutions, all their laws and their methods of making laws; nor could they have created, without any prior knowledge of existing technology, the entire technology by which they work on nature. They could not have created—entirely by themselves, and beginning from zero—the landscape as it exists at any given moment and the pattern of roads and other lines of transportation. Although it is true that much of the stock of language, governmental institutions, laws and methods of making laws, technology, landscape, and lines of transportation has been added over any period of thirty years or twenty or even ten years, those innovations move from a received point of departure from a tradition, a great deal of which remains fairly intact, and without which the present situation could not have conceivably been reached.

Many human beings are quite content with this situation. They might or might not like the substance of these traditions in particular respects, but they do not bridle against them. They accept much of the situation in which they live, and the fact that it bears some resemblance to what existed in the past does not render it less acceptable. It perhaps even helps to make it more acceptable.

If we look at some of the deeper and more intimate spheres of life—the spheres of domestic and sexual life, of religious beliefs and institutions, of knowledge and appreciation of literature, art, and science, and of entertainment—we find that the situation in these spheres is not very different from that which obtains with respect to those spheres of life which are regarded as more external. Much that has come into the present from the past century or two has been steadily reproduced, with some modifications, into the present, across the generations. There is also innovation in each of these spheres. In literature, art, and science, new works, new ideas, new forms, new substances have appeared, although the older works continue to be read, seen, and appreciated, and their ideas make up part of the present stock.

Innovations occur in every sphere of belief and conduct and in patterns of organization. The innovations do not occur equally in all parts of any society. Large proportions of the population adhere more or less to the beliefs which their elders adhered to; in many of their actions, they act more or less in ways in which many members of their society acted seventy-five or fifty or twenty-five years ago. They go to work each working day, attend church services fairly frequently, even if not weekly; they are married, reasonably faithful to their spouses, and fairly attentive to and solicitous about their children. They remain attached to the political party that they began to support thirty years ago and to which the parents of many of them inclined earlier. They work regularly, if they have the opportunity to do so; they attempt to live within their means. They are moderately patriotic, gaining gratification if their country has a high standing in the world with respect to its achievements in any particular sphere of activity. They are moderately respectful of the authority of the state; they are generally law-abiding. They are not rebellious against the very notion of doing particular things and believing in particular ideas simply because they were done and believed in the past. Some of them, in fact, think that it is good and right to act and to believe as those in the past acted and believed—as long as these actions and beliefs from the past are not inconvenient or especially uneconomical. Others are less adherent to traditional ways, and still others follow a quite anti-traditional tradition.

These practices and dispositions, which maintain patterns of action and belief from the past, are more common in the older generation than they are in the younger ones. Numerous investigations in the United States, Great Britain, France, West Germany, and other countries bear witness to this difference between generations. Although the proportion of persons with a "traditional" outlook in each age-group is often substantial, there is a more or less steady decrease as one moves downward from those persons sixty and over, through those between forty-five and fifty-nine years old and those between thirty and forty-four years old, toward those between fifteen and thirty years old. The decline in traditionality from the older to the younger age-groups does not, however, necessarily mean that the members of the younger age-group will retain their present relatively indifferent or hostile attitude toward traditional beliefs and conduct when they become older. If this were to be so, fifty years from now the adherence to traditional patterns of belief and conduct would very much be reduced among those who will then be sixty and over, in comparision with the extent of adherence of those who have been over sixty years of age during the past decade and a half. On the other hand, if the present degree of adherence to traditional patterns among those who are between fifteen and twenty years of age were to persist until they become sixty, and if the same differences between age-groups as now exists were to persist then, there would be very few persons adhering to traditional patterns of belief and conduct by the end of a century.

The latter is, however, very unlikely to be the case for one very important reason. Traditional orientations become more salient as individuals grow older. Not all of those in the younger generations, whose actions and beliefs are relatively untraditional, will continue to be so untraditional as they grow older. Even if there were a unilinear trend toward untraditionality, that trend could not be demonstrated from the evidence of the existing differences between the aged and the young at any particular time. Nevertheless, the possibility of such a unilinear trend toward untraditionality or toward the establishment of an anti-traditional tradition over the past century and a half cannot be overlooked. But even if this trend exists, it is certainly not moving very quickly toward complete realization.

There are limits on the possibility of such a thoroughgoing attrition of traditionality. One limit is that human beings cannot live utterly independently of all traditions; such a thing is physiologically, linguistically, technologically, and intellectually impossible. The other chief limitation is that there are many human beings who, through strong inner necessity, cling to the beliefs and conduct into which they were inducted in their childhood and youth. They are sustained by this adherence. Respect for traditional religious beliefs and observance of the norms of conduct traditionally espoused by religious institutions and authorities comfort them and give them assurance. Life in a family is not experienced by them as a burden without valuable compensations. They have a need to respect authority in the large society. They want to live in an orderly world, and the institutions of church, family, and state give them the assurance that at least some parts of the world are ordered. Even—perhaps especially—if they are distressed by the actual condition of the world, they want to believe in the rightness of the normative order of the world. They want some fixed points of judgment; relativism or nihilism in standards of moral judgment is abhorrent to them. An anti-traditional tradition is not acceptable as a surrogate. They want to live in and believe in the primary institutions of family, church, and state; they believe in the value of their country and of their nationality.

This need to live in an ordered world is inherent in the human mind. It is so strong that it often causes those who are subject to this need to affirm institutions that are shaky and to accept beliefs that are not true according to "scientific" or "rational" arguments. There is also a tendency, which is not equally strong in all human beings, for this need to become more pronounced with advancing age.

II

These things being said, it is also undeniable that there are many persons who do not act in accordance with traditional patterns, who deny the validity or legitimacy of the institutions that require such conduct, and to whom traditional patterns of belief make no sense. There is no ground to be found in denying that this tendency has grown in our Western societies over the many years.

General experience and systematic research show that the phenomenon of untraditionality or anti-traditionality is more common among those in their younger years than among those who are older. The traditional orientation has been under severe criticism for at least two centuries; in fact, the criticism goes back much further. In the present century, there has developed, alongside this criticism of traditionality made by progressivistic thinkers of the eighteenth and nineteenth centuries, the proposition that traditionality is an outlook of the older generations, and that the desire for freedom from tradition and traditionality is natural to young persons. This assertion of the necessary association of youthfulness and anti-traditionality first appeared in the youth movement in Germany around the turn of the century; paradoxically, the youth movement often declared its independence from the traditionality of its elders by honoring much older Germanic traditions. In France the assertion appeared a little later, and there it took the similarly paradoxical form of criticizing the tradition of rationalism and scientism on behalf of patriotism.

In this relatively new variant of the criticism of traditionality, youth has been elevated into the position of being the representative of a new movement, rejecting the false idols of the recent past; the hope of overcoming a deadening traditionality has also been fastened on youth. Young persons themselves took up this program. The movements of the *Wandervogel* and of other currents of the youth movement around the end of the nineteenth century and the beginning of the twentieth century were a self-conscious self-designation of the important cultural phenomenon of being distinctively youthful. There had been some more restricted manifestations of youthful self-consciousness early in the nineteenth century; literary movements, for example, accepted the designation of "youth" or "young"—for instance, *"Jungdeutschland."* It was, however, only in the youth movement of the end of the last century and of the early part of the present century that youthfulness and the rejection of traditionality on behalf of "life," or "authenticity," "vitality," etc., became closely associated with each other. Youthfulness, "life," "vitality," and the rejection of tradition seemed to go naturally together.

There was some justification for the assertion that there was such a link. Young persons are, by their nature as newcomers into society, less committed to already-existent patterns of conduct and belief; they have not yet assimilated all the main traditions of their society; they are less at ease in them than their elders who have been living in them, the same elders who contributed to their maintenance and who have benefited by them. The virtues of genuineness, spontaneity, freshness, and lofty aspirations have been put forward for contrast with the mature virtues of deliberate restraint, caution, and the inhibition of impulse and ambition. The former were believed to be characteristic of youth, the latter of more advanced age. This belief was to a large extent a creation of intellectuals. It was a view shared by some young intellectuals in the years just before and just after the First World War.

The idea of a conflict between youthfulness and traditionality was reanimated about a decade after the end of the Second World War. This time the movement took place on a much broader front. The earlier movement of youth against traditionality became more widespread, deeper, and more comprehensive. It was no longer primarily an intellectuals' affair; it spread among young persons in all sectors of society—to university students, young factory workers, office workers, and even schoolchildren. It became more expressive, more passionate. It became more active and sometimes even violent. The ideal of youthful spontaneity of expression and of the primacy of feeling and impulse was far deeper and less inhibited than had been the praise of "naturalness" in the youth movement of the early part of the century.

The culture and style of life of young persons had always been somewhat different from that of their elders. That was taken for granted. In the period since the Second World War, however, "youth culture" became a more recognized phenomenon, with its own patterns of consumption, its own institutions, its own music, its own commerce, and its own heroes. The spiritual resistance to incorporation into traditional institutions and beliefs has, of course, been very uneven, and it is far from universal, least of all in any extreme form, in the youthful generations since the 1960s.

There are intelligent and well-educated persons who welcome this movement against traditionality, and they would like to see it come to full culmination. They welcome youth culture; they do not see it as a passing phase in the life of the individual. They know, of course, that life consists of more than music of a certain type or certain bizarre modes of dress. Nevertheless they affirm the underlying tendency of the youth culture to strike out on a wholly new path without submission to the idols of the older generation. They would like all of society to be spontaneous and free from the oppression of institutions attached to the past.

These persons who sing songs of praise to youth culture have not given sufficient thought to what could be the result of the fulfillment of the anti-traditional trend of our society through the universalization of the more extreme forms of youth culture. They do not see what has been caused in many lives by aimlessness, fitful pursuit of intense but short-lived and destructive pleasures, and by an attitude of negation that is exhilarating at first but that ends in a joyless bitterness, except in the few who make a profitable profession of derogation or who do it with great talent.

The negative attitude toward the traditional institutions of society and toward traditional beliefs has sometimes been sustained by a political movement or by an ideological scheme. The political movements of anti-traditionality have often been pernicious in their consequences, but for their members they have afforded the satisfaction of being part of something larger than themselves; their members became "engaged"—for at least as long as the movement had not disintegrated or had not come to power with results that sorely disappointed them. Under these conditions, the movements of anti-traditionality have had some value for those who participated in them or who sympathized with them. The ideological transfiguration of negative anti-traditionality also has given a coherent picture of the world and a pattern of the right mode of life to those who could share it. It imposed a certain amount of mental discipline and it ordered their world, at least subjectively. Nevertheless, ideologies, taken seriously, are like straw fires—they flare up and die out. When these ideological straw fires die out, they leave their adherents in a condition of abject disappointment. For a time, at least, if they do not pass on to a more affirmative attitude toward traditional beliefs and institutions, they are left in a state of mind in which nothing has meaning or value.

The negative attitude toward traditional institutions and beliefs, not encased in an ideology or in a political movement, is a much more common phenomenon among the youth of Western societies. It is a condition of aesthetic revolt and a resistance to being incorporated, or being "co-opted," into the traditional institutions of family and work. Once the initial enthusiasm has been attenuated, it becomes a condition which the French sociologists have called anomie—a condition of normlessness, of purposelessness. It does not permit a satisfying membership in any collectivity. It isolates the individual, drives him toward transient pleasures that must be intensified constantly to be maintained. It demands an unending succession of quick pleasures. It causes routines to be experienced as sheer boredom. It allows no cumulativeness of experience and of becoming wise through reflection on that experience; it offers no prospect of quiet satisfaction. It causes regularity in domestic life, in friendship, and in work to be experienced as unbearably boring. The time between intermittent thrills and ecstasy is filled by a gnawing restlessness and discontent. These thrills and ecstatic states can only be intermittent at best, because it is not in the nature of thrill or ecstasy to be long lasting. Ecstatic or thrilling experiences are such only when they are occasional moments which break out of the routines of everyday life. They are bound to be intermittent, and the periods between moments of intensity, for people who live for such moments, are extremely distasteful.

It is one of the blemishes of contemporary societies that many young persons have fallen into anomie. They have become disconnected from institutions and from the beliefs that go along with them. This condition of disconnectedness gives those who have fallen into it no satisfactory routines of work or family, no long-term perspective of an occupational career, no satisfaction of family life, no satisfaction of forming a household and participating in the guidance of offspring. It is a condition of extreme or excessive individualism, of a hedonism on a treadmill of continuously receding pleasures.

Historically, the youth culture of the present day has a close affinity with the bohemianism that flourished among aspiring young artists and writers. Bohemianism, too, was a style of life rejecting bourgeois respectability, regular employment for wages or salary, regular domestic arrangements, regular attendance at religious services, moderate political views without the great passion of ideological political movements, and, above all, the philistine outlook that was indifferent to the great works of art and literature.

Each of the great cities of the world had its own bohemia around the turn of the century and continued to until after the Second World War. Robert Park once said that "bohemia" was "both a state of mind and a place." Bohemias were quarters of large cities, where bohemians could live near one another, where they could read or view each other's work, sustain each other by their common spirit of resistance to bourgeois morals and their devotion to the life of art and personal freedom. The bohemian mode of life, with its unconventional apparel, its disregard for domestic amenities, its enjoyment of the sense of community, was a forerunner of the youth culture of the present. Youth culture has gone very much further than bohemianism, but bohemianism and youth culture clearly belong to the same category of hostility to traditionality. The youth culture of recent decades is, however, no longer segregated, as bohemianism was, among a group of young writers and artists living in a particular quarter of a city. Although youth culture entails withdrawal from the routines of society, it now runs throughout the whole range and breadth of society. Youth culture is no longer even confined to youth.

Although in this age of relativism in moral judgments, it might seem that I am espousing or, much worse, attempting to impose the moral values of philistinism and condemning the free existence of the bohemian style of life. This is not so at all. I am condemning this bohemian style of life because it injures those who live it if they persist in it over a long period. Bohemianism is quite suitable for young persons and for those who wish to follow the free, institutionally unhampered life of artists and writers; writers, once they are moderately successful, usually renounce much of their bohemianism; the unsuccesful writers also usually renounce the bohemian mode of life as they grow older and, being unsuccessful, cease to write.

The culture which began as youth culture has ceased to be the culture of youth alone. Persons who were youths twenty years ago are no longer so youthful, yet they have brought many of the attitudes of youth culture with them into adulthood.

III

At the center of any relatively satisfying existence must be work in which reward is roughly commensurate with exertion and in which there is a discipline of punctuality and of competent performance. The individual's life becomes ordered around a life of work. The regular receipt of an earned income enables the individual who has earned it by his exertions to learn through experience that he must ration the pleasures that he can purchase through his income. Even where the work is not wholly gratifying, the regular receipt of income is itself gratifying. The purchase of the goods and services, scheduled through time, affords the prospect of future satisfactions. Except for a few geniuses in the art of leisure and consumption, regularity of work and reasoned expenditures of income are indispensable to an ordered life. They are also indispensable to the pleasures of leisure.

One of the major problems of modern societies has been the inadequate induction of the younger generation into this kind of life. Where it is difficult for young persons to find work that provides the possibility of a satisfactory orderliness of life, a crucial stage of life is missed and its absence leaves a deficiency for which it is hard to compensate in later life. Once the equation of steady exertion and steady reward is prevented from coming into existence, the person who has never learned that equation has lost the opportunity of entry into a life of earned and moderate gratification.

If nothing has to be earned, then the objects of desire become limitless. The search for intense gratification becomes predominant. The prospect of moderate satisfaction holds no attraction for a person placed in this condition. After some years of searching for intense pleasures, it is not easy to acquire the discipline needed to work for rewards which bring only modest satisfaction.

The productivity of the modern economy, the strength of trade unions, improvements in the technology of communication, the common solicitude for the weak and unprotected, and the indulgent attitude of parents and their sense of powerlessness in the guidance of their offspring have led to a situation which is injurious to young persons in all of our Western societies. The improved income of employees of all sorts has rendered the earnings of adolescents no longer necessary in working-class families. More affluent parents of all classes can be more indulgent to their children. The absence of pressure to obtain employment on the one side, the paucity of opportunities for employment on the other make if very difficult for young persons to acquire the benefits of regular and remunerated work.

Not having seized the opportunity, or having been refused this opportunity, for assimilation into the outlook that accepts moderate satisfaction as a reasonable value, the victim of this deprivation—for victimization is what this spuriously happy condition is—is barred from the world of traditional institutions and beliefs. This encourages the demand for intense pleasures. The craving for intense pleasures renders the workaday world intolerable. As a result, the institutions which are part of the workaday world appear to be intolerably tyrannical and oppressive. The authorities who speak for the workaday world and the institutions with which they are associated become repugant. The way of life which they recommend has no attractions. Rebelliousness and refractoriness, without an ideology and without a political movement, further aggravate the dissatisfaction.

Moral preaching, filled with clichés, is repellent to those who have eschewed or have been unable to enter the workaday world. The preachers, lay and ecclesiastical, speak to deaf ears. Insofar as they are heard at all, they sound like the enemies of intense pleasure. Their voices are regarded as the voices of killjoys, of the hard, puritanical authorities whom the young are already rejecting.

Young persons are indeed the victims—not at all, however, in the way in which radicals assert that they are the victims—of the capitalistic culture. They are the victims of a false idea of the good life. The falsity lies in the belief in the supreme value of intense, exciting, exhilarating pleasure and in the possibility of its complete attainment. It lies also in the belief that work is a burden and leisure without work an unqualified good. They are in fact the victims of the ideals which are distorted in the slogan "consumers' society" and which the more radical among them use as a criticism of present-day Western society.

IV

The desire and the capacity for intense pleasure are very great in adolescence and youth. Sensitivity, physical and mental, is at its height at this age. That is why the transition to adult life always encounters some resistance; the prospect of a life without unlimited, intense, and unqualified pleasure is extremely repulsive.

In addition to this displacement of desire onto intense pleasure, there is another reason for the aversion against traditional patterns of conduct and belief and against traditional institutions of family, work, religion, or state. This is the weakness of the authorities who purport to espouse traditional values. By weakness I mean visible uncertainty of conviction about, or even implicit disavowal of, the value of traditional institutions, conduct, and belief. It is not that all persons in authority—political leaders, clergymen, parents, school and university officials and teachers—unanimously and explicitly disavow the institutions for which they have legal and moral responsibility. Far from it. They do, nonetheless, not wish to appear to be "out of touch with the young." They, too, have been affected by the cult of youth. Unlike Max Weber—who in an address to German students at a time when youth was thought to possess salvationary powers, said, "I have never allowed myself to be impressed in any discussion by reference to dates recorded on birth certificates"—they have become impressed with the date of birth of those to whom they address themselves. In our contemporary Western societies, there has been a displacement of appreciation onto youthfulness. Youthfulness is viewed, from a romantic angle, as the best period of life, and the aspirations and demands of youth are treated as imperative. This is a view that is today widely shared. The old as well as the young accept it. Even where the older generation does not completely accept it, it does not want to be thought of as rejecting it.

Those who are in powerful positions in political, economic, and cultural institutions in modern Western societies find themselves subject to much harsh criticism, to some extent simply because they occupy those positions of power. They are very sensitive to these criticisms; the attention which they give to polls of public opinion is obvious evidence of that. The criticisms are severe and diverse, because the most active and demanding members of modern societies, of all ages and strata, have a strong sense of their own dignity and rights, and they are correspondingly distrustful of authority. The powerful are by no means in total disagreement with these very attitudes which are so critical of them.

Here, too, the young generation is a victim, not of exploitation by industrialists and financiers, politicians and churchmen, teachers and parents, but of the lack of courage and forthrightness in these groups. So many concessions have been made to progressive ideas in the raising of children, in the construction of curricula in the schools, and in the flattery of the desires of the young, that the young have no grounds to respect them.

How could it be otherwise? The shuffling off of traditions, to the extent that it is at all possible, was not begun by the present younger generation. It has been going on for a long time, and leading figures of the currently and recently dominant older generation in many institutions in which authority is expected to be exercised are themselves, in many respects, permeated by the outlook of anti-traditionality that censures them. Of course, they are not unqualifiedly anti-traditional, but they, too, hold traditional beliefs and institutions somewhat in suspicion, even while being attached to them and enjoying their benefits.

V

How can this cleavage be bridged? How can the young be addressed so that they will not be alienated from the traditions that are repugnant to them but that they need for their well-being? How can the experience of the older generation and the wisdom of many generations be communicated in an acceptable way to the young? Disregarding for the moment the difficulties of communication under present circumstances—when the young who receive attention are those who occupy buildings, spray slogans on walls, hold demonstrations and marches, and, at the most extreme, provide a reservoir from which terrorists are recruited—traditional beliefs and conduct cannot be shored up simply by addresses on television and interviews and articles in newspapers and reviews. The core of society has been the family, the school, the church, and, in a different form, the economy. If the authorities of those institutions which have been the main custodians and sustaining forces of traditional patterns of belief and conduct default of their obligations, can one expect much help from the others, including university teachers, who operate the institutions which form opinion?

The intellectuals—I have in mind primarily university teachers and literary men—are very crucial in this process. With the great increase in the numbers of young persons attending universities and other institutions of higher education, university teachers have acquired an influence on the opinion of the greatly enlarged educated classes that they did not possess earlier. At the same time, university teachers have been the principal objects of attack of the politically most active participants in youth culture. They have, however, contributed mightily toward it. University teachers, in particular, are in the most continuous and direct contact with the more intellectually interested sector of the younger generation. In the social sciences and the humanistic disciplines, attitudes hostile to tradition have now been nurtured and propagated for many years. About sixty years ago, Werner Sombart said sociology was an "oppositional science." This might not be true of sociology as such—leaving aside the question of whether it is a science—but it is certainly true of many sociologists. It is not true of all of them, but there can be no doubt that those sociologists who are oppositional—which means in opposition to traditional beliefs and actions—are even more so nowadays than they were in the past, when the socialistic opponents of the existing society laid great urgency on the transformation of economic institutions, even though they seldom thought of attacking the ethos of work.

The same is true, although to a lesser extent, in political studies. One major stream of denunciation of traditional patterns of belief and conduct flows from the humanistic disciplines, where new doctrines of literary criticism and an ill-understood sociology have been combined with a splatter of Marxism to provide the intellectual facade of a surreptitious offensive against traditional attitudes toward culture, authority, and society.

Perhaps it is like expecting the poacher to become the gamekeeper, or expecting the fox to become the watchman over the hen house, to say that the turning of the direction of the younger generation is dependent, at least as far as the more intellectual part of the younger generation is concerned, on university teachers. This would be a baseless hope if there were not many university teachers who are opposed in principle to these trends but who believe themselves to be powerless to stand out against their aggressively oppositional colleagues in matters of appointment and in the making up of the syllabi of courses of study.

University teachers are not alone in their responsibility and opportunities for speaking directly to the younger generation. Schoolteachers, especially teachers in the secondary schools, along with administrators in the schools and in governments, have no less great responsibilities and opportunities to guide the younger generation into a readiness to accept the tasks of living under the strain of obligations and to appreciate the possibilities of pleasure as a reward for the carrying out of obligations rather than as an alternative to it. Teachers and school officials have a great part to play in supporting those parents who are horrified by the detachment of their offspring from traditional ways. They also have a part to play in protecting the schools from being diverted from their proper paths. Employers, too, have a crucial part to play in finding employment for young persons and assimilating them into the ethics of conscientious work. Finally, politicians have their responsibilities cut out for them; they must not seek to placate the most anti-traditional blocs of their membership by turning the schools and universities over to them.

These are all necessary, but the brunt of the task of renewing and strengthening attachment to traditional beliefs and conduct belongs to the parents themselves, and the teachers, and, behind them, the educational administrators in schools and governments. Those who deal directly with the young must deal with them with transparent honesty and with an obvious faith in their own convictions. Young persons must be treated with respect and consideration, but they must not be flattered. They must be told of the dangers of some of the paths they follow, and they must be spoken to in a straightforward way, with understanding and sympathy.

This is the crux of the matter. The hostility against tradition is hostility against demands for the acceptance of obligation in family, work, society, and the state. Hostility against authority is hostility against those who demand the acceptance of obligations.

VI

I think it is inevitable that much of the practical wisdom of life that individuals accumulate in the course of many years of experience is bound to be lost. The wisdom of life is one of the most universally valid kinds of knowledge; it is not rigorously tested scientifically but is put into aphoristic and concrete form. It makes little sense to those to whom it is addressed and who have not had experiences of the kind and quality that have given rise to it. The same is true of written wisdom. It is best appreciated when enough experiences have left a deposit in memory. There is a continuous seepage of wisdom, because young persons are too inexperienced to have been able to create it for themselves and hence too inexperienced to accept it and to bear it in mind in their own subsequent actions.

This has always been so. The world of the young, unencumbered by memories and reflection, has never been wholy the world of their elders, who have much stored in their memories. The two worlds are especially different nowadays, when the affluence of contemporary Western societies allows or even forces young persons not to have the experience of work. What was once thought to be privilege—the privilege of leisure—has become a burden on those who have received it and a hindrance to a satisfactory life.

VII

At present there are all sorts of substantive issues on which the younger generation seems to be separated from its elders: problems of the protection of the natural environment from pollution; the use of nuclear energy for the production of electrical power, defense, and disarmament; state grants for higher education as against loans. These are serious issues in themselves and very complicated ones. They are further complicated by the more general antagonism against the whole order of Western societies. This antagonism is not confined to youth, and it is certainly not characteristic of the whole of the younger generation.

It would be a mistake to think that if views on particular issues could be refuted, the fundamental anti-traditional attitude which underlies them would be dissipated. That fundamental attitude can be affected only by a shift in the balance of the diverse elements which make up the outlook of those who are at present so resistant to traditionality.

In every outlook, there are multiple possibilities of development. There are many conflicts among these elements within the minds of those who accept and those who actively espouse the outlook. There is a heterogeneity of outlook within each person; there are tendencies in different directions within the same mind. There is often a latent respect for traditions existing alongside a more as- cendant anti-traditionality within the same person. Obviously the balance is not the same in all cases. There are, however, many persons whose courage and confidence in tradition would be strengthened by a more self-confident, more respect-worthy enun- ciation of the value of traditional conduct and traditional beliefs. And in strengthening these persons, we strengthen the hope for the future.

STUDY QUESTIONS

1. What, in your opinion, is tradition's role in moral education?
2. Is respect for tradition an antiprogressive force? How do you view the relationship between tradition and progress?
3. What does Shils mean by normlessness? How is normlessness related to "anomie"? Do you agree that an antitraditionalist attitude usually results in normlessness and anomie?
4. Does Shils offer grounds for distinguishing between worthy and unworthy traditions? Are some traditions immoral?

SUGGESTED READINGS

Bluestein, Jeffrey. *Parents and Children. The Ethics of the Family.* Oxford: Oxford University Press, 1983.

Lamm, Norman, ed. *The Good Society: Jewish Ethics in Action.* New York: Viking Press, 1974.

McKee, Patrick. *Philosophical Foundations of Gerontology.* New York: Human Sciences Press, 1982.

O'Neil, Onora, and William Ruddick, eds. *Having Children: Philosophical and Legal Reflections on Parenthood.* New York: Oxford University Press, 1979.

Russell, Bertrand. *Marriage and Morals.* New York: Liveright Publishing Corp., 1929.

Shils, Edward. *Tradition.* Chicago: University of Chicago Press, 1981.

Chapter

8

MORALITY AND SOCIETY

One striking development in contemporary moral philosophy is the increasing attention we pay to questions in practical ethics: Is abortion right or wrong? Are doctors ever authorized to give lethal injections to dying, pain-ridden patients who request their own death? Do animals have moral rights? The practical ethics movement originated in the late sixties when philosophers began to participate in national debates on issues such as free speech, civil disobedience, enthanasia, and abortion. The recent interest in applying ethical theory to specific practical problems is not a novel development, for philosophers since Plato and Aristotle have continuously concerned themselves with questions of everyday morality. The period between 1940 and 1970 is something of a historical exception: During those post–World War II decades, Western philosophy became increasingly analytical and methodologically rigorous. Clarification and theory were of primary concern; applied ethics was secondary. This interest in theory and method has not waned, but in the past fifteen years philosophers have reentered the arena of applied ethics with a vengeance. The philosopher Michael Walzer says, about the new popularity of applied ethics,

... when in our books and college courses we argue about distributive justice, killing in war, deception in politics, medical ethics, ... we are ... engaged in a common human activity ... temporarily discontinued at American universities at some cost. Now it is apparently about to be resumed. ... It presses us back toward older moralities, or forward to newer ones, in which personal choice and utilitarian calculation are subjected to the discipline of public philosophy.

In a disciplined approach to a controversial issue, we argue formally for a particular point of view. Consider, for example, the argument offered by those who oppose abortion:

(1) It is wrong to kill an innocent human being.
(2) The fetus is an innocent human being.

.˙. It is wrong to kill a fetus.

In this argument, the conclusion follows logically from the two premises, so anyone who wishes to disagree with the conclusion must be prepared to give reasons to doubt one of the two premises. Most defenders of abortion go after premise (2), which asserts that the fetus is a human being. In her article "A Defense of Abortion," Judith Jarvis Thomson challenges premise (1): She designs an imaginative analogy that illustrates occasions, analogous to abortion, when killing an innocent human being is morally permissible. President Reagan's article opposing abortion marshals the classical reasons for accepting both premises. But, in particular, Reagan argues for the status of the fetus as a human being whose life is sacrosanct.

Arguments pro and con are essential to any position paper in ethics; another ingredient is harder to specify. Linda Bird Francke's "Abortion: A Personal Moral Dilemma" deals with the painful human factor in the ethical dilemma. In a concrete predicament we may not have the luxury of being certain that what we are doing is right.

Though this final chapter primarily considers ethical issues that relate to social policy, the focus of many of the articles is personal. In "Famine, Affluence, and Morality," Peter Singer concludes that readers themselves have a serious moral obligation to do all they can to fight world hunger. James Rachels advises readers to become vegetarians on moral grounds. Students who disagree with these conclusions will need to analyze the arguments to see if they can find false premises or faulty reasoning. This may be harder than it seems. A number of philosophers have found Singer's argument concerning world famine surprisingly difficult to refute. And quite a few philosophers have become vegetarians, or, more commonly, guilty meat eaters, after reviewing the arguments for animal rights.

This said, we should note that moralists like Singer, who seek to apply clear-cut utilitarian principles in calling for action on the world famine problem, face a serious challenge from other utilitarians who claim that the consequences of carrying out Singer's type of policy are worse than the consequences of "callous" inaction. Garrett Hardin argues that international famine relief can be responsible for a cycle of increasing misery. In effect, Hardin argues, a well-meaning and good-hearted moralist like Singer may do far more harm than good.

Some of the articles in this chapter discuss the relative decline of private ethics compared to the increasing interest in social ethics. Daniel Callahan calls contemporary society "minimalistic." In the minimalist society neighbors are moral strangers, and altruism and self-sacrifice cease to be moral duties. Callahan is concerned that, in their eagerness to argue for protection of rights and civil liberties, moral philosophers neglect private virtue, thereby contributing to a moral minimalism. Callahan argues that the new minimalism is in part an effect of widespread misinterpretations of the philosophy of John Stuart Mill.

The decline of private ethics is not all that recent. Joseph Wood Krutch ("The Importance of Private Ethics") noticed and deplored the shift away from concern with private ethics toward concern with social morality more than twenty years ago. Christina Hoff Sommers ("Where Have All the Good Deeds Gone?") observes that the shift Krutch speaks of has led to the obsolescence of the "moral amateur" and the rise of a professional class of social workers who have taken over moral responsibility (for example, in care for the aged) in many areas where the nonprofessional private person had been the primary moral agent. She points out that the literature in applied ethics is now correspondingly biased in favor of social policy issues (euthanasia, recombinant DNA research, capital punishment) to the relative neglect of concern with private ethics. Like Krutch and Callahan, Sommers wants to see greater attention paid to private ethics.

Abortion: A Personal Moral Dilemma

LINDA BIRD FRANCKE

Linda Bird Francke is a magazine and newspaper editor. She is also a frequent contributor to popular journals such as *McCalls, Ms.,* and *Harper's Bazaar.*

In 1976, Linda Bird Francke published an anonymous editorial in the *New York Times* describing what having an abortion was like. She has now written a book on the subject under her own name. In the Introduction (reprinted here), she includes the *New York Times* editorial and reveals herself as its author. Francke gives us a perspective on abortion that most of the discussions pro and con miss: the concrete experience of a woman who faced an unwanted pregnancy and chose to abort.

"Jane Doe," thirty-eight, had an abortion in New York City in 1973. The mother of three children, then three, five, and eleven, Jane had just started a full-time job in publishing. She and her husband, an investment banker, decided together that another baby would add an almost unbearable strain to their lives, which were already overfull. What Jane had not anticipated was the guilt and sadness that followed the abortion. She wrote about the experience shortly thereafter and filed the story away. Three years later she reread it and decided it might be helpful to other women who experience the ambivalence of abortion. The *New York Times* ran it on their Op-Ed page in May 1976. This is what she wrote:

> We were sitting in a bar on Lexington Avenue when I told my husband I was pregnant. It is not a memory I like to dwell on. Instead of the champagne and hope which had heralded the impending births of the first, second and third child, the news of this one was greeted with shocked silence and Scotch. "Jesus," my husband kept saying to himself, stirring the ice cubes around and around. "Oh, Jesus."
>
> Oh, how we tried to rationalize it that night as the starting time for the movie came and went. My husband talked about his plans for a career change in the next year, to stem the staleness that fourteen years with the same investment-banking firm had brought him. A new baby would preclude that option.
>
> The timing wasn't right for me either. Having juggled pregnancies and child care with what freelance jobs I could fit in between feedings, I had just taken on a full-time job. A new baby would put me right back in the nursery just when our youngest child was finally school age. It was time for *us*, we tried to rationalize. There just wasn't room in our lives now for another baby. We both agreed. And agreed. And agreed.
>
> How very considerate they are at the Women's Services, known formally as the Center for Reproductive and Sexual Health. Yes, indeed, I could have an abortion that very Saturday morning and be out in time to drive to the country that afternoon. Bring a first morning urine specimen, a sanitary belt and napkins, a money order or $125 cash—and a friend.
>
> My friend turned out to be my husband, standing awkwardly and ill at ease as men always do in places that are exclusively for women, as I checked in at nine A.M. Other men hovered around just as anxiously, knowing they had to be there, wishing they weren't. No one spoke to each other. When I would be cycled out of there four hours later, the same men would be slumped in their same seats, locked downcast in their cells of embarrassment.
>
> The Saturday morning women's group was more dispirited than the men in the waiting room. There were around fifteen of us, a mixture of races, ages and backgrounds. Three didn't speak English

551

at all and a fourth, a pregnant Puerto Rican girl around eighteen, translated for them.

There were six black women and a hodge-podge of whites, among them a T-shirted teenager who kept leaving the room to throw up and a puzzled middle-aged woman from Queens with three grown children.

"What form of birth control were you using?" the volunteer asked each one of us. The answer was inevitably "none." She then went on to describe the various forms of birth control available at the clinic, and offered them to each of us.

The youngest Puerto Rican girl was asked through the interpreter which she'd like to use: the loop, diaphragm, or pill. She shook her head "no" three times. "You don't want to come back here again, do you?" the volunteer pressed. The girl's head was so low her chin rested on her breastbone. "*Sí*," she whispered.

We had been there two hours by that time, filling out endless forms, giving blood and urine, receiving lectures. But unlike any other group of women I've been in, we didn't talk. Our common denominator, the one which usually floods language and economic barriers into familiarity, today was one of shame. We were losing life that day, not giving it.

The group kept getting cut back to smaller, more workable units, and finally I was put in a small waiting room with just two other women. We changed into paper bathrobes and paper slippers, and we rustled whenever we moved. One of the women in my room was shivering and an aide brought her a blanket.

"What's the matter?" the aide asked her. "I'm scared," the woman said. "How much will it hurt?" The aide smiled. "Oh, nothing worse than a couple of bad cramps," she said. "This afternoon you'll be dancing a jig."

I began to panic. Suddenly the rhetoric, the abortion marches I'd walked in, the telegrams sent to Albany to counteract the Friends of the Fetus, the Zero Population Growth buttons I'd worn, peeled away, and I was all alone with my microscopic baby. There were just the two of us there, and soon, because it was more convenient for me and my husband, there would be one again.

How could it be that I, who am so neurotic about life that I step over bugs rather than on them, who spend hours planting flowers and vegetables in the spring even though we rent out the house and never see them, who make sure the children are vaccinated and inoculated and filled with vitamin C, could so arbitrarily decide that this life shouldn't be?

"It's not a life," my husband had argued, more to convince himself than me. "It's a bunch of cells smaller than my fingernail."

But any woman who has had children knows that certain feeling in her taut, swollen breasts, and the slight but constant ache in her uterus that signals the arrival of life. Though I would march myself into blisters for a woman's right to exercise the option of motherhood, I discovered there in the waiting room that I was not the modern woman I thought I was.

When my name was called, my body felt so heavy the nurse had to help me into the examining room. I waited for my husband to burst through the door and yell "stop," but of course he didn't. I concentrated on three black spots in the acoustic ceiling until they grew in size to the shape of saucers, while the doctor swabbed my insides with antiseptic.

"You're going to feel a burning sensation now," he said, injecting the Novocaine into the neck of the womb. The pain was swift and severe, and I twisted to get away from him. He was hurting my baby, I reasoned, and the black saucers quivered in the air. "Stop," I cried. "Please stop." He shook his head, busy with his equipment. "It's too late to stop now," he said. "It'll just take a few more seconds."

What good sports we women are. And how obedient. Physically the pain passed even before the hum of the machine signaled that the vacuuming of my uterus was completed, my baby sucked up like ashes after a cocktail party, Ten minutes start to finish. And I was back on the arm of the nurse.

There were twelve beds in the recovery room. Each one had a gaily flowered draw sheet and a soft green or blue thermal blanket. It was all very feminine. Lying on these beds for an hour or more were the shocked victims of their sex, their full wombs now stripped clean, their futures less encumbered.

It was very quiet in that room. The only voice was that of the nurse, locating the new women who had just come in so she could monitor their blood pressure, and checking out the recovered women who were free to leave.

Juice was being passed about, and I found myself sipping a Dixie cup of Hawaiian Punch. An older woman with tightly curled bleached hair was just getting up from the next bed, "That was no goddamn snap," she said, resting before putting on her miniskirt and high white boots. Other women came and went, some walking out as dazed as they had entered, others with a bounce that signaled they were going right back to Bloomingdale's.

Finally then, it was time for me to leave. I checked out, making an appointment to return in two weeks for an IUD insertion. My husband was slumped in the waiting room, clutching a single yellow rose wrapped in a wet paper towel and stuffed into a baggie.

We didn't talk the whole way home, but just held hands very tightly. At home there were more yellow roses and a tray in bed for me and the children's curiosity to divert.

It had certainly been a successful operation. I didn't bleed at all for two days just as they had predicted, and then I bled only moderately for another four days. Within a week my breasts had subsided and the tenderness vanished, and my body felt mine again instead of the eggshell it becomes when it's protecting someone else.

My husband and I are back to planning our summer vacation and his career switch.

And it certainly does make more sense not to be having a baby right now—we say that to each other all the time. But I have this ghost now. A very little ghost that only appears when I'm seeing something beautiful, like the full moon on the ocean last weekend. And the baby waves at me. And I wave at the baby. "Of course, we have room," I cry to the ghost. "Of course, we do."

I am "Jane Doe." Using a pseudonym was not the act of cowardice some have said it was, but rather an act of sympathy for the feelings of my family. My daughters were too young then to understand what an abortion was, and my twelve-year-old son (my husband's stepson) reacted angrily when I even broached the subject of abortion to him. Andrew was deeply moralistic, as many children are at that age, and still young enough to feel threatened by the actions of adults; his replies to my "suppose I had an abortion" queries were devastating. "I think abortion is okay if the boy and girl aren't married, and they just made a mistake," he said. "But if you had an abortion, that would be different. You're married, and there is no reason for you not to have another baby. How could you just kill something—no matter how little it is—that's going to grow and have legs and wiggle its fingers?

"I would be furious with you if you had an abortion. I'd lose all respect for you for being so selfish. I'd make you suffer and remind you of it all the time. I would think of ways to be mean. Maybe I'd give you the silent treatment or something.

"If God had meant women to have abortions, He would have put buttons on their stomachs."

I decided to wait until he was older before we discussed it again.

There were other considerations as well. My husband and I had chosen not to tell our parents about the abortion. My mother was very ill at the time and not up to a barrage of phone calls from her friends about "what Linda had written in the newspaper." And there were my parents-in-law, who had always hoped for a male grandchild to carry on the family name. So I avoided the confessional and simply wrote what I thought would be a helpful piece for other women who might have shared my experience.

The result was almost great enough to be recorded on a seismograph. Interpreting the piece as anti-abortion grist, the Right-to-Lifers reproduced it by the thousands and sent it to everyone on their mailing lists. In one Catholic mailing, two sentences were deleted from the article: one that said I was planning to return to the clinic for an IUD insertion, and the other the quote from a middle-aged woman, "That was no goddamn snap." Papers around the country and in Canada ran it, culminating in its appearance in the Canadian edition of the *Reader's Digest*, whose staff took it upon their editorial selves to delete the last paragraph about the "little ghost" because they considered it "mawkish." They also changed the title from "There Just Wasn't Room in Our Lives for Another Baby" to "A Successful Operation" in the hopes that it would change their magazine's pro-abortion image.

Hundreds of letters poured into the *New York Times*, some from Right-to-Lifers, who predictably called me a "murderer," and others from pro-choice zealots who had decided the article was a "plant" and might even have been written by a man. Women wrote about their own abortions, some of which had been positive experiences and some disastrous. One woman even wrote that she wished her own mother had had an abortion instead of subjecting her to a childhood that was "brutal and crushing." Many of the respondents criticized me, quite rightly, for not using birth control in the first place, I was stunned, and so was the *New York Times*. A few weeks later they ran a sampling of the letters and my reply, which follows:

The varied reactions to my abortion article do not surprise me at all. They are all right. And they are all wrong. There is no issue so fundamental as the giving of life, or the cessation of it. These decisions are the most personal one can ever make and each person facing them reacts in her own way. It is not black-and-white as the laws governing abortion are forced to be. Rather it is the gray area whose core touches our definition of ourselves that produces "little ghosts" in some, and a sense of relief in others.

I admire the woman who chose not to bear her fourth child because she and her husband could not afford to give that child the future they felt necessary. I admire the women who were outraged that I had failed to use any form of contraception. And I ache for the woman whose mother had given birth to her even though she was not wanted, and thus spent an empty, lonely childhood. It takes courage to take the life of someone else in your own hands, and even more courage to assume responsibility for your own.

I had my abortion over two years ago. And I wrote about it shortly thereafter. It was only recently, however, that I decided to publish it. I felt it was important to share how one person's abortion had affected her, rather than just sit by while the pro and con groups haggled over legislation.

The effect has indeed been profound. Though my husband was very supportive of me, and I, I think, of him, our relationship slowly faltered. As our children are girls, my husband anguished at the possibility that I had been carrying a son. Just a case of male macho, many would argue. But still, that's the way he feels, and it is important. I hope we can get back on a loving track again.

Needless to say, I have an IUD now, instead of the diaphragm that is too easily forgotten. I do not begrudge my husband his lack of contraception. Condoms are awkward. Neither do I feel he should have a vasectomy. It is profoundly difficult for him to face the possibility that he might never have that son. Nor do I regret having the abortion. I am just as much an avid supporter of children by choice as I ever was.

My only regret is the sheer irresponsibility on my part to become pregnant in the first place. I pray to God that it will never happen again. But if it does, I will be equally thankful that the law provides women the dignity to choose whether to bring a new life into the world or not.

I had obviously and unintentionally touched a national nerve. With abortion becoming an everyday occurrence since the Supreme Court ruling in 1973, which overturned the right of individual states to intervene in a woman's decision to abort in the first trimester (twelve weeks) of pregnancy and to intervene in the second trimester (twenty-four weeks) only to ensure medical practices "reasonably related to maternal health," American women of all ages, races, and backgrounds were facing the same sort of dilemma I had. . . .

. . . So much has happened in the short time since abortion was legalized that only now is there an opportunity to draw breath and begin to evaluate what the 1973 Supreme Court decision has wrought, and what repercussions the 1977 Supreme Court decision upholding states' rights to withhold abortion funding for the poor will have. Abortion is not new by any means. But confronting the fact of it without furtiveness and danger is. The quantum leap from women's age-old need and desire to control their reproductive lives to their sanctioned ability finally to do so has raised questions of ethics and morality that have yet to be answered. Perhaps they never will be.

STUDY QUESTIONS

1. The Right-to-Life Movement reprinted and distributed Francke's editorial. Pro-Choice advocates criticized it and suggested it was a plant written by a man. Are these reactions on both sides justified?
2. Francke suffers from a persistent sense of guilt and sadness; occasionally she sees the ghost of her unborn child. Does the fact that she is married and economically secure make her more susceptible to guilt and regret than, say, an unmarried and economically unviable young woman? Is Francke, in your opinion, indeed more guilty since she could, after all, have nurtured and supported a healthy child in relative comfort?

Abortion and the Conscience of the Nation

RONALD REAGAN

Ronald Reagan (b. 1911) is the President of the United States.

President Ronald Reagan points out that since the Supreme Court legalized abortion in 1973 "more than 15 million unborn children have had their lives snuffed out . . . ten times the number of Americans lost in all our nation's wars." And yet, abortion on demand is not a right guaranteed by the Constitution; the American people have never voted in favor of it, and probably believe it is wrong. Reagan has no doubt that the fetus is a human being and finds no reason to exclude fetuses and infants with birth defects from the general protection of laws. Concretely, the rights of the fetus and the newborn are such that no one may kill a fetus or starve a baby with Down's Syndrome to death in a publicly funded hospital. Reagan decries the "deadly logic" of those who conclude that some human beings are not fit to live; the sanctity of life takes priority over an ethic that emphasizes the quality of life. He is disturbed to find that many of the same people who worry about

ABORTION AND THE CONSCIENCE OF THE NATION Reprinted by permission of Thomas Nelson Publishers from the book *Abortion and the Conscience of the Nation.* Copyright © 1984 by Human Life Foundation, Inc.

558

saving timber wolves or bald eagles react indifferently to killing the unborn. He also rejects the idea that unwanted children will inevitably be unhappy, pointing out that a great number of families are seeking to adopt.

The 10th anniversary of the Supreme Court decision in *Roe v. Wade* is a good time for us to pause and reflect. Our nationwide policy of abortion-on-demand through all nine months of pregnancy was neither voted for by our people nor enacted by our legislators—not a single State had such unrestricted abortion before the Supreme Court decreed it to be a national policy in 1973. But the consequences of this judicial decision are now obvious: since 1973, more than 15 million unborn children have had their lives snuffed out by legalized abortions. That is over ten times the number of Americans lost in all our nation's wars.

Make no mistake, abortion-on-demand is not a right granted by the Constitution. No serious scholar, including one disposed to agree with the Court's result, has argued that the framers of the Constitution intended to create such a right. Shortly after the *Roe v. Wade* decision, Professor John Hart Ely, now Dean of Stanford Law School, wrote that the opinion "is not constitutional law and gives almost no sense of an obligation to try to be." Nowhere do the plain words of the Constitution even hint at a "right" so sweeping as to permit abortion up to the time the child is ready to be born. Yet that is what the Court ruled.

As an act of "raw judicial power" (to use Justice White's biting phrase), the decision by the seven-man majority in *Roe v. Wade* has so far been made to stick. But the Court's decision has by no means settled the debate. Instead, *Roe v. Wade* has become a continuing prod to the conscience of the nation.

Abortion concerns not just the unborn child, it concerns every one of us. The English poet, John Donne, wrote: ". . . any man's death diminishes me, because I am involved in mankind; and therefore never send to know for whom the bell tolls; it tolls for thee."

We cannot diminish the value of one category of human life—the unborn—without diminishing the value of all human life. We saw tragic proof of this truism last year when the Indiana courts

allowed the starvation death of "Baby Doe" in Bloomington because the child had Down's Syndrome.

Many of our fellow citizens grieve over the loss of life that has
followed *Roe v. Wade*. Margaret Heckler, soon after being nomi-
nated to head the largest department of our government, Health
and Human Services, told an audience that she believed abortion
to be the greatest moral crisis facing our country today. And the
revered Mother Teresa, who works in the streets of Calcutta minis-
tering to dying people in her world-famous mission of mercy, has
said that "the greatest misery of our time is the generalized abortion of children."

Over the first two years of my Administration I have closely
followed and assisted efforts in Congress to reverse the tide of
abortion—efforts of Congressmen, Senators and citizens responding to an urgent moral crisis. Regrettably, I have also seen the
massive efforts of those who, under the banner of "freedom of
choice," have so far blocked every effort to reverse nationwide
abortion-on-demand.

Despite the formidable obstacles before us, we must not lose
heart. This is not the first time our country has been divided by a
Supreme Court decision that denied the value of certain human
lives. The *Dred Scott* decision of 1857 was not overturned in a day,
or a year, or even a decade. At first, only a minority of Americans
recognized and deplored the moral crisis brought about by denying
the full humanity of our black brothers and sisters; but that minority persisted in their vision and finally prevailed. They did it by
appealing to the hearts and minds of their countrymen, to the truth
of human dignity under God. From their example, we know that
respect for the sacred value of human life is too deeply engrained
in the hearts of our people to remain forever suppressed. But the
great majority of the American people have not yet made their
voices heard, and we cannot expect them to—any more than the
public voice arose against slavery—*until* the issue is clearly framed
and presented.

What, then, is the real issue? I have often said that when we talk
about abortion, we are talking about two lives—the life of the
mother and the life of the unborn child. Why else do we call a
pregnant woman a mother? I have also said that anyone who
doesn't feel sure whether we are talking about a second human life

should clearly give life the benefit of the doubt. If you don't know whether a body is alive or dead, you would never bury it. I think this consideration itself should be enough for all of us to insist on protecting the unborn.

The case against abortion does not rest here, however, for medical practice confirms at every step the correctness of these moral sensibilities. Modern medicine treats the unborn child as a patient. Medical pioneers have made great breakthroughs in treating the unborn—for genetic problems, vitamin deficiencies, irregular heart rhythms, and other medical conditions. Who can forget George Will's moving account of the little boy who underwent brain surgery six times during the nine weeks before he was born? Who is the *patient* if not that tiny unborn human being who can feel pain when he or she is approached by doctors who come to kill rather than to cure?

The real question today is not when human life begins, but, *What is the value of human life?* The abortionist who reassembles the arms and legs of a tiny baby to make sure all its parts have been torn from its mother's body can hardly doubt whether it is a human being. The real question for him and for all of us is whether that tiny human life has a God-given right to be protected by the law—the same right we have.

What more dramatic confirmation could we have of the real issue than the Baby Doe case in Bloomington, Indiana? The death of that tiny infant tore at the hearts of all Americans because the child was undeniably a live human being—one lying helpless before the eyes of the doctors and the eyes of the nation. The real issue for the courts was *not* whether Baby Doe was a human being. The real issue was whether to protect the life of a human being who had Down's Syndrome, who would probably be mentally handicapped, but who needed a routine surgical procedure to unblock his esophagus and allow him to eat. A doctor testified to the presiding judge that, even with his physical problem corrected, Baby Doe would have a "non-existent" possibility for "a minimally adequate life"—in other words, that retardation was the equivalent of a crime deserving the death penalty. The judge let Baby Doe starve and die, and the Indiana Supreme Court sanctioned his decision.

Federal law does not allow Federally-assisted hospitals to decide that Down's Syndrome infants are not worth treating, much less to decide to starve them to death. Accordingly, I have directed the Departments of Justice and HHS to apply civil rights regulations to protect handicapped newborns. All hospitals receiving Federal funds must post notices which will clearly state that failure to feed handicapped babies is prohibited by Federal law. The basic issue is whether to value and protect the lives of the handicapped, whether to recognize the sanctity of human life. This is the same basic issue that underlies the question of abortion.

The 1981 Senate hearings on the beginning of human life brought out the basic issue more clearly than ever before. The many medical and scientific witnesses who testified disagreed on many things, but not on the *scientific* evidence that the unborn child is alive, is a distinct individual, or is a member of the human species. They did disagree over the *value* question, whether to give value to a human life at its early and most vulnerable stages of existence.

Regrettably, we live at a time when some persons do *not* value all human life. They want to pick and choose which individuals have value. Some have said that only those individuals with "consciousness of self" are human beings. One such writer has followed this deadly logic and concluded that "shocking as it may seem, a newly born infant is not a human being."

A Nobel Prize winning scientist has suggested that if a handicapped child "were not declared fully human until three days after birth, then all parents could be allowed the choice." In other words, "quality control" to see if newly born human beings are up to snuff.

Obviously, some influential people want to deny that every human life has intrinsic, sacred worth. They insist that a member of the human race must have certain qualities before they accord him or her status as a "human being."

Events have borne out the editorial in a California medical journal which explained three years before *Roe v. Wade* that the social acceptance of abortion is a "defiance of the long-held Western ethic of intrinsic and equal value for every human life regardless of its stage, condition, or status."

Every legislator, every doctor, and every citizen needs to recognize that the real issue is whether to affirm and protect the sanctity of all human life, or to embrace a social ethic where some human lives are valued and others are not. As a nation, we must choose between the sanctity of life ethic and the quality of life ethic.

I have no trouble identifying the answer our nation has always given to this basic question, and the answer that I hope and pray it will give in the future. America was founded by men and women who shared a vision of the value of each and every individual. They stated this vision clearly from the very start in the Declaration of Independence, using words that every schoolboy and schoolgirl can recite:

> We hold these truths to be self-evident, that all men are created equal, that they are endowed by their Creator with certain unalienable rights, that among these are life, liberty, and the pursuit of happiness.

We fought a terrible war to guarantee that one category of mankind—black people in America—could not be denied the inalienable rights with which their Creator endowed them. The great champion of the sanctity of all human life in that day, Abraham Lincoln, gave us his assessment of the Declaration's purpose. Speaking of the framers of that noble document, he said:

> This was their majestic interpretation of the economy of the Universe. This was their lofty, and wise, and noble understanding of the justice of the Creator to His creatures. Yes, gentlemen, to all His creatures, to the whole great family of man. In their enlightened belief, nothing stamped with the divine image and likeness was sent into the world to be trodden on . . . They grasped not only the whole race of man then living, but they reached forward and seized upon the farthest posterity. They erected a beacon to guide their children and their children's children, and the countless myriads who should inhabit the earth in other ages.

He warned also of the danger we would face if we closed our eyes to the value of life in any category of human beings:

> I should like to know if taking this old Declaration of Independence, which declares that all men are equal upon principle and making exceptions to it where will it stop. If one man says it does not mean a Negro, why not another say it does not mean some other man?

When Congressman John A. Bingham of Ohio drafted the Four-teenth Amendment to guarantee the rights of life, liberty, and property to all human beings, he explained that *all* are "entitled to the protection of American law, because its divine spirit of equality declares that all men are created equal." He said the rights guaran-teed by the amendment would therefore apply to "any human being." Justice William Brennan, writing in another case decided only the year before *Roe v. Wade*, referred to our society as one that "strongly affirms the sanctity of life."

Another William Brennan—not the Justice—has reminded us of the terrible consequences that can follow when a nation rejects the sanctity of life ethic:

> The cultural environment for a human holocaust is present whenever any society can be misled into defining individuals as less than human and therefore devoid of value and respect.

As a nation today, we have *not* rejected the sanctity of human life. The American people have not had an opportunity to express their view on the sanctity of human life in the unborn. I am convinced that Americans do not want to play God with the value of human life. It is not for us to decide who is worthy to live and who is not. Even the Supreme Court's opinion in *Roe v. Wade* did not explicitly reject the traditional American idea of intrinsic worth and value in all human life; it simply dodged this issue.

The Congress has before it several measures that would enable our people to reaffirm the sanctity of human life, even the smallest and the youngest and the most defenseless. The Human Life Bill expressly recognizes the unborn as human beings and accordingly protects them as persons under our Constitution. This bill, first introduced by Senator Jesse Helms, provided the vehicle for the Senate hearings in 1981 which contributed so much to our under-standing of the real issue of abortion.

The Respect Human Life Act, just introduced in the 98th Con-gress, states in its first section that the policy of the United States is "to protect innocent life, both before and after birth." This bill, sponsored by Congressman Henry Hyde and Senator Roger Jep-sen, prohibits the Federal government from performing abortions or assisting those who do so, except to save the life of the mother. It also addresses the pressing issue of infanticide which, as we have seen, flows inevitably from permissive abortion as another step in the denial of the inviolability of innocent human life.

I have endorsed each of these measures, as well as the more difficult route of constitutional amendment, and I will give these initiatives my full support. Each of them, in different ways, attempts to reverse the tragic policy of abortion-on-demand imposed by the Supreme Court ten years ago. Each of them is a decisive way to affirm the sanctity of human life.

We must all educate ourselves to the reality of the horrors taking place. Doctors today know that unborn children can feel a touch within the womb and that they respond to pain. But how many Americans are aware that abortion techniques are allowed today, in all 50 states, that burn the skin of a baby with a salt solution, in an agonizing death that can last for hours?

Another example: two years ago, the *Philadelphia Inquirer* ran a Sunday special supplement on "The Dreaded Complication." The "dreaded complication" referred to in the article—the complication feared by doctors who perform abortions—is the *survival* of the child despite all the painful attacks during the abortion procedure. Some unborn children *do survive the late-term abortions* the Supreme Court has made legal. Is there any question that these victims of abortion deserve our attention and protection? Is there any question that those who *don't* survive were living human beings before they were killed?

Late-term abortions, especially when the baby survives, but is then killed by starvation, neglect, or suffocation, show once again the link between abortion and infanticide. The time to stop both is now. As my Administration acts to stop infanticide, we will be fully aware of the real issue that underlies the death of babies before and soon after birth.

Our society has, fortunately, become sensitive to the rights and special needs of the handicapped, but I am shocked that physical or mental handicaps of newborns are still used to justify their extinction. This Administration has a Surgeon General, Dr. C. Everett Koop, who has done perhaps more than any other American for handicapped children, by pioneering surgical techniques to help them, by speaking out on the value of their lives, and by working with them in the context of loving families. You will not find his former patients advocating the so-called quality of life ethic.

I know that when the true issue of infanticide is placed before the American people, with all the facts openly aired, we will have no trouble deciding that a mentally or physically handicapped baby has the same intrinsic worth and right to life as the rest of us. As the New Jersey Supreme Court said two decades ago, in a decision upholding the sanctity of human life, "a child need not be perfect to have a worthwhile life."

Whether we are talking about pain suffered by unborn children, or about late-term abortions, or about infanticide, we inevitably focus on the humanity of the unborn child. Each of these issues is a potential rallying point for the sanctity of life ethic. Once we as a nation rally around any one of these issues to affirm the sanctity of life, we will see the importance of affirming this principle across the board.

Malcolm Muggeridge, the English writer, goes right to the heart of the matter: "Either life is always and in all circumstances sacred, or intrinsically of no account; it is inconceivable that it should be in some cases the one, and in some the other." The sanctity of innocent human life is a principle that Congress should proclaim at every opportunity.

It is possible that the Supreme Court itself may overturn its abortion rulings. We need only recall that in *Brown v. Board of Education* the Court reversed its own earlier "separate-but-equal" decision. I believe if the Supreme Court took another look at *Roe v. Wade*, and considered the real issue between the sanctity of life ethic and the quality of life ethic, it would change its mind once again.

As we continue to work to overturn *Roe v. Wade*, we must also continue to lay the groundwork for a society in which abortion is not the accepted answer to unwanted pregnancy. Pro-life people have already taken heroic steps, often at great personal sacrifice, to provide for unwed mothers. I recently spoke about a young pregnant woman named Victoria, who said, "In this society we save whales, we save timber wolves and bald eagles and Coke bottles. Yet, everyone wanted me to throw away my baby." She has been helped by Sav-a-Life, a group in Dallas, which provides a way for unwed mothers to preserve the human life within them when they might otherwise be tempted to resort to abortion. I think also of House of His Creation in Coatesville, Pennsylvania, where a loving couple has taken in almost 200 young women in the past ten years. They have seen, as a fact of life, that the girls are *not* better off having abortions than saving their babies. I am also reminded of the remarkable Rossow family of Ellington, Connecticut, who have opened their hearts and their home to nine handicapped adopted and foster children.

The Adolescent Family Life Program, adopted by Congress at the request of Senator Jeremiah Denton, has opened new opportunities for unwed mothers to give their children life. We should not rest until our entire society echoes the tone of John Powell in the dedication of his book, *Abortion: The Silent Holocaust*, a dedication to every woman carrying an unwanted child: "Please believe that you are not alone. There are many of us that truly love you, who want to stand at your side, and help in any way we can." And we can echo the always-practical woman of faith, Mother Teresa, when she says, "If you don't want the little child, that unborn child, give him to me." We have so many families in America seeking to adopt children that the slogan "every child a wanted child" is now the emptiest of all reasons to tolerate abortion.

I have often said we need to join in prayer to bring protection to the unborn. Prayer and action are needed to uphold the sanctity of human life. I believe it will not be possible to accomplish our work, the work of saving lives, "without being a soul of prayer." The famous British Member of Parliament, William Wilberforce, prayed with his small group of influential friends, the "Clapham Sect," for *decades* to see an end to slavery in the British empire. Wilberforce led that struggle in Parliament, unflaggingly, because he believed in the sanctity of human life. He saw the fulfillment of his impossible dream when Parliament outlawed slavery just before his death.

Let his faith and perseverance be our guide. We will never recognize the true value of our own lives until we affirm the value in the life of others, a value of which Malcolm Muggeridge says: ". . . however low it flickers or fiercely burns, it is still a Divine flame which no man dare presume to put out, be his motives ever so humane and enlightened."

Abraham Lincoln recognized that we could not survive as a free land when some men could decide that others were not fit to be free and should therefore be slaves. Likewise, we cannot survive as a free nation when some men decide that others are not fit to live and should be abandoned to abortion or infanticide. My Administration is dedicated to the preservation of America as a free land, and there is no cause more important for preserving that freedom than affirming the transcendent right to life of all human beings, the right without which no other rights have any meaning.

STUDY QUESTIONS

1. What, in Reagan's view, does recognizing the human status of the fetus entail?

2. How does Reagan tie together the issue of abortion with the issues surrounding the care of handicapped infants.

3. An argument "begs the question" when it assumes what it is supposed to prove. Can we accuse Reagan of begging the question when he assumes the fetus's humanity at every stage of pregnancy? Is his contention—that a fetus at the earliest stages (when it is a small sphere of cells) is a human being with a full set of moral and legal rights—really all that certain?

4. If the majority of Americans opposed abortion, would the Supreme Court be wrong to legalize it?

5. Reagan quotes Mother Teresa who says that "the greatest misery of our time is the generalized abortion of children." Why do you think someone like Mother Teresa, who is very much aware of the plight of the world's poor, would see abortion as the source of the greatest misery?

6. We consider slave societies to be morally benighted. Will future generations be likely to consider the present generation morally benighted because it allows the practice of abortion?

A Defense of Abortion

JUDITH JARVIS THOMSON

Judith Jarvis Thomson (b. 1929) is a professor of philosophy at the Massachusetts Institute of Technology. She is the author of *Acts and Other Events* (1977).

In her defense of abortion Thomson accepts, for the sake of argument, that the fetus is an innocent human being with a right to live. Her strategy is to show that killing an innocent human being is not always wrong. She asks you to imagine yourself waking up one morning and finding that you have been kidnapped, taken to a hospital, and attached to the circulatory system of a famous violinist who will die if you unplug yourself. Apparently, a group of music lovers canvassed local medical records and determined that you alone have the right blood type. Thomson argues that you have the right to unhook yourself even if this will cause the violinist's death. According to Thomson, you might allow the violinist to use your kidneys out of kindness, but you are certainly not *obligated* to do so and may rightfully pull the plug on him. To the objection that in pregnancy the mother in some sense invites the fetus to use her body, Thomas replies that this is more like the negligence of opening a window that permits easy intrusion by an unwanted visitor. You still have the

I am very much indebted to James Thomson for discussion, criticism, and many helpful suggestions.

A DEFENSE OF ABORTION From *Philosophy and Public Affairs*, Vol. 1, no. 1 (Fall 1971). Copyright © 1971 by Princeton University Press. Reprinted by permission of Princeton University Press.

right to cast out the intruder. Thomson concedes that abortion is sometimes a selfish act, but denies that we must refrain from unselfishness; an act may be "self-centered, callous, indecent, but not unjust." No law requires anyone to be even a "Minimally Decent Samaritan." Yet prohibiting abortion forces women to be Good Samaritans.

Thomson's argument does not give blanket permission to abort. Some cases require minimal decency and entail no right to abort. She considers this consequence a merit of her argument. Finally, the right to abort is not the right to kill: If a fetus can be saved once it is taken from its mother's body then she has no right to demand its death.

Most opposition to abortion relies on the premise that the fetus is a human being, a person, from the moment of conception. The premise is argued for, but, as I think, not well. Take, for example, the most common argument. We are asked to notice that the development of a human being from conception through birth into childhood is continuous; then it is said that to draw a line, to choose a point in this development and say "before this point the thing is not a person, after this point it is a person" is to make an arbitrary choice, a choice for which in the nature of things no good reason can be given. It is concluded that the fetus is, or anyway that we had better say it is, a person from the moment of conception. But this conclusion does not follow. Similar things might be said about the development of an acorn into an oak tree, and it does not follow that acorns are oak trees, or that we had better say they are. Arguments of this form are sometimes called "slippery slope arguments"—the phrase is perhaps self-explanatory—and it is dismaying that opponents of abortion rely on them so heavily and uncritically.

I am inclined to agree, however, that the prospects for "drawing a line" in the development of the fetus look dim. I am inclined to think also that we shall probably have to agree that the fetus has already become a human person well before birth. Indeed, it comes as a surprise when one first learns how early in its life it begins to acquire human characteristics. By the tenth week, for example, it already has a face, arms and legs, fingers and toes; it has internal organs, and brain activity is detectable.[1] On the other hand, I think that the premise is false, that the fetus is not a person from the moment of conception. A newly fertilized ovum, a newly implanted clump of cells, is no more a person than an acorn is an oak tree. But I shall not discuss any of this. For it seems to me to be of great interest to ask what happens if, for the sake of argument, we allow the premise. How, precisely, are we supposed to get from there to the conclusion that abortion is morally impermissible? Opponents of abortion commonly spend most of their time establishing that the fetus is a person, and hardly any time explaining the step from there to the impermissibility of abortion. Perhaps they think the step too simple and obvious to require much comment. Or perhaps instead they are simply being economical in argument. Many of those who defend abortion rely on the premise that the fetus is not a person, but only a bit of tissue that will become a person at birth; and why pay out more arguments than you have to? Whatever the explanation, I suggest that the step they take is neither easy nor obvious, that it calls for closer examination than it is commonly given, and that when we do give it this closer examination we shall feel inclined to reject it.

I propose, then, that we grant that the fetus is a person from the moment of conception. How does the argument go from here? Something like this, I take it. Every person has a right to life. So the fetus has a right to life. No doubt the mother has a right to decide what shall happen in and to her body; everyone would grant that. But surely a person's right to life is stronger and more stringent than the mother's right to decide what happens in and to her body, and so outweighs it. So the fetus may not be killed; an abortion may not be performed.

It sounds plausible. But now let me ask you to imagine this. You wake up in the morning and find yourself back to back in bed with an unconscious violinist. A famous unconscious violinist. He has

---

[1] Daniel Callahan, *Abortion: Law, Choice and Morality* (New York, 1970), p. 373. This book gives a fascinating survey of the available information on abortion. The Jewish tradition is surveyed in David M. Feldman, *Birth Control in Jewish Law* (New York, 1968), Part 5, the Catholic tradition in John T. Noonan, Jr., "An Almost Absolute Value in History," in *The Morality of Abortion*, ed. John T. Noonan, Jr. (Cambridge, Mass., 1970).

been found to have a fatal kidney ailment, and the Society of Music Lovers has canvassed all the available medical records and found that you alone have the right blood type to help. They have therefore kidnapped you, and last night the violinist's circulatory system was plugged into yours, so that your kidneys can be used to extract poisons from his blood as well as your own. The director of the hospital now tells you, "Look, we're sorry the Society of Music Lovers did this to you—we would never have permitted it if we had known. But still, they did it, and the violinist now is plugged into you. To unplug you would be to kill him. But never mind, it's only for nine months. By then he will have recovered from his ailment, and can safely be unplugged from you." Is it morally incumbent on you to accede to this situation? No doubt it would be very nice of you if you did, a great kindness. But do you *have* to accede to it? What if it were not nine months, but nine years? Or longer still? What if the director of the hospital says, "Tough luck, I agree, but you've now got to stay in bed, with the violinist plugged into you, for the rest of your life. Because re-member this. All persons have a right to life, and violinists are persons. Granted you have a right to decide what happens in and to your body, but a person's right to life outweighs your right to decide what happens in and to your body. So you cannot ever be unplugged from him." I imagine you would regard this as out-rageous, which suggests that something really is wrong with that plausible-sounding argument I mentioned a moment ago.

In this case, of course, you were kidnapped; you didn't volunteer for this operation that plugged the violinist into your kidneys. Can those who oppose abortion on the ground I mentioned make an exception for a pregnancy due to rape? Certainly. They can say that persons have a right to life only if they didn't come into existence because of rape; or they can say that all persons have a right to life, but that some have less of a right to life than others, in particular, that those who came into existence because of rape have less. But these statements have a rather unpleasant sound. Surely the ques-tion of whether you have a right to life at all, or how much of it you have, shouldn't turn on the question of whether or not you are the product of a rape. And in fact the people who oppose abortion on the ground I mentioned do not make this distinction, and hence do not make an exception in case of rape.

Nor do they make an exception for a case in which the mother has to spend the nine months of her pregnancy in bed. They would agree that would be a great pity, and hard on the mother; but all the same, all persons have a right to life, the fetus is a person, and so on. I suspect, in fact, that they would not make an exception for a case in which, miraculously enough, the pregnancy went on for nine years, or even the rest of the mother's life.

Some won't even make an exception for a case in which continuation of the pregnancy is likely to shorten the mother's life; they regard abortion as impermissible even to save the mother's life. Such cases are nowadays very rare, and many opponents of abortion do not accept this extreme view. All the same, it is a good place to begin: a number of points of interest come out in respect to it.

1. Let us call the view that abortion is impermissible even to save the mother's life "the extreme view." I want to suggest first that it does not issue from the argument I mentioned earlier without the addition of some fairly powerful premises. Suppose a woman has become pregnant, and now learns that she has a cardiac condition such that she will die if she carries the baby to term. What may be done for her? The fetus, being a person, has a right to life, but as the mother is a person too, so she has a right to life. Presumably they have an equal right to life. How is it supposed to come out that an abortion may not be performed? If mother and child have an equal right to life, shouldn't we perhaps flip a coin? Or should we add to the mother's right to life her right to decide what happens in and to her body, which everybody seems to be ready to grant—the sum of her rights now outweighing the fetus' right to life?

The most familiar argument here is the following. We are told that performing the abortion would be directly killing[2] the child, whereas doing nothing would not be killing the mother, but only letting her die. Moreover, in killing the child, one would be killing an innocent person, for the child has committed no crime, and is not aiming at his mother's death. And then there are a variety of ways in which this might be continued. (1) But as directly killing an innocent person is always and absolutely impermissible, an

---

[2]The term "direct" in the arguments I refer to is a technical one. Roughly, what is meant by "direct killing" is either killing as an end in itself, or killing as a means of some end, for example, the end of saving someone else's life. See footnote 5, for an example of its use.

abortion may not be performed. Or, (2) as directly killing an innocent person is murder, and murder is always and absolutely impermissible, an abortion may not be performed.[3] Or, (3) as one's duty to refrain from directly killing an innocent person is more stringent than one's duty to keep a person from dying, an abortion may not be performed. Or, (4) if one's only options are directly killing an innocent person or letting a person die, one must prefer letting the person die, and thus an abortion may not be performed.[4]

Some people seem to have thought that these are not further premises which must be added if the conclusion is to be reached, but that they follow from the very fact that an innocent person has a right to life.[5] But this seems to me to be a mistake, and perhaps the simplest way to show this is to bring out that while we must certainly grant that innocent persons have a right to life, the theses in (1) through (4) are all false. Take (2), for example. If directly killing an innocent person is murder, and thus is impermissible, then the mother's directly killing the innocent person inside her is murder, and thus is impermissible. But it cannot seriously be thought to be murder if the mother performs an abortion on herself to save her life. It cannot seriously be said that she *must* refrain, that she *must* sit passively by and wait for her death. Let us look again at the case of you and the violinist. There you are, in bed with the violinist, and the director of the hospital says to you, "It's all most

---

[3] Cf. *Encyclical Letter of Pope Pius XI on Christian Marriage*, St. Paul Editions (Boston, n.d.), p. 32: "however much we may pity the mother whose health and even life is gravely imperiled in the performance of the duty allotted to her by nature, nevertheless what could ever be a sufficient reason for excusing in any way the direct murder of the innocent? This is precisely what we are dealing with here." Noonan (*The Morality of Abortion*, p. 43) reads this as follows: "What cause can ever avail to excuse in any way the direct killing of the innocent? For it is a question of that."

[4] The thesis in (4) is in an interesting way weaker than those in (1), (2), and (3): they rule out abortion even in cases in which both mother *and* child will die if the abortion is not performed. By contrast, one who held the view expressed in (4) could consistently say that one needn't prefer letting two persons die to killing one.

[5] Cf. the following passage from Pius XII, *Address to the Italian Catholic Society of Midwives*: "The baby in the maternal breast has the right to life immediately from God.—Hence there is no man, no human authority, no science, no medical, eugenic, social, economic or moral 'indication' which can establish or grant a valid juridical ground for a direct deliberate disposition of an innocent human life, that is a disposition which looks to its destruction either as an end or as a means to another end perhaps in itself not illicit.—The baby, still not born, is a man in the same degree and for the same reason as the mother" (quoted in Noonan, *The Morality of Abortion*, p. 45).

distressing, and I deeply sympathize, but you see this is putting an additional strain on your kidneys, and you'll be dead within the month. But you *have* to stay where you are all the same. Because unplugging you would be directly killing an innocent violinist, and that's murder, and that's impermissible." If anything in the world is true, it is that you do not commit murder, you do not do what is impermissible, if you reach around to your back and unplug yourself from that violinist to save your life.

The main focus of attention in writings on abortion has been on what a third party may or may not do in answer to a request from a woman for an abortion. This is in a way understandable. Things being as they are, there isn't much a woman can safely do to abort herself. So the question asked is what a third party may do, and what the mother may do, if it is mentioned at all, is deduced, almost as an afterthought, from what it is concluded that third parties may do. But it seems to me that to treat the matter in this way is to refuse to grant to the mother that very status of person which is so firmly insisted on for the fetus. For we cannot simply read off what a person may do from what a third party may do. Suppose you find yourself trapped in a tiny house with a growing child. I mean a very tiny house, and a rapidly growing child—you are already up against the wall of the house and in a few minutes you'll be crushed to death. The child on the other hand won't be crushed to death; if nothing is done to stop him from growing he'll be hurt, but in the end he'll simply burst open the house and walk out a free man. Now I could well understand it if a bystander were to say, "There's nothing we can do for you. We cannot choose between your life and his, we cannot be the ones to decide who is to live, we cannot intervene." But it cannot be concluded that you too can do nothing, that you cannot attack it to save your life. However innocent the child may be, you do not have to wait passively while it crushes you to death. Perhaps a pregnant woman is vaguely felt to have the status of house, to which we don't allow the right of self-defense. But if the woman houses the child, it should be remembered that she is a person who houses it.

I should perhaps stop to say explicitly that I am not claiming that people have a right to do anything whatever to save their lives. I think, rather, that there are drastic limits to the right of self-defense. If someone threatens you with death unless you torture someone else to death, I think you have not the right, even to save your life, to do so. But the case under consideration here is very different. In our case there are only two people involved, one whose life is threatened, and one who threatens it. Both are innocent: the one who is threatened is not threatened because of any fault, the one who threatens does not threathen because of any fault. For this reason we may feel that we bystanders cannot intervene. But the person threatened can.

In sum, a woman surely can defend her life against the threat to it posed by the unborn child, even if doing so involves its death. And this shows not merely that the theses in (1) through (4) are false; it shows also that the extreme view of abortion is false, and so we need not canvass any other possible ways of arriving at it from the argument I mentioned at the outset.

2. The extreme view could of course be weakened to say that while abortion is permissible to save the mother's life, it may not be performed by a third party, but only by the mother herself. But this cannot be right either. For what we have to keep in mind is that the mother and the unborn child are not like two tenants in a small house which has, by an unfortunate mistake, been rented to both: the mother *owns* the house. The fact that she does adds to the offensiveness of deducing that the mother can do nothing from the supposition that third parties can do nothing. But it does more than this: it casts a bright light on the supposition that third parties can do nothing. Certainly it lets us see that a third party who says "I cannot choose between you" is fooling himself if he thinks this is impartiality. If Jones has found and fastened on a certain coat, which he needs to keep him from freezing, but which Smith also needs to keep him from freezing, then it is not impartiality that says "I cannot choose between you" when Smith owns the coat. Women have said again and again "This body is *my* body!" and they have reason to feel angry, reason to feel that it has been like shouting into the wind. Smith, after all, is hardly likely to bless us if we say to him, "Of course it's your coat, anybody would grant that it is. But no one may choose between you and Jones who is to have it."

We should really ask what it is that says "no one may choose" in the face of the fact that the body that houses the child is the mother's body. It may be simply a failure to appreciate this fact. But it may be something more interesting, namely the sense that one has a right to refuse to lay hands on people, even where it would be just and fair to do so, even where justice seems to require that somebody do so. Thus justice might call for somebody to get Smith's coat back from Jones, and yet you have a right to refuse to be the one to lay hands on Jones, a right to refuse to do physical violence to him. This, I think, must be granted. But then what should be said is not "no one may choose," but only "*I* cannot choose," and indeed not even this, but "*I* will not *act*," leaving it open that somebody else can or should, and in particular that anyone in a position of authority, with the job of securing people's rights, both can and should. So this is no difficulty. I have not been arguing that any given third party must accede to the mother's request that he perform an abortion to save her life, but only that he may.

I suppose that in some views of human life the mother's body is only on loan to her, the loan not being one which gives her any prior claim to it. One who held this view might well think it impartiality to say "I cannot choose." But I shall simply ignore this possibility. My own view is that if a human being has any just, prior claim to anything at all, he has a just, prior claim to his own body. And perhaps this needn't be argued for here anyway, since, as I mentioned, the arguments against abortion we are looking at do grant that the woman has a right to decide what happens in and to her body.

But although they do grant it, I have tried to show that they do not take seriously what is done in granting it. I suggest the same thing will reappear even more clearly when we turn away from cases in which the mother's life is at stake, and attend, as I propose we now do, to the vastly more common cases in which a woman wants an abortion for some less weighty reason than preserving her own life.

3. Where the mother's life is not at stake, the argument I mentioned at the outset seems to have a much stronger pull. "Everyone has a right to life, so the unborn person has a right to life." And isn't the child's right to life weightier than anything other than the mother's own right to life, which she might put forward as ground for an abortion?

This argument treats the right to life as if it were unproblematic. It is not, and this seems to me to be precisely the source of the mistake.

For we should now, at long last, ask what it comes to, to have a right to life. In some views having a right to life includes having a right to be given at least the bare minimum one needs for continued life. But suppose that what in fact *is* the bare minimum a man needs for continued life is something he has no right at all to be given? If I am sick unto death, and the only thing that will save my life is the touch of Henry Fonda's cool hand on my fevered brow, then all the same, I have no right to be given the touch of Henry Fonda's cool hand on my fevered brow. It would be frightfully nice of him to fly in from the West Coast to provide it. It would be less nice, though no doubt well meant, if my friends flew out to the West Coast and carried Henry Fonda back with them. But I have no right at all against anybody that he should do this for me. Or again, to return to the story I told earlier, the fact that for continued life that violinist needs the continued use of your kidneys does not establish that he has a right to be given the continued use of your kidneys. He certainly has no right against you that *you* should give him continued use of your kidneys. For nobody has any right to use your kidneys unless you give him such a right; and nobody has the right against you that you shall give him this right—if you do allow him to go on using your kidneys, this is a kindness on your part, and not something he can claim from you as his due. Nor has he any right against anybody else that *they* should give him continued use of your kidneys. Certainly he had no right against the Society of Music Lovers that they should plug him into you in the first place. And if you now start to unplug yourself, having learned that you will otherwise have to spend nine years in bed with him, there is nobody in the world who must try to prevent you, in order to see to it that he is given something he has a right to be given.

Some people are rather stricter about the right to life. In their view, it does not include the right to be given anything, but amounts to, and only to, the right not to be killed by anybody. But here a related difficulty arises. If everybody must refrain from killing that violinist, then everybody must refrain from doing a great many different sorts of things. Everybody must refrain from slitting his throat, everybody must refrain from shooting him— and everybody must refrain from unplugging you from him. But does he have a right against everybody that they shall refrain from unplugging you from him? To refrain from doing this is to allow him to continue to use your kidneys. It could be argued that he has a right against us that *we* should allow him to continue to use your kidneys. That is, while he had no right against us that we should give him the use of your kidneys, it might be argued that he anyway has a right against us that we shall not now intervene and deprive him of the use of your kidneys. I shall come back to third-party interventions later. But certainly the violinist has no right against you that *you* shall allow him to continue to use your kidneys. As I said, if you do allow him to use them, it is a kindness on your part, and not something you owe him.

The difficulty I point to here is not peculiar to the right to life. It reappears in connection with all the other natural rights; and it is something which an adequate account of rights must deal with. For present purposes it is enough just to draw attention to it. But I would stress that I am not arguing that people do not have a right to life—quite to the contrary, it seems to me that the primary control we must place on the acceptability of an account of rights is that it should turn out in that account to be a truth that all persons have a right to life. I am arguing only that having a right to life does not guarantee having either a right to be given the use of or a right to be allowed continued use of another person's body—even if one needs it for life itself. So the right to life will not serve the opponents of abortion in the very simple and clear way in which they seem to have thought it would.

4. There is another way to bring out the difficulty. In the most ordinary sort of case, to deprive someone of what he has a right to is to treat him unjustly. Suppose a boy and his small brother are jointly given a box of chocolates for Christmas. If the older boy takes the box and refuses to give his brother any of the chocolates, he is unjust to him, for the brother has been given a right to half of them. But suppose that, having learned that otherwise it means nine years in bed with that violinist, you unplug yourself from him. You surely are not being unjust to him, for you gave him no right to use your kidneys, and no one else can have given him any such right. But we have to notice that, in unplugging yourself, you are killing him; and violinists, like everybody else, have a right to life, and thus in the view we were considering just now, the right not to be killed. So here you do what he supposedly has a right you shall not do, but you do not act unjustly to him in doing it.

The emendation which may be made at this point is this: the

right to life consists not in the right not to be killed, but rather in the right not to be killed unjustly. This runs a risk of circularity, but never mind: it would enable us to square the fact that the violinist has a right to life with the fact that you do not act unjustly toward him in unplugging yourself, thereby killing him. For if you do not kill him unjustly, you do not violate his right to life, and so it is no wonder you do him no injustice.

But if this emendation is accepted, the gap in the argument against abortion stares us plainly in the face: it is by no means enough to show that the fetus is a person, and to remind us that all persons have a right to life—we need to be shown also that killing the fetus violates its right to life, i.e., that abortion is unjust killing. And is it?

I suppose we may take it as a datum that in a case of pregnancy due to rape the mother has not give the unborn person a right to the use of her body for food and shelter. Indeed, in what pregnancy could it be supposed that the mother has given the unborn person such a right? It is not as if there were unborn persons drifting about the world, to whom a woman who wants a child says "I invite you in."

But it might be argued that there are other ways one can have acquired a right to the use of another person's body than by having been invited to use it by that person. Suppose a woman voluntarily indulges in intercourse, knowing of the chance it will issue in pregnancy, and then she does become pregnant; is she not in part responsible for the presence, in fact the very existence, of the unborn person inside her? No doubt she did not invite it in. But doesn't her partial responsibility for its being there itself give it a right to the use of her body?[6] If so, then her aborting it would be more like the boy's taking away the chocolates, and less like your unplugging yourself from the violinist—doing so would be depriving it of what it does have a right to, and thus would be doing it an injustice.

And then, too, it might be asked whether or not she can kill it even to save her own life: If she voluntarily called it into existence, how can she now kill it, even in self-defense?

---

[6] The need for a discussion of this argument was brought home to me by members of the Society for Ethical and Legal Philosophy, to whom this paper was originally presented.

The first thing to be said about this is that it is something new. Opponents of abortion have been so concerned to make out the independence of the fctus, in order to establish that it has a right to life, just as its mother does, that they have tended to overlook the possible support they might gain from making out that the fetus is *dependent* on the mother, in order to establish that she has a special kind of responsibility for it, a responsibility that gives it rights against her which are not possessed by any independent person— such as an ailing violinist who is a stranger to her.

On the other hand, this argument would give the unborn person a right to its mother's body only if her pregnancy resulted from a voluntary act, undertaken in full knowledge of the chance a pregnancy might result from it. It would leave out entirely the unborn person whose existence is due to rape. Pending the availability of some further argument, then, we would be left with the conclusion that unborn persons whose existence is due to rape have no right to the use of their mothers' bodies, and thus that aborting them is not depriving them of anything they have a right to and hence is not unjust killing.

And we should also notice that it is not at all plain that this argument really does go even as far as it purports to. For there are cases and cases, and the details make a difference. If the room is stuffy, and I therefore open a window to air it, and a burglar climbs in, it would be absurd to say, "Ah, now he can stay, she's given him a right to the use of her house—for she is partially responsible for his presence there, having voluntarily done what enabled him to get in, in full knowledge that there are such things as burglars, and that burglars burgle." It would be still more absurd to say this if I had had bars installed outside my windows, precisely to prevent burglars from getting in, and a burglar got in only because of a defect in the bars. It remains equally absurd if we imagine it is not a burglar who climbs in, but an innocent person who blunders or falls in. Again, suppose it were like this: people-seeds drift about in the air like pollen, and if you open your windows, one may drift in and take root in your carpets or upholstery. You don't want children, so you fix up your windows with fine mesh screens, the very best you can buy. As can happen, however, and on very, very rare occasions does happen, one of the screens is defective; and a seed drifts in and takes root. Does the person-plant who now develops have a right to the use of your house? Surely not—despite the fact that you voluntarily opened your windows, you knowingly kept carpets and upholstered furniture, and you knew that screens were sometimes defective. Someone may argue that you are responsible for its rooting, that it does have a right to your house, because after all you *could* have lived out your life with bare floors and furniture, or with sealed windows and doors. But this won't do—for by the same token anyone can avoid a pregnancy due to rape by having a hysterectomy, or anyway by never leaving home without a (reliable!) army.

It seems to me that the argument we are looking at can establish at most that there are *some* cases in which the unborn person has a right to the use of its mother's body, and therefore *some* cases in which abortion is unjust killing. There is room for much discussion and argument as to precisely which, if any. But I think we should sidestep this issue and leave it open, for at any rate the argument certainly does not establish that all abortion is unjust killing.

5. There is room for yet another argument here, however. We surely must all grant that there may be cases in which it would be morally indecent to detach a person from your body at the cost of his life. Suppose you learn that what the violinist needs is not nine years of your life, but only one hour: all you need to do to save his life is to spend one hour in that bed with him. Suppose also that letting him use your kidneys for that one hour would not affect your health in the slightest. Admittedly you were kidnapped. Admittedly you did not give anyone permission to plug him into you. Nevertheless it seems to me plain you *ought* to allow him to use your kidneys for that hour—it would be indecent to refuse.

Again, suppose pregnancy lasted only an hour, and constituted no threat to life or health. And suppose that a woman becomes pregnant as a result of rape. Admittedly she did not voluntarily do anything to bring about the existence of a child. Admittedly she did nothing at all which would give the unborn person a right to the use of her body. All the same it might well be said, as in the newly emended violinist story, that she *ought* to allow it to remain for that hour—that it would be indecent in her to refuse.

Now some people are inclined to use the term "right" in such a way that it follows from the fact that you ought to allow a person to use your body for the hour he needs, that he has a right to use your body for the hour he needs, even though he has not been given that right by any person or act. They may say that it follows also that if you refuse, you act unjustly toward him. This use of the term is perhaps so common that it cannot be called wrong; nevertheless it seems to me to be an unfortunate loosening of what we would do better to keep a tight rein on. Suppose that box of chocolates I mentioned earlier had not been given to both boys jointly, but was given only to the older boy. There he sits, stolidly eating his way through the box, his small brother watching enviously. Here we are likely to say "You ought not to be so mean. You ought to give your brother some of those chocolates." My own view is that it just does not follow from the truth of this that the brother has any right to any of the chocolates. If the boy refuses to give his brother any, he is greedy, stingy, callous—but not unjust. I suppose that the people I have in mind will say it does follow that the brother has a right to some of the chocolates, and thus that the boy does act unjustly if he refuses to give his brother any. But the effect of saying this is to obscure what we should keep distinct, namely the difference between the boy's refusal in this case and the boy's refusal in the earlier case, in which the box was given to both boys jointly, and in which the small brother thus had what was from any point of view clear title to half.

A further objection to so using the term "right" that from the fact that A ought to do a thing for B, it follows that B has a right against A that A do it for him, is that it is going to make the question of whether or not a man has a right to a thing turn on how easy it is to provide him with it; and this seems not merely unfortunate, but morally unacceptable. Take the case of Henry Fonda again. I said earlier that I had no right to the touch of his cool hand on my fevered brow, even though I needed it to save my life. I said it would be frightfully nice of him to fly in from the West Coast to provide me with it, but that I had no right against him that he should do so. But suppose he isn't on the West Coast. Suppose he has only to walk across the room, place a hand briefly on my brow—and lo, my life is saved. Then surely he ought to do it, it would be indecent to refuse. Is it to be said "Ah, well, it follows that in this case she has a right to the touch of his hand on her brow, and so it would be an injustice in him to refuse"? So that I have a right to it when it is easy for him to provide it, though no right when it's hard? It's rather a shocking idea that anyone's rights should fade away and disappear as it gets harder and harder to accord them to him.

So my own view is that even though you ought to let the violinist use your kidneys for the one hour he needs, we should not conclude that he has a right to do so—we should say that if you refuse, you are, like the boy who owns all the chocolates and will give none away, self-centered and callous, indecent in fact, but not unjust. And similarly, that even supposing a case in which a woman pregnant due to rape ought to allow the unborn person to use her body for the hour he needs, we should conclude that she is self-centered, callous, indecent, but not unjust, if she refuses. The complaints are no less grave; they are just different. However, there is no need to insist on this point. If anyone does wish to deduce "he has a right" from "you ought," then all the same he must surely grant that there are cases in which it is not morally required of you that you allow that violinist to use your kidneys, and in which he does not have a right to use them, and in which you do not do him an injustice if you refuse. And so also for mother and unborn child. Except in such cases as the unborn person has a right to demand it—and we were leaving open the possiblity that there may be such cases—nobody is morally *required* to make large sacrifices, of health, of all other interests and concerns, of all other duties and commitments, for nine years, or even for nine months, in order to keep another person alive.

6. We have in fact to distinguish between two kinds of Samaritan: the Good Samaritan and what we might call the Minimally Decent Samaritan. The story of the Good Samaritan, you will remember, goes like this:

> A certain man went down from Jerusalem to Jericho, and fell among thieves, which stripped him of his raiment, and wounded him, and departed, leaving him half dead.
>
> And by chance there came down a certain priest that way; and when he saw him, he passed by on the other side.
>
> And likewise a Levite, when he was at the place, came and looked on him, and passed by on the other side.
>
> But a certain Samaritan, as he journeyed, came where he was; and when he saw him he had compassion on him.
>
> And went to him, and bound up his wounds, pouring in oil and wine, and set him on his own beast, and brought him to an inn, and took care of him.

And on the morrow, when he departed, he took out two pence, and gave them to the host, and said unto him, "Take care of him; and whatsoever thou spendest more, when I come again, I will re-pay thee."

(Luke 10:30–35)

The Good Samaritan went out of his way, at some cost to himself, to help one in need of it. We are not told what the options were, that is, whether or not the priest and the Levite could have helped by doing less than the Good Samaritan did, but assuming they could have, then the fact they did nothing at all shows they were not even Minimally Decent Samaritans, not because they were not Samaritans, but because they were not even minimally decent.

These things are a matter of degree, of course, but there is a difference, and it comes out perhaps most clearly in the story of Kitty Genovese, who, as you will remember, was murdered while thirty-eight people watched or listened, and did nothing at all to help her. A Good Samaritan would have rushed out to give direct assistance against the murderer. Or perhaps we had better allow that it would have been a Splendid Samaritan who did this, on the ground that it would have involved a risk of death for himself. But the thirty-eight not only did not do this, they did not even trouble to pick up a phone to call the police. Minimally Decent Samaritan-ism would call for doing at least that, and their not having done it was monstrous.

After telling the story of the Good Samaritan, Jesus said "Go, and do thou likewise." Perhaps he meant that we are morally required to act as the Good Samaritan did. Perhaps he was urging people to do more than is morally required of them. At all events it seems plain that it was not morally required of any of the thirty-eight that he rush out to give direct assistance at the risk of his own life, and that it is not morally required of anyone that he give long stretches of his life—nine years or nine months—to sustaining the life of a person who has no special right (we were leaving open the possibility of this) to demand it.

Indeed, with one rather striking class of exceptions, no one in any country in the world is *legally* required to do anywhere near as much as this for anyone else. The class of exceptions is obvious. My main concern here is not the state of the law in respect to abortion, but it is worth drawing attention to the fact that in no state in this country is any man compelled by law to be even a Minimally Decent Samaritan to any person; there is no law under which charges could be brought against the thirty-eight who stood by while Kitty Genovese died. By contrast, in most states in this country women are compelled by law to be not merely Minimally Decent Samaritans, but Good Samaritans to unborn persons inside them. This doesn't by itself settle anything one way or the other, because it may well be argued that there should be laws in this country—as there are in many European countries—compelling at least Minimally Decent Samaritanism.[7] But it does show that there is a gross injustice in the existing state of the law. And it shows also that the groups currently working against liberalization of abortion laws, in fact working toward having it declared unconstitutional for a state to permit abortion, had better start working for the adoption of Good Samaritan laws generally, or earn the charge that they are acting in bad faith.

I should think, myself, that Minimally Decent Samaritan laws would be one thing, Good Samaritan laws quite another, and in fact highly improper. But we are not here concerned with the law. What we should ask is not whether anybody should be compelled by law to be a Good Samaritan, but whether we must accede to a situation in which somebody is being compelled—by nature, perhaps—to be a Good Samaritan. We have, in other words, to look now at third-party interventions. I have been arguing that no person is morally required to make large sacrifices to sustain the life of another who has no right to demand them, and this even where the sacrifices do not include life itself; we are not morally required to be Good Samaritans or anyway Very Good Samaritans to one another. But what if a man cannot extricate himself from such a situation? What if he appeals to us to extricate him? It seems to me plain that there are cases in which we can, cases in which a Good Samaritan would extricate him. There you are, you were kidnapped, and nine years in bed with that violinist lie ahead of you. You have your own life to lead. You are sorry, but you simply cannot see giving up so much of your life to the sustaining of his.

---

[7] For a discussion of the difficulties involved, and a survey of the European experience with such laws, see *The Good Samaritan and the Law*, ed. James M. Ratcliffe (New York, 1966).

You cannot extricate yourself, and ask us to do so. I should have thought that—in light of his having no right to the use of your body—it was obvious that we do not have to accede to your being forced to give up so much. We can do what you ask. There is no injustice to the violinist in our doing so.

7. Following the lead of the opponents of abortion, I have throughout been speaking of the fetus merely as a person, and what I have been asking is whether or not the argument we began with, which proceeds only from the fetus' being a person, really does establish its conclusion. I have argued that it does not.

But of course there are arguments and arguments, and it may be said that I have simply fastened on the wrong one. It may be said that what is important is not merely the fact that the fetus is a person, but that it is a person for whom the woman has a special kind of responsibility issuing from the fact that she is its mother. And it might be argued that all my analogies are therefore irrelevant—for you do not have that special kind of responsibility for that violinist, Henry Fonda does not have that special kind of responsibility for me. And our attention might be drawn to the fact that men and women both *are* compelled by law to provide support for their children.

I have in effect dealt (briefly) with this argument in section 4 above; but a (still briefer) recapitulation now may be in order. Surely we do not have any such "special responsibility" for a person unless we have assumed it, explicitly or implicitly. If a set of parents do not try to prevent pregnancy, do not obtain an abortion, and then at the time of birth of the child do not put it out for adoption, but rather take it home with them, then they have assumed responsibility for it, they have given it rights, and they cannot *now* withdraw support from it at the cost of its life because they now find it difficult to go on providing for it. But if they have taken all reasonable precautions against having a child, they do not simply by virtue of their biological relationship to the child who comes into existence have a special responsibility for it. They may wish to assume responsibility for it, or they may not wish to. And I am suggesting that if assuming responsibility for it would require large sacrifices, then they may refuse. A Good Samaritan would not refuse—or anyway, a Splendid Samaritan, if the sacrifices that had to be made were enormous. But then so would a Good Samaritan assume responsibility for that violinist; so would Henry Fonda,

587

if he is a Good Samaritan, fly in from the West Coast and assume responsibility for me.

8. My argument will be found unsatisfactory on two counts by many of those who want to regard abortion as morally permissible. First, while I do argue that abortion is not impermissible, I do not argue that it is always permissible. There may well be cases in which carrying the child to term requires only Minimally Decent Samaritanism of the mother, and this is a standard we must not fall below. I am inclined to think it a merit of my account precisely that it does *not* give a general yes or a general no. It allows for and supports our sense that, for example, a sick and desperately frightened fourteen-year-old schoolgirl, pregnant due to rape, may *of course* choose abortion, and that any law which rules this out is an insane law. And it also allows for and supports our sense that in other cases resort to abortion is even positively indecent. It would be indecent in the woman to request an abortion, and indecent in a doctor to perform it, if she is in her seventh month, and wants the abortion just to avoid the nuisance of postponing a trip abroad. The very fact that the arguments I have been drawing attention to treat all cases of abortion, or even all cases of abortion in which the mother's life is not at stake, as morally on a par ought to have made them suspect at the outset.

Secondly, while I am arguing for the permissibility of abortion in some cases, I am not arguing for the right to secure the death of the unborn child. It is easy to confuse these two things in that up to a certain point in the life of the fetus it is not able to survive outside the mother's body; hence removing it from her body guarantees its death. But they are importantly different. I have argued that you are not morally required to spend nine months in bed, sustaining the life of that violinist; but to say this is by no means to say that if, when you unplug yourself, there is a miracle and he survives, you than have a right to turn round and slit his throat. You may detach yourself even if this costs him his life; you have no right to be guaranteed his death, by some other means, if unplugging yourself does not kill him. There are some people who will feel dissatisfied by this feature of my argument. A woman may be utterly devastated by the thought of a child, a bit of herself, put out for adoption and never seen or heard of again. She may therefore want not merely that the child be detached from her, but more, that it die. Some opponents of abortion are inclined to regard this as beneath contempt—thereby showing insensitivity to what is surely a powerful source of despair. All the same, I agree that the desire for the child's death is not one which anybody may gratify, should it turn out to be possible to detach the child alive.

At this place, however, it should be remembered that we have only been pretending throughout that the fetus is a human being from the moment of conception. A very early abortion is surely not the killing of a person, and so is not dealt with by anything I have said here.

STUDY QUESTIONS

1. How do you react to Thomson's violinist analogy? Do you think she answers the most serious objections that can be brought against it?
2. What moral responsibility, if any, does a pregnant woman have for the fetus? What is the basis for such a responsibility? Does it make a difference whether the pregnancy is wanted? Imposed?
3. Thomson distinguishes among Good Samaritans, Splendid Samaritans, and Minimally Decent Samaritans. Which are we obligated to be? How does the distinction between being a Good Samaritan and a Minimally Decent Samaritan apply to the woman with an unwanted pregnancy?

Famine, Affluence, and Morality

PETER SINGER

A biographical sketch of Peter Singer is found on page 303.

Singer describes the mass starvation in many parts of the world and argues that affluent persons are morally obligated to contribute part of their time and income toward alleviating hunger. He assumes that passivity, when people are able to act to prevent evil, is morally wrong. Nowadays we can help people over great distances; instant communication and air travel have transformed the world into a "global village." If, says Singer, bystanders see a child drowning in a shallow pond, they ought to save that child even if it means muddying their clothes. Failure to do so is gross moral negligence. Singer compares the citizens of the affluent West to these bystanders.

As I write this, in November 1971, people are dying in East Bengal from lack of food, shelter, and medical care. The suffering and death that are occurring there now are not inevitable, not unavoidable in any fatalistic sense of the term. Constant poverty, a cyclone, and a civil war have turned at least nine million people into destitute refugees; nevertheless, it is not beyond the capacity of the

FAMINE, AFFLUENCE, AND MORALITY From *Philosophy and Public Affairs*, Vol. 1, no. 3 (Spring 1972). Copyright © 1972 by Princeton University Press. Reprinted by permission of Princeton University Press.